Seldom Seen, Rarely Heard

PSYCHOLOGY, GENDER, AND THEORY

Rachel T. Hare-Mustin and Jeanne Marecek
Series Editors

Focusing on emerging ideas in psychology, gender theory, and the politics of knowledge, this scholarly/trade series examines contemporary developments broadly associated with postmodernism and with feminist critiques of psychology and other social science disciplines. Among the topics explored are gender relations; the social construction of gender, class, race/ethnicity, and other categories of difference/hierarchy; and critical reformulations of therapy theory and practice. We seek manuscripts that propose or exemplify new ways of doing psychology, that reconsider the foundational assumptions of psychology—both in scholarship and practice. Of interest as well are works that examine ways in which the discipline of psychology and its work practices not only reflect arrangements of power and privilege in society but also produce knowledge serving to justify those arrangements.

Seldom Seen, Rarely Heard: Women's Place in Psychology, edited by
Janis S. Bohan

FORTHCOMING

Sex Is Not a Natural Act and Other Essays,
Leonore Tiefer

Seldom Seen, Rarely Heard

Women's Place in Psychology

edited by Janis S. Bohan

Metropolitan State College of Denver

Westview Press

BOULDER • SAN FRANCISCO • OXFORD

Psychology, Gender, and Theory

Published in 1992 in the United States of America by Westview Press, Inc., 5500 Central Avenue, Boulder, Colorado 80301–2877, and in the United Kingdom by Westview Press, 36 Lonsdale Road, Summertown, Oxford OX2 7EW

Library of Congress Cataloging-in-Publication Data
Seldom seen, rarely heard : women's place in psychology / edited by
    Janis S. Bohan.
        p. cm. — (Psychology, gender, and theory)
    Includes bibliographical references.
    ISBN 0-8133-1394-5. 0-8133-1395-3 (pbk.).
    1. Women—Psychology. 2. Feminism. 3. Feminist psychology.
4. Sex role. I. Bohan, Janis S. II. Series.
HQ1206.S4465 1992
150'.82—dc20   92-13751
                                                                                 CIP

Printed and bound in the United States of America

The paper used in this publication meets the requirements
of the American National Standard for Permanence of Paper
for Printed Library Materials Z39.48-1984.

10   9   8   7   6   5   4   3   2   1

To Ann Cook and Marjorie Whittaker Leidig
sine quibus non

CONTENTS

PREFACE AND
ACKNOWLEDGMENTS

A number of years ago, I undertook as a sabbatical project the task of discovering psychology's lost "foremothers." I expected the project to be a fairly straightforward process of research and revision, learning about these women and inserting their names and work into course outlines, perhaps doing some writing about them and the exclusionary nature of psychology's histories. My involvement in this work stemmed from a long-standing interest in the history of psychology, an interest that one day had come face-to-awakened-face with the absence of women and their work from depictions of psychology's evolution. While that exclusion, once confronted, seemed both outrageous and understandable, I was intrigued by the tolerance of the discipline for this distortion, even among many of us who were involved with feminist issues in other spheres. I set out with a mission: to discover the invisible, important women of psychology's history, who both my intuition and historical data on the prevalence of women in psychology convinced me must be there.

My journey of discovery led me into areas I had never anticipated. As I searched for psychology's lost women, I discovered women's history, a vast literature that illuminated for me the plethora of forces that have rendered women invisible—not only in the academic disciplines but to history in general, as history is usually written. My quest for principles to explain how history could be so distorted led me to historiographic scholarship that clarified the contextual forces shaping the writing of history. And my wish to understand how knowledge is shaped by context led me, in turn, to the postmodernist, especially the constructionist, literature. I came away with a view of knowledge entirely different from that with which I began; the understanding provided by this new perspective made sense of women's place in psychology. More important, it provided me with a set of conceptual tools that could be used to re-view psychology, to construct a psychology that is inclusive of women.

As is apparent from the range of the book's coverage, my initial interest in psychology's earlier prominent women has broadened considerably. As I strived to understand psychology's historical neglect of women, I repeatedly confronted the parallels and linkages between this historical distortion and psychology's persistent mistreatment of women, both as subjects of interest and as participants in the discipline. Reconstructing psychology to be women-inclusive, I have come to realize, entails a far more extensive effort than simply adding women to its histories; contemporary psychology is also exclusionary, is also a product of misogynist sociohistorical contexts, is also subject to the influence of political forces that shape the development of psychological "knowledge." Although it is often easier to recognize these shaping forces from the wisdom of hindsight, an application of the same contextual analysis to contemporary treatments of women provides a lens through which a re-vision of psychology is possible—a vision of psychology that includes women as integral.

My mission has changed, broadened, become more expansive and more compelling. And it has become more constructive. It is now less a critique of exclusion, more a search for inclusion; it is less a historical endeavor, more an attempt to understand the place of women in contemporary psychology. This book reflects the stages of my journey, and it offers the tools of understanding I've discovered to others interested in the questions inspired by my own odyssey.

As is always the case with such undertakings, this book was not completed by my own efforts alone. I have been inspired and encouraged throughout its development by the insights and challenges provided by my students and colleagues. The burdensome task of seeking out information and resources would have been overwhelming without the help of Imelda Mulholland, who, as a librarian and a friend, provided support without which I could not have completed this book. Donna Arlton and Diane Hollenbeck did and re-did the most tedious of typing chores (onerous tasks like bibliographies and permission letters), freeing me to work on the text. Carole Horle's assistance was invaluable; her reading of the nearly completed manuscript provided a thoughtful perspective from outside my own mind, which by this time saw wisdom even in incoherence. I am grateful, also, to the series editors, Rachel Hare-Mustin and Jeanne Marecek, who have been generous in their support and immeasurably helpful in their feedback as the book has progressed. And, most assuredly, the book would never have been possible were my work not supported and my life enriched by caring friends.

Janis S. Bohan

Seldom Seen,
Rarely Heard

INTRODUCTION

Women's place in psychology: seldom seen, rarely heard. Why is that, and how has it come to be? This book explores those questions, seeking an answer that accommodates both the reality of women's marginalization in psychology and the hope for redress. The problem we are addressing here is women's virtual invisibility in psychology, both as scholars and as subjects of concern. Women and women's perspective are notably absent from psychology's mainstream research and theory, from the discipline's self-presentation in curricula, from its histories, and from prominent professional and lay depictions of what psychology is and does. The task before us is to reveal the women of psychology, to construct a foundation for a women-inclusive psychology.

Throughout my discussions in this book, I will use the term *re-placing* women in psychology to describe the process we undertake here. This term is derived from usage by historian Gerda Lerner (1979), who spoke of "placing" women in history (see also Furumoto, 1985; Furumoto & Scarborough, 1986 [included in this book]). My intent in coining the neologism *re-placing* is to underscore the fact that our charge is not, at base, to place women in psychology; women have always been present in psychology. They have often been invisible; their perspective and the issues that shape their lives have been neglected; they have confronted exclusionary practices and structures, have occasionally been misrepresented or denied acknowledgment, have frequently been trivialized—but women have not, despite all that, been absent from psychology. The project at the heart of this book, then, is not to create a place for women but to illuminate the place they have always held, not to place women anew but to assert their continuing presence in and impact on psychology.

Psychology as it has heretofore been defined and portrayed has effectively screened women, women's concerns, and women's work from visibility; the re-placement of women will require a new construal of the field of psychology. The necessity for a foundational reconstruction of psychology is amply demonstrated by the abundance of recent scholarship documenting the exclusionary consequences of psychology as it has op-

1

erated to date. An extensive literature identifies the scope of psychology's marginalization of women, including the exclusion of women and women's issues from the formulation, design, and content of psychological research; psychology's (mis)representation of the experience of women as deviant from the male norm; the androcentric bias of psychology curricula; gender bias in psychological theory and practice; and women's absence from psychology's histories.

This marginalization persists even in the face of growing feminist consciousness in academia and in psychology at large. The treatment of the women of psychology in the field's histories serves as an illustrative case in point. Despite the fact that it has been nearly two decades since women's absence from histories was first called to the attention of the psychological community, the majority of history and systems texts still do not present the work of major women pioneers in the field. When these women are mentioned, their work is minimally described and often presented as ancillary material. Comparable reticence in responding to the challenge raised by the highlighting of women's marginalization has been demonstrated in other areas as well. Feminist challenges to research methodologies go largely unrecognized; much psychological theory retains its androcentric bias; standard curriculum persists in its neglect of women's issues and women's contributions to the field; clinical theory and practice retain assumptions grounded in gender bias and the pathologizing of women; women continue to be underrepresented among the power elite, despite their growing majority in the discipline (e.g., Bronstein & Quina, 1988; Caplan, 1991; Fine, 1985; Hare-Mustin & Marecek, 1988 [included in this book]; Lykes & Stewart, 1986; Ostertag & McNamara, 1991; Walker, 1991; Wine, 1982).

We are discussing here two closely related issues: the marginalization of women as scholars, as participants in the discipline of psychology, and the neglect of women and women's concerns in psychological theory, research, and practice. What unites the variety of works addressing these issues is their common origin in social structures. Psychology as a discipline is itself a social system, a particular sociohistorically situated context that itself embodies the norms of the broader society. Assumptions about gender operative in society as a whole are reflected and reproduced in psychology's endeavors. Women are invisible as scholars not because they lack merit (as the myth of the academy as a meritocracy would have us believe) but because academia is a social system reflective of the broader society. Psychology has neglected women's experience in its formulations not because men's experience is adequate to an understanding of all humanity (as the notion of science as objective purveyor of truth would suggest) but because male is taken as the norm in society.

Thus, the pervasive patriarchal forces that operate to marginalize women in society are the same forces that make psychology's women scholars invisible and are the same forces that allow psychological theory and research to neglect and disparage women. The discipline's failure to confront this fact, to acknowledge that it is subject to social influence, derives from the field's paradigm-induced insularity. Psychology's self-definition as an objective and value-neutral science has precluded the field's acknowledging its own contextually derived gender biases. Only as the intricate connections between social norms and professional activities have been unraveled by feminist scholars have the underpinnings of women's exclusion become obvious.

And with this unraveling, promising harbingers of change have appeared in the generally gloomy picture of persistent neglect. The place of women in the history of psychology has recently become the focus of considerable scholarship, highlighting the lives, work, and impact of the women who have participated in psychology's development, as well as the forces that have rendered them invisible (e.g., Bohan, 1990, 1992; Furumoto, 1985; Furumoto & Scarborough, 1986; O'Connell & Russo, 1980, 1983, 1988, 1990; Russo & Denmark, 1987; Scarborough & Furumoto, 1987). In other areas of scholarship as well, feminist psychologists have offered woman-aware approaches to psychology curricula, developing novel courses and providing resources for the integration of women's perspectives and women's work into standard course content (e.g., Bohan, 1992; Bronstein & Quina, 1988; Freedman, Golub, & Krauss, 1982; Furumoto, 1985, 1988; Golub et al., 1983; Moke & Bohan, 1992).

Beyond the domain of historical and curricular issues, feminist psychologists have proposed alternative approaches to psychological practice, approaches that validate women's experience and challenge traditional, normative assumptions about gender. Research methodologies have come under scrutiny, both for the exclusion of women as subjects and women's issues as subject matter and for the inherently "masculinist" assumptions undergirding traditional epistemological commitments. Psychological theory, too, has encountered this revisionist bent, with critiques challenging both the neglect of women's realities in theory formulation and the tacit, prescriptive assumptions about gender that pervade psychological theory (e.g., Brown, 1991; Burman, 1990; Crawford & Gentry, 1989; Crawford & Marecek, 1989a, 1989b [included in this book]; Deaux, 1984; Eichenbaum & Orbach, 1983; Fine & Gordon, 1989; Grady, 1981; Henley, 1985; H. Lerner, 1989; Lewin, 1984; Lott, 1985; Marecek, 1989; Torrey, 1987; Wallston, 1981; Wallston & Grady, 1985 [included in this book]).

Despite this burgeoning scholarship, the task of re-placing women in psychology remains a daunting one. Two problems continue to hamper our efforts. First, relevant work that might provide a theoretical scaffolding for the reconstructive effort is scattered throughout the psychological and feminist literature, appearing in a variety of journals, books, and conference proceedings and addressed to a variety of constituencies. Ready access to this literature is hampered by such diversity, even as that same diversity represents a major strength of the work.

Second, efforts toward re-placing women in psychology presently lack an explicit overarching conceptual synthesis to join the assortment of writings into a unitary body of scholarship. The fundamental hindrance to incorporating women, women's perspective, and women's work resides in the fact that psychology's self-definition, the discipline's own understanding of its substance and its processes, is grounded in assumptions that by their very nature act to marginalize women, a topic that will be elaborated at length as the book proceeds. Without an alternative theoretical foundation, efforts at re-placing women lack the coherence necessary for a thoroughgoing, women-inclusive re-vision of psychology.

This book proposes such an alternative, a model that attempts to make sense of women's place in psychology, including their invisibility. To achieve this re-viewing of psychology, the book offers a synthesis of the insights of feminist psychology with postmodernist views of knowledge, as reflected in social constructionism and concepts from historiography. From this perspective, women's place is seen as a product of two constructions (two understandings of "truth" or reality): the understanding (or construction) of gender within the society as a whole and the changing self-definition (or construction) of the discipline. The intersection of these two constructions is seen as creating the space that women have filled in psychology (Bohan, 1990).

The organization of the book provides the elements of this model. The reader will become acquainted with the basic principles of constructionism and will then explore their application to the question of women's place in and impact upon psychology. The Prologue outlines the constructionist model; the readings that follow have been selected to represent and elaborate upon the central points raised in the Prologue. These readings are organized into four parts, each part representing one element in the structure suggested by the book's conceptual model. The first part raises the issue at hand: psychology has consistently marginalized women— women's issues, women's experience, and women's work. The second group of readings introduces a social constructionist model as a tool for understanding the source and impact of this exclusion. The last two parts then apply the constructionist perspective to explore issues of gender in psychology and to ask what are the consequences for the discipline and for women of this process of re-placing women in psychology. The material thus moves in a sequence that parallels the arguments introduced in the Prologue. In addition, readings within each part are presented in chronological sequence in order to convey a sense of the process by which ideas and worldviews change—a working illustration of the construction of reality, itself embedded in these discussions of constructionism.

References

Bohan, Janis S. (1990). Contextual history: A framework for re-placing women in the history of psychology. *Psychology of Women Quarterly, 14,* 213–227.

Bohan, Janis S. (Ed.) (1992). *Re-placing women in psychology: Readings toward a more inclusive history.* Dubuque, IA: Kendall/Hunt.

Bohan, Janis S. (1992). "The Women of Psychology": Making women a matter of course. *Women's Studies Quarterly, 20* (1 & 2), 59–69.

Bronstein, Phyllis A., & Quina, Kathryn. (Eds.). (1988). *Teaching a psychology of people: Resources for gender and sociocultural awareness.* Washington, DC: American Psychological Association.

Brown, Laura S. (1991). Ethical issues in feminist therapy. *Psychology of Women Quarterly, 15,* 323–336.

Burman, Erica. (Ed.). (1990). *Feminists and psychological practice.* London: Sage.

Caplan, Paula J. (1991). What's happening these days with the DSM? *Feminism and Psychology, 1,* 317–319.

Crawford, Mary, & Gentry, Margaret. (Eds.). (1989). *Gender and thought: Psychological perspectives.* New York: Springer-Verlag.

Crawford, Mary, & Marecek, Jeanne. (1989a). Feminist theory, feminist psychology: A bibliography of epistemology, critical analysis, and applications. *Psychology of Women Quarterly, 13,* 477–491.

Crawford, Mary, & Marecek, Jeanne. (1989b). Psychology reconstructs the female, 1968–1988. *Psychology of Women Quarterly, 13,* 147–165.

Deaux, Kay. (1984). From individual differences to social categories: Analysis of a decade's research on gender. *American Psychologist, 39,* 105–116.

Eichenbaum, Luise, & Orbach, Susie. (1983). *Understanding women: A feminist psychoanalytic approach.* New York: Basic Books.

Fine, Michelle. (1985). Reflections on a feminist psychology of women. *Psychology of Women Quarterly, 9,* 167–183.

Fine, Michelle, & Gordon, Susan M. (1989). Feminist transformations of/despite psychology. In Mary Crawford & Margaret Gentry (Eds.), *Gender and thought: Psychological perspectives* (pp. 146–174). New York: Springer-Verlag.

Freedman, Rita J., Golub, Sharon, & Krauss, Beatrice. (1982). Mainstreaming the psychology of women into the core curriculum. *Teaching of Psychology, 9,* 165–168.

Furumoto, Laurel. (1985). Placing women in the history of psychology course. *Teaching of Psychology, 12,* 203–206.

Furumoto, Laurel. (1988). The new history of psychology. *G. Stanely Hall Lectures* (vol. 9, pp. 9–34). Washington, DC: American Psychological Association.

Furumoto, Laurel, & Scarborough, Elizabeth. (1986). Placing women in the history of psychology: The first American women psychologists. *American Psychologist, 41,* 35–42.

Golub, Sharon, Freedman, Rita J., Krauss, Beatrice, Carpenter, Ronda, Quina, Kathryn, & Russo, Nancy F. (1983). *Resources for introducing psychology of women into the psychology core curriculum.* Washington, DC: American Psychological Association.

Grady, Kathleen. (1981). Sex bias in research design. *Psychology of Women Quarterly, 5,* 628–636.

Hare-Mustin, Rachel T., & Marecek, Jeanne. (1988). The meaning of difference: Gender theory, postmodernism, and psychology. *American Psychologist, 43,* 455–464.

Henley, Nancy M. (1985). Review: Psychology and gender. *Signs: Journal of Women in Culture and Society, 11,* 101–119.

Lerner, Gerda. (1979). *The majority finds its past: Placing women in history.* New York: Oxford University Press.

Lerner, Harriet. (1989). *Women in therapy: Visions and revisions.* New York: Harper & Row.

Lewin, Miriam. (1984). *In the shadow of the past: Psychology portrays the sexes.* New York: Columbia University Press.

Lott, Bernice. (1985). The potential enrichment of social/personality psychology through feminist research and vice versa. *American Psychologist, 40,* 155–164.

Lykes, M. Brinton, & Stewart, Abigail. (1986). Evaluating the feminist challenge to research in personality and social psychology: 1963–1983. *Psychology of Women Quarterly, 10,* 393–412.

Marecek, Jeanne. (Ed.). (1989). Theory and method in feminist psychology [special issue]. *Psychology of Women Quarterly, 13*(4).

Moke, Pamela, & Bohan, Janis S. (1992). Re-constructing curriculum: Psychology's paradigm and the virtues of iconoclasm. *Women's Studies Quarterly, 20* (1 & 2), 7–27.

O'Connell, Agnes N., & Russo, Nancy F. (Eds.). (1980). Eminent women in psychology: Models of achievement [special issue]. *Psychology of Women Quarterly, 5*(1).

O'Connell, Agnes N., & Russo, Nancy F. (1983). *Models of achievement: Reflections of eminent women in psychology.* New York: Columbia University Press.

O'Connell, Agnes N., & Russo, Nancy F. (1988). *Models of achievement: Reflections of eminent women in psychology,* vol. 2. Hillsdale, NJ: Lawrence Erlbaum.

O'Connell, Agnes N., & Russo, Nancy F. (1990). *Women in psychology: A bio-bibliographic sourcebook.* New York: Greenwood.

Ostertag, Patricia A., & McNamara, J. Regis. (1991). "Feminization" of psychology: The changing sex ratio and its implications for the profession. *Psychology of Women Quarterly, 15,* 349–369.

Russo, Nancy F., & Denmark, Florence L. (1987). Contributions of women to psychology. *Annual Review of Psychology, 38,* 279–298.

Scarborough, Elizabeth, & Furumoto, Laurel. (1987). *Untold lives: The first generation of American women psychologists.* New York: Columbia University Press.

Torrey, Jane W. (1987). Phases of feminist re-vision in the psychology of personality. *Teaching of Psychology, 14,* 155–160.

Walker, Lenore E. (1991). The feminization of psychology. *Psychology of Women: Newsletter of APA Division 35, 18*(2), 1, 4.

Wallston, Barbara S. (1981). What are the questions in the psychology of women? A feminist approach to research. *Psychology of Women Quarterly, 5,* 597–617.

Wallston, Barbara S., & Grady, Kathleen. (1985). Integrating the feminist critique and the crisis in social psychology: Another look at research methods. In Virginia E. O'Leary, Rhoda K. Unger, & Barbara S. Wallston (Eds.), *Women, gender, and social psychology* (pp. 7–33). Hillsdale, NJ: Lawrence Erlbaum.

Wine, Jeri D. (1982). Gynocentric values and feminist psychology. In Angela R. Miles & Geraldine Finn (Eds.), *Feminism in Canada: From pressure to politics* (pp. 67–87). Montreal: Black Rose.

1

PROLOGUE: RE-VIEWING PSYCHOLOGY, RE-PLACING WOMEN—AN END SEARCHING FOR A MEANS

In order to create a conceptual foundation for understanding women's relationship to the discipline, I will explore in this Prologue the connections among three domains of thought: feminist psychology, social constructionism, and historiography. The understanding of women's place in psychology that derives from this merger will allow us to enter into the reconstructive process of considering what a women-inclusive psychology will/should look like.

This book begins with a recognition that psychology has not treated women well. I refer in part but not solely to the neglect of and discrimination against women in the field's theory, research, and practice (e.g., Brodksy, 1980; Grady, 1981; Hare-Mustin, 1983; H. Lerner, 1989; Lewin, 1984; Lott, 1985a; Newman, 1985; Sherif, 1979a; Squire, 1989; Weisstein, 1968, 1971). I refer as well to the neglect of women and their work practiced by the discipline itself: women's invisibility in psychology's histories (e.g., Bohan, 1990a, 1992; Denmark, 1980; O'Connell & Russo, 1980, 1990; Stevens & Gardner, 1982), the neglect of women's research and theoretical work (e.g., Bronstein & Quina, 1988; Fine, 1985; Lykes & Stewart, 1986), the persistent paucity of women among the higher ranks of faculty and the discipline's power elite (Ostertag & McNamara, 1991; Russo & Denmark, 1987; Walker, 1991), and the discounting of the potentially paradigmatic impact of feminist challenges to psychology's fundamental assumptions and practices (e.g., Fine & Gordon, 1989; K. Gergen, 1985; M. Gergen, 1988; Marecek, 1989; Moke & Bohan, 1992; Squire, 1989; Wine, 1982).

Although such disregard has been well documented, it is appropriate to consider the scope and magnitude of its impact as a starting point for this book. The first group of readings contains pivotal and often provocative works that have called attention to the problem, illuminating the extent of the distortion caused by the mis-representation (in both senses of that word) of women in/by psychology. The questions that emerge from this literature are crucial and legion: How did this occur? Why has women's invisibility been itself invisible to the discipline (historically, even to most of the discipline's women)? And how do we proceed radically to dismantle the foundations of this neglect and replace them with under-girding more hospitable to women? What does such a reconstruction require and what will it engender? It is questions such as these that we must confront if our efforts are to transform psychology. How, in short, can we make sense both of women's invisibility and of the project to develop a women-inclusive psychology?

The avowed goal of this book is to *re-place* women[1] in psychology— that is, to make visible the place they have always held. As the extent of the literature sampled here testifies, that task entails far more than simply adding women to the existing content of psychology's subject matter, the range of its theories, the variety of its methods, the nature of its practice, and the personages of its histories. The approach to re-placement sug-gested here is grounded in my certainty that a thorough integration of women must involve a fundamentally altered perspective on the field and on history. This assumption, and hence the approach proffered here, is informed in part by historian Gerda Lerner's model for the construction of a historical narrative that includes women.

Gerda Lerner (1979) delineated three stages in the placement (or re-placement) of women in history. In the first two stages, which Lerner dubs "compensatory" and "contribution" history, women's inclusion is predi-cated upon their relationship to dominant (male-defined) conceptions of what is important to history. These "add women and stir" approaches, which homogenize women and their work into the existent blend of historical discussion, are necessary initial steps but are inadequate to the comprehensive integration of women into history. In order to appreciate fully women's role in and importance to history, Lerner averred, it is essential to transcend these forms of history and to assume a stance from which history is viewed through the lens of women's distinctive experi-ence, focusing on that experience as crucial to an adequate depiction of history. An understanding of women's place in the history of psychology, pursued from Lerner's women-focused perspective, requires not simply the addition of the names and works of important women to the litany of this field's "great men," in Boring's (1950b) revealing usage. It demands, rather, that we seek to understand why women's place in the discipline has been as it has *from the point of view of women's experience.*

Lerner's challenge provides a basis for the approach offered here, where re-placing women in psychology is grounded in the primacy of women's experience. The conclusion suggested by this model is that we can make sense of women's place in psychology (including their invisibility) by recognizing and explicating the manner in which women's experience has formed a unique context, shaping their relationship to the field of psychology throughout its history. By extension, a sensible re-placement of women is also possible if that effort derives from the realization that women's context is central to the determination of their place in psychology.

This effort at re-placing women, then, requires two elements. First, it demands an understanding of the centrality of context as it underpins the construction of knowledge, of history, and of the field of psychology itself. Second, it requires an awareness of the relevant contexts that have shaped those constructions, in this case the (constructed) history of (a constructed) psychology as seen from women's perspective. My aim in this Prologue is to outline these elements and their relationship to each other.

Social Constructionism and Contextual History

For the moment, let us take as given that women have been rendered invisible to mainstream psychology by a complex array of social, historical, and professional circumstances. Given this reality, is it possible to look beyond principles explaining each of those circumstances to discover a metatheory that makes sense of the overall pattern of dynamics that has shaped women's place in psychology? Such a metatheory would have to explain the nature of psychology itself in regard to women, insofar as qualities endemic to the discipline have conjoined with external forces in the marginalization of its women. It would also have to explain the impact on psychology (as a discipline and as a community of individuals) of broader sociohistorical circumstances that have contributed to women's invisibility. And it would have to explain why those many tiers of influence have, for long periods and even among women, been invisible to the very people whose understandings were shaped by them—namely, psychologists themselves. Social constructionism provides such a metatheory, a set of concepts that can support our efforts. I offer here a brief introduction to those concepts; subsequent readings will concentrate on certain elements of the overall approach, progressively reinforcing its utility in the process of understanding women's relationship to psychology.

The Critique of Positivism

Roughly contemporaneous with the belated acknowledgment of the need to re-place women in psychology as in other disciplines, recent scholarship in epistemology, historiography, and the sociology of knowledge has brought into question traditional conceptions of the philosophy and history of science in general, as well as their application to psychology. These challenges, while disorienting because of their disruption of long-held and comfortable presuppositions, are nevertheless exhilarating because of the promise they hold of restructuring psychology and in the process creating an understanding of how women and their work might be properly integrated. Among the most cogent criticisms of traditional (modernist) conceptions of knowledge are the following:

The Inadequacy of Sensory Knowledge. The modernist, Western conception of science has held that knowledge of truth can be gained by sensory means, through objective observation. The accuracy and utility of our understanding, according to this view, depend upon the assiduous application of well-defined methods, designed to ensure the precision and objectivity of such observation. These assumptions, which are fundamental to our conception of the scientific method, remain the explicit (if unexamined) cornerstone of psychology's epistemological base, despite centuries-old challenges from the philosophy of science.

Critics of this epistemological position have argued that knowledge (if by that is meant absolute and certain apprehension of the nature of reality) cannot be achieved by sensory means. There can be no "objective observation," no "raw data" when human knowledge is always and inevitably filtered through multiple layers of perception and cognition, each level of which can be demonstrated to be subject to distortion. Nevertheless, nineteenth-century science rested on an epistemology termed *positivism*, which asserts that only that which can be affirmed with absolute certainty may be accepted as knowledge and that scientific observation is the only sure route to certain (or apodictic) knowledge (Polkinghorne, 1983).

The natural sciences initially embraced with eagerness this conception of truth as accessible to observation, and psychology followed, joining in what Gergen termed "the dance of scientific respectability" (1976, p. 374), captured in its self-conscious attempt to ally itself with those sciences and thus to share in their advancing prestige. Ironically, this philosophy of science, dominant in the nineteenth century as psychology emerged, was soon to be rejected by the very sciences psychology chose to emulate. "Psychology," asserted Koch, "still bases its understanding of vital questions of method on an extrinsic philosophy of science which . . . is twenty years or more out of date" (1959, p. 787), an observation that suggests that our steadfast adherence to the positivist prescription now places the discipline a full half century behind the epistemological times.

Context Stripping: The Constriction of Vision. Those who question the appropriateness of positivism as the foundational epistemology for psychology urge that the strictures imposed by this epistemology inevitably limit psychology's vision and its usefulness. Psychology's adherence to the positivist agenda (in truth, a very simplistic and misrepresented version of positivism at that, as we shall see) has dictated the discipline's subject matter, the scope and definition of acceptable questions, the range of its methodology, and the nature of interpretations and applications generated by psychological theory and research (Crawford & Marecek, 1989b; Giorgi, 1971; Koch, 1981; McGuire, 1973; Morawski, 1985a, 1988; Toulmin & Leary, 1985; Unger, 1983, 1988). In attempting to model its methods after the natural sciences, positivist psychology has selected as topics for investigation only those that are amenable to atomistic analysis and direct observation; where salient variables can be isolated, operationally defined, and systematically manipulated; and where results of such manipulation can be expressed in quantitative terms and subjected to statistical analysis. Questions that do not meet these criteria are deemed meaningless (as opposed to empirically testable, this terminology a legacy of logical positivism). Yet, the most intensely meaningful (in the sense of important, crucial) questions cannot be accommodated by this conceptual procrustean bed and are therefore dismissed as inappropriate for psychological inquiry.

In an attempt to fit complex human questions to the demands of the positivist model, experimental procedures are specifically designed to strip context (Crawford & Marecek, 1989b; Mishler, 1976). The intent is to eliminate the effects of all but the variables of interest, deeming all others confounding or contaminating ("nuisance" variables, which, as Unger [1983] pointed out, are extraneous only insofar as they are not the variables central to the current investigation).

The impact of context stripping reaches beyond research design to mold psychological theory as well. The disregard for (even intentional elimination of) context has fostered an unquestioning acceptance of person-blame explanations, which take the individual as the unit of analysis. Such explanations locate the determinants of human behavior and experience within the person rather than in the context of behavior, thus blinding psychology to the pervasive impact of contextual forces on human experience (cf. Albee, 1986; Caplan & Nelson, 1973; Fine, 1985; Mednick, 1989; Prilleltensky, 1989; Sampson, 1990; Squire, 1989; West & Zimmerman, 1987). As a result of this penchant for context stripping, the reality of human experience—namely, that it always occurs in context, is always framed by a plethora of fluid and ill-defined borders—is lost.

Thus, psychology has selected its topics, methods, interpretations, and applications for their compatibility with the demands of positivist epistemology, whether or not they contribute to a richer understanding of human experience. In Koch's apt words, the "stipulation that psychology be adequate to *science* outweighed [the] commitment that it be adequate to [humanity]. . . . Respectability held more glamour than insight, caution than curiosity, feasibility than fidelity and fruitfulness" (1959, p. 783).

The repercussions of this epistemological myopia, reflected on both methodological and theoretical planes, extend beyond its direct impact on the discipline. Caplan and Nelson (1973) argued cogently that our obsession with methodology has created a discipline whose primary goal is the application of techniques rather than the investigation of issues of genuine import to our understanding of human behavior and experience. Compelling human questions are inevitably excluded from consideration by a psychology that so rigidly defines the narrow boundaries of its subject matter and method (cf. Sampson, 1990). Hence, psychology's actual and potential impact on the betterment of the human condition has been severely delimited by this methodological tunnel vision. In a particularly literary passage, McGuire conveyed his dismay that "in our unholy determination to confront reality and put our theory to the test of nature, we have plunged through reality, like Alice through the mirror, into a never-never land in which we contemplate not life but data" (1973, p. 453).

The Denial of Values. Despite the positivist insistence to the contrary, critics argue, science is not and cannot be value-free—indeed, it should not be. Science, being a human endeavor, is unavoidably infused with the values questions that are an inextricable part of human experience and that therefore permeate scientific institutions and activities. Howard (1985) drew a distinction between two sets of values that might influence scientific endeavor: epistemic and nonepistemic values. In a feminist variation on this theme, Longino (1983, 1986) differentiated between constitutive and contextual values. Nonepistemic, or contextual, values are those issues commonly inferred from the term "values," entailing what are essentially ethical issues that reflect personal, social, and cultural preferences. Epistemic, or constitutive, values, on the other hand, are concerned precisely with the business of science and involve judgments about "right" ways of attaining knowledge: which methods are to be valued as legitimate techniques for ferreting out truth, which theories meet the criterion of "good" fit to understood reality, and so forth. Positivism dictates that although nonepistemic, or contextual, values contribute to problem selection, they play no role in the proper conduct of scientific inquiry.

Those who question the positivist ideal of value-free science contend that science (particularly social science) is unavoidably infused with both epistemic and nonepistemic values. Positivist assumptions notwithstanding, nonepistemic, or contextual, values are clearly implicated in every stage of scientific endeavor. Quite apparently, the very act of asking certain questions and not others reveals the researcher's values. "There can be no such thing as disinterested research," Myrdal asserted; "there are no answers except to questions" (1969, pp. 160–161).

Even presumably epistemic, or constitutive, judgments, the critique continues, are intertwined with nonepistemic values. The methods adopted by science reveal assumptions about reality and about human nature. The terms selected, the structure of explanatory language, the interpretations offered, explicit and implicit suggestions for applications—all reveal perspectives that can only be viewed as value-laden. Marecek concisely summarized the point: "A method is an interpretation" (1989, p. 370). (See also Buss, 1975; Crawford & Marecek, 1989b; McHugh, Koeske, & Frieze, 1986; Sampson, 1983; Unger, 1983; Wallston, 1981.)

As illustrative of the unacknowledged values that suffuse psychological concepts, consider the following: To ask a question about gender differences implies that such differences, should they exist, are of import. To select a method that stresses experimental control and quantitative measures implies that human behavior can be viewed from the atomistic stance that isolates variables without thereby affecting the whole of the phenomenon under study. To choose to measure dysphoria and interpersonal stress as indices of PMS reflects the implicit assumption that women's biological cycles correspond only to negative psychological states (or do not correspond to them; the point is the same). To study the family structure of poor (but not of wealthy) families reveals underlying assumptions as to who constitutes the "problem population" in need of attention. To choose interventions that minimize gender differences where they occur (assertiveness training for women, for example) discloses the tacit belief that gender differences (if indeed they exist at all) are in need of correction, and in this as in most cases, that it is women who must change to "correct" the difference. To take the self-contained individual as psychology's subject matter excuses psychologists from addressing needed social change.

Failure to recognize the inevitable valuation implicit in scientific endeavor results in distortions of the process, the outcome, and the uses of psychology. For the issue is partly but not solely that values inescapably shape human life, for the psychologist as for the subject. The converse is also true: science shapes human values and human lives as well. This dialectic interplay of unacknowledged values is dramatically clear in psychology, where description and prescription are inextricably linked. An apparently straightforward psychological description of what "is" implies, by virtue of the tacit values embodied in this description, what "should be." That prescription, in turn, influences social behavior (cf. Buss, 1975; Caplan & Nelson, 1973; Gergen, 1973, 1976, 1979; Giorgi, 1970; Kahn & Yoder, 1989). To illustrate, note how readily discernible are the values (and hence the prescriptions) underlying such psychological constructs as ego strength, self-esteem, locus of control, and conformity.

Objectivity as Separation. Finally, the challenge to psychology's traditional epistemology continues, positivism imposes a demand for objectivity that is unattainable. Objectivity, in the positivist construal, derives from a separation between the knower (the psychologist) and the object (in psychology, the "subject"), such that the knower and the object are considered as entirely separate and independently functioning events (see Morawski, 1985a, for a discussion of psychology's construction of this subject-as-object). Implied here is the assumption that the psychologist is untouched by any qualities of the subject, that the subject is unchanged by the process of being observed, and that the psychologist has control of the situation (including the subject) so that all extraneous variables (including the researcher's own troublesome subjectivity) can be eliminated or technically managed.

Critics of this perspective insist that science, especially the human sciences, cannot be "objective" in this sense. Indeed, this assumption of subject-object duality cannot be upheld in the natural sciences regardless of the nature of the object under study; even in physics, the Heisenberg uncertainty principle vitiates any notion of an objective observer operating separately from the object of observation. In the human sciences, this duality, this presumed separation between scientist and subject/object, disregards the unavoidable relationship between the two, wherein the psychologist and the subject mutually and reciprocally influence each other. Human subjects share with human psychologists human traits, and psychologists are perforce both the subject and the object of their own understandings.

Among the principles that psychologists must turn back upon themselves is the very fact of human subjectivity. Psychologists cannot, by definition, be objective about (in the sense of separated from) experiences that are their own as much as they are those of the subject/object. Gender is a prime example: no one, neither psychologist nor subject, can be separate from the meaning and impact of gender and the issues it raises in her or his own life. Conversely, human subjects cannot remain untouched by the process of observation. Humans are not objects without awareness but sentient beings cognizant both of their place as objects of study and of their relationship with the researcher.

When psychology attempts to manage methodologically the discomforting reality of the psychologist's subjectivity (through double-blind designs, measures of interrater reliability, and so on), we revert to a stripping of context. The reality left unacknowledged by such methodological gimmickry is that human beings behave differently, experience reality differently, when observed and when observing; context matters, and eliminating it changes things. To excise that fact from our descriptions of human experience is to abstract a context-free, and therefore barren and misleading, depiction of that experience.

Squire (1989) argued that psychology has avoided the difficulties inherent in using subjective individuals to study the subjective experiences of others by disregarding this fundamental philosophical dilemma. Instead, we have elaborated techniques and invoked arguments of scientific objectivity to erase from view the inescapable paradox. This strategy, however, is doomed as soon as it is exposed. The ultimate mutuality and reflectivity of human experience are unavoidable adjuncts to psychological knowledge; in their face, suggestions of "objective" psychology are rendered meaningless (Gadlin & Ingle, 1975; Sampson, 1981; Squire, 1989; Zaner, 1985).

To admit to the impossibility of objectivity in this dualistic sense is not to abdicate rationality. On the contrary, clinging to the belief that such objectivity is possible inhibits the search for rational understanding. By taking into account our inevitable subjectivity, we are empowered to use it in a productive manner; it becomes a conscious and intentional component to our constructions of knowledge rather than an unrecognized, and therefore potentially an insidiously forceful, contaminant to our understanding. Conceptualizing objectivity as intersubjectivity (Fee, 1981; Keller, 1980), for instance, provides a view of knowledge that affirms both the inevitability of human subjectivity and the merits of shared criteria for knowledge.

In combination, the deficiencies of the positivist paradigm must lead us to question the merits of this epistemology as a means of coming to know. Indeed, it seems clear from these arguments that it is simply not possible, as positivism would have it, to discover an externally existing truth, one residing outside of values, untouched by method, known objectively by a disinterested scientist. And a psychology that aims to do so is at the mercy of unexamined values and unacknowledged subjectivity.

Positivism and the Exclusion of Women

While limiting to psychology as a whole, the tenets of positivism outlined above have had particular salience in defining women's place in psychology. The assumptions that give form to positivist psychology suffuse all realms of psychological endeavor. If we analyze these assumptions, searching for their impact on women, we discover that they embody beliefs and generate practices that have served specifically to marginalize women in the discipline (Bohan, 1991a). Let me briefly discuss each in turn, unpacking the often subtle exclusionary elements contained therein.

Context Stripping. The denial of context entailed by the positivist paradigm supports a belief that science operates in a sociohistorical vacuum and that psychology itself is free from contextual influences. The failure to attend to the social, political, and economic context that pervades and surrounds psychology has allowed us to disregard the myriad ways in which those forces have precluded women's greater participation and visibility in the discipline (Bohan, 1990a; O'Connell & Russo, 1983, 1988; Scarborough & Furumoto, 1987). Psychology operating in vacuo needn't concern itself with sexism in the broader society, for such events are not believed capable of penetrating the barrier of scientific purity.

Further, in contrast to the atomistic, decontextualized stance of positivism, the topic areas that have been and continue to be of paramount importance to a disproportionate percentage of women in psychology are by their very nature complex, contextually grounded concerns. The construction of gender has consigned women to roles that are interpersonal in nature, and this relational focus is reflected in their roles in psychology. Women have been primarily involved with psychological topics focusing on relationships, on social systems, and on complex events shaping human experience (O'Connell & Russo, 1983, 1988; Russo & Denmark, 1987; Scarborough & Furumoto, 1987). How, one might ask, does one address in the laboratory questions about institutionalized sexism; about the impact of society's tolerance for violence against women; about the complex interactions within the family, which is inherently a complex, context-dependent social system? Precisely because the issues that have occupied women are at base contextual ones, context stripping has had a marginalizing effect on women. Stripping psychology of context results in stripping psychology of much of women's work.

Even work in the psychology of women (indeed, even some psychology intended to support feminist aims) has not been immune to the consequences of psychology's penchant for disregarding context. In particular, feminist psychology has often embraced the discipline's predilection for invoking internal dynamics to explain psychological phenomena, thereby minimizing attention to the power of context. This identification with a person-blame orientation has resulted in theoretical explanations and research interpretations focusing on individual responsibility and intrapsychic attributions and has thereby failed to grant adequate importance to the contexts defining women's reality, including the androcentric biases that shape social experience (Bohan, in press; Crawford & Marecek, 1989b; Fine, 1985; Kahn & Yoder, 1989; Lott, 1981, 1988; Squire, 1989; Westkott, 1988; Wine, 1982). Thus we see that even those striving to review gender find themselves enmeshed in the implicit assumptions of the disciplinary paradigm.

Denial of Values. The refusal to acknowledge that science (psychology) is value-laden has allowed psychologists to cling to the perception that psychology is a value-free endeavor, that the outcome of science is the factual representation of reality. If women's work or women as individuals were of consequence, the argument continues, the value-free science of psychology would surely have recognized and acknowledged that fact. The widespread belief in this myth of meritocracy provides a piece to the puzzle of women's own historical failure to recognize and confront their marginalization. Convinced (by their positivist education) that psychology was value-neutral, women could easily take their invisibility as an accurate reflection of their contributions rather than as a value-based distortion derived from positivist values incompatible with their work and aims. The refusal to acknowledge psychology's ineradicable valuing has acted to excuse the discipline from confronting the difficult values issues that are in fact raised by psychological research, among them issues of sexism, racism, and classism and the role of psychology in maintaining those institutions (cf. Caplan & Nelson, 1973; Kahn & Yoder, 1989; Prilleltensky, 1989; Wine, 1982).

Gendered constructs in psychology are clearly among the concepts that bear prescriptive as well as descriptive weight. Consider the explicit evaluative connotations of the older notion of sex role appropriateness, taken as a worthy goal (Spence, 1981), and the measurement of masculinity and femininity as if they were actual and estimable qualities of the individual (Morawski, 1985b). Similarly, judgments regarding optimal functioning permeate such recent constructs as androgyny (Hare-Mustin & Marecek, 1988; Lott, 1988; Mednick, 1989; Sherif, 1979b), fear of success (Kahn & Yoder, 1989; Mednick, 1989; Sassen, 1980; Spence, 1981), and essentialist views represented by concepts such as "cultural feminism" (Bohan, 1991b, in press; Broughton, 1983; Friedman, Robinson, & Friedman, 1987; Hare-Mustin & Marecek, 1988; Kahn & Yoder, 1989; Kerber et al., 1986; Lott, 1988, 1990; Mednick, 1989; Scott, 1988). Again, even concepts derived by women and initially intended as corrective to psychology's gender biases may conceal potentially adverse prescriptions.

Objectivity as Duality. The emphasis placed by the positivist model upon distancing, control, and the dispassionate consideration of the objectively observed facts of the matter has been challenged as an inherently "masculinist" way of knowing, neatly corresponding as it does with our construction of masculine gender: separateness (individuality, independence), control over self and environment, and a search for rational truth unimpeded by emotional distractions (e.g., Keller, 1985; Squire, 1989). This confounding of masculinity with objective knowing suggests that this (presented as the only legitimately scientific) way of knowing is not available to women. Further, it implies that knowledge gained from any other approach is not real science, hence, is not worthy knowledge. When nondualistic (connected) knowing is further identified as a distinctively "women's way of knowing" (e.g., Belenky et al., 1986)—again conflating gender and epistemology—the consequent genderization of knowledge marginalizes any knowledge developed by women.

Finally, and directly related to the invisibility of much of women's work in psychology, this valuing of objectivity as separation serves to exclude from accredited psychological knowledge the plethora of areas within the discipline where knowledge derives precisely and explicitly from connection rather than from separation. Not surprisingly, those are exactly the areas where women have predominated—the applied specialties in general, clinical practice in particular.

It appears then that the positivist model fails psychology on multiple grounds. It is insufficient as an explanation of the source and meaning of "knowledge," for it fails to account for certain undeniable aspects of human knowledge making. Positivism is further indicted by the exclusionary implications of its philosophical presuppositions, rendering it particularly inadequate if we aspire to a women-inclusive psychology.

The Social Construction of Knowledge

We must begin our work here, then, from a recognition that the epistemological paradigm that has underlain our discipline is inadequate to the task, is in fact obstructive to the development of a psychology where women are integral. In order to fashion such a psychology, we must first come to an alternative understanding of the meaning of knowledge, one that confronts the shortcomings of positivism and provides a new grounding for knowledge making, a foundation that embraces rather than excludes the reality and the meaning of women's presence in psychology.

The fusion of meanings that I hope to create here—a fusion among feminism, psychology, and epistemology—is based on a view of knowledge that provides such a foundation: social constructionism. This approach recognizes that reality cannot be directly and objectively apprehended and contends that what we take as knowledge is not in fact an objective description of a freestanding reality; rather, we construct models of "reality," which we then agree through social interchange to accept as knowledge. These conceptions of reality are at every stage constructed (rather than discovered) by truth seekers and by the process of truth seeking itself and are unavoidably influenced by the social context within which they are derived. Berger and Luckmann's (1967) treatise is foundational to this awareness; their conceptions are echoed in recent elaborations of social constructionism in psychology (e.g., Buss, 1975; Gergen, 1985; Hare-Mustin & Marecek, 1988; Morawski, 1984, 1985a, 1988; Sampson, 1983; Sarason, 1981; Scarr, 1985; Toulmin, 1982; Wittig, 1985). An excellent example of constructionism as applied to gender is found in Crawford and Marecek's (1989b) historical analysis of psychological treatments of gender. Their discussion, which incorporated much of the critique of psychological epistemology outlined here, pointed to an emerging perspective on women's issues that they termed a "transformationist" framework. This framework represents a clear constructionist analysis of gender issues in psychology.

From a perspective informed by constructionism, knowledge is inextricably bound up in context—the context of the object known, the context from which the knower acts, and the context shaping the process of knowledge making. Stark explained, "Ideas are engendered in, and grow out of, social interaction, and . . . they show, in their concrete content, the reflected image of the social reality within which they have come to life" (1958, p. 45).

Indeed, the very fact of psychology's foundational commitment to the positivist paradigm is illustrative of this process. Psychology's attachment to positivism is explicable by reference to sociohistorical context, being clearly a reflection of the elevated status of the natural sciences at the time that psychology's pioneers sought legitimation for their own new science. At the time, philosophy was declining in prestige and the natural sciences ascending; Charles Rosenberg (1976) likened the reverence accorded science in the nineteenth century to religious devotion. In order to achieve the position of prestige thus accorded to science, psychology aspired to a methodological association with the natural sciences, then operating from a positivist base. Thus, psychology's self-definition, the construction of psychology itself, was shaped by the then-dominant societal values, namely, the nineteenth century's devotion to science. A psychology established in another sociohistorical milieu might well have evolved a radically different self-definition, with substantive consequences for its theoretical and methodological allegiances.

Knowledge, then—or "whatever passes for knowledge," to quote Berger and Luckmann (1967, p. 3)—is socially constructed, created within the nexus of social interchange, and validated by its congruence with shared understandings. What is seen as a legitimate question and the terms in which the question is couched; which methods are deemed appropriate and adequate to address that question and how those are justified, administered, and assessed; how we interpret the process and the product of those methods; and the implications and applications of our conclusions—all these pieces of "knowledge" are suspended in a complex and mutable fabric of social interaction and social meaning.

The Role of Paradigms. Thomas Kuhn's (1970) pivotal work adds an important dimension to the constructionist view of science. Science, Kuhn argued, does not consist in the oft-idealized open and unrestrained search for knowledge, whose cumulative and linear progress leads to ever-closer approximations to truth. Rather, at every point in the scientific endeavor, scientists are embedded in social and cognitive structures that influence each step of their process.

For Kuhn, science proceeds within a paradigm, the dominant model or worldview of a given scientific community. Only those questions, methods, concepts, conclusions, and interpretations that are congruent with the fundamental assumptions of the paradigm can make sense to those enmeshed in its web of meaning; "true" is defined precisely in terms of coherence with this foundational perspective.

Scientists operate as a community (defined by a shared paradigm), wherein novitiate members of the discipline are socialized into the world-view of their future profession through an educational process whose primary raison d'être consists in communicating the parameters of the accepted paradigm to fledgling members of the community. Once thus initiated, each scientist operates within this worldview, not seeing it as a peculiar worldview at all but rather as self-evident truth.

From this point of view, what science "knows" can only mean that which a given scientific community at a given time accepts as truth within its currently dominant paradigm and which it therefore passes on as truth through the process of educating new members of the profession. Kuhn (1970) suggested that it is only when gross or multiple anomalies occur, items that simply cannot be accommodated by the existing paradigm, that a sense of disquiet emerges, and scientists begin to view the paradigm itself as an object of study rather than as the very basis from which their work emanates. If another paradigm presents itself, one that can make sense of these anomalies and that also promises (though it may not immediately provide) resolution of other important problems, a scientific revolution may ensue, culminating in a paradigm shift that renders all previous questions, methods, and answers suspect and that provides a new model within which "normal" (i.e., paradigmatic) science can again proceed.

A paradigm serves a positive and constructive function for a science, acting as it does to encourage the continuing and progressively refined pursuit of knowledge through further articulation of the paradigm. Precisely because it offers a structure within which to do science, the existence of such a framework facilitates the systematic and detailed elaboration of the accepted paradigm, thus rendering anomalies strikingly apparent. But a paradigm also acts to constrain the unbridled search for truth by constricting the scope of acceptable topics, methods, and interpretations, limiting them to those compatible with the extant paradigm.

Psychology as Paradigmatic. I have suggested here that psychology operates within a paradigm, grounded in its acceptance of positivist epistemology, which in turn generates a particular construal of reality as well as determining the discipline's subject matter and methodology. Although some writers have concurred with this judgment (e.g., Buss, 1975, 1978; Gergen, 1985; Giorgi, 1970; Sampson, 1978; Unger, 1983), others have argued that psychology is preparadigmatic, having not yet attained the scientific maturity requisite to the achievement of a discipline-wide paradigm. Kuhn (1970) himself suggested that the social sciences as a group are preparadigmatic. Psychology, this latter position asserts, has no clearly defined and broadly accepted set of basic principles that define the nature and scope of the discipline (e.g., Koch, 1969; Schultz & Schultz, 1987), which to Kuhn constitutes the hallmark of a paradigmatic science.

A reconciliation of these views can be found in the work of Laudan (1984), who suggested that paradigms need not necessarily function holistically; rather, methodological aspects of a paradigm may operate separately from conceptual or theoretical components. Psychology, from this point of view, might adhere to an epistemological paradigm even in the absence of a universally accepted paradigm delineating the discipline's subject matter and theoretical alliances. If we apply this analysis to psychology, the discipline's allegiance to positivism indeed reveals an implicit paradigmatic commitment. Although the paradigm may be on the face of it solely a methodological one, method in fact shapes concepts and theories as well. Thus, psychology's positivist paradigm molds all phases of the discipline's activity, as we shall see.

The contention that psychology is indeed based on a paradigm—a positivist one—is bolstered by arguments pointing to the manifestations within psychology of the inherently limiting nature of paradigmatic "normal" science, as discussed by Kuhn. In psychology, the presence of such a narrow definition of the field is revealed in the charge that psychology's slavish adherence to positivist methodology has constrained its subject matter and its methods. This concern, elaborated above, suggests exactly a situation described by Kuhn, where unquestioned assumptions have directed the discipline, assumptions taken by its members not as one of many potential worldviews but as obvious "truth"—in this case, as the one legitimate epistemology.

Also evident in psychology is the preeminent role granted to the educational process, which serves within a paradigmatic discipline to socialize future members of the profession to a tacit acceptance of the worldview held by its members. Again, the paradigm that emerges when we apply this criterion to psychology is the positivist-empiricist model that underlies psychology's every effort. It has been argued that the espoused goal of psychological education is precisely indoctrination into the discipline's positivist-empiricist paradigm. This process of socialization begins with the introductory course, whose major aim, in Bakan's words, has been "to impress students with the possibility of a so-called scientific psychology" (1977, p. 228). Gergen agreed: "From the introductory text to the advanced handbook, this commitment [to positivist empiricism] is restated with unrelenting constancy" (1979, p. 197). Friedrich unselfconsciously asserted that "a primary goal in most introductory psychology courses is teaching students to view psychology as a science" (1990, p. 20) and presented a technique for recruiting students to this view, explaining his approach in terms of "teaching and persuasion in the classroom" (1990, p. 22). His use of the word "persuasion" is exactly in keeping with Kuhn's assertion that recruitment to a paradigm is accomplished by persuasion rather than by proof of its validity.

Paradigms and Social Constructionism. Kuhn (1970) argued that developments within science are largely free of external, societal influences. This "internalist" perspective (Wertheimer, 1980) is one now open to widespread criticisms from the sociology of knowledge. Cohen (1973), for example, argued that Kuhn's failure to recognize the dialectic interplay between science and society vitiates his depiction of paradigm shifts in science, for it fails to acknowledge either the impact of socially defined worldviews on the emergence and acceptance of a new scientific paradigm or the reciprocal consequences of scientific paradigms for the society in which their interpretations and their products are promulgated.

It is possible, however, to merge the internalist perspective, which views paradigms as operative within a scientific community, with the "externalist" view (Wertheimer, 1980), which proposes a continual dialectical exchange between science and society. Social constructionism as presented here asserts, in keeping with (internalist) Kuhnian thought, that what we take as knowledge is constrained by the parameters of supposed truth (the paradigm) embraced by the professional community in which that supposed knowledge is generated, from which it takes its legitimacy, and education into which is the guarantor of adherence to the dominant paradigm. In keeping with (externalist) arguments from the sociology of knowledge, the community that shapes and defines knowledge is here seen as extending beyond the scientific community to include also the broader social and historical milieu within which the scientist (and her or his professional community) operates. The scientist thus functions within a two-tiered social structure, an understanding of which Stark (1958) termed the micro- and macrosociology of knowledge, referring to the immediate professional and the broader cultural-historical systems, respectively. Although thoroughgoing positivist science would purport to be immune to such extrinsic influences, the scientist's (psychologist's) work is nonetheless demonstrably influenced by these forces.

History as Constructed. It is apparent that the principles presented above can be applied to historical narrative as effectively as to other forms of knowledge (Bohan, 1990b). From a constructionist perspective, the telling of history cannot be an unadorned presentation of past events. The initial impediment to history's being "factual" in this sense is that we cannot, by definition, know history directly. We have access not to historical happenings themselves but only to accounts from others who were present or to residual measures, such as concrete consequences of events. When we recognize that even those who actually experienced an event can only interpret (rather than know) what happened, even this most direct of historical information is seen to be constructed. Beyond this primary construction, as this initial interpretation is reported and recorded through time, history becomes ever more distant from actual events, ever more influenced by the particular biases acting upon the procurement and analysis of historical "data," inevitably influenced at every step by the personal and social context within which history is transmitted (cf. Collingwood, 1946; Harvey, 1965; Kuhn, 1977; Nowell-Smith, 1977; Stocking, 1965; Weinstein, 1988).

Historical narrative is constructed in a complex web of interrelated contexts. The historian is an individual with individual values; she or he is also a participant in a series of social networks, each of which exerts an influence on the construction of history. The professional community within which a historian works directs and shapes how history is written, acting through the medium of criteria for relevance, accuracy, and adequacy that are implicit in the profession's current paradigms (Kuhn, 1977). More broadly, the values of the society in which the historian works guide the selection, analysis, and interpretation of historical information. Simultaneously and in concert, the multifaceted context encompassed by the term *Zeitgeist* influences the particular construction of history offered and its acceptance by the larger community.

The Context of Psychological History. Furumoto's (1988) discussion of the need in psychology for critical history is expressly relevant here. Furumoto argued that psychology has lagged behind the natural sciences in its awareness of the need to recognize contextual forces that shape both the making and the telling of history. Furumoto issued a twofold charge to historians of psychology: to attend to context as it has shaped the events of psychology's past and to be sensitive to the contexts framing the creation of historical narratives.

Examples of each of these expressions of history's context-dependent nature will serve to illustrate the constructionist notion that historical knowledge is constructed knowledge. If we look first to our understanding of the events of psychology's past, we discover developments that can best be understood when viewed through a contextual lens. As an illustration of a critical contextual analysis of such events, we can re-view psychology's implementation of positivism, unpacking the apparently straightforward acceptance of a popular epistemology to discover the particular meanings it held for psychology. This process reveals that the conception of positivist science adopted by psychology—namely, that science is, can be, and should be value-free—is itself a distortion, comprehensible as a product of social construction.

Positivist philosophy had its roots in the work of Auguste Comte (1798–1857), who argued for a "positive" scientific philosophy intended to lead the world beyond the "negative" governmental and societal arrangements of his time. Far from urging a value-free science, this philosophy was in fact deeply value-infused. Beyond its explicit elitist recommendations for a cadre of scientist-leaders (reminiscent of Plato's "philosopher kings"), Comte's position contended that scientific enterprise must remain firmly anchored in and aspire to a religious or moral philosophy (Samelson, 1974). The vast separation between this original conception of positivist science and psychology's later understanding and application of positivism (now stripped of these explicit values) is remarkable testimony to the process by which ideas can be shaped to fit the context in which they are used. In this case, a narrow conception of positivist epistemology was disembodied from its valuational corpus in order more readily to meld with the societal and disciplinary milieu of the nineteenth- and twentieth-century science to which it has been applied. Psychology constructed a version of positivism in keeping with its own aims.

Another illustration will demonstrate the application of a critical analysis to Furumoto's second point, the manner in which contexts shape the development and transmission of historical knowledge. Recent scholarship has demonstrated how grave have been the misconceptions held by generations of psychologists regarding the work of Wilhelm Wundt, arguably considered to be psychology's founder. Wundt's research, theories, and prominent concerns were misrepresented by Edward Titchener, the primary medium for the introduction and espousal of Wundt's work in this country (Blumenthal, 1977; Danzinger, 1979; Leary, 1979). Titchener, an avowed Lockean empiricist, disregarded Wundt's phenomenological tendencies, purged Wundt's theory of the Kantian tradition to which Wundt himself had declared his allegiance, and ignored Wundt's social psychological interests in favor of a focus on controlled laboratory experimentation. This truncated version of Wundt's system is what Titchener presented to American psychology as the views of the master. Titchener's personal stance was buttressed by the overriding values both of his immediate professional community (psychology, striving to be science) and of the broader community (nineteenth-century America, enamored of science).

Further elaboration of this illustration also demonstrates the breadth of impact such an idiosyncratic construction can have. One of Titchener's devoted students was E. G. Boring, whose text, *A History of Experimental Psychology* (1950a), dedicated to Titchener, was for decades recognized as the most authoritative work in the field. Titchener's initial misrepresentation of Wundt was compounded by Boring's own agenda, which aimed to reaffirm and validate the merits of experimental psychology in the face of growing encroachment by applied specialties, a commitment revealed by the book's title (O'Donnell, 1979). Wundt's experimental work was compatible with this aim, but his phenomenological orientation and his social psychology were not. Hence, the vision of Wundt's system that shaped the new discipline of psychology in America was a personal and social construction, a depiction altered by the values and interests of one man and transmitted by another, both of whom operated in the context of a discipline, a society, and a historical time prone to accept this rendering as truth.

Social Constructionism and Psychology

In psychology, postpositivism as represented by the social constructionist approach has recently found a receptive audience among those disenchanted by the shortcomings of our commitment to positivism. Constructionism promises a more flexible approach to questions of epistemology and a broader view of the meaning of knowledge. The constructionist focus on context appeals to those who doubt the validity and the utility of constructs derived from the isolation of variables that do not, in fact, appear as isolated in actual human experience. The unavoidably value-laden character of psychology's subject matter has made appealing this avowal of science's inevitable valuing, and many have welcomed the opportunity to subject to scrutiny, rather than to circumvent, the values questions that pervade psychological topics. The recognition that objectivity is an illusion, particularly as it applies to psychology, is yet another challenging, if freeing, concession, for it demands that psychology and psychologists acknowledge the impact upon their work of their own human-ness, their own irrefutable subjectivity.

Feminist scholars have been among the most vocal critics of the modernist approach to knowledge (Crawford & Marecek, 1989a). Moved by the apparent inadequacy of traditional understandings in accounting for women's experience, feminists across the disciplines have actively confronted both the exclusionary (often misogynist) underpinnings of modernism and the flaws inherent in the application of a natural sciences epistemology to human questions.[2]

The critique of positivism afforded by constructionism is compelling. It resonates with the vague discontent that has long plagued psychology, particularly among those less convinced of psychology's need to be scientific in the modernist-positivist sense than of its call to be relevant to the human condition. Constructionism offers a new vision of knowledge; notions such as truth and historical fact cease to wield the power they possessed within a positivist worldview. In making knowledge less certain, less concretized, constructionism reveals the long-obscured possibility of diverse ways of knowing. And, of central importance here, to the degree that traditional ways of seeing reality and viewing psychology have effectively screened women from psychology's view, the promise of new forms of knowledge is invigorating. It is this flexibility, the openness to alternative modes of understanding, that renders the constructionist perspective so relevant to the process of reconstructing psychology and of re-writing history to incorporate women. Constructionism provides the opportunity and the conceptual tools for making sense of women's place in psychology to date and for constructing a women-inclusive psychology for the future.

Constructing Women's Context

Underlying the organization of this book is the suggestion that the construal of knowledge and of history proffered by the social constructionist perspective can be used as a framework for re-placing women in psychology. This application of constructionism focuses on the context created by women's experience vis-à-vis psychology, clarifying how this context has created and supported the distinctive place of women in the discipline throughout its history. Two broad domains of scholarship have direct relevance here. The first addresses psychology's beginnings and the question of women's place there; these early experiences, as seen from women's perspective, form the backdrop for the role that women have played in psychology's evolution. The second deals with the field's subsequent history, including both the historical events that have framed psychology's activities and the qualities inherent in psychology itself.

Psychology's Beginnings:
Where Were the Women?

American psychology was born around the turn of the century, a period that witnessed massive social change. Technology, thriving on the material success of the industrial revolution, stood as the model for progress; science, revered as the impressively successful infrastructure of technology, held the hope for a future of economic and social improvement.

The universities were growing apace, their direction diverging from the traditional focus on the classics toward modernized curricula addressing the demands of the new technology and emulating their esteemed model, the European (especially German) research university. Industrialization had ushered in not only new technologies but also (and of greatest relevance to women) changes in the function of the family and the activities of its members. These changes led, in turn, to alterations in the relations between the sexes and in the definition of their appropriate roles (Berkin & Norton, 1979; Bernard, 1979, 1981; Ehrenreich & English, 1978; G. Lerner, 1979; R. Rosenberg, 1976).

To re-create the context of women's experience as the beginning of psychology approached, we need only imagine living in a society where scientists implored a receptive public to understand "truths" such as these:

> Deficiency in reproductive power . . . can be reasonably attributed to the overtaxing of [women's] brains. (Spencer, 1867, p. 485)

> Some of the [intellectual] powers [that characterize women] are characteristic of . . . a past and lower state of civilization. The chief distinction in the intellectual powers of the two sexes is shown by man's attaining to a higher eminence, in whatever he takes up, than can woman. (Darwin, 1871, pp. 326–327)

> The "woman's rights movement" is an attempt to rear, by the process of "unnatural selection," a race of monstrosities—hostile alike to men, to normal women, to human society, and to the future development of our race. ("Biology," 1878, p. 213)

> All that is distinctly human is man; all that is truly woman is merely reproductive. (Allen, 1889, p. 263)

Such scientific wisdom was reinforced by the lay press: the *Saturday Review* described educated women as "defeminated," "hermaphrodite," "mongrel," a "species of vermin," "one of the most intolerable monsters of creation" (Delamont & Duffin, 1978, p. 180), and *The Mothers Magazine* condemned women's rights advocates as "Amazonians [who] are their own executioners," assuring that "they have unsexed themselves in public estimation, and there is no fear that they will perpetuate their race" ("Female orators," 1838, p. 27).

These comments are illustrative of attitudes regarding gender that were prevalent at the turn of the century when psychology emerged in America; they illustrate how American society understood the inherent nature and thus the proper place of women. In the terms used in this discussion, these comments illustrate how society at that time constructed

gender. The construction of gender formed one element of the sociohistorical background against which psychology entered the American scene;
subsequent constructions of gender have likewise contributed to the
setting within which the discipline has matured.

The contexts framing women's position at psychology's beginning can
be conceptualized as concentric circles. In the outermost circle lie the
prescriptions for women's behavior, the understanding of gender as constructed within the society at large. Within these general perceptions of
women's "nature," we find specific ideas about women and education,
important here because psychology was from its beginnings a highly
academic field. Inside this circle of expectations regarding women's intellectual activities, we find attitudes regarding women's participation in the
fields deemed most academic and most "masculine," namely, science.
These presumptions formed a determining contextual force for would-be
women psychologists, for psychology aspired to a place among the sciences. At the innermost circle, the practices and institutions of psychology
itself created context that was influential in defining the direction and
scope of women's place in the discipline. We will consider each of these
levels of context in turn.

Women in Society. By the late nineteenth century in America, industrialization and mass production had brought an end to the relative
financial self-sufficiency of families, moving productivity from the home
to the factory. As production grew more distant from the domestic realm,
a distinction solidified between two spheres of human functioning: the
public sphere of commerce and production, where impersonal monetary
reality reigned, and the private realm of home and family, where nurturance and personal care flourished.

Within the parameters of this "doctrine of spheres," the prescribed
role for women, or "woman's sphere," was encompassed by the tenets of
the "cult of true womanhood" (Welter, 1966).[3] The woman who would
aspire to true womanhood must demonstrate certain cardinal virtues:
piety, purity, submissiveness, and domesticity. The most obvious quality
of these demands is their restrictiveness, intended as they were to affirm
women's legitimate and natural sphere as the home. That women were ill
represented in the professions during this era is not surprising, given these
terribly limiting prescriptions alone.

Paradoxically, these same attributions provided initial entry for women
into the public sphere. Demands for piety were transformed into the moral
imperative reflected in women's broad participation in social reform
activities; domesticity was transferred to roles that Adams (1971) termed
"housekeeping" for society; submissiveness translated into subordinate
roles in the public realm. These initial entrées gradually evolved into the

"women's work" that came to characterize women's participation in many fields, including psychology (Rossiter, 1982).

Women's confinement to this submissive, domestic role had heretofore been justified by appeals to religion and custom. Now, in the face of the nineteenth century's devotion to science, scientific expertise was invoked to address the "woman problem" and to explain the evident differences between women and men. It should not be surprising, given our earlier discussion of values and objectivity in science, that scientific conclusions regarding women's inherent "nature" (some of which are quoted above) looked suspiciously like the answers previously offered without scientific validation, now made all the more powerful by the appellation "scientific." Shields succinctly expressed the consequences: "That science played hand-maiden to social values cannot be denied" (1975, p. 753).

The roles designated for men and women were ardently believed to be imposed by nature rather than dictated by convention. This certainty (that is, the constructed "knowledge" about masculinity and femininity) rested on the late-nineteenth-century preference for biology (nature) over socialization (nurture) in explaining human behavior. This predilection was in keeping with the ascendancy of the principles of evolution initially proposed by Darwin (1859, 1871) and later elaborated and extended by others (e.g., Geddes & Thomson, 1889; Spencer, 1873, 1891).

The apparently broad applicability of evolutionary theory was widely viewed as heralding the possibility of a full understanding of human experience, including complex human behavior. The principles of evolution were invoked to buttress gender role prescriptions, providing an excellent illustration of the dialectic so compatible with a constructionist approach: Darwin's work reciprocally enjoyed ready acceptance precisely because of its congruence with the already-prevalent respect for the natural sciences and simultaneously because it could be seen as compatible with preexisting societal beliefs regarding the sexes.

Thus, although this understanding of gender can, in retrospect, be readily seen as a socially and historically situated construction, it was not seen as such at the time but was taken as self-evidently true. Such is the nature of the social construction of reality: gender was what it was "known" to be.

Women in Education. When psychology first appeared in the United States, women were only beginning to emerge from the quagmire of restrictions and impediments that had prohibited women's full participation in the academy, both as students and as professionals (Bernard, 1964; R. Rosenberg, 1979, 1988; Rossiter, 1982; Solomon, 1985). Resistance to women's involvement in academia had a dual effect on the place made available to women in psychology: first, women found it difficult to receive the education necessary for participation in this very academic discipline;

and second, even the rare woman Ph.D. in psychology found employment opportunities for women scarce within academia, where most psychologists were employed, and largely nonexistent elsewhere. This obstruction of women's progress in academia was rooted in dominant societal beliefs, nourished by legitimation from science (including psychological science). Let us consider a few of the scientific doctrines invoked in the service of these practices.

The "variability hypothesis" argued that women as a group are less variable than are men, evidencing a narrower range of mental abilities; they are hence unable to achieve at the highest levels (Darwin, 1859, 1871; Spencer, 1867; Thorndike, 1906). Further, women's brains were said to be less evolved than men's and their intellectual skills therefore more primitive ("Biology," 1878; Spencer, 1867, 1873). In addition, women were believed to be inherently frail, their reproductive systems being especially vulnerable to damage from stress or overwork. The rigors of education would therefore be a grave threat to women's reproductive capability and thus to the perpetuation of the species (Cattell, 1909; Clarke, 1873; Hall, 1905; Spencer, 1867).

Social Darwinism, the extension of Darwin's theory propounded by Spencer (1873, 1891) and employed in support of these proscriptions, offers an excellent illustration of the creation of presumed truth. Spencer's phrase, "survival of the fittest," became the watchword for an ideology that viewed white, male, upper-class society as the pinnacle of evolution, a perception verified within this framework by the very fact of this group's dominance. Men's greater achievement was taken as demonstration of their intellectual superiority; women's manifest lack of achievement was taken as evidence of their intellectual inferiority.

Social Darwinism invoked doctrines that had originally argued for the improvement of species through gradual change, manipulating those principles to justify the status quo—particularly the subordination of women and other "lower" groups. The resultant description of what amounted to a social caste system had, in true constructionist fashion, prescriptive impact: as a result of their presumed incapacity to benefit from education, "less-evolved" groups (women and minorities) were "justifiably" excluded from participation in the very institutions that would have exposed them to opportunities to demonstrate their capabilities. In short, they were victims of the social construction of their inferiority.

Women in Science. As discussed above, the "new psychology" undertook to disavow its philosophical origins and to portray itself as a member of the prestigious family of natural sciences. This phenomenon is itself an excellent illustration of the power of social context, which shaped in this case the discipline's own self-definition and hence its future direction and at the same time greatly influenced women's place in psychology. Because psychology chose to define itself as a science, the women who would enter psychology faced the biases that obstructed women's participation in the sciences.

The perception that science and femininity are incongruent, that "woman scientist" is, in Rossiter's words, a "contradiction in terms" (1982, p. xv), meant that the woman who chose a career in science was violating the culture's dictates for properly feminine behavior. Consider the terms that typically describe scientific endeavor: tough, rigorous, impersonal, unemotional, detached, objective. These attributions are quite clearly incompatible with the characterizations of "true womanhood" outlined above.

Further, although academia represented the best hope of employment for women scientists, women academics were forced to contend with limited resources and restricted opportunities, which militated against scientific productivity. Women scientists were concentrated in women's colleges, where they contended with inadequate laboratory facilities; they had no graduate students to serve as research assistants or to promulgate their theories; teaching and advising loads, as well as expectations for college and community involvement, were greater than in research institutions; and there was little incentive to produce, for no more prestigious or lucrative position was available to them (Bernard, 1964; Harris, 1978; R. Rosenberg, 1988; Solomon, 1985). Furthermore, women who entered academia were often required to choose between career and family, even obligated to resign if they married (Scarborough & Furumoto, 1987). Thus the woman who chose a career in science opted for a position that violated the culture's expectations for her behavior as a woman; those same expectations further insured that she would not receive support for her activities as a scientist, her inability to function at optimal levels of productivity further reinforcing the perception that women are not suited for science.

Women found themselves unwelcome in both the informal and the formal exchanges of their male peers and were thereby excluded from the collegial networks that form an essential part of professional growth (Furumoto, 1988). Women were explicitly denied participation in all-male clubs; in "smokers" where professional issues were often discussed (because no self-respecting woman would smoke); and at other social occasions where men unself-consciously excluded (even denigrated) women, as in one professional society's self-proclaimed "misogynist dinner" (Rossiter, 1982). The self-conscious process of professionalization within the sciences further limited women's potential by eliminating women from professional organizations, for reasons unrelated to their capabilities (Furumoto, 1987; Rossiter, 1982).

Women in Psychology: A Case in Point. Regrettably, within psychology itself are found manifestations of these very obstructions. Arguments that women were less highly evolved and thus possessed only primitive mental abilities, that women were by nature confined to the mediocre range of mental abilities, that women should be excluded from high academic rank and from professional organizations, that women were obligated to reproduce for the sake of the species, and that education would threaten women's fertility—all these were views propounded by the most noted psychologists of the day, including James M. Cattell, G. S. Hall, Edward Thorndike, and E. B. Titchener (Boring, 1967; Cattell, 1909; Furumoto, 1988; Hall, 1903, 1905, 1906; R. Rosenberg, 1982; Rossiter, 1982; Thorndike, 1906, 1910). Paradoxically, some of these same men (especially Cattell and Hall) figured prominently in women's gradual admission to higher education and to psychology (Diehl, 1986; Rossiter, 1982; Shields & Mallory, 1987).

Psychology's role in the perpetuation of this misogynist construction of gender was not without exceptions. Some of psychology's pioneer women devoted their efforts to debunking the myths entailed in such concepts. Especially noteworthy were Helen (Thompson) Woolley's pioneering research on sex differences in mental traits (1903, 1010, 1914), Leta Hollingworth's research on the effects of menses (1914a), and Hollingworth's investigation of sex differences in mental abilities and her challenges to the variability hypothesis (1913, 1914b, 1916a, 1916b, 1918, 1922). This work was instrumental in calling into question those appeals to "nature" that had previously characterized psychological explanations of gender. If even gender, that most obvious of differences, is not biologically determined, the question came, can any complex human behavior be attributed to biology alone? Rossiter (1982) has credited these early demonstrations of the social bases of gender with acting as catalysts for the shift from the (Darwinian-based) biological determinism of the late nineteenth century to the environmental determinism that underpinned behaviorism a few decades later.

Beyond the Beginnings:
Women's Place in Psychology

Subsequent to these early years, the place of psychology's women has continued to be shaped by the two-tiered context that frames social construction. On the one hand, the sociohistorical context within which psychology has functioned has influenced psychology's self-definition and thereby the nature of the discipline and of women's role within it. On the other hand, qualities inherent to psychology as a field have shaped women's place within the discipline. Over the years, this nexus of constraining and enabling forces has defined women's role in psychology, commensurate always with the contemporary societal construction of gender.

Sociohistorical Context. Women's place in psychology has continually been determined by a confluence of beliefs about gender and the self-definition of the field, changing in response to the needs of society at large. A few illustrations will demonstrate this point.

The widespread testing that resulted from the universal draft in World War I stimulated test development and administration, a specialty that became increasingly a female bailiwick as testing assumed a secondary "technician" status (Furumoto, 1987; O'Connell & Russo, 1983). The poor results achieved on the tests administered to World War I draftees gave rise to the child development and progressive education movements. These movements provided professional opportunities for some women, who were otherwise largely excluded from research and academic settings, precisely because such activities were regarded as appropriate to women's natural abilities (O'Connell & Russo, 1983; Russo & Denmark, 1987).

After World War I, applied psychology flourished. Women's disproportionate representation among the applied specialities again reflects the gendering of psychological subfields, as applied psychology was neatly in keeping with women's presumed natural proclivity for service to others. However, even though women were more numerous in the applied fields, the continuing control exercised by (male-dominated) academic psychology over all arms of the discipline served to reinforce women's subordinate position (Furumoto, 1987; Scarborough & Furumoto, 1987). And academia, particularly the prestigious research universities, remained a male bastion. As recently as the 1950s, psychology's best-known historian, E. G. Boring, acknowledged women's continuing exclusion from academia, suggesting that women psychologists seek careers elsewhere. His recommendation was that women write books dealing with topics appropriate to women's interests—"the young, the helpless and the distressed" (1951, p. 680)—though he conceded that such work would not procure professional recognition.

In the years between psychology's beginnings (when psychology's women pioneers had addressed issues of gender) and the recent resurgence of interest in women's issues, psychology's women engaged in the breadth of activities and interests that characterized the expanding field, their efforts largely directed toward earning and justifying their positions by complying with the predominant expectations and paradigmatic models of the discipline. Their work was shaped by the social construction of their proper role within psychology, itself a reflection of the construction of gender in society at large, an influence that was not acknowledged by themselves or by the discipline. During this heyday of psychology's expansion, its professionalization, and its popularization, both women's issues and individual women were invisible and largely indistinguishable components of a psychology constructed in part from gendered notions but largely blind to the role of gender in those constructions.

During the 1960s and 1970s, however, the new context provided by the nascent women's movement generated a new awareness of gender, of women's issues, and of the role of psychology in addressing these concerns. This awareness has stimulated and has in turn been informed by an extensive and expanding body of research. Although mainstream psychology has responded poorly to the task of incorporating feminist perspectives (Lykes & Stewart, 1986; Squire, 1989), major elements of the discipline have been transformed by this second wave of feminism.

Simultaneously, some segments of psychology have participated in a critique of the positivist model, turning from exclusive reliance on controlled laboratory situations to broader naturalistic and human science models. The restructured professional milieu resulting from these events has supported the emergence of entire new fields of study, has challenged long-held conceptions of psychology's purpose as well as its methods, and has altered the face of the discipline, if only in circumscribed arenas. These developments, as was true of those that preceded them in prior decades, reflect changes in the cultural construction of gender, in psychology's own self-definition, and hence in psychology's construction of women's place in the discipline.

Women's Place in the Community of Psychology. Across the span of these historical changes and throughout the history of the discipline, women's place in psychology has been measured by their invisibility, a product of the criteria used by the field as measures of eminence. Eminence requires recognition; an individual's work must be known, be evaluated as important, and be widely disseminated in order for one to be judged eminent in the field. For a variety of reasons, such visibility has often been unattainable to the women of psychology, even where their contributions have been significant.

The Meaning and Making of Eminence: The Exclusion of Women. The determination of eminence in psychology rests largely on research (in the positivist tradition) and publication; reciprocally, a consistent record of research and publication is its own best sustenance. This phenomenon of "accumulative advantage" (Allison & Stewart, 1974) operates to women's disadvantage, because the resources and opportunities available to women have been limited and their access to professional recognition correspondingly curtailed. In fact, in contrast to the benefits of self-sustaining growth in eminence, women and their work have suffered from a progressive diminution of recognition in historical accounts of psychology's growth, such that women's work once acknowledged frequently vanishes from later editions of texts (Scarborough & Furumoto, 1987; Stevens & Gardner, 1982).

Exacerbating the selective consequences of the phenomenon of accumulative (dis)advantage is the fact that much of women's work is concentrated in fields and topic areas that are more applied, less prestigious, and less central to the discipline's self-definition than is the work more characteristic of men. Simply put, "women who are psychologists are not the kind of psychologists who get cited in the scientific literature" (Stevens & Gardner, 1982, vol. 1, p. 9). In this vein, Scarborough & Furumoto (1987) pointed out that histories of psychology have traditionally been intellectual histories, presentations of the field as an academic and research science rather than as an applied profession. This focus has effectively screened a large body of women's work from such histories.

The relative devaluation of the applied subfields where women predominate may derive from the very fact of the preponderance of women in practitioner roles. Touhey (1974) has demonstrated a direct linkage between the entry of women into a field and that field's subsequent decline in prestige. The lesser prestige and consequent invisibility of applied psychology may also result from applied psychology's status as subordinate to academia (Furumoto, 1987). Not only does academic/research activity afford opportunities for research and publication, the sine qua non of visibility in psychology, but all psychologists, including those aspiring to practice in applied specialties, must earn their credentials in academic programs.

In addition, positions available for practitioners have often been viewed as relatively menial (supervised staff positions, test administration, direct contact with needy clients) and thus as appropriate to women's socially constructed subordinate position (Furumoto, 1987; Scarborough & Furumoto, 1987). Brumberg and Tomes (1982) pointed out that the least prestigious roles in any professional realm tend to be positions most in touch with human suffering, the "dirty work" of the field. Doctors and nurses, sociologists and social workers are cases in point. In psychology, the applied specialties function to provide direct services, and as in other professions, these least visible, least prestigious positions have been assumed disproportionately by women. The more prestigious positions, those academic and research positions that do not involve direct interaction with needy clients, are occupied predominantly by men.

Note the circularity of this phenomenon: Women are selectively shunted (by the construction of gender) into applied fields. Work in applied fields is in turn judged (in the constructed self-definition of psychology) as less meritorious. These devalued positions are, to close the circle, identified as women's work in the discipline, largely invisible in its recorded histories.

But what of the women, limited in number though they may be, who participate in the academic and research activities of psychology? Even when women's work meshes with the research orientation of the field, their efforts, for a variety of reasons, often go unrecognized. Among the factors contributing to this neglect are the following:

Social custom and women's place. Women's subordinate position in society is mirrored in psychology. Women have been relegated to the roles of research assistant and junior author; their efforts have received only footnote acknowledgment; women's work has been misattributed; women have found less advocacy for their promotion within professional circles; and women are still underrepresented in academia, disproportionately found in lower-status, less-visible positions (O'Connell & Russo, 1980, 1983, 1988; Ostertag & McNamara, 1991; Russo & Denmark, 1987; Scarborough & Furumoto, 1987; Stevens & Gardner, 1982; Walker, 1991).

Further, women's traditional role within the family imposes a handicap, for the woman who seeks to advance in her career is competing for recognition among colleagues who are able to devote greater time and energy to the professional activities that are, for her, only one of a complex set of demands (Bryan & Boring, 1947; O'Connell & Russo, 1980). Simeone summarizes: "Married men have the benefit of a two-person career, when one considers the direct and indirect assistance of a wife, while married women are more likely to be part of a two-career couple" (1987, p. 138).

Names and citations. Conventions in the use of names have proven detrimental to women's prestige. The practice of changing one's name at marriage has meant that the continuity of many women's career visibility has been sacrificed. Further, the joint work of husband and wife psychologists—and even the woman's independent work—has often been identified with a name and the name with the man of the pair (Bernstein & Russo, 1974; O'Connell & Russo, 1983; Stevens & Gardner, 1982). Consider the following names: Clark, Harlow, Hollingworth, Sherif, Spence. Each is shared by a psychologist couple; each is likely to conjure up the man's first name.

In addition, psychology's citation format, which uses only initials of first names, makes it impossible to identify women's work and thus may have the insidious effect of supporting a presumption of male authorship. For this reason, references cited in my contributions to this book include full first names, in an attempt to illustrate both the ease with which this problem can be corrected and the impact this apparently minor change has on the reader's awareness of women's contributions.

Collegial expectations. Finally, women's work has not achieved visibility commensurate with its worth precisely because the institutions of psychology and the members of the field have failed to recognize and acknowledge women as significant contributors to psychology, a reflection of the general societal disregard for women and women's activities. Members of the profession are largely unaware of women's work (Anin, Boring, & Watson, 1968; Brodsky, Nevill, & Kimmel, 1976; Simeone, 1987; Stevens & Gardner, 1982), and a self-fulfilling prophecy is thus engaged: it is assumed that women contribute little of import; hence, the work they produce is discounted; women's consequent invisibility serves to reinforce the notion that women do little of significance, and so the cycle continues.

The problem, it seems, is partly but not solely that women's opportunities have been restricted and that they have been largely prevented by these restrictions from contributing to the field. Scarborough & Furumoto have argued that women's exclusion reflects not only such socially and historically explicable forces as these but also "prejudice against women and women's work." "Devaluation of whatever is produced by women," they argue, "continues as a widespread though often unacknowledged attitude. There is little reason to believe that historians are exempted from this cultural handicap" (1987, p. 185). The handicap to which Scarborough and Furumoto refer is precisely the social construction of "knowledge" and of "history," wherein unexamined assumptions are taken as data and unacknowledged values direct both inquiry and interpretation. Why, indeed, should psychology be exempt from this "knowledge"-making process?

Synthesis

Scattered throughout the discussion thus far have been references to the interface among the concepts of social constructionism, historiography, and the re-placing of women in psychology. By way of conclusion, I offer here some explicit summary comments regarding that confluence, notions that find further elaboration in the readings that follow.

The Construction of Gender

Fundamental to this effort at re-placing women is the awareness that the meaning of gender is socially constructed, as is true of other pieces of knowledge. Our understanding of what it means to be masculine or feminine is a product of the social interchange that generates agreement, even certainty, about the nature of reality. The construction of gender reflects what Berger & Luckmann (1967) have termed primary socialization; it is an understanding so early-instilled and so pervasive in our experience that it passes essentially unnoticed and hence unquestioned. Given the encompassing quality of gender concepts, their construction inevitably influences much of our lives, much of our "knowledge"—even aspects of existence that seem irrelevant to gender (although just which things are relevant to gender is a part of that very construction).

Following from the constructionist view, different historical epochs and different cultural milieus necessarily produce differing constructions of gender. These constructions determine how that society relates to women and to men, what place is created for each of them within the culture. Institutions of society, in turn, incorporate and embellish these constructions, their own practices and paradigms reflecting the attitudes of society at large as filtered through the self-definition of such institutions. Academic disciplines are included here; the practices and institutions of psychology are gendered, both implicitly and explicitly. Psychology has participated in the particular construction of gender that conflates gender and sex, defines gender as difference, and sees gender as a quality of persons rather than a manifestation of context.

The Construction of Psychology

Psychology itself is constructed. The discipline was created and is continually re-created by its own self-definition, by self-conscious declarations regarding its subject matter, its methods, its role and mission in society. Alterations in this self-definition derive only in part from developments internal to psychology. As society has changed, making different demands upon and holding changing expectations for the field, psychology's self-definition has been transformed in response. The construction that results from this process, the view psychology holds of its own meaning, is unavoidably shaped by the sociohistorical context in which that self-definition is created (cf. Brumberg & Tomes, 1982).

The Construction of History

The social constructionist literature provides a compelling argument that our understanding of psychology's past is not a simple narrative about factual events but a construction. Just as historical events are themselves explicable in terms of the context of their occurrences, so too is any historical rendering of those events framed by the situatedness of its own construction. What we have in a published history of psychology is not an objective depiction of past persons and happenings but an interpretation, a hypothesis about events that occurred in a complex context that may not be fully appreciated by subsequent historians. The narrative depicting those events, in turn, is necessarily selective, unavoidably value-laden, and inescapably shaped by its own sociohistorical location.

The Construction of Women's Place
in Psychology's History

The conclusion that emerges from these arguments is multifaceted yet clear: the place of women in psychology and in the history of psychology is constructed; it is a product of the intersection of the construction of gender, the construction of psychology, and the construction of history. When we look at the stultifying definition of women's sphere in the years of psychology's emergence, it is not surprising to find women scarce at psychology's beginnings nor to discover their work largely unrecognized. If we consider how gender has been constructed throughout the evolution of the discipline, it is not surprising to discover women selectively shunted into particular subfields and devalued positions within psychology nor to find them largely invisible to the discipline as a whole. Beliefs about women, passing as "knowledge," have influenced their access to education, their entrance into the public sphere, the availability and quality of employment opportunities, the areas of psychology where they have prospered and those where they have found scant welcome, the recognition of themselves and their work, and their slow fade from the screen of psychology's history.

Further, the historical rendering of women's place has been shaped by the context within which history has been written. When we view the historical record as constructed, its creation grounded in the dominant worldview of the society (including its construction of gender) and the reigning paradigm of the discipline (including its gendered components, both obvious and implicit), it is not surprising to find women largely absent from psychology's histories as well as from contemporary portrayals of the discipline. Our understanding of women, of the female gender, has been constructed in a manner that leads to women's invisibility in history, as history is usually written, and their exclusion from mainstream renditions of psychology. The roles that women have filled in psychology are not ones whose activities fill history books or the professional literature. Nor is the obvious circularity of the process of exclusion-invisibility-exclusion difficult to comprehend from the perspective of a gendered view of psychology's history: women's constructed invisibility makes them appear irrelevant to the discipline and thus serves, in turn, to support their continuing exclusion.

Feminist Reconstruction and Psychology

Against the often bleak background of the consequences for women of the construction of gender and of psychology, a brighter possibility emerges. The interface between constructionism and feminism has provided impetus for a body of feminist discourse that foresees a reconstruction of the very concept of knowledge and of the processes of knowledge seeking embodied in science. If knowledge is not discovered but created, feminists ask, in what manner has that process of construction reflected the androcentric bias of society as a whole? From this question has sprung a rich literature contesting traditional assumptions about knowledge and epistemology, reflected in incisive challenges to scientific method in both the natural sciences (e.g., Bleier, 1984; Fee, 1981; Harding & O'Barr, 1987; Keller, 1985) and the social sciences (e.g., Bernard, 1973; Henley, 1985; Keller & Flax, 1988; Lott, 1985b; Marecek, 1989; McHugh, Koeske, & Frieze, 1986; Sherif, 1979a; Unger, 1983, 1989; Wallston, 1981; Westkott, 1979; Wittig, 1985).

This feminist critique of science directly confronts psychology's commitment to positivism, revealing its inherent inadequacies and thereby pointing up a plethora of anomalies that leave that commitment open to serious question. In Kuhn's (1970) view, it is the discomfiture arising from just such anomalies that generates the disciplinary crisis that precedes a paradigm shift. Given the dissatisfaction with traditional modes of psychological science reflected in the feminist and the constructionist literature, psychology might well be ripe for such a scientific revolution. The burgeoning presence of feminist thought in psychology, then, might well serve as the catalyst for major changes in the discipline's methods, its subject matter, and the direction of its future efforts. If this scenario is actualized, the process of re-placing women will indeed have had a transformative impact on the future of psychology.

Conclusion

In the readings that follow, the model outlined here finds elaboration through the thoughts of a number of scholars whose work has individually confronted long-held conceptions about psychology and whose writings in combination create a new vision for the discipline. Collectively, these works detail the reality of women's marginalization in psychology as it has been construed to date, the utility of social constructionism as a system for understanding women's place in the field, and the consequences for the discipline of constructing a women-inclusive psychology. To the extent that the composite impact of these readings creates an understanding of why women have been seldom seen and rarely heard by psychology, to the extent that they construct a context supportive of women's meaningful re-placement in psychology, the book will have served its purpose.

Notes

1. For an explanation of the term *re-place*, see Introduction, page 1.

2. For example: Acker, Barry, & Esseveld, 1983; Bernard, 1973; Bleier, 1984, 1986; Brumberg & Tomes, 1982; Diner, 1979; Fausto-Sterling, 1985; Fee, 1986; Fine, 1985; Harding, 1986; Harding & Hintikka, 1983; Harding & O'Barr, 1987; Keller, 1985; Langland & Gove, 1981; Lewin, 1984; Lott, 1985a, 1985b; Morawski, 1982, 1988; O'Leary, Wallston, & Unger, 1985; Scarr, 1985; Scott, 1988; Sherman & Beck, 1979; Unger, 1981, 1982, 1983, 1985, 1988, 1989; Westkott, 1979; Wittig, 1985.

3. Gerda Lerner (1979) differentiated between expectations for "the lady and the mill girl," emphasizing that the qualities deemed essential for true womanhood never applied (either descriptively or prescriptively) to working-class women. In terms of women's place in psychology, however, it is "the lady" and perceptions of her nature that were of central significance. Middle- and upper-middle-class women were, almost without exception, the only ones who had access to educational opportunities and the freedom from obligatory labor that allowed them to pursue a career in psychology (Furumoto, 1987; Furumoto & Scarborough, 1986; Scarborough & Furumoto, 1987).

References

Acker, Joan, Barry, Kate, & Esseveld, Joke. (1983). Objectivity and truth: Problems in doing feminist research. *Women's Studies International Quarterly, 6,* 423–436.

Adams, Margaret. (1971). The compassion trap. In Vivian Gornick & Barbara Moran (Eds.), *Women in sexist society* (pp. 401–416). New York: Basic Books.

Albee, George W. (1986). Toward a just society: Lessons from observations on the primary prevention of psychopathology. *American Psychologist, 41,* 891–898.

Allen, Grant. (1889). Woman's place in nature. *Forum, 7,* 258–263.

Allison, Paul D., & Stewart, John A. (1974). Productivity differences among scientists: Evidence for accumulative advantage. *American Sociological Review, 39,* 596–606.

Anin, Edith L., Boring, Edwin G., & Watson, Robert I. (1968). Important psychologists, 1600–1967. *Journal of the History of the Behavioral Sciences, 4,* 303–315.

Bakan, David. (1977). Political factors in the development of American psychology. *Annals of the New York Academy of Sciences, 291,* 222–232.

Belenky, Mary F., Clinchy, Blythe M., Goldberger, Nancy R., & Tarrule, Jill M. (1986). *Women's ways of knowing: The development of self, voice and mind.* New York: Basic Books.

Berger, Peter L., & Luckmann, Thomas. (1967). *The social construction of reality.* New York: Doubleday.

Berkin, Carol R., & Norton, Mary Beth. (1979). *Women of America: A history.* Boston: Houghton Mifflin.

Bernard, Jessie. (1964). *Academic woman.* Cleveland: World Publishing Co.

Bernard, Jessie. (1973). My four revolutions: An autobiographical history of the ASA. In Joan Huber (Ed.), *Changing women in a changing society* (pp. 11–29). Chicago: University of Chicago Press.

Bernard, Jessie. (1979). The mother role. In Jo Freeman (Ed.), *Women: A feminist perspective* (pp. 122–133). Palo Alto: Mayfield.

Bernard, Jessie. (1981). *The female world.* New York: Free Press.

Bernstein, Maxine D., & Russo, Nancy F. (1974). The history of psychology revisited: Or, up with our foremothers. *American Psychologist, 29,* 130–134.

Biology and "women's rights." (1878). *Popular Science Monthly, 14,* 201–213.

Bleier, Ruth. (1984). *Science and gender: A critique of biology and its theories on women.* New York: Pergamon.

Bleier, Ruth. (Ed.). (1986). *Feminist approaches to science.* New York: Pergamon.

Blumenthal, Arthur. (1977). Wilhelm Wundt and early American psychology: A clash of two cultures. *Annals of the New York Academy of Sciences, 291,* 13–20.

Bohan, Janis S. (1990a). Contextual history: A framework for re-placing women in the history of psychology. *Psychology of Women Quarterly, 14,* 213–227.

Bohan, Janis S. (1990b). Social constructionism and contextual history: An expanded approach to the history of psychology. *Teaching of Psychology, 17,* 82–89.

Bohan, Janis S. (1991a, August). Positivism and curriculum: Tacit assumptions and the exclusion of women. Paper presented at the annual convention of the American Psychological Association, San Francisco.

Bohan, Janis S. (1991b, November). Gilligan, Chodorow, and women's ways of knowing: Denial of diversity? Paper presented at the meeting of the American Education Research Association Special Interest Group: Research on Women and Education, San Jose, Calif.

Bohan, Janis S. (Ed.). (1992). *Re-placing women in psychology: Readings toward a more inclusive history.* Dubuque, IA: Kendall/Hunt.

Bohan, Janis S. (in press). Regarding gender: Essentialism, constructionism, and feminist psychology. *Psychology of Women Quarterly.*

Boring, Edwin G. (1950a). *A history of experimental psychology* (2nd ed.). New York: Appleton-Century-Crofts. (Original work published 1929).

Boring, Edwin G. (1950b). Great men and scientific progress. *Proceedings of the American Philosophical Society, 94,* 339–351.

Boring, Edwin G. (1951). The woman problem. *American Psychologist, 6,* 679–682.

Boring, Edwin G. (1967). Titchener's experimentalists. *Journal of the History of the Behavioral Sciences, 3,* 315–325.

Brodsky, Annette A. (1980). A decade of feminist influence on psychotherapy. *Psychology of Women Quarterly, 4,* 331–344.

Brodsky, Annette A., Nevill, Dorothy, & Kimmel, Ellen. (1976). A progress report on the Visiting Woman Psychologist Program. *Professional Psychology, 7,* 214–221.

Bronstein, Phyllis A., & Quina, Kathryn. (Eds.). (1988). *Teaching a psychology of people: Resources for gender and sociocultural awareness.* Washington, DC: American Psychological Association.

Broughton, John M. (1983). Women's rationality and men's virtues: A critique of gender dualism in Gilligan's theory of moral development. *Social Research, 50,* 597–642.

Brumberg, Joan J., & Tomes, Nancy. (1982). Women in the professions: A research agenda for American historians. *Reviews in American History, 10,* 275–276.

Bryan, Alice, & Boring, Edwin G. (1947). Women in American psychology: Factors affecting their careers. *American Psychologist, 2,* 3–20.

Buss, Alan R. (1975). The emerging field of the sociology of psychological knowledge. *American Psychologist, 30,* 988–1002.

Buss, Alan R. (1978). The structure of psychological revolutions. *Journal of the History of the Behavioral Sciences, 14,* 57–64.

Caplan, Nathan, & Nelson, Stephen D. (1973). On being useful: The nature and consequences of psychological research on social problems. *American Psychologist, 28,* 199–211.

Cattell, James M. (1909). The school and the family. *Popular Science Monthly, 74,* 91–92.

Clarke, Edward H. (1873). *Sex and education: Or, a fair chance for the girls.* Boston: J. R. Osgood. Reprinted: Medicine and Society series. New York: Arno Press, 1972.

Cohen, Hyman R. (1973). Dialectics and scientific revolutions. *Science and Society, 37,* 326–336.

Collingwood, R. G. (1946). The a priori impossibility of a science of man. In R. G. Collingwood (Ed.), *The idea of history* (pp. 205–231, 315–320). New York: Oxford University Press.

Crawford, Mary, & Marecek, Jeanne. (1989a). Feminist theory, feminist psychology: A bibliography of epistemology, critical analysis, and applications. *Psychology of Women Quarterly, 13,* 477–491.

Crawford, Mary, & Marecek, Jeanne. (1989b). Psychology reconstructs the female, 1968–1988. *Psychology of Women Quarterly, 13,* 147–165.

Danzinger, Kurt. (1979). The social origins of modern psychology. In Alan Buss (Ed.), *Psychology in social context* (pp. 27–45). New York: Irvington.

Darwin, Charles. (1859). *On the origin of species by means of natural selection: Or, the preservation of favoured races in the struggle for life.* London: John Murray.

Darwin, Charles. (1871). *The descent of man and selection in relation to sex.* London: John Murray.

Delamont, Sara, & Duffin, Lorna. (Eds.). (1978). *The nineteenth-century woman.* New York: Barnes & Noble.

Denmark, Florence L. (1980). Psyche: From rocking the cradle to rocking the boat. *American Psychologist, 35,* 1057–1065.

Diehl, Lesley A. (1986). The paradox of G. Stanley Hall: Foe of co-education and educator of women. *American Psychologist, 41,* 868–878.

Diner, Hasia. (1979). Women and history: Doing good history. In Eloise C. Snyder (Ed.), *The study of women: Enlarging perspectives on social reality* (pp. 296–317). New York: Harper & Row.

Ehrenreich, Barbara, & English, Diedra. (1978). *For her own good: 150 years of experts' advice to women.* New York: Anchor Press.

Eichenbaum, Luise, & Orbach, Susie. (1983). *Understanding women: A feminist psychoanalytic approach.* New York: Basic Books.

Fausto-Sterling, Anne. (1985). *Myths of gender.* New York: Basic Books.

Fee, Elizabeth. (1981). Is feminism a threat to scientific objectivity? *International Journal of Women's Studies, 4,* 378–392.

Fee, Elizabeth. (1986). Critiques of modern science: The relationship of feminism to other radical epistemologies. In Ruth Bleier (Ed.), *Feminist approaches to science* (pp. 42–56). New York: Pergamon.

Female orators. (1838). *The Mothers Magazine, 4,* 27.

Fine, Michelle. (1985). Reflections on a feminist psychology of women. *Psychology of Women Quarterly, 9,* 167–183.

Fine, Michelle, & Gordon, Susan M. (1989). Feminist transformations of/despite psychology. In Mary Crawford & Margaret Gentry (Eds.), *Gender and thought: Psychological perspectives* (pp. 146–174). New York: Springer-Verlag.

Friedman, William J., Robinson, Amy B., & Friedman, Britt L. (1987). Sex differences in moral judgments? A test of Gilligan's theory. *Psychology of Women Quarterly, 11,* 37–46.

Friedrich, James. (1990). Writing affects thinking: Empirical evidence. *Teaching of Psychology, 17,* 23–27.

Furumoto, Laurel. (1987). On the margins: Women and the professionalization of psychology in the United States, 1890–1940. In Mitchell G. Ash & William R. Woodward (Eds.), *Psychology in twentieth-century thought and society* (pp. 93–113). Cambridge, MA: Cambridge University Press.

Furumoto, Laurel. (1988). Shared knowledge: The experimentalists 1904–1929. In Jill G. Morawski (Ed.), *The rise of experimentalism in American psychology* (pp. 94–113). New Haven: Yale University Press.

Furumoto, Laurel, & Scarborough, Elizabeth. (1986). Placing women in the history of psychology: The first American women psychologists. *American Psychologist, 41,* 35–42.

Gadlin, Howard, & Ingle, Grant. (1975). Through the one-way mirror: The limits of experimental self-reflection. *American Psychologist, 30,* 1003–1009.

Geddes, Patrick, & Thomson, J. Arthur. (1889). *The evolution of sex.* London: Scott.

Gergen, Kenneth J. (1973). Social psychology as history. *Journal of Personality and Social Psychology, 26,* 309–320.

Gergen, Kenneth J. (1976). Social psychology, science and history. *Personality and Social Psychology Bulletin, 2,* 373–383.

Gergen, Kenneth J. (1979). The positivist image in social psychological theory. In Alan Buss (Ed.), *Psychology in social context* (pp. 193–212). New York: Irvington.

Gergen, Kenneth J. (1985). The social constructionist movement in modern psychology. *American Psychologist, 40,* 266–275.

Gergen, Mary M. (1988). *Feminist thought and the structure of knowledge.* New York: New York University Press.

Giorgi, Amadeo. (1970). *Psychology as human science.* New York: Harper & Row.

Giorgi, Amadeo. (1971). Phenomenology and experimental psychology, I & II. In Amadeo Giorgi, William Fischer, & Rolf VonEckartsberg (Eds.), *Duquesne studies in phenomenological psychology,* vol. 1 (pp. 6–29). Pittsburgh: Duquesne University Press.

Grady, Kathleen E. (1981). Sex bias in research design. *Psychology of Women Quarterly, 5,* 628–636.

Hall, G. Stanley. (1903). Coeducation in the high school. *Proceedings of the National Education Association,* 446–460.

Hall, G. Stanley. (1905). *Adolescence.* New York: D. Appleton.

Hall, G. Stanley. (1906). The question of coeducation. *Munsey's Magazine, 34,* 588–592.

Harding, Sandra. (1986). *The science question in feminism.* Ithaca, NY: Cornell University Press.

Harding, Sandra, & Hintikka, Merrill. (Eds.). (1983). *Discovering reality: Feminist perspectives on metaphysics, epistemology, methodology and the philosophy of science.* Boston: D. Reidel.

Harding, Sandra, & O'Barr, Jean. (1987). *Sex and scientific inquiry.* Chicago: University of Chicago Press.

Hare-Mustin, Rachel T. (1983). An appraisal of the relationship between women and psychotherapy, 80 years after the case of Dora. *American Psychologist, 38,* 593–601.

Hare-Mustin, Rachel T., & Marecek, Jeanne. (1988). The meaning of difference: Gender theory, postmodernism, and psychology. *American Psychologist, 43,* 455–464.

Harris, Barbara J. (1978). *Beyond her sphere: Women and the professions in American history.* Westport, CT: Greenwood Press.

Harvey, O. J. (1965). The history of psychology as sociology of thought. *Journal of the History of the Behavioral Sciences, 1,* 196–202.

Henley, Nancy M. (1985). Review: Psychology and gender. *Signs: Journal of Women in Culture and Society, 11,* 101–119.

Hollingworth, Leta S. (1913). The frequency of amentia as related to sex. *Medical Record, 84,* 753–756.

Hollingworth, Leta S. (1914a). *Functional periodicity: An experimental study of the mental and motor abilities of women during menstruation.* New York: Teachers College.

Hollingworth, Leta S. (1914b). Variability as related to sex differences in achievement. *American Journal of Sociology, 19,* 510–530.

Hollingworth, Leta S. (1916a). Sex differences in mental traits. *Psychological Bulletin, 13,* 377–385.

Hollingworth, Leta S. (1916b). Social devices for impelling women to bear and rear children. *American Journal of Sociology, 22,* 19–29.

Hollingworth, Leta S. (1918). Comparison of the sexes in mental traits. *Psychological Bulletin, 25,* 427–432.

Hollingworth, Leta S. (1922). Differential action on the sexes of forces which tend to segregate the feebleminded. *Journal of Abnormal and Social Psychology, 17,* 35–37.

Howard, George S. (1985). The role of values in the science of psychology. *American Psychologist, 40,* 255–265.

Kahn, Arnold S., & Yoder, Janice D. (1989). The psychology of women and conservatism: Rediscovering social change. *Psychology of Women Quarterly, 13,* 417–432.

Keller, Evelyn F. (1980). Feminist critique of science: A forward or backward move? *Fundamentia Scientiae, 1,* 341–349.

Keller, Evelyn F. (1985). *Reflections on gender and science.* New Haven: Yale University Press.

Keller, Evelyn F., & Flax, Jane. (1988). Missing relations in psychoanalysis: A feminist critique of traditional and contemporary accounts of analytic theory and practice. In Stanley B. Messer, Louis A. Sass, & Robert L. Woolfolk (Eds.), *Hermeneutics and psychological theory: Interpretive perspectives on personality, psychotherapy, and psychopathology* (pp. 334–366). New Brunswick, NJ: Rutgers University Press.

Kerber, Linda K., Greeno, Catherine G., Maccoby, Eleanor E., Lana, Zell, Stack, Carol B., & Gilligan, Carol. (1986). On *In a different voice:* An interdisciplinary forum. *Signs: Journal of Women in Culture and Society, 11,* 304–333.

Koch, Sigmund. (1959). Epilogue. In Sigmund Koch (Ed.), *Psychology: The study of a science,* vol 3. (pp. 729–788). New York: McGraw-Hill.

Koch, Sigmund. (1969). Psychology cannot be a coherent science. *Psychology Today,* September, 14, 16, 64, 66–68.

Koch, Sigmund. (1981). The nature and limits of psychological knowledge: Lessons of a century *qua* "science." *American Psychologist, 36,* 257–269.

Kuhn, Thomas S. (1970). *The structure of scientific revolutions* (2nd ed.). Chicago: University of Chicago Press.

Kuhn, Thomas S. (1977). *The essential tension: Selected studies in scientific tradition and change.* Chicago: University of Chicago Press.

Langland, Elizabeth, & Gove, Walter. (Eds.). (1981). *A feminist perspective in the academy: The difference it makes.* Chicago: University of Chicago Press.

Laudan, Larry. (1984). *Science and values: An essay on the aims of science and their role in scientific debate.* Berkeley: University of California Press.

Leary, David E. (1979). Wundt and after: Psychology's shifting relations with the natural sciences, social sciences, and philosophy. *Journal of the History of the Behavioral Sciences, 15,* 231–241.

Lerner, Gerda. (1979). *The majority finds its past: Placing women in history.* New York: Oxford University Press.

Lerner, Harriet. (1989). *Women in therapy: Visions and revisions.* New York: Harper & Row.

Lewin, Miriam. (1984). *In the shadow of the past: Psychology portrays the sexes.* New York: Columbia University Press.

Longino, Helen E. (1983). Beyond "bad science": Skeptical reflections on the value-freedom of scientific inquiry. *Science, Technology, and Human Values, 8,* 7–17.

Longino, Helen E. (1986). Can there be a feminist science? (Working paper no. 163). Wellesley, MA: Wellesley College Center for Research on Women.

Lott, Bernice. (1981). A feminist critique of androgyny: Toward the elimination of gender attributions for learned behavior. In Clara Mayo & Nancy M. Henley (Eds.), *Gender and non-verbal behavior* (pp. 171–180). New York: Springer.

Lott, Bernice. (1985a). The devaluation of women's competence. *Journal of Social Issues, 41*, 43–60.

Lott, Bernice. (1985b). The potential enrichment of social/personality psychology through feminist research and vice versa. *American Psychologist, 40*, 155–164.

Lott, Bernice. (1988). Separate spheres revisited. *Contemporary Social Psychology, 13*, 55–62.

Lott, Bernice. (1990). Dual natures or learned behavior: The challenge to feminist psychology. In Rachel Hare-Mustin & Jeanne Marecek (Eds.), *Making a difference: Psychology and the construction of gender* (pp. 65–101). New Haven: Yale University Press.

Lykes, M. Brinton, & Stewart, Abigail. (1986). Evaluating the feminist challenge to research in personality and social psychology: 1963–1983. *Psychology of Women Quarterly, 10*, 393–412.

McGuire, William. (1973). The yin and yang of progress in social psychology. *Journal of Personality and Social Psychology, 26*, 446–456.

McHugh, Maureen C., Koeske, Randi D., & Frieze, Irene H. (1986). Issues to consider in conducting non-sexist psychological research. *American Psychologist, 41*, 879–890.

Marecek, Jeanne. (Ed.). (1989). Theory and method in feminist psychology [special issue]. *Psychology of Women Quarterly, 13*(4).

Mednick, Martha T. (1989). On the politics of psychological constructs: Stop the bandwagon, I want to get off. *American Psychologist, 44*, 1118–1123.

Mendelsohn, Everett. (1977). The social construction of scientific knowledge. In Everett Mendelsohn & Peter Weingart (Eds.), *The social production of scientific knowledge* (pp. 3–26). Boston: Reidel.

Mishler, Elliot G. (1979). Meaning in context: Is there any other kind? *Harvard Educational Review, 49*, 1–19.

Moke, Pamela, & Bohan, Janis S. (1992). Re-constructing curriculum: Psychology's paradigm and the virtues of iconoclasm. *Women's Studies Quarterly, 20* (1 & 2), 7–27.

Morawski, Jill G. (1982). On thinking about history as social psychology. *Personality and Social Psychology Bulletin, 8*, 393–401.

Morawski, Jill G. (1984). Historiography as a metatheoretical text for social psychology. In Kenneth Gergen and Mary M. Gergen (Eds.), *Historical social psychology* (pp. 37–60). Hillsdale, NJ: Lawrence Erlbaum.

Morawski, Jill G. (1985a). Contextual discipline: The making and unmaking of sociality. In Ralph L. Rosnow & Marianthi Georgoudi (Eds.), *Contextualism and understanding in behavioral science* (pp. 47–67). New York: Praeger.

Morawski, Jill G. (1985b). The measurement of masculinity and femininity: Engendering categorical realities. *Journal of Personality, 53*, 196–223.

Morawski, Jill G. (1988). Impossible experiments and practical constructions: The social bases of psychologists' work. In Jill G. Morawski (Ed.), *The rise of experimentalism in American psychology* (pp. 72–93). New Haven: Yale University Press.

Myrdal, Gunnar. (1969). Biases in social research. In Arne Tiselius & Sam Nillson (Eds.), *The place of values in a world of facts* (pp. 155–161). New York: Wiley.

Newman, Louise. (Ed.). (1985). *Men's ideas/Women's realities*. New York: Pergamon.

Nowell-Smith, P. H. (1977). The constructionist theory of history. *History & Theory: Studies in the Philosophy of History, 16*, 1–28.

O'Connell, Agnes N., & Russo, Nancy F. (Eds.). (1980). Eminent women in psychology: Models of achievement [special issue]. *Psychology of Women Quarterly, 5*(1).

O'Connell, Agnes N., & Russo, Nancy F. (1983). *Models of achievement: Reflections of eminent women in psychology*. New York: Columbia University Press.

O'Connell, Agnes N., & Russo, Nancy F. (1988). *Models of achievement: Reflections of eminent women in psychology*, vol. 2. Hillsdale, NJ: Lawrence Erlbaum.

O'Connell, Agnes N., & Russo, Nancy F. (1990). *Women in psychology: A biobibliographic sourcebook*. New York: Greenwood.

O'Donnell, John M. (1979). The crisis of experimentalism in the 1920's: E. G. Boring and his uses of history. *American Psychologist, 34*, 289–295.

O'Leary, Virginia E., Unger, Rhoda K., & Wallston, Barbara S. (Eds.). (1985). *Women, gender, and social psychology*. Hillsdale, NJ: Lawrence Erlbaum.

Ostertag, Patricia A., & McNamara, Regis. (1991). "Feminization" of psychology: The changing sex ratio and its implications for the profession. *Psychology of Women Quarterly, 15*, 349–369.

Polkinghorne, Donald. (1983). *Methodology for the human sciences: Systems of inquiry*. Albany: State University of New York Press.

Prilleltensky, Isaac. (1989). Psychology and the status quo. *American Psychologist, 44*, 795–802.

Rosenberg, Charles. (1976). *No other gods: On science and American sociological thought*. Baltimore: Johns Hopkins University Press.

Rosenberg, Rosalind. (1979). The academic prism: The new view of American women. In Carol R. Berkin & Mary Beth Norton (Eds.), *Women of America: A history* (pp. 318–341). New York: Houghton Mifflin.

Rosenberg, Rosalind. (1982). *Beyond separate spheres: Intellectual roots of modern feminism*. New Haven: Yale University Press.

Rosenberg, Rosalind. (1988). The limits of access: A history of coeducation in America. In John M. Faragher & Florence Howe (Eds.), *Women and higher education in American history* (pp. 107–128). New York: Norton.

Rossiter, Margaret W. (1982). *Women scientists in America: Struggles and strategies to 1940*. Baltimore: Johns Hopkins University Press.

Russo, Nancy F., & Denmark, Florence L. (1987). Contributions of women to psychology. *Annual Review of Psychology, 38*, 279–298.

Samelson, Franz. (1974). History, origin myth and ideology: The "discovery" of social psychology. *Journal of the Theory of Social Behavior, 4*, 217–231.

Sampson, Edward E. (1977). Psychology and the American idea. *Journal of Personality and Social Psychology, 35*, 767–782.

Sampson, Edward E. (1978). Scientific paradigms and social values: Wanted: a scientific revolution. *Journal of Personality and Social Psychology, 36*, 1332–1343.

Sampson, Edward E. (1983). Deconstructing psychology's subject. *Journal of Mind and Behavior, 4*, 135–164.

Sampson, Edward E. (1990). Social psychology and social control. In Ian Parker & John Shotter (Eds.), *Deconstructing social psychology* (pp. 117–126). London: Routledge.

Sarason, Seymore B. (1981). An asocial psychology and a misdirected clinical psychology. *American Psychologist, 40,* 1203–1211.

Sassen, Georgia. (1980). Success anxiety in women: A constructionist interpretation of its social significance. *Harvard Educational Review, 50,* 13–24.

Scarborough, Elizabeth, & Furumoto, Laurel. (1987). *Untold lives: The first generation of American women psychologists.* New York: Columbia University Press.

Scarr, Sandra. (1985). Constructing psychology: Making facts and fables for our time. *American Psychologist, 40,* 499–512.

Schultz, Duane, & Schultz, Ellen. (1987). *A history of modern psychology* (4th ed.). San Diego: Harcourt Brace Jovanovich.

Scott, Joan W. (1988). Deconstructing equality versus difference: On the uses of post-structuralist theory. *Feminist Studies, 14,* 33–50.

Sherif, Carolyn W. (1979a). Bias in psychology. In Julia Sherman & Evelyn T. Beck (Eds.), *The prism of sex: Essays in the sociology of knowledge* (pp. 93–133). Madison: University of Wisconsin Press.

Sherif, Carolyn W. (1979b). What every intelligent person should know about psychology and women. In Eloise C. Snyder (Ed.), *The study of women: Enlarging perspectives on social reality* (pp. 143–183). New York: Harper & Row.

Sherman, Julia, & Beck, Evelyn T. (Eds.). (1979). *The prism of sex: Essays in the sociology of knowledge.* Madison: University of Wisconsin Press.

Shields, Stephanie A. (1975). Functionalism, Darwinism and the psychology of women: A study in social myth. *American Psychologist, 30,* 739–753.

Shields, Stephanie A., & Mallory, Mary E. (1987). Leta Stetter Hollingworth speaks on "Columbia's Legacy." *Psychology of Women Quarterly, 11,* 285–300.

Simeone, Angela. (1987). *Academic women: Working towards equality.* South Hadley, MA: Bergin & Garvey.

Solomon, Barbara M. (1985). *In the company of educated women: A history of women and higher education in America.* New Haven: Yale University Press.

Spence, Janet T. (1981). Changing conceptions of men and women: A psychologist's perspective. In Elizabeth Langland & Walter Gove (Eds.), *A feminist perspective in the academy: The difference it makes* (pp. 130–148). Chicago: University of Chicago Press.

Spencer, Herbert. (1867). *The principles of biology.* New York: Appleton.

Spencer, Herbert. (1873). Psychology of the sexes. *Popular Science Monthly, 4,* 30–38.

Spencer, Herbert. (1891). *The study of sociology.* New York: Appleton.

Squire, Corinne. (1989). *Significant differences: Feminism in psychology.* London: Routledge.

Stark, Werner. (1958). *The sociology of knowledge: An essay in aid of a deeper understanding of the history of ideas.* London: Routledge & Kegan Paul.

Stevens, Gwendolyn, & Gardner, Sheldon. (1982). *The women of psychology,* vols. 1 & 2. Cambridge, MA: Schenkman.

Stocking, George W. (1965). On the limits of "presentism" and "historicism" in the historiography of the behavioral sciences. *Journal of the History of the Behavioral Sciences, 1*, 211–218.

Thorndike, Edward L. (1906). Sex in education. *Bookman, 23*, 211–214.

Thorndike, Edward L. (1910). *Educational psychology.* New York: Teachers College, Columbia University.

Touhey, John C. (1974). Effects of additional women professionals on ratings of occupational prestige and desirability. *Journal of Personality and Social Psychology, 29*, 86–89.

Toulmin, Stephen. (1982). The construal of reality: Criticism in modern and postmodern science. *Critical Inquiry, 9*, 93–111.

Toulmin, Stephen, & Leary, David E. (1985). The cult of empiricism in psychology, and beyond. In Sigmund Koch & David E. Leary (Eds.), *A century of psychology as science* (pp. 594–617). New York: McGraw–Hill.

Unger, Rhoda K. (1981). Sex differences: Historical perspectives and methodological implications. *Developmental Review, 1*, 187–206.

Unger, Rhoda K. (1982). Advocacy versus scholarship revisited: Issues in the psychology of women. *Psychology of Women Quarterly, 7*, 5–17.

Unger, Rhoda K. (1983). Through the looking glass: No wonderland yet! (The reciprocal relationship between methodology and models of reality). *Psychology of Women Quarterly, 8*, 9–32.

Unger, Rhoda K. (1985). Epistemological consistency and its scientific implications. *American Psychologist, 40*, 1413–1414.

Unger, Rhoda K. (1988). Psychological, feminist, and personal epistemology: Transcending contradiction. In Mary M. Gergen (Ed.), *Feminist thought and the structure of knowledge* (pp. 124–141). New York: New York University Press.

Unger, Rhoda K. (1989). *Representations: Social constructions of gender.* Amityville, NY: Baywood.

Walker, Lenore E. (1991). The feminization of psychology. *Psychology of Women: Newsletter of APA division 35, 18*(2), 1, 4.

Wallston, Barbara S. (1981). What are the questions in the psychology of women? A feminist approach to research. *Psychology of Women Quarterly, 5*, 597–617.

Weinstein, Fred. (1988). The problem of subjectivity in history. In William M. Ryan (Ed.), *Psychology and historical interpretation* (pp. 166–186). New York: Oxford University Press.

Weisstein, Naomi. (1968). *Kinder, Küche and Kirche as scientific law: Psychology constructs the female.* Boston: New England Free Press.

Weisstein, Naomi. (1971). Psychology constructs the female, or the fantasy life of the male psychologist (with some attention to the fantasies of his friends the male biologist and the male anthropologist). *Social Education, 35*, 362–373.

Welter, Barbara. (1966). The cult of true womanhood. *American Quarterly, 18*, 151–174.

Wertheimer, Michael. (1980). Historical research—Why? In Josef Brozek & Ludwig J. Pongratz (Eds.), *Historiography of modern psychology* (pp. 5–23). Toronto: Hogrefe.

West, Candace, & Zimmerman, Don. (1987). Doing gender. *Gender & Society, 1,* 125–151.

Westkott, Marcia. (1979). Feminist criticism of the social sciences. *Harvard Educational Review, 49,* 422–430.

Westkott, Marcia. (1988). *Female relationality and the idealized self.* Unpublished manuscript, University of Colorado, Boulder.

Wine, Jeri. (1982). Gynocentric values and feminist psychology. In Angela R. Miles & Geraldine Finn (Eds.), *Feminism in Canada: From pressure to politics* (pp. 67–87). Montreal: Black Rose.

Wittig, Michele A. (1985). Metatheoretical dilemmas in the psychology of gender. *American Psychologist, 40,* 800–811.

Woolley, Helen (Thompson). (1903). *The mental traits of sex.* Chicago: University of Chicago Press.

Woolley, Helen (Thompson). (1910). A review of recent literature on the psychology of sex. *Psychological Bulletin, 7,* 335–342.

Woolley, Helen (Thompson). (1914). The psychology of sex. *Psychological Bulletin, 11,* 353–379.

Zaner, Richard M. (1985). The logos of psyche: Phenomenological variations on a theme. In Sigmund Koch & David E. Leary (Eds.), *A century of psychology as science* (pp. 618–637). New York: McGraw-Hill.

PART 1
THROUGH A FEMINIST PRISM: WOMEN'S PLACE IN PSYCHOLOGY

Psychology has nothing to say about what women are really like, what they need and what they want, essentially because psychology does not know. (Weisstein, 1971, p. 364)

Despite its "not knowing," psychology has had a great deal to say about women. And, as Weisstein deftly pointed out, what psychology has said has had more to do with unspoken assumptions and cultural biases than with the reality of women's experience. The title of Weisstein's article is "Psychology Constructs the Female"; her choice of title has proven prescient. Recent theoretical and empirical scholarship persuasively demonstrates that gender is indeed a construction, a product of sociohistorical context, and as such is irretrievably bound up in the biases and assumptions that pervade both societal Zeitgeist and disciplinary paradigm.

The burgeoning recognition that psychology has not treated women well, an awareness both reflected in and incited by works such as Weisstein's, is the subject of the readings in Part 1. I use the phrase "treated women" advisedly, for the multiplicity of its connotations points to the plethora of forms of ill-treatment women have been accorded by psychology. Psychological theory and research have variously ignored, discounted, distorted, minimized, and demeaned the experiences of women; clinical practice has hewed to dominant (misogynist) interpretations of mental health and gender identity, trivializing and pathologizing women; women's place in the discipline, as students and professionals, has been marginalized and their importance to psychology disregarded.

The articles included in this part elaborate on this assertion, exploring the variety of ways in which psychology has willingly regarded culturally embedded assumptions about gender as if they were facts and how this penchant has distorted crucial questions of women's experience. Weisstein's article, the first reading in this part, has become a classic, and although it is now two decades old, the issues raised remain salient and her commentary compelling. Beyond pointing out how psychology's practices, its research, and its interpretations have been shaped by the unacknowledged (and sexist) presuppositions of a largely male-defined psychology, Weisstein's discussion initiates the constructionist analysis that will characterize later writings. Without deploying explicitly constructionist terminology, she builds a powerful case for the conclusion that psychology's "understanding" of women has indeed been a sociohistorically situated construction. Upon analysis, this purported body of knowledge reveals unquestioned, albeit unverified, presuppositions about human experience in general, women's experience in particular.

Writing about a theme that appeared in the Prologue to this book and that will recur in later discussions, Weisstein took to task psychology's predilection for invoking internal dynamics as explanatory of human behavior, thereby minimizing the impact of social context. Although such intrapsychic attribution is problematic across the board, it is particularly troublesome in explanations of women's experience, for it disregards the gendered qualities of social context, qualities that are precisely those reproduced by the sexist and misogynist attitudes of psychologists. Further, she argued, theories elaborating on these internal dynamics and their consequences for behavior have failed to submit their notions to adequate empirical testing. This strategy distorts psychology's presentation of women by allowing theory to be shaped not by evidence but by unrecognized social forces, particularly presumptions about gender. When such insidious influences are allowed to operate unchecked by appeals to reality, Weisstein cautioned, the result is theories that mimic social norms—not scientific understandings but affirmations of cultural biases.

The warning sounded by Weisstein is reiterated in Stephanie Shields's article, whose subtitle, "A Study in Social Myth," encapsulates the issue at hand: psychology's portrayal of women is composed more of belief than of reality. Shields's particular focus was on the treatment of women in the early years of American psychology, where the impact of social opinion on presumably objective scientific activity is, in retrospect, strikingly obvious. Shields neatly unpacked the foundational assumptions of the psychology of this formative era, particularly the role of Darwinism and its psychological offspring, functionalism, in determining how psychology would address the "woman question." This analysis was played out against the further background of broader societal understandings of gender, thus illustrating how both the construction of gender in the society at large and the paradigm(s) operative within the discipline cooperate in framing the address to issues touching on social norms. In this case, as Shields's examination demonstrated, the two streams of influence converged, forming an apparently irresistible (or unresisted) current that led psychology—and indeed other sciences—to support then-prevalent notions regarding gender. The added credibility given these beliefs by the appellation "scientific" served well to reinforce a particular (and particularly misogynist) construction of gender. In Shields's apt words, "That science played handmaiden to social values cannot be denied" (1975, p. 753).

The parallel between Weisstein's commentary on midcentury psychology's treatment of women and Shields's analysis of turn-of-the-century psychology is apparent. The persistent leitmotif is that psychology (science, broadly) has supported, reinforced, even conspired in the propagation of societal norms demeaning to women. The construction of gender can be seen as both determinant and product of psychology's endeavors: the psychology of women has been framed by societal understandings of gender, and psychology has (at least often) contributed to the maintenance and elaboration of those same understandings.

Despite the perspicacity of work such as Weisstein's and Shields's, it is evident upon perusal of the subsequent psychological literature that such challenges went largely unnoticed by mainstream psychology, certainly generating no ground swell of revisionist activity in psychological laboratories, classrooms, or arenas of praxis. On the contrary, the dynamic pointed out by Shields as characteristic of turn-of-the-century psychology, what might be termed the "science as handmaiden" syndrome, has persisted largely unabated, and the discipline has continued to reflect in its work the power of social forces devaluing women.

For those working to apply feminist analysis to psychology's practices, the neglect of quite persuasive evidence demonstrating psychology's misogynist myopia points to deeper issues. Psychology, these analyses argue, rests at its most fundamental levels upon assumptions that act to distort women's experience, their place in the discipline, and their treatment in psychological theory, research, and practice. Attempting to ferret out the nature and impact of these assumptions, feminist psychologists undertook to unravel psychology's philosophical commitments—commitments implicit in its theoretical, methodological, historiographic and pragmatic allegiances—searching among these underpinnings for the elements of psychology's foundation that acted perniciously to marginalize women.

Among the discoveries of this work we find truly fundamental challenges to psychology's modus operandi. Moving well beyond the obvious exclusion of women from professional circles, from research activities, and from the subjects about whom theories are written and for whom practice is shaped, this work exposes psychology's fundamental indifference to women. This indifference is reflected and magnified in a parallel disdain for modes of psychological inquiry and practice that deviate from the norm. It is apparent that standards for mainstream psychological endeavor incorporate assumptions that act insidiously to marginalize women, even when they are not explicitly about marginalizing women.

Carolyn Wood Sherif's article introduces this discussion, documenting gender bias in psychology within a framework of asking broader questions about the activities and the purposes of psychology. By addressing questions of epistemology and methodology, by unpacking the presumptions about human experience entailed by standard psychological theories and practices, Sherif pushed the question of women's exclusion beyond the concrete reality of women's invisibility to the conceptual infrastructure that has generated and sustained that exclusion. It is essential but inadequate, Sherif's article suggested, simply to document bias against women. In order effectively to ameliorate that problem and its attendant distortions, we must understand what it is about psychology, purporting to offer an objective perspective on human experience, that in reality supports an approach that is very biased indeed. Psychology's failure to acknowledge its inevitable valuing has, Sherif argued, allowed the discipline to serve as "handmaiden," perpetuating social myths and upholding the status quo.

Now-familiar themes in Sherif's deconstruction of psychology's paradigmatic commitments were her arguments for the centrality of context, the detrimental consequences of intrapersonal attribution, and the delimiting impact upon psychological activities of particular social constructions of "reality." Sherif's challenge to the business-as-usual of psychology was accompanied by a parallel call to action, a charge that reflects a similarly broad perspective: simply adding women subjects to research, women psychologists to histories, and women's experience to theories is not sufficient to a thorough revision of psychology; psychology's philosophical grounding must be queried as well. To this end, Sherif proposed conceptual and practical strategies for reconstructing psychology in a manner that would accommodate the criticisms raised by analyses such as hers.

The unifying thread that joins the work of Weisstein, Shields, and Sherif is psychology's unreflective adherence to tacit assumptions that operate to marginalize women, women's issues, and women's work in psychology. And it is to this confrontation with the inescapable role of philosophical assumptions, the interdependence of "methods and models of reality," that Rhoda Unger invited us. Addressing specifically the manner in which psychological method shapes our understandings of reality, Unger presented a persuasive argument for this relationship as fundamental. This argument was actually twofold: one thread explored the conflation of method and worldview, the other elaborated on implications of this relationship for psychology's treatment of women.

First, Unger's article carefully dissected psychological methods, exposing their subtle implications for the understanding of human experience. A method is a theory, this analysis suggested; the terminology, the technique, the interpretation of results all reveal a particular perspective on the nature of reality. The personal and social implications of differing models of reality (qua methodology), Unger insisted, are directly derivative from the assumptions entailed therein. Hence, using different methods implies operating from differing worldviews and will unavoidably lead to differing implications and applications, differing social and personal consequences.

A second, derivative layer of analysis embedded in Unger's discussion was taken from the perspective of the sociology of knowledge and specifically addressed the question of women's place in psychology. So-called knowledge, this argument averred, is in actuality a product of social context (the echo of our prior discussions of constructionism is strong here); psychology's "knowledge" of women has been shaped by social context both internal to the discipline (its adherence to a particular methodological paradigm and the commensurate view of reality) and external to psychology (the social norms to which psychology has often served as handmaiden). If models of reality are reflected in method and if traditional psychological methods have marginalized women, then it follows that in order to create a women-inclusive psychology, we must expand our methodological options. Unger rounded out this discussion with recommendations for a reflexive psychology, one which recognizes its inextricable valuing and its embeddedness in context.

In the final article in this part, Bernice Lott brings us full circle. From Weisstein's original indictment of psychology's (mis)understanding of women as misogynist "fantasy," we discover that almost fifteen years later the monotonous theme is still playing: women are still devalued, and that devaluation still reflects stereotyped beliefs regarding women, present in the culture and reflected in psychology's own undertakings. Particularly striking in Lott's discussion is the discrepancy between reality (the reality of women's competence, of women's experience) and perception. In the face of evidence to the contrary, people (especially men) persist in perceiving women as less competent. Indeed, even competent women tend to devalue their own abilities, attributing them to external forces. While Lott's discussion illustrated a pattern of findings far more complex than this simple summary allows, the overwhelming impression left by her work is this: Our beliefs about women's competence (tightly interwoven with our construction of gender) are so firm that contrary evidence has little impact on them. Although the specific topic here was competence, the implication is far broader. Our socially constructed certainty about the "reality" of gendered qualities is so firmly rooted and so well buttressed by social norms and social institutions that it stands fast even in the face of gales of disconfirming information.

To extend Lott's analysis to psychology as a field, we must ask what role this discipline has played in creating and sustaining that mythical knowledge and how the practices presently undertaken by psychology obstruct its dismantling. If, as Weisstein argued, psychology's understanding of women is nothing more than fantasy sustained by misogynist egocentrism; if psychology has, in Shields's words, simply served as handmaiden to social norms; if our histories and our methods reflect these same socially constructed distortions passing for meaningful understanding, as Sherif and Unger argued, how do we go about creating a women-inclusive psychology that values women and their work?

The readings included here amply demonstrate psychology's poor treatment of women. If in our attempt to illuminate this ill-treatment we appeal to charges of sexism, misogyny, and male domination of the field, our answer will be correct and inadequate. Those claims, although surely accurate, simply push the question back a step, and it becomes this: How do sexism, misogyny, and male dominance shape psychology's treatment of women? What are the mechanisms by which these demonstrably pervasive forces create a discipline where women are marginalized? How can we understand women's place in psychology in such a way that our understanding informs and invigorates a reconstruction of the field? We must move beyond documenting the problem to a deeper understanding of the social constructions and paradigmatic structures that undergird it. The articles in this part lay a foundation for that understanding.

References

Shields, Stephanie A. (1975). Functionalism, Darwinism and the psychology of women: A study in social myth. *American Psychologist, 30,* 739–753.

Weisstein, Naomi. (1971). Psychology constructs the female, or the fantasy life of the male psychologist (with some attention to the fantasies of his friends the male biologist and the male anthropologist). *Social Education, 35,* 362–373.

2

PSYCHOLOGY CONSTRUCTS THE FEMALE, OR THE FANTASY LIFE OF THE MALE PSYCHOLOGIST

(With Some Attention to the Fantasies
of His Friends the Male Biologist
and the Male Anthropologist)

Naomi Weisstein

It is an implicit assumption that the area of psychology which concerns itself with personality has the onerous but necessary task of describing the limits of human possibility. Thus when we are about to consider the liberation of women, we naturally look to psychology to tell us what "true" liberation would mean: what would give women the freedom to fulfill their own intrinsic natures. Psychologists have set about describing the true natures of women with a certainty and a sense of their own infallibility rarely found in the secular world. Bruno Bettelheim, of the University of Chicago, tells us (1965) that "We must start with the realization that, as much as women want to be good scientists or engineers, they want first and foremost to be womanly companions of men and to be mothers." Erik Erikson of Harvard University (1964), upon noting that young women often ask whether they can "have an identity before they know whom they will marry, and for whom they will make a home,"

This article is a revised and expanded version of "Kinder, Küche, Kirche as Scientific Law: Psychology Constructs the Female," published by the New England Free Press, 791 Tremont Street, Boston, MA (1968). Copyright © Naomi Weisstein. Reprinted by permission of the author.

explains somewhat elegiacally that "Much of a young woman's identity is already defined in her kind of attractiveness and in the selectivity of her search for the man (or men) by whom she wishes to be sought. . . ." Mature womanly fulfillment, for Erikson, rests on the fact that a woman's ". . . somatic design harbors an 'inner space' destined to bear the offspring of chosen men, and with it, a biological, psychological, and ethical commitment to take care of human infancy." Some psychiatrists even see the acceptance of woman's role by women as a solution to societal problems. "Woman is nurturance. . . ," writes Joseph Rheingold (1964), a psychiatrist at Harvard Medical School, ". . . anatomy decrees the life of a woman . . . when women grow up without dread of their biological functions and without subversion by feminist doctrine, and therefore enter upon motherhood with a sense of fulfillment and altruistic sentiment, we shall attain the goal of a good life and a secure world in which we live it." (p. 714)

These views from men who are assumed to be experts reflect, in a surprisingly transparent way, the cultural consensus. They not only assert that a woman is defined by her ability to attract men, they see no alternative definitions. They think that the definition of a woman in terms of a man is the way it should be; and they back it up with psychosexual incantation and biological ritual curses. A woman has an identity if she is attractive enough to obtain a man, and thus, a home; for this will allow her to set about her life's task of "joyful altruism and nurturance."

Business certainly does not disagree. If views such as Bettelheim's and Erikson's do indeed have something to do with real liberation for women, then seldom in human history has so much money and effort been spent on helping a group of people realize their true potential. Clothing, cosmetics, home furnishings, are multi-million dollar businesses: if you don't like investing in firms that make weaponry and flaming gasoline, then there's a lot of cash in "inner space." Sheet and pillowcase manufacturers are concerned to fill this inner space:

> Mother, for a while this morning, I thought I wasn't cut out for married life. Hank was late for work and forgot his apricot juice and walked out without kissing me, and when I was all alone I started crying. But then the postman came with the sheets and towels you sent, that look like big bandana handkerchiefs, and you know what I thought? That those big red and blue handkerchiefs are for girls like me to dry their tears on so they can get busy and do what a housewife has to do. Throw open the windows and start getting the house ready, and the dinner, maybe clean the silver and put new geraniums in the box. *Everything to be ready for him when he walks through that door.* (Fieldcrest 1966; emphasis added.)

Of course, it is not only the sheet and pillowcase manufacturers, the cosmetics industry, the home furnishings salesmen who profit from and make use of the cultural definitions of man and woman. The example above is blatantly and overtly pitched to a particular kind of sexist stereotype: the child nymph. But almost all aspects of the media are normative, that is, they have to do with the ways in which beautiful people, or just folks, or ordinary Americans, or extraordinary Americans should live their lives. They define the possible; and the possibilities are usually in terms of what is male and what is female. Men and women alike are waiting for Hank, the Silva Thins man, to walk back through that door.

It is interesting but limited exercise to show that psychologists and psychiatrists embrace these sexist norms of our culture, that they do not see beyond the most superficial and stultifying media conceptions of female nature, and that their ideas of female nature serve industry and commerce so well. Just because it's good for business doesn't mean it's wrong. What I will show is that it *is wrong;* that there isn't the tiniest shred of evidence that these fantasies of servitude and childish dependence have anything to do with women's true potential; that the idea of the nature of human possibility which rests on the accidents of individual development or genitalia, on what is possible today because of what happened yesterday, on the fundamentalist myth of sex organ causality, has strangled and deflected psychology so that it is relatively useless in describing, explaining or predicting humans and their behavior. It then goes without saying that present psychology is less than worthless in contributing to a vision which could truly liberate—men as well as women.

The central argument of my article, then, is this. Psychology has nothing to say about what women are really like, what they need and what they want, essentially because psychology does not know. I want to stress that this failure is not limited to women; rather, the kind of psychology which had addressed itself to how people act and who they are has failed to understand, in the first place, why people act the way they do, and certainly failed to understand what might make them act differently.

The kind of psychology which has addressed itself to these questions divides into two professional areas: academic personality research, and clinical psychology and psychiatry. The basic reason for failure is the same in both these areas: the central assumption for most psychologists of human personality has been that human behavior rests on an individual and inner dynamic, perhaps fixed in infancy, perhaps fixed by genitalia, perhaps simply arranged in a rather immovable cognitive network. But this assumption is rapidly losing ground as personality psychologists fail again and again to get consistency in the assumed personalities of their subjects (Block, 1968). Meanwhile, the evidence is collecting that what a person does, and who he believes himself to be, will in general be a function of what people around him expect him to be, and what the overall situation in which he is acting implies that he is. Compared to the influence of the social context within which a person lives, his or her history and "traits," as well as biological makeup, may simply be random variations, "noise" superimposed on the true signal which can predict behavior.

Some academic personality psychologists are at least looking at the counter evidence and questioning their theories; no such corrective is occurring in clinical psychology and psychiatry. Freudians and neo-Freudians, Adlerians and neo-Adlerians, classicists and swingers, clinicians and psychiatrists, simply refuse to look at the evidence against their theory and practice. And they support their theory and practice with stuff so transparently biased as to have absolutely no standing as empirical evidence.

To summarize: the first reason for psychology's failure to understand what people are and how they act is that psychology has looked for inner traits when it should have been looking for social context; the second reason for psychology's failure is that the theoreticians of personality have generally been clinicians and psychiatrists, and they have never considered it necessary to have evidence in support of their theories.

Theory Without Evidence

Let us turn to this latter cause of failure first: the acceptance by psychiatrists and clinical psychologists of theory without evidence. If we inspect the literature of personality, it is immediately obvious that the bulk of it is written by clinicians and psychiatrists, and that the major support for their theories is "years of intensive clinical experience." This is a tradition started by Freud. His "insights" occurred during the course of his work with his patients. Now there is nothing wrong with such an approach to theory *formulation;* a person is free to make up theories with any inspiration which works: divine revelation, intensive clinical practice, a random numbers table. But he is not free to claim any validity for his theory until it has been tested and confirmed. But theories are treated in no such tentative way in ordinary clinical practice. Consider Freud. What he thought constituted evidence violated the most minimal conditions of scientific rigor. In *The Sexual Enlightenment of Children* (1963), the classic document which is supposed to demonstrate empirically the existence of a castration complex and its connection to a phobia, Freud based his analysis not on the little boy who had the phobia, but on the reports of the father of the little boy, himself in therapy, and a devotee of Freudian theory. I really don't have to comment further on the contamination in this kind of evidence. It is remarkable that only recently has Freud's classic theory on the sexuality of women—the notion of the double orgasm—been actually tested physiologically and found just plain wrong. Now those who claim that fifty years of psychoanalytic experience constitute evidence enough of the essential truths of Freud's theory should ponder the robust health of the double orgasm. Did women, until Masters and Johnson (1966), believe they were having two different kinds of orgasm? Did their psychiatrists intimidate them into reporting something that was not true? If so, were there other things they reported that were also not true? Did psychiatrists ever learn anything different than their theories had led them to believe? If clinical experience means anything at all, surely we should have been done with the double orgasm myth long before the Masters and Johnson studies.

But certainly, you may object, "years of intensive clinical experience" is the only reliable measure in a discipline which rests for its findings on insight, sensitivity, and intuition. The problem with insight, sensitivity, and intuition is that they can confirm for all time the biases that one started out with. People used to be absolutely convinced of their ability to tell which of their number were engaging in witchcraft. All it required was some sensitivity to the workings of the devil.

Years of intensive clinical experience is not the same thing as empirical evidence. The first thing an experimenter learns in any kind of experiment which involves humans is the concept of the "double blind." The term is taken from medical experiments, where one group is given a drug which is presumably supposed to change behavior in a certain way, and a control group is given a placebo. If the observers or the subjects know which group took which drug, the result invariably comes out on the positive side for the new drug. Only when it is not known which subject took which pill, is validity remotely approximated. In addition, with judgments of human behavior, it is so difficult to precisely tie down just what behavior is going on, let alone what behavior should be expected, that one must test again and again the reliability of judgments. How many judges, blind, will agree in their observations? Can they replicate their own judgments at some later time? When, in actual practice, these judgment criteria are tested for clinical judgments, then we find that the judges cannot judge reliably, nor can they judge consistently: they do no better than chance in identifying which of a certain set of stories were written by men and which by women; which of a whole battery of clinical test results are the products of homosexuals and which are the products of heterosexuals (Hooker, 1957); and which of a battery of clinical test results *and* interviews (where questions are asked such as "Do you have delusions?"—Little & Schneidman, 1959) are products of psychotics, neurotics, psychosomatics, or normals. Lest this summary escape your notice, let me stress the implications of these findings. The ability of judges, chosen for their clinical expertise, to distinguish male heterosexuals from male homosexuals on the basis of three widely used clinical projective tests—the Rorschach, the TAT, and the MAP—was *no better than chance*. The reason this is such devastating news, of course, is that sexuality is supposed to be of fundamental importance in the deep dynamic of personality; if what is considered gross sexual deviance cannot be caught, then what are psychologists talking about when they, for example, claim that at the basis of paranoid psychosis is "latent homosexual panic"? They can't even identify what homosexual anything is, let alone "latent homosexual panic."[1] More frightening, expert clinicians cannot be consistent on what diagnostic category to assign to a person, again on the basis of both tests and interviews; a number of normals in the Little & Schneidman study were described as psychotic, in such categories as "schizophrenic with homosexual tendencies" or "schizoid character with depressive trends." But most disheartening, when the judges were asked to rejudge the test protocols some weeks later, their diagnoses of the same subjects on the basis of the same protocol differed markedly from their initial judgments. It is obvious that even simple descriptive conventions in clinical psychology cannot be consistently applied; that these descriptive conventions have any explanatory significance is therefore, of course, out of the question.

As a graduate student at Harvard some years ago, I was a member of a seminar which was asked to identify which of two piles of a clinical test, the TAT, had been written by males and which by females. Only four students out of twenty identified the piles correctly, and this was after one and a half months of intensively studying the differences between men and women. Since this result is below chance—that is, this result would occur by chance about four out of a thousand times—we may conclude that there is finally a consistency here; students are judging knowledgeably within the context of psychological teaching about the differences between men and women; the teachings themselves are simply erroneous.

You may argue that the theory may be scientifically "unsound" but at least it cures people. There is no evidence that it does. In 1952, Eysenck reported the results of what is called an "outcome of therapy" study of neurotics which showed that, of the patients who received psychoanalysis the improvement rate was 44%; of the patients who received psychotherapy the improvement rate of 64%; and of the patients who received no treatment at all the improvement rate was 72%. These findings have never been refuted; subsequently, later studies have confirmed the negative results of the Eysenck study. (Barron & Leary, 1955; Bergin, 1963; Cartwright and Vogel, 1960; Truax, 1963; Powers and Witmer, 1951). How can clinicians and psychiatrists, then, in all good conscience, continue to practice? Largely by ignoring these results and being careful not to do outcome-of-therapy studies. The attitude is nicely summarized by Rotter (1960) (quoted in Astin, 1961): "Research studies in psychotherapy tend to be concerned with psychotherapeutic procedure and less with outcome ... to some extent, it reflects an interest in the psychotherapy situation as a kind of personality laboratory." Some laboratory.

The Social Context

Thus, since clinical experience and tools can be shown to be worse than useless when tested for consistency, efficacy, agreement, and reliability, we can safely conclude that theories of a clinical nature advanced about women are also worse than useless. I want to turn now to the second major point in my article, which is that, even when psychological theory is constructed so that it may be tested, and rigorous standards of evidence are used, it has become increasingly clear that in order to understand why people do what they do, and certainly in order to change what people do, psychologists must turn away from the theory of the causal nature of the inner dynamic and look to the social context within which individuals live.

Before examining the relevance of this approach for the question of women, let me first sketch the groundwork for this assertion.

In the first place, it is clear (Block, 1968) that personality tests never yield consistent predictions; a rigid authoritarian on one measure will be an unauthoritarian on the next. But the reason for this inconsistency is only now becoming clear, and it seems overwhelmingly to have much more to do with the social situation in which the subject finds himself than with the subject himself.

In a series of brilliant experiments, Rosenthal and his co-workers (Rosenthal and Jacobson, 1968; Rosenthal, 1966) have shown that if one group of experimenters has one hypothesis about what it expects to find, and another group of experimenters has the opposite hypothesis, both groups will obtain results in accord with their hypotheses. The results obtained are not due to mishandling of data by biased experimenters; rather, somehow, the bias of the experimenter creates a changed environment in which subjects actually act differently. For instance, in one experiment, subjects were to assign numbers to pictures of men's faces, with high numbers representing the subject's judgment that the man in the picture was a successful person, and low numbers representing the subject's judgment that the man in the picture was an unsuccessful person. One group of experimenters was told that the subjects tended to rate the faces high; another group of experimenters was told that the subjects tended to rate the faces low. Each group of experimenters was instructed to follow precisely the same procedure: they were required to read to subjects a set of instructions, and to *say nothing else*. For the 375 subjects run, the results showed clearly that those subjects who performed the task with experimenters who expected high ratings gave high ratings, and those subjects who performed the task with experimenters who expected low ratings gave low ratings. How did this happen? The experimenters all used the same words; it was something in their conduct which made one group of subjects do one thing, and another group of subjects do another thing.[2]

The concreteness of the changed conditions produced by expectation is a fact, a reality: even with animal subjects, in two separate studies (Rosenthal & Fode, 1960; Rosenthal & Lawson, 1961), those experimenters who were told that rats learning mazes had been especially bred for brightness obtained better learning from their rats than did experimenters believing their rats to have been bred for dullness. In a very recent study, Rosenthal & Jacobson (1968) extended their analysis to the natural class-room situation. Here, they tested a group of students and reported to the teachers that some among the students tested "showed great promise." Actually, the students so named had been selected on a random basis. Some time later, the experimenters retested the group of students: those students whose teachers had been told that they were "promising" showed real and dramatic increments in their IQ's as compared to the rest of the students. Something in the conduct of the teachers towards those whom the teachers believed to be the "bright" students made those students brighter.

Thus, even in carefully controlled experiments, and with no outward or conscious difference in behavior, the hypotheses we start with will influence enormously the behavior of another organism. These studies are extremely important when assessing the validity of psychological studies of women. Since it is beyond doubt that most of us start with notions as to the nature of men and women, the validity of a number of observations of sex differences is questionable, even when these observations have been made under carefully controlled conditions. Second, and more important, the Rosenthal experiments point quite clearly to the influence of social expectation. In some extremely important ways, people are what you expect them to be or at least they behave as you expect them to behave. Thus, if women, according to Bettelheim, want first and foremost to be good wives and mothers, it is extremely likely that this is what Bruno Bettelheim, and the rest of society, want them to be.

There is another series of brilliant social psychological experiments which point to the overwhelming effect of social context. These are the obedience experiments of Stanley Milgram (1965) in which subjects are asked to obey the orders of unknown experimenters, orders which carry with them the distinct possibility that the subject is killing somebody.

In Milgram's experiments, a subject is told that he is administering a learning experiment, and that he is to deal out shocks each time the other "subject" (in reality, a confederate of the experimenter) answers incorrectly. The equipment appears to provide graduated shocks ranging upwards from 15 volts through 450 volts; for each of four consecutive voltages there are verbal descriptions such as "mild shock," "danger, severe shock," and, finally, for the 435 and 450 volt switches, a red XXX marked over the switches. Each time the stooge answers incorrectly the subject is supposed to increase the voltage. As the voltage increases, the stooge begins to cry in pain; he demands that the experiment stop; finally, he refuses to answer at all. When he stops responding, the experimenter instructs the subject to continue increasing the voltage; for each shock administered the stooge shrieks in agony. Under these conditions, about 62.5% of the subjects administered shock that they believed to be possibly lethal.

No tested individual differences between subjects predicted how many would continue to obey, and which would break off the experiment. When forty psychiatrists predicted how many of a group of 100 subjects would go on to give the lethal shock, their predictions were orders of magnitude below the actual percentages; most expected only one-tenth of one percent of the subjects to obey to the end.

But even though *psychiatrists* have no idea how people will behave in this situation, and even though individual differences do not predict which subjects will obey and which will not, it is easy to predict when subjects will be obedient and when they will be defiant. All the experimenter has to do is change the social situation. In a variant of the experiment, Milgram had two stooges present in addition to the "victim"; these worked along with the subject in administering electric shocks. When these two stooges refused to go on with the experiment, only ten percent of the subjects continued to the maximum voltage. This is critical for personality theory. It says that behavior is predicted from the social situation, not from the individual history.

Finally, an ingenious experiment by Schachter and Singer (1962) showed that subjects injected with adrenaline, which produces a state of physiological arousal in all but minor respects identical to that which occurs when subjects are extremely afraid, became euphoric when they were in a room with a stooge who was acting euphoric, and became extremely angry when they were placed in a room with a stooge who was acting extremely angry.

To summarize: If subjects under quite innocuous and non-coercive social conditions can be made to kill other subjects and under other types of social conditions will positively refuse to do so; if subjects can react to a state of physiological fear by becoming euphoric because there is somebody else around who is euphoric or angry because there is some-body else around who is angry; if students become intelligent because teachers expect them to be intelligent, and rats run mazes better because experimenters are told the rats are bright, then it is obvious that a study of human behavior requires, first and foremost, a study of the social contexts within which people move, the expectations as to how they will behave, and the authority which tells them who they are and what they are supposed to do.

Biologically-Based Theories

Biologists also have at times assumed they could describe the limits of human potential from the observations of animal rather than human behavior. Here, as in psychology, there has been no end of theorizing about the sexes, again with a sense of absolute certainty. These theories fall into two major categories.

One biological theory of differences in nature argues that since females and males differ in their sex hormones, and sex hormones enter the brain (Hamburg & Lunde in Maccoby, 1966), there must be innate behavioral differences. But the only thing this argument tells us is that there are differences in physiological state. The problem is whether these differences are at all relevant to behavior.

Consider, for example, differences in testosterone levels. A man who calls himself Tiger[3] has recently argued (1970) that the greater quantities of testosterone found in human males as compared with human females (of a certain age group) determines innate differences in aggressiveness, competitiveness, dominance, ability to hunt, ability to hold public office, and so forth. But Tiger demonstrates in this argument the same manly and courageous refusal to be intimidated by evidence which we have already seen in our consideration of the clinical and psychiatric tradition. The evidence does not support his argument, and in some cases, directly contradicts it. Testosterone level co-varies neither with hunting ability, nor with dominance, nor with aggression, nor with competitiveness. As Storch has pointed out (1970), all normal male mammals in the reproductive age group produce much greater quantities of testosterone than females; yet many of these males are neither hunters nor are they aggressive. Among some hunting mammals, such as the large cats, it turns out that more hunting is done by the female than the male. And there exist primate species where the female is clearly more aggressive, competitive, and dominant than the male (Mitchell, 1969; and see below). Thus, for some species, being female, and therefore, having less testosterone than the male of that species means hunting more, or being more aggressive, or being more dominant. Nor does having *more* testosterone preclude behavior commonly thought of as "female": there exist primate species where females do not touch infants except to feed them; the males care for the infants (Mitchell, 1969; see fuller discussion below). So it is not clear what testosterone or any other sex-hormonal difference means for differences in nature of sex-role behavior.

In other words, one can observe identical sex-role behavior (e.g., "mothering") in males and females despite known differences in physiological state, i.e., sex hormones. What about the converse to this? That is, can one obtain differences in behavior given a single physiological state? The answer is overwhelmingly yes, not only as regards non-sex-specific hormones (as in the Schachter and Singer 1962 experiment cited above), but also as regards gender itself. Studies of hermaphrodites with the same diagnosis (the genetic, gonadal, hormonal sex, the internal reproductive organs, and the ambiguous appearances of the external genitalia were identical) have shown that one will consider oneself male or female depending simply on whether one was defined and raised as male or female (Money, 1970; Hampton & Hampton, 1961):

"There is no more convincing evidence of the power of social interaction on gender-identity differentiation than in the case of congenital hermaphrodites who are of the same diagnosis and similar degree of hermaphroditism but are differently assigned and with a different postnatal medical and life history." (Money, 1970, p. 432.)

Thus, for example, if out of two individuals diagnosed as having the adrenogenital syndrome of female hermaphroditism, one is raised as a girl and one as a boy, each will act and identify her/himself accordingly. The one raised as a girl will consider herself a girl; the one raised as a boy will consider himself a boy; and each will conduct her/himself successfully in accord with that self-definition.

So, identical behavior occurs given different physiological states; and different behavior occurs given an identical physiological starting point. So it is not clear that differences in sex hormones are at all relevant to behavior.

There is a second category of theory based on biology, a reductionist theory. It goes like this. Sex-role behavior in some primate species is described, and it is concluded that this is the "natural" behavior for humans. Putting aside the not insignificant problem of observer bias (for instance, Harlow, 1962, of the University of Wisconsin, after observing differences between male and female rhesus monkeys, quotes Lawrence Sterne to the effect that women are silly and trivial, and concludes that "men and women have differed in the past and they will differ in the future"), there are a number of problems with this approach.

The most general and serious problem is that there are no grounds to assume that anything primates do is necessary, natural, or desirable in humans, for the simple reason that humans are not non-humans. For instance, it is found that male chimpanzees placed alone with infants will not "mother" them. Jumping from hard data to ideological speculation researchers conclude from this information that *human* females are necessary for the safe growth of human infants. It would be as reasonable to conclude, following this logic, that it is quite useless to teach human infants to speak, since it has been tried with chimpanzees and it does not work.

One strategy that has been used is to extrapolate from primate behavior to "innate" human preference by noticing certain trends in primate behavior as one moves phylogenetically closer to humans. But there are great difficulties with this approach. When behaviors from lower primates are directly opposite to those of higher primates, or to those one expects of humans, they can be dismissed on evolutionary grounds—higher primates and/or humans grew out of that kid stuff. On the other hand, if the behavior of higher primates is counter to the behavior considered natural for humans, while the behavior of some lower primate is considered the natural one for humans, the higher primate behavior can be dismissed also, on the grounds that it has diverged from an older, prototypical pattern. So either way, one can select those behaviors one wants to prove as innate for humans. In addition, one does not know whether the sex-role behavior exhibited is dependent on the phylogenetic rank, or on the environmental conditions (both physical and social) under which different species live.

Is there then any value at all in primate observations as they relate to human females and males? There is a value but it is limited: its function can be no more than to show some extant examples of diverse sex-role behavior. It must be stressed, however, that this is an extremely limited function. The extant behavior does not begin to suggest all the possibilities, either for non-human primates or for humans. Bearing these caveats in mind, it is nonetheless interesting that if one inspects the limited set of existing non-human primate sex-role behaviors, one finds, in fact, a much larger range of sex-role behavior than is commonly believed to exist. "Biology" appears to limit very little; the fact that a female gives birth does not mean, even in non-humans, that she necessarily cares for the infant (in marmosets, for instance, the male carries the infant at all times except when the infant is feeding [Mitchell, 1969]); "natural" female and male behavior varies all the way from females who are much more aggressive and competitive than males (e.g., Tamarins, see Mitchell, 1969) and male "mothers" (e.g., Titi monkeys, night monkeys, and marmosets, see Mitchell, 1969)[4] to submissive and passive females and male antagonists (e.g. rhesus monkeys).

But even for the limited function that primate arguments serve, the evidence has been misused. Invariably, only those primates have been cited which exhibit exactly the kind of behavior that the proponents of the biological basis of human female behavior wish were true for humans. Thus, baboons and rhesus monkeys are generally cited: males in these groups exhibit some of the most irritable and aggressive behavior found in primates, and if one wishes to argue that females are naturally passive and submissive, these groups provide vivid examples. There are abundant counter examples, such as those mentioned above (Mitchell, 1969): in fact, in general, a counter example can be found for every sex-role behavior cited, including, as mentioned in the case of marmosets, male "mothers."

But the presence of counter examples has not stopped florid and overarching theories of the natural or biological basis of male privilege from proliferating. For instance, there have been a number of theories dealing with the innate incapacity in human males for monogamy. Here, as in most of this type of theorizing, baboons are a favorite example, probably because of their fantasy value: the family unit of the hamadryas baboon, for instance, consists of a highly constant pattern of one male and a number of females and their young. And again, the counter examples, such as the invariably monogamous gibbon, are ignored.

An extreme example of this maiming and selective truncation of the evidence in the service of a plea for the maintenance of male privilege is a recent book, *Men in Groups* (1969) by Tiger (see above and footnote 3). The central claim of this book is that females are incapable of honorable collective action because they are incapable of "bonding" as in "male bonding." What is "male bonding"? Its surface definition is simple: ". . . a particular relationship between two or more males such that they react differently to members of their bonding units as compared to individuals outside of it" (pp. 19–20). If one deletes the word male, the definition, on its face, would seem to include all organisms that have any kind of social organization. But this is not what Tiger means. For instance, Tiger asserts that females are incapable of bonding; and this alleged incapacity indicates to Tiger that females should be restricted from public life. Why is bonding an exclusively male behavior? Because, says Tiger, it is seen in male primates. All male primates? No, very few male primates. Tiger cites two examples where male bonding is seen: rhesus monkeys and baboons. Surprise, surprise. But not even all baboons: as mentioned above, the hamadryas social organization consists of one-male units; so does that of the Gelada baboon (Mitchell, 1969). And the great apes do not go in for male bonding much either. The "male bond" is hardly a serious contribution to scholarship; one reviewer for *Science* has observed that the book ". . . shows basically more resemblance to a partisan political tract than to a work of objective social science," with male bonding being ". . . some kind of behavioral phlogiston" (Fried, 1969, p. 884).

In short, primate arguments have generally misused the evidence: primate studies themselves have, in any case, only the very limited function of describing some possible sex-role behavior; and at present, primate observations have been sufficiently limited so that even the range of possible sex-role behavior for non-human primates is not known. This range is not known since there is only minimal observation of what happens to behavior if the physical or social environment is changed. In one study (Itani, 1963), different troops of Japanese macaques were observed. Here, there appeared to be cultural differences: males in 3 out of the 18 troops observed differed in their amount of aggressiveness and infant-caring behavior. There could be no possibility of differential evolution here; the differences seemed largely transmitted by infant socialization. Thus, the very limited evidence points to some plasticity in the sex-role behavior of non-human primates; if we can figure out experiments which massively change the social organization of primate groups, it is possible that we might observe great changes in behavior. At present, however, we must conclude that, since given a constant physical environment non-human primates do not seem to change their social conditions very much by themselves, the "innateness" and fixedness of their behavior is simply not known. Thus, even if there were some way, which there isn't, to settle on the behavior of a particular primate species as being the "natural" way for humans, we would not know whether or not this were simply some function of the present social organization of that species. And finally, once again it must be stressed that even if non-human primate behavior turned out to be relatively fixed, this would say little about our behavior. More immediate and relevant evidence, i.e., the evidence from social psychology, points to the enormous plasticity in human behavior, not only from one culture to the next, but from one experimental group to the next. One of the most salient features of human social organization is its variety; there are a number of cultures where there is at least a rough equality between men and women (Mead, 1949). In summary, primate arguments can tell us very little about our "innate" sex-role behavior; if they tell us anything at all, they tell us that there is no one biologically "natural" female or male behavior, and that sex-role behavior in non-human primates is much more varied than has previously been thought.

Conclusion

In brief, the uselessness of present psychology (and biology) with regard to women is simply a special case of the general conclusion: one must understand the social conditions under which women live if one is going to attempt to explain the behavior of women. And to understand the social conditions under which women live, one must be cognizant of the social expectations about women.

How are women characterized in our culture, and in psychology? They are inconsistent, emotionally unstable, lacking in a strong conscience or superego, weaker, "nurturant" rather than productive, "intuitive" rather than intelligent, and, if they are at all "normal," suited to the home and the family. In short, the list adds up to a typical minority group stereotype of inferiority (Hacker, 1951): if they know their place, which is in the home, they are really quite lovable, happy, childlike, loving creatures. In a review of the intellectual differences between little boys and little girls, Eleanor Maccoby (1966) has shown that there are no intellectual differences until about high school, or, if there are, girls are slightly ahead of boys. At high school, girls begin to do worse on a few intellectual tasks, such as arithmetic reasoning, and beyond high school, the achievement of women now measured in terms of productivity and accomplishment drops off even more rapidly. There are a number of other, non-intellectual tests which show sex differences; I chose the intellectual differences since it is seen clearly that women start becoming inferior. It is no use to talk about women being different but equal; all of the tests I can think of have a "good" outcome and a "bad" outcome. Women usually end up at the "bad" outcome. In light of social expectations about women, what is surprising is not that women end up where society expects they will; what is surprising is that little girls don't get the message that they are supposed to be stupid until high school; and what is even more remarkable is that some women resist this message even after high school, college, and graduate school.

My article began with remarks on the task of the discovery of the limits of human potential. Psychologists must realize that it is they who are limiting discovery of human potential. They refuse to accept evidence, if they are clinical psychologists, or, if they are rigorous, they assume that people move in a context-free ether, with only their innate dispositions and their individual traits determining what they will do. Until psychologists begin to respect evidence, and until they begin looking at the social contexts within which people move, psychology will have nothing of substance to offer in this task of discovery. I don't know what immutable differences exist between men and women apart from differences in their genitals; perhaps there are some other unchangeable differences; probably there are a number of irrelevant differences. But it is clear that until social expectations for men and women are equal, until we provide equal respect for both men and women, our answers to this question will simply reflect our prejudices.

Notes

1. It should be noted that psychologists have been as quick to assert absolute truths about the nature of homosexuality as they have about the nature of women. The arguments presented in this article apply equally to the nature of homosexuality; psychologists know nothing about it; there is no more evidence for the "naturalness" of heterosexuality than for the "naturalness" of homosexuality. Psychology has functioned as a pseudo-scientific buttress for our cultural sex-role notions, that is, as a buttress for patriarchal ideology and patriarchal social organization: women's liberation and gay liberation fight against a common victimization.

2. I am indebted to Jesse Lemisch for his valuable suggestions in the interpretation of these studies.

3. Schwarz-Belkin (1914) claims that the name was originally *Mouse*, but this may be a reference to an earlier L. Tiger (putative).

4. All these are lower-order primates, which makes their behavior with reference to humans unnatural, or more natural; take your choice.

References

Astin, A. W., "The Functional Autonomy of Psychotherapy." *American Psychologist*, 1961, *16*, 75–78.

Barron, F., & Leary, T., "Changes in Psychoneurotic Patients with and without Psychotherapy." *Journal of Consulting Psychology*, 1955, *19*, 239–245.

Bergin, A. E., "The Effects of Psychotherapy: Negative Results Revisited." *Journal of Consulting Psychology*, 1963, *10*, 244–250.

Bettelheim, B., "The Commitment Required of a Woman Entering a Scientific Profession in Present-Day American Society." *Woman and the Scientific Professions*, the MIT Symposium on American Women in Science and Engineering, 1965.

Block, J., "Some Reasons for the Apparent Inconsistency of Personality." *Psychological Bulletin*, 1968, *70*, 210–212.

Cartwright, R. D., & Vogel, J. L., "A Comparison of Changes in Psychoneurotic Patients during Matched Periods of Therapy and No-therapy." *Journal of Consulting Psychology*, 1960, *24*, 121–127.

Erikson, E., "Inner and Outer Space: Reflections on Womanhood." *Daedalus*, 1964, *93*, 582–606.

Eysenck, H. J., "The Effects of Psychotherapy: an Evaluation." *Journal of Consulting Psychology*, 1952, *16*, 319–324.

Fieldcrest—Advertisement in the *New Yorker*, 1965.

Fried, M. H., "Mankind Excluding Woman," review of Tiger's *Men in Groups, Science, 165,* 1969, 883–884.

Freud, S., *The Sexual Enlightenment of Children.* Collier Books Edition, 1963.

Goldstein, A. P., & Dean, S. J., *The Investigation of Psychotherapy: Commentaries and Readings.* New York: John Wiley & Sons, 1966.

Hacker, H. M., "Women as a Minority Group." *Social Forces,* 1951, *30,* 60–69.

Hamburg, D. A. & Lunde, D. T., "Sex Hormones in the Development of Sex Differences in Human Behavior." In Maccoby (ed.). *The Development of Sex Differences.* Stanford University Press, 1966, 1–24.

Hampton, J. L., & Hampton, J. C.: "The Ontogenesis of Sexual Behavior in Man." In W. C. Young (ed.), *Sex and Internal Secretions,* 1961, 1401–1432.

Harlow, H. F., "The Heterosexual Affectional System in Monkeys." *The American Psychologist,* 1962, *17,* 1–9.

Hooker, E., "Male Homosexuality in the Rorschach." *Journal of Projective Techniques,* 1957, *21,* 18–31.

Itani, J. "Paternal Care in the Wild Japanese Monkeys, *Macaca Fuscata.*" In C. H. Southwick (ed.), *Primate Social Behavior,* Princeton: Van Nostrand, 1963.

Little, K. B., & Schneidman, E. S., "Congruences among Interpretations of Psychological and Anamnestic Data." *Psychological Monographs,* 1959, *73,* 1–42.

Maccoby, Eleanor E., "Sex Differences in Intellectual Functioning." In Maccoby (ed.), *The Development of Sex Differences.* Stanford University Press, 1966, 25–55.

Masters, W. H., & Johnson, V. E., *Human Sexual Response.* Boston: Little Brown, 1966.

Mead, M., *Male and Female: A Study of the Sexes in a Changing World.* New York: William Morrow, 1949.

Milgram, S., "Some Conditions of Obedience and Disobedience to Authority." *Human Relations,* 1965a, *18,* 57–76.

Milgram, S., "Liberating Effects of Group Pressure." *Journal of Personality and Social Psychology,* 1965b, *I,* 127–134.

Mitchell, G. D., "Paternalistic Behavior in Primates." *Psychological Bulletin,* 1969, *71,* 339–417.

Money, J., "Sexual Dimorphism and Homosexual Gender Identity." *Psychological Bulletin,* 1970, *74,* 6, 425–440.

Powers, E., & Witmer, H., *An Experiment in the Prevention of Delinquency.* New York: Columbia University Press, 1951.

Rheingold, J., *The Fear of Being a Woman.* New York: Grune & Stratton, 1964.

Rosenthal, R., "On the Social Psychology of the Psychological Experiment: The Experimenter's Hypothesis as Unintended Determinant of Experimental Results." *American Scientist,* 1963, *51,* 268–283.

Rosenthal, R., *Experimenter Effects in Behavioral Research.* New York: Appleton-Century-Crofts, 1966.

Rosenthal, R. & Jacobson, L., *Pygmalion in the Classroom: Teacher Expectation and Pupil's Intellectual Development.* New York: Holt, Rinehart & Winston, 1968.

Rosenthal, R., & Lawson, R., "A Longitudinal Study of the Effects of Experimenter Bias on the Operant Learning of Laboratory Rats." Unpublished Manuscript, Harvard University, 1961.

Rosenthal, R., & Fode, K. L., "The Effect of Experimenter Bias on the Performance of the Albino Rat." Unpublished Manuscript, Harvard University, 1960.

Rotter, J. B., "Psychotherapy." *Annual Review of Psychology,* 1960, *11,* 381–414.

Schachter, S., & Singer, J. E., "Cognitive, Social and Physiological Determinants of Emotional State." *Psychological Review,* 1962, *60,* 379–399.

Schwarz-Belkin, M. "Les Fleurs de Mal." In *Festschrift for Gordon Piltdown.* New York: Ponzi Press, 1914.

Storch, M., "Reply to Tiger," 1970. Unpublished Manuscript.

Tiger, L., *Men in Groups.* New York: Random House, 1969.

Tiger, L., "Male Dominance? Yes. Alas. A Sexist Plot? No." *New York Times Magazine,* Section N, Oct. 25 1970.

Truax, C. B., "Effective Ingredients in Psychotherapy: an Approach to Unraveling the Patient-therapist Interaction." *Journal of Counseling Psychology,* 1963, *10,* 256–263.

3

FUNCTIONALISM, DARWINISM, AND THE PSYCHOLOGY OF WOMEN: A STUDY IN SOCIAL MYTH

Stephanie A. Shields

The psychology of women is acquiring the character of an academic entity as witnessed by the proliferation of research on sex differences, the appearance of textbooks devoted to the psychology of women, and the formation of a separate APA division, Psychology of Women. Nevertheless, there is almost universal ignorance of the psychology of women as it existed prior to its incorporation into psychoanalytic theory. If the maxim "A nation without a history is like a man without a memory" can be applied, then it would behoove the amnesiacs interested in female psychology to investigate its pre-Freudian past.

This article focuses on one period of that past (from the latter half of the 19th century to the first third of the 20th) in order to clarify the important issues of the time and trace their development to the position they occupy in current psychological theory. Even a limited overview leads the reader to appreciate Helen Thompson Woolley's (1910) early appraisal of the quality of the research on sex differences:

> There is perhaps no field aspiring to be scientific where flagrant personal bias, logic martyred in the cause of supporting a prejudice, unfounded assertions, and even sentimental rot and drivel, have run riot to such an extent as here. (p. 340)

Stephanie A. Shields, "Functionalism, Darwinism, and the Psychology of Women: A Study in Social Myth." *American Psychologist, 30,* 739–754. Copyright 1975 by the American Psychological Association. Reprinted by permission.

The Functionalist Milieu

Although the nature of woman had been an academic and social concern of philosopher psychologists throughout the ages, formal psychology (its inception usually dated 1879) was relatively slow to take up the topic of female psychology. The "woman question" was a social one, and social problems did not fall within the sharply defined limits of Wundt's "new" psychology. The business of psychology was the description of the "generalized adult mind," and it is not at all clear whether "adult" was meant to include both sexes. When the students of German psychology did venture outside of the laboratory, however, there is no evidence that they were sympathetic to those defending the equality of male and female ability (cf. Wundt, 1901).

It was the functionalist movement in the United States that fostered academic psychology's study of sex differences and, by extension, a prototypic psychology of women. The incorporation of evolutionary theory into the practice of psychology made the study of the female legitimate, if not imperative. It would be incorrect to assume that the psychology of women existed as a separate specialty within the discipline. The female was discussed only in relation to the male, and the function of the female was thought to be distinctly different from and complementary to the function of the male. The leitmotiv of evolutionary theory as it came to be applied to the social sciences was the evolutionary supremacy of the Caucasian male. The notion of the supplementary, subordinate role of the female was ancillary to the development of that theme.

The influence of evolutionary theory on the psychology of women can be traced along two major conceptual lines: (a) by emphasizing the biological foundations of temperament, evolutionary theory led to serious academic discussion of maternal instinct (as one facet of the general topic of instinct); and (b) by providing a theoretical justification of the study of individual differences, evolutionary theory opened the door to the study of sex differences in sensory, motor, and intellectual abilities. As a whole, the concept of evolution with its concomitant emphasis on biological determinism provided ample "scientific" reason for cataloging the "innate" differences in male and female nature.

This article examines three topics that were of special significance to the psychology of women during the functionalist era: (a) structural differences in the brains of males and females and the implications of these differences for intelligence and temperament, (b) the hypothesis of greater male variability and its relation to social and educational issues, and (c) maternal instinct and its meaning for a psychology of female "nature." As the functionalist paradigm gave way to behaviorism and psychoanalytic theory, the definition and "meaning" of each of these issues changed to fit the times. When issues faded in importance, it was not because they were resolved but because they ceased to serve as viable scientific "myths" in the changing social and scientific milieu. As the times change, so must the myths change.

The Female Brain

The topic of female intelligence came to 19th-century psychology via phrenology and the neuroanatomists. Philosophers of the time (e.g., Hegel, Kant, Schopenhauer) had demonstrated, to their satisfaction, the justice of woman's subordinate social position, and it was left to the men of science to discover the particular physiological determinants of female inadequacy. In earlier periods, woman's inferiority had been defined as a general "state" intimately related to the absence of qualities that would have rendered her a male and to the presence of reproductive equipment that destined her to be female. For centuries the mode of Eve's creation and her greater guilt for the fall from grace had been credited as the cause of woman's imperfect nature, but this was not an adequate explanation in a scientific age. Thus, science sought explanations for female inferiority that were more in keeping with contemporary scientific philosophy.

Although it had long been believed that the brain was the chief organ of the mind, the comparison of male and female mental powers traditionally included only allusions to vague "imperfections" of the female brain. More precise definition of the sites of these imperfections awaited the advancement of the concept of cortical localization of function. Then, as finer distinctions of functional areas were noted, there was a parallel recognition of the differences between those sites as they appeared in each sex.

At the beginning of the 19th century, the slowly increasing interest in the cerebral gyri rapidly gathered momentum with the popularization of phrenology. Introduced by Franz Joseph Gall, "cranioscopy," as he preferred to call it, postulated that the seat of various mental and moral faculties was located in specific areas of the brain's surface such that a surfeit or deficiency could be detected by an external examination of the cranium. Phrenology provided the first objective method for determining the neurological foundation of sex differences in intelligence and temperament that had long been promulgated. Once investigation of brain structure had begun, it was fully anticipated that visible sex differences would be found: Did not the difference between the sexes pervade every other aspect of physique and physiological function? Because physical differences were so obvious in every other organ of the body, it was unthinkable that the brain could have escaped the stamp of sex.

Gall was convinced that he could, from gross anatomical observation, discriminate between male and female brains, claiming that "if there had been presented to him in water, the fresh brains of two adult animals of any species, one male and the other female, he could have distinguished the two sexes" (Walker, 1850, p. 317). Gall's student and colleague, Johann Spurzheim, elaborated on this basic distinction by noting that the frontal lobes were less developed in females, "the organs of the perceptive faculties being commonly larger than those of the reflective powers." Gall also observed sex differences in the nervous tissue itself, "confirming" Malebranche's belief that the female "cerebral fibre" is softer than that of the male, and that it is also "slender and long rather than thick" (Walker, 1850, p. 318). Spurzheim also listed the cerebral "organs" whose appearance differed commonly in males and females: females tended to have the areas devoted to philoprogenetiveness and other "tender" traits most prominent, while in males, areas of aggressiveness and constructiveness dominated. Even though cranioscopy did not survive as a valid system of describing cortical function, the practice of comparing the appearance of all or part of the brain for anatomical evidence of quality of function remained one of the most popular means of providing proof of female mental inferiority. Most comparisons used adult human brains, but with the rise of evolutionary theory, increasing emphasis was placed on the value of developmental and cross-species comparisons. The argument for female mental inferiority took two forms: some argued that quality of intellect was proportional to absolute or relative brain size; others, more in the tradition of cortical localization, contended that the presence of certain mental qualities was dependent upon the development of corresponding brain centers.

The measurement of cranial capacity had long been in vogue as one method of determining intellectual ability. That women had smaller heads than men was taken by some as clear proof of a real disparity between male and female intelligence. The consistently smaller brain size of the female was cited as another anatomical indicator of its functional inferiority. More brain necessarily meant better brain; the exception only proved this rule. Alexander Bain (1875) was among those who believed that the smaller absolute brain size of females accounted for a lesser mental ability. George Romanes (1887) enumerated the "secondary sex characteristics" of mental abilities attributable to brain size. The smaller brain of women was directly responsible for their mental inferiority, which "displays itself most conspicuously in a comparative absence of originality, and this more especially in the higher levels of intellectual work" (p. 655). He, like many, allowed that women were to some degree compensated for intellectual inferiority by a superiority of instinct and perceptual ability. These advantages carried with them the germ of female failure, however, by making women more subject to emotionality.

Proof of the male's absolute brain-size superiority was not enough to secure his position of intellectual superiority, since greater height and weight tended to offset the brain-size advantage. Reams of paper were, therefore, dedicated to the search of the most "appropriate" relative measures, but results were equivocal: if the ratio of brain weight to body weight is considered, it is found that women possess a proportionately larger brain than men; if the ratio of brain surface to body surface is computed, it is found to favor men. That some of the ratios "favored" males while others "favored" females led some canny souls to conclude that there was no legitimate solution to the problem. That they had ever hoped for a solution seems remarkable; estimates of brain size from cranial capacity involve a large margin of error because brains differing as much as 15% have been found in heads of the same size (Elliott, 1969, p. 316).

Hughlings Jackson has been credited as the first to regard the frontal cortex as the repository of the highest mental capacities, but the notion must have held popular credence as early as the 1850s because that period saw sporadic references to the comparative development of the frontal lobes in men and women. Once the function of the frontal lobes had been established, many researchers reported finding that the male possessed noticeably larger and more well-developed frontal lobes than females. The neuroanatomist Hischke came to the conclusion in 1854 that woman is *homo parietalis* while man is *homo frontalis* (Ellis, 1934). Likewise, Rudinger in 1877 found the frontal lobes of man in every way more extensive than those of women, and reported that these sex differences were evident even in the unborn fetus (Mobius, 1901).

At the turn of the century, the parietal lobes (rather than the frontal lobes) came to be regarded by some as the seat of intellect, and the necessary sex difference in parietal development was duly corroborated by the neuroanatomists. The change in cerebral hierarchy involved a bit of revisionism:

> the frontal region is not, as has been supposed smaller in woman, but rather larger relatively. . . . But the parietal lobe is somewhat smaller, [furthermore,] a preponderance of the frontal region does not imply intellectual superiority . . . the parietal region is really the more important. (Patrick, 1895, p. 212)

Once beliefs regarding the relative importance of the frontal and parietal lobes had shifted, it became critical to reestablish congruence between neuroanatomical findings and accepted sex differences. Among those finding parietal predominance in men were Paul Broca,[1] Theodore Meynert, and the German Rudinger (see Ellis, 1934, p. 217).

Other neuroanatomical "deficiencies" of the female were found in (a) the area of the corpus callosum, (b) the complexity of the gyri and sulci, (c) the conformation of gyri and sulci, and (d) the rate of development of the cortex of the fetus (Woolley, 1910, p. 335). Franklin Mall (1909) objected to the use of faulty research methods that gave spurious differences the appearance of being real. Among the most serious errors he noted was the practice of making observations with a knowledge of the sex of the brain under consideration.

The debate concerning the importance of brain size and anatomy as indicators of intelligence diminished somewhat with the development of mental tests; nevertheless, the brain-size difference was a phenomenon that many felt obligated to interpret. Max Meyer (1921) attempted to settle the matter by examining the various measures of relative difference that had been employed. After finding these methods far too equivocal, he concluded, in the best behavioristic terms, that sex differences in intelligence were simply "accidents of habits acquired."

Characteristics of the female brain were thought not simply to render women less intelligent but also to allow more "primitive" parts of human nature to be expressed in her personality. Instinct was thought to dominate woman, as did her emotions, and the resulting "affectability" was considered woman's greatest weakness, the reason for her inevitable failure. Affectability was typically defined as a general state, the manifestation of instinctive and emotional predispositions that in men were kept in check by a superior intellect.[2]

One of the most virulent critics of woman was the German physiologist Paul Mobius (1901), who argued that her mental incapacity was a necessary condition for the survival of the race. Instinct rendered her easily led and easily pleased, so much the better for her to give her all to bearing and rearing children. The dependence of woman also extracted a high price from man:

> All progress is due to man. Therefore the woman is like a dead weight on him, she prevents much restlessness and meddlesome inquisitiveness, but she also restrains him from noble actions, for she is unable to distinguish good from evil. (p. 629)

Mobius observed that woman was essentially unable to think independently, had strong inclinations to be mean and untrustworthy, and spent a good deal of her time in an emotionally unbalanced state. From this he was forced to conclude that "If woman was not physically and mentally weak, if she was not as a rule rendered harmless by circumstances, she would be extremely dangerous" (Mobius, 1901, p. 630). Diatribes of this nature were relatively common German importations; woman's severest critics in this country seldom achieved a similar level of acerbity. Mobius and his ilk (e.g., Weininger, 1906) were highly publicized and widely read in the United States, and not a little of their vituperation crept into serious scientific discussions of woman's nature. For example, Porteus and Babcock (1926) resurrected the brain-size issue, discounting the importance of size to intelligence and instead associating it with the "maturing of other powers." Males, because of their larger brains would be more highly endowed with these "other powers," and so more competent and achieving. Proposals such as these which were less obviously biased than those of Mobius, Weininger, and others, fit more easily into the current social value system and so were more easily assimilated as "good science" (cf. Allen, 1927, p. 294).

The Variability Hypothesis

The first systematic treatment of individual differences in intelligence appeared in 1575. Juan Huarte attributed sex differences in intelligence to the different humoral qualities that characterized each sex, a notion that had been popular in Western thought since ancient Greece. Heat and dryness were characteristic of the male principle while moisture and coolness were female attributes. Because dryness of spirit was necessary for intelligence, males naturally possessed greater "wit." The maintenance of dryness and heat was the function of the testicles, and Huarte (1959) noted that if a man were castrated the effects were the same "as if he had received some notable dammage in his very braine" (p. 279). Because the principles necessary for cleverness were only possessed by males, it behooved parents to conduct their life-style, diet, and sexual intercourse in such a manner as to insure the conception of a male. The humoral theory of sex differences was widely accepted through the 17th century, but with the advent of more sophisticated notions of anatomy and physiology, it was replaced by other, more specific, theories of female mental defect: the lesser size and hypothesized simpleness of the female brain, affectability as the source of inferiority, and complementarity of abilities in male and female. It was the developing evolutionary theory that provided an overall explanation for why these sex differences existed and why they were necessary for the survival of the race.

The theory of evolution as proposed by Darwin had little to say regarding the intellectual capacity of either sex. It was in Francis Galton's (Charles Darwin's cousin) anthropometric laboratory that the investigation of intellectual differences took an empirical form (Galton, 1907). The major conclusion to come from Galton's research was that women tend in all their capacities to be inferior to men. He looked to common experience for confirmation, reasoning that:

If the sensitivity of women were superior to that of men, the self interest of merchants would lead to their being always employed; but as the reverse is the case, the opposite supposition is likely to be the true one. (pp. 20–21)

This form of logic—women have not excelled, therefore they cannot excel—was often used to support arguments denigrating female intellectual ability. The fact of the comparative rarity of female social achievement was also used as "evidence" in what was later to become a widely debated issue concerning the range of female ability.

Prior to the formulation of evolutionary theory, there had been little concern with whether deviation from the average or "normal" occurred more frequently in either sex. One of the first serious discussions of the topic appeared in the early 19th century when the anatomist Meckel concluded on pathological grounds that the human female showed greater variability than the human male. He reasoned that because man is the superior animal and variability a sign of inferiority, this conclusion was justified (in Ellis, 1903, p. 237). The matter was left at that until 1871. At that time Darwin took up the question of variability in *The Descent of Man* while attempting to explain how it could be that in many species males had developed greatly modified secondary sexual characteristics while females of the same species had not. He determined that this was originally caused by the males' greater activity and "stronger passions" that were in turn more likely (he believed) to be transmitted to male offspring. Because the females would prefer to mate with the strong and passionate, sexual selection would insure the survival of those traits. A tendency toward greater variation per se was not thought to be responsible for the appearance of unusual characteristics, but "development of such characters would be much aided, if the males were more liable to vary than the females" (Darwin, 1922, p. 344). To support this hypothesis of greater male variability, he cited recent data obtained by anatomists and biologists that seemed to confirm the relatively more frequent occurrence of physical anomaly among males.

Because variation from the norm was already accepted as the mechanism of evolutionary progress (survival and transmission of adaptive variations) and because it seemed that the male was the more variable sex, it soon was universally concluded that the male is the progressive element in the species. Variation for its own sake took on a positive value because greatness, whether of an individual or a society, could not be achieved without variation. Once deviation from the norm became legitimized by evolutionary theory; the hypothesis of greater male variability became a convenient explanation for a number of observed sex differences, among them the greater frequency with which men achieved "eminence." By the 1890s it was popularly believed that greater male variability was a principle that held true, not only for physical traits but for mental abilities as well:

> That men should have greater cerebral variability and therefore more origi-
> nality, while women have greater stability and therefore more "common
> sense," are facts both consistent with the general theory of sex and verifiable
> in common experience. (Geddes & Thomson, 1890, p. 271)

Havelock Ellis (1894), an influential sexologist and social philosopher, brought the variability hypothesis to the attention of psychologists in the first edition of *Man and Woman*. After examining anatomical and patholog-ical data that indicated a greater male *variational tendency* (Ellis felt this term was less ambiguous than *variability*), he examined the evidence germane to a discussion of range of intellectual ability. After noting that there were more men than women in homes for the mentally deficient, which indicated a higher incidence of retardation among males, and that there were more men than women on the roles of the eminent, which indicated a higher incidence of genius among males, he concluded that greater male variability probably held for all qualities of character and ability. Ellis (1903) particularly emphasized the wide social and educa-tional significance of the phenomenon, claiming that greater male vari-ability was "a fact which has affected the whole of our human civilization" (p. 238), particularly through the production of men of genius. Ellis (1934) was also adamant that the female's tendency toward the average did not necessarily imply inferiority of talent; rather, it simply limited her expertise to "the sphere of concrete practical life" (p. 436).

The variability hypothesis was almost immediately challenged as a "pseudo-scientific superstition" by the statistician Karl Pearson (1897). Though not a feminist, Pearson firmly believed that the "woman question" deserved impartial, scientific study. He challenged the idea of greater male variability primarily because he thought it contrary to the fact and theory of evolution and natural selection. According to evolutionary theory (Pearson, 1897), "the more intense the struggle the less is the variability, the more nearly are individuals forced to approach the type fittest to their surroundings, if they are to survive" (p. 258). In a "civilized" community one would expect that because men have a "harder battle for life," any difference in variation should favor women. He took Ellis to task by arguing it was (a) meaningless to consider secondary sex characteristics (as Ellis had done), and likewise, (b) foolish to contrast the sexes on the basis of abnormalities (as Ellis had done). By redefining the problem and the means for its solution, he was able to dismiss the entire corpus of data that had been amassed: "the whole trend of investigations concerning the relative variability of men and women up to the present seems to be erroneous" (Pearson, 1897, p. 261). Confining his measurements to "normal variations in organs or characteristics not of a secondary sexual character," he assembled anthropometric data on various races, from Neolithic skeletons to modern French peasants. He also challenged the adequacy of statistical comparison of only the extremes of the distribution, preferring to base his contrasts on the dispersion of measures around the mean. Finding a slight tendency toward greater female variability, he concluded that the variability hypothesis as stated remained a "quite unproven principle."

Ellis countered Pearson in a lengthy article, one more vicious than that ordinarily due an intellectual affront.[3] Pearson's greatest sins (according to Ellis) were his failure to define "variability" and his measurement of characteristics that were highly subject to environmental influence. Ellis, of course, overlooked his own failure to define variability and his inclusion of environmentally altered evidence.

In the United States the variability hypothesis naturally found expression in the new testing movement, its proponents borrowing liberally from the theory of Ellis and the statistical technique of Pearson. The favor that was typically afforded the hypothesis did not stem from intellectual commitment to the scientific validity of the proposal as much as it did from personal commitment to the social desirability of its acceptance. The variability hypothesis was most often thought of in terms of its several corollaries: (a) genius (seldom, and then poorly, defined) is a peculiarly male trait; (b) men of genius naturally gravitate to positions of power and prestige (i.e., achieve eminence) by virtue of their talent; (c) an equally high ability level should not be expected of females; and (d) the education of women should, therefore, be consonant with their special talents and special place in society as wives and mothers.

Woman's Education

The "appropriate" education for women had been at issue since the Renaissance, and the implications of the variability hypothesis favored those who had been arguing for a separate female education. Late in the 18th century, Mary Wollstonecraft Godwin (1759–1797) questioned the "natural" roles of each sex, contending that for both the ultimate goal was the same: "the first object of laudable ambition is to obtain a character as a human being, regardless of the distinction of sex" (Wollstonecraft, 1955, p. 5). Without education, she felt, women could not contribute to social progress as mature individuals, and this would be a tragic loss to the community. Though not the first to recognize the social restrictions arbitrarily placed on women, she was the first to hold those restrictions as directly responsible for the purported "defective nature" of women.

She emphasized that women had never truly been given an equal chance to prove or disprove their merits. Seventy years later, John Stuart Mill (1955) also took up the cause of women's education, seeing it as one positive action to be taken in the direction of correcting the unjust social subordination of women. He felt that what appeared as woman's intellectual inferiority was actually no more than the effort to maintain the passive-dependent role relationship with man, her means of support:

> When we put together three things—first, the natural attraction between the sexes; secondly, the wife's entire dependence on the husband . . . and lastly, that the principal object of human pursuit, consideration, and all objects of social ambition, can in general be sought or obtained by her only through him, it would be a miracle if the object of being attractive to men had not become the polar star of feminine education and formation of character. (pp. 232–233)[4]

Although Mill objected to fostering passivity and dependency in girls, other educators felt that this was precisely their duty. One of the more influential of the 19th century, Hannah More, rejected outright the proposal that women should share the same type of education as men, because "the chief end to be proposed in cultivating the understanding of women" was "to qualify them for the practical purposes of life" (see Smith, 1970, p. 101). To set one's sights on other than harmonious domesticity was to defy the natural order. Her readers were advised to be excellent women rather than indifferent men; to follow the "plain path which Providence has obviously marked out to the sex . . . rather than . . . stray awkwardly, unbecomingly, and unsuccessfully, in a forbidden road" (Smith, 1970, pp. 100–101). Her values were consonant with those held by most of the middle class, and so her *Strictures on the Modern System of Female Education* (More, 1800) enjoyed widespread popularity for some time.

By the latter part of the century, the question had turned from whether girls should be educated like boys to how much they should be educated like boys. With the shift in emphasis came the question of coeducation. One of the strongest objections to coeducation in adolescence was the threat it posed to the "normalization" of the menstrual period. G. Stanley Hall (1906) waxed poetic on the issue:

> At a time when her whole future life depends upon normalizing the lunar month, is there not something not only unnatural and unhygienic, but a little monstrous, in daily school associations with boys, where she must suppress and conceal her instincts and feelings, at those times when her own promptings suggest withdrawal or stepping a little aside to let Lord Nature do his magnificent work of efflorescence. (p. 590)

Edward Clarke (see Sinclair, 1965, p. 123) had earlier elucidated the physiological reason for the restraint of girls from exertion in their studies: by forcing their brains to do work at puberty, they would use up blood later needed for menstruation.

Hall proposed an educational system for girls that would not only take into consideration their delicate physical nature but would also be tailored to prepare them for their special role in society. He feared that women's competition with men "in the world" would cause them to neglect their instinctive maternal urges and so bring about "race suicide." Because the glory of the female lay in motherhood, Hall believed that all educational and social institutions should be structured with that end in mind. Domestic arts would therefore be emphasized in special schools for adolescent girls, and disciplines such as philosophy, chemistry, and mathematics would be treated only superficially. If a girl had a notion to stay in the "male" system, she should be able to but, Hall warned, such a woman selfishly interested in self-fulfillment would also be less likely to bear children and so be confined to an "agamic" life, thus failing to reproduce those very qualities that made her strong (Hall, 1918).

Throughout Hall's panegyric upon the beauties of female domestic education, there runs an undercurrent of the *real* threat that he perceived in coeducation, and that was the "feminization" of the American male. David Starr Jordan (1902) shared this objection but felt that coeducation would nevertheless make young men more "civilized" and young women less frivolous, tempering their natural pubescent inclinations. He was no champion of female ability though, stressing that women "on the whole, lack originality" (p. 100). The educated woman, he said, "is likely to master technic rather than art; method, rather than substance. She may know a good deal, but she can do nothing" (p. 101). In spite of this, he did assert that their training is just as serious and important as that of men. His position strongly favored the notion that the smaller range of female ability was the cause of lackluster female academic performance.

The issue of coeducation was not easily settled, and even as late as 1935, one finds debates over its relative merits (*Encyclopedia of the Social Sciences*, 1935, pp. 614–617).

The Biological Bases of Sex Differences

The variability hypothesis was compatible not only with prevailing attitudes concerning the appropriate form of female education but also with a highly popular theory of the biological complementarity of the sexes. The main tenet of Geddes and Thomson's (1890) theory was that males are primarily "catabolic," females "anabolic." From this difference in metabolism, all other sex differences in physical, intellectual, and emotional makeup were derived. The male was more agile, creative, and variable; the female was truer to the species type and therefore, in all respects, less variable. The conservatism of the female insured the continuity of the species. The authors stressed the metabolic antecedents of female conservatism and male differentiation rather than variational tendency per se, and also put emphasis on the complementarity of the two natures:

> The feminine passivity is expressed in greater patience, more open-mindedness, greater appreciation of subtle details, and consequently what we call more rapid intuition. The masculine activity lends a greater power of maximum effort, of scientific insight, or cerebral experiment with impressions and is associated with an unobservant or impatient disregard of minute details, but with a more stronger grasp of generalities. (p. 271)

The presentation of evolutionary theory anchored in yin-yang concepts of function represents the most positive evaluation of the female sex offered by 19th-century science. Whatever woman's shortcomings, they were necessary to complete her nature, which itself was necessary to complete man's: "Man thinks more, woman feels more. He discovers more, but remembers less; she is more receptive, and less forgetful" (Geddes & Thomson, 1890, p. 271).

Variability and the Testing Movement

Helen Thompson (later Woolley) put Geddes and Thomson's and other theories of sex differences in ability to what she felt was a crucial experimental test (see Thompson, 1903). Twenty-five men and 25 women participated in nearly 20 hours of individual testing of their intellectual, motor, and sensory abilities. Of more importance than her experimental results (whether men or women can tap a telegraph key more times per minute has lost its significance to psychology) was her discussion of the implications of the resulting negligible differences for current theories of sex differences. She was especially critical of the mass of inconsistencies inherent in contemporary biological theories:

> Women are said to represent concentration, patience, and stability in emotional life. One might logically conclude that prolonged concentration of attention and unbiased generalization would be their intellectual characteristics, but these are the very characteristics assigned to men. (p. 173)

In the face of such contradictions, she was forced to conclude that "if the author's views as to the mental differences of sex had been different, they might as easily have derived a very different set of characteristics" (pp.

173–174). Thompson singled out the variability hypothesis for special criticism, objecting not only to the use of physical variation as evidence for intellectual variation but also to the tendency to minimize environmental influences. She held that training was responsible for sex differences in variation, and to those who countered that it is really a fundamental difference of instincts and characteristics that determines the differences in training, she replied that if this were true, "it would not be necessary to spend so much time and effort in making boys and girls follow the lines of conduct proper to their sex" (p. 181).

Thompson's recommendation to look at environmental factors went unheeded, as more and more evidence of woman's incapability of attaining eminence was amassed. In the surveys of eminent persons that were popular at the turn of the century, more credence was given to nature (à la Hall) than nurture (à la Thompson) for the near absence of eminent women (Cattell, 1903; Ellis, 1904). Cattell (1903) found a ready-made explanation in the variability hypothesis: "Women depart less from the normal than man," ergo "the distribution of women is represented by a narrower bell-shaped curve" (p. 375). Cora Castle's (1913) survey of eminent women was no less critical of woman's failure to achieve at the top levels of power and prestige.

One of the most influential individuals to take up the cause of the variability hypothesis was Edward Thorndike. Much of the early work in the testing movement was done at Columbia University, which provided the perfect milieu for Thorndike's forays into the variability problem as applied to mental testing and educational philosophy. Thorndike based his case for the acceptance of the variability hypothesis on the reevaluation of the results of two studies (Thompson, 1903; Wissler, 1901) that had not themselves been directed toward the issue. Thorndike insisted that greater male variability only became meaningful when one examined the distribution of ability at the highest levels of giftedness. Measurement of more general sex differences could only "prove that the sexes are closely alike and that sex can account for only a very small fraction of human mental differences in the abilities listed" (Thorndike, 1910, p. 185). Since the range of female ability was narrower, he reasoned, the talents of women should be channeled into fields in which they would be most needed and most successful because "this one fundamental difference in variability is more important than all the differences between the average male and female capacities" (Thorndike, 1906):

> Not only the probability and the desirability of marriage and the training of children as an essential feature of woman's career, but also the restriction of women to the mediocre grades of ability and achievement should be reckoned with by our educational systems. The education of women for . . . professions

> . . . where a very few gifted individuals are what society requires, is far less
> needed than for such professions as nursing, teaching, medicine, or architec-
> ture, where the average level is the essential. (p. 213)

He felt perfectly justified in this recommendation because of "the patent
fact that in the great achievements of the world in science, as, invention,
and management, women have been far excelled by men" (Thorndike,
1910, p. 35). In Thorndike's view, environmental factors scarcely mattered.

Others, like Joseph Jastrow (1915), seemed to recognize the tremendous influence that societal pressures had upon achievement. He noted
that even when women had been admitted to employment from which
they had previously been excluded, new prejudices arose: "allowances
and considerations for sex intrude, favorably or unfavorably; the avenues
of preferment, though ostensibly open are really barred by invisible
barriers of social prejudice" (pp. 567–568). This was little more than lip
service because he was even more committed to the importance of
variational tendency and its predominance over any possible extenuating
factors: the effects of the variability of the male and the biological conservatism of the female "radiates to every distinctive aspect of their contrasted
natures and expressions" (p. 568).

A small but persistent minority challenged the validity of the variability hypothesis, and it is not surprising that this minority was composed
mainly of women. Although the "woman question" was, to some degree,
at issue, the larger dispute was between those who stressed "nature" as
the major determinant of ability (and therefore success) and those who
rejected nature and its corollary, instead emphasizing the importance of
environmental factors. Helen Thompson Woolley, while remaining firmly
committed to the investigation of the differential effects of social factors
on each sex, did not directly involve herself in the variability controversy.
Leta Stetter Hollingworth, first a student and then a colleague of Thorndike's at Teachers College of Columbia University, actively investigated
the validity of the hypothesis and presented sound objections to it. She
argued that there was no real basis for assuming that the distribution of
"mental traits" in the population conforms without exception to the
Gaussian distribution. The assumption of normality was extremely important to the validity of the variability hypothesis, because only in a
normal distribution would a difference in variability indicate a difference
in range. It was the greater range of male ability that was used to "prove"
the ultimate superiority of male ability. Greater range of male ability was
usually verified by citing lists of eminent persons (dominated by men)
and the numbers and sex of those in institutions for the feebleminded
(also dominated by men). Hollingworth (1914) saw no reason to resort to
biological theory for an explanation of the phenomenon when a more

parsimonious one was available in social fact. Statistics reporting a larger
number of males among the feebleminded could be explained by the fact
that the supporting data had been gathered in institutions, where men
were more likely to be admitted than women of an equal degree of
retardation. The better ability of feebleminded women to survive outside
the institutional setting was simply a function of female social role:

> Women have been and are a dependent and non-competitive class, and when
> defective can more easily survive outside of institutions, since they do not
> have to compete *mentally* with normal individuals, as men do, to maintain
> themselves in the social *milieu*. (Hollingworth, 1914, p. 515)

Women would therefore be more likely to be institutionalized at an older
age than men, after they had become too old to be "useful" or self-
supporting. A survey of age and sex ratios in New York institutions
supported her hypothesis: the ratio of females to males increased with the
age of the inmates (Hollingworth, 1913). As for the rarity of eminence
among women, Hollingworth (1914) argued that because the social role of
women was defined in terms of housekeeping and child-rearing functions,
"a field where eminence is not possible," and because of concomitant
constraints placed on the education and employment of women by law,
custom, and the demands of the role, one could not possibly validly
compare the achievements of women with those of men who "have
followed the greatest possible range of occupations, and have at the same
time procreated unhindered" (p. 528). She repeatedly emphasized (Hollingworth, 1914, 1916) that the true potential of woman could only be
known when she began to receive social acceptance of her right to choose
career, maternity, or both.

Hollingworth's argument that unrecognized differences in social training had misdirected the search for *inherent* sex differences had earlier
been voiced by Mary Calkins (1896). Just as Hollingworth directed her
response particularly at Thorndike's formulation of the variability hypothesis, Calkins objected to Jastrow's (1896) intimations that one finds "greater
uniformity amongst women than amongst men" (p. 431).

Hollingworth's work was instrumental in bringing the variability issue
to a crisis point, not only because she presented persuasive empirical data
to support her contentions but also because this was simply the first major
opposition that the variability hypothesis had encountered. Real resolution
of this crisis had to await the development of more sophisticated testing
and statistical techniques. With the United States' involvement in World
War I, most testing efforts were redirected to wartime uses. This redirec-
tion effectively terminated the variability debate, and although it resumed
during the postwar years, the renewed controversy never attained the

force of conviction that had characterized the earlier period. "Variational tendency" became a statistical issue, and the pedagogic implications that had earlier colored the debate were either minimized or disguised in more egalitarian terms.

After its revival in the mid-1920s, investigation of the variability hypothesis was often undertaken as part of larger intelligence testing projects. Evidence in its favor began to look more convincing than it ever had. The use of larger samples, standardized tests, and newer methods of computing variation gave an appearance of increased accuracy, but conclusions were still based on insubstantial evidence of questionable character. Most discussions of the topic concluded that there were not enough valid data to resolve the issue and that even if that data were available, variation within each sex is so much greater than the difference in variation between sexes that the "meaning" of the variability hypothesis was trivial (Shields, Note 1).

Maternal Instinct

The concept of maternal instinct was firmly entrenched in American psychology before American psychology itself existed as an entity. The first book to appear in the United States with "psychology" in its title outlined the psychological sex differences arising from the physical differences between men and women. Differences in structure were assumed to imply differences in function, and therefore differences in abilities, temperament, and intelligence. In each sex a different set of physical systems was thought to predominate: "In man the arterial and cerebral systems prevail, and with them irritability; in woman the venous and ganglion systems and with the pasticity and sensibility" (Rausch, 1841, p. 81). The systems dominant in woman caused her greatest attributes to lie in the moral sphere in the form of love, patience and chastity. In the intellectual sphere, she was not equally blessed, "and this is not accidental, not because no opportunity has offered itself to their productive genius . . . but because it is their highest happiness to be mothers" (Rausch, 1841, p. 83).[5]

Although there was popular acceptance of a maternal instinct in this country, the primary impetus for its incorporation into psychology came by way of British discussion of social evolution. While the variability hypothesis gained attention because of an argument, the concept of maternal instinct evolved without conflict. There was consistent agreement as to its existence, if not its precise nature or form. Typical of the evolutionary point of view was the notion that woman's emotional nature (including her tendency to nurturance) was a direct consequence of her reproductive physiology. As Herbert Spencer (1891) explained it, the female's energies were directed toward preparation for pregnancy and lactation, reducing the energy available for the development of other qualities. This resulted in a "rather earlier cessation of individual evolution" in the female. Woman was, in essence, a stunted man. Her lower stage of development was evident not only in her inferior mental and emotional powers but also in the resulting expression of the parental instinct. Whereas the objectivity of the male caused his concern to be extended "to all the relatively weak who are dependent upon him" (p. 375), the female's propensity to "dwell on the concrete and proximate rather than on the abstract and remote" made her incapable of the generalized protective attitude assumed by the male. Instead, she was primarily responsive to "infantile helplessness."

Alexander Sutherland (1898) also described a parental instinct whose major characteristic (concern for the weak) was "the basis of all other sympathy," which is itself "the ultimate basis of all moral feeling" (p. 156). Like his contemporaries (e.g., McDougall, 1913, 1923; Shand, 1920; Spencer, 1891), Sutherland revered maternal sentiment but thought the expression of parental instinct in the male, that is, a protective attitude, was a much more significant factor in social evolution, an attitude of benevolent paternalism more in keeping with Victorian social ethic than biological reality. The expression of the parental instinct in men, Sutherland thought, must necessarily lead to deference toward women out of "sympathetic regard for women's weakness." He noted that male protectiveness had indeed wrought a change in the relations between the sexes, evident in a trend away from sexual motivations and toward a general improvement in moral tone, witness the "large number of men who lead perfectly chaste lives for ten or twenty years after puberty before they marry," which demonstrated that the "sensuous side of man's nature is slowly passing under the control of sympathetic sentiments" (p. 288).[6]

Whatever facet of the activity that was emphasized, there was common agreement that the maternal (or parental) instinct was truly an instinct. A. F. Shand (1920) argued that the maternal instinct is actually composed of an ordered "system" of instincts and characterized by a number of emotions. Despite its complexity, "maternal love" was considered to be a hereditary trait "in respect not only of its instincts, but also of the bond connecting its primary emotions, and of the end which the whole system pursues, namely, the preservation of the offspring" (p. 42). The sociologist L. T. Hobhouse (1916) agreed that maternal instinct was a "true" instinct, "not only in the drive but in some of the detail." He doubted the existence of a corresponding paternal instinct, however, since he had observed that few men have a natural aptitude with babies.

The unquestioning acceptance of the maternal instinct concept was just as prevalent in this country as it was in Britain. William James (1950) listed parental love among the instincts of humans and emphasized the strength with which it was expressed in women. He was particularly impressed with the mother-infant relationship and quoted at length from a German psychologist concerning the changes wrought in a woman at the birth of her child: "She has, in one word, transferred her entire egoism to the child, and lives only in it" (p. 439). Even among those who employed a much narrower definition of instinct than James, maternal behavior was thought to be mediated by inherent neural connections. R. P. Halleck (1895) argued that comparatively few instincts are fully developed in humans, because reason intervenes and modifies their expression to fit the circumstances. Maternal instinct qualified as a clear exception, and its expression seemed as primitive and unrefined as that of infants' reflexive behavior.

Others (e.g., Jastrow, 1915; Thorndike, 1914a, 1914b) treated instinct more as a quality of character than of biology. Edward Thorndike (1911) considered the instincts peculiar to each sex to be the primary source of sex differences: "it appears that if the primary sex characters—the instincts directly related to courtship, love, child-bearing, and nursing—are left out of account, the average man differs from the average woman far less than many men differ from one another" (p. 30). Thorndike taught that the tendency to display maternal concern was universal among women, although social pressures could "complicate or deform" it. He conceded that males share in an instinctive "good will toward children," but other instincts, such as the "hunting instinct," predominated (Thorndike, 1914b). He was so sure of the innate instinctual differences between men and women that it was his contention (Thorndike, 1914b) that even "if we should keep the environment of boys and girls absolutely similar these instincts would produce sure and important differences between the mental and moral activities of boys and girls" (p. 203). The expression of instincts therefore was thought to have far-reaching effects on seemingly unrelated areas of ability and conduct. For example, woman's "nursing instinct," which was most often exhibited in "unreasoning tendencies to pet, coddle, and 'do for' others," was also "the chief source of woman's superiorities in the moral life" (Thorndike, 1914a, p. 203). Another of the female's instinctive tendencies was described as "submission to mastery":

Women in general are thus by original nature submissive to men in general. Submissive behavior is apparently not annoying when assumed as the instinctive response to its natural stimulus. Indeed, it is perhaps a common satisfier. (Thorndike, 1914b, p. 34)

The existence of such an "instinct" would, of course, validate the social norm of female subservience and dependence. An assertive woman would be acting contrary to instinct and therefore contrary to *nature*. There is a strikingly similarity between Thorndike's description of female nature and that of the Freudians with their mutual emphasis on woman's passivity, dependency, and masochism. For Thorndike, however, the *cause* of such a female attitude was thought to be something quite different from mutilation fears and penis envy.

The most vocal proponent of instinct, first in England and later in this country, was William McDougall (1923). Unlike Shand, he regarded "parental sentiment" as a primary instinct and did not hesitate to be highly critical of those who disagreed with him. When his position was maligned by the behaviorists, his counterattack was especially strong:

> And, when we notice how in so many ways the behavior of the human mother most closely resembles that of the animal-mother, can we doubt that . . . if the animal-mother is moved by the impulse of a maternal instinct, so also is the woman? To repudiate this view as baseless would seem to me the height of blindness and folly, yet it is the folly of a number of psychologists who pride themselves on being strictly "scientific." (p. 136)

In McDougall's system of instincts, each of the primary instincts in humans was accompanied by a particular emotional quality. The parental instinct had as its primary emotional quality the "tender emotion" vaguely defined as love, tenderness, and tender feeling. Another of the primary instincts was that of "pairing," its primary emotional quality that of sexual emotion or excitement, "sometimes called love—an unfortunate and confusing usage" (p. 234). Highly critical of what he called the "Freudian dogma that all love is sexual," McDougall proposed that it was the interaction of the parental and pairing instincts that was the basis of heterosexual "love." "Female coyness," which initiated the courtship ritual, was simply the reproductively oriented manifestation of the instincts of self-display and self-abasement. The appearance of a suitable male would elicit coyness from the female, and at that point the male's parental instinct would come into play:

> A certain physical weakness and delicacy (probably moral also) about the normal young woman or girl constitute in her a resemblance to a child. This resemblance . . . throws the man habitually into the protective attitude, evokes the impulse and emotion of the parental instinct. He feels that he wants to protect and shield and help her in every way. (p. 425)

Once the "sexual impulse" had added its energy to the relationship, the young man was surely trapped, and the survival of the species was insured. McDougall, while firmly committed to the importance of instinct all the way up the evolutionary ladder, never lost his sense of Victorian delicacy: while pairing simply meant reproduction in lower animals, in humans it was accorded a tone of gallantry and concern.

The fate of instinct at the hands of the radical behaviorists is a well-known tale. Perhaps the most adamant, as well as notorious, critic of the instinct concept was J. B. Watson (1926). Like those before him who had relied upon observation to prove the existence of maternal instinct, he used observation to confirm its nonexistence:

> We have observed the nursing, handling, bathing, etc. of the first baby of a good many mothers. Certainly there are no new ready-made activities appearing except nursing. The mother is usually as awkward about that as she can well be. The instinctive factors are practically nil. (p. 54)

Watson attributed the appearance of instinctive behavior to the mother's effort to conform to societal expectations of her successful role performance. He, like the 19th-century British associationist Alexander Bain, speculated that not a little of the mother's pleasure in nursing and caring for the infant was due to the sexually stimulating effect of those activities.[7]

Even the most dedicated behaviorists hedged a bit when it came to discarding the idea of instinct altogether. Although the teleology and redundancy of the concept of instinct were sharply criticized, some belief in "instinctive activity" was typically retained (cf. Dunlap, 1919–1920). W. B. Pillsbury (1926), for example, believed that the parental instinct was a "secondary" instinct. Physical attraction to the infant guided the mother's first positive movements toward the infant, but trial and error guided her subsequent care. Instinct was thought of as that quality which set the entire pattern of maternal behavior in motion.

In time instinct was translated into *drive* and *motivation*, refined concepts more in keeping with behavioristic theory. Concomitantly, interest in the maternal instinct of human females gave way to the study of mothering behavior in rodents. The concept of maternal instinct did find a place in psychoanalytic theory, but its definition bore little resemblance to that previously popular. Not only did maternal instinct lose the connotation of protectiveness and gentility that an earlier generation of psychologists had ascribed to it, but it was regarded as basically sexual, masochistic, and even destructive in nature (cf. Rheingold, 1964).

The Ascendancy
of Psychoanalytic Theory

The functionalists, because of their emphasis on "nature," were predictably indifferent to the study of social sex roles and cultural concepts of masculine and feminine. The behaviorists, despite their emphasis on "nurture," were slow to recognize those same social forces. During the early 1930s, there was little meaningful ongoing research in female psychology: the point of view taken by the functionalists was no longer a viable one, and the behaviorists with their emphasis on nonsocial topics (i.e., learning and motivation) had no time for serious consideration of sex differences. While the functionalists had defined laws of behavior that mirrored the society of the times, behaviorists concentrated their efforts on defining universal laws that operated in any time, place, or organism. Individual differences in nature were expected during the functionalist era because they were the sine qua non of a Darwinian view of the world and of science. The same individual differences were anathema to early learning-centered psychology because, no longer necessary or expedient, they were a threat to the formulation of universal laws of behavior.

In the hiatus created by the capitulation of functionalism to behaviorism, the study of sex differences and female nature fell within the domain of psychoanalytic theory—the theory purported to have all the answers. Freudian theory (or some form of it) had for some years already served as the basis for a psychology of female physiological function (cf. Benedek & Rubenstein, 1939). The application of principles popular in psychiatry and medicine (and their inescapable identification with pathology) to academic psychology was easily accomplished. Psychoanalytic theory provided psychology with the first comprehensive theoretical explanation of sex differences. Its novelty in that respect aided its assimilation.

Psychology proper, as well as the general public, had been well-prepared for a biological, and frankly sexual, theory of male and female nature. Havelock Ellis, although himself ambivalent and even hostile toward Freudian teachings, had done much through his writing to encourage openness in the discussion of sexuality. He brought a number of hitherto unmentionable issues to open discussion, couching them in the commonly accepted notion of the complementarity of the sexes, thus insuring their popular acceptance. Emphasis on masculinity and femininity as real dimensions of personality appeared in the mid-1930s in the form of the Terman Masculinity-Femininity Scale (Terman & Miles, 1968). Although Lewis Terman himself avoided discussion of whether masculinity and femininity were products of nature or nurture, social determinants of masculinity and femininity were commonly deemphasized in favor of the notion that they were a type of psychological secondary sexual characteristic. Acceptance of social sex role soon came to be perceived as an indicator of one's mental health.

The traps inherent in a purely psychoanalytic concept of female nature were seldom recognized. John Dewey's (1957) observation, made in 1922, merits attention, not only for its accuracy but because its substance can be found in present-day refutations of the adequacy of psychoanalytic theory as an explanation of woman's behavior and "nature":

> The treatment of sex by psycho-analysts is most instructive, for it flagrantly exhibits both the consequences of artificial simplification and the transformation of social results into psychic causes. Writers, usually male, hold forth on the psychology of women, as if they were dealing with a Platonic universal entity, although they habitually treat men as individuals, varying with structure and environment. They treat phenomena which are peculiarly symptoms of civilization of the West at the present time as if they were the necessary effects of fixed nature impulses of human nature. (pp. 143–144)

The identification of the psychology of women with psychoanalytic theory was nearly complete by the mid-1930s and was so successful that many psychologists today, even those most deeply involved in the current movement for a psychology of women, are not aware that there was a psychology of women long before there was a Sigmund Freud. This article has dealt only with a brief period in that history, and then only with the most significant topics of that period. Lesser issues were often just as hotly debated, for example, whether there is an innate difference in the style of handwriting of men and women (cf. Allen, 1927; Downey, 1910).

And what has happened to the issues of brain size, variability, and maternal instinct since the 1930s? Where they are politically and socially useful, they have an uncanny knack of reappearing, albeit in an altered form. For example, the search for central nervous system differences between males and females has continued. Perhaps the most popular form this search has taken is the theory of prenatal hormonal "organization" of the hypothalamus into exclusively male or female patterns of function (Harris & Levine, 1965). The proponents of this theory maintain an Aristotelian view of woman as an incomplete man:

> In the development of the embryo, nature's first choice or primal impulse is to differentiate a female. . . . The principle of differentiation is always that to obtain a male, something must be added. Subtract that something, and the result will be a female. (Money, 1970, p. 428)

The concept of maternal instinct, on the other hand, has recently been taken up and refashioned by a segment of the woman's movement.

Pregnancy and childbirth are acclaimed as important expressions of womanliness whose satisfactions cannot be truly appreciated by males. The idea that women are burdened with "unreasoning tendencies to pet, coddle, and 'do for' others" has been disposed of by others and replaced by the semiserious proposal that if any "instinctive" component of parental concern exists, it is a peculiarly male attribute (Stannard, 1970). The variability hypothesis is all but absent from contemporary psychological work, but if it ever again promises a viable justification for existing social values, it will be back as strongly as ever. Conditions which would favor its revival include the renaissance of rugged individualism or the "need" to suppress some segment of society, for example, women's aspirations to positions of power. In the first case the hypothesis would serve to reaffirm that there are those "born to lead," and in the latter that there are those "destined to follow."

Of more importance than the issues themselves or their fate in contemporary psychology is the recognition of the role that they have played historically in the psychology of women: the role of social myth. Graves (1968, p. v) included among the functions of mythologizing that of justification of existing social systems. This function was clearly operative throughout the evolutionist-functionalist treatment of the psychology of women: the "discovery" of sex differences in brain structure to correspond to "appropriate" sex differences in brain function; the biological justification (via the variability hypothesis) for the enforcement of woman's subordinate social status; the Victorian weakness and gentility associated with maternity; and pervading each of these themes, the assumption of an innate emotional, sexless, unimaginative female character that played the perfect foil to the Darwinian male. That science played handmaiden to social values cannot be denied. Whether a parallel situation exists in today's study of sex differences is open to question.

Notes

The author would like to thank Judith Abplanalp, Carolyn Sherif, and Dale Harris for helpful comments concerning earlier drafts of this manuscript.

1. Ellis (1934) claimed that Broca's opinion changed over time. Broca "became inclined to think that it [the hypothesized male superiority of intellect] was merely a matter of education—of muscular . . . not merely mental, education—and he thought that if left to their spontaneous impulses men and women would tend to resemble each other, as happens in the savage condition" (p. 222).

2. Burt and Moore (1912, p. 385), inspired by contemporary theories of cortical localization of function, proposed a neurological theory of female affectability. On the basis of the popular belief that the thalamus was "the centre for the natural expression of the emotions" while "control of movements and the

association of ideas" was localized in the cortex and the common assumption that the male was more inclined to be intellectual and rational and the female more passionate and emotional, they concluded that in the adult male the cortex would tend to be "more completely organized," while in the adult female "the thalamus tends to appear more completely organized." They came to the general conclusion that "the mental life of man is predominantly cortical; that of woman predominantly thalamic."

3. One of Ellis's biographers (Calder-Marshall, 1959, pp. 97–98) has suggested that Ellis was "wildly jealous" of Karl Pearson's influence on Olive Schreiner, the controversial South African writer. Schreiner first met Pearson in 1885, over a year after she had met Ellis, and according to Calder-Marshall "was vastly attracted to him [Pearson] in what she considered to be a selfless Hintonian sense. . . . She regarded him as a brilliant young man, dying of tuberculosis, whose few remaining years it was her selfless duty to solace" (Pearson died in 1936). Calder-Marshall summed up the triangle in few, but insinuating, phrases: "Exactly what was happening between Karl Pearson and Olive Schreiner during these months [August 1885–December 1886] is a matter more for any future biographer of Olive Schreiner . . . it is enough to know that Olive did her best to remain loyal to both her friends without telling too many lies, and that while Olive remained the most important person in Havelock's life, the most important person in Olive's life was Karl Pearson from the time she first met him to a considerable time after she left England" (p. 98). Ellis's rivalry with Pearson could explain his bitter and supercilious treatment of Pearson's venture into "variational tendency," since Ellis was not one to easily accept an assault on his ego. For his part Pearson "despised the Hinton group, including Ellis. He thought they were flabby-minded, unhealthy and immoral" (p. 97). But these opinions, while possibly influencing him to write on variation originally, did not intrude upon a fair-minded scientific discussion of the matter.

4. One of the severest critics of Mill's defense of women was Sigmund Freud. He felt Mill's propositions were in direct contradiction to woman's "true" nature: "It is really a stillborn thought to send women into the struggle for existence exactly as men. . . . I believe that all reforming action in law and education would break down in front of the fact that, long before the age at which a man can earn a position in society, Nature has determined woman's destiny through beauty, charm, and sweetness. Law and custom have much to give women that has been withheld from them, but the position of women will surely be what it is: in youth an adored darling and in mature years a loved wife" (quoted in Reeves 1971, pp. 163–164).

5. This sentiment was echoed by Bruno Bettelheim (1965) over 100 years later: "as much as women want to be good scientists or engineers, they want first and foremost to be womanly companions of men and to be mothers" (p. 15).

6. Similar observations were made concerning women. Sutherland (1898) noted that because social morality had developed to such a high level, women "now largely enter upon marriage out of purely sympathetic attractions, in which sex counts for something, but with all its grosser aspects gone." He happily reported another's finding that "sexual desire enters not at all into the minds of a very large proportion of women when contemplating matrimony" (p. 288).

7. Bain's (1875) position was similar except that he believed that there *was* an innate tendency to nurture that initiated the entire cycle of positive affect-positive action. The instinct was thought to be a natural "sentiment," which was fostered by the long period of gestation and the "special energies" required of the mother to sustain the infant. The positive affect arising from activity connected with the infant then brought about increased nurturance and increased pleasure. At least part of this pleasure was thought to be physical in nature.

Reference Note

1. Shields, S. A. *The variability hypothesis and sex differences in intelligence.* Unpublished manuscript, 1974. (Available from Department of Psychology, Pennsylvania State University.)

References

Allen, C. N. Studies in sex differences. *Psychological Bulletin,* 1927, 24, 294–304.

Bain, A. *Mental science.* New York: Appleton, 1875.

Benedek, T., & Rubenstein, B. B. The correlations between ovarian activity and psychodynamic processes. II. The menstrual phase. *Psychosomatic Medicine,* 1939, 1, 461–485.

Bettelheim, B. The commitment required of a woman entering a scientific profession in present-day American society. In J. A. Mattfield & C. G. Van Aken (Eds.), *Women and the scientific professions.* Cambridge, MA: M.I.T. Press, 1965.

Burt, C., & Moore, R. C. The mental differences between the sexes. *Journal of Experimental Pedagogy,* 1912, 1, 355–388.

Calder-Marshall, A. *The sage of sex.* New York: Putnam, 1959.

Calkins, M. W. Community of ideas of men and women. *Psychological Review,* 1896, 3, 426–430.

Castle, C. A. A statistical study of eminent women. *Columbia Contributions to Philosophy and Psychology,* 1913, 22(27).

Cattell, J. McK. A statistical study of eminent men. *Popular Science Monthly,* 1903, 62, 359–377.

Darwin, C. *The descent of man* (2nd ed.). London: John Murray, 1922. (Originally published, 1871; 2nd edition originally published, 1874.)

Dewey, J. *Human nature and conduct.* New York: Random House, 1957.

Downey, J. E. Judgment on the sex of handwriting. *Psychological Review,* 1910, 17, 205–216.

Dunlap, J. Are there any instincts? *Journal of Abnormal and Social Psychology,* 1919–1920, 14, 307–311.

Elliott, H. C. *Textbook of neuroanatomy* (2nd ed.). Philadelphia: Lippincott, 1969.

Ellis, H. *Man and woman: A study of human secondary sexual characters.* London: Walter Scott; New York: Scribner's, 1894.

Ellis, H. Variation in man and woman. *Popular Science Monthly,* 1903, 62, 237–253.

Ellis, H. *A study of British genius.* London: Hurst & Blackett, 1904.

Ellis, H. *Man and woman, a study of secondary and tertiary sexual characteristics* (8th rev. ed.). London: Heinemann, 1934.

Encyclopedia of the Social Sciences. New York: Macmillan, 1935.

Galton, F. *Inquiries into the human faculty and its development.* London: Dent, 1907.

Geddes, P., & Thomson, J. A. *The evolution of sex.* New York: Scribner & Welford, 1890.

Graves, R. Introduction. In *New Larousse encyclopedia of mythology* (Rev. ed.). London: Paul Hamlyn, 1968.

Hall, G. S. The question of coeducation. *Munsey's Magazine,* 1906, *34,* 588–592.

Hall, G. S. *Youth, its education, regimen and hygiene.* New York: Appleton, 1918.

Halleck, R. *Psychology and psychic culture.* New York: American Book, 1895.

Harris, G. W., & Levine, S. Sexual differentiation of the brain and its experimental control. *Journal of Physiology,* 1965, *181,* 379–400.

Hobhouse, L. *Morals in evolution.* New York: Holt, 1916.

Hollingworth, L. S. The frequency of amentia as related to sex. *Medical Record,* 1913, *84,* 753–756.

Hollingworth, L. S. Variability as related to sex differences in achievement. *American Journal of Sociology,* 1914, *19,* 510–530.

Hollingworth, L. S. Social devices for impelling women to bear and rear children. *American Journal of Sociology,* 1916, *22,* 19–29.

Huarte, J. *The examination of mens wits* (trans. from Spanish to Italian by M. Camilli; trans. from Italian to English by R. Carew). Gainesville, FL: Scholars' Facsimiles and Reprints, 1959.

James, W. *The principles of psychology.* New York: Dover, 1950.

Jastrow, J. Note on Calkins' "Community of ideas of men and women." *Psychological Review,* 1896, *3,* 430–431.

Jastrow, J. *Character and temperament.* New York: Appleton, 1915.

Jordan, D. S. The higher education of women. *Popular Science Monthly,* 1902, *62,* 97–107.

Mall, F. P. On several anatomical characters of the human brain, said to vary according to race and sex, with especial reference to the weight of the frontal lobe. *American Journal of Anatomy,* 1909, *9,* 1–32.

McDougall, W. *An introduction to social psychology* (7th ed.). London: Methuen, 1913.

McDougall, W. *Outline of psychology.* New York: Scribner's, 1923.

Meyer, M. *Psychology of the other-one.* Columbia: Missouri Book, 1921.

Mill, J. S. *The subjection of women.* London: Dent, 1955.

Mobius, P. J. The physiological mental weakness of woman (A. McCorn, Trans.). *Alienist and Neurologist,* 1901, *22,* 624–642.

Money, J. Sexual dimorphism and homosexual gender identity. *Psychological Bulletin,* 1970, *74,* 425–440.

More, H. *Strictures on the modern system of female education. With a view of the principles and conduct prevalent among women of rank and fortune.* Philadelphia, PA: Printed by Budd and Bertram for Thomas Dobson, 1800.

Patrick, G. T. W. The psychology of women. *Popular Science Monthly*, 1895, *47*, 209–225.

Pearson, K. Variation in man and woman. In *The chances of death* (Vol. 1). London: Edward Arnold, 1897.

Pillsbury, W. B. *Education as the psychologist sees it*. New York: Macmillan, 1926.

Porteus, S., & Babcock, M. E. *Temperament and race*. Boston: Gorham Press, 1926.

Rausch, F. A. *Psychology; Or, a view of the human soul including anthropology* (2nd rev. ed.). New York: Dodd, 1841.

Reeves, N. *Womankind*. Chicago: Aldine-Atherton, 1971.

Rheingold, J. *The fear of being a woman*. New York: Grune & Stratton, 1964.

Romanes, G. J. Mental differences between men and women. *Nineteenth Century*, 1887, *21*, 654–672.

Shand, A. F. *The foundations of character*. London: Macmillan, 1920.

Sinclair, A. *The better half: The emancipation of the American woman*. New York: Harper & Row, 1965.

Smith, P. *Daughters of the promised land*. Boston: Little, Brown, 1970.

Spencer, H. *The study of sociology*. New York: Appleton, 1891.

Stannard, U. Adam's rib, or the woman within. *Trans-Action*, 1970, *8*, 24–35.

Sutherland, A. *The origin and growth of the moral instinct* (Vol. 1). London: Longmans, Green, 1898.

Terman, L., & Miles, C. C. *Sex and personality*. New York: Russell and Russell, 1968.

Thompson, H. B. *The mental traits of sex*. Chicago: University of Chicago Press, 1903.

Thorndike, E. L. Sex in education. *The Bookman*, 1906, *23*, 211–214.

Thorndike, E. L. *Educational psychology* (2nd ed.). New York: Teachers College, Columbia University, 1910.

Thorndike, E. L. *Individuality*. Boston: Houghton Mifflin, 1911.

Thorndike, E. L. *Educational psychology* (Vol. 3). New York: Teachers College, Columbia University, 1914. (a)

Thorndike, E. L. *Educational psychology briefer course*. New York: Teachers College, Columbia University, 1914. (b)

Walker, A. *Woman physiologically considered*. New York: J. & H. G. Langley, 1850.

Watson, J. B. Studies on the growth of the emotions. In *Psychologies of 1925*. Worcester, MA: Clark University Press, 1926.

Weininger, O. *Sex and character* (trans.). London: Heinemann, 1906.

Wissler, C. The correlation of mental and physical tests. *Psychological Review Monograph Supplements*, 1899–1901, *3*(6, Whole No. 16).

Wollstonecraft, M. *A vindication on the rights of woman*. New York: Dutton, 1955.

Woolley, H. T. Psychological literature: A review of the recent literature on the psychology of sex. *Psychological Bulletin*, 1910, *7*, 335–342.

Wundt, W. *Ethics*. Vol. 3: *The principles of morality, and the departments of the moral life* (M. F. Washburn, Trans.). London: Sonnenschein, 1901.

4

BIAS IN PSYCHOLOGY

Carolyn Wood Sherif

Almost a decade ago, Naomi Weisstein fired a feminist shot that ricocheted down the halls between psychology's laboratories and clinics, hitting its target dead center. The shot was a paper, of course; and thanks to the woman's movement, it later found its way into print under the title "Psychology Constructs the Female, or The Fantasy Life of the Male Psychologist." Her thesis was that "psychology has nothing to say about what women are really like, what they need and what they want, essentially because psychology does not know."[1]

Weisstein's critique focused on the male-centeredness of psychology and upon theories that attribute women's lower status in society and personal problems to psychological qualities that make both appear to be inevitable. She correctly directed attention to social-psychological research demonstrating the impact of social circumstances upon an individual's private experiences and actions.

Still earlier, a woman whose academic study had been in psychology made similar critical points in *The Feminine Mystique*.[2] The year that book appeared I spoke at a symposium at Rice University on the status of the "educated woman," declaring that ignorance about women pervaded academic disciplines in higher education, where the "requirements for the degree seldom include thoughtful inquiry into the status of women, as part of the total human condition."[3] A reading of Georgene Seward's *Sex and the Social Order*[4] had long ago convinced me that the orthodox methods of studying and interpreting sex differences were capable of delivering only mischievous and misleading trivia. Apart from the hoary sex-differences tradition (euphemistically called the "study of individual differ-

Carolyn Wood Sherif, "Bias in Psychology." In Julia Sherman & Evelyn T. Beck (Eds.), *The Prism of Sex: Essays in the Sociology of Knowledge* (pp. 93–133). Copyright 1979 by the University of Wisconsin Press. Reprinted by permission.

ences"), psychology's treatment of the sexes contained several brands of psychoanalytic thought and a growing accumulation of research on socialization to "sex-appropriate behaviors," which was actually the old sex-difference model mixed with psychoanalytic notions and served in a new disguise.

Since the 1960s, the woman's movement has provided the needed context for critical examination of biased theoretical assumptions and working practices in psychology's diverse areas. While referring to that critical literature and the more positive efforts to proceed toward reconstruction, I will concentrate here on examining the following questions, which I believe must be answered if there is to be an equitable pursuit of knowledge about human individuals in psychology:

1. Why have demonstrations of theoretical and research bias, some dating to the earliest days of academic psychology, been no more effective than they have been in correcting theory and research practice? Is the problem simply that there have not been enough women in psychology, or is there something in psychology's assumptions and working practices that also needs attention?
2. What are the dominant beliefs in psychology about the proper ways to pursue knowledge? Where do they come from and what supports them, despite the documented fact that they can encourage biased perspectives?
3. What assumptions about the human individual lie beneath the diversity of psychological theories and their associated procedures for studying that individual?
4. What can we learn from an examination of the state of psychology today that will further an equitable pursuit of knowledge?

Ethnocentrism, Androcentrism, and Sexist Bias in Psychology

The growth of academic psychology over the past century has been compellingly a United States' phenomenon, despite European origins and the non-American backgrounds of a number of its stimulating theorists and researchers. A few decades after William James at Harvard and Wilhelm Wundt at Leipzig started psychological laboratories (1875, according to Boring's history),[5] their students had started psychology departments or laboratories at major universities, including the newly forming women's colleges. Work by women Ph.D.'s began to appear, and two of them (Mary Calkins and Margaret Washburn) served early in this century as presidents of the American Psychological Society, which had formed toward the end of the nineteenth century. In Cattell's *American Men of Science* of 1903, three women were included among fifty psychologists starred as "eminent," two ranked in twelfth and nineteenth ranks (Mary Calkins and C. Ladd-Franklin, respectively), and the third among the last twenty (Margaret Washburn).[6] Not a high proportion, to be sure.

The problem of bias in psychological research was encountered early in the discipline's history, as E. G. Boring's *History of Experimental Psychology* makes clear. "Laboratory atmospheres," or the little Geister within the Zeitgeist (to use his favorite term), were repeatedly found to affect the results coming from different laboratories on the same problem, whether the problem concerned such issues as the presence or absence of images in thought, insightful learning vs. slow trial-and-error learning, or the accumulating research on sex difference. In his history, Boring dismissed sex bias once and for all when assessing the results of Francis Galton's psychological assessments on 9,337 persons at the 1884 International Health Exhibition: "No important generalizations as regards human individual differences appeared, however, unless we should note Galton's erroneous conclusion that women tend in all their capacities to be inferior to men."[7]

Helen Thompson Woolley had critically exposed the bias in sex-difference research, dismissing much of it as drivel, in 1903 and 1910.[8] Leta S. Hollingworth completed doctoral research at Columbia on whether performance on several tasks suffered during menstruation, finding no decrement despite the contrary conviction of her major professor, E. L. Thorndike. Like Mary Calkins earlier, she repeatedly wrote against the hypothesis that women's intellectual capacities varied less than men's. She penned an article in 1916 called "Social Devices for Impelling Women to Bear and Rear Children" that can still rock complacent heels.[9]

And surely someone must have read the dissertation by Mary Putnam Jacobi that won the distinguished Boylston Prize from Harvard University in 1876 on the question, "Do women require mental and bodily rest during menstruation, and to what extent?" Dr. Jacobi began her dissertation with the following caution: "An inquiry into the limits of activity and attainments that may be imposed by sex is very frequently carried on in the same spirit as that which hastens to ascribe to permanent differences in race all the peculiarities of a class, and this because the sex that is supposed to be limiting in its nature, is nearly always different from that of the person conducting the inquiry."[10] Then she reviewed historical evidence both on medical views of menstruation and on women as workers. She collected complete case histories on 268 women, including on their health, took physiological measures during one to three months, and conducted a small performance experiment. She concluded that, yes, short rest periods during the working day would be helpful for menstruating women, as they also would be for women and men during the rest of the month, all of whom would benefit even more by an eight-hour day in place of the twelve or more hours they then labored.

Admittedly, I have chosen cases of women who were keenly aware of the actualities of sex bias, and who were vigorously protesting its manifestations. If, instead, we were to look at the work of the other forty-seven eminent psychologists on Cattell's list in 1903 or at the bulk of writings on sex differences during the early part of this century or at the writings of Sigmund Freud, we would find tons of exemplars for the conclusion reached by my colleague and former student, Stephanie Shields, in her highly original paper reviewing the early years to document social myth in psychology. Her conclusion was as follows: "That science played handmaiden to social values cannot be denied."[11] A similar conclusion could be reached by examining the literature in psychology on race. Yet some mental testers will deny that racism has anything to do with contemporary controversies over intelligence testing.[12]

One could go on and on with further examples of theoretical and research controversies involving bias in psychology on large and on small problems. But I come to a major question: If the possibility and the existence of sexist bias was recognized by the turn of this century, why and how could academic and nonacademic psychology continue to perpetuate its myths up to the present?

Hierarchy in Psychology

It has been thirty-four years since I entered psychology as a graduate student, having learned as an undergraduate at Purdue University that there was such a thing as social psychology. My desire to be a social psychologist was then unorthodox. Nevertheless, I was accepted, even welcomed into the psychology department of the University of Iowa as a graduate assistant. It was 1943, during World War II, when qualified male applicants to graduate programs were scarcer than hen's teeth. As we should know, women are valued more when men are scarce, as today's volunteer army demonstrates. My first lessons at Iowa concerned the status criteria and norms valued by psychologists.

At the peak of the status hierarchy were the experimentalists. At that time and place, being an experimentalist meant being self-consciously scientific, reading the philosophy of science as expounded by logical positivists, and studying hungry rats learning the way to food, or humans responding to a puff of air to the eyelid. One way to determine who "counts" to an elite is to learn whose arguments the elite attends to and whose viewpoints they try to demolish. At the time, the only people worthy of attention from experimentalists were other experimentalists.

The next rung in the hierarchy was occupied by the "mental testers" and statistical buffs, who represented a quite different tradition in psychology but had to be listened to by experimentalists who wanted to analyze their data in the currently fashionable way. The testing tradition, which began in Great Britain, had been fueled by the practical success of the French psychologists Binet and Simon in developing a workable test for singling out school children with potential learning problems. The Stanford version of their test, the development of group tests, and their use during World War I put testers of all kinds into an orbit that is now a $120 million industry by conservative estimate.[13] Interestingly enough, a survey of the interests of women psychologists just after World War II revealed that proportionally more were in the ranks of the testers than of the experimentalists.[14] So perhaps it is no accident that the two women (Anne Anastasi and Leona Tyler) who were elected presidents of the American Psychological Association in the past decade were recognized as experts in the mental testing tradition of differential psychology as well as active contributors to the professional organization. Somewhat more predictably, their terms followed immediately upon that of the first and only black president of the association (Kenneth B. Clark).

On the next lowest rung of the hierarchy at Iowa in 1943 were the developmental psychologists, whose work at the time focused heavily on preschool children. They were housed in the same building, but under the separate roof of the Institute for Child Welfare (a less prestigious locale, you may be sure), and included the only women faculty. Although regarded as the "child study people," they were headed by an experimentalist from the same major university as the psychology chairman; hence, a few of them were regarded as acceptable by experimentalists. But the testers and the developmentalists had more to talk about, since Iowans were in the forefront of the attack on a fixed, inherited "intelligence," battling Minnesotans and Californians who defended the alleged constancy of IQ.

One distinguished member of the Child Welfare faculty was Kurt Lewin. Lewin had published the famous studies on the effects of adult modes of interaction on the behavior of small boys in leisure-time groups, the authoritarian, democratic, and laissez-faire leadership experiments.[15] At the time, he was often in Washington, involved in the equally well-known studies on group decision. (These studies demonstrated that women volunteers in Red Cross activities were not easily persuaded by lectures to alter long-ingrained food customs, but were quite capable of changing the family diet to include unpopular foods to help the war effort when presented with the problem of food shortages and encouraged to arrive at a joint decision to make the change.)[16] Like many of their experimental colleagues in Washington, in military service, or with the Office of War Information, the experimentalists at Iowa regarded these as "applied" activities, necessary at the time but not the stuff of which a science is made. At the bottom of the Iowa ladder and also classified as "applied" were the one other social psychologist and the clinical psychologists.

The hierarchy was male, of course. Thirty years ago, it was the experimentalists at the top, the testers and statisticians next, then the developmentalists, and finally the social psychologists, including some interested in what was called personality, along with the clinicians. After World War II, there were notable changes, the most striking being the enormous increase in number of clinical psychologists, with federal funds to support their activities and student training. Today, about 40 percent of APA members are clinical psychologists. The numbers and the standing of social psychologists changed, less through their following the example of Kurt Lewin than through their self-conscious efforts to be accepted as *experimental* social psychologists and their quoting Lewin's injunction against historicalism, one of his least defensible points. A host of new specialties was born of postwar prosperity. You name it, we have it, including in 1973 a division on psychology of women and by 1976 a division "interested in religion."

So why do I bring up the hierarchy of three decades ago? It is my contention that each of the fields and specialities in psychology sought to improve its status by adopting (as well and as closely as stomachs permitted) the perspectives, theories, and methodologies as high on the hierarchy as possible. The way to "respectability" in this scheme has been the appearance of rigor and scientific inquiry, bolstered by highly restricted notions of what science is about. The promise was that theirs was the true path to general psychological principles, applicable with slight modification to any human being and, in some cases, to any organism, even rats, monkeys, and chimpanzees.

Never mind that in practice, psychology treated women, blacks, and other minorities, as well as residents of certain other countries, as more "different" than a well-behaved laboratory chimpanzee. We are talking of myth, or more accurately, the ideology of psychology's elite. In that perspective, work outside of the laboratory was suspect. Research in naturalistic settings was regarded as necessarily less "pure," even "contaminated." Efforts to change social life or individual circumstances were regarded as merely "applied" work, typically as premature attempts to apply psychological principles.

The irony is that the preservation of psychology's hierarchy and the expansion of the entire enterprise was supported by those psychologists making inroads into major institutions—educational, business, industrial, military, governmental, the growing mass media, and the "mental health" institutions and industry—in short, the "applied" psychologists.Without their inroads, psychology would have been small potatoes in academia, but it need not have worried. The growing number of psychologists in major institutions needed the academic hierarchy to support its claims at being scientific.

Dominant Beliefs Conducive
to Bias in Psychology

Certain of its dominant beliefs about the proper way to pursue knowledge have made psychological research peculiarly prone to bias in its conception, execution, and interpretation. It is on these that I shall focus here—and I shall be highly critical. If I thought that these were the only beliefs in psychology or that they characterized everything within its bounds, I would not still be a psychologist. But I have seen a number of battles and skirmishes over psychological findings, many of them possible because of fundamental flaws in the orthodox modes of seeking knowledge.

A historical perspective is useful in understanding the issues. One year after psychology's entry onto the academic scene, the Centennial Exposition of 1876 opened in Philadelphia. As the Smithsonian's 1976 recreation vividly reminds us, rhapsodic praise of science and technology was a major theme. From its birth, academic psychology cast its lot within the bright promise of a scientific future. Similarly, founders of the notion of psychotherapy—all physicians, including Sigmund Freud—were immersed in the same promise. Freud reserved special indignation for those critics, like Havelock Ellis, who suggested that he was dealing in allegory and myth rather than in science.[17] In this respect alone, Freud was brother under the skin to the best-known psychologist of our day, B. F. Skinner.

I shall not be exploring the larger historical trends toward faith in science. Instead, I am concerned with the subsidiary impulse of psychologists to seek acceptance and prestige for their new discipline through imitating the more established scientific disciplines. Over time, those who became the most prominent psychologists were those who imitated the most blindly, grasping what brought prestige in their society even though it was more a caricature of the more established sciences.

Undeniably, the prestigious and successful sciences in the late nineteenth and early twentieth century were those securely focused on the physical world and the physical processes of the organic world. Psychologists, in their strivings to gain status with other scientists, did not pause long on issues raised by the differences between studying a rock, a chemical compound, or an animal, on one hand, and a human individual, on the other. Instead, methods that had been successful in the physical and biological sciences were embraced as models for psychology. Researchers were soon deep into analogy, comparing the human individual to the chemical compound or to the animal as the subject of research, with all of the power that such an analogy gives to the scientific investigator, at least if the animal is captive and small. Unlike the natural scientist, however, the psychologists had only social power over the research subject, not the greater power to explore, observe, and analyze that had unlocked so many of nature's secrets for the physical sciences.

Beliefs About What is "Basic"

The methodology promoted in psychology, in its strivings for social acceptability and prestige, rested on the assumption that the causes of an event can be determined by breaking down the event into component parts, or elements, and studying those parts and their relationships to one another. The more "basic" these parts or elements are, the more "basic" is the inquiry.

What psychology defined as basic was dictated by slavish devotion to the more prestigious disciplines. Thus, a physiological or biochemical part or element was defined as more basic than a belief that Eve was created from Adam's rib, not because the former can necessarily tell us more about a human individual, but because physiology and biochemistry were more prestigious than religious history or sociology. On the environmental side, a physical element that could be counted or that one of the physical sciences had already measured was regarded as more "basic" than poverty; thus, the social disciplines that wrote about poverty in any way other than by counting income had even less standing than psychology. Turning to the humanities for an understanding of what is basic in being human was considered absurd. What could scholars in English or Spanish, in history or classics, possibly tell psychologists? Psychologists did look to history and philosophy to find out about the history and philosophy of science, but then, that was all about mathematics, physics, and chemistry, and therefore respectable.

Narrowing the Space and Time Framework

The event to be studied and the elements to be considered basic or peripheral were to be those that occurred in the here-and-now of the researcher's observation or of the other techniques for data collection. In many respects, Kurt Lewin's call for ahistoricalism in psychology—that is, for concerning oneself with history only as it forces were revealed in the immediate situation at the time of study—was merely confirmation of existing research practice.[18] Nonetheless, it provided justification for developmental, social, and personality psychologists to view as "scientific" the conduct of research on human individuals about whose past, personal loyalties, and social ties, about whose place in a larger historical-cultural nexus, they knew next to nothing. Consequently, they seldom looked for or found evidence of history, culture, or organizational ties in the specific research situations they studied. Mary Putnam Jacobi's surveys of the history of cultural and medical thought about menstruation and of the historical experiences of working women were now to be considered excess baggage in a study of particular women at a particular period of time. Even her case histories would come to be seen as unnecessary, except insofar as they contained evidence of physiologic malfunction, since physiological factors were defined as basic.

"Objective" Language as a Disguise for Ignorance or Bias

By the mid-twentieth century the elementism practiced by orthodox psychology became thoroughly blended with the language of applied mathematical statistics, especially as applied to biological and agricultural research. Thus, the elements became abstract "variables." The psychologist in pursuit of knowledge was attempting to seek causation by discovering lawful relationships among variables. Paraphrasing E. L. Thorndike, the psychologist came to believe that "anything that exists, exists in some quantity, hence can be measured" and hence is a variable.[19]

In causation, not all variables are created equal, however. Some are designated "independent variables," and it is to these that one looks for causality, despite textbook cautions to the contrary. One may find the independent variable in nature, as when an agronomist selects garden plots with soil rich or poor in nitrogen in which to plant corn. The yield or height of the growing corn is then the "dependent" variable caused by the independent variable (rich or poor soil), unless the soil or the seed or the air contain other "contaminating" variables.

It goes without saying that a person's sex is considered an independent variable, not a dependent one, despite the fact that everyone and no one knows what that means. Psychologists seem to think they know, when they pronounce that the sex of the researcher or the sex of the research subject, or both, are independent variables in research; but it should not take a Renée Richards to demonstrate that the assumption of causality by the "independent variable" of sex is misleading. Why? Because the "variable" called sex is like a railroad boxcar: everyone knows what it is called and what it is used for, but no one knows what is inside. Older psychologists had no doubt that it contained "biology." Modern psychologists follow suit, or add culture, or subtract biology as well. Result? Utter confusion in almost all discussions of the variable "sex" or of sex differences.

Glorifying the Experiment: An Example

The highly abstract belief that knowledge is to be gained by studying parts, elements, or variables and by seeking lawfulness in their relationships, is translated into reality during psychological research. The most prestigious way to make this translation is the experiment. In the experiment, certain selected "independent," presumably causative, elements are deliberately varied, while other possible choices are controlled or kept in a constant state.

What this description of the experiment means is that in the human experiment much of what goes on is simply ignored. The researcher may choose the independent variable by selecting persons according to sex, race, etc., or according to their performance on a psychological test. But the experiment is considered much more valid if the researcher attempts to create the independent variable by "manipulating" the circumstances in the research situation—for example, by controlling what people see or hear or do. Thus created, the variable is somehow regarded as purer, less "contaminated" by past experiences. History is ignored, and the researcher has the illusion of creating history at the moment.

While I was looking for an example of an experiment, the mail brought the current issue of the *Journal of Personality and Social Psychology*, the most widely read and cited journal in that area of psychology. The second article, by the journal editor and his students, concerned the effects of three "independent variables" upon reactions to messages intended to persuade college students for or against some viewpoint, for example, for or against faculty tenure. Other independent variables were also introduced in a series of eight separate experiments. All of these experiments studied the ratings of messages on thirty-six different topics made by persons described as follows: "Subjects were either unpaid undergraduate volunteers who were enrolled in introductory psychology courses or were paid respondents to classified advertisements in the university newspaper. . . . Subjects were recruited without regard to sex and were assigned randomly to a persuasion . . . group and to an identification number within that group. . . . a total of 616 subjects provided data."[20]

Eighteen of the messages concerned past presidents of the United States, and eighteen others concerned arbitrarily selected social issues— that is, the researchers simply picked them. The experiments are presented as a novelty, with considerable pride, because the messages were presented to subjects by computer on video screen, and the subjects responded to them by pushing the computer's buttons. "The computerized method assures a standardized experimental procedure for each subject . . . it minimizes interaction of the subject with a human experimenter. These characteristics are responsible for a desirably high degree of situational control and assurance that possible sources of experimenter bias are minimized."[21] But it was the researchers who selected the topics, presented them in certain orders, varied the contents of the screen, etc. Moreover, the researchers were forced to add the caution that "although the relationship of experimenter to subject is mediated by the computer, that relationship nonetheless exists."[22] They make less issue about the undeniable possibility of significant effects from interacting with a computer.

The researchers present their findings on the persuasive effects of the messages in typical fashion, as the means or averages of all the students' single ratings on each issue after they had read the message. The individual differences among the students, including what their opinions about the presidents or the social issues were before the messages were presented, were treated in the statistical analysis as a "random-effect" factor.

In short, this experiment typifies the assumption in a great deal of experimentation that "general laws" about the relationships among variables can be obtained by comparing averages of the responses made by a sizable number of individuals, who are regarded as being without a background, personal history, or gender that might have anything to do with their response in the situation. In this case, the situation itself is described only in terms of the equipment, which is shown in a photograph. Its duration appears to have been well within the academic hour.

Are These the Beliefs of "Hard Science"?

Doing "basic" research on "variables" that are given numbers, and hence can be treated statistically, and, especially, performing experiments are sometimes called the "hard science" ways of seeking knowledge in psychology. What these beliefs describe, instead, are efforts by some members of a newer, less established discipline to imitate what they, as outsiders, see as the ways the physical sciences achieved knowledge successfully. It is the physical sciences that are called "hard sciences," as we all know, and the human disciplines that are "soft."

The adoption of the "hard" and "soft" analogy within psychology and within other social disciplines obscures the real issues, which are about the ways to extend scientific methods to the study of human beings by other human beings. Those who use these adjectives have almost always been men trying to put down other men and their work, attempting to enhance their own status by associating their own efforts with the more prestigious physical or natural sciences.[23] For this reason, I think it particularly misleading to suggest that "hard" also implies "masculine," while "soft" implies "feminine." After all, in the physical sciences there have been a few women, and some of the women minority in the "soft" disciplines follow the hard line.

Within psychology, the "hard" vs. "soft" name-calling is also to be heard when issues of "scientific" vs. "humanistic" psychology are discussed. Again, the controversies do not divide the men from the women; they have been quite divisive of male psychologists. But "humanistic" psychologists need to cease accepting their opponents' definitions of what is "scientific" and start to assess science as a human endeavor. The self-consciously scientific experimental psychologists need to start thinking about the unique problems raised in the history of science when human individuals turn to studying other individuals.

Meanwhile, the equitable pursuit of knowledge will be better served if we recognize psychologists' self-annointment as "hard" researchers for what it is: a put-down of critics who do not accept their orthodoxies. Those who proclaim the hardness of their methods and their hardware the loudest are the most guilty of producing research findings with the durability of a marshmallow. And now, we shall see why.

Critique of Psychological Orthodoxy's Beliefs on Its Objectivity

I have intended my description of the standard in psychological research, which admittedly was almost a caricature, to make clear that the standard research situation is loaded with opportunity for bias. The opportunity starts when a researcher decides what to study and it continues to widen during decisions about how to study the subject. What is the individual being studied to do during the research? The researcher decides, of course, often in highly arbitrary ways dictated by custom in previous research, not by what the person does or is doing in daily life. What are to be included as the all-important independent variables? Which aspects of the individual's behavior are to be noticed and which ignored during the research experience? The researcher makes all of these decisions, often forgetting at times that he or she is a human being who is part of the research situation too.

Research as an Interpersonal
and Cultural Event

Now we can see, I trust, why Robert Rosenthal and many others after him were able to demonstrate in the late 1950s and the 1960s the phenomenon of researcher bias—specifically, that the researcher's expectations of the outcome in research affect what is actually found.[24] Rosenthal's findings should have come as no surprise. Studies of interviewing had already shown that middle-class interviewers obtained answers from working-class respondents that differed from those obtained by working-class interviewers, that white interviewers got answers from black respondents differing from those obtained by black interviewers, and that women respond differently to men and to women, as men respond differently to women and to men.[25]

Why should the effect of one human being upon another be a surprise, especially the effect of a much more powerful researcher upon a person who has agreed to cooperate in an institutional setting that defines the person as "subject"? Did someone believe that the psychology of researcher and the psychology of subject, both human beings, are altogether different?

There was also the failure to recognize other sociocultural aspects of the research situation. The research setting, whether experiment or interview, packs a cultural wallop through its physical location, especially if defined as a place to do research, and through the plethora of equipment, clipboards, forms, tape recorders, and audiovisual equipment that researchers pack about. Two-way mirrors, intended to hide the researcher, in fact alert the person observed that his or her actions are being watched and evaluated. A simple button placed in the room in the event that the subject wants to leave becomes a signal to "panic" ("if it's there, it's there to be used"). The supposedly neutral and objective paper-and-pencil test or information blank turns out to be a signal to the individual that someone who knows more than she does is evaluating something about her, perhaps even her worth as a person—an unnerving thought at best and at worst a promoter of apprehension or of an active effort to appear "socially desirable." Finally, evidence has accumulated indicating that people who volunteer for research tend to be those with more interest in psychology, research, and science, who do respond to the research situation differently from a person somehow mousetrapped in the research situation. The difference is typically in a direction congenial to the researcher's interest, although it need not be, especially since the researcher has often been unaware of the impact of these research impedimenta or of the active attempts by subjects to evaluate and deal with the research situation.[26]

The impact of the research situation is nowhere more convincingly shown than in Stanley Milgram's study of obedience by research subjects to a researcher's commands to deliver increasingly more severe electric shocks to another person who is ostensibly another innocent subject. Actually, the latter played a prescribed role, exhibiting discomfort and objecting to the procedures, though never actually being shocked. Once a "subject," man or woman, agreed to participate in the experiment, typically for pay, the highly institutional setting, the white-coated experimenter, and the structured procedures took precedence, at least for 65 percent of the subjects, so long as the apparent victim was out of sight in the next room. Milgram understood the power of that institutional setting, its equipment, and the authoritative researcher. He showed that obedience dropped sharply when the procedures called for closer proximity to the apparent victim, and that another person refusing to cooperate blew the game. The standard personality tests purporting to measure proclivities toward aggression proved worthless in predicting reactions to the research situation. On the other hand, certain past experiences in the subject's life did appear to relate to his or her decision on whether to continue shocking the victim or whether to stop, as 35 percent of Milgram's subjects did even in his most compelling situation. These past experiences related much more to the individual's perspectives on authority, on science, and on self than they did to abstractly defined personality characteristics.[27]

More Culture in Study of Persons

The final cultural wallop packed by a research situation concerns the activity performed by the research subject. What is the individual to do for research? How does she or he regard the task—as easy or difficult, fun or boring, familiar or strange? The researcher's choice of what is to be done, and hence, of what behaviors are to be examined, is critical.

By now, we know that the standard procedures developed in an influential line of research to study achievement motivation were biased by the choice of tasks and of instructions that were male-oriented. They were inappropriate for studying achievement orientations of women who had been brought up to believe that certain activities and institutions— e.g., the military—were off-limits for women.[28] We also know that the effort to patch up that theory on achievement by adding a new motiva- tion—avoidance or fear of success—produced over two hundred studies with conflicting results.[29]

Both efforts failed largely because the researchers, in defining the research situation, forgot that outside of it and for years, success had been defined by others who count in our eyes—our reference persons and groups—and that what success meant has been quite different for the reference persons and groups of different men and women in our society. In fact, *success* has been defined so differently that both women and men who have tried to achieve success in ways ruled more appropriate for the other gender—for example, career women or male ballet dancers—have been targets for derogatory labels and negative adjectives so widely used as to be social stereotypes. Especially in a society where some of these divisions have begun to change, indeed where some people are actively rejecting both the definitions and the possibility of "success" in traditional terms, what kind of a theory on motivations to achieve, or fears of failure, or motives to avoid success, can ignore the issues of who defines success or failure for whom, and whether individuals accept those definitions as their own? A little history, a little sociology and economics, a little attention to the historic pleas of feminists and antiracist movements, would have helped.

Another example of bias induced by the selection of activities is a whole line of research on influenceability or suggestibility. One of the old saws in many social psychology texts up through 1974 (though not in any of the four authored by the Sherifs) was that women are more susceptible to persuasive influences or suggestions than men. The research evidence to lay that old saw to rest was collected by my former student Ben Tittler over ten years ago, when he showed that both men and women were more suggestible when the topic at hand was of very little concern to them (e.g., the reputation of General von Hindenburg) than when the topic was deeply and personally involving (e.g., the appropriate personal qualities for men and women). More recently, Judy Morelock's Ph.D. research at Pennsylvania State University has demonstrated that whether men or women are easily influenced by persuasive suggestions depends upon the gender of the researcher in relation to the topic—specifically, that women are more suggestible with a male researcher when the topic is socially defined as one of male interest, while men respond in parallel fashion when a woman researcher tries to influence them on a topic socially defined as interesting to women. Finally, Alice Eagley has performed the arduous task of surveying all available research on short-term persuasion and suggestion, and has found no basis whatsoever for the blanket conclusion that one sex is more suggestible than the other.[30] There is, however, a great deal of evidence that anyone may be suggestible or influenced when he or she is placed in an ambiguous situation where one's responsiveness to the situation itself seems more important at the time than personal integrity or self-definition as individual man or woman. When some aspect of the person's self becomes highly involved or is at stake, neither sex is readily or easily influenced by the opinions or persuasiveness of another person during a brief encounter, especially if that other person is a stranger.[31]

Short Course in How to Perpetuate Social Myth

The lesson for those who want to perpetuate sex bias in psychological research is clear: Restrict the framework for study to a narrow span of time. Attend only to what you decide is important, ignoring as much else as possible. Label these important aspects in the language of "variables," both to sound objective and to mask your ignorance. Arrange the research situation as you choose. If you are biased, the situation will be. Record your selectively chosen data and discuss them as though dealing with eternal verities.

If anyone tries to refer to historical, cultural, or organizational circumstances outside of your own narrow framework, either (1) derogate such talk as referring to "soft" facts and "soft" disciplines which you see as being of little relevance to your carefully controlled variables and findings; or (2) suggest that everyone has different interests, and that yours happens to be in psychology, whatever its limitations, not in history, culture, etc. In either case, you will have removed the most effective and, ultimately, the only effective means by which your critic can expose your bias and show what you have done wrong. You will have put the critic in the position either of confining the discussion to your limited framework, or of going out to do another study to show that your research does not hold up—that it cannot be replicated or that it crumbles when another variable is introduced.

Suppose that your critic does the latter. The attempt to replicate a study with a few well-chosen variations is the means many psychologists choose if they want to do serious battle in order to gain victory within the establishment's walls. The history of our field and the analysis of the "social psychology of the psychological experiment" that I just reviewed both suggest that the critic's chance of scoring a critical point is very high. Findings in the area will become "controversial."

Now, what should you, the researcher, do to your critic? By far the best tactic is to withdraw from the field, murmuring about the weaknesses of the research design that has become controversial. Find another way to score your point with a research design so different that the ongoing controversy is no longer relevant.

In fact, that is exactly what has happened over and over again in psychology on many topics, but almost invariably on topics where sex bias is charged. For example, most research from Putnam-Jacobi's and Hollingworth's to the present shows insignificant variations in women's performance attributable to the menstrual cycle on a variety of laboratory tasks. So proponents of the view that menstruation is debilitating by definition switched grounds. Instead of looking at what women do, the started looking at the way women said they *felt*—at their reported moods and especially their bad ones. The switch amounted to saying, in effect, that bad moods *are* debilitating, whether women perform differently or not. Then new critics showed quite convincingly that the culture is loaded with stereotyped notions about menstruation and bad moods, some authors almost seeming to say that women report bad moods because they think they are supposed to. The debilitator school chuckles tolerantly and points to hormonal fluctuations during the cycle. Can such hormonal "storms" be ignored?

Meanwhile, women who experience discomfort during menstruation are wondering whether to blame the experience on their *really* being the "weaker sex," or on their society, or on themselves. Women who experience no discomfort wonder what all the fuss is about. Fortunately, a small minority of researchers is beginning to realize that an unbiased view of this universal, greatly neglected cyclic phenomenon can be developed only over considerable time through enlarging the framework for study. That framework has to include historical perspective and study, as well as unbiased physiological study that sees hormonal variations as normal and universal for both genders, each with characteristic patterns. It has to include a vastly expanded perspective on what women and men do, their relationships to one another and in a variety of periodic activities, as these relate to the most underdeveloped problem area in psychological research—namely, how people feel and experience themselves, and why, when, and how these self-experiences affect their actions.

If the issues of bias in psychological research were as simple as turning the methods and instruments prized by psychology into the service of defeating bias, many battles would have been won long ago. My short course in how to perpetuate myths has already been learned too well by too many to allow such a defeat. The long course in how to destroy myths has to begin with the essentials: Broaden the framework within which knowledge is sought, then persist in the difficult tasks of relating events within that broadened framework through a variety of methods and research techniques. This is the only course toward an unbiased psychology. Otherwise, those who hold biased viewpoints, either wittingly or unwittingly, will return a decade later, dredge up the old research evidence, reinterpret it by clothing it in new words, and start the argument again before public audiences who like the message. This is what happened in the so-called race and intelligence controversy, which many psychologists believed had been laid to rest a generation ago.

Buttresses in Society
for Psychology's Orthodoxy

In view of the openness of psychological research to bias, who in society buttresses the continuation of its research traditions by supporting them or by drawing upon their conclusions? It is popular in academia to say "no one"; but such scholarly aloofness is far from true, historically. Since World War I, the military has been one of the strongest sources of support for psychological tests on what psychologists called "intelligence," then came to define as "what my test measures." Tests of "abilities" and of variously labeled aptitudes followed. Another source of support has been our vast educational system, from preschool through graduate school, in order to place students into educational tracks and channel them into different slots for future training or education. In fact, the goals of education became defined in terms of test performance, rather than tests serving as a means of seeing whether the educational establishment was meeting its own goals or those considered desirable in society.

The logical extension of the so-called intelligence or ability tests to the assessment of various aspects of the personality and of motivation followed, especially after World War II. These tests became so standard that incoming freshmen at the University of Minnesota accepted the practice of taking the Minnesota Multiphasic Personality Inventory along with placement tests in academic subjects. They were widely used in government and industry, which also adopted large batteries of aptitude tests for use in selecting employees and in promotion. Desirous of an "instant criterion" for selecting able and docile employees, these institutions did not, typically, develop tests demonstrably predictive of success in a job, but purchased commercial tests often developed for entirely different purposes. The use of such tests, both in educational placement and in fateful decisions about employment, have figured recently in several court decisions on affirmative action practices.[32] I am told also that a well-known vocational interest test for high school students has ceased printing its separate tests for women and men, which were on pink and blue forms.

Aside from the testing industry, the military and other agencies of government have poured huge sums into research on problems that concerned them at the moment. During and after World War II, the popular topic was propaganda; then came studies of small groups and leadership; and by the early sixties all the money was for cross-cultural research and studies on how to change people's attitudes. The relationship between what was supported, what psychologists in those periods studied, and what problems were concerning government and the military is clear, though seldom discussed. Similarly, the record of what is supported in the study of child development mirrors the social problems of concern to authorities at the time and the programs they hope to justify be research. A whole new research industry whose sole aim is to evaluate social programs by the government has recently been born in academia and in commercial firms. Such evaluation research is prone to bias in the direction of confirming what policymakers want to perpetuate and what they hope fails, as one of the earliest papers on the topic makes abundantly clear.[33] More recently, we learn from daily papers that, all the while, the CIA has been supporting research through a variety of phony foundations and social agencies.

Finally, the emergence of clinical psychology as the largest specialty by psychologists after World War II reflects the fact that wars are very hard on people, creating problems that last far beyond their duration. Clinical psychology grew from the lack of enough psychiatrists to handle war-related human problems and from the growing numbers of human casualties at the community level who raised community, hence governmental issues. And once we had the problems and a growing army of professionals, the definition of what is to be done with human problems in living changed: many now required, not friends, not better working conditions, not a social worker, not a job interview, not a minister or loving parent, but a therapist. Benefitting from the aura already created by the medical profession, clinical psychologists came into demand, in preference to a minister or a social worker or a counselor, because their claims to expertise rested on a discipline that said it was scientific, that based its procedures on research findings.

It has become customary for women to deplore the practices of testing for psychological assessment, placement, and hiring, but to regard these practices as not especially biased against their gender. This misconception probably arose because the early intelligence testers in this country made the deliberate decision not to construct tests indicating overall male-female differences in intelligence. The decision was dictated perhaps less by lack of sex bias) though indeed, it was made when the suffrage movement was at its height), than by the necessity of having a test that correlated with the only available criterion of validity—performance in elementary school, in which the sexes did not differ systematically. Nevertheless, this sagacious decision by the early testers did not apply to those women, or men, who happened to have been born into a poor family or came from a minority group with problems and opportunities differing markedly from those more fortunate.

The extension of the early testers' logic to issues of aptitudes, personal motivation, and interests has been loaded with gender bias. Society has persisted in attempting to define women and men as creatures with entirely different capabilities and fates, despite the historic social trends in employment, family, and other activities of the kind documented so well by Jessie Bernard in discussing "tipping points."[34] The indiscriminate use of tests developed primarily for males is both biased and inappropriate as society changes. Necessarily their use assumes that the standards based on male performance in the past will be retained when the very institutions in which performance is to occur will have changed by admitting women. The situation is remarkably similar to that in cross-cultural research when the researcher attempts to use the methods and procedures developed in the United States to study, say, India.

The Indian psychologist Durganand Sinha has commented on this practice perceptively. "Psychology," he said, "appears to be method-bound. Sometimes it is ridiculed as a science without content but with plenty of methodology. Modelling itself after physical sciences and in its zeal for precision and universality of its principles, it has not only adopted a micro approach but has fought shy of highly complex social processes. When the study of a social phenomenon is not easily amenable to its methods, it is ignored." Sinha then goes on to relate his own experiences in attempting to apply standard research methods and procedures in Indian villages, giving examples of the need for "culturally appropriate models, tools and techniques."[35] With the same logic, we may see that particular methods and procedures which may have been useful to a society content with its unequal division of labor and unequal opportunities in education are misleading when the same society finds its institutions changing to include those hitherto relegated to different or markedly inferior status.

Thus, U.S. society contains many major and central institutions with interests bolstering psychology's claims to be scientific and bolstering the particular version of scientific methodology adopted as its most prestigious resource. I do not intend at all to pose a dichotomy between so-called basic and so-called applied research. On the contrary, both have been constrained by a particular vision of what is worth doing and how to do that scientifically. That particular vision is not the only one available, nor does it lead to unbiased definition of problems, results, or conclusions. Its most powerful weapons against charges of bias have been, not dazzling scientific accomplishments, but its support by elites in psychology and the larger society based on consensus of opinion.

Assumptions (Theories)
About the Individual

At the basis of the natural science model of psychological research there are assumptions about the individual that, when formally stated, we would call psychological theory. In fact, there is no generally accepted perspective in psychology, much less a generally accepted theory. There is, instead, a jungle of rival schools, situation-specific and person-specific generalizations, and mini-theories developed to explain what went on in a particular experiment. Nevertheless, the rival schools share some or many common assumptions about how to pursue knowledge, they use each other's methods, and their interests reveal certain patterns.

I think it is not unfair to say that experimental orthodoxy in psychology has most purely revealed a lack of interest in research problems or theoretical statements that concern women and men in the problems of living in their families, with friends, and in working and raising children. From the beginning, experimental psychology's assumptions about the individual have regarded individual and social differences as something to be treated as "error," in the sense that its experiments and its laws would not try to explain them. Individuals are different, that's all. The result has been an experimental psychology that appears to treat everyone equitably, but in fact makes decisions arbitrarily about when to study women or men, blacks or whites, rich or poor, in terms of the researcher's convenience, their likelihood of performing appropriately for the researcher, or the source of research funds.

Watching Out for Other Animals

Many (though fortunately not all) experimentalists have also adopted a peculiarly American view of the evolutionary process, one that places less emphasis on Darwin's original interest in explaining the origins of the *different* species than on continuity in evolutionary development. The emphasis on continuity is sometimes so extreme that the human individual is seen as differing from individuals in other species only in terms of increased quantity and complexity of the human central nervous system, and in a few other details, including the undeniable absence of a tail.

Such views are the basis for the enthusiasm exhibited by some psychologists for the current fad called sociobiology. Their enthusiasm is also aided by near total ignorance of elementary anthropology, especially about kinship systems.[36] The uncritical assumption that the human individual is a somewhat more complicated white rat or hairless ape has been criticized valiantly by European researchers and by outstanding researchers in this country.[37] But our texts are still full of animal research placed side by side with human research on, say, the "maternal drive." It is now considered necessary to include a well-placed warning that, of course, one should not ignore the complicating factors that differentiate human mothers from rat mothers. But new students and often their teachers proceed to analyze the human mother on the basis of what rats have done when separated from their pups by an electrified grid.

The importance of a genuinely comparative study of animal behavior does not need defense. But the uncritical acceptance of the assumption that apparent similarity in behaviors by a human individual and by individuals in another species is evidence for a "biological" basis in the human behavior is both erroneous and an obstacle to the equitable pursuit of knowledge. In the larger sense, all human behavior has a biological basis. Little is added to that statement by seeking surface resemblances between the human being and other animals, while ignoring the processes underlying the analogous actions.[38]

As others have said, the cat and the human individual both act, but the human knows that he or she is acting, thinks about it, and can talk about it. It is of interest that chimpanzees are bright enough to learn to communicate by gestures or through a computer, painfully taught by human beings. It is nonsense to conclude that the chimpanzee is learning in the same way that a human child learns to communicate. By about the age two, any normal human child in any culture outstrips the chimpanzee without special instruction, provided only that there are other human individuals about who speak.[39]

It should not be necessary to reiterate such observations, except that the simple and universal phenomenon of human consciousness, of awareness of self in relation to others, is not at all central in orthodox psychology's assumptions or its methodology. How else can we explain that some psychologists still have great difficulty in believing that what the human research subject thinks, how he or she sizes up the research situation and the research, how he or she hopes to appear to the researcher, are critical events in the sequence that leads to the researcher's so-called hard data?

Why else should it be a mystery to some that a woman and a man in the same situation might size up the situation differently? Instead, the orthodox proclivity is to attribute any differences in the reactions by a man and a woman in what researchers see as the "same" situation to some hypothetical attribute, often biologically determined. If, as often happens, they react in the same way, that similarity is seen as irrelevant to the subject's gender.

The Study of Sex Differences and Trait Theory

The reason that only differences between the genders are considered of research or theoretical significance is not hard to uncover. Many psychologists, including Julia Sherman in her notable survey of research on women as well as Eleanor Maccoby and Carol Jacklin in their survey of early childhood literature on sex differences, have noted the remarkable tendency not to publish, to ignore, or even to distort findings of no differences.[40] Jessie Bernard has commented trenchantly on the study of individual differences in psychology, warning us once again of the dangers of looking only at arithmetic averages and ignoring overlaps in the frequency distributions of individual measures.[41] They and many others have analyzed the reasons for the resulting distortions in the literature, which are undeniably biased against women. That is why any difference is better for publication than no difference.

In reviewing the literature, Maccoby and Jacklin complained that the nature of most of the research on sex differences forced them into being "trait' psychologists.[42] Jessie Bernard correctly cautioned psychologists against their usual practice of reporting a difference between averages with language that implied the uniform possession of attributes, for example, by saying that girls are less aggressive than boys when what was found was that more boys than girls performed an aggressive action or that some boys performed more aggressively than most boys, thus creating a higher average for boys than for girls. In fact, the shape of the distribution of individual differences is seldom even described in research on sex differences. It is assumed to be a "normal" curve for each gender.

The entire literature on sex differences reflects certain assumptions of its founding father, Sir Francis Galton, who also is responsible for the research tradition comparing racial and national differences. Of course, Galton found that women are inferior, just as he found the British superior to those of their subject peoples who visited the Exposition. He was interested in proving the superiority of British males to women and to the colored peoples they ruled, founding a Eugenics Society for the purpose of improving and purifying British blood, even if it had to be contaminated by that of women. Later psychologists improved the research model he developed to make the tests more "workable," but it is still the same model with the same assumptions about what a human individual is.

The image of the human individual is that of a bundle of abilities, capacities, skills, and personal traits. The assumption is that the psychologist can develop a test of each of these traits, either through a set of tasks to be performed or a set of questions to be answered. With little concern about the research situation itself, and certainly not assigning it major importance, the researcher selects the tasks or tests, judging what is appropriate to study. The more abilities or traits one can measure, the merrier, of course. In fact, most research concentrates on a few at a time.

The assumed validity of the test rests theoretically upon some criterion measure—for example, the actual performance by a child in school, his/her actual frequency of aggressive actions in a sample day, or actual performance on the job. In fact, such criterion tests of validity are seldom available in research on sex differences. Instead, psychologists have devised a host of subterfuges to escape them. The criterion is established in the same situation in which the test is given, then called "internal validity," while "external validity" outside of the research situation is merely fervently hoped for. Or they talk of "construct validity," in which one test correlates with another test called by the same name.

The score on the test or the level of task performance is taken as indication that the person *is* intelligent, or aggressive, or submissive, or anxious, or *has* this or that motive. By verbal magic, a specific set of actions

in a specific research situation is transformed into the label for something
that the person has, is, or possesses as a trait.

In the early days, it was assumed that any differences so obtained
between males and females were biologically determined. Wasn't sex a
biological variable? The two sexes evolved through biological evolution,
didn't they? What's the problem in finding cause in biology? By the 1930s
many psychologists had been exposed to the findings of cultural anthropology, especially to the early writings of Margaret Mead and Ruth
Benedict. Becoming reluctant to assign all sex differences to biology, when
the two genders differed so noticeably from one culture to another, they
began the more usual practice of assigning some to cultural socialization,
or to both biological and cultural influences in some undetermined mix.
But they had bought into a theoretical and research model that, in itself,
contained no possibility of assessing the cause of anything. On the
contrary, the assumptions and the research procedures were ideal for
promulgating or perpetuating myths.

Even in developmental psychology, the search for causation was not
included in the rationale for testing "traits," so it was added, in the form
of partial information about the child's family or how teachers treat boys
and girls. Great joy is expressed by environmentalists if these agents can
be blamed for sex differences that result. But what one comes out with is
a girl or boy that *has* such-and-such a trait in some degree, to which the
psychologist attributes the cause for the behavior that had initially provided the basis for the trait attribution. It is a beautifully circular argument
with no escape route.

When research efforts have turned to whether the traits allegedly
discovered in research are evident in the behavior of the same individuals
on a variety of tests or across several situational contexts, the results have
included many negative outcomes. Consistency in behaviors defining the
alleged traits is hard to come by. Yet every generation of researchers
manages to turn up one finding that may provide a clue out of the trait
trap, whether concerning gender differences or not. When a person
believes that he or she possesses a personal characteristic and when,
furthermore, that characteristic is personally important to him or her, then
that person is more likely to be consistent in manner of behaving across
different situations.[43] In short, the key to consistent social behavior appears
to lie in whether or not and to what extent the person values consistency
in that respect.

Going a step further, let us recall Woodworth's caution long ago about
the characteristics of trait names. Although usually regarded as qualities
describing the *person*, most are in fact adverbs or evaluations of social
interaction. If a person behaves aggressively, isn't it often toward another
person? Can one be submissive by oneself, or doesn't one need someone

or something else to submit to? Thus, it would seem that what the person *has* is not a trait, but some or many highly charged convictions about what kind of a person he or she is or wants to be, relative to others, in certain activities and circumstances. Such a notion leads to quite a different view of the human individual.

It would seem logical to extend these implications to greater exploration of the individual's self-system, which is linked in all major theoretical statements since the time of William James to the person's establishment of relationships—conceptual and motivational—with other persons, social values, groups, and institutions. Such a direction seems preferable to attempting to build on the old trait theory to develop a set of traits to be emulated by the individual seeking androgyny. Emphasizing personal flexibility, this work has concentrated on demonstrating the superiority of a person who feels she or he exhibits traits traditionally incorporated in both the stereotypical masculine and feminine roles in our society.[44] In view of the extreme susceptibility to bias in the trait theory model for research, I would feel more comfortable with a definition based, not on traits, but on cross-disciplinary study of the human self-system. Similarly, I am troubled by the rush of young researchers attempting to prove that females are not inferior to males in such-and-such an ability or such-and-such a trait, especially when it is by no means clear what difference it makes.

Behavioristic Images of the Individual

The many versions of behavioristic theorizing since John Watson's triumphant proclamations of its advent should have altered the study of sex differences a great deal more than they have. Watson and behaviorists since him proclaimed that psychologists had to concentrate on observing concrete actions relative to specific environmental circumstances, eliminating reliance on the plethora of instincts, drives, traits, and other hypothetical and unobservable concepts that psychologists used to explain the causes of behavior. The strong environmental determinism in behavioristic theories has been appealing to some feminists, but the virtual dominance of behavioristic theories in psychology over several decades has not reduced the frequency of stereotypes and myths about sex differences. One explanation, of course, has been that most behaviorists have been men. Yet, despite its healthy correctives to biological determinism and unbridled speculation about what goes on inside the human mind, behaviorisms as currently formulated have been inadequate to the task of explaining the psychosocial differentiation of the two genders, even in our own society.

It is worthwhile, I believe, to comment on behavioristic theories from this perspective. First of all, each has insisted that it is totally unscientific to include human consciousness or self-awareness in its explanations. The result has been failure to deal with the human experience, whether male or female. Second, though environmental determinists of one kind or another, behaviorists have been weaker than other schools in psychology in specifying the human social environment. Environmental influences have been confined to rewards and/or punishments or, in the extremity of a B. F. Skinner, to any state of affairs that increases the probable frequency of a particular response. Few behaviorists regard it as worthwhile to turn to the social disciplines in order to understand the distinctively human parts of the social environment, wherein other individuals are labeled by society as male or female, child or adult, weak or powerful. To most behaviorists, it is irrelevant or boring to emphasize that individuals develop in more or less organized groups and institutions, including families, circles of peers, churches, schools, and so on, each with social values invested in the criteria for being man or woman; that one's own groups are juxtaposed with others seen and treated as superior or inferior, powerful, less powerful, or powerless; that the very objects and technologies are symbols of differing personhoods and of different genders. This sociocultural environment does not include merely goodies for the good and punishment for the bad, but rules for evaluating how the individual *should* behave, what he or she should strive for and what avoid, what individual variations will be tolerated by individuals in different social classifications and what variations will be punished. Such general rules are the social norms of the culture, invested with values that traditionally differ for men and women.

The neglect of the human social environment by behaviorists has left their theories based on naïve notions about pleasure and pain, reward and punishment. The issues of why one individual tolerates or even wants to be dominated by another, or why a boy learns to become unemotional to the point of being unable to shed a tear, remain mysteries that their most cynical adherents toss off with flippant phrases such as, "Well, some people get their kicks out of the darndest things." The various theories of "social exchange" now current in social psychology are guilty of similar assumptions and similar neglect of the social environment, of which the give-and-take among individuals is an important part. What is exchanged are rewards and punishments, according to some inner calculus that the adherents of the theory understand because they are parts of the same culture.[45] Projections of the calculus and the rewards into the minds of another sex, another group, or another culture produce a bizarre psychology, replete with androcentric, ethnocentric, or nationalistic biases.

Furthermore, the behavioristic emphasis in psychology has produced theories capable only, in the last analysis, of explaining how certain selected aspects of the environment determine certain individual behaviors. They are quite helpless in the face of individuals who actively participate in the process of changing the social environment or of altering their own actions. Finally, they appeal at last resort to such inner forces as "self-reinforcement" or "intrinsic motivation," for which there is no provision in behaviorism. The accumulating research evidence that bribery is not the most effective means to improve learning or skills is admission of the failures of strict behaviorisms.[46]

Psychodynamic Visions of Woman's Place

Of course, the most devastating power plays through psychological theorizing ignore both the social environment and behavior as much as possible by focusing exclusively upon the internal psychological world— on so-called psychodynamics. If one were to design a theory to keep women in inferior position and at lowered worth, none is more suitable than one locating the causes of women's behavior and problems inside the woman. In many ways, the old sex-difference researchers who firmly believed in innate and inevitable female inferiorities were easier to refute than those psychodynamicists who admit some environmental influences into the picture in order to create the motivations and complexes that would hold women in bondage.

Julia Sherman's review of the research literature on psychosexual development was a healthy corrective and commentary on the unbridled influence of the forefather of psychodynamists, Sigmund Freud. Like Maccoby and Jacklin, who found themselves trapped in research inspired by trait theories, Sherman often found herself enmeshed in research (a lot of it not very good research) inspired by Freudian formulations.[47] She found her way out of it with level head, careful assessment of the evidence, and some gentle humor.

In my view, the equitable pursuit of knowledge is totally impossible within a Freudian framework, no matter how nice Freud was to individual women nor how many patients lacking money for his own fees he sent to Anna Freud or other women analysts. According to Gilman, Sigmund Freud continued to emphasize his conclusions that women are morally and ethically deficient as well as masochistic and more prone than men to neuroses as a weapon against feminists five years after U.S. women achieved the vote. "We must not allow ourselves to be deflected from such conclusions," he wrote, "by the denials of the feminists who are anxious to force us to regard the two sexes as completely equal in position and worth."[48]

Nor do I regard it as accidental that the most quoted writer on adolescence in the United States today, Erik Erikson, who loaded his writings with cultural influences and humane concern for women, concluded as follows: ". . . womanhood arrives when attractiveness and experience have succeeded in selecting what is to be admitted to the welcome of the inner space 'for keeps.'" Thereby, he defines maturity, concluding an identity search which "must keep itself open for the peculiarities of the man to be joined and of the children to be brought up" although "already defined by her kind of attractiveness and in the selective nature of her search for the man (or men) by whom she wishes to be sought." Erikson pronounced that "successive stages of life offer growing and maturing individuals ample leeway for free variation in essential sameness."[49] Hasn't there been more leeway for some than for others?

Erikson's position, like Freud's, can be understood only as the tacit assumption that all is inevitable in the world. Women and men must adjust to their destinies, which are both sexual, except that men can have all that and outer space too. If it is still necessary to pay homage to those early pioneers who, like Freud, dared to talk about sex, I suggest that we turn our attention outside of psychology to Margaret Sanger or to Havelock Ellis, who hit it right on the head when he suggested that Freud was spinner of myth. Explanations of a person's experiences and actions in terms so inevitably focused on hidden processes and complexes formed prior to earliest memories, with minimal regard for the differing cultural conditions of development, are bound to be unverifiable and open to the arbitrary interpretations of someone else's "great mind." Psychoanalytic theory has been under attack for years from several sources, but it is my hope that the movement toward equality of men and women will deliver the final blow to any attempt to explain behavior in terms of inner psychodynamics alone.

Critiques and Changes
Within Psychology

In the vast and diversified halls of psychology, there is something for almost everyone. Psychologists themselves, however, are becoming increasingly concerned about the state of their domain, especially as provoked by the considerable changes in society and the movements toward a more equitable society among blacks, students, and other war protesters and, of course, among women. Some even listen to the criticism from abroad, which is growing. The signs of change are evident in the organizing of the Association for Women in Psychology and, later, Division 35 of the American Psychological Association, and in the founding of journals like *Sex Roles* and the *Psychology of Women Quarterly*. The language in psychology journals no longer commits atrocities like that of referring to the research subject as "he" in an experiment in which all of the subjects were women. It even appears that the report of the Task Force on Sex Bias and Sex Stereotypes in Psychotherapy will not be altogether forgotten.[50]

But much business goes on as usual. Changes in thinking and in research practice are slowest of all. Therefore, I must confine my remarks to a few trends that seem to be in the direction of healthy correction. These trends are accompanied by quite a bit of in-fighting and considerable confusion. Some writers refer to the "crisis" (in social psychology), to the "jungle" (in the literature on learning), to the "misery" (of psychotherapy), in psychology.[51] Nevertheless, the signs are hopeful and the trends necessary.

1. The first is toward broadening psychologists' perspectives on the pervasive influences of cultural institutions, of ways of living and working, and of social values upon the individual in any research situation. The androcentrism of psychology until recent years is really but one sign of its narrow perspective. No amount of technical refinement and replication of findings within a restricted sociocultural and institutional setting will broaden the perspective. Comparative research within the same country, cross-cultural research, and an eye to history are the first essentials in enlarging this vision of human beings, male and female.[52] It is hoped that the several volumes on cross-cultural research forthcoming may aid in the broadening process and in delineating the problems.[53]

2. Second, there is great need for psychology to extend its cross-disciplinary borrowing beyond the biological disciplines, to which it has continually turned with pride. It needs to learn from the social disciplines and humanities, which it has treated like poor relatives for many years, about significant and enduring problems in human relationships. Such cross-disciplinary borrowing and perspectives are most natural in social psychology, which has in recent decades gotten itself into difficulties by seeking respectability within the cloistered confines of the laboratory without attending to relevant field research and the actualities of real life. The self-defined crisis in social psychology, discussed by a score of its leading practitioners, is in large part a product of attempting to be really acceptable to psychological orthodoxy while neglecting contributions from the other social disciplines on the scope and importance of the larger social environment. Women in psychology should be and are in the forefront in this relevant cross-disciplinary borrowing, in order to understand their own status and subsidiary roles in many spheres of living, including the politics of housework and childcare.[54]

3. There is another trend that some call a "cognitive revolution" in psychology. It is not a revolution except to those dyed-in-the-wool behaviorists who once really believed that human beings do not think or ponder or worry, but instead only *think* that they do. The trend toward cognitive theories (that is, theories about knowing and how we know) varies in different parts of psychology. For example, among experimentalists who used to be studying "verbal learning" and among many developmental psychologists, it is closely linked to renewed interest in language and language development. Strongly influenced by Piaget, whose work was once brushed over lightly with complaints about broad theory and anecdotal research, the study of child development has come to focus heavily on cognitive development. On the other hand, in social psychology, the interest in cognition is manifest in hundreds of studies on the attribution process, that is, how individuals make decisions about what caused behavior they observe in another or in themselves.

This generally healthy trend entails some dangers, particularly in the tendency to propose cognition as some kind of "pure" mental event that is altogether different from feeling or wanting. Psychologists are prone to separate off the latter as problems of emotion or mood, on one hand, or of motivation, on the other. In truth, the human individual is a small system, whose mind, emotions, and desires cannot be compartmentalized into neat pigeonholes to be worked over one at a time. When a person tries to know or does know something, she or he almost invariably evaluates the process and what is known. The tendency to deal with human cognition in terms of "information processing" or "pure cognition" derives prestige from analogy with computer technology. You can be sure, however, that unless evaluation, feeling, and wanting are allowed into cognitive processing for everyone, it will be women who will be accused of "irrationality." One need look only at what male psychologists have thought that they knew about women in the past to know that cognition is affected by evaluations, feelings, and desires. Yet they did not think themselves irrational. Therefore, the old dichotomy of rational vs. irrational had better be eliminated in favor of a unified perspective that sees some emotion and some motivation in every cognitive process.

4. There is growing acceptance in psychology of the necessity for a perspective on the individual that sees his or her experiences and actions as jointly and intimately affected by internal events (past experiences, thoughts, feelings, and desires) and by a continuing interaction with a social environment, which includes much more than other individuals, as I noted earlier. The spelling out of such a coordinated perspective is difficult. Available formulae (such as Kurt Lewin's that behavior is a function of the person *in* the environment) cannot tell us how to study the personal and environmental influences that jointly affect behavior. I

suspect that the tasks of translating the perspective into research practice are essential to an equitable pursuit of knowledge. Therefore, I will devote the rest of this paper to exploring the problems. They are not separate from the three trends previously noted.[55]

Needed Perspective: Coordinating Psychological and Sociocultural Influences

I will illustrate the needed perspective through research on a set of problems that are intimately related to bias in psychology, namely social stereotypes and their psychological ramifications. Social stereotypes consist of consensual and evaluative judgments on the character, attributes, and personal qualities of individuals classified into one common social category (e.g., by national origin, race, social class, or sex) by members of another social category. The agreement among individuals on such attributions is naïvely viewed as evidence of their truth. Indeed, such agreement may extend beyond the social boundaries of the judges and be shared by many of those judged.

Thus, research findings in the United Sates and in many other countries document men's stereotyped images of women and women's stereotyped images of men as well as considerable agreement between the genders on the characteristics of both. Such documentation has been interpreted in many ways, the naïve realist concluding: "Well, if everyone agrees, the stereotypes must be true of individual men and women—or most of them." The impulse of a psychologist with orthodox training in one of the perspectives already discussed would be to challenge the naïve realist: "Let me study individuals to see whether, indeed, men are more competent or aggressive than women, women more emotional, passive, or nurturant than men." Depending upon the psychologist's training, tasks, tests, or situations will be devised to assess the behaviors of individual women and men in order to test the stereotypes.

As we have seen, the test of "truth" in any specific social situation is hazardous, in that the researcher's bias (pro or con) can enter at any step: in defining the task or test, in setting up the situation, in selecting the particular behaviors that are to be recorded and assessed. Consequently, the eventual outcome of a series of such experiments is likely to be contradictory evidence. The sensible conclusion, in line with that of Maccoby and Jacklin's on young children, is that we do not know very much about gender-related differences in behavior and that many stereotyped attributions are made with little or no support from research findings on how males or females actually behave.

What the psychologist has failed to grasp is that consensual agreement on psychological or social "reality" is also one evidence in history, political science, or anthropology for the existence of social myth. Other indicators of myth include those that turn up in psychological studies to test social stereotypes: they may exist in the face of conflicting, contradictory, or ambiguous evidence. Their challenge is met by emotional refutation, even elaborate defense. Clear exceptions to the myth are celebrated as amazing phenomena, by no means altering the general rule (hence the "exceptional women" who "thinks like a man").

The study of those myths called social stereotypes in history, political science, and sociology clarifies the psychological problems, especially when the study examines the origins of social stereotypes and their changes over time. Invariably, social stereotypes reflect the history of relationships between groups or classes of people. Mutually supportive alliances promote mutually positive images of the other group or class. Competition for mutually exclusive ends, conflict, or domination-subordination promote negative, even derogatory, images.

The focus on the relationship among people, rather than on the characteristics or specific actions of individuals, is a point of departure at a historical and sociological level of analysis for reformulating a variety of issues in the psychological study of the genders. Such reformulations have already been attempted on group stereotypes through a series of three naturalistic experiments in summer camps directed by Muzafer Sherif, in a study of competitive and cooperative relationships between girls' groups by Rozet Avigdor, and in the many studies of adults in workshops by Robert R. Blake and Jane Mouton.[56] These studies all concentrated on the relationships between individuals belonging to informally organized groups whose initial contacts were arranged to preclude preexisting stereotyped views of the other group. When interacting over a period of time (e.g., a week) in repeated circumstances that pitted each group against the other toward highly desirable ends and valued status available to only one group, the group members not only became hostile and aggressive toward one another, but also formed clear-cut, negative, and stereotyped images of individuals in the other group.

The individuals on each side blamed those on the other for their conflicting relationships, attributing the blame to personal qualities shared by the other side. These images, in turn, strongly colored the perceptions and actions of individual participants, leading to derogation of observed performance by the other side that did not differ from their own, to self-justified acts of dominance and aggression, to distorted appraisals of actual events. And, it should be emphasized, these were "normal, healthy" individuals, carefully selected for the research and initially unacquainted (in the Sherif experiments).

The same individuals, however, changed their behaviors and their views of one another when the relationships between groups changed. Rozet Avigdor compared the stereotyped images held by groups of young girls when in conflict and when cooperating for common ends, showing beautifully how the particular characteristics attributed to the other group under these varying circumstances were related to the intergroup relationships. For example, in conflict, the stereotyped attributions pertained to aggressiveness, undesirable motivations, self-seeking, and the like, but not to a number of other unfavorable traits that were included on the list to be used in evaluation. The Sherif research showed that, most reluctantly, the boys in summer camps began to cooperate when faced with a series of events which affected both groups equally and whose undeniably preferred outcomes required the joint efforts of all individuals in both groups (superordinate goals). Then their images of one another changed to favorable attributions. They explained their own ability to interact with the others on the basis of changes in the other individuals.

In brief, these studies showed that major psychological phenomena associated with invidious stereotyping of others occur within specific contexts of human relationships. Stereotypes and their psychological consequences reflect those relationships. No amount of detailed study of the individuals apart from those relationships could serve to test the truth value of the stereotyped images that had formed. To the contrary, short-term tests of the perceptions, judgments, and actions of the individuals apart from the intergroup relationships might have led a psychologist to conclude that individuals on one side or the other, or both, were psychologically aberrant.

The histories of relationships between the genders differ in many ways from intergroup conflict, notably in the absence of well-defined groups of men and women separated by geographic as well as social space. On the contrary, even the most gender-polarized patriarchal societies necessarily admit women into kinship structures, men's sexual activities, and the division of productive work, including child care and food production and preparation. Thus, while gender relationships share the dominant-subordinate structure to be found in many intergroup relationships, they are also sufficiently different to make cliches about "the longest war" or about "sleeping with the enemy" misleading for analytical purposes (as contrasted with their possible utility as slogans). In fact, as Julia Sherman has suggested, the rise and change of social stereotypes among individuals classified by virtue of uniquely different and significant capabilities (comparable to the sexual capabilities of women and men) as well as by division of labor and social status remains to be studied systematically.

Steps Toward the Future

If there is a parallel between intergroup relations and relations between men and women, I believe that it lies in the primacy of the relationships between the genders, which must change if lasting changes are to occur in their respective self-definitions and the mutual views that the two genders maintain in our society. The woman's movement offered glimpses of what might happen by showing that the "raising" of one's own consciousness as a woman required rejection of others' definitions of self coupled with an understanding of the relationships in which women become enmeshed. Annette Brodsky has reported on the therapeutic value of such efforts toward redefining self.[57] As Martha Mednick has pointed out, self-definition has to be accompanied by rejection of the system of relationships that had produced acceptance of a lowered status for women. The consolidation of the renewed self-definition as woman can only occur through actions consonant with the new definition.[58] Julia Sherman has similarly emphasized the therapeutic effects of new activities with the social support of others.[59] Yet, here is where the rub lies. The rest of the world changes more slowly than the new awareness of self, and parts of both resist change or simply stay the same. Social power is not equitably distributed.[60]

The woman's movement has been responsible for wonders in the last ten years in bringing awareness of the issues to women and to men and in pointing to the permeation of sexism throughout our lives. Many women and men have accepted viewpoints, tasks, and changed relationships that they would not have dreamed of a mere decade ago; they might have laughed at the thought. Meanwhile, as in any social movement, counter-movements and reactions have also grown up and strengthened.[61]

One of the first systematic studies of an educational scheme to alter sex-related stereotypes in the public schools has reported mixed results. According to Guttentag and Bray, the educational materials had the greatest impact on kindergarten children, especially girls, followed by fifth graders, chiefly the girls; but their impact on ninth graders was most mixed of all. Some changes were evident for some ninth-grade girls, but this seemed to depend upon having a teacher truly dedicated to using the materials and on the cooperation of peer groups. In some schools the girls were so oriented toward boys that the boys' derogation of the effort soured the girls as well. On the whole, the ninth-grade boys reacted to the educational materials by being more stereotyped and negative than previously, while the girls showed some gains in the desired direction.[62] Apparently, changes by the more advantaged boys would require some changes in what they are doing, in their relationships with girls, and in how they see those relationships in the future.

Rebecca, Hefner, and Oleshansky have commented upon the requirements of work situations and the self-definitions of men and women in a
way particularly appropriate to conclude this discussion. Noting that the
emphasis has been on women and men's changing themselves, they
inquire why it is not also reasonable to emphasize changing the roles in
which men and women live and work, separately or together.[63] Institutional change seldom gets handed down from above as a free gift. Even if
it did, such suggestions imply a process of change over time, wherein
individuals change themselves as they change their practices, and their
practices as they change themselves.

The challenge to psychology as such actualities occur and as future
possibilities appear is the development of methods and practices that can
encompass the events. To meet this challenge, we shall have to be
developing ways of seeking knowledge that are not stereotyped as "hard"
or "soft," but that obtain information on a broader spectrum of the social
world, through several disciplines and with comparative methods and
techniques as well as those now commonly used. I do not propose that
every study be done in naturalistic circumstances or that we all emulate
Jane Goodall's example by spending five years to investigate the social
behaviors of chimpanzees for a dissertation. I do believe that we must
change the notion that anything of great value can be learned about
human beings in the quick study with canned procedures. These characterize the kind of research in psychology that promotion committees have
come to count, rather than to read. What goes on in our laboratories,
clinics, and classrooms must be seen for what it is, cultural phenomena
and events where we can learn about individuals, provided we understand
the times and the larger societies of which they are parts.

Notes

1. Naomi Weisstein, "Psychology Constructs the Female, or The Fantasy Life
of the Male Psychologist," in *Roles Women Play: Readings toward Women's Liberation*,
ed. Michele H. Garskof (Belmont, Calif., 1971), pp. 68–83.

2. Betty Friedan, *The Feminine Mystique* (New York, 1963).

3. Carolyn W. Sherif, "Women's Role in the Human Relations of a Changing
World," in *The Role of the Educated Woman*, ed. C. M. Class (Houston, 1964), pp.
29–41.

4. Georgene Seward, *Sex and the Social Order* (New York, 1946).

5. E. G. Boring, *A History of Experimental Psychology*, 2nd ed. (New York,
1950), p. 509.

6. Ibid., p. 548.

7. Ibid., p. 487.

8. Helen B. Thompson, *The Mental Traits of Sex* (Chicago, 1903), Helen T. Woolley, "Psychological Literature: A Review of the Recent Literature on the Psychology of Sex," *Psychological Bulletin* 7 (1910): 335–42.

9. For an account of Leta S. Hollingworth's career and the views of prominent male psychologists during the early period of her work, see Stephanie A. Shields, "Ms. Pilgrim's Progress: The Contributions of Leta Stetter Hollingworth to the Psychology of Women," *American Psychologist* 30 (1975): 852–57. The title quoted was published in *American Journal of Sociology* 22 (1916): 19–29.

10. Mary Putnam Jacobi, *The Question of Rest for Women during Menstruation* (New York, 1877), pp. 1–2.

11. Stephanie A. Shields, "Functionalism, Darwinism and the Psychology of Women," *American Psychologist* 30 (1975): 739–54.

12. See Lee J. Cronbach, "Five Decades of Public Controversy over Mental Testing," *American Psychologist* 30 (1975): 1–14.

13. *AAP Advance*, August-September 1977, p. 2.

14. Boring, *A History of Experimental Psychology*, p. 583.

15. See Ronald Lippitt and Ralph K. White, "An Experimental Study of Leadership and Group Life," in *Basic Studies in Social Psychology*, ed. Harold Proshansky and Bernard Seidenberg (New York, 1965), pp. 523–37. Lewins' first publication on this research appeared in 1939.

16. Kurt Lewin, "Studies in Group Decision," reprinted in *Group Dynamics: Research and Theory*, ed. Dorwin Cartwright and Alvin Zander, 2nd ed. (New York, 1956).

17. See Carol Tavris and Carole Offir, *The Longest War* (New York, 1977), pp. 151–52.

18. A penetrating critique of ahistoricalism and its psychologizing of the social environment was written by one of Lewins' most ardent admirers, Roger G. Barker, "On the Nature of the Environment," *Journal of Social Issues* 19 (1963): 15–38.

19. Masculinity-femininity as a "variable" or polarized dimension is one example of the mischief created in psychology by "thinking in variables" and accepting the implied dictum about measurement. See Anne Constantinople, "Masculinity-Femininity: An Exception to a Famous Dictum?" *Psychological Bulletin* 80 (1973): 389–407; and Lawrence Kohlberg, "A Cognitive-Developmental Analysis of Children's Sex-Role Concepts and Attitudes," in *The Development of Sex Differences*, ed. Eleanor E. Maccoby (Stanford, 1966), pp. 82–173. Very different views on the proper way to seek knowledge are achieved when the definition of what is "masculine" and "feminine" is sought by analyzing divisions of people and their activities in human social life. See Muzafer Sherif and Carolyn W. Sherif, *Social Psychology* (New York, 1969).

20. D. L. Ronis, M. H. Baumgardner, M. R. Leippe, J. J. Cacioppo, and A. G. Greenwald, "In Search of Reliable Persuasion Effects, I: A Computer-Controlled Procedure for Studying Persuasion," *Journal of Personality and Social Psychology* 35 (1977): 551.

21. Ibid., p. 567.

22. Ibid.

23. For a sociological analysis of conditions promoting such efforts by psychologists, see J. Ben-David and R. Collins, "Social Factors in the Origin of a New Science: The Case of Psychology," *American Sociological Review* 31 (1966): 451–65.

24. Robert Rosenthal, *Experimenter Effects in Behavioral Research* (New York, 1966).

25. See Hadley Cantril, *Gauging Public Opinion* (Princeton, 1944); Howard Schuman and Shirley Hatchett, *Black Racial Attitudes: Trends and Complexities* (Ann Arbor, 1974); Charles F. Cannell and Robert L. Kahn, "Interviewing," in *Handbook of Social Psychology,* ed. Gardner Lindzey and Elliott Aronson (Reading, Mass., 1968), vol. 2.

26. Some of the vast literature on the "social psychology of the research situation" is summarized in Robert Rosenthal and Ralph L. Rosnow, eds., *Artifact in Behavioral Research* (New York, 1969). A more recent and readable introduction is James G. Adair, *The Human Subject: The Social Psychology of the Psychological Experiment* (Boston, 1973). Both tend to ignore the earlier work on "social desirability" effects; see Allen L. Edwards, *The Social Desirability Variable in Personality Assessment and Research* (New York, 1957). Both also tend toward trying to "eliminate" or reduce the effects they have studied, rather than using their understanding toward reconstruction of psychology's methodology. For alternative perspectives with the latter aim, see Sherif and Sherif, *Social Psychology,* esp. chap. 6, and Carolyn W. Sherif, *Orientation in Social Psychology* (New York, 1976).

27. The most complete review of the obedience research is in Stanley Milgram, *Obedience to Authority* (New York, 1974). Cross-cultural comparisons leading to similar conclusions are summarized in M. E. Shanab and Khawla A. Yahya, "A Behavioral Study of Obedience in Children," *Journal of Personality and Social Psychology* 35 (1977): 530–36.

28. Aletha H. Stein and Margaret M. Bailey, "The Socialization of Achievement Orientation in Females," *Psychological Bulletin* 80 (1973): 345–66. See also Martha T. S. Mednick, Sandra J. Tangri, and Lois W. Hoffman, eds., *Women and Achievement: Social and Motivational Analysis* (Washington, D.C., 1975); Virginia O'Leary, "Some Attitudinal Barriers to Occupational Aspirations in Women," *Psychological Bulletin* 81 (1974): 809–26.

29. John Condry and Susan Dyer, "Fear of Success: Attribution of Cause to the Victim," *Journal of Social Issues* 32 (1976): 63–83; David Tresemer, "The Cumulative Record of Research on 'Fear of Success,'" *Sex Roles* 2 (1976): 217–36.

30. See Carolyn W. Sherif, Merrilea Kelly, Lewis Rodgers, Gian Sarup, and Bennet Tittler, "Personal Involvement, Social Judgment, and Action," *Journal of Personality and Social Psychology* 27 (1973): 311–28; Judith C. Morelock, "Sex Differences in Compliance," *Sex Roles; A Journal of Research,* in press; Alice H. Eagley, "Sex Differences in Influenceability," *Psychological Bulletin* 85 (1978): 86–116.

31. This analysis of the persuasion or "suggestibility" research follows that in Muzafer Sherif and Carolyn W. Sherif, *An Outline of Social Psychology* (New York, 1956); and idem, *Social Psychology.*

32. See, for example, Phyllis A. Wallace, ed., *Equal Employment and the AT&T Case* (Cambridge, Mass., 1976). Judith Long Laws's chapters in this book are

excellent examples of the broadened perspective on women's interests and motivations that becomes possible when conditions of work and living are included in the framework of study. Other chapters particularly relevant in the present context reveal sharp divisions among psychologists on the use and interpretation of tests and interviews used in hiring or promotion.

33. Donald T. Campbell, "Reforms as Experiments," *American Psychologist* 24 (1969): 409–29.

34. Jessie Bernard, *Women, Wives, Mothers: Values and Options* (Chicago, 1975).

35. Durganand Sinha, "Social Psychologists' Stance in a Developing Country," *Indian Journal of Psychology* 50 (June 1975): 98–99.

36. In reviewing Marshall Sahlin's *Use and Abuse of Biology* (Ann Arbor, 1976), M. H. Fried of Columbia's anthropology department finds it amusing that geneticists should accept the kinship genealogies used in different cultures as genetic genealogies. Sahlins had remarked that the lack of correspondence is "merely Anthropology I. Is it too much to ask that our colleagues in contingent biological fields raise their sights to a somewhat more sophisticated level?" M. A. Fried, "The Use and Abuse of Biology," *The American Scientist* 65 (1977): 352–53. Meanwhile, some of what is taught in Anthropology I is being questioned by Mary K. Martin and Barbara Voorhies, *Female of the Species* (New York, 1975), and by others, though not the lack of correspondence between social and genetic genealogies noted above.

37. Francois Jacob, professor of cell genetics at Institut Pasteur in Paris, provided an interesting view of evolutionary possibilities, including both continuities and discontinuities in species evolution. François Jacob, "Evolution and Tinkering," *Science* 196 (1977): 1161–66. Among psychologists, T. C. Schneirla and his students have consistently pursued comparative studies within an evolutionary framework encompassing both species-specific and continuity assumptions. See T. C. Schneirla, "Levels in the Biopsychology of Social Organization," *Journal of Abnormal and Social Psychology* 41 (1946); and Lester R. Aronson, Ethel Tobach, D. S. Lehrman, and J. S. Rosenblatt, eds., *Development and Evolution of Behavior: Essays in Memory of T. C. Schneirla* (San Francisco, 1970).

38. Schneirla made trenchant criticisms of attributions to "biology" or nature based on no more than surface similarities.

39. See Roger Brown, "Development of the First Language in the Human Species," *American Psychologist* 28 (1973): 107–28; Kingsley Davis, "A Final Note on a Case of Extreme Isolation," *American Journal of Sociology* 52 (1947): 432–37; Eric H. Lenneberg, *Biological Foundations of Language* (New York, 1967).

40. Julia A. Sherman, *On the Psychology of Women: A Survey of Empirical Studies* (Springfield, Ill., 1971); Eleanor E. Maccoby and Carol N. Jacklin, *The Psychology of Sex Differences* (Stanford, 1974).

41. Jessie Bernard, "Sex Differences: An Overview," in *Beyond Sex-Role Stereotypes: Readings toward a Psychology of Androgyny*, ed. Alexandra G. Kaplan and Joan P. Bean (Boston, 1976), pp. 9–26.

42. Maccoby and Jacklin have been praised for what they did not do (for example, they did not abolish differences between the sexes or conclude that there were none) and blamed for what they did not try to do (for example, examine the

research literature on adult women). They were attempting to evaluate the congruence of research findings on alleged differences in early childhood. What they found was, in the words of one reviewer, "a sprawling, unruly body of data." Jeanne H. Block, "Debatable Conclusions about Sex Differences," *Contemporary Psychology* 21 (1976): 517–22. Since most of those data were also obtained within the research model for personality traits, it seems less than judicious to suggest that the authors should have organized the data differently. In fact, the contrast between the pontifical conclusions in many texts about early childhood differences and the mess Maccoby and Jacklin exposed is genuinely amusing. Thus, while some reviewers bemoan the Maccoby-Jacklin effort, I take it as one more indication that a trait approach to personality will invariably produce a mess.

43. Gordon W. Allport, "The Ego in Contemporary Psychology," *Psychological Review*, 50 (1943): 451–78; Muzafer Sherif and Hadley Cantril, *The Psychology of Ego-Involvements* (New York, 1947); Sherif et al., "Personal Involvement, Social Judgment, and Action;" Daryl J. Bem and Andrea Allen, "On Predicting Some of the People Some of the Time: The Search for Cross-Situational Consistencies in Behavior," *Psychological Review* 81 (1974): 506–20; Hazel Markus, "Self-Schemata and Processing Information about the Self," *Journal of Personality and Social Psychology* 35, no. 2 (1977): 63–78.

44. Sandra L. Bem, "The Measurement of Psychological Androgyny," *Journal of Consulting and Clinical Psychology* 42 (1974): 155–62.

45. See Michael Billig's *Social Psychology and Intergroup Relations* (London, 1976), chap. 6, for a trenchant critique from a European perspective of the assumptions of "interpersonal games" in U.S. social science.

46. John Condry, "Enemies of Exploration: Self-Initiated Versus Other-Initiated Learning," *Journal of Personality and Social Psychology* 35 (1977): 459–77.

47. Julia A. Sherman, *On the Psychology of Women*.

48. Richard Gilman, "The FemLib Case against Sigmund Freud," *The New York Times Magazine*, 31 January 1971, pp. 42–47.

49. Erik H. Erikson, *Identity: Youth and Crisis* (New York, 1968), pp. 282–83.

50. American Psychological Association, "Report of the Task Force on Sex Bias and Sex-Role Stereotyping in Psychotherapeutic Practice," *American Psychologist* 30 (1975): 1169–75. A fuller mimeographed report is also available from the APA. The report is providing the basis for a National Conference on Psychotherapy Research sponsored by the association.

51. The *Personality and Social Psychology Bulletin*, official publication of APA's Division 8, has carried a dozen or more articles on the "crisis" in the last year. See M. Brewster Smith, "Social Psychology, Science, and History: So What?" *Personality and Social Psychology Bulletin* 2 (1976): 438–44; Muzafer Sherif, "Crisis in Social Psychology: Some Remarks towards Breaking through the Crisis" ibid. 3 (1977): 368–82. See also H. Rachlin, "A Guide through the Jungle of Animal Learning," *Contemporary Psychology* 22 (1977): 165–66; A. M. Des Lauriers, "The Greatness and the Misery of Clinical Psychology," ibid., pp. 169–70; J. F. Rychlak, "Personality Theory: Its Nature, Past, Present and—Future?" *Personality and Social Psychology Bulletin* 2 (1976): 209–25.

52. Sherif and Sherif, *Social Psychology*, chap. 1.

53. Harry C. Triandis, University of Illinois, is editor. See also idem, "Social Psychology and Cultural Analysis," *Journal for the Theory of Social Behaviour* 5 (1975): 81–106.

54. See Florence L. Denmark, "The Psychology of Women: An Overview of an Emerging Field," *Personality and Social Psychology Bulletin* 3 (1977): 356–67.

55. In fact, a coordinated interactionist perspective guided this entire chapter, which reflects my recent book, *Orientation in Social Psychology*. References to the specific researches cited in the next sections are in that book.

56. See Carolyn W. Sherif, *Orientation in Social Psychology*, Chapter 5 for summaries of this research. For complete accounts, see Muzafer Sherif, O. J. Harvey, B. Jack White, W. Robert Hood and Carolyn W. Sherif, *Intergroup Conflict and Cooperation: The Robbers Cave Experiment*. Norman, Okla.: University Book Exchange, 1961; Rozet Avigdor, Étude expérimentale de la genèse des stéréotypes. *Cahiers Internationaux de Sociologie*, 14 (1953): 154–68; Robert R. Blake, Herbert Shepard, and Jane S. Mouton, *Managing Intergroup Conflict in Industry*. Houston: Gulf Publishing Co., 1964.

57. Annette Brodksy, "The Consciousness-Raising Group as a Model for Therapy with Women," *Psychotherapy: Theory, Research, and Practice* 10 (1973): 24–29.

58. Martha Mednick, "Social Change and Sex Role Inertia: The Case of the Kibbutz," in Mednick, Tangri, and Hoffman, *Women and Achievement*, pp. 85–103.

59. Julia A. Sherman, "Social Values, Femininity, and the Development of Female Competence," *Journal of Social Issues* 32 (1976): 181–95.

60. Rhoda Unger, a psychologist trained in physiological psychology, is among those whose study of male-female interactions has led her to the concept of social power or status as the key to such a study. Phyllis Chesler, a clinical psychologist, came to similar conclusions. For an intriguing survey of the research literature on male-female interactions and an application to training, see Marlaine E. Lockhead and Katherine P. Hall, "Conceptualizing Sex as a Status Characteristic: Applications to Leadership Training Strategies," *Journal of Social Issues* 32 (1976): 111–24.

61. For a social-psychological perspective on this process, see my *Orientation in Social Psychology*.

62. Marcia Guttentag and Helen Bray, *Undoing Sex Stereotyping: Research and Resources for Educators* (New York, 1976).

63. Meda Rebecca, Robert Hefner, and Barbara Oleshansky, "A Model of Sex-Role Transcendence," *Journal of Social Issues* 32 (1976): 197–206.

5

THROUGH THE LOOKING GLASS: NO WONDERLAND YET!
(The Reciprocal Relationship Between
Methodology amd Models of Reality)

Rhoda Kesler Unger

It is difficult to find a title for an essay in an area that can encompass the whole of psychology. Hence, I take refuge in *Alice in Wonderland*, since one can find an allusion to almost anything in its pages. Nevertheless, my title does relate to the content of this article. I am going to embark with you on a very adventurous journey—a voyage into the nature of the psychological reality with which we deal.

The purpose of this exploration is to examine the extent to which "methodological" issues are actually conceptual ones. Many of the issues to be discussed here have been raised about mainstream psychology, but are relevant to the psychology of women as well (see the growing discussion of methods in our literature, e.g., Brannon, 1981; Grady, 1981; Parlee, 1981; Unger, 1981; Wallston, 1981).

I propose to examine some issues that are usually considered philosophical or metaphysical and therefore irrelevant to us in psychology. I shall discuss how conceptual frameworks of which we may not be aware affect our methodology; how models of reality influence psychological research; how particular value structures have affected specific studies; how some aspects of the feminist value structure influence our own work; some of the factors determining whether or not paradigmatic change will occur; and why women may be uniquely suited to be agents of paradig-

Rhoda Kesler Unger, "Through the Looking Glass: No Wonderland Yet! (The Reciprocal Relationship Between Methodology and Models of Reality)." *Psychology of Women Quarterly*, 8, 9–32. Copyright 1983 by Cambridge University Press. Reprinted by permission.

matic change. Finally, I will offer some suggestions for a more responsive psychology.

It is necessary first to consider some fundamental questions, such as

1. What is the nature of the human being we study?
2. How do the constraints of methodology influence what we see as the nature of that human being?
3. How do our ideology, our values, and/or our place in society influence our methods and the way we interpret them?
4. Contrariwise, how do our methods create our concepts?

These questions are basically epistemological, that is, they involve the nature of the truths we seek. It is not a mere semantic quibble whether we discover truths or create them or whether facts are absolute or relative. Arguments about methods frequently involve conflicts between different epistemological systems. We are *all* concerned about the valid means by which truth can be acquired. And, by now, we all understand how the nature of the search affects the very findings. It will clarify matters considerably if we deal with these issues as conceptual rather than methodological. For example, much of the argument about the relative value of quantitative versus qualitative methodology actually involves the issue of whether or not measurement can or should be divorced from evaluation.

Although such questions may be ultimately unresolvable, an analysis of them will be helpful for the understanding of research trends in the psychology of women and may be helpful in the formulation of future work in the field.

The Positivist Empiricist Model and Its Critique

The positivist empiricist model has been an important model for psychology and, despite occasional allusions to post-positivist science, it still guides much of the work in the field. In brief, this model restricts analysis to a few clearly observable units of behavior in order to avoid imposing one's own beliefs upon the organisms studied. The subject matter and method of investigation are conceived as independent of each other. In practice, although not in principle, behavior is removed to a laboratory in order to prevent extraneous variables (defined as anything other than the experimenter's manipulations) from influencing the behavior. This practice turns people into subjects by removing them from their situational and historical context.

Early waves of feminist psychologists concentrated upon the omissions produced by this approach. They focused attention on the neglect of women as subjects of research (Carlson & Carlson, 1961); on the effect of the sex of the experimenter or other evaluator of the person's performance (Harris, 1971; Pedersen, Shinedling & Johnson, 1968); on the tendency to make more generalizations to humans as a whole from all-male than from all-female data (Holmes & Jorgenson, 1971); and on the effect of sex biases in determining what kind of behavior gets studied with what sex (Frodi, Macaulay & Thome, 1977; McKenna & Kessler, 1977).

Such omissions, however, may be and are being remedied by feminists using traditional experimental methodology. It is the transformation of people into object-like subjects that is the essence of the theoretical critique of most empirical psychological work on humans. The ideological framework of positivist empiricism defines the relationship between researcher and subject as an impersonal one. The logic of these methods (and even their language) prescribes prediction and control. It is difficult for one who is trained in such a conceptual framework to step beyond it and ask what kind of person such a methodology presupposes.

It may be argued that the ideal subject of the psychological experiment is a narrowly calculating human being who adapts, conforms, and engages in self-interested behavior, rather than in action that has social as well as personal meaning (Elshtain, 1979). But to produce such a creature, a set of arbitrary and strongly simplifying assumptions have had to be set up; the behaviors examined have largely been restricted to those that are amenable to simple observation and/or categorization (and, therefore, devoid of much meaning to the subject); alternative behaviors have been eliminated (this is known as control); and, most importantly, those actions involving ideology and values have been defined out by fiat as operationally meaningless. Here I am reminded of one of Alice's encounters with Humpty Dumpty in *Through the Looking Glass:*

> "When *I* use a word," Humpty Dumpty said, in a rather scornful tone, "it means just what I choose it to mean—neither more or less."
>
> "The question is," said Alice, "whether you *can* make words mean so many different things."
>
> "The question is," said Humpty Dumpty, "which is to be master—that's all."

Control by definition is a key to understanding many of the issues in this area.

Given the context of observation, it is not surprising that the subject permits himself or herself to be manipulated by the experimenter's independent variables. The results of these studies may reflect not only people's desire to be helpful to the experimenter, but also the degree to which people experience themselves as overwhelmed by external conditions beyond their control.

We should not be surprised that the human element has a way of slipping through. It is characteristic of the unreflective nature of much research that the social nature of human experimentation has been seen more as a procedural problem than as an indication of a general conceptual crisis (Gadlin & Ingle, 1975). Like increased blood clotting due to the "pill," the social relationship between experimenter and subject is seen as an "unwanted side effect." Like the blood clotting properties of estrogenic substances, however, such effects are intrinsic. They are side effects only to the extent that they are not the ones desired.

It is not easy to document how many side effects due to the social relationship between subjects and researchers have been ignored. By definition, they are not an aspect for analysis. However, a study I came across recently provides an instructive example. In 1964, Berkowitz, Klanderman, and Harris published a study of subjects' productivity in a simulated work situation. When the subject and experimenter were of different sexes, the subjects worked harder for their unseen partner the sooner the experimenter saw their work, but when the subject and experimenter were of the same sex they did not do so. The investigators suggested that subjects worked harder for an opposite-sex experimenter's approval since the work would be learned about right away. This effect, however, "interfered" with the *real* purpose of the experiment, which was to determine whether effort expended in behalf of the partner varied depending on the length of time before which their effort would become known. Therefore, the sex-related effect was never followed up. Some time later, in fact, Berkowitz (1972) remarked: "In order to minimize S's desire to gain E's approval, all later experiments employed investigators of the same sex as the subject" (p. 72).

Many sex-of-subject/sex-of-stimulus-person effects are hidden away as factors that produce dilemmas for the experimenter (Unger, 1981). Such phenomena are characterized by terms such as experimenter bias, demand characteristics, or evaluation apprehension. What these phenomena actually demonstrate is that the experimental method cannot expunge human relationships. They demonstrate that the experimental method presupposes its own appropriateness and cannot adequately handle questions of its own efficacy (Gadlin & Ingle, 1975).

Sex-related effects are particularly problematic for experimental methodology for a number of conceptual reasons.

1. In traditional methodology sex is a nonmanipulable given or an independent variable. To assume that sex, or rather gender, is

      created by the measuring procedure involves assuming a different paradigm (Unger, 1979b).

2. Experimentation, with its ahistorical, asituational context, is not appropriate when the problem involves the person's sense of place in the world (Lana, 1976). As we are aware, it is virtually impossible to eliminate consideration of the role of status from any examination of the relationship between females and males (Unger, 1976, 1978).

3. When women become involved in the research process, either as subjects or researchers, it becomes impossible to continue the fiction that knowledge is a matter of objective observation. The actual and particular position of women in the world cannot be suspended (D. E. Smith, 1979).

Models of Reality
and Psychological Research

As larger numbers of women (and minority and poor people) have become involved in social science research and as more matters of concern to them have become the objects of research, it has become harder for social scientists to sustain the illusion that knowledge is abstract and value-free. We have become more and more aware that objectifying practices conceal a particular vision of people and their world. Women scholars are particularly likely to reach this conclusion because we have been largely excluded from the processes through which knowledge is obtained.

It might seem surprising that this exclusion of more than half of humanity has gone unnoticed. The reason becomes clear, however, when we recognize the implications of a view of knowledge as the discovery of universals. As Sampson (1978) has noted, such a view argues that a particular group has no more valid claim to knowledge of their world than does someone not in that group. This view of scholarship thus helps support the existing balance of power and the interests of the dominant minority.

The positivist empiricist model is, of course, not the only epistemological model available to psychologists. Psychology appears to have alternated its focus from time to time between an objectified view of the person and a concentration upon the person's subjective reality (Lana, 1976). Buss's (1978b) recent analysis of the deep structure of this kind of paradigm shift has been most useful to my thinking in the area. He suggests that two prototype statements can be used for characterizing the underlying structure of psychological paradigms: *either reality constructs the person or the person constructs reality.* Psychological revolutions represent a shift from one to the other paradigm. Thus, the most recent shift from behaviorism to cognitive psychology represents a shift from a conceptualization that stresses how various factors in an individual's past or present situation determine her or his actions (assuming an objective past or present) to a conceptualization that stresses how the individual's motivations and belief structures influence what aspects of the psychological world are attended to, remembered and utilized.

These two basic paradigms reflect different conceptions of reality. Both behaviorism and many theories about personality minimize the importance of rationality and human consciousness (Buss, 1978b). They see the individual as a consequence of certain aspects of an unchanging reality. Causality runs largely in one direction—responses to past and present stimuli direct present and future actions. There is little room in this kind of metaphysical reality for the awareness that people can change their circumstances and, therefore, potentially, themselves.

Current cognitive theory assumes that the objective conditions in a person's world fuse with his or her subjective view of these conditions (Berger & Luckmann, 1966). Although researchers in the area may disagree about the extent, they assume that some aspects of reality are socially constructed and that so-called objective reality is based upon various levels of agreement among individuals as they interact with each other. In this view, knowledge is clearly a matter of social definition.

Recent research in social cognition (*cf* Hamilton, 1979) has demonstrated that cognitive biases are very pervasive. It has recently been shown that people use much less information than is available to them (Major, 1980); that they form illusory correlations based upon statistically rare information and groups (Hamilton & Gifford, 1976); that they selectively seek information that confirms their naive hypotheses rather than disconfirming them (Hansen, 1980); and that they reconstruct memories based on stereotypic beliefs about members of groups other than their own (Snyder & Uranowitz, 1978). Any individuals who are distinctive within a group are most likely to receive extreme judgments (Taylor, Fiske, Close, Anderson & Ruderman, cited in Taylor & Fiske, 1978). And so-called normal behavior may be attended to and labeled as deviant when it is engaged in by a person who has received a socially deviant label (Langer & Imber, 1980). Erroneous relationships may be inferred and the beliefs maintained even when the initial evidential base is totally discredited (Anderson, Lepper & Ross, 1980). All of this work is noteworthy because it demonstrates the mechanisms by which sexist and racist biases may be perpetuated even after repeated scholarly demonstrations that no major differences between groups exist.

Since most people are uncritical or naive realists they are not aware of the extent to which they create the reality with which they deal. Psychologists who uncritically accept a positivistic empiricist model (reality constructs the person) may, in fact, deny that the world is dependent upon the observer's viewpoint. They see knowledge as discovered, not made. This unwillingness to accept a relativistic view of knowledge does not, of course, prevent such a view from having an impact upon their own operations on the world.

It is important to stress that it is not techniques of experimentation or quantification that I am criticizing here. They are potential tools that are devoid of much significance in themselves. What I am criticizing is our unawareness of the epistemological commitments we make when we use such tools unthinkingly. As Ruth Hubbard has written:

> We learn to examine the ways in which our experimental methods can bias our answers, but we are not taught to be equally wary of the biases introduced by our implicit, unstated, and often unconscious beliefs about the nature of reality. (1978, p. 10)

It is important to reiterate that our beliefs about reality also prescribe what we ignore or omit as well as with what we concern ourselves.

Philosophical concerns are relevant to contemporary psychology because questions about what is true are answered implicitly by the psychologist in the way she or he frames questions or phrases statements about observations (Eacker, 1972). As the information so gathered is strained through successive reworkings, psychologists come to agree that they are discovering phenomena and laws of the universe in the behavioral laboratory. For example, when a researcher writes that "the acquisition of sex-typed behavior is facilitated by reinforcement" this passive linguistic structure conceals the statement "someone is choosing to reinforce and thereby differentially change behavior in males and females." The linguistic convention omits such major questions as, reinforcement by whom? For what purpose? In whose interest? When we acknowledge the omitted questions, we realize that the phenomena and laws of behavior are of interest *only* in terms of their situational context and that this situational context is far larger than the laboratory in which they were observed.

Evidence for the Impact of Values on Research

It is more difficult to find empirical studies of the effect of conceptual bias on psychology than it is to find critiques of these biases. Nevertheless, some intriguing information does exist.

There is evidence that American psychologists still hold a predominantly objectivist viewpoint, found by Coan (1979) in an analysis of the responses of 866 members of APA on a 63-item theoretical orientation scale. Objectivism as measured by this scale comprised a number of semi-independent components including: a belief in impersonal causality; behavioral content emphasis; a preference for dealing with relatively elementary or specific variables and relationships; and a view that psychologists should seek laws and principles expressible in physical terms. A remarkably similar pattern of responses has been found among undergraduate psychology majors as well. Since King (1980) found no change in theoretical orientation scores in students before or after courses in psychology, or from freshmen to seniors, he has suggested that students come to the discipline with a consistent and rather firmly fixed system of values. These values appear to be founded upon a broader base than mere exposure to disciplinary concerns. Faculty in psychology differed from their students only in being more strong believers in strict causality.

Coan (1979) has reported some connections between the theoretical orientation of psychologists and their life circumstances and personal characteristics. For example, subjectivists are more likely to show evidence of a European background, whereas objectivism seems to be more compatible with Anglo-American culture. Subjectivists are more likely to value religion and are a little more likely to be Jewish. Coan notes that while it is possible subjectivists are more likely to have experienced a lack of accord with American society, objectivists more often report difficulties with a parent, usually the parent of their same sex. He suggests that the concern of the objectivist for achieving and maintaining control in his/her intellectual work may have its roots in childhood. He also notes that objectivists are a little more likely to have experienced sensory and motor handicaps as children that may have predisposed some of them to view human problems in physical terms.

There is one undeservedly obscure study that demonstrates that a relationship exists between the background characteristics of psychologists and the conclusions they draw from their research. Sherwood and Nataupsky (1968) found that the conclusions investigators reached about whether blacks were innately inferior to whites in intelligence could be predicted from biographical data about the investigators. Those who concluded intelligence differences were due to innate factors were more likely to be firstborn, to have had a lower number of foreign born grandparents, to have had parents with more years of education, to have spent their childhood in a rural community, and to have had higher scholastic standing as undergraduates than those who did not draw that conclusion. Taken together, these biographical data suggest that those researchers who concluded that blacks were innately inferior came from nonurban, higher socioeconomic backgrounds. It is also consistent with Coan's findings to argue that such researchers had had more acceptance in American society than their more environmentalist colleagues.

It seems likely that personal experience sensitizes people to different aspects of problems, and leads some to question the assumptions taken as self-evident by others lacking such experience. Recent studies suggest that the sex of investigators contributes to what effects they look for and, indeed, find. Thus, Signorella, Vegega, and Mitchell (1981) note that female researchers in developmental and social psychology are more likely to perform routine analyses for sex differences than are male researchers in comparable fields. And Eagly and Carli (1981) note that the sex of the researchers is a determinant of research findings in the area of influence-ability. They found that 79% of the authors of influenceability studies were male, and that men obtained larger sex differences in the direction of greater persuasibility and conformity among women. In studies authored by women there was no sex difference. The source of this sex-related bias may be the selection of research questions, the interaction between experimenter and subject, or differential biases about what research gets published and by whom it is authored.

Franz Samelson (1978) has examined historically the relationship between researchers' positions in the world and their research conclusions. He notes that although in 1920 most psychologists believed in the existence of mental differences between races, by 1940 they were looking for the sources of "irrational prejudices" toward members of other racial groups. He accounts for this change of focus in part by the movement into the psychological profession of increasing numbers of members of ethnic minority groups. (Early American psychology had been primarily Anglo-Saxon in composition.) Samelson points out, for example, that the first psychologist who tested "white and Negro" children and who did not simply conclude blacks were intellectually inferior was both an immigrant and a female.

This shift from the study of a behavior of various groups to the way various groups are perceived is an excellent exemplar of the type of paradigm shift discussed earlier. The focus shifted from assumptions about existing reality to the way that reality might be constructed. The analogy of the shift from the study of sex differences to the study of sexism is obvious!

Attitudes about nature and nurture are not independent of other sociopolitical attitudes. In a content analysis of the writings of 24 American and English scientists prominent in the nature-nurture controversy in the period 1900–1940, Pastore (1949) found that 11 of the 12 in each group classified as either hereditarian or environmentalist could correspondingly be classified as conservative or liberal-radical in their other attitudes. The scientists did not appear to be aware of the deep relationship between their political loyalties and their scientific thinking. In fact, Pastore noted parenthetically that the hereditarians he studied were least willing to accept the evidence of such a connection. Thus, as early as 1949, Pastore characterized the nature-nurture controversy as as much a sociological as a scientific one based upon evidence of these ideological connections.

What we look for determines what we find, and psychology trains us to look within the person for sources of problems. Caplan and Nelson (1973) examined six issues of the 1970 *Psychological Abstracts* for research dealing with black Americans as the most visible and frequently studied group perceived to be in a problematic relationship to the rest of society. They found that only 16% of the studies looked at causal situational variables and none examined both personal and situational factors simultaneously. Again, criticism is not aimed at the methodology of the studies, but at the relative absence of alternatives to the individualistic approach. Person-blame explanations of social issues, whether valid or not, hold the potential for reinforcing stereotypes and thereby perpetuating the condition of the target group.

Psychologists may be more willing to offer person-blame explanations than is the general public. For example, when the public (rather than psychologists) was surveyed, Kahn (1972) found that the causes of violence were more likely to be seen as social problems than as instances of individual pathology. Nine out of ten of Kahn's respondents agreed that discrimination caused violence and about 75% agreed that poverty, lack of good jobs, and poor education were among its causes. Like the professionals, however, the same respondents used individual approaches when asked for practical cures or preventive measures. The emphasis was on controlling the violent individual rather than altering his or her social circumstances (Lubek, 1979).

What is done about a problem depends on how it is seen. Another excellent example of these definitional issues involves a further encounter of Alice with Humpty Dumpty.

"What a beautiful belt you've got on!" Alice suddenly remarked. . . . "At least," she corrected herself on second thoughts, "a beautiful cravat, I should have said—no a belt, I mean—I beg your pardon!" she added in dismay, for Humpty Dumpty looked thoroughly offended, and she began to wish she hadn't chosen that subject. "If only I knew," she thought to herself, "which was neck and which was waist!"

How we determine which is neck and which is waist may be a matter of viewpoint.

Doctrinal differences within disciplines do not simply remain within those disciplines. There is evidence that the public may receive a biased picture of what social scientists believe and that communication to the public and to fellow professionals may differ in content as well as style. For example, Satariano (1979) compared views on immigration presented by social scientists in popular magazines versus articles on the same subject in professional journals during the period from 1920–1930. This was a period when immigration restriction was being intensively debated. He found that whereas there was a definite preference for the environmentalist perspective in the professional literature, the racial heredity interpretation predominated in the popular articles. Thus, readers looking to social science for an "informed opinion" about immigration were not given an accurate picture of scholarly thought on the subject. It is not clear, however, whether social science popularizers are chosen for their point of view by the communications media or whether they are more likely to volunteer themselves than scholars who may be less emotionally invested in the issues.

The popular literature about women and sex differences has been subject to this kind of bias. It is easy, for example, to document the fact that much attention is paid in the public media—in the august pages of the *New York Times* (albeit on its style page) or on the cover of *Newsweek*—to biological (particularly neural) "differences" between the sexes. It is particularly pernicious that such investigations are seen as more scientific than when environmental variables are explored.When Benbow and Stanley (1980) published their controversial article about purported innate sex differences in mathematical ability between female and male adolescents it was accorded popularized treatment in *Science* in addition to its scholarly manifestation. Subsequent objections (Schafer & Gray, 1981) received less attention from the journal and far less from the popular press, which had picked up the original study without paying attention to cautionary statements by the authors themselves that numerous interpretations were consistent with the data.

Potential Conceptual Biases in Feminist Scholarship

Biological determinism seems to be particularly notable for its unwillingness to scrutinize alternative mechanisms for the effects obtained. Its intrasigence may be explicable in terms of the role of ideology in the structuring of knowledge. Since the position appears to spring from a world view that assumes that certain aspects of physical reality construct the person, there may be difficulty encompassing a multicausal perspective, let alone one that postulates that causality operates "backwards" from the person to reality as well. Although lip service is frequently given to the concept of interaction, person-centered and situation-centered variables are rarely both examined in the same research study or even by the same researcher.

Again, I wish to stress that I am not arguing against the use of biological data. Biological variables, however, appear to possess some conceptual properties of which researchers may be unaware. For example, they are more likely to be perceived as irreversible than are social variables. Moreover, factors that operate early in the lifetime of the individual are also seen more as irreversible than are those that operate at a later developmental stage. I have reviewed a number of biological assumptions in my book *Female and Male* (Unger, 1979a) and so will stress only a few here. Important other assumptions include: the belief that female psychology is more dependent on biology than male psychology is; the belief that conditions that have a strong biological basis in women have no analog in men; and, possibly most importantly, the belief that behavioral characteristics associated with biological events occur by way of direct central nervous system regulation. Researchers are not required to specify what these hormonal or neural mechanisms are. Social perceptions and cognitions relating to such events are presumed to have little effect on behavior associated with them.

There is little empirical evidence to support these assumptions. They should be tested wherever possible. While it is important to continue to emphasize that sex differences operate in a context of interactions, it is equally important to recognize that many different kinds of interactionist hypotheses are possible that may have quite different emphases in terms of biology or culture. I am indebted to Nora Newcombe (1980) for her clear analysis of various forms of interaction. She notes that in the analysis of spatial ability it is equally interactionist to postulate:

> a. that a biologically given sex difference in spatial ability is potentiated and widened by cultural circumstances; b. that a biologically given sex difference in activity level leads to sex differences in experience, which produces sex differences in spatial ability; c. that biologically given differences in genitals elicit different responses from caretakers, and that these treatment differences lead to sex differences in spatial ability. (Newcombe, 1980, p. 807).

Each of these hypotheses generates a distinct set of empirical predictions and social implications. They are not, of course, mutually exclusive. Acceptance of a biological explanation for sex-related differences should not automatically result in the conclusion that differences are immutable or independent of social context.

It is also clear that sex differences, like race differences, are often a matter of interpretation and focus. Has the research looked at the behavior of the stimulus persons or at the reports of individuals perceiving these stimulus persons? The problem is further compounded because sometimes the persons reporting the behavior are themselves the stimulus persons. Far more self-reports of sex differences exist than do reports of such differences when actual behavior is observed by others (O'Leary, 1977; Sherif, 1979). We need to make clear the distinction between self-reports based on social expectation and those based on personal experience. Interestingly, our psychological vocabularies lack the clarity to make the necessary distinctions.

Studies on sex differences probably also suffer from prejudice against the null hypothesis (Greenwald, 1975). It is impossible to tell how many studies of sex similarities might have been found if theoretical or conceptual frameworks had justified their publication. Relabeling the area "sex comparisons" is only one step in making any finding in this area salient.

We cannot assume that all conceptual confusions and distortions are the responsibility of "other" psychologists. Female psychologists, in general, appear to share psychology's belief in objectivism to a degree only slightly less than that of their male counterparts (Coan, 1979). I have been attempting recently to delineate the belief structures of feminist psychologists and have found, contrary to my initial hypothesis, that my sample of activist people in the field is similar to my colleagues and students at a state college in their belief in the importance of nonconscious forces in the control of behavior (Unger, Note 1). In other words, even actively feminist researchers share the assumptions of the subdisciplines in which they were socialized, regardless of whether these perspectives were experimental, clinical, or social-cognitive.

Researchers in the psychology of women have often searched within the person to explain why women are different from men. Such explanations share a deep paradigmatic relationship to biological explanations. Society is seen as relatively unproblematic whereas individual behavior is seen as problematic (Israel, 1979). In both psychology of women and biology, the relatively permanent properties of people are seen to determine their behavior. Examples of concepts that derive from inside the person are fear of success and androgyny. Those who use these concepts are careful to emphasize that they arise from differential socialization of females and males and/or are supported within the individual by continual situational constraints. Nevertheless, they are commonly used as typologies by which to organize and predict other attitudinal characteristics (Wallston, 1981).

Androgyny has been viewed by some feminist theorists as a prescription for social health because of its potential for greater sex role flexibility.

I have no basis with which to quarrel with this formulation. Nevertheless, the search for sources for social change within the person has many pitfalls, as we already know from reviewing the literature on race psychology. (See Caplan and Nelson, 1973, for an excellent critique of person-centered theories in terms of their latent ideological content.)

One can also argue that lack of androgyny has not yet been defined as a source of personal problems. However, aspects of traditional femininity have been so defined, placing women in yet another version of the double bind. The creation of the social myth known as the "Cinderella syndrome" is already in progress. The energy we spend on criticizing these myths cannot be used for creating our own.

Person-centered interpretations appear to derive from biases deeply imbedded in belief structures. These biases distort reality, although the distortion is neither conscious nor intentional. Again, person-centered research is not necessarily poor research. But feminist scholars must transcend the values, norms, and prejudices of their disciplinary structures rather than accept customary conceptual structures and simply test whether traditional constructs about women are not or are not true.

Paradigm Change and the Sociology of Knowledge

The number of instances in which critiques of traditional psychology have appeared in mainstream psychological journals is striking (e.g., Buss, 1975; Caplan & Nelson, 1973; Gadlin & Ingle, 1975; Koch, 1981; Levine, 1974; Sampson, 1978; Sarason, 1973). The critiques to which I refer do not simply involve the so-called crisis in social psychology or awareness of the ahistorical and acultural bias of traditional psychology. In one way or another, these critics have also maintained that methodological problems are often conceptual ones. They have offered example after example of what Koch (1981) has so aptly termed "epistemopathology."

Despite these critiques, there are forces that make change within any area of psychology difficult to induce. These forces have been discussed extensively within the area known as the sociology of knowledge; I will briefly describe some that are particularly relevant to scholarship by and about women.

It is well to remember that it is through the approval of members of our disciplinary community, not that of the target population affected by our work, that careers are made. Mary Payer (1977), a philosopher of science, has made the distinction between knowledge and scholarship that is an important one here. She notes that questions about knowledge include: "What is real?" "What is objective?" and "How do I know this to be the case?" Scholarship provides another set of questions: "What bodies of data are held to be significant?" "What are the criteria for their acceptance?" "Who sets these standards?" "In accordance with whose needs and interests?" And, lastly, "What constitutes valid criticism?"

In scholarship experiences are not only created but are legitimized by institutionalized vocabularies and practices. Mature institutions are seen as possessing a high degree of objectivity (Payer, 1977). They are seen as existing over and beyond individuals who happen to embody them at the moment. When institutions are experienced as having a reality of their own, we lose sight of the crucial elements of history and social context. We fail to take into account our own responsibility for our creations. As Payer states: "Consequently, it *makes* the world, both theoretically and practically speaking—when we say *not* this is one view or theory of reality *we* have developed, *but* this is the way that reality is" (1977, p. 32). The reification of institutions such as scholarship enables them to make claims for universality and objectivity that individuals would be unwilling to make for themselves.

It is also important to keep in mind that not all members of a community of scholars have an equal opportunity to define what is legitimate knowledge. Humpty Dumpty's assertions have more power than Alice's. Becker (1967) speaks of a "hierarchy of credibility." In any system of ranked groups, participants take it as a given that members of the highest group have the right to define the way things really are. Matters of rank and status have an almost moral quality. We are, if we are proper members of the group, bound to accept the definition imposed on reality by the superordinate group in preference to those definitions formulated by subordinates.

Women have less legitimacy than men even when they occupy supposedly equivalent positions (Unger, 1982). Women may sometimes do some of the naming. Nonetheless, the power to name the namers rests with men (Stimpson, 1979). It has been argued that the method of independent observations insures an objective reality. As we have seen, however, scientists do not think and work independently. Scholars have been predominantly university-trained white males from privileged social backgrounds. It is likely that their views about the nature of reality have been biased by their limited experiences and that their scholarly product tells us as much about the investigator as about the subject studied (Hubbard, 1978).

Women as Agents
of Scholarly Change

If scientific knowledge is held to be the superior or only way of knowing, it serves to devalue or invalidate much of people's daily experience. Since even those females involved in scholarship have had a different subjective reality from their male counterparts, it is not surprising that they focus on different aspects of experience and/or evaluate it differently. For example, Lisa Furby (1979) notes that by virtue of social class and sex in the United States, most psychological researchers have had more objective (actual) experiences of internal control than the average person. Thus, they have more subjective (perceived) experiences of internal locus of control and may have difficulty making a distinction between people's sense of personal control and their expectations about the degree of control permitted to them by society. This level of expectation or aspiration could be defined as a "knowledge" variable. Because, however, psychologists may not recognize the role of differential personal experience in determining what we know, they may have difficulty distinguishing knowledge from motivation.

Women's position as both the subjects and objects of their own research uniquely fits them to be agents of change. Dorothy Smith (1979) makes the analogy to servants of the upper class in England who knew much about both their own lives and those of their masters, whereas the upper class had access only to their own lives. If, however, women make claims of special access to knowledge by virtue of our position in society, we must do so with the realization that paradigmatic shifts take a long time to accomplish. We must also remain aware that because of our inferior status in academia we are in a poor position from which to argue legitimacy issues. It is very easy to dismiss feminist arguments as "special pleading" or as examples of the poor worker who blames his or her tools. We cannot expect that arguments will be evaluated independently of who makes them.

These problems, of course, are not arguments that we should stop thinking. It is unlikely, however, that a paradigm will be discarded without another one to put in its place. Kuhn (1962) has documented many instances in which scholars have continued to ignore countervailing "facts" and have buttressed increasingly outmoded theories because there was no acceptable alternative model. Buss (1974–1975), working from Mannheim's theory about generations and social change, has argued that paradigm shifts are most likely to come about when a new generation without years of commitment to the existent ideology comes to power. In some ways, women scholars are in a position of being the younger generation whatever their ages. They may have less commitment to prevailing ideology both because they are in a good position to recognize its flaws and because they have not received many rewards for having been committed to it.

Toward a Reflexive Psychology

It is important that I do not conclude this article by simply reiterating the need to question *all* conceptual frameworks. I would rather present some ideas for breaking away from the fixations we have inherited from the psychology in which we were trained and socialized.

I am not arguing for a simple cognitive paradigm although, as I noted earlier, studies designed in terms of that paradigm appear to be very valuable to feminist psychology. Some of the flaws of a purely cognitive approach include its apparent inability to deal with the evaluative aspects of the self (Sherif, 1982) and confusion between the causes and reasons for behavior (Buss, 1978a; Eacker, 1972). These flaws reveal that the cognitive framework also has unexamined epistemological problems. For example, the question "why" appears to have different meanings for the observer and the actor. Simple informational hypotheses do not explain this problem.

Probably the most trenchant criticisms of the cognitive framework have been offered by Sampson (1981). He points out that by concentrating on subjective reality we may neglect the actual barriers various groups encounter. Perceptual and cognitive restructuring may also serve as a substitute for action. The uncritical acceptance of the social choices available at a given time fails to confront the issue of how such choices became available in the first place. Lastly, we may fail to consider the possible nonrationality or ineffectuality of any of the set of alternative behaviors available to some groups in terms of what a given social system has made available to them for their apparently rational selection.

I would like to join with others in arguing for a social science that admits values—not only as sources of bias, but also as means for evaluating all parts of the research process. We must accept as an assumption that to describe and to evaluate, to state what is and what ought to be, are not two entirely separable activities (Elshtain, 1979). Description is always from someone's point of view and hence is always evaluative. Description is always for a purpose. Because purposes may be unintentional or imbedded in a series of tacit unexamined prior commitments, scholars have never felt the need to defend them. Instead, critics of established views have always felt compelled to justify their "deviant" theoretical positions.

What form might a moral—i.e., value-imbued—social science take? I have borrowed some ideas from a variety of sources that may prove fruitful.

1. No particular methodology of psychology needs to be singled out for criticism. The major problem lies in unthinking acceptance of any methodology without analyzing its underlying metaphysical framework. We should be particularly concerned about any methodology that makes unwarranted claims to be the sole source of truth.

2. I have devoted more time to a paradigm that stresses that the person creates reality, not because I feel this is the only way to proceed, but because it is relatively unexplored as a resource for feminist psychology. It is especially valuable to our field because of the particularist nature of the realities it espouses. Just as it was important to criticize universal theories about humans based on studies of men, it is equally important to be aware that we are not ready to build universal theories about women. Some forms of knowledge may simply not be universal (Parlee, Note 2). In fact, the idea that some psychological relationships exist only in a relatively limited context or under limited circumstances may be an important contribution of the psychology of women to the field of psychology as a whole.

3. We need to begin to consider a paradigm in which hypotheses about subject-object relationships will not be transformed whenever we reach an impasse in what we can learn by exclusive focus on the "objective" or "subjective" world. Recently, several theories have discussed what they have termed the dialectical or reflexive nature of such a paradigm (Buss, 1978b; Elshtain, 1979; Gadlin & Ingle, 1975; Riegel, 1979). Its nature is too complex to be discussed at length here. One important element, however, is its emphasis on the reciprocal, interactive relationship between the person and reality. It emphasizes that although circumstances change people, people can also alter their circumstances.

4. A reflexive or dialectical view of understanding behavior probably also requires a different way of doing research. We must recognize that subjects' actions in a study are not different in kind from their actions in the so-called real world. Hence, experimenter and subject bias must be recognized as inevitable accompaniments of research and not as transient procedural contaminants. We can learn a great deal about the informal mechanisms controlling behavior in terms of sex and gender by examining such "biases" (Unger, 1981).

5. If we recognize that our subjects possess the ability to size up a situation and think about it, we may wish to enter into different research arrangements with them. For example, one could construct a study in which the subject is exposed to self-knowledge based on the experimenter's research findings (Buss, 1978a). This

process might assist people in escaping from previously uncon- scious causal forces. Kenneth Dion (1975) has made use of a similar technique incorporating false feedback about a confederate's eval- uation and his social biases, but I know of no studies that have provided subjects with accurate information about themselves.

It might also be possible for researcher and subject to attempt to determine the subjective meaning of the subject's behavior throughout the research process. Some efforts have been made to this end by asking respondents successive questions designed to get at different aspects of their reality (Looft, 1971). This technique is analogous to practices in clinical psychology, but is said to invalidate the research process.

6. Reflexivity assumes that the study of human behavior necessarily includes the behavior of the psychologist (Gadlin & Ingle, 1975). Any picture of reality must involve knowledge about the subject, about the researcher, and about knowledge itself. No one researcher can concern herself or himself with all aspects, but no claims about data should be made without taking into consideration all facets of the acquisition of knowledge.

7. We must build other criteria besides seeking the facts into our studies. One such criterion is the degree to which studies are helpful to the target population. This point does not mean we must do away with "pure" and only design "applied" studies. But, at the very least, we should attempt to make our subjects more self- aware than they were before they involved themselves in our procedures. It may be particularly valuable to teach as many people as possible that alternative explanations can be drawn from any set of findings. Recent social cognitive researchers (Anderson, Lepper & Ross, 1980) have suggested that the generation of alternative explanations may be the most effective means of getting people to alter preexisting cognitive biases. They suggest that it might even be possible to "innoculate" against the perseveration of erroneous beliefs by having people imagine all possible positive and negative connections that can be generated from information before being exposed to that information.

8. We must continue to be wary about proof. M. Brewster Smith (1980) has argued that many of the "classic" contributions to psychology have been valuable as exemplifications and demonstra- tions of important processes and relationships more than as starting points for cumulative parametric exploration. What accumulates from them is sensitization to and enlightenment about aspects of the contemporary human condition that we had not previously seen so clearly.

Sigmund Koch (1981) has recently noted that the quest for certainty is a major reason why psychology has failed to progress. This failure may spring both from the unwillingness to deal with complex conceptual issues and from the anxiousness of American psychologists to escape from their philosophical roots. It is an exemplification of the reflexive nature of the acquisition of knowledge that much of the material that I have drawn upon for this article was generated either by Canadian psychologists, by American males with a European background, or by females. We cannot share in the general unwillingness to acknowledge the existence of these epistemological issues or to regard philosophy as synonymous with pseudoscience if we wish to build a better scholarship. The questions will not go away. Koch (1981) has offered a quote from Bertrand Russell that appears to be most apt:

> Science tells us what we can know, but what we can know is little, and if we forget how much we cannot know we become insensitive to many things of very great importance. . . . Uncertainty in the presence of vivid hopes and fears is painful, but must be endured if we wish to live without the support of comforting fairy tales. It is not good either to forget the questions that philosophy asks, or to persuade ourselves that we have found indubitable answers to them. To teach how to live without certainty, and yet without being paralyzed by hesitation, is perhaps the chief thing that philosophy, in our age, can still do for those who study it (Russell, 1943, pp. XIII–XIV).

Or to conclude with a comforting fairytale—remember Alice's discussion near the red king as to who is the dreamer and who is the dreamed. We are the dreamers—Wonderland may yet be ours!

Notes

This article is based on the presidential address to Division 35 of APA given at the 89th Annual Convention, Los Angeles, California, August 26, 1981.

The author thanks Alice H. Eagly, Carolyn W. Sherif, and Barbara S. Wallston for their critical reading of the article

Reference Notes

1. Unger, R.K. A preliminary analysis of the Attitudes towards Reality Scale. Unpublished data, 1981.
2. Parlee, M. B. Personal communication. March, 1981.

References

Anderson, C. A., Lepper, M. R., & Ross, L. Perseverance of social theories: The role of explanation in the persistence of discredited information. *Journal of Personality and Social Psychology*, 1980, *39*, 1037–1049.

Becker, H. S. Whose side are we on? *Social Problems*, 1967, *14*, 239–247.

Benbow, C. P., & Stanley, J. C. Sex differences in mathematical ability: Fact or artifact? *Science*, 1980, *210*, 1262–1264.

Berger, P. L., & Luckmann, T. *The social construction of reality*. Garden City, New York: Anchor, 1966.

Berkowitz, L. Social norms, feelings, and other factors affecting helping and altruism. In L. Berkowitz (Ed.), *Advances in experimental social psychology* (Vol. 6). New York: Academic Press, 1972.

Berkowitz, L., Klanderman, S. B., & Harris, R. Effects of experimenter awareness and sex of subject and experimenter on reactions to dependency relationships. *Sociometry*, 1964, *27*, 327–337.

Brannon, R. Current methodological issues in paper-and-pencil measuring instruments. *Psychology of Women Quarterly*, 1981, *5*, 618–627.

Buss, A. R. Counter-culture and counter-psychology. *Interpersonal Development*, 1974–1975, *5*, 223–233.

Buss, A. R. The emerging field of the sociology of psychological knowledge. *American Psychologist*, 1975, *30*, 988–1002.

Buss, A. R. A conceptual critique of attribution theory. *Journal of Personality and Social Psychology*, 1978, *36*, 1311–1321. (a)

Buss, A. R. The structure of psychological revolutions. *Journal of the History of the Behavioral Sciences*, 1978, *14*, 57–64. (b)

Carlson, E. R., & Carlson, R. Male and female subjects in personality research. *Journal of Abnormal and Social Psychology*, 1961, *61*, 482–483.

Caplan, N., & Nelson, S. D. On being useful: The nature and consequences of psychological research on social problems. *American Psychologist*, 1973, *28*, 199–211.

Carroll, L., *Alice's adventures in Wonderland and through the looking glass*. New York: Signet, 1960.

Coan, R. W. *Psychologists: Personal and theoretical pathways*. New York: Irvington, 1979.

Dion, K. L. Women's reactions to discrimination from members of the same or opposite sex. *Journal of Research in Personality*, 1975, *9*, 294–306.

Eacker, J. N. On some elementary philosophical problems of psychology. *American Psychologist*, 1972, *27*, 553–565.

Eagly, A. H., & Carli, L. L. Sex of researchers and sex-typed communications as determinants of sex differences in influenceability: A meta-analysis of social influence studies. *Psychological Bulletin*, 1981, *90*, 1–20.

Elshtain, J. B. Methodological sophistication and conceptual confusion: A critique of mainstream political science. In J. Sherman & E. T. Beck (Eds.). *The prism of sex: Essays in the sociology of knowledge*. Madison, Wisconsin: University of Wisconsin Press, 1979.

Frodi, A., Macaulay, J., & Thome, P. R. Are women always less aggressive than men? *Psychological Bulletin*, 1977, *84*, 634–660.

Furby, L. Individualistic bias in studies of locus of control. In A. R. Buss (Ed.), *Psychology in social context*. New York: Irvington, 1979.

Gadlin, H., & Ingle, G. Through the one-way mirror: The limits of experimental self-reflection. *American Psychologist*, 1975, *30*, 1003–1009.

Grady, K. E. Sex bias in research design. *Psychology of Women Quarterly*, 1981, *5*, 628–636.

Greenwald, A. G. Consequences of prejudice against the null hypothesis. *Psychological Bulletin*, 1975, *82*, 1–20.

Hamilton, D. L. A cognitive attributional analysis of stereotyping. In L. Berkowitz (Ed.), *Advances in experimental social psychology* (Vol. 12). New York: Academic Press, 1979.

Hamilton, D. L., & Gifford, R. Illusory correlations in interpersonal perception: A cognitive basis of stereotypic judgments. *Journal of Experimental Social Psychology*, 1976, *12*, 392–404.

Hansen, R. D. Commonsense attribution. *Journal of Personality and Social Psychology*, 1980, *39*, 996–1009.

Harris, S. Influence of subject and experimenter sex in psychological research. *Journal of Consulting and Clinical Psychology*, 1971, *37*, 291–294.

Holmes, D. S., & Jorgenson, B. W. Do personality and social psychologists study men more than women? *Representative Research in Social Psychology*, 1971, *2*, 71–76.

Hubbard, R. Have only men evolved? In R. Hubbard, M. S. Henifin, & B. Fried (Eds.), *Women look at biology looking at women*. Cambridge: Schenkman, 1978.

Israel, J. From level of aspiration to dissonance. In A. R. Buss (Ed.), *Psychology in social context*. New York: Irvington, 1979.

Kahn, R. L. The justification of violence: Social problems and social resolutions. *Journal of Social Issues*, 1972, *28*, 155–175.

King, D. J. Values of undergraduate students and faculty members on theoretical orientations in psychology. *Teaching of Psychology*, 1980, *7*, 236–237.

Koch, S. The nature and limits of psychological knowledge: Lessons of a century qua "science." *American Psychologist*, 1981, *36*, 257–269.

Kuhn, T. S. *The structure of scientific revolutions*. Chicago: University of Chicago Press, 1962.

Lana, R. E. *The foundations of psychological theory*. Hillsdale, New Jersey: Lawrence Erlbaum Associates, 1976.

Langer, E. J., & Imber, L. Role of mindlessness in the perception of deviance. *Journal of Personality and Social Psychology*, 1980, *39*, 360–367.

Levine, M. Scientific method and the adversary model. *American Psychologist*, 1974, *29*, 661–677.

Looft, W. R. Sex differences in the expression of vocational aspirations by elementary school children. *Developmental Psychology*, 1971, *5*, 366.

Lubek, I. A brief social psychological analysis on aggression in social psychology. In A. R. Buss (Ed.), *Psychology in social context*. New York: Irvington, 1979.

Major, B. Information acquisition and attribution processes. *Journal of Personality and Social Psychology*, 1980, *39*, 1010–1023.

McKenna, W., & Kessler, S. J. Experimental design as a source of sex bias in social psychology. *Sex Roles*, 1977, *3*, 117–128.

Newcombe, N. Beyond nature and nurture. *Contemporary Psychology*, 1980, *25*, 807–808.

O'Leary, V. E. *Toward understanding women.* Monterey, California: Brooks/Cole, 1977.

Pastore, N. *The nature-nurture controversy.* New York: King's Crown Press, 1949.

Parlee, M. B. Appropriate control groups in feminist research. *Psychology of Women Quarterly*, 1981, *5*, 637–644.

Payer, M. E. Is traditional scholarship value free? Towards a critical theory. *Papers from the Scholar and the Feminist IV: Connecting theory, practice, and values.* New York: The Women's Center, Barnard College, 1977.

Pedersen, D. M., Shinedling, M. M., & Johnson, D. L. Effects of sex of examiner and subject on children's quantitative test performance. *Journal of Personality and Social Psychology*, 1968, *10*, 251–254.

Riegel, K. F. *Dialectical psychology.* New York: Academic Press, 1979.

Russell, B. *A history of western philosophy.* New York: Simon & Schuster, 1943.

Samelson, F. From "race psychology" to "studies in prejudice": Some observations on the thematic reversals in social psychology. *Journal of the History of the Behavioral Sciences*, 1978, *14*, 265–278.

Sampson, E. E. Scientific paradigms and social values: Wanted—a scientific revolution. *Journal of Personality and Social Psychology*, 1978, *36*, 1332–1343.

Sampson, E. E. Cognitive psychology as ideology. *American Psychologist*, 1981, *36*, 730–743.

Sarason, S. B. Jewishness, Blackishness, and the nature-nurture controversy. *American Psychologist*, 1973, *28*, 962–971.

Satariano, W. A. Immigration and the popularization of social science 1920 to 1930. *Journal of the History of the Behavioral Sciences*, 1979, *15*, 310–320.

Schafer, A. T., & Gray, M. W. Sex and mathematics. *Science*, 1981, *211*, editorial page.

Sherif, C. W. Bias in psychology. In J. Sherman & E. T. Beck (Eds.), *The prism of sex: Essays in the sociology of knowledge.* Madison, Wisconsin: University of Wisconsin Press, 1979.

Sherif, C. W. Needed concepts in the study of gender identity. *Psychology of Women Quarterly*, 1982, *6*, 375–398.

Sherwood, J. J., & Nataupsky, M. Predicting the conclusions of Negro-White intelligence research from biographical characteristics of the investigator. *Journal of Personality and Social Psychology*, 1968, *8*, 53–58.

Signorella, M. L., Vegega, M. E., & Mitchell, M. E. Subject selection and analysis for sex-related differences: 1968–1970 and 1975–1977. *American Psychologist*, 1981, *36*, 988–990.

Smith, D. E. A sociology for women. In J. Sherman & E. T. Beck (Eds.), *The prism of sex: Essays in the sociology of knowledge.* Madison, Wisconsin: University of Wisconsin Press, 1979.

Smith, M. B. Attitudes, values, and selfhood. In H. E. Howe Jr. & M. M. Page (Eds.), *Nebraska symposium on motivation 1979.* Lincoln, Nebraska: University of Nebraska Press, 1980.

Snyder, M., & Uranowitz, S. W. Reconstructing the past: Some cognitive consequences of person perception. *Journal of Personality and Social Psychology*, 1978, *36*, 941–950.

Stimpson, C. R. The power to name: Some reflections on the avant-garde. In J. Sherman & E. T. Beck (Eds.), *The prism of sex: Essays in the sociology of knowledge*. Madison, Wisconsin: University of Wisconsin Press, 1979.

Taylor, S. E., & Fiske, S. T. Salience, attention and attribution: Top of the head phenomena. In L. Berkowitz (Ed.), *Advances in experimental social psychology* (Vol. 11). New York: Academic Press, 1978.

Unger, R. K. Male is greater than female: The socialization of status inequality. *The Counseling Psychologist*, 1976, *6*, 2–9.

Unger, R. K. The politics of gender: A review of relevant literature. In J. Sherman & F. Denmark (Eds.), *Psychology of women: Future directions of research*. New York: Psychological Dimensions Inc., 1978.

Unger, R. K. *Female and male: Psychological perspectives*. New York: Harper & Row, 1979. (a)

Unger, R. K. Toward a redefinition of sex and gender. *American Psychologist*, 1979, *34*, 1085–1094. (b)

Unger, R. K. Sex as a social reality: Field and laboratory research. *Psychology of Women Quarterly*, 1981, *5*, 645–653.

Unger, R. K. Advocacy versus scholarship revisited: Issues in the psychology of women. *Psychology of Women Quarterly*, 1982, *7*, 5–17.

Wallston, B. S. What are the questions in psychology of women? A feminist approach to research. *Psychology of Women Quarterly*, 1981, *5*, 597–617.

6
THE DEVALUATION
OF WOMEN'S COMPETENCE

Bernice Lott

Women's experiences support the expectation that, across a wide range of areas, a woman and a man of comparable ability are not evaluated or rewarded equally. Men especially will tend to judge a woman less favorably than a similarly or identically credentialed or performing man. Such biased judgments are a predictable consequence, or an indicator, of sexism.

Using the language and perspective of social psychology, three independently measurable but theoretically related components of sexism may be distinguished:

1. Negative attitudes toward women—i.e., generalized hostility, dislike, misogyny, or in more familiar terms, prejudice.
2. Beliefs about women that reinforce, complement, or justify the prejudice and involve a basic assumption of their inferiority. In more familiar terms these are the stereotypes: well learned, widely shared, socially validated, almost irresistible beliefs about the nature of women.
3. Acts of exclusion directed toward women; these constitute discrimination. Such acts can be conceptualized as avoidance behaviors that achieve separation and distancing from women; they may range on a continuum from the humorous "put-down," on one end, to ultimate exclusion through physical aggression on the other. I suggest that these are highly probable responses to women, especially by men, in all situations except those in which there is

Bernice Lott, "The Devaluation of Women's Competence." *Journal of Social Issues*, 41, 43–60. Copyright 1985 by the Society for the Psychological Study of Social Issues. Reprinted with permission.

an expectation of nurturance, sexual pleasure, or some particular situation-related reward.

Why should we expect that women of high talent and competence will be immune from the sexist responses of women in general? If what is salient to the responder is the woman's gender, then the predicted response in neutral situations will be prejudice, stereotyped belief statements, and/or overt or subtle discrimination, depending upon the response mode(s) required by, or applicable to, the conditions. In any given situation, however, other stimuli may be equally or more salient, e.g., the woman's unique personal qualities or the anticipated consequences for the behaver. These may evoke other competing responses that complicate the prediction of behavior.

One of my objectives in this paper is to identify some of the conditions under which competent women are more likely to be negatively evaluated. Another objective is to bridge the distance between the reality of women's experiences and the data obtained through empirical investigations.

Experiences of Women

I begin with a chance example from the media—four advertisements that appeared in the very same issue of one of our most prestigious professional journals, *Science* (March 13, 1981). I make no claim that these are representative advertisements: they were not sampled; they simply jumped out at me, and they illustrate the problem under discussion. The first is an advertisement for a technical typewriter that, predictably, shows a young woman behind the machine. The second ad is for graduated cylinders; this time we see a man in a white lab coat pouring liquid from one cylinder to another. In the third advertisement, for the periodical *Nature*, which we are told is sent to "the world's most important science addresses," we see a woman and a man at their door on their way out for the evening; *Nature* is in the man's hands, for a quick glance, while the woman waits smiling. Finally, there is an ad for a "simultaneous observation" microscope in which see both women and men working together. There are four young women in lab coats, making observations. In the center is the man, grey-haired, and in a suit jacket; he is obviously in charge.

Another set of illustrations from the media represents what I see as a recent and particularly insidious thrust—the undermining and demeaning of women who compete successfully in previously male domains. In one advertisement (*New York Times Magazine*, Sept. 12, 1982) a female physician is shown at the bedside of a patient "making the rounds" with fully exposed "silky satin" bra and bikini; she is standing next to two male physicians who are, of course, fully and appropriately dressed. A similar full-page advertisement (*New York Times Magazine*, Feb. 21, 1982) presents a lawyer pleading a case, interrogating a witness, with glasses in one hand and legal papers in the other—dressed in her underwear.

Examples of the devaluation of women abound in the professional lives of some highly productive and creative academic women. Ruth Benedict, a brilliant and influential anthropologist, began teaching at Columbia University in 1923 as a lecturer on a series of one-year contracts. In 1931 she became an assistant professor, without tenure, and not until 1948 was she promoted to full professor (Zorn, 1974). Maria Goeppert-Mayer, winner of a Nobel Prize in Physics in 1963, was not offered a full-time faculty appointment at an American university until a year before the award, when it was rumored that she would be in the running. Then she was offered appointments by the University of Chicago (where she had labored for many years without a tenured academic position) and the University of California at San Diego; the latter offer she accepted (Dash, 1973).

Some scientists believe that Rosalind Franklin should have shared in the 1962 Nobel Prize awarded to James Watson, Maurice Wilkins, and Francis Crick for establishing the molecular structure of DNA. In an extraordinary book, Anne Sayre (1975) has documented Franklin's contributions, which were well known to Watson and the others. Sayre discusses Watson's distorted characterization of Franklin in his book *The Double Helix*, in which he referred to her throughout as "Rosy," a name that Sayre maintains

> was never used by any friend of Rosalind's, and certainly by no one to her face. But beyond this, [are] a series of minor inaccuracies of fact, each aligned in a consistent direction . . . [so that] the figure which emerged was . . . the perfect unadulterated stereotype of the unattractive, dowdy, rigid, aggressive, overbearing, steely, "unfeminine" blue-stocking, the female grotesque we have been taught either to fear or to despise. (p. 19)

A recent president of the American Association for the Advancement of Science (AAAS), the eminent astronomer E. Margaret Burbidge, had worked with her husband Geoff (also an astronomer) in England with William Fowler. Fowler suggested that on his return to the United States in 1955 the

> Burbidges accompany him to Pasadena, Margaret to Mount Wilson Observatory . . . and Geoff . . . [to] the California Institute of Technology. A letter to the director of the Mount Wilson Observatory elicited the response that the

single toilet at Mount Wilson precluded awarding [a] . . . fellowship to a
woman. With their usual adaptability [the Burbidges switched jobs]. . . . Not
until 1965 did a woman legally observe at the Hale Observatories and not
until 1979 was a woman named a Mount Wilson Carnegie Fellow. (Rubin,
1981)

In 1974, astronomers Martin Ryle and Anthony Hewish received the
Nobel Prize for Physics for their contributions to the understanding of
pulsars. Credit for the discovery of pulsars, however, has been attributed
to Jocelyn Bell (Burnell) who was a graduate student in Hewish's laboratory
(Wade, 1975). Similarly, in 1978 the Lasker Award for Basic Medical
Research, considered to be the "forerunner of the Nobel Prize," was
awarded to three men for their discoveries of opiate receptors in the brain.
As noted in *Science* ("Lasker Award," 1979), "missing from the award
citation was the name of Candace Pert," a woman who had collaborated
with one of the winners "on much of the research for which he was cited."
While such stories in *Science* have critically noted the exclusion of women
from the reward system, its own editorials have reflected the same
phenomenon. In a letter to the editors, Rochelle Albin (1979) charged that
the AAAS had failed "to assign weekly *Science* editorials to women"; she
presented as supporting evidence "the disturbing observation that, in the
last 25 issues of 1978, a sample likely to be representative of most issues,
not a single woman authored a *Science* editorial" (p. 228). And recently
Vivian Gornick (1983), after chronicling the lives of a number of women
in science, wrote: "Hundreds of women who possessed the driving spirit
. . . occupied peripheral, often humiliating, positions for twenty and thirty
years in order to do science" (p. 52).

A more positive story, finally, is that of Dr. Barbara McClintock, an
81-year-old geneticist. After more than 30 years of research, she was the
recipient in 1981 of the Albert Lasker Award, and in 1983 of the Nobel
Prize. Would recognition have come sooner if she had been a man?

One further example sharpens the evaluation dilemma faced by
women professionals. This case involved a woman faculty member recently
denied tenure at an eastern university despite support from her department (in which she was one of two women). She grieved the decision to
a hearing officer who ruled against her and upheld the administration on
the following grounds:

This hearing officer has carefully reviewed the evaluation forms of another
professor at the University [a man in the same department] . . . who was
granted tenure in spite of having received evaluations which are roughly
comparable to those received by Professor [X]. . . . It is clear that both records
were judged to be marginal in nature and that the decision in both cases could

have gone either way. Under these circumstances, I do not believe that a hearing officer is justified in overturning the decision of the academic experts who made the final decision. . . . (personal communication)

If the records of the two faculty members, one a man and the other a woman, were "roughly comparable," on what basis did the academic experts approve tenure for the former and deny it to the latter?

Research

Can we get help in understanding such a judgment from the findings reported in our professional journals?

College Student Samples

Most of the relevant experimental reports are of studies with college-student participants who are asked to evaluate bogus stimulus persons and/or their products under a number of different instructions, which are presumably persuasive enough for the students to take their task seriously. The primary manipulation in the typical paradigm is to vary the gender identification of the stimulus person, with background, credentials, experience, or product (e.g., essay, painting, work sample, etc.) identical. With the publication in 1968 of Goldberg's now-famous study, "Are Women Prejudiced Against Women?," a chain of research along these lines was launched.

Goldberg (1968), using only women participants, found that the same article was judged to be more valuable, and the author more competent, if authored by a man than by a woman. Since then, college students of both genders have been shown to: select women for a managerial position less than men (Cann, Siegfried, & Pearce, 1981; Rosen & Jerdee, 1974) and reject women even more sharply if the position is highly demanding (Rosen & Jerdee, 1974); rate men instructors (not their own) in a generally more favorable way than women (Denmark, 1979); evaluate men instructors as more intelligent and motivating than equally presented women teachers (Bernard, Keefauver, Elsworth, & Naylor, 1981); rate men instructors as more powerful and effective (Kaschak, 1981) and prefer to take a course from a man (Lombardo & Tocci, 1979); rate a female applicant for an insurance agent's job as less suitable for the job than a similarly high-scoring man (Heneman, 1977); hire a man over a woman judged equally suitable for a department store job and try harder to persuade a man than a woman to stay with the firm (Gutek & Stevens, 1979); be more willing to recommend hiring a man than a woman for a sales management traineeship and at a higher salary (Dipboye, Arvey, & Terpstra, 1977); and give more favorable evaluations to male than to female applicants for a newswriting job on such attributes as professional competence, predicted job success, value of a work sample, dedication to journalism, and writing style (Etaugh & Kasley, 1981). In some of the above studies bias against women was greater on the part of men than of women respondents.

Gender of evaluator and certain other conditions have sometimes been found to mediate the effect of stimulus-person gender. For example, two studies found that it was only among low-status writers of an identical article that a male author was evaluated more highly than a female author (Isaacs, 1981; Peck, 1978). Male students, but not female students, have been reported to give higher ratings to male than to identically described female teachers on effectiveness, concern, likability, and excellence, regardless of subject taught (Kaschak, 1977), and to describe women faculty as logical less often than men faculty (Brown, cf. Roark, 1980). In two other investigations the type of behavior performed was found to affect its evaluation. In one study (Taynor & Deaux, 1975), doing something thought of as "man's work" was rated more socially desirable than doing something ascribed to women, while a man who did the man's task was rated as more logical than a woman who did the same and, by males only, as having more ability than a woman who did the same. In the other study (Mischel, 1974), a sample of American students preferred articles in male-identified fields written by men, whereas articles in female-identified fields were evaluated more positively if written by women; these findings were not obtained for Israeli students. Another investigator (Toder, 1980) has reported that ratings for the same articles attributed to a woman or to a man were affected by whether they were made in mixed-gender or in all-woman groups. Only in the former was the average rating lower for female-authored than for male-authored articles; this was true for both woman-associated and man-associated topics. And finally, male artists of contest entries (but not of winning paintings) were judged by women evaluators as more technically competent and as having a more promising artistic future than were female artists (Pheterson, Kiesler, & Goldberg, 1971).

The years spanned by the above investigations are 1968 through 1981. During the same period a sizeable number of studies also utilizing college-student participants and the same experimental paradigm, with similar stimulus materials and comparable situations, have reported no reliable differences in evaluative judgments of women and men or, in a few instances, more positive ratings of women. Using Goldberg's original stimulus materials, or comparable ones, a failure to find significant overall sex-of-author effects has been reported by several investigators (Chobot, Goldberg, & Abramson, 1974; Gross & Geffner, 1980; Levenson, Burford, Bonno, & Davis, 1975; Mischel, 1974; Panek, Deitchman, Burkholder,

Speroff, & Haude, 1976). Three studies found no sex-of-applicant effect in simulated selection: for law-school admission of a poorly qualified candidate (Beattie & Diehl, 1979), for a business manager's job (Soto & Cole, 1975), and for ratings of candidates for a number of varied jobs (Ward, 1981). One investigator found in two studies (Harris 1975, 1976) that teaching style matters more than teacher gender, and that bogus faculty members who were described as teaching in a forceful and objective manner were judged to be more intelligent, hard-working, and competent than those described as gentle and tactful. Another study found that teacher gender did not influence choice of courses in a mock registration exercise (Barnett & Littlepage, 1979). Well-known artists and their work were judged more positively than lesser known artists, regardless of gender (Etaugh & Sanders, 1974), and evaluation of managerial skills on a task was also found not to be influenced by performer's gender (Frank & Drucker, 1977).

In some laboratory exercises, students of both genders have been found to evaluate women significantly more positively than men: on intelligence and academic success (Bailey, Zinser, & Edgar, 1975); as counselors if described as experts (Merluzzi, Banikiotes, & Missbach, 1978); as job candidates across three different jobs, if of average scholastic ability (Muchinsky & Harris, 1977); for a pay raise if a manager with mainly male subordinates (Rose & Stone, 1978); when the stimulus person was described as helping in the capture of a gunman (Taynor & Deaux, 1973); as an artist, but only by nonart students (Ward, 1981); and on competence as an attorney (Abramson, Goldberg, Greenberg, & Abramson, 1977).

Another distinguishable group of studies has also utilized college-student evaluators, but instead of responding to descriptive materials or to products such as paintings, essays, or work samples, the student participants are provided with some brief experience, within a laboratory setting, during which a person is observed. Under such experimental conditions, both male and female students have been reported to judge women significantly less favorably than men: on leader effectiveness after viewing a videotape of a small group being directed to solve a design problem (Welsh, 1979); on intelligence and likability after viewing a videotape of confederates roleplaying faculty members at a committee meeting (Lao, Upchurch, Corwin, & Grossnickle, 1975); and on effectiveness and competence, after listening to a taped interview of a highly qualified scholarship applicant (Deaux & Taynor, 1973). In one study (Sanders & Schmidt, 1980), student volunteers sorted cards in accord with quotas set by a bogus graduate student (who was referred to but never appeared). More work was done for the male than for the female quota setter, especially by male participants. Again, however, not all investigations in this second category have yielded similar results. No overall differences in evaluations of women and men were reported in two situations in which the stimulus person was not only observed but actually interacted with, on ratings of counselors (Heppner & Pew, 1977), and on judgments of confederate supervisors (Lee & Alvares, 1977). And in two studies, in which participants observed films of applicants for a job performing an unskilled task, women received higher ratings than men (Hamner, Kim, Baird, & Bigoness, 1974), especially when the comparison was between high-performing persons (Bigoness, 1976).

Employer Samples

The most unequivocal evidence for bias against women and the fewest number of contrary findings has come from studies in which evaluations are made not by inexperienced students who have no stake in the outcomes, but by real, functioning decision makers (e.g., employers, supervisors, employment recruiters, etc.) in hypothetical or actual decision-making situations. I suggest that for such persons (but not for most college students) the evaluation of a job applicant is likely to evoke associations with previously experienced, meaningful consequences.

Most employer-sample studies have utilized industrial or business management personnel; only a small number of investigations has involved academic employers. The findings have been similar regardless of employment setting, and it is therefore instructive to examine these studies, conducted under varied conditions, for general outcome.

Participants in employer-sample studies (in both academic and business settings) are typically asked to read resumes or transcripts of interviews, and sometimes see photographs, but they do not actually meet the persons to be evaluated. Under such conditions it has been found that: personnel administrators of both genders predicted greater job success for male than for female applicants for two different jobs on a local magazine (Sharp & Post, 1980); a sample of chairmen of graduate departments in the physical sciences preferred an average male to an average female applicant (with identical credentials) for a faculty position, and consistently gave men higher ratings on educational background and hiring possibilities (Lewin & Duchan, 1971); a sample of psychology department chairmen made more offers at higher ranks to persons whose resumes they reviewed if those persons were men than women (Fidell, 1970); employers (predominantly male), interviewed by telephone, recommended more highly the hiring of a man for a semiskilled position than the hiring of a woman with identical background (Haefner, 1977); male professional interviewers gave higher ratings to male than to female applicants for the job of furniture department head (Dipboye, Fromkin, & Wiback, 1975); a sample of employers responded more quickly and positively to unsolicited resumes from male than from female job applicants (McIntyre, Moberg, & Posner, 1980); personnel directors responded more frequently and positively to job inquiries from a person using only first-name initials than one identified by a woman's name (Zikmund, Hitt, & Pickens, 1978); and public school superintendents judged a woman to be less acceptable and suitable than a man with identical credentials for a job requiring travel, less often advised a principal to influence a woman than a man to stay in a job, were less likely to promote a woman than a man who said that family responsibilities came first, and considered a child-care leave of absence less appropriate for a female than for a male counselor (Frasher, Frasher, & Wims, 1982). In one study (Kryger & Shikiar, 1978), male personnel managers were found to be more interested in interviewing a female than a male job seeker who sent credentials through the mail, but were more likely to consider the woman applicant for a lower level position than the one for which she applied.

Mediating factors have also been reported in some research with employers or their representatives. In one study, authoritarian personnel officers were found more likely than others to rank male job applicants higher than female applicants (Simas & McCarrey, 1979), and two studies have reported that type of job interacts with applicant gender in influencing applicant evaluation. Male job recruiters who read interview transcripts judged a female applicant as more acceptable than a male for an editorial assistant's job, but a male applicant as more acceptable than a female for a personnel assistant's job (Cohen & Bunker, 1975); personnel consultants judged male applicants to be more qualified for jobs considered appropriate for them (e.g., auto sales) and vice versa for women (e.g., receptionist) (Cash, Gillen, & Burns, 1977). In separate studies, the same investigators (Dipboye & Wiley, 1977, 1978) utilized videotaped interviews observed by male recruiters in which self-presentation style as well as gender of interviewee was varied, and found that applicant/interviewee gender did not influence evaluations.

Explanations and Consequences of Success

A number of investigations have been concerned not with evaluative judgments per se, but with how persons tend to explain the competence or success of women and men, respectively. The general conclusion from studies in a variety of settings in which attributions are made of others (not oneself) is that a woman's success is more likely to be explained by external factors like luck or ease of task, or by high effort, an internal but unstable factor, whereas a man's success is more likely to be attributed to high ability. The reverse is true for explanations of failure; men are said to fail because of bad luck, a hard task, or low effort, whereas women are said to fail because of low ability. Thus, in one study (Deaux & Emswiller, 1974) those who heard a tape recording of a man performing a verbal task judged him to be more skillful than those who heard a woman, although both were rated as having performed equally well. Other investigators (Feather & Simon, 1975) found that a group of Australian high-school girls judged ability as a more important cause of success for a man than a woman, and lack of ability as a more important cause of failure by a woman than a man (especially in medical school). This gender-related differential attribution for failure has been replicated and reported from a sample of male and female college students (Post, 1981), and from a sample of girls at each of four different grade levels (Etaugh & Brown, 1975). Also, in the latter study, women's success in mechanics was attributed less to ability than was men's success, and women's success across several tasks was attributed more to effort than was men's success. In still another investigation, effort was attributed more to women problem solvers than to men, regardless of level of success (Feldman-Summers & Kiesler, 1974). One investigator (Garland, 1977) has reported no support for differential attributions to women and men among college students.

In addition to the explanations offered for a woman's achievement or competence, a related issue is the consequences such a woman is likely to experience. One such consequence is for women to be judged as having more attributes stereotypically assigned to men and fewer attributes stereotypically assigned to women—i.e., to be judged more "masculine" and less "feminine" than less-competent women. For example, male and female college students, who had observed a woman experimenter in a videotape behaving in a confident and assured manner, rated her as more masculine, stronger, and harder than students who had seen an incompetent woman experimenter, and as more severe than a competent male experimenter seen by other students. Incompetent female experimenters were seen as not only weaker and softer than other experimenters but also as more feminine (Piacente, Penner, Hawkins, & Cohen, 1974). Complementary findings have been reported from the previously cited study of high-school girls (Feather & Simon, 1975) who evaluated a male stimulus person more positively, and judged him to be more powerful, wiser, more honest, and less feminine if he succeeded than if he failed; but they evaluated a successful female stimulus person *less* positively than one who failed, and as less powerful, obedient, polite, wise, honest, and feminine.

Using a behavioral measure, both male and female students in an Israeli sample (Nadler, Shapira, & Ben-Itzhak, 1982) were found to seek more help with a laboratory-presented problem from a physically unattractive than from an attractive woman. Did these participants assume that competence is negatively related to attractiveness? The attractiveness of potential male helpers made no difference to men, but was related to more help seeking by women.

Other consequences of competence for women that have been reported are as follows: judged as less well adjusted than a male candidate for law school with identical credentials (Beattie & Diehl, 1979); object of more negative comments than a similarly functioning male supervisor in a simulated work setting (Cohen, Bunker, Burton, & McManus, 1978); awarded a lower salary than an identically qualified male candidate in a workshop exercise in which evaluators were instructed to follow a strong affirmative action policy (Rosen & Mericle, 1979); more likely to be excluded from a work group than a competent man (Hagen & Kahn, 1975); and having people remember less of what a woman said than what a man said, regardless of the topic (Gruber & Gaebelein, 1979).

A small group of studies has found that consequences for competence in women are mediated by such factors as the extent to which the woman will be pursuing traditional or nontraditional interests or goals. For example, a woman of great academic promise was judged to be less likely to find a marriage partner when presented as success oriented than as nonsuccess oriented (Michelini, Eisen, & Snodgrass, 1981); men rated a competent woman lower on femininity, intelligence, kindness, and sensitivity, and liked her less if she planned to pursue a career than if she planned to stay at home with her family (Pines, 1979); and competent women expressing traditional interests were preferred to those expressing interests stereotypically associated with men (Shaffer & Wegley, 1974). In another study (Shaffer & Johnson, 1980) this tendency to find persons who are "gender consistent" more socially attractive regardless of their competence was found to hold for male as well as female stimulus-persons. And some investigations (Sanford & Hewitt, 1980; Spence, Helmreich, & Stapp, 1975; Vaughn & Wittig, 1980) have found that under certain conditions a woman's competence does not detract from her likability.

Evaluation of Familiar Persons
in Natural Settings

One small group of relevant research differs in important ways from the studies discussed thus far; the participants are asked to evaluate *real persons* with whom they have actually worked and interacted over a reasonable period of time in an ongoing natural situation (or to generalize to such a class of persons). Under such circumstances, competent women tend not to be devalued on the measures utilized by the investigators and are sometimes evaluated more positively than men. The results of this research are heartening, and suggest that actual experience with a capable woman may provide sufficient positive reinforcement so that the typically negative response to the general cue of gender is low on the hierarchy of responses; instead, stronger competing responses will be evoked by more salient cues, those unique to the particular woman evaluated. Thus, public welfare managers supervised by women were significantly more positive in their evaluations of women managers than were those not supervised by a woman (Ezell, Odewahn, & Sherman, 1981); the work behaviors of male and female supervisors were evaluated similarly by a national interview sample of adult workers (Cullen & Perrewe, 1981); student ratings of actual teachers were not reliably different on most scales for women and men (Elmore & LaPointe, 1974, 1975); prior exposure of staff and academic employees of a midwestern university (Ferber, Huber, & Spitze, 1979) to women bosses or professionals was negatively associated with preference for men over women as bosses/professionals; and social service agency workers who had female supervisors rated them more highly, in general, than those who had male supervisors (Munson, 1979).

Some ambiguous findings have also been reported. A group of primarily male supervisors was found to judge their first-level male store managers as friendlier, as having better relations with the supervisor, and as having a more difficult job than their female store managers; at the same time, they did not rate the men and women differently on a number of work-related dimensions (Deaux, 1979). In a somewhat different kind of study (Guillemin, Holmstrom, & Garvin, 1979), a content analysis was performed on all the letters of reference for candidates for a junior faculty position in a department of sociology. Male candidates were more likely than female candidates to be described in superlatives and to be represented as capable in areas such as intellectual ability, publication potential, organizational skill, and prediction of future career developments. These findings, however, were not replicated in a similar study of letters of reference for a one-year position within a psychology department (Burrows, Pfennig, & White, 1982).

Conclusions

1. *The tendency to devalue a competent woman, although not invariable, appears to be more the rule than the exception.* This devaluation may be directly focused on her performance, or potential performance, or may be reflected in explanations of her success that emphasize luck, effort, or an easy task rather than ability. Or she may be "put down" in the social sphere by being judged less likable than an equally competent man or a less-competent or nonsuccess-oriented woman, and/or judged as more "masculine" and less "feminine" than other women in terms of stereotypic attributes or characteristics.

Such reactions to competent women have been documented in a variety of settings. Women in academe, like women in art, business, or science, are likely to be judged less positively on work or social criteria than equally credentialed or similarly behaving men. In other words, equal performance by women and men does not yield equal evaluation. As Bridges and Hartmann (1975, p. 77) suggested, academic women may be at a disadvantage when compared with men; not only is their authority in question with respect to what they know (and teach), but more is expected of them in relating to students. "Male teachers who are responsive are 'really good guys': Women who are responsive are just being women. . . . Men don't have to be 'nice'; women *do.*"

Although some research has shown that devaluation is more likely in areas of activity that are nontraditional (or unusual) for persons of one's gender, this is not a consistent finding, and is more true of women than men. Thus, for example, in one study (Gilbert, Lee, & Chiddix, 1981) the stimulus person who received the highest ratings among two men and two women presenters of videotaped lectures was a man who spoke on "sex bias in the counseling of women" (a topic that has not been a traditional concern of men!). Such a highly positive response to men who are doing "women's things" is reflected dramatically in the media by such films as *Kramer vs. Kramer* and *Author, Author*, and in a new group of television and magazine commercials in which nurturant fathers and their children are used to sell a variety of products ("One Step," 1982).

2. The available data suggest that *a competent woman is most likely to be devalued* (when she is not actually known or known well by an evaluator) *when judgments are made in a serious, believable and realistic context, and when there are potential consequences for the evaluator.* Thus, studies using college-student participants who are asked to judge bogus stimulus persons or products in a classroom-exercise situation less consistently reveal biased judgments of women, while studies in which actual employers, managers, or hiring agents are asked to judge prospective employees overwhelmingly find a significant devaluation of women. That the behavior of prospective employers should manifest more sexism than the behavior of college students in simulated situations is consistent with, and predictable from, the theoretical considerations outlined at the beginning of this paper. For actual employers, the gender of an employee has real significance and potential consequences and should, therefore, be far more salient than for student role players. The empirical data reviewed here suggest that this is so.

3. Still another generalization has emerged from this review of research. *Negative evaluations of competent women are least likely in situations where persons are judging someone they know well, or with whom they have worked or interacted.* In such cases gender would be expected to be a less

salient cue than other personal, specific characteristics of the individual; sexist responses would be in competition with those made to personal qualities and, therefore, less probable. [Other reviewers (Nieva & Gutek, 1980) have suggested that evaluators of a person's actual past performance are called upon to make fewer inferences, and thus there is less opportunity for bias, than evaluators of the more ambiguous qualifications of unknown persons.] This conclusion may well be one of the strongest arguments we can make in favor of continued adherence to a clear affirmative action policy. When given a chance to perform (in a positive environment), a competent woman in academe or other settings will not only do the job well but, as the data indicate, is more likely to be judged fairly.[1] (One dilemma faced by women in the workplace is that efforts to increase familiarity with male coworkers may be misinterpreted as a sexual advance: but avoiding social contact reduces the degree to which potential evaluators can get to know them.)

The encouraging conclusion that familiarity decreases the likelihood that a competent woman will be devalued must be tempered by the reality of the experiences of the eminent academic women with which this paper began, and by the documented and well-known differentials between women and men in such areas as salary, promotion, and other institutional rewards. While it seems likely that ongoing experience with a competent woman may facilitate an accurate and unbiased judgment of her performance on the job, such a judgment may not be the only one solicited from evaluators or the only factor relevant to the making of salary or advancement decisions. When rewards are being distributed, especially in situations in which women are in direct competition with men for limited resources, factors that are not directly work-related may influence job decisions or evaluations. For example, in a field study involving interviews and analysis of job performance records of 651 employees of five different companies (Gupta, Jenkins, & Beehr, 1983), it was found that "while opinions (evaluations) may be positive, actions (promotions) still follow traditions" (p. 183). Women subordinates received the fewest promotions regardless of the evaluations of their work.

When Jessie Bernard (1978) was gathering material for her book, *Academic Women*, she wrote to her daughter about a set of "interesting tables [which] show that women who receive Ph.D. degrees average considerably higher in testable intelligence than [comparable] men" (p. 308). The hypothesis she proposed in the early sixties to explain why such very bright academic women achieved lesser status than academic men was that it was attributable to the "stag factor," i.e., women's exclusion from places where men gathered to discuss their work. She did not believe, at the time, that the exclusion of women was "by design or conspiracy." Only later did she see her earlier explanation as naive and superficial and realize that she had paid insufficient attention to discrimination. "I had not pushed my analyses far enough" (Bernard, 1978, p. 309); "I had accepted the male-delineated perspective of my [male] colleagues" (p. 311). She had not yet examined the experiences of academic women in the context of a sexist society.

This paper began with a definition of sexism in social-psychological terms, and distinguished among three components: negative attitudes toward women (prejudice), beliefs that complement the prejudice (stereotypes), and acts of exclusion (discrimination). Responses to competent women, seen in the findings of formal investigations as well as in the experiences of academic women, provide illustrations of all three components of sexism—affect, cognition, and overt behavior. From an examination of the empirical literature, it is concluded that competent women are less likely to be evaluated as highly as equally competent men, but not under all conditions. A lesser evaluation is least likely in situations where a competent woman is known to the evaluator and personal stimuli other than gender evoke positive responses. On the other hand, devaluation is most probable under conditions in which gender is a more salient cue than the person's other qualities and/or the evaluator anticipates significant consequences for the allocation of limited resources. These generalizations must be carefully and systematically tested by future research.

Notes

An earlier version of this paper was read at the 90th annual convention of the American Psychological Association, Washington, D.C., August 1982, as part of a symposium on Women's Professional Advancement in Psychology: Progress and Problems.

Correspondence regarding this article should be addressed to Bernice Lott, Department of Psychology, University of Rhode Island, Kingston, RI 02881.

1. A recent legal judgment issued on a class action discrimination suit in which I am involved as a member of the class of women faculty at my university provides a remarkable illustration of this third conclusion—that devaluation of competent women is more probable *prior* to personal knowledge of them than after. United States District Judge Bruce Selya found that the evidence to support our charge of discrimination by the university administration and board of governors was substantial and explicit with respect to salary and rank at hire, but he found that the evidence for discrimination with respect to promotion and tenure was not as clear or unambiguous. Although the plaintiffs believe the case for discrimination is strong on all counts, the judge's perception that the administration's negative, discriminatory responses to competent faculty women are more clearly evident before the women were known (i.e., at hire) than after their work

and personal qualities were known by colleagues and evaluators, is consistent with the research reviewed and the theoretical considerations presented in this paper.

References

Abramson, P. R., Goldberg, P. A., Greenberg, J. H., & Abramson, L. M. (1977). The talking platypus phenomenon: Competency ratings as a function of sex and professional status. *Psychology of Women Quarterly, 2*, 114–124.

Albin, R. S. (1979). Women and *Science* editorials. *Science, 203*, 227–228.

Bailey, R. C., Zinser, O., & Edgar, R. (1975). Perceived intelligence, motivation, and achievement in male and female college students. *Journal of Genetic Psychology, 127*, 125–129.

Barnett, L. T., & Littlepage, G. (1979). Course preferences and evaluations of male and female professors by male and female students. *Bulletin of Psychonomic Society, 13*, 44–46.

Beattie, M. Y., & Diehl, L. A. (1979). Effects of social conditions on the expression of sex-role stereotypes. *Psychology of Women Quarterly, 4*, 241–255.

Bernard, J. (1978). *Self-portrait of a family.* Boston: Beacon.

Bernard, M. E., Keefauver, L. W., Elsworth, G., & Naylor, F. D. (1981). Sex role behavior and gender in teacher-student evaluations. *Journal of Educational Psychology, 73*, 681–696.

Bigoness, W. J. (1976). Effect of applicant's sex, race, and performance on employers' performance ratings: Some additional findings. *Journal of Applied Psychology, 61*, 80–84.

Bridges, A., & Hartmann, H. (1975). Pedagogy by the oppressed. *Review of Radical Political Economics, vi(4)*, 75–79.

Burrows, P. B., Pfennig, J. L., & White, A. (1982, August). Analysis of letters of recommendation: Sex differences and setbacks. In P. B. Burrows & M. R. Walsh (Chairs), *Women's professional advancement in psychology: Progress and problems.* Symposium conducted at the 90th annual convention of the American Psychological Association, Washington, D.C.

Cann, A., Siegfried, W. D., & Pearce, L. (1981). Forced attention to specific applicant qualifications: Impact on physical attractiveness and sex of applicant biases. *Personnel Psychology, 34*, 65–76.

Cash, T. F., Gillen, B., & Burns, D. S. (1977). Sexism and "beautyism" in personnel consultant decisions. *Journal of Applied Psychology, 62*, 301–310

Chobot, D. S., Goldberg, P. A., & Abramson, L. M. (1974) Prejudice against women: A replication and extension. *Psychological Reports, 35*, 478.

Cohen, S. L., & Bunker, K. A. (1975). Subtle effects of sex role stereotypes on recruiters' hiring decisions. *Journal of Applied Psychology, 60*, 566–572.

Cohen, S. L., Bunker, K. A., Burton, A. L., & McManus, P. D. (1978). Reactions of male subordinates to the sex-role congruency of immediate supervision. *Sex Roles, 4*, 297–311.

Cullen, J. B., & Perrewe, P. L. (1981). Superior's and subordinate's gender: Does it really matter? *Psychological Reports, 48*, 435–438.

Dash, J. (1973). *A life of one's own.* New York: Harper & Row.

Deaux, K. (1979). Self-evaluations of male and female managers. *Sex Roles, 5,* 570–580.

Deaux, K., & Emswiller, T. (1974). Explanations of successful performance on sex-linked tasks: What is skill for the male is luck for the female. *Journal of Personality and Social Psychology, 29,* 80–85.

Deaux, K., & Taynor, J. (1973). Evaluation of male and female ability: Bias works two ways. *Psychological Reports, 32,* 261–262.

Denmark, F. L. (1979). The outspoken woman: Can she win? Paper presented at The New York Academy of Sciences, New York City.

Dipboye, R. L., Arvey, R. D., & Terpstra, D. E. (1977). Sex and physical attractiveness of raters and applicants as determinants of resume evaluations. *Journal of Applied Psychology, 62,* 288–294.

Dipboye, R. L., Fromkin, H. L., & Wiback, K. (1975). Relative importance of applicant sex, attractiveness, and scholastic standing in evaluation of job applicant. *Journal of Applied Psychology, 60,* 39–43.

Dipboye, R. L., & Wiley, J. W. (1977). Reactions of college recruiters to interviewee sex and self-presentation style. *Journal of Vocational Behavior, 10,* 1–12.

Dipboye, R. L., & Wiley, J. W. (1978). Reactions of male raters to interviewee self-presentation style and sex: Extension of previous research. *Journal of Vocational Behavior, 13,* 192–203.

Elmore, P. B., & LaPointe, K. A. (1974). Effects of teacher sex and student sex on the evaluation of college instructors. *Journal of Educational Psychology, 66,* 386–389.

Elmore, P. B., & LaPointe, K. A. (1975). Effect of teacher sex, student sex, and teacher warmth on the evaluation of college instructors. *Journal of Educational Psychology, 67,* 368–374.

Etaugh, C., & Brown, B. (1975). Perceiving the causes of success and failure of female performers. *Developmental Psychology, 11,* 103.

Etaugh, C., & Kasley, H. C. (1981). Evaluating competence: Effects of sex, marital status, and parental status. *Psychology of Women Quarterly, 6,* 196–203.

Etaugh, C., & Sanders, S. (1974). Evaluation of performance as a function of status and sex variables. *Journal of Social Psychology, 94,* 237–241.

Ezell, H. F., Odewahn, C. A., & Sherman, J. D. (1981). The effects of having been supervised by a woman on perceptions of female managerial competence. *Personnel Psychology, 34,* 291–300.

Feather, N. T., & Simon, J. G. (1975). Reactions to male and female success and failure in sex-linked occupations: Impressions of personality, causal attributions and perceived likelihood of different consequences. *Journal of Personality and Social Psychology, 31,* 20–31.

Feldman-Summers, S. A., & Kiesler, S. B. (1974). Those who are number two try harder: The effect of sex on attributions of causality. *Journal of Personality and Social Psychology, 30,* 846–855.

Ferber, M., Huber, J., & Spitze, G. (1979). Preference for men as bosses and professionals. *Social Forces, 58,* 466–476.

Fidell, L. S. (1970). Empirical verification of sex discrimination in hiring practices in psychology. *American Psychologist, 25,* 1094–1098.

Frank, F. D., & Drucker, J. (1977). The influence of evaluatee's sex on evaluations of a response on a managerial selection instrument. *Sex Roles, 3,* 59–64.

Frasher, J. M., Frasher, R. S., & Wims, F. B. (1982). Sex-role stereotyping in school superintendents' personnel decisions. *Sex Roles, 8,* 261–268.

Garland, H. (1977). Sometimes nothing succeeds like success: Reactions to success and failure in sex-linked occupations. *Psychology of Women Quarterly, 2,* 50–61.

Gilbert, L. A., Lee, R. N., & Chiddix, S. (1981). Influence of presenter's gender on students' evaluations of presenters discussing sex fairness in counseling: An analogue study. *Journal of Counseling Psychology, 28,* 258–264.

Goldberg, P. (1968, April). Are women prejudiced against women? *Trans-action, 5* (5), 28–30.

Gornick, V. (1983, October). Women in science: A passion for discovery, *Ms.,* 50–52, 130–135.

Gross, M. M., & Geffner, R. A. (1980). Are the times changing? An analysis of sex-role prejudice. *Sex Roles, 6,* 713–722.

Gruber, K., & Gaebelein, J. (1979). Sex differences in listening comprehension. *Sex Roles, 5,* 299–310.

Guillemin, J., Holmstrom, L. L., & Garvin, M. (1979). Judging competence: Letters of recommendation for men and women faculties. *School Review, 87,* 157–170.

Gupta, N., Jenkins, G. D. Jr., & Beehr, T. A. (1983). Employee gender, gender similarity, and supervisor-subordinate cross-evaluations. *Psychology of Women Quarterly, 8,* 174–184.

Gutek, B. A., & Stevens, D. A. (1979). Effects of sex of subject, sex of stimulus cue, and androgyny level on evaluations in work situations which evoke sex role stereotypes. *Journal of Vocational Behavior, 14,* 23–32.

Haefner, J. E. (1977). Race, age, sex, and competence as factors in employer selection of the disadvantaged. *Journal of Applied Psychology, 62,* 199–202.

Hagen, R. L., & Kahn, A. (1975). Discrimination against competent women. *Journal of Applied Social Psychology, 5,* 362–376.

Hamner, W. C., Kim, J. S., Baird, L., & Bigoness, W. J. (1974). Race and sex as determinants of ratings by potential employers in a simulated work-sampling task. *Journal of Applied Psychology, 59,* 705–711.

Harris, M. B. (1975). Sex role stereotypes and teacher evaluations. *Journal of Educational Psychology, 67,* 751–756.

Harris, M. B. (1976). The effects of sex, sex-stereotyped descriptions, and institution on evaluations of teachers. *Sex Roles, 2,* 15–22.

Heneman, H. G. (1977). Impact of test information and applicant sex on applicant evaluations in a selection simulation. *Journal of Applied Psychology, 62,* 524–526.

Heppner, P. P., & Pew, S. (1977). Effects of diplomas, awards, and counselor sex on perceived expertness. *Journal of Counseling Psychology, 24,* 147–149.

Isaacs, M. B. (1981). Sex role stereotyping and the evaluation of the performance of women: Changing trends. *Psychology of Women Quarterly, 6,* 187–195.

Kaschak, E. (1977). Sex bias in student evaluations of college professors. *Psychology of Women Quarterly, 2,* 235–243.

Kaschak, E. (1981). Another look at sex bias in students' evaluations of professors: Do winners get the recognition that they have been given? *Psychology of Women Quarterly, 5,* 767–772.

Kryger, B. R., & Shikiar, R. (1978). Sexual discrimination in the use of letters of recommendation: A case of reverse discrimination. *Journal of Applied Psychology, 63,* 309–314.

Lao, R. C., Upchurch, W. H., Corwin, B. J., & Grossnickle, W. F. (1975). Biased attitudes toward females as indicated by ratings of intelligence and likability. *Psychological Reports, 37,* 1315–1320.

Lasker award stirs controversy. (1979). *Science, 203,* 341.

Lee, D. M., & Alvares, K. M. (1977). Effects of sex on descriptions and evaluations of supervisory behavior in a simulated industrial setting. *Journal of Applied Psychology, 62,* 405–410.

Levenson, H., Burford, B., Bonno, B., & Davis, L. (1975). Are women still prejudiced against women? A replication and extension of Goldberg's study. *Journal of Psychology, 89,* 67–71.

Lewin, A. Y., & Duchan, L. (1971). Women in academia: A study of the hiring decision in departments of physical science. *Science, 173,* 892–895.

Lombardo, J. P., & Tocci, M. E. (1979). Attribution of positive and negative characteristics of instructors as a function of attractiveness and sex of instructor and sex of subject. *Perceptual and Motor Skills 48,* 491–494.

McIntyre, S., Moberg, D. J., & Posner, B. Z. (1980). Preferential treatment in preselection decisions according to sex and race. *Academy of Management Journal, 23,* 738–749.

Merluzzi, T. V., Banikiotes, P. G., & Missbach, J. W. (1978). Perceptions of counselor characteristics: Contributions of counselor sex, experience, and disclosure level. *Journal of Counseling Psychology, 25,* 479–482.

Michelini, R. L., Eisen, D., & Snodgrass, S. R. (1981). Success orientation and the attractiveness of competent males and females. *Sex Roles, 7,* 391–402.

Mischel, H. N. (1974). Sex bias in the evaluation of professional achievements. *Journal of Educational Psychology, 66,* 157–166.

Muchinsky, P. M., & Harris, S. L. (1977). The effect of applicant sex and scholastic standing on the evaluation of job applicant resumes in sex-typed occupations. *Journal of Vocational Behavior, 11,* 95–108.

Munson, C. E. (1979). Evaluation of male and female supervisors. *Social Work, 24,* 104–111.

Nadler, A., Shapira, P., & Ben-Itzhak, S. (1982). Good looks may help: Effects of helpers' physical attractiveness and sex of helper on males' and females' help-seeking behaviors. *Journal of Personality and Social Psychology, 42,* 90–99.

New York Times Magazine, (1982, Feb. 21). 47, 48.

New York Times Magazine, (1982, Sept. 12). 90.

Nieva, V. F., & Gutek, B. A. (1980). Sex effects on evaluation. *Academy of Management Review, 5,* 267–276.

One step forward. The selling of the nurturing father. (1982, February). *Ms.* 102.

Panek, P. E., Deitchman, R., Burkholder, J. H., Speroff, T., & Haude, R. H. (1976). Evaluation of feminine professional competence as a function of level of accomplishment. *Psychological Reports, 38,* 875–880.

Peck, T. (1978). When women evaluate women, nothing succeeds like success: The differential effects of status upon evaluations of male and female professional ability. *Sex Roles, 4,* 205–214.

Pheterson, G. I., Kiesler, S. B., & Goldberg, P. (1971). Evaluation of the performance of women as a function of their sex, achievement, and personal history. *Journal of Personality and Social Psychology, 19,* 114–118.

Piacente, B. S., Penner, L. A., Hawkins, H. C., & Cohen, S. L. (1974). Evaluation of the performance of experimenters as a function of their sex and competence. *Journal of Applied Social Psychology, 4,* 321–329.

Pines, A. (1979). The influence of goals on people's perceptions of a competent woman. *Sex Roles, 5,* 71–76.

Post, R. D. (1981). Causal explanations of male and female academic performance as a function of sex-role biases. *Sex Roles, 7,* 691–698.

Roark, A. C. (1980, March 17). In Science. Birthrates not affected by cycles of the moon. *Chronicle of Higher Education,* 18.

Rose, G. L., & Stone, T. H. (1978). Why good job performance may (not) be rewarded: Sex factors and career development. *Journal of Vocational Behavior, 12,* 197–207.

Rosen, B., & Jerdee, T. H. (1974). Effects of applicant's sex and difficulty of job on evaluations of candidates for managerial positions. *Journal of Applied Psychology, 59,* 511–512.

Rosen, B., & Mericle, M. F. (1979). Influence of strong versus weak fair employment policies and applicant's sex on selection decisions and salary recommendations in a management simulation. *Journal of Applied Psychology, 64,* 435–439.

Rubin, V. C. (1981, February 27). E. Margaret Burbidge, President-elect. *Science, 211,* 915–916.

Sanders, G. S., & Schmidt, T. (1980). Behavioral discrimination against women. *Personality and Social Psychology Bulletin, 6,* 484–488.

Sanford, F., & Hewitt, J. (1980). No discrimination against brilliant women. *Psychological Reports, 46,* 1267–1270.

Sayre, A. (1975). *Rosalind Franklin and DNA.* New York: Norton.

Science. (1981, March 13). *211,* 1096, 1109, 1115, 1120.

Shaffer, D. B., & Johnson, R. D. (1980). Effects of occupational choice and sex role preferences on the attractiveness of competent men and women. *Journal of Personality, 48,* 505–519.

Shaffer, D. B., & Wegley, C. (1974). Success orientation and sex-role congruence as determinants of the attractiveness of the competent woman. *Journal of Personality, 42,* 586–600.

Sharp, C., & Post, R. (1980). Evaluation of male and female applicants for sex congruent and sex incongruent jobs. *Sex Roles, 6,* 391–402.

Simas, K., & McCarrey, M. (1979). Impact of recruiter authoritarianism and applicant sex on evaluation and selection decisions in a recruitment interview analogue study. *Journal of Applied Psychology, 64,* 483–491.

Soto, D. H., & Cole, C. (1975). Prejudice against women: A new perspective. *Sex Roles, 1,* 385–393.

Spence, J. T., Helmreich, R., & Stapp, J. (1975). Likability, sex-role congruence of interest, and competence: It all depends on how you ask. *Journal of Applied Social Psychology, 5,* 93–109.

Taynor, J., & Deaux, K. (1973). When women are more deserving than men: Equity, attribution, and perceived sex differences. *Journal of Personality and Social Psychology 28,* 360–367.

Taynor, J., & Deaux, K. (1975). Equity and perceived sex differences: Role behavior as defined by the task, the mode, and the actor. *Journal of Personality and Social Psychology, 32,* 381–390.

Toder, N. L. (1980). The effect of the sexual composition of a group on discrimination against women and sex-role attitudes. *Psychology of Women Quarterly, 5,* 292–310.

Vaughn, L. S., & Wittig, M. A. (1980). Occupation, competence, and role overload as evaluation determinants of successful women. *Journal of Applied Social Psychology, 10,* 398–415.

Wade, N. (1975). Discovery of pulsars: A graduate student's story. *Science, 189,* 358–364.

Ward, C. (1981). The differential assessment of males and females as prospective employees by a sample of nonworking women. *Sex Roles, 7,* 811–820.

Welsh, M. C. (1979). Attitudinal measures and evaluation of males and females in leadership roles. *Psychology Reports, 45,* 19–22.

Zikmund, W. G., Hitt, M. A., & Pickens, B. A. (1978). Influence of sex and scholastic performance on reactions to job applicant resumes. *Journal of Applied Psychology, 63,* 252–258.

Zorn, J. (1974, November 17). No "Lady anthropologist." (Review of *Ruth Benedict* by M. Mead). *New York Times Book Review,* 20–21.

PART 2
RE-VIEWING PSYCHOLOGY: A CONSTRUCTIONIST PERSPECTIVE

When analyzed in historical context, these gender concepts are found to share ethnopsychological origins—roots in social practices and prescriptions. . . . If we choose to terminate such fruitless ventures and generate novel understandings of the social world, then we must undertake critical self-appraisal and adopt a new metatheoretical grounding. (Morawski, 1985, p. 196)

Morawski's appeal is for a constructionist metatheory as a more progressive basis for creating new understandings and new social forms. When we look to social constructionism as such a metatheory, we discover there conceptual tools that clarify women's place in psychology, the mistreatment so well depicted in our readings to this point. As Morawski insisted, ideas taken by psychology as knowledge about women can be readily disassembled to appreciate their sociohistorical framework, with so-called scientific knowledge about gender closely intertwined with each era's social norms. The article by Shields in the first part of this book neatly demonstrated this phenomenon as regards early American psychology; later readings will depict subsequent context-dependent notions. Similarly, women's place in the discipline and psychology's treatment of its own women can be seen as products of historical context, shaped both by social norms regarding women's proper sphere and by the discipline's self-definition.

In keeping with the dialectic perspective fundamental to constructionism, psychology's presentations of women and of gender can also be explored for their impact on society at large. Early psychology provided presumably scientific justification for contemporary beliefs regarding women, just as recent theory and research in the psychology of women have contributed to the scholarly basis of feminist thought. The valuation inherent in gendered constructs makes these notions particularly compelling for their impact on a wide range of human behavior. Thus, psychology's treatment of women and of gender shows just the sort of reciprocity that constructionism highlights: psychology is both framed by the social construction of gender and has participated in that construction.

Psychology's contribution to the social construction of gender is precisely the focus of Jill Morawski's article, a remarkably precise historical and conceptual analysis of psychology's treatment of "masculinity" and "femininity." Morawski dissected psychology's understanding of gender, revealing it not as an independently existing phenomenon but rather as a product of the means by which it had been measured. The subtitle tells the tale: "Engendering Categorical Realities." In unfolding this clever double entendre, Morawski detailed how the categories of masculinity and femininity had in fact been created (engendered) through the development of techniques for measuring them; simultaneously, she revealed how those very measurements, which were in no sense inherently about gender, were granted gender (engendered) through the processes of their utilization.

The origins of this scientific construction of gender-as-category are intricately intertwined with its implications, for both origin and consequence are grounded in identifiable social norms. Morawski's discussion ranged among these, touching on roots in social institutions such as marriage and family life, in psychological practices surrounding test construction, and in issues of social responsibility. The science-as-handmaiden theme lent added perspective, as Morawski traced the historical treatment of the constructs of masculinity and femininity, anchoring them in changing societal beliefs and professional expectations. The result is a study of psychology's creation of gender categories in the service of social norms, an understanding seriously questioned only when changing norms demanded reassessment of the underlying meaning of and uses for these categories. Indeed, the concept of androgyny, initially acclaimed as the long-awaited palliative to psychology's gender malaise, was demonstrated to be equally entwined with social expectations.

As Morawski concluded, this unpacking of the assumptions and mechanics of the measurement of gender has broad ramifications for psychology. The questions it raises challenge us to reconsider how psychology's practices, its language, and its response to historically situated values serve to create a vision of human experience that is less reality than artifact. If in striving to measure we actually create social categories, then psychology must assume the obligation to be reflective about the values that guide its activities. In Morawski's words, "If we choose to participate in generating novel ways of looking at the social world . . . then we must first audit our inventory of artifactual and conventional beliefs" (1985, p. 218).

The role of unquestioned beliefs in psychology's understanding of gender sounds the theme for Rachel Hare-Mustin and Jeanne Marecek's analysis of the meaning of difference in psychological gender theory. This is a conceptually dislocating article, a constructionist analysis of the fundamental meaning that has been attributed to gender: difference. Hare-Mustin and Marecek took on the range of psychological theory and research regarding gender, confronting both those approaches that stress gender difference ("alpha bias") and those that minimize difference ("beta bias"). They concluded that these two apparently disparate stances reveal a common preoccupation with gender defined by difference. The distinction between alpha and beta biases, as they revealingly demonstrated, is not a distinction between feminist and antifeminist approaches, for both alpha bias and beta bias positions can be found among both feminists and antifeminists. Nor is the question simply one of whether psychology should be looking for similarities rather than difference. Rather, the issue is that psychology has *defined* gender (that is, constructed the meaning of gender, our "knowledge" of gender) with difference as the cornerstone.

Both alpha bias and beta bias positions begin with the presumption that gender is about difference, and the questions generated by both reflect this assumption: How much difference? In what areas? With what implications? and so forth. Abjuring the argument about the reality or extent of gender differences, Hare-Mustin and Marecek explored the utility of each position, disclosing how each can serve both feminist and antifeminist aims. Thus, they argued, it is the construction of gender as difference that must be engaged if we are to move beyond the morass of conflicting and irresolvable claims to reality made by alpha- and beta-biased approaches. Hare-Mustin and Marecek argued that the construction of gender as difference acts to obscure the truly crucial questions, particularly issues of power and oppression that are disguised by rhetoric regarding gender difference. Their application of this approach to clinical work was a study in deconstruction as re-vision—the very antithesis of the science-as-handmaiden syndrome.

This deconstruction of the meaning of gender is crucial to the project of creating a women-inclusive psychology. Insofar as traditional renderings of gender define the issues to be addressed—whether by our acquiescence or our opposition to these depictions—feminist psychology, women-inclusive psychology, remains shaped by the received view. A feminist analysis of this process, exposing the power relations that have allowed mainstream psychology to define the terms of the discussion, must generate alternative meanings, alternative constructions of gender. As Hare-Mustin and Marecek urged, "constructing gender is a process, not an answer" (1988, p. 462). Our charge is to participate in the continuing reconstruction of gender to accommodate the realities of women's experience.

The construction of gender as difference reflects the androcentric bias of traditional psychology, for it maintains the position from which women are viewed in terms of men—their similarity to or difference from the male "norm." Without defining it in just these terms, Weisstein delineated the problem two decades ago. Since that time, feminist psychologists have struggled with the dilemma of how to create a psychology that is not infused with the subtle remnants of that traditional perspective. Their efforts, running parallel to nonfeminist (if not always identifiably antifeminist) mainstream treatments of gender, are the subject matter of Mary Crawford and Jeanne Marecek's article. This paper is in essence a constructionist historical analysis of two decades' psychological consideration of women. Beginning where Weisstein left off, Crawford and Marecek undertook a critical reflection on psychology's treatments of gender in general and of women in particular during the deluge of research and theory that followed Weisstein's exposé.

Among the discoveries of Crawford and Marecek's odyssey through the gender literature are trends that appear promising for the substantial reconstruction of psychology's treatment of women. Among these trends they detailed the growing diversity and complexity of gender theory and research, a substantial trend away from the (now obviously) simplistic questions about "sex differences" that characterized earlier work. This growing intricacy is paralleled by a movement away from tacit acceptance of the male as norm and growing validation of women's experience on its own terms. The abandonment of (androcentric) sex differences work and the adoption of a more inclusive psychology of gender have further demanded substantial alterations in the field's most fundamental practices and normative assumptions. Beyond challenging traditional renderings of gender, this work has stimulated the development of alternative methodologies and has fostered a broader perspective on issues of race, class, and ethnic bias in the discipline.

This is a hopeful and empowering realization: not only are we beginning to reconstruct psychology's understanding of women but in the process we are instigating significant changes in the discipline that promise a more expansive and inclusive psychology overall. As Crawford and Marecek's analysis showed, the process continues as research and theory move beyond gender per se toward a "transformation" of the discipline. Stemming from feminist research but by no means confined to it, this fundamental challenge to psychology's philosophical underpinnings and the practices deriving from them brings us to a juncture between psychological scholarship and political advocacy.

The postmodern turn in psychology, the grounding for the constructionist approach of this book, demands recognition of the inescapable connections among theory, research, social impacts, and political aims. Feminist psychology stands to profit mightily from this attention to the contextuality of knowledge, the acknowledgment of the value-laden character of psychological science, and the demands for social responsibility that postmodernism ushers in. No longer an attempt at "objective" description of the reality of sex differences, psychology's contemporary construction of the female is multiply defined, historically situated, contextually grounded, women-validating, and politically sensitive.

References

Hare-Mustin, Rachel T., & Marecek, Jeanne. (1988). The meaning of difference: Gender theory, postmodernism, and psychology. *American Psychologist, 43,* 455–464.

Morawski, Jill G. (1985). The measurement of masculinity and femininity: Engendering categorical realities. *Journal of Personality, 53,* 196–223.

7
THE MEASUREMENT OF MASCULINITY AND FEMININITY: ENGENDERING CATEGORICAL REALITIES

J. G. Morawski

When the protagonist of Virginia Woolf's *Orlando* is suddenly transformed from male to female, he/she has minimal difficulty adjusting to a new form. The recent shift from the bipolar, apparently antiquated concepts of masculinity and femininity to one of androgyny, though purportedly a major reformulation, actually intimates a similar facile accommodation. While different in kind, both changes rely on mundane oppositions—those cultural concepts that ordinarily signify masculine and feminine. Both changes constitute fairly undramatic revisions rather than radical transformations.

The study of femininity and masculinity, comprising a massive scientific project across 90 years of experimental psychology, depicts a curious recurrence of these cultural concepts. The research exemplifies the repetition, with minor modifications, of several central stipulations about masculinity and femininity. Conventional literature reviews strive to identify significant advances in gender research, to chart the "breakthroughs" or "discoveries" as it were, but they neglect what is stable and common to the studies. A perspective that acknowledges the repeated similarities is needed to begin to appreciate the virtual reification of the existence, contents, and evaluative dynamics of masculinity and femininity concepts. Such a perspective attends to the procedures through which those stipulations were defended and sustained. It illuminates some of the nonempirical reasons for maintaining certain categorical stipulations about femininity and masculinity and, in turn, intimates how these categories bolstered prescriptions for appropriate social behavior.

The contents of the masculinity and femininity categories are familiar even to those uninitiated into gender-role research. They are constituted by global polarities found in common personality dimensions: instrumental vs. expressive, agentic vs. communal, active vs. passive, independent vs. dependent characteristics. At this level the categories are straightforward and represent nothing more than what is ordinarily meant when one is said to be like a man or woman in our culture. In addition, it is presupposed that the categories are consistent within the individual and that the individual has a sincere desire to manifest them appropriately. The enduring presence of the categories is readily apparent, and in the light of recent feminist studies, so is the unhappy coincidence that the dichotomous personality signifiers indicate behavior norms for social relations between men and women. The present exploration, then, moves beyond these acknowledged conditions in order to locate the means by which scientific psychologists (while avowing an ethos of objectivity, disinterestedness, and impartiality) retained the categories. How, in the face of contradictory empirical findings and of nonobservable postulates, were they sustained? The answer involves more than just revealing unreasonable or unscientific practices, because the assumptions under question were also maintained through normal and legitimate scientific procedures. For their maintenance it was necessary that psychologists occasionally override scientific knowledge as well as the knowledge of ordinary people.

The first section of this study examines the procedures and rhetoric whereby even scientific knowledge was rendered dubious in order to uphold the reality of femininity and masculinity. The second section describes the ways in which psychologists were able to verify the nearly ephemeral gender entities as a psychological *reality* and claim *privileged* access to *observing* and *assessing* that reality. Once this psychological phenomenon was secured, the study of masculinity and femininity seemed to consist simply of healthy competition for the most efficient and elegant assessment techniques. The apparent breakdown of the extended research tradition came primarily through challenges raised by feminist scholarship, and even the subsequent revisions of androgyny theory ultimately proved insufficient to meet those challenges.

The methodology of the present study departs from conventional criticism by looking not at faulty scientific ideas but at how the research practices themselves were constructed to foster certain interests and even to confect certain realities. Historical studies have identified some of the misogynist and androcentric theories in psychology. Yet we must look beyond cranks and heresies to understand how normal scientific practices were integral to the construction and maintenance of an "engendered" psychological reality. The study does not deny the existence of gender differences but rather questions the particular forms ascribed to these differences and the means by which they were sustained. The fact that these practices confirmed the mundane realities of social life, the ethnopsychology of gender categories, makes it surprising that psychologists even had the troubles they did in locating masculinity and femininity.

Discovering Masculinity and Femininity Through Science

In his comprehensive review of sex difference research, Havelock Ellis (1894) noted the ideological distortions frequently imposed on the subject. For these ideological biases, Ellis prescribed the remedy of empirical inquiry, particularly the "new" scientific psychology which "lays the axe at the root of many pseudoscientific superstitions" (p. 513). However, he cautioned that science reveals only factual, not potential, conditions, for "our present knowledge of men and women cannot tell us what they might be or what they ought to be, but what they actually are, under the conditions of civilization" (p. 513). Within a decade, numerous American psychologists had taken up the question of sex differences. While acknowledging the precedent of Ellis's work, they professed closer alignment with the empirical spirit of providing what Helen Thompson Woolley (1903) described as the "original investigation" that his study lacked (p. 2). As did many of her cohorts, Thompson Woolley reached somewhat different conclusions than Ellis, for though she admonished pseudoscientific theorizing and anticipated the fruits of objective experimentation, she believed that modifications in social life could or would alter psychological sex differences. With agreement on the correct methods for knowledge acquisition, Ellis and Thompson Woolley disagreed on whether or not the psychology of the sexes might change, or be perfected, with the former betting on nature's desires and the latter on the effects of social organization. Nevertheless, the psychologist's task was not to explore the dynamics of social perfectibility but to better the process of knowledge production. The normative notion of bettering gender arrangements was taken to be another problem altogether.

Thompson Woolley's careful laboratory research resembles a host of similar studies, many of them conducted by women (such as Mary Whiton Calkins, Leta Hollingworth, Catherine Cox Miles, and Margaret Floy Washburn) who, with the new opportunities for higher education, turned to intellectual questions that were not far removed from their own lives

(Rosenberg, 1982). Thompson Woolley's dissertation (1903) reported experiments on sex differences in motor, affective, sensory, and intellectual abilities. Within the next three decades hundreds of studies assessed these sex differences as well as those to be found in the association of ideas, color preference, handwriting, remembering of advertisements and moving pictures, motor efficiency, nervous behavior of nursery school children, fear responses, reading speed, credulity regarding fortune telling, stammering, scope of attention, reasoning, and ideals and tastes, not to mention knowledge of psychology after the first course (see Allen, 1927, 1930; Hollingworth, 1916, 1918; Johnson & Terman 1940; Thompson Woolley, 1910, 1914).

The research on the psychology of sex created some confusion because many of the studies reported no or minor sex differences and those finding differences often indicated female superiority. Probably no study equalled the impact of the intelligence research as measured by the new mental tests. In revising the Binet-Simon Intelligence Scale, Lewis Terman (1917) tested 1,000 children and found slight superiority of girls. The results led him to consider why women had not attained eminence and ultimately to suggest that their failure "may be due to wholly extraneous factors." Even before Terman's standardized test, other investigators found few significant sex differences on measures of mental abilities. In her 1914 review of the psychology of sex, Thompson Woolley reported these findings with a cynical conclusion: "On the whole then, girls have stood better than boys in measures of general intelligence. So far as I know, no one has drawn the conclusion that girls have greater native ability than boys. One is tempted to indulge in idle speculation as to whether this admirable restraint from hasty generalization would have been equally marked had the sex findings been reversed!" (p. 365). The reported differences were often so slight that Hollingworth (1918) claimed that any reviewer who restricted himself to reporting sex differences on mental traits would "automatically tend to do himself out of his review. He would have very little to report" (p. 428).

Despite such enthusiasm, the wide-scale operation to attain objective scientific knowledge of the psychology of sex faltered, and by 1930 was mired in complications due to inconsistent findings and a paucity of studies on social factors as well as to professional difficulties of the women psychologists who undertook a substantial amount of the research (see Rosenberg, 1982). Yet, the persistent spirit behind the project was far from exhausted though the problems encountered by experimentalists were serious. For those who had posited the superiority of males on tasks involving general mental ability the ground had fallen away, for the new intelligence tests left their position unsubstantiated. While experimental studies were indicating that males and females diverged on some measures, they gave no coherent explanation of these differences. They ultimately provided no final test of theory—no indication of whether the differences were environmentally or biologically determined. And because a number of variables could not be controlled, the critical experiment to ascertain the respective natures of males and females could not be performed, at least not on conventional ethical grounds. This limitation plagued more than John B. Watson, who in his autobiography claimed "regret" at not having established "a group of infant farms" where various races could be reared under controlled conditions (1936, p. 281), a variation on his earlier proposal for a human laboratory "where squads can be kept at work. Their food, water, sex, and shelter could then be kept under very definite control" (1924, p. 214). In describing these impracticable experiments, some contemplated such perfect controls as Arcady, for their constitution required elimination of all gender-related discrimination (Hinkle, 1920; Thompson Woolley, 1903). What several decades of research apparently had disclosed is that males and females differed on some psychological measures and were similar on others, and that the decisive experiment for ascertaining the essence of gender, while resembling a nonsexist environment, was unfeasible.

The solutions to these problems were of several types. Some psychologists seemed indifferent to the experimental research and proceeded to publish theoretical statements on the psychology of men and women. These researchers frequently intimated that the actualization of psychology as a true science had not yet happened, but they took license as professionals to conjecture, to proffer scientific expertise, on an important psychological and social issue. While lacking experimental evidence, these statements nevertheless represented knowledge of the new "scientific intelligence" as Lippmann (1922) called them, the social scientific experts who had gained a public spotlight during the reform period and later through involvement in the war effort. Thus, G. Stanley Hall (1922) explained that the flapper, rather than exemplifying the demise of femininity in the American woman, actually represented "the bud of a new and better womanhood, and the evolutionary progress of civilization toward maternal femininity." He added, "Our Simon-Binet tests can grade and mark, at least for intelligence, but here they baulk, stammer, and diverge" (p. 780). Watson (1927) identified the dangerous characteristics of modern women which guaranteed that men would opt out of marriage in the next fifty years and suggested behaviorist femininity through careful hygiene for sexual attractiveness. Others turned toward the new "glandular psychology" to learn the final word on masculinity and femininity.

While these respondents exhibited what charitably could be called benign neglect of empirical evidence, others, assured that psychology as science had arrived, stipulated the means for discovering the *real* nature of masculine and feminine. A minor study published in 1922 epitomizes the general logic behind these newer explorations and, therefore, is worthy of extended quotation:

> The mental test seems to have said its utmost on the subject of sex differences, and the results have been on the whole surprisingly at variance with the insistent prejudices of the average man and woman.
>
> When common sense and science clash it is more often science that has the last word, but not always. Occasionally the worm turns, and a supposedly scientific doctrine unacceptable to common sense continues to be scrutinized until a glaring flaw is discovered either in the method or in the interpretation of results that led to the doctrine. The history of medicine is strewn with the wrecks of such doctrines, and psychology bids fair to number at least its fair share of derelict 'scientific' notions. . . .
>
> Very much the same may be said of the small differences apparent in the test scores of men and women. So far as these results suggest the interpretation that the mental differences between the two sexes are after all comparatively insignificant, they suggest something that common sense and universal experience refuse to allow. Such results again promise to stand as the mark of the inadequacy of the psychological test to get at the most important features of mental differentiation (Moore, 1922, p. 210).

Moore depicted the important feature of maleness and femaleness in "natural emotional aptitude, of an unyielding innate divergence that predominates the enthusiasms that are to be expected from the two sexes in identically the same environment" (p. 211). He proceeded to test his hypothesis by measuring these "natural aptitudes" as they were expressed in conversations of men and women on Broadway. He found that male-to-male conversations were typically about money and business while woman-to-woman conversations were about persons of the opposite sex. His hypothesis was confirmed.

In addition to natural aptitudes, other researchers looked for maleness and femaleness in such phenomena as levels of "mental energy" (Leuba, 1926), the "unconscious" (Hamilton, 1931), and in "mind"(Jastrow, 1918, p. 303). Jastrow found the intelligence test to be both "partial" and "artificial," claiming that "deeper and more comprehensive are the allied and supporting processes which gave the cutting edge to the instrument, and determine the temper of the mind, the manner and spirit of its use." Real psychological processes corresponding to masculinity and femininity in everyday life are located "in the habitat of deep psychology, where traits are at once subtle and profound. Here the feminine mind, as all minds in the specialized aspects, becomes most revealing" (p. 314). Discontented with the extant empirical research, this last group of psychologists was convinced that the *real* substance of masculinity and femininity existed but not in what was measured by the myriad mental tests. They argued from the logical premise that *if other* human sciences, notably anatomy, physiology and pathology reveal man as man and woman as woman, then "What reason is there to suspect psychology to enter a dissenting opinion?" (Jastrow, 1918, p. 303).

Producing the Subject of Psychological Science

Given these general trends in psychology, and given the rather audacious ad hoc theorizing without supporting "facts," or without any facts, it appears that some psychologists were engaging in sex role stereotyping. Perhaps they were subjects of a "cultural lag" similar to that which Eagley (1978) detected in some psychologists of a later period. But while investigations of masculinity and femininity seem to have diverged from conventional research practices, perhaps to accommodate particular sex role stereotypes, they also converged with those practices in several revealing ways. They emphasized detached objective observation and the consequential devaluation and even denigration of subjective observations. The ordinary observer or self-observer came to be seen as an incomplete psychologist at best (Watson, 1919; Robinson, 1926); he or she was unable to identify the true causes of behavior (Dashiell, 1928). The image of the incompetent subject gained support not only with the intensified dedication to rigorous objective techniques but also with concurrent assumptions about the complexity and causal interdependence of human actions (Haskell, 1977). The idea of the causal complexity of human action gained adherents throughout the early twentieth-century, and it dovetailed with another social assumption adopted by psychology: the increasing human disorder and the consequent need for rational control. While these concerns were voiced in the progressive era (Haber, 1964; Wiebe, 1967) and reinforced with the successes of applied social science in the war effort, they were amplified by psychologists in the 1920s and 1930s (O'Donnell, 1979; Samelson, 1979; Sokal, 1984). Scientists in general showed escalated concern about human ignorance and about the scientists' leadership responsibilities (Kaplan, 1956; Tobey, 1971). For instance Edward Thorndike (1920) suggested that the average citizen, the "half-educated man," should relinquish decision making to the experts.

Similar portraits of human irrationality were depicted by psychologists as were the pleas for scientific, particularly psychological, control (Danziger, 1979; Morawski, 1982, 1983, 1984b). Psychologists became more vocal about their role in bringing social problems under control (Allport, 1924; Angell, 1929; Dunlap, 1920, 1928; Terman, 1922 a and b). For many, control became a fundamental component of the definition of psychology: "Ultimately it is a desire to get *control*" (Dashiell, 1928, p. 6). Even the seemingly most detached researchers saw the world in "dire need" of control over human conduct (Hull, 1935, p. 515).

Of the institutions needing control, marriage and family life were thought to be central for they constituted the primary source for individual well-being and for socialization of adjusted adults. Researchers proceeded with several premises: that the family is universal, the nuclear family being the most natural form; that the role of the mother is primary in the socialization of children; and that childrearing failures were to be interpreted as failures of mothers. Intimated in these premises is the preference for studying only adult heterosexual relationships in the context of the nuclear family (Morawski, 1984b).

The shifts in research orientations over the four decades indicate more than innovative conceptual strategies for pursuing an empirical question; they represent an intriguing deviation from mainstream psychology. The conceptual changes proceeded from a search for corporeal differences, then to cognitive and behavioral differences, and eventually to postulates about hidden but salient, nonconscious substrates of masculinity and femininity. To some extent the changes resemble the broader transition from structuralism and introspectionism to behaviorism which was then occurring in American psychology. However, the study of the sexes deviates significantly from that pattern. The rise in behaviorism, although meeting more resistance than is typically believed, involved an extensive exorcism of nonobservable or mentalist phenomena. Even excluding extremists such as John B. Watson and Karl Lashley there was an emerging consensus that psychology consisted of the objective study of observable events. Mind, self, consciousness, and personality traits were like epiphenomena. Personality traits were taken as merely descriptive aspects of more fundamental causal mechanisms since they are, behaviorally speaking, "the individual's characteristic reactions to social stimuli, and the quality of his adaptations to the social features of his environment" (Allport, 1924, p. 101). The ascendency of objective and behavioral psychology foreshortened the search for any real mental mechanisms; even though individual differences research continued, behaviorism challenged the plausibility of interior mental entities such as ethnic and racial traits (Cravens & Burnham, 1971; Samelson, 1978, 1979).

Psychologists' particular interest in the diagnoses and eventual remediation of social disorders provides an important clue to the persistent intrigue with male and female psychological functioning. These interests help explicate the continued discourse on masculinity and femininity which often deviated from current theoretical and methodological trends and disregarded empirical findings. At least hypothetically, standardized tests promised to rectify some of the empirical problems while serving the overall practical interests in control. Hence there ensued a quiet transition from the study of sex differences to the exploration of "masculinity" and "femininity."

The Solution of
Terman and Miles

Challenged by the muddled state of masculinity and femininity research and specifically "by the lack of the definiteness with respect to what these terms should connote," Lewis Terman and Catherine Cox Miles (1936, p. vi) undertook an extensive project in the early 1920s. They were moved by the questioning of the very existence of such entities which was being made by some psychologists and anthropologists, notably Margaret Mead. Nevertheless, they began with the premise that masculinity and femininity were real. Terman and Miles understood their task to resemble the earlier efforts to eradicate misconceptions about intelligence: like Binet's transformation of intelligence research, they sought "a quantification of procedures and concepts" (p. vi). They believed that despite the failures to determine the origin of sex-related attributes and the inability to attain observer agreement on the content of these attributes, there existed considerable clarity in the composite pictures of femininity and masculinity. Hence, the only assumption Terman and Miles suspended was that about origins; however, like previous researchers they lamented the ethical impossibility of conducting the study, the experimental rearing of infants, that could reveal those origins (p. 464).

Terman and Miles (1936) constructed a test to give "a more factual basis" to ordinary concepts of masculinity and femininity by accumulating test items on which males and females differed (p. 3). A preliminary version of the test was given to members of Terman's group of gifted children, and in this pretesting they observed their first case of a high cross-sex scorer displaying homosexual tendencies, or "sexual inversion." The final product of the psychometric project was a 910-item test with seven subtests: word association, ink-blot association, general information, emotional and ethical attitudes, interests, opinions, and introvertive response. Most subtests were compiled by modifying existing tests on those phenomena according to two criteria: selection of items that best discriminate the responses of males and females, and maximization of the efficiency and economy of test administration. Items were converted to multiple-choice format where two of the response alternatives were feminine and two masculine. Validity was assessed by ascertaining overlap of score distributions for male and female samples and by correlations with independent measures of femininity and masculinity. Since there was no other psychometric measure for ascertaining validity, comparison data were obtained from clinical studies.

The contents of the test perhaps now appear as an intriguing cultural artifact, but it did discriminate successfully between females and males. Scores of the sexes differed on average by 122 points and only about 10 out of 1000 subjects of each sex had scores exceeding the mean of the other sex (Terman & Miles, 1936, p. 371). The Attitude-Interest Analysis Test (AIST), as the M-F scale was titled to mask its purpose, contains masculine response items such as those requiring negative responses to the questions "Do you like to have people tell you their troubles?", "Do you usually get to do the things that please you most?", "Do you some- times wish you had never been born?", and "Do you feel that you are getting a square deal in life?" Femininity points are attained by responding negatively to the questions "Do people ever say you are a bad loser?", "Do you feel bored a large share of the time?", and "Were you ever fond of playing with snakes?" Masculinity points are gained by replying that you dislike foreigners, religious men, women cleverer than you are, dancing, guessing games, being alone, and thin women. Femininity points are accrued by indicating dislike for sideshow freaks, bashful men, riding bicycles, giving advice, bald-headed men, and very cautious people.

AIST correlated with only a small number of other personality inven- tories and poorly with measures of marital adjustment. The scores varied considerably for different age groups (for both sexes, scores declined in older samples), and the test was susceptible to faking. Qualitative com- parison of the test results and clinical measures of abnormalities such as homosexuality and female delinquency was more promising: The AIST detected "roughly, degree of inversion of the sex temperament, and it is probably from inverts in this sense that homosexuals are chiefly recruited" (p. 467). Despite its limitations, Terman and Miles endorsed the scale and its potential. Use of the AIST promised to "help clean up the confused notions which are current with regard to what constitutes masculinity and femininity of personality. The fact seems to be that most of us have not acquired the ability to discriminate very clearly the genuinely mas- culine from the genuinely feminine" (pp. 465–466).

Convinced of the everyday inability to make such discriminations and of the detrimental effects of such judgment errors, Terman and Miles conducted a study on psychologists showing that even professionals, without the use of scientific techniques such as the AIST, were inadequate judges of masculinity and femininity (pp. 454–459). Such findings sup- ported the hypothesis that "the test scores do have behavioral correlates but that ordinary observers lack adeptness in detecting them" (p. 465). The authors confidently anticipated use of the test in clinical diagnosis and in ameliorating familial and marital maladjustments. They refrained from relating their results to the environment-heredity controversy over the origins of sex differences. However, they offered a clear conception of psychological well-being, a model equating mental health with definitive correspondence between psychological and biological sex ascriptions. The subsequent research of Terman and Miles further attests to their interest in relating mental health to gender-based psychological characteristics (Miles, 1942; Terman, 1938).

Production of M-F

Theirs was the first major attempt to assess quantitatively the existence of masculinity and femininity in the psychological realm of temperament and to do so without postulating causality or nature/nurture influences. Terman and Miles had introduced a way of accessing the reality of masculinity and femininity that became a model for constructing scales over the next 25 years. Most of the tests shared with their predecessor three assumptions: that masculinity and femininity existed but at a level that could not be readily identified by the ordinary observer; that the attributes were so psychologically charged that subjects had to be deceived of the true nature of the test lest they fake their response in order to appear socially desirable; and that femininity and masculinity were distinct qualities which were somehow related to psychological stability and deviancy, notably homosexuality and familial troubles. The first two assumptions were supported by the popularity of social theories that conceptualized human action as complex, causally interdependent, and beyond the self-knowledge attainable by the ordinary observer. Later investigations confirmed these conjectures when empirical evidence was found to contradict everyday analysis: Psychometric assessments were showing pedestrian attributions of femininity and masculinity to be in error. The third assumption, that of adjustment and mental health, corresponds with the mandates for reconstructing psychology into a more objective behavioral science that would better serve social control. As stated by two psychologists engaged in an extensive study of sex and marriage: "Some of us feel that if we were permitted to train the management, fewer of the exploring children would get hurt, and more of them would find the happiness they are looking for" (Hamilton & MacGowan, 1928, p. 287). Understanding intimate heterosexual relationships, sexuality, and family life comprised a substantial obligation for socially responsible psychologists.

Just as these assumptions directed conceptualizing about the form and location of "gendered" psyches, so Terman and Miles (1936) also indicated their content. In a quantitative analysis of the findings, they described the masculine psyche as adventurous, mechanically and object oriented, aggressive, self-asserting, fearless, and rough, and the feminine psyche as aesthetically and domestically oriented, sedentary, compassionate, timid, emotional, and fastidious. The two composite minds resemble the Victorian sex role schema of separate spheres (Lewin, 1984 b and c; Rosenberg, 1982). This reconstituted schema lent certainty to the increasingly fuzzy question of the nature of the sexes, and was similar in content to the one Robert Yerkes (1943) generated from his studies of male and female chimpanzee behavior (see Haraway, 1978). This gender schematization can be contrasted with the concurrent changes in the actual social positions of men and women and the alterations and confusions of gender images and roles (for examples, see Filene, 1974; May, 1980; Showalter, 1978). Given the social conditions of the period, the M-F scale itself may have served more than a taxonomic or descriptive function; it offered prescriptions for a moral order. Here the case of Ernest Hemingway's writing is suggestive. While portraying rigidly sex typed characters in his published fiction, his unpublished works include characters who betray, escape, or eschew conventional gender attributes (Latham, 1977). A somewhat different example of two levels of reality is apparent in writings of John B. Watson in which the strong argument for total conditioning and environmental adjustments were to provide behavior directives primarily for certain classes, including that of women (Harris, 1984). Invoking certainty can appear to arrest the flux of an uncertain social reality. Whatever the intended or unintended prescriptive function of the AIST may have been, and whatever the discrepancy between the test findings and other social indicators may mean, the form and content of the scale are significant, for they came to inform later assessment techniques and normative evaluations.

Reproduction of M-F Inventories

Although the AIST was developed according to a psychometric procedure of selecting test items for their ability to discriminate the criterion groups of men and women, it lacked theoretical coherence due to the variety of psychological phenomena tapped by the subscales. Later attempts to construct M-F instruments often focused on a more specific range of psychological phenomena and were considered in terms of particular personality theories. For instance, in the same year that Terman and Miles published their study, two quite specific inventories were reported, one by Edward K. Strong and the other by J. P. and Ruth

Guilford. Strong (1936) prepared a Masculinity-Femininity subscale for his general inventory of vocational interests, the Strong Vocational Interest Blank (SVIB). He reported that although both sexes exhibited more feminine interests with age, sex differences were a major indicator of occupational interest. Strong suspended pronouncement on the origin of these differences, and simply concluded his study by asking, "Are the differences in interest of engineers and lawyers to be found in differences in hormone secretions, or in early attachment to father instead of mother, or in the possession of certain abilities in which the sexes differ?" (p. 65). On the one hand, Strong (1943) cautiously noted that the interests of males and females were more similar than different and that because his inventory also assessed similarities, it was in this sense superior to Terman and Miles' test. On the other hand, he admitted that his inventory was limited in the psychological dimensions it assessed; in the end, he deferred to the findings of Terman and Miles. A later test of occupational preferences also incorporated a M-F subscale (Kuder, 1946).

Guilford and Guilford (1936) attained a sex temperament measure through factor analysis of a test of introversion-extroversion. Guilfords' 101-item Nebraska Personality Inventory contains five factors, one of which is M. Although initially viewing the factor as "masculine-ideal," the investigators chose the "more noncommittal letter M" (p. 121) to signify a factor that was "perhaps masculinity-femininity, or possibly a dominance or ascendance-submission factor" (p. 127). The tentative identification of the masculinity factor later was described with considerable certainty (Guilford & Zimmerman, 1956; Lewin, 1984c). Both the scales of Strong and of the Guilfords, while ostensibly appraising different psychological dimensions, indicated greater aggressiveness, dominance, and fearlessness in males and greater emotionality, subjectivity, and sympathy in females. In both cases checks on external validity were limited and inconclusive.

Masculinity and femininity comprised a subarea of interest in other inventories designed primarily to assess psychological abnormalities. S. R. Hathaway and J. C. McKinley devised the Minnesota Multiphasic Personality Inventory (MMPI) in 1940 to measure traits of importance to the practitioner who "wishes to assay those traits that are commonly characteristic of disabling psychological abnormality" (Hathaway & McKinley, 1951, p. 5). Many of their items were inspired by Terman and Miles' inventory; others were original. The MMPI manual gives no information about the construction of the M-F subscale although other evidence suggests that it was compiled using only a criterion group of 13 male homosexuals (Lewin, 1984b). In developing a subscale of psychological femininity for the California Psychological Inventory (CPI), Harrison Gough (1952) attempted to create a less obtrusive instrument than the

MMPI or SVIB. Gough selected items according to both their differentiation between male and female responses and their subtlety. The resultant
58 true-false questionnaire, containing items like "I am inclined to take
things hard," discriminated between males and females but was only
moderately successful in identifying psychological abnormalities and in
correlating with judgements of trained observers. (Femininity, as interpreted in this scale, is characterized as sensitivity, timidity, compassion,
acquiescence, subjectivity, and sentimentality.) A shortened version of the
scale, the version that was integrated into the CPI, was examined for cross-
cultural validation, accurate identification of adjustment problems, and
correlation with other M-F scales; these checks were only moderately
successful (Gough, 1966, 1975). A third scale of this type is the M-F
subscale of the Depauw Adjustment Inventory (Heston, 1948).

Most of these researchers were concerned that their tests might be
susceptible to either faking or reflecting cultural ideals. Yet they typically
concluded, as did Guilford and Guilford (1936), that their test was sufficiently complex to elude the acumen or disingenuous calculations of the
normal subject. Other researchers were not so readily convinced and
sought to eliminate two possible contaminants of the conventional scales:
(1) "cultural" biases and (2) the possibility that subjects could deceive
testers, and themselves, given the ostensibly common tendency to obscure
issues of sex identity. Solution to these problems of cultural and psychological "noise" was sought by testing symbolic representation through
projective techniques; symbolic representation was believed to be beyond
cultural constraints and the subject's awareness of self. Kate Franck (1946)
designed a projective test of M-F based on the subjects' choices of pictures
with male or female symbols. This and other studies assumed that normal
subjects would prefer opposite sex symbols. The projective study of
drawing styles indicated that men close off areas, expand the stimulus,
seek unity, and use angular and sharp lines while women leave areas
open, elaborate within the stimulus area, and blunt or enclose sharp lines
(Franck and Rosen, 1949). Men tend to create objects such as towers, tools,
and mechanical vehicles. Women tend to construct vases windows, flow-
ers, and human figures. Franck and Rosen compared their findings to Erik
Erikson's analysis of children's play constructions and to Freudian psychoanalysis; they suggested the universality of symbols, and offered
guidelines for evaluating maladjustments in role identification. Other
attempts to appraise the "hidden" or "unconscious" of masculinity and
femininity identification employed projective devices such as draw-a-
person (Caligor, 1951; Machover, 1949), the Thematic Apperception Test
(Webster, 1953), and open-ended word association (Goodenough, 1946).

During the 40-year period, 1930–1970, projective tests were not the
sole means for circumventing cultural artifacts and subject biases. Several

researchers adopted rating scales to permit the subject to evaluate self and others; by indirectly assessing social "ideals" or "stereotypes," they could check deviations from those baselines (Berdie, 1959; Reece, 1964). Berdie (1959) claimed that the adjective check list, because it enabled self-other statements, could measure not just "dimensions" of personality but also "processes" including "such things as identification, repression, self-acceptance, and perception" (p. 327). These researchers presumed the primacy of sex role identification for mental health, and that direct behavioral responses which reflect these underlying processes comprised valuable information for clinical practice. Measurement of other behavior indices of masculinity and femininity sometimes (Gray, 1957) though not always (Rosenberg & Sutton-Smith, 1959) linked sex role identification with these elusive or unconscious psychological processes.

The qualitative definitions of masculinity and femininity were consistent among these tests, though quantitative reliability checks did not always confirm such consistency (Constantinople, 1973). The tests were routinely constructed with the three core assumptions originally adopted by Terman and Miles: that masculinity and femininity were unavailable to the ordinary observer, that deception was required to deter the subject's natural tendency toward complicity, and that masculine and feminine traits were indicators of psychological adjustment. But the later scales had added grounds for making more adamant claims. By the late 1930s the idea of psychological femininity and masculinity located beyond the awareness of the person was being corroborated by depth psychology. The works of Freud, Jung, and Erikson, all of which gained popularity during the period, hypothesized that potent gender attributes were nonconscious. In addition, experimental research in general psychology was disclosing the various ways that subjects could bias responses, and these findings prompted attempts to design methods for circumventing such "faking" (Caligor, 1951). Thus, the constructs of masculinity and femininity, concepts which more than one researcher compared to atoms and genes, came to be described as knowable but not without calculated pursuit. Note how the search for the phenomena is described:

> . . . when we come to deal with what is often called the "private world" of the individual, comprising as it does, the feelings, urges, beliefs, attitudes, and desires of which he may be only dimly aware and which he is often reluctant to admit even to himself, much less to others, the problems of measurement are of a very different nature. Here the universe which we wish to assay is no longer overt and accessible but covert and jealously guarded (Goodenough, 1946, p. 456).

The subject typically complicated this search by deceptive behaviors: "A man may be an athlete, may know all about automobiles and fly a plane—

and yet be afraid of women. Everyone has known such people, for there are many, who use behavior labeled masculine or feminine by our society to hide their disorientation, often from themselves" (Franck & Rosen, 1949, p. 247).

Other test compilers checked to ensure that subjects' stereotyped ideas about masculinity and femininity did not interfere with the more "subtle" or "true" indices (Nichols, 1962; Reece, 1964). Despite such precautionary circumventions, the constructs of the gender types, when put in verbal form, did not vary much from test to test. Masculine is powerful, strenuous, active, steady, strong, self-confident, with preference for machinery, athletics, working for self, and the external/public life. Feminine is sensitive, compassionate, timid, cautious, irritable, acquiescent, sentimental, preferring artistic and sedentary activities, and the internal/private life. Nevertheless, with the near certainty of the constructs' existence few researchers pronounced on their origins.

Feminist Difference:
Complaint or Challenge?

Although problems of validity were occasionally noted, the general techniques of assessing masculinity and femininity were continued until the 1970s. A serious challenge to the tests appeared with Anne Constantinople's (1973) examination of three central postulates: the unidimensionality of femininity and masculinity, their bipolarity, and their definition in terms of sex differences in item-response. She offered convincing evidence of the theoretical vacuity of the masculinity-femininity construct. While Constantinople's critique examined M-F tests specifically, related research on sex and gender further compromised the tests' accepted validity. Theories of sex roles and sex role socialization were criticized for positing conventional norms for appropriate gender behavior (Block, 1973; Carlson, 1972), for making differential evaluations of male and female attributes (Helson, 1972; Rosenberg, 1973), and for assuming temporal stability of gender-linked traits (Angrist, 1972; Emmerich, 1973). These researchers, and those in feminist studies generally, imperiled not only the credibility of M-F scales but the very reality of "masculine" and "feminine."

An expedient solution to the resulting quandary was offered with the concept of androgyny and the accompanying techniques for its assessment. Introduced in 1974, the Bem Sex Role Inventory (BSRI) measured the ideals of masculinity and femininity in a manner enabling comparison of the degree to which an individual rates high on both attributes. It measured the degree to which an individual is "androgynous," and hence psychologically healthy (Bem, 1974, 1977). During the next few years several similar scales were created (Berzins, Welling, & Wetter, 1978; Heilbrun, 1976; Spence, Helmreich, & Stapp, 1975). Initially, the most popular of these androgyny measures, the BSRI, was recognized as successful in predicting gender-related behaviors, in expanding the range of appropriate or healthy responses (Bem, 1974, 1977), and in detecting life-span changes (Maracek, 1979; White, 1979). The concept was expediently adopted to help explain a wide range of human behaviors, especially those for which clear gender differences were found. The scale became a popular tool for explaining activities in the hospital and boardroom, in the school and romantic encounters. The very idea of androgyny was received as a solution to the ostensible "sexism" of talking about masculinity and femininity. In fact, it offered an escape from openly endorsing those gender categories and a new ideal for evaluating behavior (Bem, 1977; Kaplan, 1976; Lee & Scheurer, 1983). That ideal has little if any relevance to psychosexual matters and illustrates a heightened concern with complex cognitive competencies. While the initial M-F scale of Terman and Miles was intended to tap psycho-sexual maladjustments, the androgyny scales exhibit little relation to sexuality (Storms, 1980). Androgyny researchers have tended to eschew consideration of sexuality in favor of correlating androgyny and those complex cognitive styles believed to be essential in, for example, the workplace (see Colwill, 1982).

The concept has also received both empirical and theoretical challenges, some of which fault androgyny research with incorporating the very same presuppositions that it was intended to eliminate. The critics noted that the newer models retain, even if unintentionally, certain values associated with masculine and feminine, and thus contribute to their ossification as universals (Lott, 1981; Hefner & Rebecca, 1979). Associated with these normative stipulations are untenable prescriptions for psychological health (Kenworthy, 1979). For instance, Sampson (1977) indicated how the "self-contained individualism" assumed in the concept of the androgynous person is a dubious yet essentially unquestioned norm. Others noted how the androgyny models neglect negative attributes and gender similarities (Rosen & Rekers, 1980; White, 1979). And although purportedly sensitive to changes in gender attributes within the individual, these models do not explicate the broader cultural conditions that may mediate or transform these attributes (Kaplan, 1979; Kenworthy, 1979; Sherif, 1982; Worell, 1978). The concept of androgyny has also yielded a questionable record in empirical investigations. The findings of a recent meta-analysis of androgyny research not only confirm some of the theoretical complications but also suggest that neither the BSRI nor the PAQ even adequately predicts psychological well-being (Taylor & Hall, 1982).

The androgyny models were advanced to replace theories that were circumscribed by history and culture; yet they apparently failed to confront their own historically constituted limitations (particularly by assuming transhistorical stability). They renovate rather than replace the rejected presuppositions about the ontology, structure, and desirability of gender concepts (Morawski, 1984a). The criticisms essentially demonstrate that androgyny research proceeded without critical scrutiny of the arguable metatheoretical foundation that subtly guided the entire enterprise of explaining the psychology of gender (Sherif, 1982; Taylor & Hall, 1982; Unger, 1983). Bem (1979) has also come to question the concept. She has suggested that the androgyny concept would sow the seeds of its own destruction by immobilizing the cultural categories of masculinity and femininity and, hence, by undermining its own foundation in those very categories. Bem's (1983) reconsideration of the androgyny construct does acknowledge the historical and cultural processes involved in the construction of gender dichotomies. However, to end the repetitions and sanctioning of a particular reality requires more than acknowledging history. It demands a comprehensive reevaluation of our scientific practices, particularly the reflexivity and empowerment of psychological knowledge.

Repetition in Discoveries

Androgyny research exhibits telling resemblances to the earlier work on femininity and masculinity. Undoubtedly androgyny models no longer prescribe correspondence between biologically ascribed sex and psychologically ascribed gender roles, and they dismiss altogether the issue of sexual deviancy. These "liberating" implications have tended to obscure other qualities of the androgyny scales, most notably their retention of the categorical constructs of femininity and masculinity along with the cultural values associated with them. As such, androgyny may be viewed as extension of an enduring process of pursuing the "real." It forms part of an ostensibly progressive and maybe interminable scientific search for psychological essences by reference to somatic body types, to mind stuff, to personality matter, and eventually to roles and cognitive styles. Androgyny research is part of a pattern whereby appeals to these hypothetical constructs are invoked to locate the hypothetical constructs which were posited initially (those of the masculine and feminine). The process consists of continued indexicality of constructs where, even in the case of androgyny, the idea of gender types is substantiated by indexical relation to previously conjectured constructs. The process in turn engenders objectification and ossification of the constructs. The polarities of masculine and feminine, retaining qualities such as "instrumental" and "expressive" or "agentic" and "communal" action, become fixed, even reified. They come to represent ahistorical entities that potentially can be treated as referents of particular behaviors, traits, or ideals. Masculinity and femininity, then, become symbolic signifiers *and* the signified. Despite the apparent emancipatory implications of the androgyny theories, they, too, are embedded with limiting conditions and valuational underpinnings dictated by these polarities.

A further process operating throughout, by way of protecting the theory from external contamination, might be called "assessment control." There has developed an increasing wariness toward the commonsensical: independent reports or everyday interpretations have become a bias to be minimized or eliminated by implementing deceptive techniques and psychometric complexities. One consequence of this last procedure is the distancing of theory from everyday life. Further, regarding questions of power and privilege, distancing has significant implications for the establishment of norms of conduct. Here we approach the issue of perfectability and must recognize that any conception of betterment—be it of health, working life, or gender arrangements—requires some notion of the good. The masculinity-femininity theorists, purportedly by detaching their conceptual work from social life, have tacitly defined normative objectives by way of reference to an ideal of society and individual behavior within that society. For the earliest theorists the ideals were framed by the nineteenth-century division of labor in both the private and public realms. The test makers of the 1930s and 1940s aligned their ideals with social relations as typified by the nuclear family (hence the concern with marital adjustment, homosexuality, parenting). Their norms were also tied to perceptions of the possible collapse of these social relations. The implicit objectives of the androgyny theorists mirror the virtues of corporate democracy where self-contained individualism and role flexibility (behavioral inconsistency) are desired.

These normative stipulations need not be purposively imposed; their indirect infusion into theoretical work can be seen in the periodic occurrence of unintended reflexivity. The history of gender theorizing illustrates how psychologists' participation in and reflection upon cultural life can affect the primary stipulations in their work (Eagley, 1978; Rosenberg, 1982). Although these occurrences were not the focus of the present study, it is clear that research strategies were altered as a consequence of psychologists' experiences of the world wars, suffrage, the feminist movement of the 1960s, and general transitions in public life.

The support given to the idea of androgyny by feminist psychologists raises several obvious questions. Why did feminists not only subscribe to but participate in the reiteration of cultural concepts and consequently endorse the underlying moral edicts? On one level it is apparent how the concept was, in some senses self-serving: feminist psychologists have been primarily white, professional women who could find in androgyny theory an inspiring model for their own roles in a predominantly male world (not to mention their interests in the desired roles of their male peers). Here may be one case of unintended reflexive thinking. On another level, feminist psychologists may have been vulnerable to the lures of scientific ideals, and to the essentialist psychology that historically underlay the scientific ethos of skeptical empiricism, disinterestedness, and impartiality. Science has been extolled as the primary if not sole technique to work against prejudice and discrimination. Especially for those trained in scientific methods, it is not easy (or sometimes permissible) to acknowledge how scientific rationality itself is fallible (see Lykes & Stewart, 1983); yet the grounds of rationality are derived by social consensus and can be renegotiated and even transformed during normal scientific practice (Knorr-Cetina, 1981; Shapin, 1982). That feminist psychologists throughout the century would entrust their work to the superior rationality of scientific knowledge makes sense (as does the particular faith in psychology with its legacy of social reformism). This adherence is even more comprehensible given the resistance of the discipline to critically confronting the positivist metaphysics and naive realism which has both prefigured our observations of psychological reality as well as foreshortened our understanding of epistemological alternatives.

Toward New Theory

The exploration of masculinity and femininity is but one aspect of the history of gender research, and although highly informative work on the subject is now appearing (Lewin, 1984a; Rosenberg, 1982; Shields, 1975, 1982), further investigation is needed. Such historical ventures, along with those on the history of the actual practices of gender relations, offer correctives to current research (Morawski, 1984a). The history reviewed here suggests a reconsideration of the entire project of developing theory through a critical unpacking of our habits of theorizing and the generation of new theoretical frameworks. Such reconsideration begins with a critical and historical framework. It is critical in the sense of holding that all attempts to establish knowledge claims should be evaluated not simply in terms of empirical confirmation but also in terms of the very criteria of reliable knowledge and rationality that are attributed to the knower (psychologist). It is historical in the sense that knowledge claims must be understood as historical products, as constructions guided by particular interests and problematics. Neither of these provisions necessarily implies any radical relativism (Rorty, 1982, pp. 160–175).

Given this general superstructure, several issues fundamental to constructing gender theory must be considered. Most obvious is the need to take the broader context, and consequently reflexivity, seriously (Unger, 1983). The comprehensive social context must be understood if, borrowing Sherif's (1982) illustrations, we are to understand why the androgynous person may not be a political feminist or how social power relates to gender-linked behaviors. Such contextualist understanding requires sociological, anthropological, and historical studies (Morawski, 1983; Sherif, 1982) and is inescapably political (Parlee, 1979). A corollary is the need for the researcher to undertake critical self-appraisal as well as assessment of the stipulated canons of rationality (Addelson, 1983; Harding, 1984; Jaggar, 1984) and of the social and political facets of his or her work (Buss, 1979; Eagley, 1978; Flanagan, 1981; Sampson, 1977). Masculinity and femininity research demonstrates how the scientific questions of gender necessarily imply political questions in that even the androgyny theorists posit an idealization of society. Mere tacit endorsement of this idealization (in the case of androgyny an idealization where advances in technology and welfare may mitigate the bases for some gender distinctions) harbors debatable stipulations about the kind of world we are promoting.

The second major area of reconsideration concerns replacing conceptions of human nature that have either distorted or impeded research on gender. In light of the history of gender and of psychology generally, it seems prudent if not profitable at least to consider a working conception of human beings *as* human beings. And if we require any metaphors of powers or essences, those atoms of psychological actions, we consider that they be located in the act of the search, in *language* and its context of use. Simply assuming that human beings are active social agents involved with moral ambitions and with the construction of psychological realities generates numerous possibilities for future research. Some contributions in this direction include the study of the phenomenology of gender labeling (Kessler & McKenna, 1978), dialectics of sex role transcendence (Hefner & Rebecca, 1979), alternatives to the orthodox psychoanalytic theories of socialization (Chodorow, 1978; Dinnerstein, 1976; see Steele, in press), and gender styles in moral decision making (Gilligan, 1982). These basic conceptions also imply reappraisal of the conventional modes of assessment control: it is necessary to examine how we empower certain voices (the researcher's) and not others with inordinate privilege, and how we define authority and rationality (Addelson, 1983; Harding, 1984). Whether this empowering is seen as the hegemony of masculine science or as a concomitant of everyday life, in gender research it has profoundly affected theory as well as empirical findings.

These general architectonics simply intimate possibilities for theory construction which are informed by a systematic rereading of the historical

record. They address some of the repeatedly evaded temporal, epistemological, and moral dimensions of research. Yet if we choose to participate
in generating novel ways of looking at the social world as, at least
hypothetically, scientists have sought new ways of viewing the natural
world, then we must first audit our inventory of artifactual and conventional beliefs.

References

Addelson, K. P. (1983). The man of professional wisdom. In S. Harding & M. B.
    Hintikka (Eds.), *Discovering reality* (pp. 165–186). Boston: D. Reidel.
Allen, C. (1927). Studies in sex differences. *Psychological Bulletin, 24,* 294–304.
Allen, C. (1930). Recent studies in sex differences. *Psychological Bulletin, 27,* 394–
    407.
Allport, F. H. (1924). *Social psychology.* Boston: Houghton Mifflin.
Angell, J. R. (1929, April 19). Yale's Institute of Human Relations. *Yale Alumni
    Weekly* (pp. 889–891).
Angrist, S. (1972). The study of sex roles. In J. M. Bardwick (Ed.), *Readings on the
    psychology of women* (pp. 101–106). New York: Harper & Row.
Bem, S. L. (1974). The measurement of psychological androgyny. *Journal of Con-
    sulting and Clinical Psychology, 42,* 155–162.
Bem, S. L. (1977). On the utility of alternative procedures for assessing psycholog-
    ical androgyny. *Journal of Consulting and Clinical Psychology, 45,* 196–205.
Bem, S. L. (1979). Theory and measurement of androgyny: A reply to Pedhazur-
    Tetenbaum and Locksley-Colten critiques. *Journal of Personality and Social
    Psychology, 37,* 1047–1054.
Bem, S. L. (1983). Gender schema theory and its implications for child develop-
    ment: Raising gender-aschematic children in a gender-schematic society. *Signs,
    8,* 598–616.
Berdie, R. F. (1959). A femininity adjective check list. *Journal of Applied Psychology,
    43,* 327–333.
Berzins, J. I., Welling, M. A., & Wetter, R. E. (1978). A new measure of psychological
    androgyny based on the Personality Research Form. *Journal of Consulting and
    Clinical Psychology, 46,* 126–138.
Block, J. H. (1973). Conceptions of sex role: Some cross-cultural and longitudinal
    perspectives. *American Psychologist, 28,* 512–526.
Buss, A. R. (Ed.). (1979). *Psychology in social context.* New York: Irvington.
Caligor, L. (1951). The determination of the individual's unconscious conception
    of his own masculinity-femininity identification. *Journal of Projective Tech-
    niques and Personality Assessment, 15,* 494–509.
Carlson, R. (1972). Understanding women: Implications for personality theory and
    research. *Journal of Social Issues, 28,* 17–32.
Chodorow, N. (1978). *The reproduction of mothering: Psychoanalysis and the sociology
    of gender.* Berkeley: University of California.

Colwill, N. L. (1982). *The new partnership: Women and men in organizations*. Palo Alto, CA: Mayfield.

Constantinople, A. (1973). Masculinity-femininity. An exception to a famous dictum. *Psychological Bulletin, 80*, 389–407.

Cravens, H., & Burnham, J. C. (1971). Psychology and evolutionary naturalism in American thought, 1890–1940. *American Quarterly, 23*, 635–657.

Danziger, K. (1979). The social origins of modern psychology. In A. R. Buss (Ed.), *Psychology in social context* (pp. 27–45). New York: Irvington.

Dashiell, J. F. (1928). *Fundamentals of objective psychology*. Boston: Houghton Mifflin.

Dinnerstein, D. (1976). *The mermaid and the minotaur: Sexual arrangements and human malaise*. New York: Harper & Row.

Dunlap, K. (1920). Social need for scientific psychology. *Scientific Monthly, 11*, 502–517.

Dunlap, K. (1928). The applications of psychology to social problems. In C. Murchison (Ed.), *Psychologics of 1925* (pp. 353–379). Worcester: Clark University Press.

Eagley, A. H. (1978). Sex differences in influenceability. *Psychological Bulletin, 85*, 86–116.

Ellis, H. H. (1894). *Man and woman: A study of human secondary characters*. London: Walter Scott.

Emmerich, W. (1973). Socialization and sex role development. In P. B. Baltes & K. W. Schaie (Eds.), *Life-span developmental psychology: Personality and socialization*. New York: Academic Press.

Filene, P. G. (1974). *Him/her/self: Sex roles in modern America*. New York: Harcourt Brace Jovanovich.

Flanagan, O. J., Jr. (1981). Psychology, progress, and the problem of reflexivity: A study in the epistemological foundations of psychology. *Journal of the History of the Behavioral Sciences, 17*, 375–386.

Franck, K. (1946). Preference for sex symbols and their personality correlates. *Genetic Psychology Monograph, 33*, 73–123.

Franck, K., & Rosen, E. (1949). A projective test of masculinity-femininity. *Journal of Consulting Psychology, 13*, 247–256.

Gilligan, C. (1982). *In a different voice: Psychological theory and women's development*. Cambridge: Harvard University Press.

Goodenough, F. L. (1946). Semantic choice and personality structure. *Science, 104*, 451–456.

Gough, H. G. (1952). Identifying psychological femininity. *Educational and Psychological Measurement, 12*, 427–439.

Gough, H. G. (1966). A cross-cultural analysis of the CPI Femininity Scale. *Journal of Consulting Psychology, 30*, 136–141.

Gough, H. G. (1975). *California psychological inventory: Manual* (rev. ed.). Palo Alto: Consulting Psychologists Press.

Gray, S. W. (1957). Masculinity-femininity in relation to anxiety and social acceptance. *Child Development, 28*, 203–214.

Guilford, J. P., & Guilford, R. B. (1936). Personality factors S, E, and M and their measurement. *Journal of Psychology, 2*, 109–127.

Guilford, J. P., & Zimmerman, W. S. (1956). *The Guilford-Zimmerman temperament survey: Manual of instructions and interpretations.* Beverly Hills, CA: Sheridan Supply.

Haber, S. (1964). *Efficiency and uplift: Scientific management in the progressive era, 1890–1920.* Chicago: University of Chicago Press.

Hall, G. S. (1922). Flapper Americana novissima. *Atlantic Monthly, 129,* 771–780.

Hamilton, G. V. (1931). The emotional life of modern woman. In S. D. Schmalhausen & V. F. Calverton (Eds.), *Woman's coming of age* (pp. 207–229). New York: Horace Liveright.

Hamilton, G. V., & MacGowan, K. (1928). Marriage and love affairs. *Harpers, 157,* 277–287.

Haraway, D. (1978). Animal sociology and a natural economy of the body politic. Part I: A political physiology of dominance. *Signs, 4,* 21–36.

Harding, S. (1984). Is gender a variable in conceptions of rationality? A survey of issues. In Carol C. Gould (Ed.), *Beyond domination: New perspective on women and philosophy* (pp. 43–63). Totowa, NJ: Rowman & Allanheld.

Harris, B. (1984). Give me a dozen healthy infants: John B. Watson's popular advice on childrearing, woman, and the family. In M. Lewin (Ed.), *In the shadow of the past: Psychology portrays the sexes.* New York: Columbia University Press.

Haskell, T. L. (1977). *The emergence of professional social science.* (Urbana: University of Illinois Press.

Hathaway, S. R., & McKinley, J. C. (1951). *Manual for the Minnesota multiphasic personality inventory* (rev. ed). Minneapolis: University of Minnesota Press.

Hefner, R., & Rebecca, M. (1979). The future of sex roles. In M. Richmond-Abbott (Ed.), *The American woman: Her past, her present, her future* (pp. 243–264). New York: Holt, Rinehart & Winston.

Heilbrun, A. B., Jr. (1976). Measurement of masculine and feminine sex role identities as independent dimensions. *Journal of Consulting and Clinical Psychology, 44,* 183–190.

Helson, R. (1972). The changing image of the career woman. *Journal of Social Issues, 28,* 33–46.

Heston, J. C. (1948). A comparison of four masculinity-femininity scales. *Educational and Psychological Measurement, 8,* 375–387.

Hinkle, B. M. (1920). On the arbitrary use of the terms "masculine" and "feminine." *Psychoanalytic Review, 7,* 15–30.

Hollingworth, L. S. (1916). Sex differences in mental traits. *The Psychological Bulletin, 13,* 377–384.

Hollingworth, L. S. (1918). Comparison of the sexes in mental traits. *Psychological Bulletin, 15,* 427–432.

Hull, C. L. (1935). The conflicting psychologies of learning—A way out. *The Psychological Review, 42,* 491–516.

Jaggar, A. (1984). Human biology in feminist theory: Sexual equality reconsidered. In Carol Gould (Ed.), *Beyond domination: New perspectives on women and philosophy* (pp. 21–42). Totowa, NJ: Rowman & Allanheld.

Jastrow, J. (1918). The feminine mind. In J. Jastrow (Ed.), *The psychology of conviction* (pp. 280–325). New York: Houghton Mifflin.

Johnson, W. B., & Terman, L. B. (1940). Some highlights in the literature of psychological sex differences published since 1920. *Journal of Psychology, 9,* 327–336.

Kaplan, A. G. (1976). Androgyny as a model of mental health for woman: From theory to therapy. In A. G. Kaplan & J. P. Bean (Eds.), *Beyond sex role stereotypes: Readings toward a psychology of androgyny* (pp. 352–362). Boston: Little Brown.

Kaplan, A. G. (1979). Clarifying the concept of androgyny: Implications for therapy. *Psychology of Women Quarterly, 3,* 223–230.

Kaplan, S. (1956). Social engineers as saviors: Effects of World War I on some American liberals. *Journal of the History of Ideas, 17,* 347–369.

Kenworthy, J. A. (1979). Androgyny in psychotherapy: But will it sell in Peoria? *Psychology of Women Quarterly, 3,* 231–240.

Kessler, S. J., & McKenna, W. (1978). *Gender: An ethnomethodological approach.* New York: John Wiley & Sons.

Knorr-Cetina, K. D. (1981). *The manufacture of knowledge.* New York: Pergamon Press.

Kuder, G. F. (1946). *Revised manual for the Kuder preference record.* Chicago: Science Research Associates.

Latham, A. (1977, October 16). A farewell to machismo. *New York Times,* 6 (pp. 52–55, 80–82, 90–99).

Lee, A., & Scheurer, V. L. (1983). Psychological androgyny and aspects of self-image in women and men. *Sex Roles, 9,* 289–306.

Leuba, J. H. (1926). The weaker sex. *Atlantic Monthly, 137,* 454–460.

Lewin, M. (Ed.), (1984a). *In the shadow of the past: Psychology portrays the sexes.* New York: Columbia University Press.

Lewin, M. (1984b). Psychology measures femininity and masculinity, II: From "13 Gay Men" to the instrumental-expressive distinction. In M. Lewin (Ed.), *In the shadow of the past: Psychology portrays the sexes* (pp. 197–204). New York: Columbia University Press.

Lewin, M. (1984c). Rather worse than folly? Psychology measures femininity and masculinity, I: From Terman and Miles to the Guilfords. In M. Lewin (Ed.), *In the shadow of the past: Psychology portrays the sexes* (pp. 155–178). New York: Columbia University Press.

Lippmann, W. (1922). *Public opinion.* New York: Macmillan.

Lott, B. (1981). A feminist critique of androgyny: Toward the elimination of gender attributions for learned behavior. In C. Mayo & N. M. Henley (Eds.), *Gender and nonverbal behavior* (pp. 171–180). New York: Springer-Verlag.

Lykes, M. B., & Stewart, A. J. (1983). Evaluating the feminist challenge in psychology: 1963–1983. Paper presented at the 91st Annual Meeting of the American Psychological Association, Anaheim, CA.

Machover, K. (1949). *Personality projection in the drawing of the human figure.* Springfield, IL: Charles C. Thomas.

Maracek, J. (1979). Social change, positive mental health, and psychological androgyny. *Psychology of Women Quarterly, 3,* 241–247.

May, E. T. (1980). *Great expectations: Marriage and divorce in post-Victorian America.* Chicago: University of Chicago Press.

Miles, C. C. (1942). Psychological study of a young man pseudohermaphrodite reared as a female. In J. F. Dashiell (Ed.), *Studies in personality contributed in honor of Lewis M. Terman* (pp. 209–228). New York: McGraw-Hill.

Moore, H. T. (1922). Further data concerning sex differences. *Journal of Abnormal and Social Psychology, 17,* 210–214.

Morawski, J. G. (1982). On thinking about history as social psychology. *Personality and Social Psychology Bulletin, 8,* 393–401.

Morawski, J. G. (1983). Psychology and the shaping of policy. *Berkshire Review, 18,* 92–107.

Morawski, J. G. (1984a). Historiography as metatheoretical text for social psychology. In K. J. Gergen & M. Gergen (Eds.), *Historical social psychology* (pp. 37–60). New York: Erlbaum.

Morawski, J. G. (1984b). Not quite new worlds: Psychologists' conceptions of the ideal family in the twenties. In M. Lewin (Ed.), *In the shadow of the past: Psychology portrays the sexes* (pp. 97–125). New York: Columbia University Press.

Nichols, R. C. (1962). Subtle, obvious, and stereotype measures of masculinity-femininity. *Educational and Psychological Measurement, 22,* 449–461.

O'Donnell, J. M. (1979). The "Crisis of Experimentalism" in the twenties: E. G. Boring and his uses of historiography. *American Psychologist, 34,* 289–295.

Parlee, M. B. (1979). Psychology and women. *Signs, 5,* 121–133.

Reece, M. (1964). Masculinity and femininity: A factor analytical study. *Psychological Reports, 14,* 123–139.

Robinson, E. S. (1926). *Practical psychology: Human nature in everyday life.* New York: Macmillan Co.

Rorty, R. (1982). *The consequences of pragmatism.* Minneapolis: University of Minnesota.

Rosen, A. C., & Rekers, G. A. (1980). Toward a taxanomic framework for variables of sex and gender. *Genetic Psychology Monographs, 102,* 191–218.

Rosenberg, B. G., & Sutton-Smith, B. (1959). The measurement of masculinity and femininity in children. *Child Development, 30,* 373–380.

Rosenberg, M. (1973). The biologic basis for sex role stereotypes. *Contemporary Psychoanalysis, 29,* 374–391.

Rosenberg, R. L. (1982). *Beyond separate spheres: Intellectual origins of modern feminism.* New Haven: Yale University Press.

Samelson, F. (1978). From "Race psychology" to "studies in prejudice." Some observations on the thematic reversals in social psychology. *Journal of the History of the Behavioral Sciences, 14,* 265–278.

Samelson, F. (1979). Putting psychology on the map: Ideology and intelligence testing. In A. R. Buss (Ed.), *Psychology in social context* (pp. 103–167). New York: Irvington.

Sampson, E. E. (1977). Psychology and the American ideal. *Journal of Personality and Social Psychology, 35,* 767–782.

Shapin, S. (1982). History of science and its sociological reconstructions. *History of Science, 20,* 157–207.

Sherif, C. W. (1982). Needed concepts in the study of gender identity. *Psychology of Women Quarterly, 6,* 375–398.

Shields, S. (1975). Functionalism, Darwinism, and the psychology of women. *American Psychologist*, 31, 739–751.

Shields, S. A. (1982). The variability hypothesis: The history of a biological model of sex differences in intelligence. *Signs*, 7, 769–797.

Showalter, E. (Ed.), (1978). *These modern women: Autobiographical essays from the twenties*. Old Westbury, New York: The Feminist Press.

Sokal, M. M. (1984). James McKeen Cattell and American psychology in the 1920s. In J. Brozek (Ed.), *Explorations in the history of psychology in the United States* (pp. 273–323). Lewisburg, PA: Bucknell University Press.

Spence, J. T., Helmreich, R., & Stapp, J. (1975). Ratings of self and peers on sex role attributes and their relation to self-esteem and conceptions of masculinity and femininity. *Journal of Personality and Social Psychology*, 32, 29–39.

Steele, R. (in press), Paradigm lost: Psychoanalysis after Freud. In C. Buxton (Ed.), *Points of view in the modern history of psychology*. New York: Academic Press.

Storms, M. D. (1980). Theories of sexual orientation. *Journal of Personality and Social Psychology*, 1980, 38, 783–792.

Strong, E. K., Jr. (1936). Interests of men and women. *Journal of Social Psychology*, 7, 49–67.

Strong, E. K., Jr. (1943). *Vocational interests of men and women*. Palo Alto: Stanford University Press.

Taylor, M. C., & Hall, J. A. (1982). Psychological androgyny: Theories, methods, and conclusions. *Psychological Bulletin*, 92, 347–366.

Terman, L. (1917). *The Stanford revision and extension of the Binet-Simon Scale for Measuring Intelligence*. Baltimore: Warwick and York.

Terman, L. M. (1922a). The control of propaganda as a psychological problem. *Scientific Monthly*, 14, 234–252.

Terman, L. M. (1922b). The psychological determinist, or democracy and the I. Q. *Journal of Educational Research*, 6, 57–62.

Terman, L. M. (1938). *Psychological factors in marital happiness*. New York: McGraw-Hill.

Terman, L. M., & Miles, C. C. (1936). *Sex and personality*. New York: McGraw-Hill.

Thorndike, E. L. (1920). Psychology of the half-educated man. *Harpers*, 140, 666–670.

Tobey, R. C. (1971). *The American ideology of National Sciences, 1919–1930*. Pittsburgh: University of Pittsburgh Press.

Unger, R. K. (1983). Through the looking glass: No wonderland yet! (The reciprocal relationship between methodology and models of reality.) *Psychology of Women Quarterly*, 8, 9–32.

Watson, J. B. (1919). *Psychology from the standpoint of a behaviorist*. Philadelphia: J. B. Lippincott.

Watson, J. B. (1924). *Behaviorism*. New York: Norton.

Watson, J. B. (1927). The weakness of women. *Nation*, 125, 9–10.

Watson, J. B. (1936). Autobiography. In C. Murchison (Ed.), *A history of psychology in autobiography* (pp. 271–282). Worcester: Clark University Press.

Webster, H. (1953). Derivation and use of the masculinity-femininity variable. *Journal of Clinical Psychology*, 9, 33–36.

White, M. S. (1979). Measuring androgyny in adulthood. *Psychology of Women Quarterly, 3,* 293–307.

Wiebe, R. (1967). *The search for order, 1877–1920.* New York: Hill & Wang.

Woolley, H. B. T. (1903). *The mental traits of sex: An experimental investigation of the normal mind in men and women.* Chicago: University of Chicago Press.

Woolley, H. B. T. (1910). A review on the recent literature on the psychology of sex. *Psychological Bulletin, 7,* 335–342.

Woolley, H. B. T. (1914). The psychology of sex. *Psychological Bulletin, 11,* 353–379.

Worell, J. (1978). Sex roles and psychological well-being: Perspectives on methodology. *Journal of Consulting and Clinical Psychology, 46,* 777–791.

Yerkes, R. M. (1943). *Chimpanzees: A laboratory colony.* New Haven: Yale University Press.

8

THE MEANING OF DIFFERENCE: GENDER THEORY, POSTMODERNISM, AND PSYCHOLOGY

Rachel T. Hare-Mustin
and Jeanne Marecek

Conventional meanings of gender typically focus on difference. They emphasize how women differ from men and use these differences to support the norm of male superiority. The overlooking of gender differences occurs as well. Until recently, psychology accepted the cultural meaning of gender as difference, and psychological research offered scientific justification for gender inequality (Lott, 1985a; Morawski, 1985; Shields, 1975; Weisstein, 1971). Theories of psychotherapy similarly supported the cultural meanings of gender (Hare-Mustin, 1983).

The connection between meaning and power has been a focus of postmodernist thinkers (Foucault, 1973; Jameson, 1981). Their inquiry into meaning focuses especially on language and the process of representation. Our concern here is with language as the medium of cognitive life and communication, rather than as the rules by which sentences are strung together. Language is not simply a mirror of reality or a neutral tool (Bruner, 1986; Taggart, 1985; Wittgenstein, 1960; 1953/1967). Language highlights certain features of the objects it represents, certain meanings of the situations it describes. Once designations in language become accepted, one is constrained by them. Language inevitably structures one's

Rachel T. Hare-Mustin and Jeanne Marecek, "The Meaning of Difference: Gender Theory, Postmodernism, and Psychology." *American Psychologist*, 43, 455–464. Copyright 1988 by the American Psychological Association. Reprinted by permission.

own experience of reality as well as the experience of those to whom one communicates.

Language and meaning making are important resources held by those in power. Indeed, Barthes (1957/1972) has called language a sign system used by the powerful to label, define, and rank. Throughout history, men have had greater influence over language than women. This is not to say that women do not also influence language, but within social groups, males have had privileged access to education and thus have had higher rates of literacy; this remains true in developing countries today (Newland, 1979). In addition, more men are published, and men control the print and electronic media (Strainchamps, 1974). The arbiters of language usage are primarily men, from Samuel Johnson and Noah Webster to H. L. Mencken and Strunk and White. Although not all men have influence over language, for those who do, such authority confers the power to create the world from their point of view, in the image of their desires. This power is obscured when language is regarded simply as description.

Two recent postmodernist movements, constructivism and deconstruction, challenge the idea of a single meaning of reality and concern themselves with the way meaning is represented. The current interest in constructivism and deconstruction is part of a widespread skepticism about the positivist tradition in science and essentialist theories of truth and meaning (Rorty, 1979). Both constructivism and deconstruction assert that meanings are historically situated and constructed and reconstructed through the medium of language.

In this article, we apply postmodernist thought to the psychology of gender. We first take up constructivism. We examine various constructions of gender, and the problems associated with the predominant meaning of gender—that of male-female difference. We then turn to deconstruction. We show how a deconstructive approach to therapeutic discourse can reframe clients' understanding of reality by revealing alternative meanings and thus can promote change. We do not propose a new theory of gender; rather, we shift to a metatheoretical perspective on gender theorizing. Our purpose is not to answer the question of what is the meaning of gender but rather to examine the question.

The Construction of Reality

Constructivism asserts that we do not discover reality, we invent it (Watzlawick, 1984). Our experience does not directly reflect what is "out there" but is an ordering and organizing of it. Knowing is a search for "fitting" ways of behaving and thinking (Von Glaserfeld, 1984). Rather than passively observing reality, we actively construct the meanings that frame and organize our perceptions and experience. Thus, our understanding of reality is a representation, that is, a "re-presentation," not a replica, of what is "out there." Representations of reality are shared meanings that derive from language, history, and culture. Rorty (1979) suggests that the notion of "accurate representation" is a compliment we pay to those beliefs that are successful in helping us do what we want to do.

Constructivism challenges the scientific tradition of positivism, which holds that reality is fixed and can be observed directly, uninfluenced by the observer (Gergen, 1985; Sampson, 1985; Segal, 1986). As Heisenberg (1952) has pointed out, a truly objective world, devoid of all subjectivity, would be unobservable. Constructivism also challenges the positivist presumption that it is possible to distinguish facts and values; for constructivists, values and attitudes determine what are taken to be facts (Howard, 1985). It is not that formal laws and theories in psychology are wrong or useless, but rather, as Kuhn (1962) asserted, that they are explanations based on a set of social conventions. Thus, whereas positivism asks what are the facts, constructivism asks what are the assumptions; whereas positivism asks what are the answers, constructivism asks what are the questions.

The positivist tradition holds that science is the exemplar of the right use of reason, neutral in its methods, socially beneficial in its results (Flax, 1987). Constructivism, and postmodernism more generally, hold that scientific knowledge, like all other knowledge, cannot be disinterested or politically neutral. In psychology, constructivism, drawing on the ideas of Bateson and Maturana, has influenced epistemological developments in systems theories of the family (Dell, 1985). Constructivist views have also been put forth in developmental psychology (Bronfenbrenner, Kessel, Kessen, & White, 1986; Scarr, 1985), in the psychology of women (Unger, 1983), and in the study of human sexuality (Tiefer, 1987). Constructivist views also form the basis of the social constructionism movement in social psychology, which draws inspiration from symbolic anthropology, ethnomethodology, and related movements in sociology and anthropology (Gergen, 1985).

Theories of gender, like other scientific theories, are representations of reality organized by particular assumptive frameworks and reflecting certain interests. In the next section, we examine gender theorizing in psychology and indicate some of the issues that a constructivist approach makes apparent.

The Construction of Gender as Difference

From a constructivist standpoint, the "real" nature of male and female cannot be determined. Constructivism focuses our attention on representations of gender, rather than on gender itself. The very term *gender* illustrates the power of linguistic categories to determine what we know of the world. The use of gender in contexts other than discussions of grammar is quite recent. Gender was appropriated by American feminists to refer to the social quality of distinctions between the sexes (Scott, 1985). Gender is used in contrast to terms like *sex* and *sexual difference* for the explicit purpose of creating a space in which socially mediated differences can be explored apart from biological differences (Unger, 1979). We still lack an adequate term for speaking of each gender. *Male-female* has the advantage of including the entire life span but implies biological characteristics and fails to distinguish humans from other species. *Men-women* is more restrictive, referring specifically to human adults but omitting childhood and adolescence. We use male-female, as well as men-women, especially when we wish to suggest the entire life span.

Just what constitutes "differentness" is a vexing question for the study of sex and gender. Research that focuses on mean differences may produce one conclusion, whereas research that focuses on range and overlap of distributions may produce another (Luria, 1986). Moreover, the size and direction of gender differences in any particular behavior, such as aggression or helping, will vary according to the norms and expectations for men and women made salient by the setting (Eagly & Crowley, 1986; Eagly & Steffen, 1986). Even more troubling, the very criteria for deciding what should constitute a difference as opposed to a similarity are disputed. How much difference makes a difference? Even anatomical differences between men and women can seem trivial when humans are compared with daffodils or ducks.

Psychological inquiry into gender has held to the construction of gender as difference. One recent line of inquiry reexamines gender with the goal of deemphasizing difference by sorting out "genuine" male-female differences from stereotypes. Some examples include Hyde's (1981) meta-analyses of cognitive differences, Maccoby and Jacklin's (1975) review of sex differences, and Eccles's work on math achievement (Eccles & Jacobs, 1986). The results of this work dispute that male-female differences are as universal, as dramatic, or as enduring as has been asserted (Deaux, 1984). Moreover, this line of inquiry sees the origins of difference as largely social and cultural, rather than biological. Thus, most differences between males and females are seen as culturally and historically fluid.

Another line of inquiry, exemplified in recent feminist psychodynamic theories (e.g., Chodorow, 1978; Eichenbaum & Orbach, 1983; Miller, 1976), takes as its goal establishing and reaffirming differences. Although these theories provide varying accounts of the origins of difference, they all emphasize deep-seated and enduring differences between women and men in "core self-structure," identity, and relational capacities. Other theorists have suggested that gender differences in psychic structure give rise to cognitive differences, for example, differences in moral reasoning and in acquiring and organizing knowledge (cf. Belenky, Clinchy, Goldberger, & Tarule, 1986; Gilligan, 1982; Keller, 1985). All these theorists represent differences between men and women as essential, universal (at least within contemporary Western culture), highly dichotomized, and enduring.

These two lines of inquiry have led to two widely held but incompatible representations of gender, one that sees few differences between males and females and another that sees profound differences. Both groups of theorists have offered empirical evidence, primarily quantitative in the first case and qualitative in the second. Rather than debating which representation of gender is "true," we shift to a meta-level, that provided by constructivism.

From the vantage point of constructivism, theories of gender are representations based on conventional distinctions. Such theories embody one or the other of two contrasting biases, alpha bias and beta bias (Hare-Mustin, 1987). Alpha bias is the tendency to exaggerate differences; beta bias is the tendency to minimize or ignore differences.

The alpha-beta schema is in some ways analogous to that in hypothesis testing. In hypothesis testing, alpha or Type I error involves reporting a significant difference when one does not exist; beta or Type II error involves overlooking a significant difference when one does exist. In our formulation, the term *bias* refers not to the probability of "error" (which would imply that there is a "correct" position), but rather to a systematic inclination to emphasize certain aspects of experience and overlook other aspects. This formulation of bias relates to the idea that all knowledge is influenced by the standpoint of the knower. "Taking a standpoint" has been seen by some feminist theorists as a positive strategy for generating new knowledge (Harding, 1986; Hartsock, 1985). Our use of the term bias underscores our contention that all ideas about difference are social constructs that can never perfectly mirror reality. Alpha and beta bias can be seen in representations of gender, race, class, age, and the like. Here we use the alpha-beta schema to examine recent efforts to theorize about gender.

Alpha Bias

Alpha bias is the exaggeration of differences. The view of male and female as different and opposite and thus as having mutually exclusive qualities transcends Western culture and has deep historical roots. Ideas of male-female opposition are present in Eastern philosophy and in the works of Western philosophers from Aristotle, Aquinas, Bacon, and Descartes to the liberal theory of Locke and the romanticism of Rousseau (Grimshaw, 1986). Women have been regarded as the repository of non-masculine traits, an "otherness" men assign to women. Alpha bias has been the prevailing view in our culture and one that has also attracted many feminist theorists.

The scientific model developed by Bacon was based on the distinction between "male" reason and its "female" opposites—passion, lust, and emotion (Keller, 1985). Because women were restricted to the private sphere, they did not have knowledge available in the public realm. When women had knowledge, as in witchcraft, their knowledge was disparaged or repudiated. As Keller points out, women's knowledge was associated with insatiable lust; men's knowledge was assumed to be chaste. In Bacon's model of science, nature was cast in the image of the female, to be subdued, subjected to the penetrating male gaze, and forced to yield up her secrets. Our purpose here is not to provide a critique of gender and science, which has been done elsewhere (cf. Keller, 1985; Merchant, 1980), but to draw attention to the long-standing association of women with nature and emotion, and men with their opposites, reason, technology, and civilization (Ortner, 1974).

In psychology, alpha bias can be seen most readily in psychodynamic theories. Freudian theory takes masculinity and male anatomy as the human standard; femininity and female anatomy are deviations from that standard. The Jungian idea of the animus and the anima places the masculine and the feminine in opposition. More recent psychodynamic theories also depict female experience as sharply divergent from male experience. For example, Erikson (1964) holds that female identity is predicated on "inner space," a somatic design that "harbors . . . a biological, psychological, and ethical commitment to take care of human infancy" (p. 586) and a sensitive indwelling. Male identity is associated with "outer space," which involves intrusiveness, excitement, and mobility, leading to achievement, political domination, and adventure-seeking. In Lacan's (1985) poststructuralist view, women are "outside" language, public discourse, culture, and the law. The female is defined not by what is, but by the absence or lack of the phallus as the prime signifier. These theories all overlook similarities between males and females and emphasize differences.

Parsons's sex role theory, which dominated the social theories of the 1950s and 1960s, also exaggerates male-female differences (Parsons & Bales, 1955). The very language of sex role theory powerfully conveys the sense that roles are fixed and dichotomous, as well as separate and reciprocal (Thorne, 1982). Parsons asserted that men were instrumental and women were expressive, that is, men were task-oriented and women were oriented toward feelings and relationships. Parsons's sex role theory was hailed as providing a scientific basis for separate spheres for men and women. Men's nature suited them for paid work and public life; women became first in "goodness" by making their own needs secondary to those of the family and altruistically donating their services to others (Lipman-Blumen, 1984). Parsons believed that separate spheres for men and women were functional in reducing competition and conflict in the family and thus preserving harmony. The role definitions that Parsons put forward became criteria for distinguishing normal individuals and families from those who were pathological or even pathogenic (cf. Broverman, Broverman, Clarkson, Rosenkrantz, & Vogel, 1970).

Alpha bias, or the inclination to emphasize differences, can also be seen in feminist psychodynamic theories such as those of Chodorow (1978), Eichenbaum and Orbach (1983), Gilligan (1982), and Miller (1976). Their emphasis on women's special nature and the richness of women's inner experience has been an important resource for cultural feminism. Cultural feminism is a movement within feminism that encourages women's culture, celebrates the special qualities of women, and values relations among women as a way to escape the sexism of the larger society.

According to Chodorow (1978), boys and girls undergo contrasting experiences of identity formation during their early years under the social arrangement in which women are the exclusive caretakers of infants. Her influential work, which is based on object relations theory, argues that girls' identity is based on similarity and attachment to their mothers whereas boys' identity is predicated on difference, separateness, and independence. These experiences are thought to result in broad-ranging gender differences in personality structures and psychic needs in adulthood. Women develop a deep-seated motivation to have children; men develop the capacity to participate in the alienating work structures of advanced capitalism. Thus, according to Chodorow, the social structure produces gendered personalities that reproduce the social structure. Although Chodorow locates the psychodynamics of personality development temporally and situationally in Western industrial capitalism, much of the work in psychology based on her ideas overlooks this point. Her work is taken to assert essential differences between women and men and to view these, rather than the social structure, as the basis for gender roles (cf. Chernin, 1986; Eichenbaum & Orbach, 1983; Jordan & Surrey, 1986; Schlachet, 1984). In any case, both Chodorow's theory and the work of her followers emphasize differences and thus exemplify alpha bias.

In her study of women's development, Gilligan (1982) harks back to Parsons's duality, viewing women as relational and men as instrumental and rational. Her theory of women's moral development echoes some of the gender differences asserted by Freud (1925/1964) and Erikson (1964). She describes female identity as rooted in connections and relationships and female morality as based on an ethic of care. However, unlike Freud, she views women's differences from men in a positive light.

A final example of alpha bias comes from the theories of certain French feminists such as Cixous and Irigaray. They have asserted that differences in the structure of the body and in early childhood experience give rise to differences in language and in the sexual desires of men and women (Donovan, 1985).

Beta Bias

Beta bias, the inclination to ignore or minimize differences, has been less prominent in psychological theory, and thus our treatment of it is necessarily briefer. Until recently, beta bias has gone unnoticed in theories of personality and adult development. Prior to the last decade, most generalizations that psychologists made about human behavior were based on observations of males (Wallston, 1981). The male was the norm against which human behavior was measured, and male experience was assumed to represent all experience. Generalizations about human development based only on the male life course represents a partial view of humanity and overlook the many differences in men's and women's experiences.

Overlooking the social context and differences in social evaluation reflects beta bias. Women and men typically have different access to economic and social resources, and their actions have different social meanings and consequences. Beta bias can be seen in recent social policies and legislation that try to provide equal benefits for men and women, such as comparable parental leave and no-fault divorce (Weitzman, 1985). Beta bias can also be seen in educational and therapeutic programs that ignore aspects of the social context. They groom women for personal or professional success by providing training in what are deemed "male" behaviors or skills, such as assertiveness, authoritative speech patterns, or "male" managerial styles. Such programs make the presumption that a certain manner of speaking or acting will elicit the same reaction regardless of the sex of the actor. This can be questioned (Gervasio & Crawford, 1987; Marecek & Hare-Mustin, 1987). For example, asking for a date, a classic task in assertiveness training, is judged differently for a woman than a man (Muehlenhard, 1983).

Beta bias can also be seen in theories that represent male and female roles or traits as counterparts, as in the theory of psychological androgyny. When the idea of counterparts implies symmetry and equivalence, it obscures differences in power and social value. Bem's (1976) theory of psychological androgyny, which involves the creation of a more "balanced" and healthy personality by integrating positive masculine and feminine qualities, implies the equivalence of such qualities (Morawski,

1985; Worrell, 1978), but in fact, the masculine qualities she includes are more highly valued and adaptive (Bem, 1976). This is not to say that every quality associated with males is regarded as positive. Aggression, for instance, is deplored outside of combat situations.

Beta bias occurs in systems approaches to family therapy such as the systems and structural theories of Haley (1976) and Minuchin (1974). The four primary axes along which hierarchies are established in all societies are class, race, gender, and age. Within families, class and race usually are constant, but gender and age vary. However, family systems theories disregard gender and view generation (that is, age) as the central organizing principle in the family (Hare-Mustin, 1987). In so doing, they ignore the fact that mothers and fathers, though they may be of the same generation, do not necessarily hold comparable power and resources in the family. Systems theories put forward a neutered representation of family life (Libow, 1985).

The Question of Utility

Rather than debate the correctness of various representations of gender, the "true" nature of which cannot be known, constructivism examines their utility or consequences. How do representations of gender provide the meanings and symbols that organize scientific and therapeutic practice in psychology? What are the consequences of representations of gender that either emphasize or minimize male-female difference? The alpha-beta schema affords a framework for discussing the utility of gender theories.

Because alpha bias has been the prevailing representation of gender, we first examine its utility. Alpha bias has had a number of effects on our understanding of gender. The idea of gender as male-female difference and the idea of masculinity and femininity as opposite and mutually exclusive poles on a continuum of personality—as in the Terman-Miles M-F Personality Scale (Terman & Miles, 1936), the Femininity Scale of the California Psychological Inventory (Gough, 1964), and other measures (see Constantinople, 1973)—mask inequality between men and women as well as conflict between them. For example, by construing rationality as an essential male quality and relatedness as an essential female quality, theories like those of Gilligan and Parsons conceal the possibility that those qualities result from social inequities and power differences. Many differences of men and women can be seen as associated with their position in the social hierarchy (Eagly, 1983). Men's propensity to reason from principles may stem from the fact that the principles were formulated to promote their interests; women's concern with relationships can be understood as the need to please others that arises from a lack of power

(Hare-Mustin & Marecek, 1986). Typically, those in power advocate rules, discipline, control, and rationality, whereas those without power espouse relatedness and compassion. Thus, in husband-wife conflicts, husbands call on rules and logic, whereas wives call on caring. When women are in the dominant position, however, as in parent-child conflicts, they emphasize rules, whereas children appeal for sympathy and understanding. Such a reversal suggests that these differences can be accounted for by an individual's position in the social hierarchy rather than by gender.

In her interpretations of women's narratives, Gilligan (1982) highlights women's concern with caring and construes it as an essential female attribute. From another point of view, this concern can be seen as the necessity for those in subordinate positions to suppress anger and placate those on whom they depend. In a careful analysis, Hayles (1986) has pointed out that the only female voice that a male world will authorize is one that does not openly express anger.

Feminist psychodynamic theories make assertions of extensive male-female personality differences throughout life. Critics have challenged the idea that a brief period in early life is responsible for broad-ranging differences in men's and women's lives and for gendering all social institutions throughout history (cf. Kagan, 1984; Lott, 1985b; Scott, 1985). Further questions have been raised as to whether changes in patterns of infant caregiving such as Chodorow (1978) and Dinnerstein (1976) have proposed are sufficient to effect social transformation. The alpha bias of feminist psychodynamic theories leads theorists to underplay the influence of economic conditions, social role conditioning, and historical change. Moreover, in focusing on the question of why *differences* exist, feminist psychodynamic theories disregard the question of why *domination* exists.

Alpha bias, the exaggerating of differences between groups, has the additional consequence of ignoring or minimizing within-group variability. Furthermore, out-groups such as women are viewed as more homogeneous than dominant groups (Park & Rothbart, 1982). Thus, men are viewed as individuals, but women are viewed as women. As a result, most psychological theories of gender have not concerned themselves with differences among women that are due to race, class, age, marital status, and social circumstances.

Another consequence of alpha bias is the tendency to view men and women as embodying opposite and mutually exclusive traits. Such a dichotomy seems a caricature of human experience. For example, to maintain the illusion of male autonomy at home and in the workplace, the contribution of women's work must be overlooked. Similarly, the portrayal of women as relational ignores the complexity of their experiences. Rearing children involves achievement, and nurturing others involves power over those in one's care (Hare-Mustin & Marecek, 1986). Gender dichotomies are historically rooted in an era, now past, when the majority of women were not part of the paid labor force (Hare-Mustin, 1988). When gender is represented as dichotomized traits, the possibility that each includes aspects of the other is overlooked.

The autonomy-relatedness dichotomy is not unique; it clearly resembles earlier gender dichotomies, such as instrumentality-expressiveness (Parsons & Bales, 1955) and agency-communion (Bakan, 1966). The idea of man/woman as a universal binary opposition is not a result of faulty definitions but of prevailing ideology, according to Wilden (1972). He has drawn attention to the way that calling the psychosocial and economic relationships of men and women "opposition" imputes a symmetry to a relationship that is unequal. Furthermore, inequality can only be maintained if interrelationships are denied. The representation of gender as opposition has its source, not in some accidental confusion of logical typing, but in the dominant group's interest in preserving the status quo. The cultural preoccupation with gender difference may be the result (Chodorow, 1979). Dinnerstein (1976) points out that women have been discontent with the double standard, but men on the whole are satisfied with it.

In our opinion, an important positive consequence of alpha bias, or focusing on differences between women and men, is that it has allowed some theorists to assert the worth of certain "feminine" qualities. This has the positive effect of countering the cultural devaluation of women and fostering a valued sense of identity in them. The focus on women's special qualities by some feminists has also prompted a critique of cultural values that extol aggression, the pursuit of self-interest, and narrow individualism. It has furnished an impetus for the development of a feminist social ethics and for a variety of philosophical endeavors (Eisenstein, 1983).

Beta bias, or minimizing differences, also has consequences for understanding gender, but its consequences have received less attention. On the positive side, equal treatment under the law has enabled women to gain greater access to educational and occupational opportunities.This enhanced access is largely responsible for the improvement in some women's status in the last two decades.

Arguing for no differences between women and men, however, draws attention away from women's special needs and from differences in power and resources between women and men. In a society in which one group holds most of the power, seemingly neutral actions usually benefit members of that group, as in no-fault divorce or parental leave. In Weitzman's (1985) research, no-fault divorce settlements were found to have raised men's standard of living 42% while lowering that of women and children 73%. Another example is the effort to promote public policies granting comparable parental leave for men and women. Such policies overlook the biological changes in childbirth from which women need to recuperate and the demands of breastfeeding, which are met uniquely by women.

Birth is, paradoxically, both an ordinary event and an extraordinary one, as well as the only visible biological link in the kinship system. The failure of the workplace to accommodate women's special needs associated with childbirth represents beta bias, in which male needs and behaviors set the norm.

In therapy, treating men and women as if they are equal is not always equitable (Gilbert, 1980; Margolin, Talovic, Fernandez, & Onorato, 1983). In marital and family therapy, equal treatment may overlook structural inequality between husband and wife. When the social status and economic resources of the husband exceed those of the wife, quid pro quo bargaining as a strategy for resolving conflicts between partners will not lead to equitable results. "Sex-fair" or "gender-neutral" therapies that advocate nonpreferential and nondifferential treatment of women and men to achieve formal equality may inadvertently foster inequality (Marecek & Kravetz, 1977).

Our purpose in examining representations of gender has not been to catalogue every possible consequence of alpha and beta bias but rather to demonstrate that representation is never neutral. From the vantage point of constructivism, theories of gender can be seen as representations that construct our knowledge and inform social and scientific practice. Representation and meaning in language are the focus of deconstruction. We now turn to the ways in which deconstruction can be used to examine the practice of therapy.

Deconstruction

Just as constructivism denies that there is a single fixed reality, the approach to literary interpretation known as deconstruction denies that texts have a single fixed meaning. Deconstruction offers a means of examining the way language operates below our everyday level of awareness to create meaning (Culler, 1982; Segal, 1986). Deconstruction is generally applied to literary texts, but it can be applied equally readily to scientific texts, or, as we suggest, to therapeutic discourse.

A primary tenet of deconstruction is that texts can generate a variety of meanings in excess of what is intended. In this view, language is not a stable system of correspondences of words to objects but "a sprawling limitless web where there is constant circulation of elements" (Eagleton, 1983, p. 129). The meaning of a word depends on its relation to other words, specifically, its difference from other words.

Deconstruction is based on the philosophy of Derrida, who has pointed out that Western thought is built on a series of interrelated hierarchical oppositions, such as reason-emotion, presence-absence, fact-value, good-evil, male-female (Culler, 1982). In each pair, the terms take their meaning from their opposition to (or difference from) each other; each is defined in terms of what the other is not. Moreover, the first member of each pair is considered "more valuable and a better guide to the truth" (Nehamas, 1987, p. 32). However, Derrida challenges both the opposition and the hierarchy, drawing attention to how each term contains elements of the other and depends for its meaning on the other. It is only by marginalizing their similarities that their meaning as opposites is stabilized and the value of one over the other is sustained.

Just as the meaning of a word partly depends on what the word is not, the meaning of a text partly depends on what the text does not say. Deconstructive readings thus rely on gaps, inconsistencies, and contradictions in the text, and even on metaphorical associations, to reveal meanings present in the text but outside our everyday level of awareness. Our intention here is not to provide a detailed explication of deconstruction but to demonstrate how it can be used to understand therapy and gender.

Therapy, Meaning, and Change

Therapy centers on meaning, and language is its medium. A deconstructivist view of the process of therapy draws attention to the play of meanings in the therapist-client dialogue and the way a therapist uses alternative meanings to create possibilities for change. From this standpoint, we examine the therapeutic process as one in which the client asks the therapist to reveal something about the client beyond the client's awareness, something that the client does not know.

Clients in therapy talk not about "actual" experiences but about reconstructed memories that resemble the original experiences only in certain ways. The client's story conforms to prevailing narrative conventions (Spence, 1982). This means that the client's representation of events moves further and further away from the experience and into a descriptive mode. Experience and its description are not the same. The client as narrator is a creator of his or her world, not a disinterested observer.

The therapist's task of listening and responding to the client's narratives is akin to a deconstructive reading of a text. Both seek to uncover hidden subtexts and multiple levels of meaning. The metaphor of therapy as healing is an idealization that obscures another metaphor, that therapists manipulate meanings. These metaphors are not contrary to each other; rather, as part of helping clients change, therapists change clients' meanings (Haley, 1976). Just as deconstructive readings disrupt the frame of reference within which conventional meanings of a text are organized, so a therapist's interventions disrupt the frame of reference within which the client sees the world. Providing new frames imparts new meanings (Watzlawick, Weakland, & Fisch, 1974). As a multiplicity of meanings becomes apparent through such therapist actions as questioning, explaining, and disregarding, more possibilities for change emerge. The deconstructive process is most apparent in psychoanalysis, but indeed, all therapy involves changing meaning as part of changing behavior.

Gender and Meaning in Therapy

Just as a poem can have many readings, a client's experience can have many meanings. However, as postmodernist scholars have pointed out, certain meanings are privileged because they conform to the explanatory systems of the dominant culture. As a cultural institution whose purpose is to help individuals adapt to their social condition, therapy largely reflects and promulgates privileged meanings. For therapists who bring a social critique to their work, therapy involves bringing out alternative or marginalized meanings. In what follows, we examine certain privileged and marginalized meanings in relation to gender issues, issues that have been the center of considerable debate among therapists and in society at large (Brodsky & Hare-Mustin, 1980).

When we look at Freud's classic case of Dora (Freud, 1905/1963) from a deconstructive perspective, we can see it as a therapist's attempt to adjust the meaning a client attaches to her experience to match the prevailing meanings of the patriarchal society in which she lives. Dora viewed the sexual attentions of her father's associate, Herr K., as unwanted and uninvited. She responded to them with revulsion. Freud framed the encounter with Herr K. as a desirable one for a 14-year-old girl and interpreted Dora's revulsion as disguised sexual arousal. When Dora refused to accept Freud's construction, he labeled her as vengeful and the therapy as a failure.

From our vantage point 90 years after Dora's encounter with Freud, the case shows how meanings embedded in the dominant culture often go unrecognized or unacknowledged. Freud evidently viewed Herr K.'s lecherous advances as acceptable behavior, although Herr K. was married and Dora was only 14 and the daughter of a close family friend. We might surmise that the cultural belief in the primacy of men's sexual needs prevented Freud from seeing Dora's revulsion as genuine.

Freud's analysis of Dora provides an example of how a therapist attempts to reaffirm privileged meanings and marginalize and discourage other meanings. The many meanings of Dora's behavior—and Freud's as well—are evident in the numerous reanalyses, film representations, and critical literary readings of the case.

Conventional meanings of gender are embedded in the language of therapy. Like all language, the language used in therapy can be thought of as metaphoric: it selects, emphasizes, suppresses, and organizes certain features of experience and thus, imparts meaning to experience. For example, "Oedipus complex" imposes the complexity of adult erotic feelings onto the experiences of small children and emphasizes male development and the primacy of the phallus. The metaphor of the "family ledger" in family therapy implies that family relations are (or should be) organized as mercantile exchanges and centered on male achievements (Boszormenyi-Nagy & Sparks, 1973).

Therapists can also use language and metaphor to disrupt dominant meanings. With respect to gender, for example, a therapist may "unpack" the metaphor of "family harmony" and expose the hierarchy by pointing out that accord within the family often is achieved through women's acquiescence and accommodation (Hare-Mustin, 1978, 1987). The stress generated by women's prescribed family roles is marginalized or overlooked (Baruch, Biener, & Barnett, 1987). In unpacking the metaphor of "family loyalty," the therapist may draw attention to the way the needs of some family members are subordinated to those of dominant members in the name of loyalty. Pogrebin (1983) has disrupted such metaphors as "preserving the family," or "the decline of the family," by suggesting that "the family" is a metaphor for male dominance when used in this way.

When the metaphor of "women's dependency" is disrupted, the dependency of men and boys on women as wives and mothers is revealed. Women have traditionally been characterized as dependent, but Lerner (1983) has questioned whether women have been dependent enough, that is, have been able to call on others to meet their needs. The therapist may draw attention to the way men's dependency on women is obscured while women's own dependency needs go unmet.

As we have shown, the resemblance of therapeutic discourse to narrative offers the possibility of using deconstruction as a resource for understanding meaning and the process of therapy. Therapy typically confirms privileged meanings, but deconstruction directs attention to marginalized meanings. Doing therapy from a feminist standpoint is like the deconstructivist's "reading as a woman" (Culler, 1982). The therapist exposes gender-related meanings that reside in culturally embedded metaphors such as "family harmony," but go unacknowledged in the conventional understanding of those metaphors. These examples also show how deconstruction reveals the meanings of gender embedded in the hierarchical opposition of male-female.

Conclusion

Postmodernism makes us aware of connections among meaning, power, and language. A constructivist view of gender theorizing in contemporary psychology reveals that gender is represented as a continuum of psychological difference. This representation serves to simplify and purify the concept of gender; it obscures the complexity of human action and shields both men and women from the discomforting recognition of inequality. Deconstruction focuses attention on hidden meanings in culturally embedded metaphors. Applying deconstruction to the discourse of therapy shows how metaphors also simplify gender by obscuring and marginalizing alternative meanings of gender. From a postmodernist perspective, there is no one "right" view of gender, but various views that present certain paradoxes.

Paradoxes in Gender Theorizing

Paradoxes arise because every representation conceals at the same time it reveals. For example, focusing on gender differences marginalizes and obscures the interrelatedness of women and men as well as the restricted opportunities of both. It also obscures institutional sexism and the extent of male authority.

The issue of gender differences has been a divisive one for feminist scholars. Some believe that differences affirm women's value and special nature; others are concerned that focusing on differences reinforces the status quo and supports inequality, given that the power to define remains with men. A paradox is that efforts to affirm the special value of women's experience and their "inner life" turn attention away from efforts to change the material conditions of women's lives and alleviate institutional sexism (Fine, 1985; Russ, 1986; Tobias, 1986). Another paradox arises from the assertion of a female way of knowing, involving intuition and experiential understanding, rather than logical abstraction. This assertion implies that all other thought is a male way of knowing, and if taken to an extreme, can be used to support the view that women are incapable of rational thought and of acquiring the knowledge of the culture.

There is a paradox faced by any social change movement, including feminism: Its critique is necessarily determined by the nature of the larger social system, and its meanings are embedded in that system. Moreover, feminist separatism, the attempt to avoid male influence by separating from men, leaves intact the larger system of male control in the society. In addition, as Sennett (1980) has observed, even when one's response to authority is defiance, that stance serves to confirm authority just as compliance does. In this regard, Dinnerstein (1976) has suggested that woman is not really the enemy of the system but its loyal opposition.

There is yet another paradox. Qualities such as caring, expressiveness, and concern for relationships are extolled as women's superior virtues and the wellspring of public regeneration. At the same time, however, they are seen as arising from women's subordination (Miller, 1976). When we extol such qualities, do we necessarily also extol women's subordination (Echols, 1983; Ringleheim, 1985)? If subordination makes women "better people," then the perpetuation of women's "goodness" would seem to require the perpetuation of inequality.

The assertion that women are "as good as" men is a source of pride for some women, but it is also a paradox arising from beta bias. Man is the hidden referent in our language and culture. As Spender (1984) points out, "women can only aspire to be as good as a man, there is no point in trying to be as good as a woman" (p. 201). Paradoxically, this attempt at denying differences reaffirms male behavior as the standard against which all behavior is judged.

In conclusion, difference is a problematic and paradoxical way to construe gender. What we see is that alpha and beta bias have similar assumptive frameworks, despite their diverse emphases. Both take the male as the standard of comparison and support the status quo. Both construct gender as attributes of individuals, not as the ongoing relations of men and women, particularly relations of domination. Neither effectively challenges the gender hierarchy. The representation of gender as difference frames the problem of what gender is in such a way that the solution produces "more of the same" (Watzlawick, Weakland, & Fisch, 1974).

The paradoxes we discover when we challenge the construction of gender as difference shake us loose from our conventional thought, revealing meanings that are present but obscured in the dominant view. Contradictions become apparent when we examine the play among meanings and entertain the question of the utility of various representations.

Postmodernism accepts randomness, incoherence, indeterminacy, and paradox, which positivist paradigms are designed to exclude. Postmodernism creates distance from the seemingly fixed language of established meanings and foster skepticism about the fixed nature of reality. Constructing gender is a process, not an answer. In using a postmodernist approach, we open the possibility of theorizing gender in heretofore unimagined ways. Postmodernism allows us to see that as observers of gender we are also its creators.

Notes

A portion of this article was presented at the meeting of the American Psychological Association, New York, August 1987.

References

Bakan, D. (1966). *The duality of human existence*. Chicago: Rand McNally.

Barthes, R. (1972). *Mythologies* (A. Lavers, Trans.). New York: Hill & Wang. (Original work published 1957)

Baruch, G. K., Biener, L., & Barnett, R. C. (1987). Women and gender in research on work and family stress. *American Psychologist, 42*, 130–136.

Belenky, M. F., Clinchy, B. M., Goldberger, N. R., & Tarule, J. M. (1986). *Women's ways of knowing: Development of self, voice, and mind*. New York: Basic Books.

Bem, S. L. (1976). Probing the promise of androgyny. In A. G. Kaplan & J. P. Bean (Eds.), *Beyond sex-role stereotypes: Readings toward a psychology of androgyny* (pp. 48–62). Boston: Little, Brown.

Boszormenyi-Nagy, I., & Sparks, G. M. (1973). *Invisible loyalties*. New York: Harper & Row.

Brodsky, A. M., & Hare-Mustin, R. T. (1980). *Women and psychotherapy: An assessment of research and practice*. New York: Guilford.

Bronfenbrenner, U., Kessel, F., Kessen, W., & White, S. (1986). Toward a critical social history of developmental psychology: A propaedeutic discussion. *American Psychologist, 41*, 1218–1230.

Broverman, I. K., Broverman, D. M., Clarkson, F. E., Rosenkrantz, P., & Vogel, S. R. (1970). Sex role stereotypes and clinical judgments of mental health. *Journal of Consulting Psychology, 34*, 1–7.

Bruner, J. (1986). *Actual minds, possible worlds*. Cambridge, MA: Harvard University Press.

Chernin, K. (1986). *The hungry self: Women, eating, and identity*. New York: Perennial Library.

Chodorow, N. (1978). *The reproduction of mothering*. Berkeley: University of California Press.

Chodorow, N. (1979). Feminism and difference: Gender, relation, and difference in psychoanalytic perspective. *Socialist Review, 9*(4), 51–70.

Constantinople, A. (1973). Masculinity-femininity: An exception to a famous dictum. *Psychological bulletin, 80*, 389–407.

Culler, J. (1982). *On deconstruction: Theory and criticism after structuralism*. Ithaca, NY: Cornell University Press.

Deaux, K. (1984). From individual differences to social categories: Analysis of a decade's research on gender. *American Psychologist, 39*, 105–116.

Dell, P. F. (1985). Understanding Bateson and Maturana: Toward a biological foundation for the social sciences. *Journal of Marital and Family Therapy, 11*, 1–20.

Dinnerstein, D. (1976). *The mermaid and the minotaur*. New York: Harper & Row.

Donovan, J. (1985). *Feminist theory: The intellectual traditions of American feminism.* New York: Ungar.

Eagleton, T. (1983). *Literary theory: An introduction.* Minneapolis: University of Minnesota Press.

Eagly, A. H. (1983). Gender and social influence: A social psychological analysis. *American Psychologist, 38,* 971–981.

Eagly, A. H., & Crowley, M. (1986). Gender and helping behavior: A meta-analytic review of the social psychological literature. *Psychological Bulletin, 100,* 283–308.

Eagly, A. H., & Steffen, V. J. (1986). Gender and aggressive behavior: A meta-analytic review of the social psychological literature. *Psychological Bulletin, 100,* 309–330.

Eccles, J., & Jacobs, J. (1986). Social forces shape math participation. *Signs, 11,* 368–380.

Echols, A. (1983). The new feminism of yin and yang. In A. Snitow, C. Stansell, & S. Thompson (Eds.), *Powers of desire: The politics of sexuality* (pp. 440–459). New York: Monthly Review Press.

Eichenbaum, L., & Orbach, S. (1983). *Understanding women: A feminist psychoanalytic approach.* New York: Basic Books.

Eisenstein, H. (1983). *Contemporary feminist thought.* Boston: G. K. Hall.

Erikson, E. H. (1964). Inner and outer space: Reflections on womanhood. *Daedelus, 93,* 582–606.

Fine, M. (1985). Reflections on a feminist psychology of women. *Psychology of Women Quarterly, 9,* 167–183.

Flax, J. (1987). Postmodernism and gender relations in feminist theory. *Signs, 12,* 621–643.

Foucault, M. (1973). *The order of things.* New York: Vintage.

Freud, S. (1963). *Dora: An analysis of a case of hysteria.* New York: Collier Books. (Original work published 1905)

Freud, S. (1964). Some psychical consequences of the anatomical distinction between the sexes. In J. Strachey (Ed. and Trans.), *Standard edition of the complete psychological works of Sigmund Freud* (Vol. 19, pp. 243–258). London: Hogarth Press. (Original work published 1925)

Gergen, K. J. (1985). The social constructionist movement in modern psychology. *American Psychologist, 40,* 266–275.

Gervasio, A. H., & Crawford, M. (1987). *Social evaluations of assertiveness: A review and reformulation.* Unpublished manuscript, Hamilton College, Clinton, NY.

Gilbert, L. A. (1980). Feminist therapy. In A. M. Brodsky & R. T. Hare-Mustin (Eds.), *Women and psychotherapy: An assessment of research and practice* (pp. 245–265). New York: Guilford.

Gilligan, C. (1982). *In a different voice: Psychological theory and women's development.* Cambridge, MA: Harvard University Press.

Gough, H. G. (1964). *California Psychological Inventory: Manual.* Palo Alto, CA: Consulting Psychologists Press.

Grimshaw, J. (1986). *Philosophy and feminist thinking.* Minneapolis: University of Minnesota Press.

Haley, J. (1976). *Problem-solving therapy.* San Francisco: Jossey-Bass.

Harding, S. (1986). *The science question in feminism.* Ithaca, NY: Cornell University Press.

Hare-Mustin, R. T. (1978). A feminist approach to family therapy. *Family Process, 17,* 181–194.

Hare-Mustin, R. T. (1983). An appraisal of the relationship of women and psychotherapy: 80 years after the case of Dora. *American Psychologist, 38,* 593–601.

Hare-Mustin, R. T. (1987). The problem of gender in family therapy theory. *Family Process, 26,* 15–27.

Hare-Mustin, R. T. (1988). Family change and gender differences: Implications for theory and practice. *Family Relations, 37,* 36–41.

Hare-Mustin, R. T., & Marecek, J. (1986). Autonomy and gender: Some questions for therapists. *Psychotherapy, 23,* 205–212.

Hartsock, N. C. M. (1985). *Money, sex, and power: Toward a feminist historical materialism.* Boston: Northeastern University Press.

Hayles, N. K. (1986). Anger in different voices: Carol Gilligan and *The Mill on the Floss. Signs. 12,* 23–39.

Heisenberg, W. (1952). Philosophic problems of nuclear science (F. C. Hayes, Trans.). New York: Pantheon.

Howard, G. (1985). The role of values in the science of psychology. *American Psychologist, 40,* 255–265.

Hyde, J. S. (1981). How large are cognitive gender differences? *American Psychologist, 36,* 892–901.

Jameson, F. (1981). *The political unconscious: Narrative as a socially symbolic act.* Ithaca, NY: Cornell University Press.

Jordan, J. V., & Surrey, J. L. (1986). The self-in-relation: Empathy and the mother-daughter relationship. In T. Bernay & D. W. Cantor (Eds.), *The psychology of today's woman: New psychoanalytic visions* (pp. 81–104). New York: Analytic Press.

Kagan, J. (1984). *The nature of the child.* New York: Basic Books.

Keller, E. F. (1985). *Reflections on gender and science.* New Haven, CT: Yale University Press.

Kuhn, T. S. (1962). *The structure of scientific revolutions.* Chicago, IL: University of Chicago Press.

Lacan, J. (1985). *Feminine sexuality* (J. Mitchell & J. Rose, Eds.; J. Rose, Trans.). New York: Norton.

Lerner, H. G. (1983). Female dependency in context: Some theoretical and technical considerations. *American Journal of Orthopsychiatry, 53,* 697–705.

Libow, J. (1985). Gender and sex role issues as family secrets. *Journal of Strategic and Systemic Therapies, 4*(2), 32–41.

Lipman-Blumen, J. (1984). *Gender roles and power.* Englewood Cliffs, NY: Prentice-Hall.

Lott, B. (1985a). The potential enrichment of social/personality psychology through feminist research and vice versa. *American Psychologist, 40,* 155–164.

Lott, B. (1985b). *Women's lives: Themes and variations.* Belmont, CA: Brooks/Cole.

Luria, Z. (1986). A methodological critique: On "In a different voice." *Signs, 11*, 316–321.

Maccoby, E. E., & Jacklin, C. N. (1975). *The psychology of sex differences.* Stanford, CA: Stanford University Press.

Marecek, J., & Hare-Mustin, R. T. (1987, March). *Cultural and radical feminism in therapy: Divergent views of change.* Paper presented at the meeting of the American Orthopsychiatric Association, Washington, DC.

Marecek, J., & Kravetz, D. (1977). Women and mental health: A review of feminist change efforts. *Psychiatry, 40,* 323–329.

Margolin, G., Talovic, S., Fernandez, V., & Onorato, R. (1983). Sex role considerations and behavioral marital therapy: Equal does not mean identical. *Journal of Marital and Family Therapy, 9,* 131–145.

Merchant, C. (1980). *The death of nature: Women, ecology, and the scientific revolution.* San Francisco: Harper & Row.

Miller, J. B. (1976). *Toward a new psychology of women.* Boston: Beacon Press.

Minuchin, S. (1974). *Families and family therapy.* Cambridge, MA: Harvard University Press.

Morawski, J. G. (1985). The measurement of masculinity and femininity: Engendering categorical realities. *Journal of Personality, 53,* 196–223.

Muehlenhard, C. L. (1983). Women's assertion and the feminine sex-role stereotype. In V. Frank & E. D. Rothblum (Eds.), *The stereotyping of women: Its effects on mental health* (pp. 153–171). New York: Springer.

Nehamas, A. (1987, October 5). Truth and consequences: How to understand Jacques Derrida. *The New Republic,* pp. 31–36.

Newland, K. (1979). *The sisterhood of man.* New York: Norton.

Ortner, S. B. (1974). Is female to male as nature is to culture? In M. Z. Rosaldo & L. Lamphere (Eds.), *Women, culture, and society* (pp. 67–87). Stanford, CA: Stanford University Press.

Park, B., & Rothbart, M. (1982). Perception of out-group homogeneity and levels of social categorization: Memory for the subordinate attributes of in-group and out-group members. *Journal of Personality and Social Psychology, 42,* 1051–1068.

Parsons, T., & Bales, R. F. (1955). *Family, socialization, and interaction process.* Glencoe, IL: Free Press.

Pogrebin, L. C. (1983). *Family politics: Love and power on an intimate frontier.* New York: McGraw-Hill.

Ringleheim, J. (1985). Women and the Holocaust: A reconsideration of research. *Signs, 10,* 741–761.

Rorty, R. (1979). *Philosophy and the mirror of nature.* Princeton, NJ: Princeton University Press.

Russ, J. (1986). Letter to the editor. *Women's Review of Books, 3*(12), 7.

Sampson, E. E. (1985). The decentralization of identity: Toward a revised concept of personal and social order. *American Psychologist, 40,* 1203–1211.

Scarr, S. (1985). Constructing psychology: Making facts and fables for our times. *American Psychologist, 40,* 499–512.

Schlachet, B. C. (1984). Female role socialization: The analyst and the analysis. In C. M. Brody (Ed.), *Women therapists for working with women* (pp. 55–65). New York: Springer.

Scott, J. (1985, December). *Is gender a useful category of historical analysis?* Paper presented at the meeting of the American Historical Association, New York.

Segal, L. (1986). *The dream of reality: Heinz von Foerster's constructivism.* New York: Norton.

Sennett, R. (1980). *Authority.* New York: Knopf.

Shields, S. A. (1975). Functionalism, Darwinism, and the psychology of women: A study in social myth. *American Psychologist, 30,* 739–754.

Spence, D. P. (1982). *Narrative truth and historical truth.* New York: Norton.

Spender, D. (1984). Defining reality: A powerful tool. In C. Kramarae, M. Schulz, & W. M. O'Barr (Eds.), *Language and power* (pp. 194–205). Beverly Hills, CA: Sage.

Strainchamps, E. (Ed.). (1974). *Rooms with no view: A woman's guide to the man's world of the media.* New York: Harper & Row.

Taggart, M. (1985). The feminist critique in epistemological perspective: Questions of context in family therapy. *Journal of Marital and Family Therapy, 11,* 113–126.

Terman, L. M., & Miles, C. C. (1936). *Sex and personality.* New York: McGraw Hill.

Thorne, B. (1982). Feminist rethinking of the family: An overview. In B. Thorne & M. Yalom (Eds.), *Rethinking the family: some feminist questions* (pp. 1–24). New York: Longmans.

Tiefer, L. (1987). Social constructionism and the study of human sexuality. In P. Shaver & C. Hendrick (Eds.), *Review of Social and Personality Psychology: Vol. 7. Sex and gender* (pp. 70–94). Beverly Hills, CA: Sage.

Tobias, S. (1986). "In a different voice" and its implications for feminism. *Women's Studies in Indiana, 12*(2), 1–2, 4.

Unger, R. K. (1979). Toward a redefinition of sex and gender. *American Psychologist, 34,* 1085–1094.

Unger, R. K. (1983). Through the looking glass: No wonderland yet! (The reciprocal relationship between methodology and models of reality). *Psychology of Women Quarterly, 8,* 9–32.

Von Glaserfeld, E. (1984). An introduction to radical constructivism. In P. Watzlawick (Ed.), *The invented reality: Contributions to constructivism* (pp. 17–40). New York: Norton.

Wallston, B. S. (1981). What are the questions in psychology of women? A feminist approach to research. *Psychology of Women Quarterly, 5,* 597–617.

Watzlawick, P. (Ed.). (1984). *The invented reality: Contributions to constructivism.* New York: Norton.

Watzlawick, P., Weakland, J. H., & Fisch, R. (1974). *Change: Principles of problem formation and problem resolution.* New York: Norton.

Weisstein, N. (1971). Psychology constructs the female. In V. Gornick & B. K. Moran (Eds.), *Woman in sexist society* (pp. 133–146). New York: Basic Books.

Weitzman, L. J. (1985). *The divorce revolution: The unexpected social and economic consequences for women and children in America.* New York: Free Press.

Wilden, A. (1972). *System and structure: Essays in communication and exchange.* London: Tavistock.

Wittgenstein, L. (1960). *Preliminary studies for the "Philosophical Investigations": The blue and brown books.* Oxford: Blackwell.

Wittgenstein, L. (1967). *Philosophical investigations.* Oxford: Blackwell. (Original work published 1953)

Worrell, J. (1978). Sex roles and psychological well-being: Perspectives on methodology. *Journal of Consulting and Clinical Psychology, 46,* 777–791.

9
PSYCHOLOGY RECONSTRUCTS THE FEMALE, 1968–1988

Mary Crawford and Jeanne Marecek

In 1968, Naomi Weisstein published a paper entitled *Kinder, Kirche, Küche as Scientific Law: Psychology Constructs the Female.*[1] Weisstein's paper presented one of the first formulations of the social construction of gender. It also documented biases, stereotypes, and fantasies in psychology's views of women. This work sets the stage for feminist efforts to reconstruct psychological knowledge about women and to develop a psychology of gender. These efforts have been rich and varied, with virtually every intellectual framework and every speciality area in psychology represented. Moreover, there is considerable diversity of opinion as to what questions are important and what forms inquiry should take. Rapid growth has left little time for critical reflection and dialogue. Yet, if the field is to mature rather than just expand, it is important that we critically engage our history.

Critical history examines the values of the field and makes value judgments about its past record. Creating such a history helps the field to develop a self-concept—a set of self-referential, self-regulating, and self-knowing structures (White in Bronfenbrenner, Kessell, Kessen, & White, 1986). Such a history will always be under revision, because the meaning of the past changes in accord with the shifts in perspective that take place as the present unfolds.

Michelle Fine's (1985) analysis of scholarship contained in *Psychology of Women Quarterly* and the *Signs* Review Essays by Mary Parlee (1975) and Nancy Henley (1985) are excellent examples of critical reflection, as are a number of more narrowly focused writings (e.g., Lykes & Stewart,

1986; Nieva & Gutek, 1981; Wallston, 1981). The goal of the critical history that we develop in this article is to examine the frameworks within which questions in the field are generated and to explore the political interests—both feminist and antifeminist—that different frameworks serve.

Not all scholarship on the psychology of women originates from a feminist perspective. Moreover, no single feminist perspective unifies all the work that is self-identified as feminist. An array of political stances is implicit in the scholarship of feminist psychologists (Hare-Mustin & Marecek, 1988; Marecek & Hare-Mustin, 1987). Not only do feminist psychologists differ in their politics, they also differ in the extent to which they believe that politics enter—or should enter—into their scholarly work. This diversity of approaches is reflected in the existence of two distinct organizations for feminist psychologists—the Association for Women in Psychology, founded in 1969 as an activist group outside the American Psychological Association (APA), and the Division of the Psychology of Women, Division 35, representing the subfield within APA since 1973.

We organize feminist inquiry on the psychology of women and gender into four frameworks. Although frameworks have been proposed to characterize feminist curriculum revision (McIntosh, 1983; Schuster & Van Dyne, 1984) and scholarship in personality psychology (Torrey, 1987), this approach has not been used to organize and clarify approaches to the production of psychological knowledge about women. In this article we describe each conceptual framework and suggest the kinds of research that exemplify it. Although we present the frameworks in sequence, they are co-existing, interdependent, and mutually informing. Thus, we will give examples of current research developed within each. We evaluate the frameworks not in terms of their correctness, but rather in terms of their utility. Before developing our analysis, however, we will briefly recapitulate prefeminist or "womanless" psychology.

In "womanless" disciplines, women's experiences are thought to be too unimportant to be a focus of inquiry. So, for example, history has been taught as an account of men's public achievements, and literature as the writings of great male authors (McIntosh, 1983). In the psychology of the past 50 years, "womanlessness" was reflected in the disproportionate use of males as experimental subjects, in the failure to examine gender differences when both sexes were used as subjects, in the assumption that conclusions drawn from the study of male behavior applied to women, and more generally in the lack of attention to gender as a category of social reality. Several feminist critiques of research methodology have called attention to the practices of "womanless" psychology and its underlying assumption that women are uninteresting or unworthy of study (e.g., Grady, 1981; McHugh, Koeske, & Frieze, 1986).

Historically, much of psychological inquiry has been virtually "womanless," not only in its subject of inquiry, but in the place allowed women in the profession itself. Women did not have control over the resources needed for the production of knowledge, and the topics and methods of accepted scholarship were defined in ways that were exclusionary at best and misogynist at worst (Lewin, 1984).

"Womanless" psychology not only omitted the consideration of women and women's experiences, it also authorized and validated the view that those activities in which men engage are the activities central to human life. It reaffirmed that the activities of women are "backstage" to the "real" action. For example, the landmark studies of achievement motivation were limited to male subjects (McClelland, Atkinson, Clark, & Lowell, 1953). Achievement was often defined narrowly to include only behaviors involved in market production; other forms of productivity and action were not considered useful to society.

Feminist psychology began with a recognition of the "womanless" state of the discipline and a basic consensus that women and gender must be integrated into theory and research. In what follows, we discuss the conceptual frameworks that feminists have devised to accomplish this integration.

Feminist Frameworks

Exceptional Women

The initial feminist critiques of the "womanless" state of various disciplines prompted a variety of responses. One response has been to retrieve evidence of women's efforts that had been expunged from the historical record. In a discipline such as history, this means including a sprinkling of female figures: Joan of Arc, Catherine the Great, Marie Curie, Dolley Madison, or Florence Nightingale. Often the personal foibles of the women are as much the focus of attention as their accomplishments.

In psychology, historical overviews may now feature Anna Freud or Karen Horney along with Wundt, Pavlov, Watson, Skinner, and Freud. More important, many women whose contributions to the history of psychology had gone unrecognized or been forgotten have been rediscovered (O'Connell & Russo, 1980, 1983; Russo & Denmark, 1987; Scarborough & Furumoto, 1987). The new subfield of the history of women in psychology is a vital one. Nonetheless, documenting the history of women's achievements in and of itself does not necessarily identify the needed changes in the current activities of the discipline.

The historical approach serves feminist interests by focusing attention on the "neglected foremothers" of psychology (Bernstein & Russo, 1974).

This may instill confidence and courage in women undertaking careers in the field, a goal that is made explicit in discussions of these women as "role models" (O'Connell & Russo, 1980, 1983; Russo & Denmark, 1987). Moreover, the recognition of "great" women and the due consideration of their achievements contribute to a more accurate record of the discipline. But, a focus on "great" women may convey an underlying message that only exceptional women are capable of "real" achievement or are worthy of serving as role models. Such a focus also may deflect critical attention from the question of what is and is not to be considered an achievement.

The quest to rediscover the record of women's accomplishments is most useful when critical attention focuses on the social context of achievement. For example, Scarborough and Furumoto (1987) detailed not only the careers of successful women, but also of brilliant women who did *not* manage sustained achievement, and they analyzed the structural obstacles those women faced. Russo and O'Connell (1980), O'Connell and Russo (1983, 1988), and Russo and Denmark (1987) discussed the impact of social factors such as employment opportunities, attitudes of male gatekeepers, and norms for familial relationships, as well as the effects of larger social movements. They also attempted to retrieve the history of minority women psychologists and discussed the reasons for their invisibility.

When accounts of the careers of exceptional women psychologists reveal exclusion and marginalization, these revelations can furnish a basis for a critique of the discipline (Russo & Denmark, 1987). Evelyn Fox Keller's (1983) biographical study of Barbara McClintock provides a ready example in the field of biology. The very absence of "exceptional" women in a discipline can be a catalyst for exploration of the structural, as opposed to personal, reasons for such absence. For example, Linda Nochlin's (1971) essay "Why are there no great women artists?" recognized and forcefully argued that exceptional achievement requires opportunities, training, financial backing, and recognition, as well as native ability.

Another feminist response to the "womanless" state of psychology has been to initiate research into the family backgrounds and personal characteristics of eminent or exceptional women. If the developmental experiences and personality traits that led to success could be pinpointed, then it might be possible to increase the number of successful women. Thus, the psychological study of exceptional women includes research on the characteristics of highly successful women, such as physicians (Lopate, 1968), corporate managers (Hennig & Jardim, 1981), academics, and scientists (Moulton, 1979). While it focuses some attention on women's contributions, this work may inadvertently reinforce a number of antifeminist views of women. First, it suggests that the only women of interest are those who do what has been traditionally considered "men's work."

As in "womanless" psychology, the implication is that only "men's work" is of interest and social importance. Moreover, when research on exceptional women focuses on personal qualities, early experience, and family backgrounds as the determinants of accomplishment, it may reinforce the belief that success is solely the product of individual ability, determination or effort. Antifeminists may use such work to argue that women who do not pursue such careers (or who do not succeed spectacularly in them) either lack the "right stuff" to succeed or opt out of success by choice (e.g., Gilder, 1986).

The focus on exceptional women obviously moves beyond prefeminist psychology in a number of important ways. As scholarship on exceptional women has matured, interest has shifted from the search for personalistic explanations for women's success to the examination of structural factors that enhance some individuals' potential and block that of others. An underrepresentation of women in a discipline points to the importance of gender as a social and political category that influences the distribution of resources (Harding, 1986). Moreover, the experiences of women in psychology illuminate the social relations of the discipline, and the ways in which these social relations determine the processes by which knowledge is sought, validated, and disseminated (Morawski, 1987).

Women as Problem or Anomaly

When research is limited either to men or to a few special women, the production of knowledge is constrained. A broader consideration of women is typical of the approach we now turn to. In this framework, women are viewed as presenting psychology with a set of problems or anomalies. Feminist scholars who adopt this framework seek to explain the deficiencies or diminished accomplishments of some (or most) women in terms of social roles and learning rather than biological factors. Early formulations such as fear of success (Horner, 1970) and math anxiety (Tobias, 1978) are examples, as are recent formulations of an "imposter phenomenon" (Clance & Imes, 1978) and a "Cinderella complex" (Dowling, 1981). In these formulations, women's shortcomings are seen as arising from gender-related motives, fears, or self-concepts that cause a woman to act against her own best interests. (Although many of these constructs have been extended to men, their prototypical "victim" remains female.)

Work that focuses on deficiencies or lack of skills as the outcome of traditional gender-role socialization is another variant of the *Women as Problem* orientation. For example, women have been seen as deficient in crucial skills such as assertiveness or the ability to speak in an authoritative public style (Lakoff, 1973). The individual deficit model has also been influential in attempting to explain women's low career status, as Nieva and Gutek (1981) point out. Women managers have been represented as lacking in business acumen, leadership qualities, or the requisite interpersonal style, as overemotional and unmotivated to succeed.

Feminist approaches to women's psychological disorders often fit within the *Women as Problem* framework, partly because much traditional theorizing on personality fits within this framework (Torrey, 1987). A dominant line of feminist argument links psychological disorders prevalent among women to gender-role socialization. For example, stereotypically feminine traits such as dependency, fearfulness, a sense of helplessness, and excessive concerns about appearance are thought to be linked to disorders prevalent among women, such as agoraphobia, depression, and anorexia nervosa (Marecek, 1988; Widom, 1984). Feminist therapists working within this framework conceive their clients as lacking certain skills or having negative or self-defeating self-concepts, attitudes, or behaviors. Therapy is seen as a regimen of "compensatory socialization" (Marecek & Hare-Mustin, 1987).

Research in this framework focuses on explanations for women's problems in terms of gender-role-related conflicts, such as role strain, role overload, and penalties for role violations. This approach emphasizes that incompatible demands placed on women may cause psychological conflict, guilt, or anxiety. The conflicts and strains of men's roles and the problems that stereotypic masculinity may cause to others are rarely topics of concern. For example, though the effect of women's labor force participation on their children is an issue of great concern to developmental psychologists, little or no concern has been expressed about the effects of men's commitment to paid work.

Examples of *Women as Problem* research are easy to generate. *Women as Problem* has been the dominant framework for the psychology of women for at least the past 10 years. Moreover, most of the "pop psych" offerings aimed at women are based on the premise that women have (or are) problems (Gervasio & Crawford, 1989; Worell, 1987).

It is important to consider the potential and the pitfalls of this framework by examining how it can serve various ideological interests. On the one hand, the *Women as Problem* framework serves feminist interests in several important ways. It focuses on ordinary women as well as on women who are special or eminent. Not only is a more representative view of women's experiences obtained, but more importantly, there is also an assumption that areas of experience that are important to women, such as domestic violence and menstruation, are worthy of study. The shift from the "inherent deficiency" model of prefeminist psychology to a "social and cultural transmission" model is also a significant advance (Crawford, 1982). Moreover, with its insistence on socialization and gender-role prescriptions as sources of women's difficulties, this line of inquiry opens the way to a social critique.

But the *Women as Problem* framework has limitations as well. Perhaps the most serious of these, echoing the misogyny of prefeminist psychology, is that men remain the norm against which women are measured (Eichler, 1988). Any observed differences between women and men can be (and often are) interpreted as evidence of female deficiency, thus reinforcing existing gender politics. Women's behavior is seen as problematic *in comparison to men's behavior;* the goal of change efforts is often to help women attain stereotypically masculine behavior. Thus, for example, the concept of fear of success came to be used to explain women's deficiencies in achievement motivation (Horner, 1970). Lakoff's (1973) "women's language" was described in explicit contrast to the more forceful and effective style of men. Assertiveness training was prescribed as a remedy for alleged skill deficiencies in women, with the implicit promise of helping (some) women compete on equal terms with men by adjusting their speech patterns to be more like men's (Gervasio & Crawford, 1989). In each case, research subsequent to the original formulations raised serious questions as to whether a sex difference actually existed. Few psychologists are aware, for example, that there is no consistent evidence for a sex difference on the paper-and-pencil assertiveness inventories used in assertiveness research and training (Hollandsworth & Wall, 1977). Thus, the original observation of a "women's problem" may have been rooted in stereotypes that overstated the extent and universality of male-female difference (Lott, 1987a; Morawski, 1985). Moreover, bias is revealed in the asymmetry of interpretation. If the stereotypical female is problematically unassertive, why is the stereotypical male not problematically overassertive?

Even when an investigator explicitly contests the meaning of difference as deficiency, findings of difference remain problematic. For example, claims of a uniquely female moral sensibility or mode of thinking (Belenky, Clinchey, Goldberger, & Tarule, 1986; Gilligan, 1982) can be appropriated by those wishing to "confirm" that women do not (and cannot) think and act like men, and thus should be barred from positions of influence in the male world of public life (Crawford, 1989b; Mednick, 1987). Hare-Mustin and Marecek (1988) argued that work that frames gender as difference will always reach an impasse both in furthering our knowledge about gender and in bringing about political change. Whether the claim is that women are deficient, equal to (i.e., not different), or better than men, the governing presumption—that man is the referent and male behavior, the norm—remains the same.

A second limitation of the *Women as Problem* orientation is that it frequently stops short of the social critique that it invites. For example, "role conflict" is often regarded as an individual problem, not a social one; and each individual is encouraged to maximize her own "adjustment" by finding a personal solution to such problems as combining marriage, motherhood, and paid employment (Crawford, 1982). The cultural emphasis on autonomy from social influences and on individual responsibility for action frequently inclines psychologists toward viewing behavior in terms of personal, internal factors rather than external social ones (Fine, 1985; Hare-Mustin & Marecek, 1985). In addition, within this approach, it is difficult to conceptualize the diversity of women's experience except in terms of multiple problems. But representing Black or Hispanic, poor, lesbian, or disabled status only as part of an additive (or multiplicative) model of socialization deficits and role conflicts renders invisible the strengths that diverse socialization and life experiences may promote (Dill, 1979). It also lends itself with unfortunate ease to racist and other discriminatory interpretations.

Warnings of the antifeminist potential of the *Women as Problem* framework are not merely academic. Indeed, the most prominent examples of this framework are explicitly antifeminist. They focus on sex differences, specifically, on what are taken to be women's deficiencies or departures from the norm, but reach back to a long tradition of similar arguments about racial and ethnic differences. Biological explanations for such differences are proposed, usually based on correlational links between such factors as genes, hormones, neurochemistry, or brain structures, and the behaviors or characteristics in question (Bleier, 1986).

Another antifeminist variant of the *Women as Problem* framework focuses on women as causing or contributing to the difficulties of others. For example, as Caplan and Hall-McCorquodale (1985) showed, clinical studies of pathological behavior involve extensive mother-blaming. Mothers have been and continue to be implicated in psychopathologies ranging from arson to incontinence, drug abuse, infanticide, and bad dreams. Indeed, women's relationships with their families have been blamed repeatedly for social ills. Erikson (1964), for example, blamed Castro's revolutionary leanings on his mother's "grandiose maternality." Equality in marriage has been blamed, especially in the popular press, for male impotence, marital conflict, the rising divorce rate, and the decay of the social order (cf. Gilder, 1987).

Black women have been the focus of both racism and sexism in woman-blaming. Sociologists, psychiatrists, and social critics have accused women of color of castrating their husbands and sons because of their own lack of "femininity" and "healthy female narcissim" (Giddings, 1984). Moynihan (1965), Gilder (1987), and others attributed the social ills of the urban Black ghetto to its "matriarchial" social organization, a characterization repudiated by black feminist theorists (Hooks, 1981).

Is it possible to develop a psychology of women that does not rest on comparisons with men, but rather keeps women's experience as its focus? One area that would seem exempt from "difference" interpretation is research on experiences related to female physiology. Yet even childbirth is sometimes defined against men's activities in war as a "different" test of courage and bravery (Lott, 1987b, p. 188) and the experience of female orgasm is compared with males' (Wiest, 1977). Other areas of focus on women, such as lesbian relationships (Peplau, 1982), or use of humor and wit (Crawford, 1989a), or "ways of knowing" (Belenky et al., 1986) are subject to similar criticism. Although they originate in the impulse to understand *women's* experiences, the implicit or explicit reference group often remains men (or heterosexual couples). Lesbian couples, for example, are described as less sex-typed than heterosexual or gay male couples (Cardell, Finn, & Marecek, 1981); or their frequency of sexual activity is compared with that of these groups (Blumstein & Schwartz, 1983). Women's humor is understood as stemming from conversational goals that differ from those of men (Crawford, 1989a) or from their lower positions in a status hierarchy (Coser, 1960); women's ways of knowing are contrasted with men's (Crawford, 1989b). Nevertheless, to the extent that *Women as Problem* research can delineate aspects of women's experience that remain invisible in other frameworks, it contains the seeds of a rich psychology of women. Examples include work on women's friendships (Johnson & Aries, 1983; McCullough, 1987) and experiences in consciousness-raising groups (Kravetz, Marecek, & Finn, 1983).

The Psychology of Gender

This approach to feminist psychology shifts the focus of inquiry from women to gender, and from gender as difference to gender as social relations. That is, gender is conceived as a principle of social organization, which structures the relations, especially the power relations, between women and men (cf. Sherif, 1982; Stacey & Thorne, 1985).

The impetus for reframing the psychology of women as the psychology of gender originates in (and can also enrich) various projects of other phases. The biographies of eminent women in psychology, as well as in other sciences, reveal not only achievement but also exclusion and marginalization. Even when they "played by the rules," women were frequently denied full participation in the scientific community and the respect accorded to male scientists (Garrison, 1981; Keller, 1983; Russo & Denmark, 1987; Scarborough & Furomoto, 1987). Recognition of a similar dynamic in other arenas of public life invites a shift of attention from individual accomplishments to the structure and organization of the social systems in which individuals operate. In a similar fashion, the analyses of gender-role-related conflicts, an important contribution of the *Women as Problem* framework, prompt a conceptual shift from *role conflicts* (construed as individual problems) to *roles* (that is, gender relations) as social problems (Crawford, 1982).

While only a few psychological studies thus far conceive gender in this way, an increasing number of feminist psychologists and other social scientists are calling for such a conceptual shift. For example, Unger (1987) urged a shift from construing gender as a noun to construing it as a verb, following West and Zimmerman (1987), who speak of "doing" gender, rather than "having" gender. That is, gender is thought of as a process, rather than a set of attributes. Deaux's (1984) review of a decade of psychological research on sex and gender concludes that research thus far has been limited by the "static nature of assumptions—that sex-related phenomena are best approached either through biological categories via stable traits, or in terms of relatively stable stereotypic conceptions." In place of static constructs, Deaux urges psychologists to "deal with the *processes* involved . . . processes through which gender information is presented and acted upon" (p. 113). More recently, Deaux and Major (1987) have proposed a process model of gender in social interaction.

An example can best illustrate the promise of analyses that focus on how gender is produced by social structure and processes. Carol Brooks Gardner (1980) investigated "street remarks," comments passed between unacquainted individuals in public settings. Note that this study of ordinary people in everyday settings would probably not have been conceived within the *Exceptional Women* framework. Within the *Women as Problem* framework, researchers might have chosen to analyze street remarks directed at women as a function of the attractiveness, age, dress, or appearance of the recipient, thus suggesting that women are individually responsible for eliciting them. Instead, Gardner noted the types of street remarks men made, the positive and negative constructions given to them, women's strategies for dealing with them, and the outcomes of various conversational sequences. Her analysis focused on the functions that men's street remarks serve: they test the limits of women's capacity for expressive self-control; they reaffirm that a woman's physical appearance is an object of male scrutiny and approval; and, with hostility and threats of violence frequent in such interchanges, they serve to reiterate that women are at risk if they go unescorted in public places.

Earlier, we observed that the *Exceptional Women* and the *Women as Problem* frameworks can overemphasize the individual and exaggerate self-determination and the power of personal effort. The *Psychology of Gender* framework, however, can run the opposite risk of overemphasizing the effects of the social structure. A view of gender-role conditioning as a global determinant of the experiences of all females may obscure the diversity of women's lives and the points of similarity between women's and men's lives. Not all women experience "role conflict," nor do all who experience it find it debilitating. Not all women speak and think in a "different voice." Some individuals resist the shaping forces of the social structure. In a sense, those individuals are, as Nancy Datan (1987) put it, "socialization failures." If we do not allow for the possibility of resistance to social forces or rebellion, our theories cannot explain the very existence of feminism. Moreover, the social structure does contain conflicting messages, including some that reinforce feminist values and actions (Lott, 1987b).

Gender is not the only axis along which social relations are organized. In some instances, similarities of class, age, or race may be as strong or stronger than gender similarities. In using gender as the lens through which to view the social structure, theorists must acknowledge that other lenses yield equally viable, though also partial, portrayals (Scott, 1985). A compelling example of the importance of recognizing interactions of gender, class, and race can be drawn from the feminist critique of violence against women. Feminists have pointed out that all women live with the threat of rape and have alleged the universality of victim-blaming. Yet, as Cole (1986) pointed out, victim-blaming interacts with both race and gender:

> It is tempting to say that all women are bound by the recurring suggestion, innuendo, or outright assertion that whatever abuse they suffer, it is basically the woman's fault: "She shouldn't have been walking down that dark street"; or "If you wear a blouse like that, you're asking for it." Yet throughout U.S. history, there has been a glaring exception to this "rule"; it is the prevailing assumption that rape is most often committed by black men and that the victims are white women. In this case, blame is laid on the "oversexed" black male. (p. 27)

An important difference between the *Psychology of Gender* framework and those previously described is that the conception of gender as a process cannot be readily accommodated within conventional methods of psychological research. When social organization and social relations are the subjects of inquiry, laboratory experiments are not necessarily the best means of study. Laboratory methods are designed to "decontextualize" the variables under study, that is, to isolate them from the contaminating influences of ongoing "real-life" processes. But gender is constructed and reconstructed through precisely these processes (Deaux & Major, 1987).

The *Psychology of Gender* framework is potentially valuable in overcoming the class, race, and ethnic biases in psychological research. It is easy to ignore (or "control") factors such as class race, ethnicity, age and disability, as well as gender, when basing a science largely on the behavior of college students in laboratory settings (Fine & Gordon, 1989). But once gender is conceptualized as a system of social relations, and methods are expanded to encompass that definition, other systems become both more visible and more amenable to study. Thus, a recent special issue of *Psychology of Women Quarterly* (Amaro & Russo, 1987) focused on the combined influences of gender and ethnicity on the psychological well-being of Hispanic women.

When scholars begin to question the adequacy of the discipline's most distinctive methods, they begin to look to other disciplines for fresh approaches. Thus, feminist psychologists are currently exploring methods from literary criticism (Crawford & Chaffin, 1986; Hare-Mustin & Marecek, 1988; Wetherell, 1986), symbolic anthropology (Bem, 1987), and sociology (Unger, 1987).

Feminism in psychology has not been limited to attempts to "remove sex bias from" or "add women to" an otherwise stable paradigm. Instead, there are incipient challenges to psychology's definition and normative practices. Disciplinary boundaries blur—but not without challenge and reassertion of disciplinary lines. For example, when we discuss Gardner's (1980) work on street remarks with other psychologists, a common reaction is that, although it is interesting research, it "isn't psychology," a judgment made on methodological grounds. Yet psychology does have a rich tradition of inquiry outside the positivist model of laboratory manipulation of isolated variables: field research, observational techniques, content analysis of open-ended responses, participant-observation, and case studies are a few examples.

Incipient challenges (both conceptual and methodological) are articulated and developed in the framework we turn to next. Intellectual ferment and a sense of broaching the unimagined characterize this fourth framework for feminist psychology.

Transformation

In this framework, attention focuses on the normative practices and philosophical premises of the discipline. This framework is in rudimentary stages in psychology of women and in psychology in general. Our notions of its scope and direction borrow heavily from the groundbreaking work of feminist philosophers and historians of science (e.g., Haraway, 1978; Harding, 1986; Merchant, 1980), whose challenge to basic tenets of science are applicable to psychology. In what follows, we indicate three of the issues that have concerned scholars working within this framework.

The Myth of Objectivity. The notion that facts exist apart from values, thus making it possible to obtain "value-free" knowledge (or practice therapy in value-free ways) is disputed. Because we necessarily speak, think, and perceive from a standpoint generated by our experience, position in the social hierarchy, and ideological commitments, objectivity is impossible to attain (Hartsock, 1985; Unger, 1983; Wallston, 1981). Empiricism, once thought to free our efforts to comprehend the world from bias, cannot do so. Indeed, claims of objectivity only serve to disguise the politics of meaning. From this vantage point, the value of feminist psychology is *not* that it is more objective than conventional psychology and thus better able to discover the "truth" about women's experience. Rather feminism holds the promise of helping psychology to be more self-conscious about its values and to change them as needed in order to promote equality and social justice.

The critique of the values of the discipline is also informed by work done in the other frameworks. For example, the biographies of "neglected foremothers" reveal that science is not the democratic community of ideas that is portrayed in our cultural myths, and point to the need to redefine the discipline to recognize the activities and contributions of women. Work on androgyny reveals the persistent reification of masculinity and femininity implicit in the concept of androgyny as well as other trait-based conceptions of gender (Lott, 1981; Morawski, 1985). Other work has analyzed key concepts in clinical theory from the standpoint of women's experience and shown them to be constructed from a masculinist point of view. Concepts that have been subjected to such critique include dependency (Lerner, 1983; Stiver, 1984), autonomy (Hare-Mustin & Marecek, 1985), and anger (Miller, 1983).

These endeavors serve to undermine the view that psychology is "objective" or value-free. Psychology, like any other mode of inquiry, rests on a set of background beliefs and assumptions. Psychology, like any discipline, actively, if covertly, selects its objects of study and devises a canon, in which the objects of study are ranked from more to less important. In a recent ranking of divisions of the American Psychological Association, the Division of the Psychology of Women (which ironically is one of the larger divisions) was perceived as 33rd out of 40 in importance and in the lowest category of interest (Harari & Peters, 1987).

A Method is a Theory. The methods of a discipline reflect certain values and assumptions about the phenomena under study. Methods limit what can be known about the phenomena. Feminists have criticized the methods of experimental psychology for context-stripping, that is, for isolating social phenomena from the situations in which they normally take place (Fine, 1985; Parlee, 1979; Sherif, 1979). The experimental paradigm has also been criticized for emphasizing discovery of universal (and static) laws of behavior. If one holds truth to be historically and culturally situated, then methods should focus on dynamic processes and regard historical and cultural influences not as "nuisance variance" but as legitimate objects of study (Hoffnung, 1985).

The traditional research paradigm positions the experimenter as the expert and the subject as object of manipulation and observation. Such a paradigm is consonant with a mechanistic view of behavior. Some feminists have called for a revision of the research paradigm to one of mutual collaboration, in which the research participant is acknowledged as the primary interpreter of her or his experience and the research initiator is acknowledged as emotionally involved and as changed by the process of doing the research. As yet, there has been little movement in this direction in studies published in either feminist (Fine, 1985) or mainstream psychology journals (Fine & Gordon, 1989; Lykes & Stewart, 1986).

Critique of Politics of Psychology. Once psychology is seen as imbued with the values of the culture at large, then one can engage in debate as to the merits of those values. Feminists have been astute in identifying the gender politics of psychology: the assumption that the male is the norm and that women are deficient. Moreover, a critique of objectivity leads to a critique of the politics of psychology. Objectivity is a political tool of science: it is used to legitimize the expertise of social scientists and thus to buttress their power position in society.

One of the headiest developments in feminist theory is its social critique. Feminist philosophers, political theorists, and historians of science have debated the values of liberal humanism for feminist theory and praxis. Points of contention include the discourse on the self (Sherif, 1982); the extolling of individualism and autonomy over cooperation and collectivity (Hare-Mustin & Marecek, 1985); the focus on competing rights, rather than responsibilities, as the basis of moral behavior (Broughton, 1983; Gilligan, 1982); and the equating of self-fulfillment with liberation from social restraints and freedom from obligation to others (Ehrenreich, 1983; Gervasio & Crawford, 1989). These ideological concerns have implications for how we construe gender, what strategies we devise to help women achieve equality, and whether we focus on individual "reformist" solutions or on collective, more revolutionary changes.

Psychology has participated in producing and reinforcing the ideology of liberal humanism. This is most readily apparent in various definitions of mental health, theories of personality, and modes of psychotherapy (cf. Wallach & Wallach, 1983), and in the persistent tendency to define mental health as a matter of individual characteristics, rather than collective conditions (Albee 1981). It also is true of the way research issues are defined and constructed, for example how the self is conceived in research on identity and self-concept (Sampson, 1985).

We have described this phase in terms of its self-reflexive study of the values, assumptions, and normative practices of the discipline. But psychology (and psychology of women) cannot study only itself: self-scrutiny and self-criticism ideally should lead to a reconstructed discipline and new methods of inquiry. What would such inquiry look like?

It is difficult to imagine work so different from the "normal science" that most active feminist psychologists have been trained in. An attempt to specify exactly how the work of the future will proceed would be neither wise nor useful. We predict that the research within this framework will be characterized by the addition of sophisticated nonexperimental methods, recognition of the perspectives and personal involvements of both the investigator and the participants, and attention to and incorporation of social/political aspects of the work (Wallston, 1986).

An example of current work that has many of these characteristics is Kitzinger's (1986) study of lesbians' accounts of their lesbianism. Kitzinger used a modification of the Q-sort method to derive five general types of explanations or justifications in the women's accounts. Types of accounts included lesbianism as personal fulfillment and self-actualization; political choice; and "cross to bear." She then checked the validity of her interpretations by sharing them with the participants. She also included her own Q-sort in the results. Finally, she analyzed at length the potential gains and costs for the individual of maintaining each type of account, while acknowledging the validity of each account from the perspective of those who gave it. This research is more indebted to a social constructionist paradigm than to prefeminist "normal science."

Conclusion

Although the nature of written presentations forces us to present our frameworks in a linear sequence, we view them as co-existing. If they are related to each other at all sequentially, the sequence is circular rather than linear. The approaches are interactive and to some extent each is recursive on the others. Each approach can illuminate the assumptions of others and reveal how those assumptions permeate inquiry. All are well beyond "womanless" psychology. And, perhaps most important, each approach allows for work proceeding from feminist assumptions, as well as for work proceeding from antifeminist assumptions.

Because psychology is a cultural institution, doing psychological research is inevitably a political act. A central activity of feminist scholarship has been to draw attention to the politics of science. But this work has thus far been developed primarily for the biological sciences. By discussing the political and social implications of various psychologies of women and gender, we have attempted to show not that one approach is more feminist than the others, but rather that all have the potential for application in feminist and antifeminist ways. The multiplicity of approaches allows for healthy dialogue and cross-fertilization among them, and the reflexivity of the *Transformation* approach assures that the politics underlying the methods, topics, and governing assumptions of our scholarship are analyzed directly and self-consciously, rather than remaining unacknowledged.

Notes

This article was written while Mary Crawford was Jane Watson Irwin Visiting Professor of Psychology at Hamilton College and Jeanne Marecek was Fulbright Senior Lecturer at the University of Peradeniya, Sri Lanka. Order of authorship was determined alphabetically.

We thank Rhoda Unger for her comments on an earlier draft and the participants at the 1988 Nags Head Sex and Gender Conference for their lively discussion of the ideas in this article.

1. This paper has been published in several versions and reprinted a total of 30 times. See, for example, Weisstein (1969, 1970, 1971a, 1971b). It has become a classic in the field.

References

Albee, G. (1981). Prevention of sexism. *Professional Psychology, 12*, 20–28.

Amaro, H., & Russo, N. F. (1987). Hispanic women and mental health: Contemporary issues in research and practice. *Psychology of Women Quarterly, 11* (Special Issue), 391–535.

Belenky, M. F., Clinchey, B. M., Goldberger, N. R., & Tarule, J. M. (1986). *Women's ways of knowing: Development of self, voice, and mind.* New York: Basic.

Bem, S. L. (1987). Gender schema theory and the romantic tradition. In P. Shaver & C. Hendrick (Eds.), *Sex and gender* (pp. 251–271). Beverly Hills: Sage.

Bernstein, M. D., & Russo, N. F. (1974). The history of psychology revisited: Or, up with our foremothers. *American Psychologist, 29,* 130–134.

Bleier, R. (1986). Sex differences research: Science or belief? In R. Bleier (Ed.), *Feminist approaches to science* (pp. 147–164). New York: Pergamon.

Blumstein, P. W., & Schwartz, P. (1983). *American couples.* New York: William Morrow.

Bronfenbrenner, U., Kessel, F., Kessen, W., & White, S. (1986). Toward a critical social history of developmental psychology. *American Psychologist, 41*, 1218–1230.

Broughton, J. M. (1983). Women's rationality and men's virtues: A critique of gender dualism in Gilligan's theory of moral development. *Social Research, 50,* 597–642.

Caplan, P. J., & Hall-McCorquodale, I. (1985). Mother-blaming in major clinical journals. *American Journal of Orthopsychiatry, 55*, 345–353.

Cardell, M., Finn, S., & Marecek, J. (1981). Sex-role identity, sex-role behavior, and satisfaction in heterosexual, lesbian, and gay male couples. *Psychology of Women Quarterly, 5,* 488–494.

Clance, P. R., & Imes, S. A. (1978). The imposter phenomenon in high-achieving women: Dynamics and therapeutic intervention. *Psychotherapy: Theory, Research, and Practice, 15,* 241–247.

Cole, J. B. (Ed.). (1986). *All American women: Lines that divide, ties that bind.* New York: Free.

Coser, R. L. (1960). Laughter among colleagues: A study of the social functions of humor among the staff of a mental hospital. *Psychiatry, 23,* 81–95.

Crawford, M. (1982). In pursuit of the well-rounded life: Women scholars and family concerns. In M. Kehoe (Ed.), *Handbook for women scholars* (pp. 89–96). San Francisco: Americas Behavioral Research Corporation.

Crawford, M. (1989a). Humor in conversational context: Beyond biases in the study of gender and humor. In R. K. Unger (Ed.), *Representations: Social constructions of gender.* New York: Baywood.

Crawford, M. (1989b). Agreeing to differ: Feminist epistemologies and women's ways of knowing. In M. Crawford & M. Gentry (Eds.), *Gender and thought.* New York: Springer-Verlag.

Crawford, M., & Chaffin, R. (1986). The reader's construction of meaning: Cognitive research on gender and comprehension. In E. Flynn & P. Schweikart (Eds.), *Gender and reading: Essays on reader, text, and context.* Baltimore: Johns Hopkins University Press.

Datan, N. (1987, April). *Illness and imagery: Feminist cognition, socialization, and gender identity.* Paper presented at the Psychological Perspectives on Gender and Thought Conference, Hamilton College, Clinton, NY.

Deaux, K. (1984). From individual differences to social categories: Analysis of a decade's research on gender. *American Psychologist, 39,* 105–116.

Deaux, K., & Major, B. (1987). Putting gender into context: An interactive model of gender-related behavior. *Psychological Review, 94,* 369–389.

Dill, B. T. (1979). The dialectics of black womanhood. *Signs, 11,* 692–709.

Dowling, C. (1981). *The Cinderella complex.* New York: Pocket Books.

Ehrenreich, B. (1983). *The hearts of men: American dreams and the flight from commitment.* Garden City, NJ: Anchor Press/Doubleday.

Eichler, M. (1988). *Nonsexist research methods: A practical guide.* Winchester, MA: Allyn & Unwin.

Erikson, E. H. (1964). Inner and outer space: Reflections on womanhood. *Daedalus, 93,* 582–606.

Fine, M. (1985). Reflections on a feminist psychology of women. *Psychology of Women Quarterly, 9,* 167–183.

Fine, M., & Gordon, S. M. (1989). Feminist transformations of/despite psychology. In M. Crawford & M. Gentry (Eds.), *Gender and thought: Psychological perspectives* (pp. 146–174). New York: Springer-Verlag.

Gardner, C. B. (1980). Passing by: Street remarks, address rights, and the urban female. *Language and social interaction (Sociology Inquiry, 50)* 328–356.

Garrison, D. (1981). Karen Horney and feminism. *Signs: Journal of Women in Culture and Society, 6,* 672–691.

Gervasio, A. H., & Crawford, M. (1989). Social evaluations of assertiveness: A critique and speech act reformulation. *Psychology of Women Quarterly, 13,* 1–25.

Giddings, P. (1984). *When and where I enter: The impact of black women on race and sex in America.* New York: Morrow.

Gilder, G. (1986, September). Jobs: Women in the workforce. *The Atlantic,* p. 20.

Gilder, G. (1987). *Me and marriage.* Gretna, LA: Pelican.

Gilligan, C. (1982). *In a different voice: Psychological theory and women's development.* Cambridge, MA: Harvard University Press.

Grady, K. E. (1981). Sex bias in research design. *Psychology of Women Quarterly, 5,* 628–636.

Harari, H., & Peters, J. M. (1987). The fragmentation of psychology: Are APA divisions symptomatic? *American Psychologist, 42,* 822–824.

Haraway, D. (1978). Animal sociology and a natural economy of the body politic, Part II: The past is the contested zone: Human nature and theories of production and reproduction in primate behavior studies. *Signs: Journal of Women in Culture and Society, 4,* 37–60.

Harding, S. (1986). *The science question in feminism.* Ithaca, NY: Cornell University Press.

Hare-Mustin, R. T., & Marecek, J. (1985). Autonomy and gender: Some questions for therapists. *Psychotherapy, 23,* 205–212.

Hare-Mustin, R. T., & Marecek, J. (1988). The meaning of difference: Gender theory, post-modernism, and psychology. *American Psychologist, 43,* 455–464.

Hartsock, N. C. M. (1985). *Money, sex, and power.* Boston: Northeastern University Press.

Henley, N. (1985). Review Essay: Psychology and gender. *Signs: Journal of Women in Culture and Society, 11,* 101–119.

Hennig, M., & Jardim, A. (1981). *The managerial woman.* Garden City, NY: Anchor Press.

Hoffnung, M. (1985). Feminist transformation: Teaching experimental psychology. *Feminist Teacher, 2,* 31–35.

Hollandsworth, J. G., & Wall, K. E. (1977). Sex differences in assertive behavior: An empirical investigation. *Journal of Counseling Psychology, 24,* 217–222.

Hooks, B. (1981). *Ain't I a woman?* Boston: South End Press.

Horner, M. S. (1970). Femininity and successful achievement: A basic inconsistency. In J. M. Bardwick, E. Douvan, M. S. Horner, & D. Gutman (Eds.), *Feminine personality and conflict* (pp. 45–74). Belmont, CA: Brooks/Cole.

Johnson, F. L., & Aries, E. J. (1983). The talk of women friends. *Women's Studies International Forum, 6,* 353–361.

Keller, E. F. (1983). *A feeling for the organism: The life and work of Barbara McClintock.* New York: Freeman.

Kitzinger, C. (1986). Introducing and developing Q as a feminist methodology: A study of accounts of lesbianism. In S. Wilkinson (Ed.), *Feminist social psychology: Developing theory and practice* (pp. 77–96). Philadelphia: Open University Press.

Kravetz, D., Marecek, J., & Finn, S. E. (1983). Factors influencing women's participation in consciousness-raising groups. *Psychology of Women Quarterly, 7,*
257–271.

Lakoff, R. (1973). Language and women's place. *Language and Society, 2,* 45–80.

Lerner, H. G. (1983). Female dependency in context: some theoretical and technical
considerations. *American Journal of Orthopsychiatry, 53,* 697–705.

Lewin, M. (Ed.). (1984). *In the shadow of the past: Psychology portrays the sexes.*
New York: Columbia University Press.

Lopate, C. (1968). *Women in medicine.* Baltimore: Johns Hopkins University Press.

Lott, B. (1981). A feminist critique of androgyny: Toward the elimination of gender
attributions for learned behavior. In C. Mayo & N. M. Henley (Eds.), *Gender
and nonverbal behavior* (pp. 171–180). New York: Springer-Verlag.

Lott, B. (1987a, August). *Masculine, feminine, androgynous, or human?* Paper presented at the meeting of the American Psychological Association, New York,
NY.

Lott, B. (1987b). *Women's lives: Themes and variations in gender learning.* Monterey,
CA: Brooks/Cole.

Lykes, M. B., & Stewart, A. S. (1986). Evaluating the feminist challenge to research
in personality and social psychology: 1963–1983. *Psychology of Women Quarterly, 10,* 393–412.

Marecek, J. (1988). *Psychological disorders of women.* Unpublished manuscript,
Swarthmore College.

Marecek, J., & Hare-Mustin, R. T. (1987, March). *Cultural and radical feminism in
therapy: Divergent views of change.* Paper presented at the meeting of the
American Orthopsychiatric Association, Washington, DC.

McClelland, D. C., Atkinson, J. W., Clark, R. A., & Lowell, E. (1953). *The
achievement motive.* New York: Appleton-Century-Crofts.

McCullough, M. (1987, November). *Women's friendships across cultures: Black and
white friends speaking.* Paper presented at meeting of the Speech Communication Association, Boston, MA.

McHugh, M., Koeske, R., & Frieze, I. H. (1986). Issues to consider in conducting
nonsexist psychological research: A guide for researchers. *American Psychologist, 41,* 879–890.

McIntosh, P. (1983). *Interactive phases of curricular re-vision: A feminist perspective.*
Working paper no. 124. Wellesley, MA: Wellesley College Center for Research
on Women.

Mednick, M. T. S. (1987, July). *On the politics of psychological constructs: Stop the
bandwagon—I want to get off.* Paper presented at the Third Interdisciplinary
Congress on Women, Dublin, Ireland.

Merchant, C. (1980). *The death of nature.* New York: Harper & Row.

Miller, J. B. (1983). *The construction of anger in women and men.* Wellesley, MA:
Stone Center.

Morawski, J. G. (1985). The measurement of masculinity and femininity: Engendering categorical realities. *Journal of Personality, 53,* 196–223.

Morawski, J. G. (1987, August). *Toward the unimagined: Feminism and epistemology
in psychology.* Paper presented at American Psychological Association, New
York, NY.

Moulton, R. (1979). Psychological challenges confronting women in the sciences. In A. M. Brisco & S. M. Pfafflin (Eds.), *Expanding the role of women in the sciences* (pp. 321–335). New York: New York Academy of Sciences.

Moynihan, D. P. (1965). *The Negro family: The case for national action.* Washington, DC: U.S. Department of Labor.

Nieva, V. F., & Gutek, B. A. (1981). *Women and work: A psychological perspective.* New York: Praeger.

Nochlin, L. (1971). Why are there no great women artists? In V. Gornick & B. Moran (Eds.), *Woman in sexist society* (pp. 480–510). New York: Basic.

O'Connell, A. N., & Russo, N. F. (1980). Eminent women in psychology: Models of achievement. *Psychology of Women Quarterly, 5* (Special Issue), 1–144.

O'Connell, A. N., & Russo, N. F. (1983). *Models of achievement: Reflections of eminent women in psychology.* New York: Columbia University Press.

O'Connell, A. N., & Russo, N. F. (1988). *Models of achievement: Reflections of eminent women in psychology* (Vol. II). Hillsdale, NJ: Erlbaum.

Parlee, M. B. (1975). Review Essay: Psychology. *Signs, 1,* 119–138.

Parlee, M. B. (1979). Psychology and women. *Signs, 5,* 121–133.

Peplau, L. A. (1982). Research on homosexual couples: An overview. *Journal of Homosexuality, 8,* 3–8.

Russo, N. F., & O'Connell, A. N. (1980). Models from our past: Psychology's foremothers. *Psychology of Women Quarterly, 5,* 11–54.

Russo, N. F., & Denmark, F. L. (1987). Contributions of women to psychology. *Annual Review of Psychology, 38,* 279–298.

Sampson, E. E. (1985). The decentralization of identity: Toward a revised concept of personal and social order. *American Psychologist, 40,* 1203–1211.

Scarborough, E., & Furumoto, L. (1987). *Untold lives: The first generation of American women psychologists.* New York: Columbia University Press.

Schuster, M., & Van Dyne, S. (1984). Placing women in the liberal arts: Stages of curriculum transformation. *Harvard Educational Review, 54,* 413–428.

Scott, J. W. (1985, December). *Is gender a useful category of historical analysis?* Paper presented at the meeting of the American Historical Association, New York, NY.

Sherif, C. (1979). Bias in psychology. In J. A. Sherman & E. T. Beck (Eds.), *The prism of sex: Essays in the sociology of knowledge* (pp. 93–133). Madison, WI: University of Wisconsin Press.

Sherif, C. (1982). Needed concepts in the study of gender identity. *Psychology of Women Quarterly, 6,* 375–398.

Stacey, J., & Thorne, B. (1985). The missing feminist revolution in sociology. *Social Problems, 32,* 301–316.

Stiver, I. P. (1984). *The meanings of "dependency" in female-male relationships.* Wellesley, MA: Stone Center.

Tobias, S. (1978). *Overcoming math anxiety.* New York: Norton.

Torrey, J. W. (1987). Phases of feminist re-vision in the psychology of personality. *Teaching of Psychology, 14,* 155–160.

Unger, R. K. (1983). Through the looking glass: No Wonderland yet? (The reciprocal relationship between methodology and models of reality). *Psychology of Women Quarterly, 8,* 9–32.

Unger, R. K. (1987, August). *The social construction of gender: contradictions and conundrums.* Paper presented at the meeting of the American Psychological Association, New York, NY.

Wallach, M. A., & Wallach, L. (1983). *Psychology's sanctions for selfishness.* San Francisco: Freeman.

Wallston, B. S. (1981). What are the questions in psychology of women? A feminist approach to research. *Psychology of Women Quarterly, 5,* 597–617.

Wallston, B. S. (1986). *What's in a name revisited: Psychology of women versus feminist psychology.* Invited Address, Annual meeting of the Association for Women in Psychology, Oakland, CA.

Weisstein, N. (1968). *Kinder, Kirche, Küche as scientific law: Psychology constructs the female.* Boston: New England Free Press.

Weisstein, N. (1969). Woman as nigger. *Psychology Today, 3,* 20–23.

Weisstein, N. (1970). *Kinder, Kirche, Küche as scientific law: Psychology constructs the female.* In R. Morgan (Ed.), *Sisterhood is powerful.* New York: Random House.

Weisstein, N. (1971a). Psychology constructs the female, or the fantasy life of the male psychologist. In M. H. Garskof (Ed.), *Roles women play: Readings toward women's liberation.* Belmont, CA: Brooks/Cole.

Weisstein, N. (1971b). Psychology constructs the female, or the fantasy life of the male psychologist (with some attention to the fantasies of his friends, the male biologist and the male anthropologist). *Journal of Social Education, 35,* 362–373.

West, C., & Zimmerman, D. H. (1987). Doing gender. *Gender and Society, 1,* 125–151.

Wetherell, M. (1986). Linguistic repertoires and literary criticism: New directions for a social psychology of gender. In S. Wilkinson (Ed.), *Feminist social psychology: Developing theory and practice* (pp. 77–96). Philadelphia: Open University Press.

Widom, C. S. (Ed.). (1984). *Sex roles and psychopathology.* New York: Plenum.

Wiest, W. M. (1977). Semantic differential profiles of orgasm and other experiences among men and women. *Sex Roles, 3,* 399–403.

Worell, J. (1987, August). *Support and satisfaction in women's close relationships.* Presidential address (Division 12, Section 4) presented at the meeting of the American Psychological Association, New York, NY.

PART 3
RECONSTRUCTING PSYCHOLOGY, RE-PLACING WOMEN

A constructionist psychology of gender uses knowledge of what is as a means of understanding what could be. (Wittig, 1985, p. 809)

"Knowledge of what is": the reality of women's marginalization and the knowledge that "knowledge" is not Knowledge but construction. "Understanding what could be": the hope for reconstructing psychology to include women. What would a women-inclusive psychology look like? The readings in the previous parts of this book identified psychology's ill-treatment of women, explored the notion that so-called knowledge is but construction, and clarified the application of constructionist principles to the issue of women's place in psychology. In the process, we have explored as well questions of the meaning of gender and the sociohistorical embeddedness of such notions. As those readings demonstrate, the construction of gender has acted to determine both psychology's understanding of women and the realities of women's place in psychology. For psychology to treat women well will demand a reconstruction of psychology that embraces reconstructed notions of gender. The readings in this part are representative of that process of reconstruction, already underway in psychology.

Michele Wittig initiates this discussion with a far-ranging and incisive exploration of the implications for the psychology of gender of the postmodern critique. Witting pointed to the need for a metatheory to underpin gender research and theorizing, urging that a constructionist perspective affords such a foundation. In examining the viability of constructionism for this role, she highlighted the distinction between the epistemological shortcomings of positivism and the role of sociohistorical forces in shaping so-called knowledge. Although it can be argued that the two are profoundly intertwined—that is, that epistemological assumptions are themselves products of contextual forces—Wittig urged that a constructionist approach has differing implications for theory making and for research techniques. Constructionism circumscribes the explanatory range of psychological theory, self-consciously confining such theorizing to application within a specified sociohistorical frame. At the same time, constructionism expands epistemological options, rejecting many restrictions of the positivist view and embracing more expansive methodologies. Thus, gender theory is held to more stringent demands for acknowledging its situatedness than traditional theorizing has imposed, while methods for exploring gender are liberated from traditional constraints.

The metatheory that emerged from Wittig's analysis of the postmodernist challenge derives from a reconstruction of the meaning of gender, offered as prototype for a reconstruction of psychology itself. Toward this end, Wittig explored several dilemmas that have characterized gender theory and research. Her approach was dialectic, as she explored the assumptions underlying theory and research and revealed the diversity of positions made possible when assumptions are severed from their particular contextual groundings. Thus, the question of advocacy versus scholarship was re-framed, the apparent opposition embedded in this antithetical posing of the dilemma was dissolved, and Wittig proposed an activist, scholarly, change-oriented psychology of gender that escapes both the pitfalls of unchecked ideology and the sterility of "objective" intellectualism unconcerned with social impact.

Similar analyses applied to other dilemmas demonstrated the power of this approach in resolving psychology's persistent queries, problems created and sustained by the received view of what is proper to psychological science and theory. These are topics essential to psychology's very identity: science versus humanism, orthodoxy versus schism, subjectivity versus objectivity. Wittig's discussion demonstrated the power of a constructionist metatheory for addressing long-standing issues in the psychology of gender, while also exploring the connections between gender and the broad scope of psychological issues. From this position, gender ceases to appear as an ancillary, if intriguing, topic and is instead recognized as embodying concerns central to the discipline. It emerges as a topic whose ramifications suffuse a range of questions generally seen as core issues in psychology and one prototypic for the reconstruction of psychology portended by the postmodernist challenge.

A strength of Wittig's work lies in the breadth of her applications, as she moved beyond an analysis of the constructionism as applied to psychological theory to approach the implications of this framework for research. Beginning with an analysis of value presuppositions inherent in psychological science and continuing through inquiry into the interpretations and applications of findings, Wittig challenged psychological researchers to be cognizant of, and attentive to, the epistemological and sociological undergirding of their work. Again, gender becomes the exemplar for deconstructing research using these conceptual tools; again, the implications for the field of psychology extend well beyond issues of gender.

Wittig's thoroughgoing exploration of constructionism as metatheory provides a foundation for a range of projects whose collective impact is the reconstruction of psychology, the creation of women-inclusive psychology. The other readings in the part illustrate a variety of approaches to that reconstruction, engaging an assortment of forms of psychological endeavor: re-visions of research methods, of psychology's history, of curriculum of design, of psychotherapy.

Barbara Wallston and Kathleen Grady made their agenda manifest in their title: "Integrating the Feminist Critique and the Crisis in Social Psychology." The crisis to which they refer is precisely the challenge to the modernist/positivist perspective in psychology, a phenomenon dubbed "crisis" in the 1970s, roughly contemporaneous with the emergence of a strong feminist voice in psychology. The historical co-incidence of these two events is surely more than coincidence; feminist psychologists (and feminists in other disciplines as well) have been among the most vocal critics of traditional research methods, attacking the assumptions and practices that have served to marginalize women. Wallston and Grady's work explored this connection, clarifying the nature and extent of the feminist critique and elaborating on its liberating potential for psychological methodology. Their discussion addressed the most basic issues of psychological research, ranging from question formulation, design, and subject selection to the uses of statistics. Each topic, explored for its potential biases, becomes a study in the construction of knowledge—in this case, the construction of knowledge-generating practices, research methods themselves long presumed to be objective arbiters of apodictic knowledge.

The task of reconstructing psychology so as to treat women well was confronted here in the most practical of terms: How do we design and conduct research that is women-inclusive? Yet, the discussion was not entirely pragmatic. Among the indictments of traditional techniques and among the recommendations for alternative approaches, we find buried reminders of how research creates rather than discovers its own reality. Wallston and Grady pointed up the thorny issues involved in identifying and engaging the social psychology of the research process itself, striving to put in its place research that is contextually sensitive and procedures that recognize meaning (rather than sensing trouble) in the social reality of psychological research.

Feminist encouragement of alternative methodologies took its impetus from two interactive sources: a crisis within the discipline, reflected in damaging challenges to positivism, and the feminist movement, with its attendant reformative impact on the individuals and institutions of psychology. A similar confluence of forces shaped the feminist re-writing of psychological histories. Within the discipline, concerns were voiced regarding the dearth of critical approaches to psychological history and psychology's apparent indifference to developments in historiographic theory and method—a critique informed by postmodern notions of knowledge (Furumoto, 1988). Roughly simultaneously, feminist recognition of the need to attend to women's voices began to infiltrate the academic disciplines, sensitizing psychology's historians to the paucity of women in the field's histories. The depth of distortion represented by this neglect of psychology's women came to light in a spate of articles and books that began appearing in the mid-1970s and had become a substantial literature by the late 1980s. In this work, feminist frameworks were progressively joined with new historiographic awareness to document and clarify the source and impact of women's invisibility in psychology's histories.

Among the scholars whose work has begun reshaping psychology's histories to include women are Laurel Furumoto and Elizabeth Scarborough. Although their article included here represents but a portion of their extensive research into the lives and work of psychology's pioneer women (see also Furumoto, 1987, 1988; Scarborough & Furumoto, 1987), this article is an informative sample of scholarship in this area. Operating from Gerda Lerner's (1979) model for placing women in history, a framework discussed previously, these authors strive to create a vision of women's place in psychology that takes women's own experience as crucial, anchoring the discussion of women's work as well as their lives in the sociohistorical framework of their experience.

Furumoto and Scarborough's presentation of several early prominent women psychologists represents not only women-inclusive history but also critical history. Absent here are assumptions that psychology has emerged in a vacuum, replaced by a clear awareness of the situatedness of psychological endeavor. Absent, too, is the presumption that any individual's work is independent of the personal contexts that frame her life, replaced by a concern for how personal experience and values infuse professional undertakings. Absent, also, is the assumption that history is simply a telling of facts, replaced by an awareness of the multiple influences that shape the selection and interpretation of historical events. And absent, finally, is the belief that the writing of history is driven by meritocracy, replaced by an awareness of forces internal and external to the discipline that have acted to marginalize women and their work, independent of their merit.

The history that emerges from such an undertaking deviates so radically from the history typically encountered in psychology curricula that it seems a different field of study entirely. Contextual history is fascinating history, for it speaks of the human lives of people working in socially shaped institutions, striving for personally meaningful goals. The comparative sterility of traditional histories is evident, as is the richness of meaning garnered from histories of the sort Furumoto and Scarborough present. Thus, the women we meet in Furumoto and Scarborough's work are multidimensional persons, and their work makes unusual sense in light of our understanding of the contexts that framed it. Furumoto and Scarborough's work is the historical counterpart to Wittig's theoretical and Wallston and Grady's methodological reconstructive efforts. All strive to re-create psychology as women-inclusive; all do so from an explicit, sound, and powerful conceptual basis. The critique of the received view and the application of a constructionist alternative infuse all three works.

As a final approach to the question of what a women-sensitive psychology would look like, Rachel Hare-Mustin examined clinical theory and practice in light of constructionist perspectives on gender. Hare-Mustin has offered a range of insightful deconstructions of therapeutic practices in other work (e.g., Hare-Mustin, 1983, 1987, 1991; Hare-Mustin & Marecek, 1988 [included in this book]) and here discussed their application to family therapy. This article systematically considered the social construction of the family, examining the impact on that construct of contemporary social trends and revealing how "family" is construed and reconstrued as an artifact of context. Hare-Mustin proceeded to conduct a comparable cross-cultural analysis of the construction of "motherhood," examining both the situated nature of that term's meaning and the implications of its multiple renderings. Finally, she explored historical trends in the social construction of gender, touching also on the concepts of alpha and beta bias raised earlier in this volume (Hare-Mustin & Marecek, 1988). With the contextual entanglement of these concepts firmly established, Hare-Mustin approached the issue of clinical work with families.

The therapeutic work Hare-Mustin described proceeds from a position sensitive to the relativity of such notions as motherhood and family and one that is apprised of the meaning and consequences of the construction of gender. From this basis, she untangled the web of implications for therapy that derive from the dismantling of traditional biases and stereotypes. In particular, she exposed the implicit minimization of women and their place in family life, which must be confronted if therapy is to succeed in transcending the limits imposed by these confining constructions. By explicating the lingering impact on families and individuals of these (usually unexamined) assumptions, notions of family, of motherhood, and of gender can be reconstructed to reduce family stress and facilitate healthier functioning. This, then, is therapy as practiced in a psychology where the contextual forces that shape our understandings are explicitly engaged, where gender is admitted for reconstruction, and where women's reality is affirmed.

We have in these articles an assortment of illustrations of how psychology looks when women and their experience are taken seriously. The range of possibilities for such re-visioning is almost endless, and, indeed, the literature continues to grow. The common theme echoing through the multiplicity of reconstructive efforts—whether they address theory, research methods, history, or practice—is the inextricable context-embeddedness of human experience. Psychology's ill-treatment of women has derived from its immersion in a worldview that negated context; the emergence of women will stem from an affirmation of the context heretofore denied.

The recognition that women's place in psychology has been (and still is) framed by context leads us to another crucial awareness: women are not only products but also producers of context. The relationship between women's experience and their place in psychology is a dialectic one. We have seen this dynamic already in the discussion of the relationship between the feminist movement and psychological thought: feminism informed critiques of psychological method and history even as psychologists were contributing to the scholarly bases of the feminist movement. This reciprocity is central to our understanding of women's place in psychology, for it implies that psychology is also both producer and product of women's participation in the discipline. To the extent that women will re-shape psychology through the operation of this dialectic, the articles included here provide a sketch of what women's impact will be. If the vision suggested here is realized, then psychological theory and research, history, curriculum, and practice will be fundamentally altered by feminist efforts at reconstruction.

References

Furumoto, Laurel. (1987). On the margins: Women and the professionalization of psychology in the United States, 1890–1940. In Mitchell G. Ash & William R. Woodward (Eds.), *Psychology in twentieth-century thought and society* (pp. 93–113). Cambridge, MA: Cambridge University Press.

Furumoto, Laurel. (1988). The new history of psychology. *G. Stanley Hall Lectures* (vol. 9. pp. 9–34). Washington, D.C.: American Psychological Association.

Hare-Mustin, Rachel T. (1983). An appraisal of the relationship between women and psychotherapy, 80 years after the case of Dora. *American Psychologist, 38,* 593–601.

Hare-Mustin, Rachel T. (1987). The problem of gender in family therapy theory. *Family Process, 26,* 15–27.

Hare-Mustin, Rachel T. (1991). Sex, lies, and headaches: The problem is power. *Journal of Feminist Family Therapy, 3*, 39–61.

Hare-Mustin, Rachel T., & Marecek, Jeanne. (1988). The meaning of difference: Gender theory, postmodernism, and psychology. *American Psychologist, 43*, 455–464.

Lerner, Gerda. (1979). *The majority finds its past: Placing women in history.* New York: Oxford University Press.

Scarborough, Elizabeth, & Furumoto, Laurel. (1987). *Untold lives: The first generation of American women psychologists.* New York: Columbia University Press.

Wittig, Michele A. (1985). Metatheoretical dilemmas in the psychology of gender. *American Psychologist, 40*, 800–811.

10
METATHEORETICAL DILEMMAS IN THE PSYCHOLOGY OF GENDER

Michele Andrisin Wittig

Evaluating the validity of underlying premises in the social and behavioral sciences has long been a concern among philosophers of science (e.g., A. Kaplan, 1964; B. Kaplan, 1967; Kuhn, 1962/1970; Luckmann, 1973/1978; Polanyi, 1958; Popper, 1935/1959; Toulmin, 1953) and sociologists of science (e.g., Barber & Hirsch, 1963; Barnes, 1974; Merton, 1957). North American psychologists have become increasingly attentive to such metatheoretical issues (for example, Brewer & Collins, 1981; Buss, 1979; Campbell, 1974; Gergen, 1973; Koch, 1981; Rosnow, 1981; Rychlak, 1977; Sampson, 1977, 1978; Secord, 1982; Staats, 1981). Much of this concern was predated by work in the European psychological community (for example, Joynson, 1974; Moscovici, 1972; Piaget, 1970/1977). Metatheorists within psychology explicitly examine ontological, epistemological, and methodological assumptions of the discipline and their consequences for knowledge acquisition and use.

Within the last 15 years, social, cognitive, personality, clinical, and developmental psychology; psychobiology; and the psychology of individual differences have all been touched by these discussions. During this same period of resurgent concern with metatheory in psychology, a psychology of gender was established (see Henley, in press, and Wallston, in press, for historical overviews). Theory development and empirical work in the new discipline have much in common with the more well-established areas of psychology (e.g., Golden, 1981). Social/cognitive psychology, in particular, has been a major source of conceptual and methodological borrowing to construct a psychology of gender (e.g., Lykes & Stewart, 1983).

Metatheoretical questions found a central place in the emergent discipline (for example, Deaux, 1984, 1985; Henley, in press; Parlee, 1975, 1979; Sherif, 1979, 19481; Sherman & Beck, 1979; Unger, 1979, 1983; Vaughter, 1976; Walker, 1981; Wallston, 1981). An examination of assumptions and validity criteria has been undertaken in part to legitimize and demarcate the new endeavor. Metatheoretical clarity is sought in the interest of establishing the psychology of gender as something more than a collection of work whose sole claim to distinction is the use of sex or gender[1] as a variable. In the present article, a constructionist metatheory is extrapolated from extant writings in the philosophy of psychology. The derived perspective is then used as the basis for resolving four metatheoretical dilemmas in the psychology of gender. The issues examined are prototypical, and the psychology of gender is intended to be illustrative. Therefore, in discussing suggested resolutions to the dilemmas, implications for the more general philosophical controversy in psychology itself are drawn.

Overview of Some Metatheoretical Issues

Kimble (1984), who conducted one of the few empirical studies of psychologists' beliefs about their discipline's underlying premises, concluded that American psychology encompasses two disparate cultures. The results of his survey suggested that "tough-minded" and "tender-minded" groups disagree in three important areas: scientific versus humanistic values, objectivism versus intuition as sources of basic knowledge, and nomothetic versus idiographic approaches to the study of behavior. Although Kimble's data showed considerable overlap between the two cultures on many dimensions, his results were consistent with the view of many that psychology is conceptually pluralistic (e.g., Royce, 1982).

For example, Kimble's data supported the conclusion that psychology does not have consensus about its definition (i.e., what it takes as its proper subject matter), its validity criteria (e.g., what would constitute adequate description, explanation, and prediction), or its methodology. Nevertheless, his results suggested that the assumption of value-free psychological inquiry has been largely replaced by a more Kuhnian (Kuhn, 1962/1970) perspective. A central tenet of the Kuhnian view is that shifts in belief systems, rather than in objective evidence alone, characterize major changes in (social and behavioral) scientific knowledge. But there is little agreement about the practical implications of this perspective, for example, what values psychological theory and method should encompass.

If value-free psychological research is impossible, how are researchers in psychology to integrate values with their explanation-seeking in a manner that does not render the enterprise a mere reflection of those values? Recent work in the sociology of knowledge and in epistemology provides partial answers to this complex metatheoretical question. The first approach uses empirical validation; the second employs formal analysis.

Distinction Between Sociological and Epistemological Issues

The sociology of knowledge is concerned with factors that affect the accessibility of knowledge and the evaluation of contributions to knowledge in all areas of endeavor, both intuitive and scientific (e.g., Barber & Hirsch, 1963; Barnes, 1974; Merton, 1957). These factors include social categories (e.g., education, social class, race, and sex); other indicators of the contributor's status (e.g., credentials, rank, degrees, honors, awards, and affiliations); organizational supports (e.g., sources of funding for the work); and professional networks (e.g., mentors). Within academic psychology, for example, research on hiring (Fidell, 1970) and peer review of manuscripts submitted for publication (Peters & Ceci, 1982) has demonstrated that positive evaluations are distributed disproportionately to those having the acceptable ascribed and achieved status, whereas the substantive products of those holding outgroup or marginal status tend to be undervalued, even when the content of the contributions is held constant. Studies of the evaluation of paintings (Phetersen, Kiesler, & Goldberg, 1971), novels (Ross, 1982), and essays on topics as diverse as dietetics and law (Goldberg, 1968) have documented the existence of a bias associated with the sex of the contributor.

In contrast to the concerns of the sociology of knowledge, there is the question of epistemological bias: the effects that both the assumptions underlying one's beliefs about the world and one's methods for understanding the world have on the conclusions drawn (e.g., A. Kaplan, 1964; Koch, 1981; Reinharz, 1982). *Webster's New International Dictionary* defines *epistemology* as "the theory or science of the method and grounds of knowledge, especially with respect to its limits and validity" (Gove, 1966, p. 765). Although epistemological assumptions operate in all endeavors, they are of particular concern in those fields that strive for objectivity.

The hypothetical extremes of logical positivism and subjective relativism provide an illustration of the diversity of such assumptions. Those who advocate logical positivism claim that scientific facts and fact-finding are value neutral and that values may be introduced only at the levels of hypothesis formation and the development and implementation of policy. Advocates of subjective relativism believe that fact-finding, analysis, and conclusions are purely subjective and, therefore, are only capable of validating the researcher's prejudices.

In Myrdal's (1969) view, logical positivism is limiting to a physical or natural scientist but debilitating to the social scientist. According to this perspective, the knowledge base of the physical sciences, as compared to that of sociology or psychology, is less susceptible to compromise when the effects of values on fact-finding are ignored. For example, physicists who ignore the effect of the social values under which they operate do not thereby compromise the adequacy of their theories or experiments. In psychology, however, the adequacy of the very knowledge base of psychology is affected by the psychologist's values because both the modes of explanation and the objects of research are value sensitive.

In summary, both the sociology of knowledge and epistemology are concerned with biases and values. The sociology of knowledge focuses on how social processes affect both access to knowledge and the acceptability of knowledge. In contrast, epistemological inquiry is concerned with the relationship between presuppositions underlying the process of knowledge acquisition and their consequences for the validity of the derived knowledge.

In the last two decades, many efforts have been made to specify the relation between the sociological and epistemological bases of explanation in psychology. Some authors argue that the dichotomy between empirical and analytic propositions, on which much of the distinction between the sociology of knowledge and epistemology rests, is a false one (e.g., Gergen, 1973, 1978, 1982, 1983; Gergen & Morawski, 1980). Gergen (1983) suggested that the acquisition of knowledge in psychology is socially constructed to such a degree that general psychology itself is best viewed as a form of social process whose knowledge is mere social artifact. As Gergen himself noted (1983), the skepticism inherent in such a view contains the seeds of suspicion of its own explanations.

In contrast, the "constructionist" perspective outlined below retains the distinction between the sociology of knowledge and epistemology. Furthermore, although acknowledging the socially constructed nature of psychological knowledge, adherents of the constructionist viewpoint attempt to delimit the influence of sociological factors.

Recent Constructionist Efforts

According to the Kuhnian (Kuhn, 1962/1970) perspective, predicting events is clouded by the fact that what constitutes the nature of the events is merely consensual for that group of scientists. It may not be representative of the world as it is or as it is viewed by other groups. Thus, Kuhn acknowledged both epistemological and sociological barriers.

In their widely used methodological text, Cook and Campbell (1979) subscribed to an "evolutionary critical-realist perspective" (p. 28). Its central assumptions are that causal relationships exist and that, although these cannot be perceived entirely accurately, the search for manipulable causes has value. With respect to methodology, Cook and Campbell emphasized a central role for experimentation as being especially suited to revealing such causes. The combination of experimentation and quasi-experimentation provides the basis for an explanatory psychology.

In their article on methodology, Feldman and Hass (1970) argued that laboratory experimentation and correlational field work are equivalent in long-range value. The former affords both direct inferences about what people can do in response to manipulations of situational variables and indirect inferences about the behavior of individuals in their natural context. The latter yields direct, though not clearly causal, inferences about what people actually do and indirect inferences about the causes of their behavior.

Recently, Manicas and Secord (1983) presented a variant of the "realist" theory of psychological inquiry. Although these authors borrowed from positivism the belief in the integrity of the search for causal relations, they were not as sanguine as Cook and Campbell about the capacity of experimentation to enable a researcher to predict behavior. Their proposal was critical of the emphasis on establishing functional relationships between variables so as to predict events, either partially or probabilistically. In Manicas and Secord's view, this goal is unattainable because everyday behavior is controlled by a complex array of interactive factors and occurs in an "open" system. Thus, validity cannot be based on a strict correspondence between theory and facts. Rather, the focus is on specifying scientific laws that identify the causal properties of structures that operate in the world to produce behavioral tendencies. This requires an interdisciplinary effort to understand the multiple structures within which behavior occurs. In this effort, social psychology is a mediating discipline, attempting to coordinate the individual's motives, beliefs, competencies, understandings, and values with the social structure that defines the individual's roles and position. Likewise, each discipline is expected to develop its own verification criteria, depending on the characteristics of its research domain.

Bhaskar (1982), from whom Manicas and Secord (1983) borrowed to develop their metatheory, proposed a "transformational" psychology, characterized by causal explanation and criticism, including self-criticism. In this framework, the explanation-seeking process and the types of causal paths emphasized are viewed as recursive. This is a consequence of the fact that much of human action has the capacity to both transform its context and be transformed by it. However, the products of such an analysis are emergent because the outcomes of such complex, bidirectional causal paths can seldom be known in advance.

Although Bhaskar used the term *transformational* to describe the entire process whereby challenges are made to extant explanations, Bronfenbrenner (1977) used it to describe research oriented toward change (along the lines of Lewin's, 1946, action research). In a complementary vein, Campbell (1969) viewed reforms as opportunities for experiments. In all such research, new person-environment combinations are constructed and studied. Although not always explicit in the writings of these researchers, there is the suggestion that these new combinations are not developed at random but are consistent with some socially progressive aim.

In summary, a constructionist perspective assigns to psychological theory a role that is at once more circumscribed and expanded than in the "received" view of science. It attempts to explain, though not necessarily predict, human behavior. Its explanatory function is more limited in that it does not attempt to find universal principles and deterministic laws that can be applied to subsets of the whole of human activity by merely adding appropriate qualifiers. However, the range of phenomena that the revised epistemic addresses is expanded. For example, the constructionist view must now account for more complex causal relationships and idiographic aspects of human action (e.g., expectancies, intentions, purposes, subjective meanings, and values) as well as the nomothetic concerns (cf. Harré, 1978; Menzel, 1978; Mishler, 1979).

With respect to methodology, a constructionist perspective retains respect for experimental and quasi-experimental designs, but is also favorable to biographical, interpretive, and other person-oriented approaches. Argyle (1978) has questioned whether the latter methods provide causal explanations or enhance prediction beyond those cases or instances on which the predictions are developed. In a similar vein, Schuler (1982) observed that specifying research methods that respect an expanded definition and higher standard of external validity without sacrificing internal validity is a formidable task because methods that favor one tend to lessen the other.

In response to such criticism, constructionists encourage methodological precision via experimental designs that create at least partially controlled ("closed") systems and via interpretive methods that are built on, rather than substitute for, the insights derived under controlled conditions of experimental psychology (Manicas & Secord, 1983).

Summary of the New Heuristic

The viewpoints just outlined represent a shift in psychology toward a constructionist perspective. This metatheory encompasses several propositions.

1. Positivist and neopositivist views of how psychological knowledge is acquired are inadequate. Knowledge about behavior is constructed, not merely deduced. Such constructions are affected by the historical, personal, social, and cultural context. Judgments of the meaning, validity, and usefulness of a particular analysis of human behavior are themselves socially influenced.

2. Explanations of human behavior that are derived under controlled conditions without knowledge of individuals in their social contexts (including their motives, expectancies, intentions, and capacity to change) are incomplete at best.

3. Behavior is multiply caused (both with respect to the number of causative factors and the systems involved). Behavior and our knowledge of it are reciprocally related, and the causal relations change in complex, unpredictable ways. This dynamic is the focus of analysis.

4. Although correspondence of theory and data is sought, verification criteria do not demand such correspondence. For some domains, accurate prediction from explanatory principles is largely unattainable. Rather, the truth of a theory resides in how well it represents the domain it attempts to explain.

5. Methods that are sensitive to bidirectional and multiple causality and subjective meanings are likely to advance our knowledge and understanding of the interactional processes involved.

6. Research that coordinates the study of psychological processes with social structural and biological processes is favored. However, explanations derived from research at one level of analysis do not necessarily have validity at another level. Distinct validation criteria may need to be established for different levels of inquiry.

A Metatheory for
the Psychology of Gender

Constructionism appears to be gaining a following among contemporary psychologists. But major difficulties arise in putting it into practice. The psychology of gender provides a concrete example of an endeavor that is attempting to incorporate recognition of the social construction of its explanations with validation criteria that are consistent with the epistemological limits outlined above. Each of the four dilemmas chosen for analysis are described in terms of the psychology of gender and are then generalized to the larger discipline. In attempting to develop resolutions to the dilemmas, a dialectic approach is used (e.g., Buss, 1979; Hefner, Rebecca, & Oleshansky, 1975; Riegel, 1973; Rychlak, 1976; Sztompka, 1979). A variant of Sztompka's application of the technique is employed. It consists of examining assumptions underlying opposing viewpoints. The assumptions these viewpoints have in common are differentiated from those that are unique to each view. The underlying premises that are apparently contradictory are then juxtaposed to form new combinations of assumptions. A resolution is developed from among the new combinations. Because other syntheses could have been produced by different decompositions and restructuring, the proposed resolution to each dilemma is not the only one that could have been derived.

Dilemma One: Scholarship or Advocacy?

Unger (1982) identified the tension between scholarship and advocacy as a major problem in the psychology of gender. According to the pure scholarship approach, the researcher is a contributor to knowledge, intent on documenting what exists and neutral with respect to the way the knowledge is used. At the opposite extreme is the researcher who is committed to eliminating sexism wherever it is found and sees little value in scholarship except insofar as it serves to overthrow patriarchy.

One criticism of advocacy in psychology is that, to the extent that researchers function simultaneously as advocates, their ability to discern facts is compromised and their "evidence" serves primarily to justify already held beliefs (e.g., Baron, 1981; Hatch, 1982). As Campbell (1969) observed, excessive advocacy makes the researcher blind to reality testing. Some have suggested that explanations offered in the psychology of gender are based primarily on political expediency and have exceeded acceptable bounds (e.g., Adelson, 1978, 1980a, 1980b). The controversy is not about whether researchers may also be activists. Rather, it is about the extent to which theory and research in psychology are influenced by the researcher's affects, wishes, interests, and values (Riegel, 1972) and the consequences of this influence on the validity of derived knowledge.

In Table 1, a forced choice between scholarship and advocacy is avoided. Instead, the dilemma is viewed as a set of assumptions about the content and function of psychological activity. The distinction between content and function is adapted from Sztompka (1979). Thus, in Table 1, "content" and "function," rather than "scholarship" and "advocacy" are contrasted. This substitution allows one to recombine assumptions and

TABLE 1   Dilemma One: Scholarship or Advocacy?

| | Content | |
Function	Propositions about what is	Propositions about what should be
Change oriented	An emancipatory psychology of gender	Ideology
Change neutral	Intellectualism	

synthesize a transcendant viewpoint: an emancipatory psychology of gender, represented in the upper left hand entry of Table 1.

Such a psychology uses information about the world as it is, but is oriented progressively toward change. It is consistent with the spirit of Saul Alinsky, who suggested in his book, *Rules for Radicals* (1975), that "the basic requirement for understanding . . . change is to recognize the world as it is" (pp. 11–12). Constructing what could be requires knowledge of what is. To the extent that such a psychology seeks knowledge not only of what is, but also of "competencies or powers" (Manicas & Secord, 1983, p. 496), it is both descriptive of the world and oriented toward change.

The proposed recombination of alternatives is based on a distinction between descriptive and normative aspects of both the content and function of the research endeavor. Consistent with the constructionist view of the bidirectionality of knowledge and behavior, such a psychology of gender recognizes that scholarship informs political action and that the political stance of the researcher affects aspects of the research endeavor. Scholarship, as contained in the discipline's propositions and research results, has both intellectual and political functions. For example, propositions in the psychology of gender are both an attempt to understand the functioning of gender in the world as it is and an articulation of what could be.

Advocacy in the psychology of gender also involves both descriptive and normative aspects. Advocacy contributes to description insofar as it influences the content of theory and the very choices of topics, procedures, and methods of scholarship. Advocacy functions normatively when the implications of the scholarship (e.g., its meaning, consequences for theory, or utility for social policy change) are specified. In addition, the form and direction of the researcher's advocacy are both informative and instrumental. For example, in the psychology of gender, advocating attention to specific research problems informs others of what the researcher believes the functioning of gender in the world could be. The results of such research can be used as the basis for deciding whether and in what ways to intervene. Campbell (1969) observed that social issues researchers may properly be advocates for the importance of social problems and the need for research to solve them, as well as for honest evaluation and investigation of other possible solutions in the face of failure.

In addition, in an emancipatory psychology, explanations involving self-determination rather than control by others are developed and tested relative to other explanations. Furthermore, it is recognized that predictions may become self-fulfilling prophesies. Therefore, although actions that promote autonomy are valued, an emancipatory psychology "does not tell us what to do, if and when (and to the extent that we are) free" (Bhaskar, 1982, p. 299).

In summary, an emancipatory psychology attempts to avoid both ideology and intellectualism. Having emancipatory aims and advocating research on specific problems do not violate this dictum. But a priori conceptions of the "proper" relation of gender to behavior are to be avoided. Rather, this relationship is best viewed as an evolving one. Insofar as it is successful in these respects, such a psychology is ideology neither for nor against women or men. But neither is it a purely intellectual endeavor.

Dilemma Two: Science or Humanism?

As Kimble's (1984) survey suggested, psychology's two cultures are distinguished by the degree to which they subscribe to scientific versus humanistic values. According to the former value system, a scientific psychology seeks corroboration, prediction, and control via empirically based methods and standardized procedures. In contrast, the humanist values insight over data gathering and is suspicious of data-collection procedures that impose uniformity of treatment over those that are sensitive to individual and situational diversity. Whereas one group emphasizes psychology's roots in the natural sciences, the other focuses on the reflexivity resulting from any attempt to understand one's own species (Luckmann, 1973/1978).

In an effort to develop a third alternative, some authors have suggested that one can make choices about methods and procedures independently. Thus, the empirical methods of science can be combined with humanistic techniques appropriate to the problem, object of study, or domain (Luckmann, 1973/1978; Sztompka, 1979). Table 2 shows how the methodological and procedural aspects of both the scientific and humanistic assumptions can be separated and rearranged. The upper left entry contains a proposed resolution of the dilemma.

In its choice of methods, a psychological analysis of gender strives for corroboration and eschews procedures that objectify and dehumanize. The canons of science are accommodated to the humanity of its object of

TABLE 2 Dilemma Two: Science or Humanism?

	Methodology	
Procedure	Favors empiricism	Opposes empiricism
Allows interpretive techniques	Distinctively psychological analysis of gender	Antiscience
Does not allow interpretive techniques	Scientism	

study and the problems that are proper to it (e.g., Reinharz, 1979, 1982; Wallston, 1981). Scientific values dictate a reliance on empirical methods, and humanism contributes procedures that recognize and respect the common humanity of the investigator and the subjects of the investigation.

Such a psychology recognizes the particular value of empirical approaches and uses the procedures for organizing information and observations that are employed in the natural sciences when the problem is amenable to such techniques. Thus, it does not embrace antiscience. But procedures are adapted and individualized, and new ones are developed as necessary to the problem under study. In this way, the endeavor avoids scientism, whereby psychology is reduced to natural science. Most researchers in psychology recognize that exclusive reliance on the methods of the natural sciences does not provide a proper basis for psychology. The challenge is to gain consensus concerning the strength of the conclusions to be drawn, given the power of the techniques employed.

Dilemma Three: Orthodoxy or Schism?

The third dilemma concerns the nature of the relationship of the psychology of gender to psychology itself. Kahn and Jean (1983) considered aspects of this dilemma in their article on the fate of the psychology of women. In its extreme form, this problem can be viewed as a choice between orthodoxy (whereby the researcher becomes an uncritical insider) and schism (by which the researcher functions as an external critic). These alternatives imply a forced choice between psychology about gender on the one hand and feminism juxtaposed against psychology on the other.

In psychology about gender, the endeavor is reminiscent of Kuhn's (1962/1970) "normal" or "paradigmatic" science. The researcher develops theories, methods, and explanations in a manner consistent with how these tasks are approached in other areas of psychology. The research process relies implicitly, if not explicitly, on the belief that sound research is nonsexist research and that no additional considerations are needed to render the endeavor nonsexist. In feminism against psychology, the focus

TABLE 3   Dilemma Three: Orthodoxy or Schism?

Concern with gender bias	Legitimacy of psychology	
	Psychology as legitimate	Psychology as illegitimate
Addresses gender bias	A transformational psychology of gender	Separatism
Ignores gender bias	Subdiscipline	

is on overcoming perceived distortions, omissions, and misinformation in psychology. The object of study is sexism in psychology, and nonfeminist psychology is viewed as a mere reflection of sexism in the culture; its findings are considered artifactual and its explanations reductive. Neither choice is sufficiently self-critical.

This dilemma can be rephrased as a judgment about the legitimacy of psychology as a discipline and a decision about whether to focus on gender bias. Assumptions underlying these two aspects of the dilemma are presented in Table 3. One resolution of the dilemma between ortho-doxy and schism is a transformational psychology of gender that rejects and retains different aspects of each position (see upper left entry). Its focus on gender is consistent with a feminist value base. It attempts to counteract biases of omission by addressing questions relating to the experiences and concerns of girls and women (Reinharz, 1982). At the same time, from its epistemic base in psychology, it views psychology as a legitimate source of knowledge that can contribute to a nonsexist society. A transformational psychology of gender attempts to construct a nonsexist psychology from within the discipline, so as to avoid both gender bias and dissociation from psychology.

Such a psychology is critical and challenges existing explanations (Bhaskar, 1982). These characteristics are evident in Carolyn Sherif's (1979) article on bias in psychology. In this article, several shortcomings of mainstream psychology were enumerated, including (a) trait descrip-tions that ignore the social interactional basis for the alleged trait; (b) the failure of behaviorism to include in its explanations consciousness, self-awareness, and the capacity of persons to change their environments and alter their actions, as well as its failure to specify important aspects of the social environment, including value-laden cultural norms; and (c) the failure of psychodynamic theories to incorporate the social environment.

A transformational psychology of gender challenges extant explana-tions concerning gender differences and women's experiences and behav-ior (Lykes and Stewart, 1983; Reinharz, 1982; Weisstein, 1968). Such work emphasizes the development of more egalitarian social interactions and social structures and favors explanations that direct researchers toward interventions that would achieve these goals.

A transformational psychology of gender is also self-critical. For example, if the researcher assumes that gender equality is a worthy emancipatory goal, he or she still needs to critically evaluate which of several specifications of gender equality constitutes its best implementation in various concrete situations. Alternative formulations include gender blindness, equality of opportunity, equality of outcomes, treating like persons alike, treating unlike persons differently but with respect for their common claim to equity, and conditions that maximize self-valuing for all. Choosing among these alternatives requires not only impartial research but also value judgments about the kind of society wanted. Such decision making requires knowledge of what the respective effects will be and what kind of society is likely to result from such decisions (Kaufmann, 1973). This is a recursive process involving persons in their roles as citizens, researchers, and social policymakers.

Consider the concepts of androgyny and self-valuation. Androgyny (Bem, 1974; Constantinople, 1973; Spence, 1981; Spence, Helmreich, & Stapp, 1974) emerged out of dissatisfaction with the unidimensional, bipolar conceptualization of masculinity and femininity. But a transformational psychology does not view androgyny or any other predetermined conception of the self as ideal. Although self-valuing is a goal, concrete specifications of what traits are valuable cannot be made primarily on the basis of psychological theory and research. Decisions about goals are required in a transformational psychology of gender, but it is appropriate that the material specification of these goals have a *pro tem* quality and that they be subject to reevaluation.

Dilemma Four:
Subjectivity Versus Objectivity

Dilemma four addresses the problem of the researcher as a source of values as well as a source of knowledge (e.g., Wallston, 1981). Value judgments are assumed to introduce subjectivity and undermine objectivity. Allowing the research endeavor to be affected by one's emancipatory values while adhering to social scientific standards of objectivity is thought to be impossible. Thus, feminists (who value the personal dignity of women, equitable treatment of the sexes, and the political, economic, and social equality of women and men; Gove, 1966) are contrasted with social scientists (who strive to achieve unbiased knowledge).

One resolution to this dilemma recasts the problem as a distinction between "values and bias" rather than between "subjectivity and objectivity" (Sztompka, 1979, p. 223). In Table 4, beliefs about values and bias

TABLE 4   Dilemma Four: Subjectivity or Objectivity?

	Values	
Bias	Impossibility of avoiding value presuppositions	Possibility of avoiding value presuppositions
Possibility of unbiased knowledge	A committed psychology of gender	Objectivism
Impossibility of unbiased knowledge	Subjectivism	

are analyzed. The term *committed* is used to describe the proposed resolution and distinguish it from the stances of the objectivist and the subjectivist.

A committed psychology of gender rejects the claim that the psychology of gender must be biased because it involves value presuppositions. It also rejects the conclusion that it is possible to avoid value judgments. Extracting aspects of each alternative, a committed psychology of gender nevertheless attempts to coordinate the nature of its explanation seeking to the object of its explanation. It integrates value presuppositions that remain true to its identity as an empirically based discipline with values derived from its focus on human behavior. Consistent with Manicas and Secord's (1983) metatheory, criteria of theory evaluation are generated that accommodate the characteristics of the domain it attempts to explain.

For example, it is recognized that even a psychological science cannot prove the truth or falsity of any particular value judgment. Nevertheless, one can test the conditions and consequences of the realization of values and assess the usefulness of various means for achieving the goals of various social policies (Nagel, 1963). Allport's (1954) classic work stands as a model of such research, attempting to evaluate the best way to achieve already valued goals by clarifying causal and means-end relationships (Smith, 1979).

But how are values to be distinguished from biases in such a metatheory? In Sabini and Silver's (1982) view, bias is a conflict between the subjective view a person has and that which he or she ought to have. For example, a person's subjective judgments may be judged to be distorted because his other values or goals are not considered appropriate. The question thus becomes how to decide when values are inappropriate and thus biased.

Max Weber's (1949) discussion of the distinction between values and facts provides a framework for an answer to this question. He used the term "value-rationality" to connote the idea that, although a person's value commitment is a priori, such commitment can be rationally pursued.

In a psychology committed to maintaining a distinction between value and bias, the validity of value judgments requires a community in which all proponents have access to the judgment process and their credibility is not a function of social caste. The sociology of knowledge, discussed earlier, suggests that such conditions do not occur automatically. This is not to say that extending the opportunities for participation and eliminating social group prejudice guarantees valid inferences, but without these, the activity itself is subverted (e.g., Hull, Scott, & Smith, 1982; Wallston, 1981). As Kaufmann (1973) suggested, "there is no better way to discover objections and alternatives than exposure to the views of others, including people of the opposite sex, and of radically different backgrounds" (p. 230).

Clarification of values in psychology often requires criticism, not only by those who share the particular explanatory framework, but also by those who subscribe to alternate paradigms. Rein (1976) has suggested than an important part of being good critics for each other is caring about each other's work. This is most likely to be true of those who share one another's values. However, as Hennigan, Flay, and Cook (1980) have suggested, the elimination of bias may not be achievable at the level of like-minded individuals, but may be at the level of the system. Therefore, the committed psychologist in particular is especially well advised to seek the evaluation of critical others.

Specifying and Evaluating Explanatory Frameworks

In the metatheory for the psychology of gender just outlined, an attempt is made to reconcile the sociological and epistemological bases for evaluating explanations. Implicit in the proposed resolutions to the dilemmas is the view that such evaluations enter at many levels. These levels will now be explicitly examined in order to clarify the ways in which values act at each level. The levels of evaluation are assumed to be interactive and are separated here for analytical purposes only.

Level I: Value Presuppositions. Value presuppositions are those values that are not questioned by the research. They constitute the assumptions, or "givens," on which the research is based (Garfinkel, 1981). Nevertheless, value presuppositions themselves are subject to scrutiny, according to how restrictive, useful, ethical, or just they are. For example, using the criterion of restrictiveness, value presuppositions in research may be evaluated by asking "What values does this research challenge, and which ones does it presume to be 'given'?"

Level II: Question Construction and Testing. The kind of question asked is guided by the value presuppositions and, in turn, influences the methods used to answer the question. As Garfinkel (1981) has suggested, if value presuppositions (at Level I) are viewed as establishing the outer boundaries of explanations, the form of the question asked and the methods used to test it (at Level II) can be viewed as establishing the domain for which an explanation is sought. Cook and Campbell (1979) used the terms *discriminant* and *convergent* validity testing to describe the complementary aspects of such a process.

For example, one basis for assessing the value of the way a research question is constructed and tested is the extent to which it can reveal causal relationships. Given this underlying premise (at Level I), the validity of the relationship of research questions to their tests (at Level II) can be assessed using various criteria. Cook and Campbell's (1979) discussion of threats to various types of internal and external validity assumes the search for causal relationships to be valuable (at Level I) and assesses the degree to which given designs allow for the unambiguous testing of such relationships (at Level II). Nevertheless, standard statistical procedures may be employed (at Level II), without subscribing to the "received" epistemology (at Level I) with respect to the symmetry of explanation and prediction.

Level III: Interpretation and Use of Results. In accord with the Kuhnian critique, statements of results are now viewed as being influenced by the particular social/historical context in which they are made. It is also widely acknowledged that the interpretations of results are value based. For example, the question of the utility of results may be evaluated in some areas of research by asking "does the result of the research suggest some intervention?" Because, at Level II, the form of explanation sought is not value free, it has an effect on the interventions that are derivable from the result obtained. These interventions presuppose some value structures and challenge others.

Another source of influence on Level III judgments of the validity of results is subjective differences in thresholds for what constitutes support for or against a given hypothesis. In Putnam's (1981) view, such differences make it likely that researchers interpreting the same data will derive different conclusions from them. Putnam argued that a scientist's antecedent beliefs about the world (Level I) affect his or her consequent beliefs in hypotheses (Level III) and that the reasonableness of prior hypotheses differs among researchers.

Sex/Gender as a Subject Variable and a Social Stimulus Variable

To illustrate the relationship among Levels I, II, and III in psychological research on gender, two research strategies in the study of cognition and gender will be described. In one, the focus is on traits, especially two broad sets of skills (verbal and spatial-mathematical). In such research, sex or gender has usually been viewed as a personal attribute that is associated with certain behavior patterns. A second research program takes the social situational significance of sex or gender as the basic phenomenon to be studied. In the latter perspective, a person's sex or gender usually constitutes one of a number of aspects of the social environment to which other persons respond.

These two sets of concerns, along with their respective coordinated methods, results, and their distinctive accompanying intervention agendas, constitute two research strategies that coexist in the cognitive psychology of gender. They will be labeled the *trait* approach and the *situation* approach. Although measures of psychological gender are commonly employed in both approaches, for simplicity of presentation and economy of space, sex rather than gender will be used in the examples of each of these constructionist strategies.

At Level I, the level of value presuppositions, the adherent of the trait perspective may be aware that sex differences in performance on cognitive skills tests are small (by comparison to variation within sex) and that, overall, such differences account for small amounts of variation in performance (e.g., Hyde, 1981). Small as they are on average, however, the differences at the ends of the distribution of skill level reflect proportions of three boys to every girl in remedial reading programs (Finnuchi & Childs, 1981) and seven or eight junior high school boys to every girl scoring 600 or above on the SAT Math test (e.g., Benbow & Stanley, 1980, 1983; Fox, Tobin, & Brody, 1979).

Some trait researchers may attach greater importance to the sex differences in representation at the ends of the distribution than to the proportion of variance accounted for by sex. Some may be concerned with the preponderance of boys in reading disabilities classes and others with the small number of girls who score high in math, depending on the researcher's value presuppositions. Nevertheless, in the trait approach to the psychology of gender, the focal questions are about the development of the particular skill under study and the origins and consequences of the gender differences.

At Level II of this perspective, such questions guide theory development, hypothesis formation, research design, and analysis. They become the phenomenon that requires explanation. The interrelationship of the biological, social, and psychological systems may be assessed (e.g., Allen, Wittig, & Butler, 1981; Wittig, 1976, 1979; Wittig & Petersen, 1979). Alternative structural models hypothesizing bidirectional causal paths may be tested to identify precursors of sex differences in cognitive functioning (e.g., Eccles [Parsons], 1983).

Decisions and outcomes from Levels I and II form the boundary conditions of plausible intervention strategies at Level III. For example, one may attempt to improve girls' and women's competence at masculine sex-typed tasks. This work may lead to the development and evaluation of educational programs for women with high math aptitude so as to increase their entrance into and advancement in less feminine-stereotyped jobs (for example, Wittig, Sasse, & Giacomi, 1984). The trait approach challenges the social structure at Level III, the level of intervention.

This trait perspective, wherein sex or gender is viewed as a subject variable, may be compared with the social situational approach that emphasizes sex or gender as an aspect of the social situation. In the latter research strategy, one might begin (at Level I) by questioning a value system that pays graduates with baccalaureates in male-dominated majors substantially more than those with baccalaureates in female-dominated fields.

At Level II of the social structural approach, this devaluation of skills at which girls and women excel becomes the phenomenon to be explained. It guides theory development, hypothesis formation, research design, and analysis. It may lead to the study of sex bias in judgments of competence (e.g., Vaughn & Wittig, 1981) and in reward allocation (e.g., Sagan, Pondel, & Wittig, 1981; Wittig, 1985; Wittig, Marks, & Jones, 1981) when actual performance levels are held constant. Designs that vary the sex and status of actors independently, so that their relative importance in predicting aspirations, expectancies, performance, and evaluations can be assessed, are favored.

At Level III of this strategy, interventions are developed that are consistent with the value judgments that were made at Level I and the questions that determined the research strategy at Level II. A researcher might attempt to develop unbiased job analyses for groups that are concerned with wage and salary differentials across sex-segregated occupations. Determining comparability of performance in qualitatively different jobs (e.g., Tangri, 1981; Treiman & Hartmann, 1981) exemplifies Level III of the social structural approach.

In summary, we need knowledge of individuals' cross-situational similarities as well as of the effects of situations on individuals if we are to understand the reciprocal causation that characterizes persons in situations. Both are needed to understand developmental processes (Scarr, 1984). Both approaches to the psychology of gender challenge the social structure within their respective research strategies.

Conclusions

A constructionist psychology of gender uses knowledge of what is as a means of understanding what could be. In this endeavor, a wide range of procedures is employed to acquire knowledge that is corroborative and able to provide causal explanation and some degree of prediction. The legitimacy of such corroboration depends in part on the participation of individuals of diverse backgrounds. Such a psychology is critical and attempts to reconstruct psychology, and itself as part of psychology, from within the discipline. It is committed to avoiding bias, but it is not itself value free. The American Psychological Association's Division 35 guidelines for nonsexist research (McHugh, Koeske, & Frieze, 1981) reflect this perspective. An important criterion of the validity of theory and research in this endeavor is the extent to which they contribute to our understanding of gender as a cause and consequence of the social structure.

Notes

This article is based on the author's presidential address to the Psychology of Women Division of the American Psychological Association (APA) at the APA meeting in August 1982 in Washington, DC. Revisions were presented as colloquia at the University of California, Santa Cruz (April 1983), Claremont Graduate School (October, 1983), and the University of California, Los Angeles (May, 1984).

Thanks are expressed to Lee Cooper, Bernard Kaplan (who honored the manuscript with an extensive critique), Kenneth Pope, Gillian Turner, Mary Roth Walsh, Barbara Strudler Wallston, and anonymous reviewers for their comments on earlier versions of this manuscript. The author is indebted to Don E. Dulany and Louis A. Ryan for introducing the author to issues addressed herein.

1. Assignment by *gender* is a social categorization emphasizing psychological attributes. Although assignment by *sex* also functions as a social label, it connotes an anatomical dichotomy (Sherif, 1981).

References

Adelson, J. (1978). The slippery slope. *Social Research, 45,* 411–415.
Adelson, J. (1980a, March 24). Androgyny advocates pose a threat to scientific objectivity. *Behavior Today,* p. 1.
Adelson, J. (1980b, June 2). The intimidation is obvious. *Behavior Today,* p. 3.
Alinsky, S. (1975). *Rules for radicals.* New York: Vintage Books.
Allen, M. J., Wittig, M. A., & Butler, K. (1981). Comment on Thomas and Jamison's A test of the X-linked genetic hypothesis for sex differences on Piaget's water level task. *Developmental Review, 1,* 284–288.
Allport, G. W. (1954). *The nature of prejudice.* Cambridge, MA: Addison-Wesley.
Argyle, M. (1978). Discussion chapter: An appraisal of the new approach to the study of social behaviour. In M. Brenner, P. Marsh, & M. Brenner (Eds.), *The social contexts of method* (pp. 237–255). New York: St. Martin's Press.
Barber, B., & Hirsch, W. (Eds.). (1963). *The sociology of science.* New York: Free Press of Glencoe.

Barnes, B. (1974). *Scientific knowledge and sociological theory*. Boston: Routledge & Kegan Paul.

Barnes, J. A. (1977). *Ethics of inquiry in social science*. London: Oxford University Press.

Baron, R. (1981, Fall). The spring of our discontent: Some observations on the less-than-shocking view that science and politics don't mix. *Newsletter of the American Psychological Association Division on Developmental Psychology*, pp. 28–33.

Bem, S. (1974). The measurement of psychological androgyny. *Journal of Consulting and Clinical Psychology, 42*(2), 155–162.

Benbow, C. P., & Stanley, J. C. (1980). Sex differences in mathematics ability: Fact or artifact? *Science, 210*, 1262–1264.

Benbow, C. P., & Stanley, J. C. (1983). Sex differences in mathematical reasoning ability: More facts. *Science, 222*, 1029–1030.

Bhaskar, R. (1982). Emergence, explanation, and emancipation. In P. F. Secord (Ed.), *Explaining human behavior: Consciousness, human action, and social structure* (pp. 275–310). Beverly Hills, CA: Sage.

Brewer, M. B., & Collins, B. E. (Eds.). (1981). *Scientific inquiry and the social sciences*. San Francisco: Jossey-Bass.

Bronfenbrenner, U. (1977). Toward an experimental ecology of human development. *American Psychologist, 32*, 513–531.

Buss, A. R. (1979). *A dialectical psychology*. New York: Irvington Press.

Campbell, D. T. (1969). Reforms as experiments. *American Psychologist, 24*, 409–429.

Campbell, D. T. (1974). Evolutionary epistemology. In P. A. Schilpp (Ed.), *The philosophy of Karl Popper* (pp. 413–463). La Salle, IL: Open Court.

Constantinople, A. (1973). Masculinity-femininity: An exception to the famous dictum? *Psychological Bulletin, 80*, 389–487.

Cook, T. D., & Campbell, D. T. (1979). *Quasi-experimentation: Design and analysis issues for field settings*. Chicago: Rand-McNally.

Deaux, K. (1984). From individual differences to social categories: Analysis of a decade's research on gender. *American Psychologist, 39*, 105–116.

Deaux, K. (1985). Sex and gender. In M. R. Rosenzweig & L. W. Porter (Eds.), *Annual Review of Psychology* (Vol. 36, pp. 49–81). Palo Alto, CA: Annual Reviews, Inc.

Eccles (Parsons), J. (1983). Expectancies, values, and academic behaviors. In J. T. Spence (Ed.), *Achievement and achievement motives: Psychological and sociological approaches* (pp. 75–146). San Francisco: W. H. Freeman.

Feldman, C. F., & Hass, W. A. (1970). Controls, conceptualization, and the interrelation between experimental and correlational research. *American Psychologist, 25*, 633–635.

Fidell, L. S. (1970). Empirical verification of sex discrimination in hiring practices in psychology. *American Psychologist, 25*, 1094–1098.

Finnuchi, J., & Childs, B. (1981). Are there really sex differences in dyslexia? In A. Ansara, N. Geschwind, A. Galaburda, M. Albert, & N. Gartrell (Eds.), *Sex differences in dyslexia* (pp. 1–10). Towson, MD: The Orton Dyslexia Society.

Fox, L. H., Tobin, D., & Brody, L. (1979). Sex-role socialization and achievement in mathematics. In M. A. Wittig & A. C. Petersen (Eds.), *Sex-related differences in cognitive functioning: Developmental issues* (pp. 303–332). New York: Academic Press.

Garfinkel, A. (1981). *Forms of explanation.* New Haven: Yale University Press.

Gergen, K. J. (1973). Social psychology as history. *Journal of Personality and social Psychology, 26,* 309–320.

Gergen, K. J. (1978). Experimentation in social psychology: A reappraisal. *European Journal of Social Psychology, 8,* 507–527.

Gergen, K. J. (1982). *Toward transformation in social knowledge.* New York: Springer-Verlag.

Gergen, K. J. (1983, August). *Social constructionism, psychology, and science.* Paper presented at the meeting of the American Psychological Association, Anaheim, CA.

Gergen, K. J., & Morawski, J. (1980). An alternative metatheory for social psychology. In L. Wheeler (Ed.), *Review of personality and social psychology* (pp. 326–352). Beverly Hills: Sage.

Goldberg, P. A. (1968, April). Are women prejudiced against women? *Transaction,* pp. 28–30.

Golden, C. (1981, April). *Psychoanalysis, feminism, and object relations theory.* Paper presented at the meeting of the Association for Women in Psychology, Boston, MA.

Gove, P. B. (Ed.). (1966). *Webster's third new international dictionary of the English language.* Springfield, MA: G. & C. Merriam Co.

Harré, R. (1978). Accounts, actions, and meanings—The practice of participatory psychology. In M. Brenner, P. Marsh, & M. Brenner (Eds.), *The social contexts of method* (pp. 44–65). New York: St. Martin's Press.

Hatch, O. G. (1982). Psychology, society, and politics, *American Psychologist, 37,* 1031–1037.

Hefner, R., Rebecca, M., & Oleshansky, D. (1975). The development of sex role transcendance. *Human Development, 18,* 143–158.

Henley, N. M. (in press). Review essay: Psychology and gender. *Signs.*

Hennigan, K. M., Flay, B. R., & Cook, T. D. (1980). "Give me the facts:" Some suggestions for using social science knowledge in national policy-making. In R. F. Kidd & M. Saks (Eds.), *Advances in applied social psychology* (Vol. 1, pp. 113–147). Hillsdale, NJ: Erlbaum.

Hull, G. T., Scott, P. B., & Smith, B. (1982). *But some of us are brave: Black women's studies.* Old Westbury, NY: Feminist Press.

Hyde, J. S. (1981). How large are cognitive gender differences? A meta-analysis using ω^2 and d. *American Psychologist, 36,* 892–901.

Joynson, R. B. (1974). *Psychology and common sense.* London: Routledge & Kegan Paul.

Kahn, A. S., & Jean, P. J. (1983). Integration and elimination or separation and redefinition: The future of the psychology of women as a discipline. *Signs, 8*(4), 659–671.

Kaplan, A. (1964). *The conduct of inquiry.* San Francisco: Chandler.

Kaplan, B. (1967). Meditations on genesis. *Human Development, 10,* 65–87.

Kaufmann, W. (1973). *Without guilt and justice.* New York: Wyden.

Kimble, G. (1984). Psychology's two cultures. *American Psychologist, 39,* 833–839.

Koch, S. (1981). The nature and limits of psychological knowledge. *American Psychologist, 36,* 257–269.

Kuhn, T. S. (1970). *The structure of scientific revolutions* (2nd ed.). Chicago: University of Chicago Press. (Original work published 1962)

Lewin, K. (1946). Action research and minority problems. *Journal of Social Issues, 2,* 34–46.

Luckmann, T. (1973/1978). Philosophy, social sciences, and everyday life. In T. Luckmann (Ed.), *Phenomenology and sociology* (2nd ed., pp. 217–256). New York: Penguin.

Lykes, M. B., & Stewart, A. (1983, August). *Evaluating the feminist challenge in psychology: 1963–1983.* Paper presented at the meeting of the American Psychological Association, Anaheim, CA.

Manicas, P. T., & Secord, P. F. (1983). Implications for psychology of the new philosophy of science. *American Psychologist, 38,* 399–413.

McHugh, M., Koeske, R., & Frieze, I. (1981). *Guidelines for nonsexist research* [Task force report of APA Division 35]. (Available from I. Frieze, University of Pittsburgh, Pittsburgh, PA, 15260)

Menzel, H. (1978). Meaning—Who needs it? In M. Brenner, P. Marsh, & M. Brenner (Eds.), *The social contexts of method* (pp. 140–171). New York: St. Martin's Press.

Merton, R. K. (1957). *Social theory and social structure.* New York: Free Press of Glencoe.

Mishler, E. (1979). Meaning in context: Is there any other kind? *Harvard Educational Review, 49*(1), 1–19.

Moscovici, S. (1972). Society and theory in social psychology. In J. Israel & H. Tajfel (Eds.), *The context of social psychology: A critical assessment* (pp. 17–68). London: Academic Press.

Myrdal, G. (1969). Biases in social research. In A. Tiselius & S. Nilsson (Eds.), *The place of values in a world of facts* (pp. 155–161). New York: Wiley.

Nagel, E. (1963). Malicious philosophies of science. In B. Barber & W. Hirsch (Eds.), *The sociology of science* (pp. 623–639). New York: Free Press of Glencoe.

Parlee, M. B. (1975). Psychology: Review essay. *Signs, 1,* 119–138.

Parlee, M. B. (1979). Psychology and women: Review essay. *Signs, 5,* 121–133.

Peters, D. P., & Ceci, S. J. (1982). Peer review practices of psychological journals: The fate of published articles, submitted again. *Behavioral and Brain Sciences, 5,* 187–195.

Pheterson, G. I., Kiesler, S. B., & Goldberg, P. A. (1971). Evaluation of the performance of women as a function of their sex, achievement, and personal history. *Journal of Personality and Social Psychology, 19,* 114–118.

Piaget, J. (1977). *Psychology and epistemology: Towards a theory of knowledge* (A. Rosin, Trans.). New York: Penguin. (Original work published 1970).

Polanyi, M. (1958). *Personal knowledge.* New York: Harper & Row.

Popper, K. (1959). *The logic of scientific discovery.* New York: Basic Books. (Original work published as *Logik des Forschung.* Vienna: Springer-Verlag, 1935).

Putnam, H. (1981). The impact of science on modern conceptions of rationality. *Synthese, 46,* 359–382.

Rein, M. (1976). *Social science and public policy.* New York: Penguin.

Reinharz, S. (1979). *On becoming a social scientist: From survey research and participant observation to experiential analysis.* San Francisco: Jossey-Bass.

Reinharz, S. (1982, August). The future of feminist psychology. In R. K. Unger (Chair), *The future of the psychology of women: Separation, integration, or elimination?* Symposium conducted at the meeting of the American Psychological Association, Washington, DC.

Riegel, K. (1972). The influence of economic and political ideologies on the development of developmental psychology. *Psychological Bulletin, 78,* 129–141.

Riegel, K. (1973). Dialectical operations: The final period of cognitive development. *Human Development, 16,* 346–380.

Rosnow, R. (1981). *Paradigms in transition.* New York: Oxford University Press.

Ross, C. (1982). Rejected published work: Similar fate for fiction. *Behavioral and Brain Sciences, 5,* 236.

Royce, J. (1982). Philosophic issues, Division 24, and the future. *American Psychologist, 37,* 258–266.

Rychlak, J. F. (1976). *Contributions to human development: Vol. 2. Dialectic: Humanistic rationale for behavior and development.* New York: Karger.

Rychlak, J. F. (Ed.). (1977). *The psychology of rigorous humanism.* New York: Wiley.

Sabini, J. P., & Silver, M. (1982). Some senses of subjective. In P. F. Secord (Ed.), *Explaining human behavior: Consciousness, human action, and social structure* (pp. 71–91). Beverly Hills: Sage.

Sagan, K., Pondel, M., & Wittig, M. A. (1981). The effect of anticipated future interaction on reward allocation in same- and opposite-sex dyads. *Journal of Personality, 49,* 439–449.

Sampson, E. E. (1977). Psychology and the American ideal. *Journal of Personality and Social Psychology, 35,* 767–782.

Sampson, E. E. (1978). Scientific paradigms and social values: Wanted—a scientific revolution. *Journal of Personality and Social Psychology, 36,* 1332–1343.

Scarr, S. (1984, Spring). The danger of having pet variables. *Newsletter of the APA Division on Developmental Psychology,* pp. 24–34.

Schuler, H. (1982). *Ethical problems in psychological research.* (Woodruff, M. S., & Wicklund, R. A., Trans). New York: Academic Press.

Secord, P. F. (1982). Interfacing the personal and the social. In P. F. Secord (Ed.), *Explaining human behavior: Consciousness, human action, and social structure* (pp. 13–34). Beverly Hills, CA: Sage.

Sherif, C. (1979). Bias in psychology. In J. A. Sherman & E. T. Beck (Eds.), *The prism of sex: Essays in the sociology of knowledge* (pp. 93–133). Madison, WI: University of Wisconsin Press.

Sherif, C. (1981). Needed concepts in the study of gender identity. *The Psychology of Women Quarterly, 6,* 375–398.

Sherman, J. A., & Beck, E. T. (Eds.). (1979). *The prism of sex: Essays in the sociology of knowledge.* Madison: University of Wisconsin Press.

Smith, M. B. (1979). Attitudes, values, and selfhood. In H. E. Howe, Jr. (Ed.), *Nebraska Symposium on Motivation:* Vol. 27. *Beliefs, attitudes, and values* (pp. 305–355). Lincoln: University of Nebraska Press.

Spence, J. T. (1981). Changing conceptions of men and women: A psychologist's perspective. In E. Langland & W. Gove (Eds.), *A feminist perspective in the academy: The difference it makes.* Chicago: University of Chicago Press.

Spence, J. T., Helmreich, R. L., & Stapp, J. T. (1974). The Personal Attributes Questionnaire: A measure of sex-role stereotypes and masculinity-femininity (Ms. No. 617). *JSAS Catalogue of Selected Documents in Psychology, 4,* 43.

Staats, A. W. (1981). Paradigmatic behaviorism, unified theory construction methods, and the zeitgeist of separatism. *American Psychologist, 36,* 239–256.

Sztompka, P. (1979). *Sociological dilemmas.* New York: Academic Press.

Tangri, S. S. (1981, August). How did we get from there to here: From protectionism to comparable worth. In A. T. Viviano (Chair), *Can the law reach? Sex bias in wage compensation.* Symposium conducted at the meeting of the American Psychological Association, Los Angeles.

Toulmin, S. (1953). *The philosophy of science.* London: Hutchinson.

Treiman, D. J., & Hartmann, H. (Eds.). (1981). *Women, work, and wages: Equal pay for jobs of equal value.* Washington, DC: National Academy Press.

Unger, R. (1979). Toward a redefinition of sex and gender. *American Psychologist, 34,* 1085–1094.

Unger, R. (1982). Advocacy versus scholarship revisited: Issues in the psychology of women. *Psychology of Women Quarterly, 7,* 5–17.

Unger, R. (1983). Through the looking glass: No wonderland yet! *Psychology of Women Quarterly, 8,* 9–32.

Vaughn, L. S., & Wittig, M. A. (1981). Women's occupation, competence, and role overload as determinants of evaluation by others. *Journal of Applied Social Psychology, 10,* 398–415.

Vaughter, R. (1976). Review essay: Psychology. *Signs, 2,* 120–146.

Walker, B. M. (1981). Psychology and feminism—If you can't beat them, join them. In D. Spender (Ed.), *Men's studies modified: The impact of feminism in the academic disciplines.* Oxford, England: Pergamon Press.

Wallston, B. S. (1981). What are the questions in the psychology of women: A feminist approach to research. *Psychology of Women Quarterly, 5,* 597–617.

Wallston, B. S. (in press). Social psychology of women and gender. *Journal of Applied Social Psychology.*

Weber, M. (1949). *The methodology of the social sciences.* Glencoe, IL: Free Press.

Weisstein, N. (1968). *Kinder, küche, kirche as scientific law: Psychology constructs the female.* Boston: New England Free Press.

Wittig, M. A. (1976). Psychological sex differences: How much of a difference do genes make? *Sex Roles, 2*(1), 63–74.

Wittig, M. A. (1979). Genetic influences on intellectual functioning: Theoretical and methodological issues. In M. A. Wittig & A. C. Petersen (Eds.), *Sex-related differences in cognitive functioning: Developmental issues* (pp. 21–65). New York: Academic Press.

Wittig, M. A. (1985). Sex-role norms and gender-related attainment values: Their role in attributions of success and failure. *Sex Roles, 12,* 1–13.

Wittig, M. A., Marks, G. S., & Jones, G. (1981). Luck versus effort attributions: Effect on reward allocation. *Personality and Social Psychology Bulletin, 7,* 71–78.

Wittig, M. A., & Petersen, A. C. (Eds.). (1979). *Sex-related differences in cognitive functioning: Developmental issues.* New York: Academic Press.

Wittig, M. A., Sasse, S. H., & Giacomi, J. (1984). Predictive validity of five cognitive skills tests among women receiving engineering training. *Journal of Research in Science Teaching, 21,* 537–546.

11
INTEGRATING THE FEMINIST CRITIQUE AND THE CRISIS IN SOCIAL PSYCHOLOGY: ANOTHER LOOK AT RESEARCH METHODS

Barbara Strudler Wallston
and Kathleen E. Grady

The major issues raised by the study of women and gender (and social psychology) have been expounded independently but have much in common. The lack of cross-citation among these literatures is not surprising, given the narrow scope of most of our reading as well as the nature of the scientific enterprise with respect to citation (cf. Kuhn, 1970; Merton, 1968; Over, 1981). Thus, a number of discussions of problems in social psychology (e.g., Baumgardner, 1976; Buss, 1975; Sampson, 1977; Weissberg, 1976) stress the importance of the social context and its influence on the research process with no recognition of the parallel feminist critiques (e.g., Parlee, 1975; Sherif, 1979; Shields, 1975; Vaughter, 1976; Weisstein, 1970; Wittig, 1982). Engendering cross-fertilization for the benefit of methodology in social psychology and in the psychology of women is one of our goals in this chapter. However, we begin with a consideration of how the study of women and gender has contributed to the debate.

The study of women and gender has the potential for a dual effect on methods in social psychology. On the one hand, the numerous feminist critiques of sample selection, control groups, and interpretation of results can lead to a more careful application of existing methods. Thus, they can make our science more "scientific." At the same time, there is a clear call for a broadening of available methods, more intensive descriptive research, more attention to understudied issues (such as rape, parenting, paid and family work), and an increased awareness of the political and cultural context for research.

The increasing emphasis on descriptive and correlational methods by researchers addressing issues of sex and gender has generated a debate about "hard" vs. "soft" methods that has often used the unfortunate labels of "masculine" vs. "feminine" (Bernard, 1973; Carlson, 1972). We believe that the gender of the researchers and the novelty of the questions asked are so badly confounded that it is impossible to assert that women researchers have affinity for particular methods. The scientifically sound use of observation and description to study relatively new questions with rigorous tests reserved for a more highly developed "state of the art" may better describe the current state of psychology research. In fact, some of our most distinguished colleagues have now, after a lifetime of rigorous empirical research, begun to employ more qualitative methods to address novel or intransigent questions (cf., Festinger, 1980; Schachter, 1982).

Although the potential for contribution in methodology is tremendous, the actual impact on the field of social psychology has been less than in more substantive areas. Sherif's (1979) excellent discussion of bias in psychology and, in particular, the issue of status hierarchies in psychology suggests some reasons why this may be the case. Sherif notes that social psychology was at the bottom of the status hierarchy in 1943 and that the improved status of social psychology has come about through "self-conscious efforts to be accepted as experimental social psychologists. . . . The way to respectability in this scheme has been the appearance of rigor and scientific inquiry, bolstered by highly restricted notions of what science is about" (p. 98). We believe this continued emphasis on narrowly defined experimentalism has been one of the reasons that feminist methodological innovations and critiques have not had a substantial impact on social psychology.

In this chapter we have organized methodological issues into question formulation, sample selection, design, operationalization, the social psychology of the research process, statistics, and interpretation. These areas overlap extensively, and some of the distinctions, as well as the topic order, are clearly arbitrary. Over the months we have spent writing this chapter, everything written about methods or feminism has at some point seemed relevant. The resulting selection of citations has consequently been somewhat arbitrary.

One major goal has been the attempt to integrate the perspectives of the feminist critique and the "crisis" literature. As will become clear, it is our opinion that social psychology is getting older *and* better. Rather than simply rehashing criticisms, we try to highlight ways in which the study of women and gender has contributed to this process.

Question Formulation

How do we derive questions? Few of our research courses focus on the issue and our textbooks give little attention to question derivation. In general, we undervalue question generation (cf. Wallston, 1981), which is part of the art of scientific inquiry. McGuire (1973) has brought this to our attention as the first of seven koan "the sound of one hand clapping. . . . and the wrong hand" (p. 450). He notes that hypothesis testing has received 90% of our attention, while hypothesis generation has been neglected, "probably due to the suspicion that so complex a creative process as hypothesis formation is something that cannot be taught" (pp. 450–451).

In an unusual vein, and one that we applaud, Wrightsman and Deaux (1981) devote three pages of the methods chapter in their recent text revision to question formulation, and they note this in the preface as an important change. Unlike the traditional coverage of this issue, which assumes that questions are logical derivations from theory, Wrightsman and Deaux note theory as only one source of questions. They also give examples of observations of phenomena outside of the laboratory from which ideas have developed which are then translated into questions (and possibly theory) that are testable.

Frequently our questions in psychology reflect areas that are important and/or problematic to us. It is more than coincidence, for example, that much dual career research has been developed by members of dual career couples (e.g., Bryson, Bryson, Licht, & Licht, 1976; Rapoport & Rapoport, 1978; Wallston, Foster, & Berger, 1978). In social psychology, the emphasis on research on achievement and the nature of the definition of achievement certainly reflect the background and interest of the researchers (see Sutherland & Veroff [1985]). On the other hand, competence and achievement in parenting, homemaking, and volunteer activities have not been studied (cf. Wallston & O'Leary, 1981). This emphasis reflects the general valuing of traditionally male achievement in our culture (cf. Lenney, 1977; Mednick, Tangri, & Hoffman, 1975; Unger, 1979) and the socialization of researchers (female and male) into this value perspective.

Experience is a good source of questions. It may provide the best insights and most creative ideas. Unger (1981b) has noted that personal experience leads to questioning assumptions that others take as self-evident. Thus, as long as most psychologists are white, middle-class males, many important questions will remain outside the experience of most psychologists. Samelson (1978), in an historical analysis, has suggested that the change in psychological focus from the study of race differences to the study of racial prejudice could be accounted for by the entry of ethnic minority group members into the psychological profession. Unger (1981b) points out an analogous shift from the study of sex differences to the study of sexism. Thus, there are scientific, in addition to justice, arguments for changing the racist, classist, and sexist procedures by which students are selected and socialized. For example, Sherwood and Nataupsky (1968) have shown that the biographical characteristics of investigators were predictive of their conclusions regarding race differences in intelligence. Changing the faces of our student body is a first step. Allowing them to ask questions of interest to them, even or especially when those questions are beyond our experience, may be even more important in broadening our understanding of human behavior.

McGuire's (1973) initial suggestions for hypothesis generation sources are worth reiteration: "case study, paradoxical incident, analogy, hypothetic deductive method, functional analysis, rules of thumb, conflicting results, accounting for exceptions, and straightening out complex relationships" (p. 451). Wallston (1981) explicates three additional principles for question generation: (1) experience which can be expanded by observation and discussion with others is a rich source of questions; (2) public policy issues (cf. Tangri & Strasburg, 1979) should be a focus of research; (3) situational as well as personological factors must be considered as potential causes of behavior when generating questions.

Methods for expanding our experience are critical to the formulation of good questions. Vaughter (1976) has argued for a participatory model in which research subjects and the public become an integral part of the scientific enterprise. The work of Plas and her colleagues (Plas & Bellet, 1983) to develop measures of Indian children's value-attitude orientations exemplifies such an approach. The Anglo research team lived on an Indian reservation with Indian families in order to better understand the culture. Questions they developed for the scale were reviewed by elders of the tribe to check face validity for the relevant population. Although less extreme, the recent work by Azjen and Fishbein (1980) has stressed the importance of eliciting salient beliefs from a representative sample of the relevant population in order to evaluate attitudes. Ethnographers regularly validate their perceptions against those of research participants (cf. Corsaro, 1981, Leinhardt, 1978; Wallston, 1983).

Research on sex and gender particularly illustrates the failure to give sufficient consideration to situational factors (cf. Riger & Galligan, 1980;

Wallston, 1978), although other areas (e.g., Caplan & Nelson, 1973) have shown this failure as well. Condry and Dyer (1976), for example, have presented an important reinterpretation of the fear of success literature from a situational rather than a motivational interpretation. Allen (1979) similarly notes that research on black women's attainment has focused on personal characteristics and background rather than scrutinizing institutional and societal practices that systematically deny equal opportunity to black women. In fact, Caplan and Nelson (1973) found that only 16% of the studies of blacks included in six issues of the 1970 *Psychological Abstracts* examined situational causes rather than taking a personological approach (cf. Unger, 1981b). This tendency on the part of psychologists may reflect observers' tendencies to overattribute the causes of women's behavior to personal factors and men's behavior to environmental factors (cf. Hansen & O'Leary, 1983; O'Leary & Hansen [1985]; Wallston & O'Leary, 1981). Not only have personal factors been overused to explicate female behavior, but sex (which is a personal factor) has been used as an explanatory variable, although it is frequently confounded with situational factors such as status or power (cf. Dion [1985]; Eagly & Wood [1985]; Henley, 1977; Miller & Zeitz, 1978; Piliavin & Unger [1985]; Unger, 1979).

To summarize, we have argued that questions and theory are undervalued in psychology. We have suggested some appropriate sources of good questions. Because a researcher's experience is often a source of questions, it is important to broaden the experiential base of future researchers. The study of women and gender illustrates how the addition of female researchers has broadened the nature of the questions that are asked. Minority researchers and those from other social class and ethnic backgrounds would similarly enhance our understanding of human experience.

Design

We have already argued that the design should reflect the question. This is not to imply that there is a single design appropriate to each question (cf. Wallston, 1983). In fact, we can draw the best conclusions when several different methodologies are used to test the same hypothesis. Such triangulation (cf. Jick, 1979; Wallston, 1983) helps confirm that our findings are not tied to the specific methodology used. The important point is that some methodologies are not inherently better than others (cf. Labouvie, 1975), although fads in our field tend to suggest that they are. As Glass and Ellett (1980) note in their discussion of evaluation research, the best design is a compromise between the possibilities afforded by the situation and the research goal. Although choosing the situation allows some flexibility, practical constraints are involved in all research design.

Most of us have been socialized to think in terms of 2 × 2 analysis of variance models (cf. Rucci & Tweney, 1980). This limited design does not allow the investigation of complex processes when more than two variables with two levels of each may be important. Thus, our ideas regarding design, particularly to the extent that they are narrow, limit the kinds of questions we ask.

As social psychologists, we have been trained to value the quantitative over the qualitative, and experimental (manipulation) over correlational (measurement only) designs (cf. Wallston, 1983). Higbee, Millard, and Folkman (1980) found that 74% of journal articles in four mainline social psychology journals in 1978–79 utilized experimental methodology. There are stages of knowledge where qualitative and observational techniques may be particularly appropriate (cf. Depner, 1981), especially when we are investigating a new area and need to develop appropriate questions. Although such restrictions of the use of methods may be too limiting (cf. Trend, 1978), if we move too quickly toward manipulating one or two experimental variables, we run the risk of ignoring the most important variables because we have not sufficiently described the phenomenon of interest.

Taking advantage of powerful effects in the real world that cannot be simulated in the laboratory may necessitate giving up some control (cf. Cook & Campbell, 1979; Ellsworth, 1977). In most research we must consider the trade-off between internal and external validity (cf. Labouvie, 1975). Correlational studies in which the relationship between variables is investigated without assuming directional causality may be more appropriate for some questions (cf. Wallston, 1983).

Frieze's (1979) important work on battered women demonstrates this problem. Investigating these important theoretical and applied issues is not possible using experimental methodology; thus, she cannot make definitive causal statements. However, this creative work also combines the more qualitative intensive interviews with structured questions to provide quantitative data. It is exemplary at fitting the method to the questions.

Wallston, Foster, and Berger's (1978) utilization of experimental methods in combination with questions about the real-life experience of dual-career couples illustrates how different methods may complement each other. In a survey study, in addition to their personal job-seeking experience, respondents were provided with job-seeking situations and asked what they would do. The sex of hypothetical job seekers was experimentally manipulated through different forms of the situations. The hypotheses generated on the basis of responses to these situations provided a different approach to the actual experiences of these dual-career couples, in which sex was confounded with factors such as age, experience, and the ability to obtain a job offer. Interpretations were possible that would have been unlikely without this combination of methods.

Grady, Kegeles, and Lund (1981) maintained a simple experimental design in a year-long field study while gathering extensive medical, experiential, and attitude data before and after the experimental manipulation. The resulting medical, sociological, and attitude data not only enrich the understanding of the experimental effects and generate new hypotheses for subsequent research, but also help to interpret the findings for researchers in public health and place them in an interdisciplinary context.

These three research examples show the value of combining methods and techniques. They illustrate the richness that is possible when we go beyond limited 2 × 2 laboratory experiments. They also show the value of fitting the design to the question and context of interest.

We spend a great deal of time teaching our students to understand the difference between an independent and a dependent variable. We fail to remember that the choice of which variable fits which category is frequently arbitrary, even with experimental designs. After a great deal of research concluding that "what is beautiful is good" (cf. Berscheid & Walster, 1974; Wallston & O'Leary, 1981), several researchers reversed the independent and dependent variables to show that our perceptions of beauty may vary depending on other characteristics of the individual (e.g., Gross & Crofton, 1977) and the situation (Unger, Hilderbrand, & Madar, 1982). These studies do not refute the initial ones; rather, they illustrate the complexities of human behavior and judgment where unidirectional causation of B by A rarely gives the full picture of the phenomenon. Our designs need to better reflect these complexities. Our focus should be on "how to accommodate the complexities and limitations of reality without trivializing the study" (Wachtel, 1980, p. 403).

Our experimental methods have been appropriately critiqued as context stripping (cf. Bronfenbrenner, 1977; Mishler, 1979; Parlee, 1979; Petronovich, 1979; Unger, 1981b; Wallston, 1983). The laboratory, as a context, has particularly been called into question and much has been made of the move from laboratory to field research. This is, however, frequently a false dichotomy or an oversimplification. Unger (1981a) suggests that whether or not subjects are aware of being studied may be the more important distinction. Tunnell (1977) defines several dimensions of naturalness—natural behavior, natural setting, and natural treatment— along which research varies. Each natural dimension adds to the external validity of our work, with the potentially concomitant loss of internal validity.

Unger (1981a) points out that more sex-of-subject effects are found in field than in laboratory studies. Several potential explanations are provided: (1) sex is more likely to be confounded with other factors in the field; (2) the awareness of being studied in the laboratory may create social desirability demands, which decrease sex effects; (3) the laboratory creates a norm of social objectivity, minimizing the operation of sex roles (Eagly, 1978). Clearly the context is important for all research (cf. Mishler, 1979), and we must expand our awareness of our laboratory context and how it influences the carrier variable, sex, in particular.

The study of women and gender has emphasized the narrowness and limitations of our research designs. As we have discussed, factorial designs may severely limit the number of variables we can study before such selection is appropriate. We need to recognize the value of correlational methods and of qualitative approaches to research. This experiment may be the "crowning glory" of our research methods (Sherif, 1981), but it can be used prematurely or inappropriately. We must pay increased attention to the contexts of our research. Triangulation of methods is a particularly fruitful, though costly, approach.

Sample Selection

The description of subjects included in research reports provides a starting point for explicating some of the issues in sampling procedures. The information contained in these descriptions may reflect mini-theories or hunches about which variables (other than those selected to be independent variables) influence the outcomes of the research. A perusal of recent issues of journals in experimental social psychology suggests that there is remarkable consistency in the variables mentioned. Three major descriptors occur repeatedly and often exclusively: undergraduate status, sex, and whether the participants were paid or volunteer. Before considering how the study of women and gender can broaden this rather narrow view of subject characteristics, it may be useful to speculate on why these three descriptors are so common.

The specification that subjects are college students suggests a recognition of the problems of generalizability from this population. Indeed, the most frequently reiterated criticism of subject selection in psychology in general is its reliance on undergraduates as subjects. As long ago as 1946, McNemar accused psychology of creating a "science of the behavior of sophomores" (p. 333). Twenty-three years later, Schultz (1969) criticized the practice of using college students enrolled in introductory psychology classes and documented its continued practice.

There are obvious difficulties in assuming that college students represent the population as a whole. In addition, descriptions also often proceed to specify the size of the college or university and the region of the country, and occasionally its public or private status, e.g., a large midwestern university, a small eastern private college. These descriptions imply an additional consensus that there may be problems in assuming that any one population of college students represents college students as a whole. The emphasis on size and region may indicate the existence of mini-theories about the quality of education, student intelligence, race, religion, traditionality, or social class of the students. Some reports give the specific name of the institution, allowing the reader to draw conclusions about what aspects of that institutional setting may have influenced the data.

The frequency with which the conditions under which subjects were recruited are mentioned is quite probably related to the traumatic ethical questions that raged throughout the sixties. The literature on differences between volunteer and nonvolunteer subjects (Ora, 1966; Rosenthal & Rosnow, 1969) may be remembered, or on a broader level, cognitive dissonance and related theories may have shaped the thinking of social psychologists at least to the extent of recognizing a potential difference between subjects who are paid or who volunteer.

The specification of the proportion of the subjects who are female or male suggests a set of amorphous assumptions about between-sex differences and within-sex similarities. The assumption that sex represents a meaningful difference, that women and men form groups within which the members are alike—an undifferentiated entity—is simply unlikely to be true, according to Parlee (1975). The assumption that merely selecting for equal numbers of female and male subjects will "control for" sex is also unlikely to be true (Parlee, 1981a). Our sampling takes place within particular societal institutions that are known to make numerous distinctions on the basis of sex (Grady, 1981). The resulting problems of sample representativeness and its relationship to the theory being tested are left to the reader to resolve with the passing mention of sex as a descriptor. In fact, Wallston (1983) suggests that studies that analyze sex as an independent variable must be considered quasi-experiments, because comparisons of males and females always involve nonequivalent control groups. All the attendant threats to validity must be considered in understanding any resultant sex differences.

Thus, the most common descriptors for sample populations are deceptively simple given the number of assumptions that may underlie them. Some may argue that these factors are mentioned out of mere convention, passed on during scientific training. It is our contention that the convention reflects theoretical considerations, the origins of which may be lost in the mists of history. Our speculations about their meaning can certainly be supplemented or replaced. In the search for universal truths, it is often easy to glide over the particularities of our sample.

Because sex is so often mentioned in subject descriptions, it has become possible (and quite popular) to do archival studies of the representation of female and male subjects in research. Most clearly apparent is the overrepresentation of male subjects found in several studies over two decades (Carlson & Carlson, 1960; Schultz, 1969; Schwabacher, 1972; Smart, 1966). In fact, Holmes and Jorgensen (1971) found that "males appear as subjects twice as often as females, a ratio even greater than that favoring college student subjects over non-college student subjects" (p. 3).

Researchers interested in women and gender have quite reasonably asked why males are more numerous. There are many possible reasons, all of which threaten generalizability at least as much as does the use of college students. As O'Leary (1977) points out, sex is generally considered a "nuisance variable to be controlled, not investigated" (p. 3). Because there are large literatures on sex differences potentially related to almost any topic, many researchers avoid the tedious task of having to review them by studying their phenomena of interest using single-sex designs. Why they use single-sex designs of men and boys only is another question. Availability would seem a likely reason except that Holmes and Jorgensen (1971) found that the overrepresentation of male subjects was as great or even greater with non-college student subjects. Thus, it is not simply because men have been overrepresented in the past among college students or available subject pools.

The topics chosen for study seem to bear some relationship to the sex of the sample selected. McKenna and Kessler (1977), correcting for the standard male overrepresentation, found that in aggression studies more than the expected number used all male subjects and more than the expected number of interpersonal attraction studies used all female subjects. If many topics are sex linked in the mind of the researcher, one must still explain why more "male" topics are studied. The answer to this question may relate to our earlier point about basing research questions on the investigator's own experience.

Researchers may also have implicit theories about the nature of women and men that guide them to choose one or the other as subjects, either generally or because of the particular research method to be used. A quite famous and prolific researcher once explained in a colloquium that he used only female subjects (referred to in his research reports by the so-called generic "he") because they are more cooperative subjects and are more likely to keep their appointments. Researchers responding to Prescott and Foster (1974) about reasons for using single-sex designs expressed fastidiousness about the social desirability or etiquette of applying their techniques to women: "I manipulated anxiety and I frankly couldn't bring myself to do this with college girls"; "Cultural values regarding sex roles make it easier to expose males to aversive stimulation." These "cultural values" may make certain things easier, just as compliant subjects do, but they shape the field in subtle and important ways.

Another researcher bias that may account for overrepresentation of male subjects may be an assumption about representativeness or generalizability. Although Reardon and Prescott (1977) subsequently found some improvement, both Schwabacher (1972) and McKenna and Kessler (1977) found that researchers were more likely to specify the sex of the subjects in the abstracts of research reports if a female sample had been used. Further, the conclusions drawn from research using all male subjects, according to Schwabacher (1972), are more likely to be generalized and discussed as "individuals are . . ." whereas research based on female subjects is likely to be discussed as "women/girls/females are. . . ." Dan and Beekman (1972) attribute these tendencies to widespread androcentric assumptions: "The habit of mind which allows that males are more representative of the human race than females should be recognized as a potentially serious bias in our psychological research and theory" (p. 1078).

Whatever the reasons for biases in sample selection in the past, the new questions being raised by researchers studying women and gender have to some extent required the study of new populations, not only more girls and women but specific subgroups. It was bound to happen, for example, that rape research would finally move out of the laboratory with its countless studies of college students' attributions of blame/guilt, attractiveness of the victim, etc., to field studies of women who had been raped (e.g., Janoff-Bulman, 1979), or of women who had been attacked but were successful in avoiding rape (Bart, 1981). The social problems and policy issues raised by the women's movement could quite clearly not be addressed through the exclusive use of college student populations. They create a press for more "real world" research. The novelty of the questions, as discussed earlier, also requires intensive description from people actually involved. A cursory review of subject descriptions suggests that field studies that use non-college populations generally provide a more thorough description of subjects, including at least age, race, and some socioeconomic variables. Thus, whatever pressures for field research have resulted from the study of women and gender may also have contributed to the pressure for more thorough descriptions of subjects.

Another critical issue of sample selection is the choice of an appropriate control group. In an excellent paper on this topic, Parlee (1981a) describes ways in which selection of control groups reflect the scientist's implicit theoretical framework. She illustrates her points by citing a controversy between biomedical and social scientists over which control group of women to add to an ongoing study of aging in a sample of highly educated, professionally successful men. The social scientists suggested a

group of women "matched" on social status variables; the biomedical
scientists suggested the sisters of the men already in the study to "match"
on physiological characteristics. The results and conclusions about sex
differences in aging would have been quite different depending on which
control was used. Thus, although the topic of control groups is usually
considered "only" a methodological issue, Parlee underlines its conceptual
significance in defining "what phenomena are and are not of interest and
about what types of explanation are sought and are permissible" (1981a,
p. 639). The basic issues raised about control groups are, as she points
out, long-standing concerns of philosophers and historians of science; her
specific and practical statements about their implications for feminist
psychology and the discipline as a whole, however, bring a new urgency
to a consideration of their implications.

Overall, then, the study of women and gender has heightened awareness of how samples are selected beyond the standard criticism of the use
of college students. The overrepresentation of male subjects has received
considerable attention, and researchers have been asked to justify their
selection by sex. However, the larger issues of the meaning of selection by
sex and "controlling for" sex have barely been addressed and are potentially of far more significance for social psychology. Further, the public
policy aspects of many of the issues raised by feminist psychologists have
contributed to the press for more field studies based on affected populations.

Operationalization

Social psychologists are appropriately self-critical about construct
validity and the operations we actually choose for testing what we want
to test. Certainly, there has been plenty of room for criticism when
automobile honking is called aggression and pressing a button is called
control. However, a whole new set of issues has become apparent with
the study of women and gender. A recognition of the pervasiveness of
sex-based distinctions and experiences has led to a reevaluation of the
methods and materials of social psychology, along new dimensions.

The specific problem of sex-typing of messages, tasks, and materials
is part of the larger problem of understanding what our operationalizations
mean to respondents. In some cases, sex-typing of stimulus materials
means the same to subjects of both sexes. This similarity of meaning has
been confirmed repeatedly with the evaluation bias literature. When Phil
Goldberg (1968) discovered that women undergraduates evaluated essays
differently depending on whether they were attributed to a male or female
author, he called his article "Are women prejudiced against women?"

Subsequent research has indicated that both men and women are "prejudiced" against women to approximately the same degree. A failure to recognize the power of this widely shared cultural reaction has led to a major misinterpretation of the first findings of "fear of success" (Horner, 1972). Because Horner gave her verbal cue "At the end of first term finals, John/Mary found him/herself at the top of the medical school class" matching sex of subject and sex of stimulus person, she was unable to untangle cultural reactions to the stimulus person's sex from personal ones based on the subject's sex. Subsequent research indicates that cultural reactions predominated and that both female and male subjects wrote bizarre explanations for Mary's success (Condry & Dyer, 1976; Monahan, Kuhn & Shaver, 1974). Based on this similarity of meaning, Kay Deaux and others have developed research programs to test attributions to sex-typed stimulus materials, resulting in substantial contributions both to attribution theory and to the psychology of women and gender (Deaux & Taynor, 1973; Taynor & Deaux, 1973).

There are occasions when the sex-typing of materials or tasks means different things to subjects of different sexes. Because of differences in experiences, training, and education, tasks may differ in complexity, novelty, or interest-level for female and male subjects. The NASA survival task, for example, may be experienced differently by people who were not Boy Scouts in the past than by people who were. If the researcher is not interested in sex differences, then this experimental difference becomes a serious confound. In a re-examination of areas in which sex differences had been touted, researchers found that "math ability" was being tested with problems what were sex-typed in interest and that different results could be obtained when the same concept was tested with a problem described as cookie-making rather than carpentry (Milton, 1959). Similarly, Sistrunk and McDavid (1971) found sex differences in conformity depending on whether the stimulus items were masculine or feminine, with no sex differences on neutral items. Although Eagly and Carli (1981) do not confirm that there was an overall preponderance of masculine items in influencability research, they also note that masculine topics tended to be associated with greater female persuasibility. They provide useful information about the sex-typing of messages that can help to explore these relationships further or to avoid the confound. Sandra Bem has used the sex-typing of tasks to advantage in her androgyny research. She has confirmed that such tasks as playing with a kitten, peer-counseling, and the standard Asch conformity situation were indeed sex-role-typed, evoking different behavior from individuals who described themselves differently on the Bem Sex Role Inventory (Bem, 1975; Bem, Martyna, & Watson, 1976).

Problems of sex bias introduced by response categories may be most easily demonstrated in the construction of questionnaires and interviews. Because the researcher and the respondent share a common culture, the categories constructed may fairly easily capture a shared meaning. Nonetheless, it is widely recognized that there is a serious threat to validity in imposing researcher-generated response categories on subjects' descriptions of their own behavior. The study of women and gender has further suggested that the researcher may be imposing categories limited by his or her own sex-biased expectations of male and female behavior. The particular wording of questions and the allowable response categories may reflect very narrow, stereotyped views of sex roles.

Bart (1971) provides an excellent example of an outrageously narrow view of sex roles in sexual behavior. In a study of pregnant women and "normals," researchers asked whether the respondent's role in sexual intercourse was "passive," "responsive," "resistant," "aggressive," "deviant," or "other." Obviously, different results might have been obtained if the allowable response included at least "active" but perhaps also "encouraging," "playful," "creative," and so forth. It is quite clear that different categories would have been constructed had men constituted part of the sample.

The existence of sex bias in the researcher, charged by many feminist psychologists, does not preclude the possibility of sex bias in the respondent. Indeed, sexism and its effects are part of our shared culture. It may be that most of the women subjects in the example above would not describe their sexual role in any way other than the categories provided. However, that issue deserves to be resolved empirically.

McKenna and Kessler (1977) have uncovered a more subtle form of sex bias in operationalization, one that involves both the type of response and the type of experimental manipulation. One might assume that the simple choice of whether to use a paper and pencil dependent measure or another kind of behavioral measure would depend on a variety of theoretical and practical considerations. The sex of the subjects would seem an unlikely factor to take into account. Yet in a review of over 50 studies of aggression and interpersonal attraction, they found that paper and pencil measures are used significantly more often with female subjects in both topic areas. In addition, they have found that in aggression studies, independent variables differ by subject sex. "Passive" manipulations, such as the content of the story, the sex of the other person, or the order of exposure to treatment conditions, are much more common with female subjects. In contrast, male subjects are more likely to be treated by others in a hostile manner, frustrated or threatened. McKenna and Kessler also note that in the interpersonal attraction literature they have found no studies in which "physical attraction of other" was an independent variable with all-female subjects.

In an article on sex bias in psychology, Carolyn Sherif asks, "Did someone believe that the psychology of the researcher and the psychology of the subject, both human beings, are altogether different?" (1979, p. 105). Even as we study labeling, we label. Ellsworth (1977), discussing research applications, says ". . . to conduct research on the unconsidered assumption that the name of the variable guarantees that it is the thing we are interested in is foolhardy at best" (p. 607). Sherif (1979) criticizes the practice of transforming "a specific set of actions in a specific research situation . . . into the label for something that the person has, is, or possesses as a trait" (p. 115).

The study of the psychology of women has contributed to the ongoing "crisis" literature about the trivial nature of operationalizations and the sweeping generalizations that often result. Close examinations of both stimulus and response materials have revealed overt and subtle forms of sex bias that influence the results and their interpretation. The sex-typing of materials, often seen as a confound, has also led to the development of new areas of study. Overall, in our judgment, the psychology of women has contributed to the more relativist attributional approach in social psychology, in which the conditions under which people label are at least as interesting as the labels themselves. Further it has applied this approach to the conduct of the researchers as well as of the subjects.

The Social Psychology
of the Research Process

The social psychology of the psychological experiment has received sporadic attention since the 1950s. The standard concerns include at least experimenter bias (particularly expectancy effects), the interference of the setting or equipment with experimental and mundane realism, order effects, the influence of other participants, and the effects of deception. Most of the criticisms or cautions articulated have been directed to laboratory research, but research outside the laboratory can be evaluated along these dimensions as well.

Herb Kelman (1968) once stated that the difference between observing a rock and a human being is that the rock can't observe back. Many research situations attempt to constrain the subject's behavior to be as rock-like as possible. Subjects are put in cubicles and given checklists or buttons to press. One particular aspect of their behavior in public situations is observed and all others ignored. A fixed set of "demographics" is collected in interviews without giving attention to other features of the subjects' life situations.

Another strategy is to make the experimenter's behavior as rock-like as possible, familiar in the use of tape recorders, pre-coded interviews, etc. In an experiment that Sherif (1979) describes, a computer presents the persuasive communications, a method the experimenters describe as resulting in "a desirably high degree of situational control and assurance that possible sources of experimenter bias are minimized" (p. 102). Sherif points out that the experimenters have arbitrarily selected the topics, presented them in certain orders, varied the contents of the screen, etc. The authors of the report fail to comment on how the use of this novel, mechanical device itself might have affected the research situation:

> In short, this experiment typifies the assumption in a great deal of experimentation that "general laws" about the relationship among variables can be obtained by comparing averages of the responses made by a sizable number of individuals, who are regarded as being without a background, personal history, or gender that might have anything to do with their response in the situation. In this case, the situation itself is described only in terms of the equipment, which is shown in a photograph. Its duration appears to have been well within the academic hour (Sherif, 1979, p. 103).

Sherif argues that these forms of "control" ignore the social psychology of the research situation, although research is inevitably a social process. She concludes that the generation of more data of the same type, using less and less human contact in the methods in an effort to minimize the social context, is not going to resolve any of the complex—or even interesting—questions about human behavior.

Unger (1981b) also urges a direct confrontation regarding the social nature of human experimentation and deplores the view that the human element presents "procedural" difficulties: "Like increased blood clotting due to the 'pill,' the social relationship between experimenter and subject is seen as an 'unwanted side effect.' Like the blood clotting properties of estrogenic substances, however, such effects are intrinsic. They are side-effects only to the extent that they are not the ones desired" (p. 5).

Many points already made in this chapter relate to a recognition of the social psychology of the research process. Research on women and gender cannot easily ignore the biosocial aspects of experimenter and subject, and social psychological research in this area contributes somewhat to the trend away from the aspiration to transform experimenter and subject to inanimate objects. There is not much to add, but there are a couple of implications we would like to draw.

One implication for research includes increased attention to the most minute details of the research setting as well as to the total *gestalt* created. Many researchers conceptualize their research settings as a stage that must be "dressed" properly to create the desired impact. The scenery, the props, the lighting—all contribute to the overall effect. It is generally assumed that constancy in these features renders them unimportant. Even though some environmental psychologists are studying the effects of physical features of the environment on social interaction (see Evans, 1981), it is probably not necessary for every social psychological research report to provide information on temperature, humidity, noise level, color of the walls, etc. However, some description of the physical as well as social aspects of the situation—the "instrumentation" of social psychology in a larger sense—would be useful.

In addition, as described previously, we know that the background of the experimenter influences the kinds of questions asked and the results obtained, particularly that training in theory and methods influences the competence with particular techniques as well as questions asked and results obtained; that the experimenter as a stimulus person presents a certain demeanor that influences the process and outcome of research; and that all of these factors interact with the individual characteristics and behavior of subjects. Shouldn't the reader of the research report have access to these critical aspects of the research situation? Research reports could include a section describing the experimenter(s) comparable to the section on subject description, a suggestion also made by Lewis and Wehren (1981). Wallston (1982) provides a section of self-description in an evaluative review article in order to help the reader evaluate her evaluations. Such tradition-breaking intrusions of social psychological sensibilities begin to respond to the criticisms and concerns of decades.

Statistics

Although statistics are a tool and should be viewed as such, psychologists have a tendency to glorify them (cf. Meehl, 1978; Sherif, 1981). In fact, analysis of variance has become the statistic of choice for psychologists in general (cf. Edgington, 1974) and for social psychologists in particular.

Some researchers involved in the study of sex and gender have called for the inclusion of qualitative techniques to complement the use of quantitative approaches (cf. Wallston, 1983; Weiss, 1981). Moreover, this dichotomy may be less clear-cut than we like to believe (cf. Cook & Campbell, 1979; Wallston, 1983). Cook and Campbell (1979) note that all science involves qualitative judgment. Determining whether a given rival hypothesis will explain the data necessarily utilizes qualitative contextual information.

Wallston (1983) notes that "our belief or disbelief of our findings is frequently a subjective judgment which dictates continuing statistical analysis, the decision to attempt a replication or to publish" (p. 32). Our decision as to when a question is answered is clearly qualitative and subjective. Shields (1975) has illustrated this particularly well with her history of the study of sex differences in the brain. Whenever conclusions suggested female superiority, a new interpretation and further questions and research were generated, because the conclusions did not fit the bias or experiences of the male researchers. Researchers in sex and gender explicitly call for testing our findings against our own experience (Parlee, 1979) as well as that of the research participant (Kidder, 1981), but write-ups of studies rarely include such discussions. They are part of our informal, rather than our formal, science.

In fact, Koch's (1981) interesting discussion of psychology as science suggests that a distrust of one's own experience is part of our current "pathology" of knowledge. We have given up or ignored the criterion that knowledge should make sense. The study of sex and gender may help instigate a move back to this approach. Of course, testing knowledge against our experience if our perspective is sexist will lead to sexist knowledge, as the brain research described by Shields (1975) shows. This criterion alone, without the inclusion of feminist scientists, will not change the nature of our conclusions.

Glass and Ellett (1980) similarly note the qualitative nature of scientific judgments: "A large part of scientific judgment is knowing which circumstances are important and which are not. Such forms of knowing are largely tacit and qualitative. . . . In these respects, the most hidebound quantitative and statistical scientist is like the naturalistic investigator" (p. 224). Glass and Ellett further discuss generalization as a qualitative process. Statistics ignore the problem of populations that are ever changing: "Reasoning from 'some to all' lacks any sort of mathematical warrant. . . . Samples are always characterized by innumerable specific circumstances" (p. 224). We have already discussed issues of sample selection. Others have discussed the need for selecting representative situations (cf. Petronovich, 1979; Tyler, 1981; Wallston, 1983). The point here is that decisions regarding external validity and construct validity are qualitative, while statistical conclusion validity (cf. Cook & Campbell, 1979) and internal validity involve judgments that can be informed by statistics.

When judgments can be informed by statistics, the nature of the statistic may restrict the nature of the question or the answer. In an historical analysis of the acceptance of analysis of variance (ANOVA) in psychology, Rucci and Tweney (1980) have shown that by 1952 ANOVA was fully established as the most frequent technique. Clearly, this choice of statistic influences design, and the influence is reciprocal. Rucci and Tweney (1980) note that factorial designs were used more after 1940 and one cannot ascertain whether ANOVA influenced the design choice or the use of factorial design influenced the ready adoption of ANOVA. At any rate, there is clear restriction on the types of questions we ask when ANOVA is our statistic of choice, although ANOVA may be used in nonexperimental research (cf. Goldstein, 1979; Wallston, 1983) when the number of variables is limited.

Higbee, Millard, and Folkman (1980) explored the use of analysis of variance in four social psychology journals, (*Journal of Personality and Social Psychology, Journal of Experimental Social Psychology, Social Psychology Quarterly, Journal of Social Psychology*) in 1978–79. They contrasted their findings with Christie's (1965) review of *Journal of Abnormal and Social Psychology* for 1949 and 1959, and Higbee and Wells' (1972) data on *Journal of Personality and Social Psychology* in 1969. There was an increase in the use of analysis of variance from 1949 to 1969. The changes were differential by journal in 1978–79, but analysis of variance is clearly the most used statistic and is used nearly as much as all other statistics combined.[1] More than 60% of the articles included analysis of variance in contrast to the less than 40% that included some form of correlational analysis in 1978–79. Parametric directional tests (F and t) were used in more than 80% of the studies.

Thus, new correlational approaches that allow multiple variables and causal inferences (cf. Boruch, 1983) have not yet attained much popularity in social psychology. Whether these techniques are used more in studies of sex and gender, or in non-mainstream journals where such studies are published, is an empirical question (cf. Stein et al., 1984). There has been a broad call for the use of such approaches (e.g., Cook, Dintzer & Mark, 1980; McGuire, 1973). Whether the journals reflect what research is being done or whether these mainstream journals effectively screen out alternate methods and statistics is not clear. Certainly there are numerous biases in the publication process (e.g., Lindsey, 1978; Miller & Zeitz, 1978) which could be operating.

The reification of statistics is also clear from the Higbee et al. (1980) analysis. Over time, more statistics were used per article. Moreover, the category "description only" was empty for the 1978–79 sample. There were no nonstatistical studies in 1978–79 in these four journals. Given our need for description (cf. Wallston, 1981) and the nonproductivity of statistics (Meehl, 1978), these may be unfortunate trends for the future development of psychology. In fact, Diamond and Morton (1978) found that empirical landmarks in social psychology were less likely to use analysis of variance techniques than has become common today.

The study of sex differences has also shown that statistics are formulated to test differences and not to investigate similarities (cf. Grady, 1979; Jacklin, 1979b). Jacklin (1979b) provides interesting illustrations of these issues from developmental psychology. DiPietro (1981) has found a relatively large difference between boys and girls in rough and tumble play, but from the alternative perspective, focusing on similarities, 80% of the boys were indistinguishable from 80–85% of the girls. The frequently cited sex difference in verbal ability accounts for only 1% of the variance (Plomin & Foch, 1981). Similarly, sex differences in influenceability account for only 1% of the variance (Eagly & Carli, 1981), while cognitive gender differences account for 1%–4% of the variance (Hyde, 1981). Deaux (1982) has suggested that 5% may prove to be the upper boundary for subject sex main effect size in social and cognitive behavior.

We need to develop means of discussing similarities. Unger (1981a) has suggested the label "sex comparison." Without a statistically significant difference, articles are less likely to be published, so the file drawer problem (Rosenthal, 1979) is particularly acute in research on sex differences. Moreover, Unger (1981a) notes that published literature finding no differences may be lost because of the nature of computer searches. Statistics once again constrain our questions.

For a more complete discussion of methodological issues relevant to sex difference research, see Jacklin (1979b). One further point she makes involves the failure to use statistics when they are appropriate. Separate analyses on male and female data are inappropriately used to draw conclusions regarding sex differences when statistically significant effects are found for one sex but not the other. Statistics comparing male and female data are necessary for such conclusions. Thus, when used appropriately, statistics can assist in drawing conclusions.

In an analysis of research articles in developmental psychology, Lewis and Wehren (1981) found that studies characterized as social were more likely to hypothesize sex differences, analyze for sex differences, and find significant differences compared to studies on non-social topics. Although sex differences were hypothesized in only 10% of the studies, there were analyses of sex differences in 28% of the studies. This finding may relate to the journal policy of *Developmental Psychology*, requesting tests of sex differences. However, Signorella, Vegega, and Mitchell (1981) have sampled articles from developmental and social psychology journals. They found that female first authors (20%) were more likely than male first authors (14%) to hypothesize sex-related differences. Also, authors in social journals (19%) were more likely than authors in developmental journals (14%) to propose such hypotheses. While only 16% of the articles hypothesized sex differences, an additional 39% analyzed for sex differences without theory or research based predictions. Such analyses were somewhat more likely in developmental (44%) than in social (32%) journals. Rather than reflecting increased attention to sex as a variable, Signorella et al. (1981) note, the increases represent increased reporting of routine analyses which are likely to yield more Type I errors.

Those statistics which have become popular, beyond focusing on differences, also emphasize whether a relationship exists and ignore the magnitude of the relationship (cf. Jacklin, 1979b; Parlee, 1981b).[2] Research on sex differences has helped to illustrate the importance of this distinction, since the magnitude of sex differences, as discussed above, is frequently quite small (Hyde, 1981; Jacklin, 1979b). Eagly and Wood [1985] illustrate the value of knowledge of effect size for drawing conclusions across studies. Meta-analysis is an important approach (cf. Cooper & Rosenthal, 1980; Glass, McGaw, & Smith, 1981) which may increase the reporting of effect size in research articles; research on sex and gender has helped stimulate interest in such techniques (e.g., Cooper, 1979; Eagly & Carli, 1981; Hall, 1978; Jacklin, 1979b; Plant, Souther, & Jacklin, 1977).

The distinction between significance and effect size parallels the difference between statistical and practical significance. Any size difference may be of some interest theoretically. When we are interested in the implications of our theories, we must take the practical significance into account (cf. Petronovich, 1979). We cannot gauge the importance of a finding from a test of statistical significance (Petronovich, 1979) or even from a knowledge of effect size. Although the latter takes us a step further, we do not know to what extent our control of variables in the laboratory has artificially restricted or enhanced effect size. Differential findings of sex differences in field and laboratory research (cf. Eagly & Wood [1985]; Unger, 1981a) illustrate this issue. Moreover, Yeaton and Sechrest (1981) note that the nature of the variable is important in determining the meaning of equivalent effect sizes. Petronovich (1979) notes that a complete science will include statements regarding the probable importance of variables.

The study of women and gender has raised issues relating to the nature of statistics and their utilization. The consistent theme is the relation among the statistics we use, the questions we ask, and the inferences we draw. To the extent that statistics restrict our questions, we must work on the development of alternative statistics and the more adequate use of available statistics. We must overcome the tendency to overrely on the statistic with which we are the most comfortable, analysis of variance. We must also put statistics back in their proper perspective. They are a tool to assist our inferences from our research. Petronovich (1979) appropriately emphasizes that adequacy of inference is a function of how the data are produced (cf. Huck & Sandler, 1979), not how they are analyzed.

Statistics are only one aspect of the research process, and they need to be viewed in that light.

Conclusions

Overall, then, what has the study of women and gender contributed to methodology in social psychology? Perhaps most noticeably, it has infused some passion into the field. It is possible that this passion has or will be a partial antidote for the "crisis in social psychology." Social psychology has always thrived on controversy. Some of the best questions and research effort have been inspired by awesome social questions or events: Nazism, Kitty Genovese, segregation and other aspects of racism, and now sexism. As phenomena have presented themselves, social psychology and its methods have tried to be responsive.

What happens to science in the midst of all this passion? Occasionally it suffers, and occasionally it benefits. If a result is going to be used to inform public policy, or if a result is interpreted in a way that is bound to be unpopular with a large group of people, then the methods had better be defensible, the statistics absolutely appropriate and of the highest quality, and the interpretation tight and circumscribed. The result may then be a press toward more technically adequate science. Certainly the critiques of social psychological methods from a feminist perspective that have been referred to in this chapter may contribute toward that end.

On the other hand, complete responsiveness to policymakers and a vested interest in outcomes can obviously produce bad science—even though such responsiveness may contribute to decent social policy. Some of the social questions that need to be resolved simply cannot be answered through the methods of social science. The gap between what is known and what needs to be known is often bridged with flawed research. The eagerness with which the public policy makers and the media embrace results interpreted (or misinterpreted) as relevant to controversial issues makes one shudder for science and yearn for a continuation of irrelevant research.

In addition to infusing passion, the study of women and gender can change social psychology in other ways. It has attracted new people to the field with new questions and perspectives. The novelty of these questions has increased attention to qualitative methods for exploratory research, broadening the scope of inquiry as well as its tools. The focus of those studying the psychology of women and gender tends to be on situational rather than personological factors—a focus that can enhance a truly social psychology. The "context-stripping" of social psychology, which has been widely criticized, may be repaired by some of the approaches offered by social psychologists studying the psychology of women: the inclusion of more qualitative data, the triangulation or combination of methods, and the efforts to make research relevant across disciplines and to the real-world situation of women. Social psychology is being forced to examine assumptions in question generation, design, subject selection, and methods of gathering and analyzing data. The result may be a more thoughtful and considered science of social behavior.

Although most of the current literature seems to indicate at best a divergence, and at worst an adversary relationship between "mainstream" social psychology and the study of women and gender, it is important to remember that feminism and science have been historical allies against king and church, superstition and dogma (Ehrenreich & English, 1979; Grady, 1981). Eighteenth century feminists eagerly turned to science as a means of discovering truth and furthering social change. They believed that the objectivity of the scientific method could overcome sex bias. Scientists believed that the objectivity of the scientific method was impervious to sex bias. The discovery of sex bias along with numerous other inadequacies and limitations in the methods themselves has raised serious questions about the meaning and usefulness of social science. In attempting to resolve these questions, the historical alliance may yet survive and function for the mutual benefit of science and feminism.

Acknowledgments

We appreciate the comments of Jeanne Plas, Howard Sandler, and Rhoda Kesler Unger on an earlier version of this manuscript. Equal work was done on this chapter by both authors.

Notes

1. Comparisons of percentages across years is somewhat difficult as articles use more than one statistic and the percentages, therefore, add up to more than 100% and are not comparable.

2. Howard Sandler, a methodologist who reviewed the chapter, commented that researchers have statistics of effect size and power available but we are lazy about using them.

References

Ajzen, I., & Fishbein, M. (1980). *Understanding attitudes and predicting social behavior*. Englewood Cliffs, NJ: Prentice-Hall.

Allen, W. R. (1979). Family roles, occupational statuses, and achievement orientations among black women in the United States. *Signs, 4,* 670–686.

Baumgardner, S. R. (1976). Critical history and social psychology's "crisis." *Personality and Social Psychology Bulletin, 2,* 460–465.

Bart, P. B. (1971). Sexism and social science: From the gilded cage to the iron cage, or, the perils of Pauline. *Journal of Marriage and the Family, 33,* 734–735.

Bart, P. B. (1981). A study of women who both were raped and avoided rape. *Journal of Social Issues, 37*(4), 123–137.

Bem, S. L. (1975). Sex role adaptability: One consequence of psychological androgyny. *Journal of Personality and Social Psychology, 31*(4), 634–643.

Bem, S. L., Martyna, W., & Watson, C. (1976). Sex typing and androgyny: Further explorations of the expressive domain. *Journal of Personality and Social Psychology, 34*(5), 1016–1023.

Bernard, J. (1973). My four revolutions: An autobiographical history of the ASA. *American Journal of Sociology, 78,* 773–791.

Berscheid, E., & Walster, E. (1974). Physical attractiveness. In L. Berkowitz (Ed.), *Advances in experimental social psychology* (Vol. 7). New York: Academic Press.

Boruch, R. F. (1983). Causal models: Their import and their triviality. In B. L. Richardson & J. Wirtenberg (Eds.) *Sex role research: Measuring social change.* New York: Praeger.

Bronfenbrenner, U. (1977). Toward an experimental ecology of human development. *American Psychologist, 32,* 513–531.

Bryson, R. B., Bryson, J. B., Licht, M. H., & Licht, B. G. (1976). The professional pair: Husband and wife psychologists. *American Psychologist, 31,* 10–16.

Buss, A. R. (1975). The emerging field of the sociology of psychological knowledge. *American Psychologist, 30,* 988–1002.

Caplan, N., & Nelson, S. D. (1973). On being useful: The nature and consequences of psychological research on social problems. *American Psychologist, 28,* 199–211.

Carlson, R. (1972). Understanding women: Implications for personality theory and research. *Journal of Social Issues, 28*(2), 17–32.

Carlson, E. R., & Carlson, R. (1960). Male and female subjects in personality research. *Journal of Abnormal and Social Psychology, 61*(3), 482–483.

Christie, R. (1965). Some implications of research trends in social psychology. In O. Klineberg & R. Christie (Eds.), *Perspectives in social psychology.* New York: Holt, Rinehart, & Winston.

Condry, J. C., & Dyer, S. L. (1976). Fear of success: Attribution of cause to the victim. *Journal of Social Issues, 32,* 63–83.

Cook, T. D., & Campbell, D. J. (1979). *Quasi-experimentation: Design and analysis issues for field settings.* Chicago: Rand McNally.

Cook, T. D., Dintzer, L., & Mark, M. M. (1980). The causal analysis of concomitant time series. In L. Bickman (Ed.) *Applied social psychology annual* (Vol. 1). Beverly Hills, CA: Sage.

Cooper, H. M. (1976). Statistically combining independent studies: A meta-analysis of sex differences in conformity research. *Journal of Personality and Social Psychology, 37,* 131–146.

Cooper, H. M., & Rosenthal, R. (1980). Statistical versus traditional procedures for summarizing research findings. *Psychological Bulletin, 87,* 422–449.

Corsaro, W. A. (1981). Entering the child's world—Research strategies for field entry and data collection in a preschool setting. In J. L. Green & C. Wallat (Eds.), *Ethnography and language in educational settings*. Norwood, NJ: Ablex.

Dan, A. J., & Beekman, S. (1972). Male versus female representation in psychological research. *American Psychologist*, 1078.

Deaux, K. (1982, May). *From individual differences to social categories: Analysis of a decade's research on gender*. Presidential address, Midwestern Psychological Association, Minneapolis.

Deaux, K., & Taynor, J. (1973). Evaluation of male and female ability: Bias works both ways. *Psychological Reports, 32*, 261–262.

Depner, C. (1981, March). *Toward the further development of feminist psychology*. Paper presented at the annual meeting of the Association for Women in Psychology, Boston.

Diamond, S. S., & Morton, D. R. (1978). Empirical landmarks in social psychology. *Personality and Social Psychology Bulletin, 4*, 217–221.

[Dion, K. L. (1985). Sex, gender, and groups: Selected issues. In V. E. O'Leary, R. K. Unger, & B. S. Wallston (Eds.), *Women, gender, and social psychology* (pp. 293–348). Hillsdale, NJ: Lawrence Erlbaum.]

DiPietro, J. A. (1981). Rough and tumble play: A function of gender. *Developmental Psychology, 17*, 50–58.

Eagly, A. H. (1978). Sex differences in influenceability. *Psychological Bulletin, 85*, 86–116.

Eagly, A. H., & Carli, L. L. (1981). Sex of researchers and sex-typed communications as determinants of sex differences in influenceability: A meta-analysis of social influence studies. *Psychological Bulletin, 90*(1), 1–20.

[Eagly, A. H., & Wood, W. (1985). Gender and influencibility: Stereotype versus behavior. In V. E. O'Leary, R. K. Unger, & B. S. Wallston (Eds.), *Women, gender, and social psychology* (pp. 225–256). Hillsdale, NJ: Lawrence Erlbaum.]

Edgington, E. S. (1974). A new tabulation of statistical procedures used in APA Journals. *American Psychologist, 29*, 25–26.

Ehrenreich, B., & English, D. (1979). *For her own good*. Garden City, N.Y.: Anchor Books.

Ellsworth, P. C. (1977). From abstract ideas to concrete instances: Some guidelines for choosing natural research settings. *American Psychologist, 32*, 604–615.

Etaugh, C., & Spandikow, D. B. (1979). Attention to sex in psychological research as related to journal policy and author sex. *Psychology of Women Quarterly, 4*(2), 175–184.

Evans, G. W. (Ed.) (1981). Environmental stress. *Journal of Social Issues, 37*(1), whole issue.

Festinger, L. (1980). *Can the science of psychology address the question of human nature?* Invited address at the annual meeting of the American Psychological Association, Montreal, Canada.

Frieze, I. H. (1979). Perceptions of battered wives. In I. H. Frieze, D. Bar-Tal, & J. S. Carroll (Eds.), *New approaches to social problems: Applications of attribution theory*. San Francisco: Jossey-Bass.

Glass, G. V., & Ellett, F. S. (1980). Evaluation research. In M. R. Rosenzweig & L. W. Porter (Eds.), *Annual review of psychology, Volume 31*. Palo Alto, CA: Annual Reviews, Inc., 211–228.

Glass, G. V., McGaw, B., & Smith, M. L. (1981). *Meta-analysis in social research.* Beverly Hills: Sage.

Goldberg, P. (1968). Are women prejudiced against women? *Transaction, 5,* 28–30.

Goldstein, E. (1979). Effect of same-sex and cross-sex role models on the subsequent academic productivity of scholars. *American Psychologist, 34,* 407–410.

Grady, K. E. (1979). Androgyny reconsidered. In J. H. Williams (Ed.), *Psychology of women: Selected readings.* New York: Norton.

Grady, K. E. (1981). Sex bias in research design. *Psychology of Women Quarterly,* 5(4), 628–636.

Grady, K. E., Kegeles, S. S., & Lund, A. K. (1982). Experimental studies to increase BSE—Preliminary findings. In C. Mettlin & G. P. Murphy (Eds.), *Issues in cancer screening and communications.* New York: Alan R. Liss, Inc.

Gross, A. E., & Crofton, C. (1977). What is good is beautiful. *Sociometry, 40,* 85–90.

Hall, J. A. (1978). Gender effects in decoding nonverbal cues. *Psychological Bulletin,* 85, 845–857.

Hansen, R. D., & O'Leary, V. E. (1983). Actresses and actors: The effects of sex on causal attributions. *Basic and Applied Social Psychology,* 4(3), 209–230.

Henley, N. M. (1979). *Body politics: Power, sex, and nonverbal communication.* Englewood Cliffs, NJ: Prentice-Hall.

Higbee, K. L., Millard, R. J., & Folkman, J. R. (1980). *Four decades of research methods in social psychology.* Paper presented at the meeting of the Western Psychological Association.

Higbee, K. I., & Wells, M. G. (1972). Some research trends in social psychology during the 1960s. *American Psychologist, 27,* 963–966.

Holmes, D. S., & Jorgensen, B. W. (1971). Do personality and social psychologists study men more than women? *Representative Research in Social Psychology, 2,* 71–76.

Horner, M. S. (1972). Toward an understanding of achievement-related conflicts in women. *Journal of Social Issues, 28,* 157–176.

Huck, H. W., & Sandler, H. M. (1979). *Rival hypotheses: Alternative interpretations of data based conclusions.* New York: Harper & Row.

Hyde, J. S. (1981). How large are cognitive gender differences? A meta-analysis using ω^2 and d. *American Psychologist, 36,* 892–901.

Jacklin, C. N. (1979a). Epilogue. In M. A. Wittig & A. C. Petersen (Eds.). *Sex-related differences in cognitive functioning: Developmental issues.* New York: Academic Press.

Jacklin, C. N. (1979b). *Methodological issues in the study of sex-related differences.* Paper presented as Master Lecture, Annual Meeting of American Psychological Association, New York City.

Janoff-Bulman, R. (1979). Characterological versus behavioral self-blame: Inquiries into depression and rape. *Journal of Personality and Social Psychology, 37,* 1798–1809.

Jick, J. (1979). Mixing qualitative and quantitative methods: Triangulation in action. *Administrative Sciences Quarterly, 24,* 601–611.

Kelman, H. C. (1968). *A time to speak: On human values and social research.* San Francisco: Jossey-Bass.

Kidder, L. H. (1981). Face validity from multiple perspectives. In D. Brinberg & L. H. Kidder (Eds.), *New directions for methodology of social and behavioral science: Forms of validity.* New York: Jossey-Bass.

Koch, S. (1981). The nature and limits of psychological knowledge: Lessons of a century qua "science." *American Psychologist, 36,* 257–269.

Kuhn, T. S. (1970). *The structure of scientific revolutions* (2nd ed.). Chicago: University of Chicago Press.

Labouvie, E. W. (1975). The dialectical nature of measurement activities in the behavioral sciences. *Human Development, 18,* 396–403.

Leinhardt, G. (1978). Coming out of the laboratory closet. In D. Bar-Tal & L. Saxe (Eds.), *Social psychology of education.* Washington, D.C.: Hemisphere.

Lenney, E. (1977). Women's self-confidence in achievement settings. *Psychological Bulletin, 84,* 1–13.

Lewis, M., & Wehren, A. (1981). *Implicit rule systems in developmental research.* Unpublished manuscript.

Lindsey, D. (1978). *The scientific publication system in social science.* San Francisco: Jossey-Bass.

McGuire, W. J. (1973). The yin and yang of progress in social psychology: Seven koan. *Journal of Personality and Social Psychology, 26,* 446–456.

McKenna, W., & Kessler, S. J. (1977). Experimental design as a source of sex bias in social psychology. *Sex Roles, 3*(2), 117–128.

McNemar, Q. (1946). Opinion-attitude methodology. *Psychological Bulletin, 43,* 289–374.

Mednick, M. T. S., Tangri, S. S., & Hoffman, L. W. (Eds.). (1975). *Women and achievement: Social and motivational analyses.* Washington, DC: Hemisphere.

Meehl, P. E. (1978). Theoretical risks and tabular asterisks: Sir Karl, Sir Ronald, and the slow progress of soft psychology. *Journal of Consulting and Clinical Psychology, 46,* 806–834.

Merton, R. K. (1968). The Matthew Effect in science. *Science, 69,* 56–63.

Miller, F. D., & Zietz, B. (1978). A woman's place is in the footnotes. *Personality and Social Psychology Bulletin, 4,* 511–514.

Milton, G. (1959). Sex differences in problem solving as a function of role appropriateness of the problem content. *Psychological Reports, 5,* 705–708.

Mishler, E. G. (1979). Meaning in context: Is there any other kind? *Harvard Educational Review, 49,* 1–19.

Monahan, L., Kuhn, D., & Shaver, P. (1974). Intrapsychic vs. cultural explanations of the "fear of success" motive. *Journal of Personality and Social Psychology, 29,* 60–64.

O'Leary, V. E. (1977). *Toward understanding women.* Monterey, CA: Brooks/Cole Publishing Company.

[O'Leary, V. E., & Hansen, R. D. (1985). Sex-determined attributions. In V. E. O'Leary, R. K. Unger, & B. S. Wallston (Eds.), *Women, gender, and social psychology* (pp. 67–100). Hillsdale, NJ: Lawrence Erlbaum.]

Ora, J. P. (1966). *Personality characteristics of college freshman volunteers for psychological experiments*. Unpublished master's thesis, Vanderbilt University.

Over, R. (1981). Research impact of men and women social psychologists. *Personality and Social Psychology Bulletin, 7*, 596–599.

Parlee, M. B. (1975). Review essay: Psychology. *Signs, 1*, 119–138.

Parlee, M. B. (1979). Psychology and women. *Signs, 5*, 121–133.

Parlee, M. B. (1981a). Appropriate control groups in feminist research. *Psychology of Women Quarterly, 5*(4), 637–644.

Parlee, M. B. (1981b). *Issues of construct validity in social processes research*. Paper presented for the National Institute of Education.

Petronovich, L. (1979). Probabilistic functionalism: A conception of research method. *American Psychologist, 34*, 373–390.

[Piliavin, J. A., & Unger, R. K. (1985). The helpful but helpless female: Myth or reality? In V. E. O'Leary, R. K. Unger, & B. S. Wallston (Eds.), *Women, gender, and social psychology* (pp. 149–190). Hillsdale, NJ: Lawrence Erlbaum.]

Plant, W. T., Southern, M. L., & Jacklin, C. N. (1977, February). *Statistically significant sex differences in attitude, interest, and personality measures: Much ado about very little!* Paper presented at the meetings of the Western Association for Women in Psychology, San Jose, California.

Plas, J. M., & Bellet, W. (1983). Assessment of the value-attitude orientations of American Indian children. *Journal of School Psychology, 4*, 57–64.

Plomin, R., & Foch, T. T. (1981). Sex differences and individual differences. *Child Development, 52*, 383–385.

Prescott, S., & Foster, K. (1974). *Why researchers don't study women: The responses of 67 researchers*. Paper delivered at the Eighty-Second Annual Meeting of the American Psychological Association.

Rapoport, R., & Rapoport, R. N. (Eds.) (1978). *Working couples*. London: Routledge & Kegan Paul.

Reardon, P., & Prescott, S. (1977). Sex as reported in a recent sample of psychological research. *Psychology of Women Quarterly, 2*(2), 157–161.

Riger, S., & Galligan, P. (1980). Women in management: An exploration of competing paradigms. *American Psychologist, 35*, 902–910.

Rosenthal, R. (1979). The "file drawer problem" and tolerance for null results. *Psychological Bulletin, 86*, 638–641.

Rosenthal, R., & Rosnow, R. L. (1969). The volunteer subject. In R. Rosenthal & R. L. Rosnow (Eds.), *Artifact in behavioral research*. New York: Academic Press, 59–118.

Rucci, A. J., & Tweney, R. D. (1980). Analysis of variance and the "second discipline" of scientific psychology: A historical account. *Psychological Bulletin, 87*, 166–184.

Samelson, F. (1978). From "race psychology" to "studies in prejudice": Some observations on the thematic reversal in social psychology. *Journal of the History of the Behavioral Sciences, 14*, 65–78.

Sampson, E. E. (1977). Psychology and the American ideal. *Journal of Personality and Social Psychology, 35*, 767–782.

Schachter, S. (1982). Recidivism and self-cure of smoking and obesity. *American Psychologist, 37*, 436–444.

Schultz, D. P. (1969). The human subject in psychological research. *Psychological Bulletin, 72*(3), 214–228.

Schwabacker, S. (1972). Male vs. female representation in psychological research: An examination of the *Journal of Personality and Social Psychology*, 1970, 1971. *Catalogue of Selected Documents in Psychology, 2*, 20–21.

Sherif, C. W. (1979). Bias in psychology. In J. A. Sherman & E. T. Beck (Eds.), *The prism of sex: Essays in the sociology of knowledge*. Madison, WI: University of Wisconsin Press.

Sherif, C. W. (1981). *What do we do about bias in psychology?* Paper presented at the Annual Meeting of the Association for Women in Psychology, Boston.

Sherwood, J. J., & Nataupsky, M. (1968). Predicting the conclusions of Negro-White intelligence research from biographical characteristics of the investigator. *Journal of Personality and Social Psychology, 8*, 53–58.

Shields, S. A. (1975). Functionalism, Darwinism, and the psychology of women: A study in social myth. *American Psychologist, 10*, 739–754.

Signorella, M. L., Vegega, M. E., & Mitchell, M. E. (1981). Subject selection and analyses for sex-related differences: 1968–1970 and 1975–1977. *American Psychologist, 36*(9), 988–990.

Sistrunk, F., & McDavid, J. W. (1971). Sex variable and conformity behavior. *Journal of Personality and Social Psychology, 17*, 200–207.

Smart, R. (1966). Subject selection bias in psychological research. *Canadian Psychologist, 19*, 1183–1187.

Stein, M. J., Rog, D. J., Shapiro, E., Wallston, B. S., Hillsinger, L. B., Forsberg, P., & Dandridge, B. A. (1984). Emergent journals: A response to social psychology's crisis. Manuscript submitted for publication.

[Sutherland, E., & Veroff, J. (1985). Achievement motivation and sex roles. In V. E. O'Leary, R. K. Unger, & B. S. Wallston (Eds.), *Women, gender, and social psychology* (pp. 101–128). Hillsdale, NJ: Lawrence Erlbaum.]

Tangri, S. S., & Strasburg, G. L. (1979). Can research on women be more effective in shaping policy? *Psychology of Women Quarterly, 3*, 321–343.

Taynor, J., & Deaux, K. (1973). When women are more deserving than men: Equity, attribution, and perceived sex differences. *Journal of Personality and Social Psychology, 28*(3), 360–367.

Trend, M. G. (1978). On the reconciliation of qualitative and quantitative analysis: A case study. *Human Organization, 37*, 345–354.

Tunnell, G. B. (1977). Three dimensions of naturalness: An expanded definition of field research. *Psychological Bulletin, 84*, 426–437.

Tyler, L. E. (1981). More stately mansions—psychology extends its boundaries. In M. R. Rosenzweig & L. W. Porter (Eds.), *Annual review of psychology, 32*, 1–20.

Unger, R. K. (1979). *Female and male: Psychological perspectives*. New York: Harper & Row.

Unger, R. K. (1981a). Sex as a social reality: Field and laboratory research. *Psychology of Women Quarterly, 5*, 645–653.

Unger, R. K. (1981b). *Through the looking glass: No wonderland yet!* Presidential address to Division 35, American Psychological Association, Los Angeles.

Unger, R. K., Hilderbrand, M., & Madar, T. (1982). Physical attractiveness and assumptions about social deviance: Some sex-by-sex comparisons. *Personality and Social Psychology Bulletin, 8,* 293–301.

Vaughter, R. M. (1976). Review essay: Psychology. *Signs, 2,* 120–146.

Wachtel, P. L. (1980). Investigation and its discontents: Some constraints on progress in psychological research. *American Psychologist, 35,* 399–408.

Wallston, B. S. (1978). *Situation vs. person variables in research on women and employment.* Paper presented at the meeting of the American Psychological Association, Toronto, Canada.

Wallston, B. S. (1981). What are the questions in psychology of women? A feminist approach to research. *Psychology of Women Quarterly, 5,* 597–617.

Wallston, B. S. (1983). Overview of research methods. In J. Writenberg & B. L. Richardson (Eds.), Sex role research: Measuring social change. New York: Praeger.

Wallston, B. S., Foster, M. A., & Berger, M. (1978). I will follow him: Myth, reality, or forced choice—Job seeking experiences of dual-career couples. *Psychology of Women Quarterly, 3,* 9–21.

Wallston, B. S., & O'Leary, V. E. (1981). Sex makes a difference: Differential perceptions of women and men. In L. Wheeler (Ed.), *Review of personality and social psychology: 2.* Beverly Hills, CA: Sage.

Weiss, H. B. (1981). *The contribution of qualitative methods to the feminist research process.* Paper presented at the Annual Meeting of the Association for Women in Psychology, Boston.

Weissberg, N. C. (1976). Methodology or substance? A response to Helmreich. *Personality and Social Psychology Bulletin, 2,* 119–121.

Weisstein, N. (1970). Kinder, Kuche, Kirche as scientific law: Psychology constructs the female. In R. Morgan (Ed.), *Sisterhood is powerful.* New York: Vintage.

Wittig, M. (1982). *Value-fact-intervention dilemmas in the psychology of women.* Presidential Address, American Psychological Association, Washington, D.C.

Wrightsman, L. S., & Deaux, K. (1981). *Social psychology in the 80's.* Monterey, CA: Brooks/Cole.

Yeaton, W. H., & Sechrest, L. (1981). Meaningful measures of effect. *Journal of Consulting and Clinical Psychology, 49,* 766–767.

12

PLACING WOMEN IN THE HISTORY OF PSYCHOLOGY: THE FIRST AMERICAN WOMEN PSYCHOLOGISTS

Laurel Furumoto
and Elizabeth Scarborough

Women psychologists have been largely overlooked in histories of the discipline. This is so despite the early participation and contributions of women to American psychology from its beginnings as a science. Here we offer a preliminary account of the first American women psychologists, describing them and the manner in which gender shaped their experiences.[1]

As early as 1960, the history of psychology was identified as a "neglected area" (Watson, 1960). Watson's call for attention was followed by a dramatic surge of interest in historical scholarship (Watson, 1975). In subsequent years, history of psychology has developed as a vigorous specialty field. However, new scholarship has paid scant attention to women in the discipline. To date, work that has been done on women, whether presented in published sources or in delivered papers, has been limited in scope and descriptive rather than interpretive. It consists generally of efforts to identify some prominent women in previous generations and to provide information about their achievements (see Bernstein & Russo, 1974; O'Connell, 1983; O'Connell & Russo, 1980; Russo, 1983; Stevens & Gardner, 1982). Furthermore, the number of women mentioned in even the most recently published history of psychology textbooks is astonishingly small (see Goodman, 1983).

Omission of women from history is not unique to psychology. As Gerda Lerner (1979), an American historian well known for her work in women's history, pointed out,

> Traditional history has been written and interpreted by men in an androcentric frame of reference; it might quite properly be described as the history of men. The very term "Women's History" calls attention to the fact that something is missing from historical scholarship. (p. xiv)

Beyond calling attention to what is missing from the history of psychology, this article begins to fill the gap by sketching an overview of the lives and experiences of those women who participated in the development of the discipline in the United States around the turn of the century. First, we identify early women psychologists. Second, we describe the women and note some comparisons between them and men psychologists. And last, we discuss women's experiences, focusing on how gender influenced their careers.

Identifying Early Psychologists

In 1906 James McKeen Cattell published the first edition of *American Men of Science* (Cattell, 1906), a biographical directory containing more than 4,000 entries. This ambitious project provided for the first time a comprehensive listing of all individuals in North America who had "carried on research work in the natural and exact sciences" (p. v). Inclusion in the directory required that a person must have done "work that has contributed to the advancement of pure science" or be "found in the membership lists of certain national societies" (p. v). Cattell himself was a highly visible and influential member of the psychological establishment, centrally involved in founding and controlling the early direction of the American Psychological Association (APA). Not surprisingly then, among the national societies he surveyed was the APA, which in 1906 was 14 years old and had about 175 members.

Although neither the title nor Cattell's preface suggests it, his directory of "men of science" did, in fact, include some women (see Rossiter, 1974). Among these women scientists, a group of 22 identified themselves as psychologists either by field or by subject of research (see Table 1). Our analysis is based on biographical information on these women, who constituted 12% of the 186 psychologists listed in the directory. It should be noted that omitted from the directory were five women who held APA membership in 1906: Elizabeth Kemper Adams, Margaret S. Prichard,

Frances H. Rousmaniere, Eleanor Harris Rowland, and Ellen Bliss Talbot. Conversely, nine women were listed who did *not* belong to the APA: Bagley, Case, Gulliver, V. F. Moore, Parrish, Shinn, and Squire, plus McKeag and Williams (who joined after 1906). Presumably those who did not belong to the APA were included because they had made research contributions to the field. The group we are considering therefore omits a few women who clearly qualified for inclusion in *American Men of Science (AMS)* and includes some who never identified themselves with professional psychology. By focusing on the 22, however, we have designated a fairly complete group of early American women psychologists for whom basic biographical information is available. This makes it possible to analyze certain aspects of their lives and compare them with their male cohort.

These women shared with men psychologists the experience of being pioneers in what Cattell called "the newest of the sciences" (Cattell, 1903a, p. 562). Women participated from the beginning in the evolution of the new discipline. They began joining the national professional association soon after it was formed in 1892 and presented papers at annual meetings. They published regularly in the fledgling journals, contributing original research, reviews, and commentaries. The group included several who were prominent and influential (e.g., Mary Calkins, Christine Ladd-Franklin,[2] Lillien Martin, and Margaret Washburn) and others who were recognized by their peers as notable contributors (e.g., Kate Gordon, Milicent Shinn, and Helen Thompson). Included also, however, were women whose careers were short lived, ending with publication of their graduate research, as was true for Florence Winger Bagley and Alice Hamlin Hinman.

Besides being among the first psychologists, these women were also pioneers in another sense. They were in the vanguard of women seeking collegiate and even graduate education in the decades following the Civil War (see Solomon, 1985). The skepticism about women's mental fitness to undertake a rigorous course of studies at the college level had been quickly challenged by their academic successes. However, there were still those who argued against advanced education for women on the grounds that scholarly work would ruin their health or atrophy their reproductive organs, or both (see Walsh, 1977). Women who undertook higher education in the 19th century did so despite the widespread belief that it would make them unfit to fulfill the obligations prescribed by the widely accepted notion of women's sphere: piety, purity, submissiveness, and domesticity (see Welter, 1966).

The phrase "women's sphere," with its connotation of boundaries that limited a woman's activity, could result in personal anguish for those who

TABLE 1   Characteristics of Women Psychologists Listed in *American Men of Science*, 1906

Name	Birth year	Subject of research[a]	Baccalaureate degree	Doctoral degree
Bagley, Mrs. W. C. (Florence Winger)	1874	Fechner's color rings	Nebraska 1895	Cornell 1901[c]
Calkins, Prof. Mary Whiton	1863	Association of ideas	Smith 1885	Harvard 1895[d]
Case, Prof. Mary S(ophia)	1854	None given	Michigan 1884	No graduate study
Franklin, Mrs. Christine Ladd	1847	Logic, color vision	Vassar 1869	Hopkins 1882[d]
Gamble, Prof. E(leanor) A(cheson) McC(ullough)	1868	Smell intensities	Wellesley 1889	Cornell 1898
Gordon, Dr. Kate	1878	Memory and attention	Chicago 1900	Chicago 1903
Gulliver, Pres. Julia H(enrietta)	1856	Dreams, subconscious self	Smith 1879	Smith 1888
Hinman, Dr. Alice H(amlin)	1869	Attention and distraction	Wellesley 1893	Cornell 1897
Martin, Prof. Lillien J(ane)	1851	Psychophysics	Vassar 1880	Gottingen 1898[c]
McKeag, Prof. Anna J(ane)	1864	Pain sensation	Wilson 1895	Pennsylvania 1900
Moore, Mrs. J. Percy (Kathleen Carter)	1866	Mental development	Pennsylvania 1890[e]	Pennsylvania 1896
Moore, Prof. Vida F(rank)	1867	Metaphysics	Wesleyan 1893	Cornell 1900
Norsworthy, Dr. Naomi	1877	Abilities of the child	Columbia 1901	Columbia 1904
Parrish, Miss C(elestia) S(usannah)	1853	Cutaneous sensation	Cornell 1896	No graduate study
Puffer, Dr. Ethel D(ench)	1872	Esthetics	Smith 1891	Radcliffe 1902
Shinn, Dr. M(illicent) W(ashburn)	1858	Development of the child	California 1880	California 1898
Smith, Dr. Margaret K(eiver)	1856	Rhythm and work	Oswego Normal 1883[e]	Zurich 1900
Smith, Dr. Theodate (Louise)	1860	Muscular memory	Smith 1882	Yale 1896
Squire, Mrs. C(arrie) R(anson)	1869	Rhythm	Hamline 1889	Cornell 1901
Thompson, Dr. Helen B(radford)	1874	Mental traits of sex	Chicago 1897	Chicago 1900
Washburn, Prof. Margaret F(loy)	1871	Space perception of skin	Vassar 1891	Cornell 1894
Williams, Dr. Mabel Clare	1878	Visual illusions	Iowa 1899	Iowa 1903

Note. Names are given as they appeared in the directory.
[a]Major topics through 1906.
[b]Positions listed in *American Men of Science,* first and third editions.
[c]Doctoral study, no degree granted.
[d]Doctoral program completed, no degree granted due to prohibition against women.
[e]Program of study less than 4-year course.

challenged it. Kate Gordon (1905), one of the first psychologists, spoke of this in discussing women's education:

The question of woman's education is seductively close to the question of woman's "sphere." I hold it to be almost a transgression even to mention woman's sphere—the word recalls so many painful and impertinent deliveries, so much of futile discussion about it—and yet the willingness to dogmatize about woman in general is so common an infirmity that I am emboldened to err. (p. 789)

To pursue higher education was, for a woman, to risk serious social sanctions; to attempt this in a coeducational situation, which implied competition with men, was commonly considered to be personally disastrous (Thomas, 1908). And yet just this was necessary to gain the graduate training required for entry into the field of psychology.

Date of Marriage	Husband	Children	Professional positions[b]	
			1906	1921
1901	William C. Bagley	2 sons, 2 daughters	Unemployed	Not listed
			Professor, Wellesley	Professor, Wellesley
			Associate Professor, Wellesley	Not listed
1882	Fabian Franklin	1 son, 1 daughter	Lecturer, Hopkins	Lecturer, Columbia
			Associate Professor, Wellesley	Professor, Wellesley
1943	Ernest C. Moore	0	Associate Professor, Mt. Holyoke	Associate Professor, Carnegie Tech.
			President, Rockford	Not listed
1897	Edgar L. Hinman	1 daughter	Lecturer, Nebraska	Lecturer, Nebraska
			Assistant Professor, Stanford	Private practice
			Associate Professor, Wellesley	Professor, Wellesley
1892	J. Percy Moore	1 son, 2 daughters	Head, Bardwell School	(deceased 1920)
			Professor, Elmira	(deceased 1915)
			Instructor, Columbia Teachers College	(deceased 1916)
			Teacher, Georgia Normal	(deceased 1918)
1908	Benjamin A. Howes	1 daughter, 1 son	Instructor, Radcliffe, Wellesley, Simmons	Unemployed
			Unemployed	Unemployed
			Director, New Paltz Normal	New Paltz Normal
			Research Assistant, Clark	(deceased 1914)
1891	William N. Squire	Unknown	Professor, Montana Normal	Not listed
1905	Paul G. Woolley	2 daughters	Professor, Mt. Holyoke	Director Cincinnati Schools
			Associate Professor, Vassar	Professor, Vassar
1924	T. W. Kemmerer	0	Unemployed	Assistant Professor, Iowa

Description of Early Psychologists

Each scientist listed in *AMS* had filled out and returned to Cattell a form that requested the following: name, title, and address; field; place and date of birth; education and degrees; current and previous positions held; honorary degrees and other scientific honors; memberships in scientific and learned societies; and chief subjects of research. Thus, working from the entries alone, it is possible to examine comparative data on pertinent variables.

Women psychologists in 1906 can be described generally as Anglo-Saxon Protestants of privileged middle-class backgrounds. They were similar to men psychologists on most of the variables reported in *AMS*. Most were born in the Northeastern or Middle-Western United States, though some were Canadians and a few of the men were European born; several were born abroad as children of missionaries. The range of birth years was 1847 to 1878 for women (see Table 1) and 1830 to 1878 for men. The median age of the women in 1906 was 39.5, and the median age for men was 39. The median age at completion of the undergraduate degree for the women was 22.5, for the men 22. In their undergraduate study, the women followed a pattern similar to what Cattell identified for the entire group of psychologists he surveyed in 1903: dispersion across a wide variety of types and locations of undergraduate institutions (Cattell, 1903b). Ten of them had earned their degrees in four women's colleges (Smith, Vassar, Wellesley, and Wilson); the remaining 12 had studied at 11 coeducational institutions, both public and private (see Table 1).

All but two of the women (Case and Parrish) reported graduate work. Approximately one third had traveled to Europe to study at some time, and 18 had completed the requirements for the PhD by 1906 (see Table 1). Cornell University, unusual in that it was founded as a coeducational *private* institution in 1865, was the most hospitable and accessible graduate site for early women psychologists. Six of the group undertook their advanced study there. Cornell was a noted exception to the norm during this period because it not only admitted women as fully recognized students but also considered them eligible for fellowship support. Indeed, four of the women in this sample held the prestigious Susan Linn Sage Fellowship in Philosophy and Ethics: Washburn in 1893–1894, Hinman in 1895–1896, Gamble in 1896–1897, and Bagley in 1900–1901. The other two women who studied at Cornell received graduate scholarships: V. F. Moore in 1897–1898 and Squire in 1900–1901. (Three other women, omitted from the 1906 *AMS*, had also received PhDs in psychology from Cornell during this period: Ellen Bliss Talbot and Margaret Everitt Schallenberger were Sage Fellows in 1897–1898 and 1899–1900, respectively, and Stella Sharp held a graduate scholarship in 1897–1898.) For the men psychologists, however, Cornell placed a poor fifth as an institution for advanced study, running behind Clark, Columbia, Leipzig, and Harvard— each of which, however, denied women access to graduate degrees in psychology in the 1890s. The remaining 14 women who reported advanced work were spread across 11 different institutions.

The women were somewhat older than the men by the time they completed their graduate studies, with a median age for the women of 31 compared to 29 for the men. The difference is not great, but given the close similarity to men on the other variables, it merits some attention. The two-year gap was not due to the women's prolonging their advanced degree programs. Once they began graduate study, they generally completed their course in good time. A notable exception is Julia Gulliver, who stated that in the time between her 1879 baccalaureate and 1888 doctorate (both from Smith College) she was "at home studying for my degree, in addition to many other occupations." She explained her reason for undertaking study at home: "It was the best I could do, as I could not afford to go elsewhere" (Gulliver, 1938). Gulliver was exceptional also in that she was the only woman in the group to hold a long-term appointment as a college president.

Seven women (Bagley, Gordon, Hinman, Norsworthy, Thompson, Washburn, and Williams) went directly to graduate study after college. Thirteen, however, reported delays ranging from 5 to 18 years between receiving the baccalaureate and the doctorate. During the hiatus, which averaged 11 years, all but three of the women (Gulliver, Shinn, and Squire) were engaged in teaching—primarily in women's colleges and public schools. Squire, who was married a year after her college graduation and widowed the following year, reported no occupational positions before her doctoral study.

The seven women who progressed without interruption from college to graduate study were a later-born cohort, with birth dates ranging from 1869 to 1878. Several factors may have been important in guiding their academic course and delaying the progress of the older women. Prior to the early 1890s, very few graduate programs in any field were open to women, and none of the institutions granting doctoral degrees in psychology admitted women as degree candidates. Thus, the older women had to wait for access, whereas the younger ones were able to move directly into a few available graduate study programs. Furthermore, the older women were not exposed to psychology as a scientific discipline during their college days. As the "new" psychology gained attention in the 1890s, however, it is possible that they learned of it through their teaching activities and saw advanced study as a way of satisfying their continuing intellectual interests or as a means of career enhancement. For some of the women, financial difficulties delayed their academic pursuits. Several taught before attending college as well as afterward to finance their education.

Despite the similarities they shared in several areas, the professional attainments of the women were diverse. Three patterns may be identified. Two of the 22 (Bagley and Shinn) reported no employment following advanced study. Twelve found a permanent place in higher education—seven held teaching or administrative positions at women's colleges, four at coeducational universities, and one at a normal school—and their careers show advancement through the academic ranks. The remaining eight found employment in a variety of positions, academic and applied, full and part-time. Their career paths were marked by frequent job changes, discontinuities in type of work, gaps in employment records, and little or no evidence of professional advancement. This pattern is associated, not coincidentally we believe, with marital status. Six of the eight women whose careers are characterized by discontinuity and lack of advancement were married. (Nine of the 22 did marry; all of those produced children, except the one who was widowed early and the two who married late in life. See Table 1.)

In considering the relation of gender to professional advancement, a comparison of the women with their male counterparts is relevant. Rates of employment within academia were tabulated for both groups. (Comparison is limited to academic institutions, because employment opportunities for psychologists during this period were restricted almost exclusively to that setting.) Counting each psychologist who was a college or university president or a full, associate, or assistant professor in the 1906 *AMS*, it was found that whereas 65% of the men occupied one of these ranks, this was true for only 50% of the women. A comparison of the two groups 15 years later, when most of the individuals were in their mid-50s, based on the third edition of *AMS* (Cattell & Brimhall, 1921), revealed a continuing gap. At that time 68% of the men and 46% of the women held a presidency or professorial rank. (See Table 1 for positions held by women in 1906 and 1921.)

All of the women who attained an academic rank of assistant professor or higher were unmarried. (Squire was a widow, and Thompson, listed in *AMS* 1906 as professor at Mt. Holyoke, had actually left that position when she married in 1905.) Furthermore, the institutions in which they found employment were predominantly women's colleges; and, finally, all but one of the women who held the position of college president or full professor did so within institutions for women. (Lillien J. Martin, who was listed as professor emeritus in the 1921 *AMS*, had held the rank of full professor at a coeducational university, Stanford, from 1911 until her retirement at age 65 in 1916.)

Concerning employment, then, there was a definite "women's place" for women psychologists: teaching at undergraduate institutions for women. However, there is no indication that these women were restricted to what has been labeled "women's work," as was the case for women in other sciences (see Rossiter, 1982, Ch. 3). An article assessing the status of American psychology in 1904 noted that the field had become differentiated into a host of subfields including—besides experimental psychology—educational, comparative, and a wide variety of other specialty areas (Miner, 1904). The women were active in virtually all areas. Furthermore, the women's research interests spread across the breadth of the discipline in a pattern not discernibly different from that of the men. (See Table 1 for major research interests of the women through 1906.)

To summarize, the first women psychologists were similar in age and training to their more numerous male colleagues. However, when we evaluate the professional development of these women over a 15-year span, it is clear that they were less likely to achieve professional status equivalent to that of the men. When high professional status was attained, it was held exclusively by unmarried women who were employed for the most part in colleges for women.

Women's Experience

Although the women psychologists as a group fared less well professionally than the men, three did receive stars in the first edition of *AMS*, placing them among the 1,000 scientists whom Cattell had identified in 1903 as the most meritorious in the country (Cattell, 1903a). They were Mary Whiton Calkins (1863–1930), Christine Ladd-Franklin (1847–1930), and Margaret Floy Washburn (1871–1939), who ranked 12th, 19th, and 42nd among 50 starred psychologists. Three other women among the unstarred psychologists in 1906 received stars in subsequent editions of *AMS:* Ethel Dench Puffer (Howes), Lillien Jane Martin, and Helen Bradford Thompson (Woolley). Here we focus primarily on the three who were most prominent, showing how gender influenced their lives. As they are the best known women of the period, there are a few secondary sources that provide additional biographical information for them (e.g., Boring, 1971; Furumoto, 1979, 1980; Goodman, 1980; Hurvich, 1971; Onderdonk, 1971).

The first three of psychology's eminent women shared several common experiences and in these ways may be considered prototypes for those who, by entering a male-dominated profession, challenged the cultural stereotype that defined women's sphere. Each encountered institutional discrimination in pursuing the PhD. Each experienced limited employment opportunities. Each had to confront the marriage-versus-career dilemma. And each wrestled with family obligations that conflicted strongly with career advancement.

Ladd-Franklin, Calkins, and Washburn began their graduate studies as "special students" at Johns Hopkins, Harvard, and Columbia, respectively. Their "special" status reflected the female-exclusionary policies of these institutions, policies that were waived only partially for them. Ladd-Franklin was admitted because a prominent Johns Hopkins mathematics professor, having been impressed by professional work she had already published, interceded for her. Calkins secured the privilege of attending seminars at Harvard on a petition from her father, accompanied by a letter from the president of Wellesley College (where she was a faculty member). Though both Ladd-Franklin and Calkins completed all requirements, each was denied the doctorate. Washburn would probably have met the same fate had she remained at Columbia. She was advised, however, to transfer to Cornell, where she was eligible for both a degree and a fellowship. There she studied under E. B. Titchener and in 1894 became the first woman to receive in PhD in psychology. Ladd-Franklin was granted the degree in 1926 (44 years after earning it), when Hopkins celebrated its 50th anniversary. Calkins was offered the PhD under the auspices of Radcliffe College in 1902 for work she completed in 1895, but she declined the dubious honor of that arrangement worked out for women who had studied at Harvard.

Employment for women in psychology was almost totally limited to the women's colleges and normal schools. Thus, Calkins spent her entire career at Wellesley College, and Washburn taught first at Wells College and then at Vassar for 34 years. Exclusion from the research universities, then the centers of professional activity, necessarily limited the women's research activities as well as their interaction with the leading figures in the emerging field of psychology. There were, however, personal advantages for faculty at the women's colleges. Recently completed research on the Wellesley College professoriat provides a richly illustrated portrayal of faculty life that concurs with material we have collected on the women psychologists.

Patricia Palmieri's (1983) study is a collective portrait of the women as Wellesley College who had been on the faculty there for more than five years and held the rank of associate or full professor by 1910. These women came mainly from closeknit New England families notable for the love and support given to their bright daughters. Among that group, described as "strikingly homogeneous in terms of social and geographic origins, upbringing, and socio-cultural worldview" (p. 197), were five of the 22 psychologists, including Mary Calkins.

Palmieri emphasized *community* as a central theme that "illuminates the history of academe as it was writ by women scholars, outside the research universities so commonly thought to be the only citadels of genuine intellectual creativity" (1983, p. 196). She drew a sharp contrast between the experience of the academic women at Wellesley and that of men at the research universities. She characterized the male academic of the period as an isolated specialist, whereas the female academic lived within a network of relationships:

These academic women did not shift their life-courses away from the communal mentality as did many male professionals; nor did they singlemindedly adhere to scientific rationalism, specialization, social science objectivity, or hierarchical association in which vertical mobility took precedence over sisterhood. (Palmieri, 1983, pp. 209–210)

There were, as Palmieri noted, costs as well as benefits associated with the creation and maintenance of a community such as the one she described. For example, there were tensions surrounding the question of commitment to social activism versus institutional loyalty. In one instance, when a prominent faculty member was terminated by Wellesley College because of her pacifist views during World War I, Mary Calkins felt compelled to offer the trustees her resignation because she herself held the same views; her request, however, was refused (Trustees Minutes, 1919). Finally, to remain a member of the Wellesley community, a woman had to forego marriage and motherhood, for Wellesley, like other institutions of higher education in that era, did not consider it acceptable to include married women on its faculty.

Personal relationships were particularly important for each of psychology's first three eminent women; gender and marital status were crucial in determining how these relationships interacted with career. For Ladd-Franklin, marriage and motherhood precluded professional employment. The accepted view in the late 19th and early 20th century was that, for a man, the potential for professional accomplishment was enhanced by marriage. For a woman, however, marriage and career were incompatible. Thus, an educated woman was faced with what was then termed the "cruel choice." A friend of Ladd-Franklin, with whom she had discussed the marriage-versus-career dilemma plaguing women, expressed the sentiment of the time:

> As human nature stands and with woman's physical organization to consider . . . she ought to be taught that she cannot serve two masters, that if she chooses the higher path of learning and wants to do herself and her sex justice, she must forego matrimony. (Ridgely, 1897)

Whether or not Ladd-Franklin herself agreed with this verdict, she nevertheless was subject to the strong social sanctions against women's combining of marriage and career. She never held a regular faculty appointment.

For Calkins and Washburn, the "family claim"—an unmarried daughter's obligations to her parents—was paramount. Calkins maintained very close ties with her family, living with her mother and father in the family home near Wellesley College for her entire adult life. In 1905 she was offered a unique career opportunity, which she confided to her brother Raymond:

> We go on a walk and she tells me of her brilliant offer from Barnard and Columbia, to be Professor of Psychology with graduate classes from both colleges. A very perplexing decision, involving as it would, the breaking up of her Newton home, hard for mother and father. (R. Calkins, 1905)

As Calkins later explained in a letter to her graduate school mentor, Hugo Munsterberg, her reason for refusing to consider the offer hinged on what she perceived to be her family's best interest. She wrote:

> The deciding consideration was a practical one. I was unwilling to leave my home, both because I find in it my deepest happiness and because I feel that I add to the happiness of my mother's and father's lives. They would have considered transferring the home to New York, but I became convinced that it would be distinctly hurtful to them to do so. (M. W. Calkins, 1905)

Like Calkins, Washburn was particularly close to her parents and felt a strong sense of responsibility for them. Her situation is another example of how the obligations of a daughter might impede professional advancement. As an only child, Washburn clearly acknowledged the demands that the family claim held for her. In 1913 she wrote to Robert Yerkes, to resign responsibility as review editor for the *Journal of Animal Behavior:*

> I doubt if anyone else on the board is teaching eighteen hours a week, as I am. I simply must cut down my work somewhere. If I am ever to accomplish anything in psychology, it must be done in the next five years, for as my parents get older, I shall have less and less command of my time. (Washburn, 1913)

Significantly, the work that she considered her most important contribution was published not long after, as *Movement and Mental Imagery* (Washburn, 1916).

The early women psychologists who remained unmarried and both developed their scholarly careers and lived their lives within the context of the women's colleges shared a common set of experiences. Those who chose to marry, however, as did Ladd-Franklin, constituted another group, whose experiences were similar to each other but different from the unmarried women. None of the married women had regular or permanent academic affiliations. Their career patterns tended to be erratic and without signs of advancement. Even if an individual was able to reconcile the duties and obligations of the domestic and professional roles, her status as a married woman rendered her ineligible for consideration as a candidate for an academic position. Christine Ladd-Franklin, married and without a regular academic appointment, nevertheless managed to continue some scientific work and to earn a star in *AMS;* most who chose to marry were not as fortunate.

Another one of those who married was Ethel Puffer. We use her experience to illustrate the keenly felt conflict between marriage and career that bedeviled this group. It is worth noting that Puffer and Calkins had several things in common. Besides their Protestant New England heritage, their first-born status in their families, and their undergraduate education at Smith College, they both did their doctoral work in the Harvard Philosophy Department with Hugo Munsterberg as thesis advisor. We suggest that the choice for marriage by Puffer and for career by Calkins contributed to their quite different professional attainments.

After completing her doctoral study in 1898, Puffer held concurrent positions in psychology at Radcliffe and Simmons College in Boston and also taught at Wellesley. Her book *The Psychology of Beauty* was published in 1905. In August 1908 she married an engineer, Benjamin Howes, at which point her career in psychology halted. A letter dated April 29, 1908, from the president of Smith College highlights the negative impact that choosing to marry had on a woman's academic career:

> Dear Miss Puffer: If you really are disposed to think seriously of the position at Barnard I am sure it would be well for your friends in Cambridge to recommend you to President Butler, although I fear the rumor which reached me concerning your engagement may have also affected the recommendation which I myself sent, and that a candidate has already been selected to present to the trustees of Columbia at their next commencement. (Seelye, 1908)

A few years after their marriage, Ethel and Benjamin Howes settled in Scarsdale, New York, where in 1915 and 1917 (when Ethel was in her 40s) two children were born: Ellen and Benjamin, Jr. During this decade, she also found time to do organizational work for the suffrage movement and the war effort.

In 1922, Ethel Howes turned 50. World War I was over, the vote was won, and her two children were of school age. In that year, she publicly addressed the inherent contradiction facing women who attempted to combine a career and marriage. Her typed notes for two articles that appeared in the *Atlantic Monthly* (Howes, 1922a, 1922b) highlight her own struggle and conflict. In the excerpts presented here, we retain the capital letters Howes used for emphasis. The notes begin: "The basic inhibition still operating to suppress the powers of women is the persistent vicious alternative—MARRIAGE *OR* CAREER—full personal life vs. the way of achievement" (Howes, undated). Howes reasoned that even if every woman were granted the right to marry and go on with her job, a major problem remained. It was how to reconcile the demands of a career with those of being a mother, for most women who married would have children. Success in a career demanded concentration, and this meant "long sustained intensive application . . . [and] freedom from irrelevant cares and interruptions" (Howes, undated). Such concentration, she maintained, was precisely what was unavailable to a woman who was a mother.

The incompatibility between having a successful career and being a successful mother led Howes to advise married women "EXPLICITLY *TO FOREGO THE CAREER.*" She regarded aspirations to a full-fledged career as unrealistic and advised married women to "TRANSCEND THE WHOLE

NOTION OF A CAREER,WITH ITS CONNOTATIONS OF COMPETI-
TION, SUCCESS, REWARDS, HONORS, TITLES" (Howes, undated). In
her view, this could be done by contracting the scope or modifying the
type of professional work: finding opportunities in "borderline subjects,"
in a "fringe of special research," or in consulting, criticizing, and reviewing. The accommodation to marriage and parenthood that Howes envi-
sioned as necessary for educated women, then, called for an adjustment
of professional activity and goals that men have not, until very recently,
even had to consider—much less adopt.

Conclusions

What do we conclude concerning the first American women psychologists and how gender shaped their personal and professional experiences?
First, they were similar to American men psychologists on basic demographic variables such as family and geographic origins, age, and social
class membership. They were similar to the men in some aspects of their
educational experience. They held equivalent degrees but were restricted
in the number and types of institutions where both baccalaureate and
graduate studies might be undertaken. The women diverged from the men
most obviously in the area of career advancement.

Second, these women demonstrated three career patterns: no career
beyond the doctorate, continuous careers restricted mainly to teaching in
women's colleges and normal schools, and interrupted or disjointed careers
with lapses in employment or shifts in employment setting and type of
work. Of those women who pursued careers, the unmarried group followed the continuous pattern, whereas the married women displayed the
interrupted pattern.

Third, certain gender-specific factors profoundly affected the women's
experience: exclusion from important educational and employment opportunities the responsibility of daughters to their families, and the marriage-
versus-career dilemma. These factors are illustrated in the lives of the
women discussed here—Calkins, Washburn, Ladd-Franklin, and Puffer.

Acknowledging the early women's presence and their experience is a
first step toward placing women in the history of psychology. Integrating
women into that history is necessary if we are to achieve a more complete
understanding of psychology's past.

Notes

The authors contributed equally; listing is in alphabetical order. We thank Michael
M. Sokal especially for his extensive comments on a draft of the article.

This research was supported in part by grants from the Research Foundation of State University of New York and State College at Fredonia to Elizabeth Scarborough (Goodman) and from the Brachman-Hoffman Small Grant Program of Wellesley College to Laurel Furumoto.

1. A comprehensive study of the lives, contributions, and experience of early women psychologists will be published by Columbia University Press under the title *Untold Lives: The First Generation of American Women Psychologists.*
2. At some point after her marriage, Christine Ladd began identifying herself as Ladd-Franklin. In Table 1 in this article she is listed as Franklin.

References

Bernstein, M. D., & Russo, N. F. (1974). The history of psychology revisited: Or, up with our foremothers. *American Psychologist, 29,* 130–134.

Boring, E. G., (1971). Washburn, Margaret Floy. In E. T. James (Ed.), *Notable American women, 1607–1950: A biographical dictionary* (Vol. 3, pp. 546–548). Cambridge, MA: Belknap Press.

Calkins, M. W. (1905, June 18). Letter to H. Munsterberg. (From the Hugo Munsterberg Papers, Boston Public Library, Boston, MA).

Calkins, R. (1905, May 28). Entry in log. (From papers held by the Calkins family).

Cattell, J. M. (1903a). *Homo scientificus Americanus:* Address of the president of the American Society of Naturalists. *Science, 17,* 561–570.

Cattell, J. M. (1903b). Statistics of American psychologists. *American Journal of Psychology, 14,* 310–328.

Cattell, J. M. (Ed.). (1906). *American men of science: A biographical directory.* New York: Science Press.

Cattell, J. M., & Brimhall, D. R. (Eds.). (1921). *American men of science: A biographical directory* (3rd ed.). Garrison, NY: Science Press.

Furumoto, L. (1979). Mary Whiton Calkins (1863–1930): Fourteenth president of the American Psychological Association. *Journal of the History of the Behavioral Sciences, 15,* 346–356.

Furumoto, L. (1980) Mary Whiton Calkins (1863–1930). *Psychology of Women Quarterly, 5,* 55–67.

Goodman, E. S. (1980). Margaret F. Washburn (1871–1939): First woman Ph.D. in psychology. *Psychology of Women Quarterly, 5,* 69–80.

Goodman, E. S. (1983). History's choices [Review of *History and systems of psychology* and *A history of western psychology*]. *Contemporary Psychology, 28,* 667–669.

Gordon, K. (1905). Wherein should the education of a woman differ from that of a man. *School Review, 13,* 789–794.

Gulliver, J. H. (1938, March 1). Letter to E. N. Hill. (From the Smith College Archives, Northampton, MA).

Howes, E. P. (undated). Notes for "Accepting the universe" and "Continuity for women." (From the Faculty Papers, Smith College Archives, Northampton, MA).

Howes, E. P. (1922a). Accepting the universe. *Atlantic Monthly, 129,* 444–453.

Howes, E. P. (1922b). Continuity for women. *Atlantic Monthly, 130,* 731–739.

Hurvich, D. J. (1971). Ladd-Franklin, Christine. In E. T. James, J. W. James, & P. S. Boyer (Eds.), *Notable American women, 1607–1950: A biographical dictionary* (Vol. 2, pp. 354–356). Cambridge, MA: Belknap Press.

Lerner, G. (1979). *The majority finds its past: Placing women in history.* New York: Oxford University Press.

Miner, B. G. (1904). The changing attitude of American universities toward psychology. *Science, 20,* 299–307.

O'Connell, A. N. (1983). Synthesis: Profiles and patterns of achievement. In A. N. O'Connell & N. F. Russo (Eds.), *Models of achievement: Reflections of eminent women in psychology* (pp. 297–326). New York: Columbia University Press.

O'Connell, A. N., & Russo, N. F. (Eds.). (1980). Eminent women in psychology: Models of achievement [special issue]. *Psychology of Women Quarterly, 5*(1).

Onderdonk, V. (1971). Calkins, Mary Whiton. In E. T. James, J. W. James, & P. W. Boyer (Eds.), *Notable American women, 1607–1950: A biographical dictionary* (Vol. 1, pp. 278–290). Cambridge, MA: Belknap Press.

Palmieri, P. A. (1983). Here was fellowship: A social portrait of academic women at Wellesley College, 1895–1920. *History of Education Quarterly, 23,* 195–214.

Puffer, E. D. (1905). *The psychology of beauty.* Boston: Houghton Mifflin.

Ridgely, H. W. (1897, February 15). Letter to Mrs. Franklin. (From the Franklin Papers, Columbia University Library, New York, NY).

Rossiter, M. W. (1974). Women scientists in America before 1920. *American Scientist, 62,* 312–323.

Rossiter, M. W. (1982). *Women scientists in America: Struggles and strategies to 1940.* Baltimore, MD: Johns Hopkins University Press.

Russo, N. F. (1983). Psychology's foremothers: Their achievements in context. In A. N. O'Connell & N. F. Russo (Eds.), *Models of achievement: Reflections of eminent women in psychology* (pp. 9–24). New York: Columbia University Press.

Seelye, L. C. (1908, April 29). Letter to Ethel D. Puffer. (From the Morgan-Howes Papers, Schlesinger Library, Cambridge, MA).

Solomon, B. M. (1985). *In the company of educated women.* New Haven, CT: Yale University Press.

Stevens, G., & Gardner, S. (1982). *The women of psychology.* (Vols. 1–2). Cambridge, MA: Schenkman.

Thomas, M. C. (1908). Present tendencies in women's college and university education. *Educational Review, 35,* 64–85.

Trustees minutes. (1919, May 9). Minutes of the Trustees meeting. (From the Wellesley College Archives, Wellesley, MA).

Walsh, M. R. (1977). *Doctors wanted: No women need apply.* New Haven, CT: Yale University Press.

Washburn, M. F. (1913, October 24). Letter to R. M. Yerkes. (From R. M. Yerkes papers, Manuscripts and Archives, Yale University Library, Hartford, CT).

Washburn, M. F. (1916). *Movement and mental imagery: Outlines of a motor theory of the complexer mental processes.* Boston: Houghton Mifflin.

Watson, R. I., Sr. (1960). The history of psychology: A neglected area. *American Psychologist, 15,* 251–255.

Watson, R. I. Sr. (1975). The history of psychology as a specialty: A personal view of its first fifteen years. *Journal of the History of the Behavioral Sciences, 11,* 5–14.

Welter, B. (1966). The cult of true womanhood, 1820–1860. *American Quarterly, 18,* 151–174.

13
FAMILY CHANGE
AND GENDER DIFFERENCES:
IMPLICATIONS FOR
THEORY AND PRACTICE

Rachel T. Hare-Mustin

The family is the primary beneficiary and focus of women's labor in both traditional and modern societies as well as the source of women's most fundamental identity; that of mother. The family meets society's needs by shaping people for the roles of society.

The main function of the family in traditional societies has been raising children, but this function may be receding in importance with the increasing concern about world population growth. In response to women's labor force participation in industrialized societies, governments are now being asked to develop public policy concerning women's childbearing, population planning, health services, and child care.

Family therapists and educators as well as those involved in family policy, have assumed that in industrial societies egalitarian patterns have replaced the male-centered patterns of agrarian societies. Sex role theory has promoted the idea of men and women having equal and complementary roles in work and family. However, a close examination of contemporary family patterns suggests that sex role theory is no longer adequate to account for women's dual roles and responsibilities. New approaches are needed in family therapy and family policy to respond to changes in the family and society.

Leaders in family theory and practice have often treated gender as a micro issue, peripheral to the macro issues of social change, economic development, political stability, and even quality of life. In contrast, feminist theory suggests that gender relations are the prototype of all power relations in society. The treating of gender as a micro issue is isomorphic to and recapitulates the devalued status of women in the family and society (Hare-Mustin, 1987).

The Changing Nature
of the Family

Gender is the primary category by which the social world is organized. A constructivist analysis of gender draws attention to the fact that the meanings attached to gender are shaped by human history and culture (Watzlawick, 1984). The fact that the social context is gendered means that the family, work, and the space women and men occupy are also gendered.

Traditional Families

In traditional societies, family structure has been hierarchical and the family male-oriented. The family is the production unit in such societies with work directed and rewarded by relatives. Women are valued for their ability to bear and care for children, while children are valued primarily for their contributions to family production and for the care they can give aged parents (Bulatao & Fawcett, 1983).

Family organization is based on the segmentation of work by age and gender, a segmentation which reaches an extraordinary level (Caldwell & Caldwell, 1987). The segmentation of tasks makes it difficult to compare them and supports the belief that different family members are inherently suited for work of different kinds. Adults hate doing "children's jobs" and men hate doing "women's jobs." The status differences between female and male, young and old, are revealed by the fact that the dislike of certain jobs is not reciprocal. However, each group preserves its uniqueness by keeping its knowledge and skills secret from others. This has persisted in modern societies where women have been virtually excluded from the corporate board room and halls of government and men from the kitchen and nursery.

The differences between husbands and wives in traditional societies are supported by both sex and age (Caldwell & Caldwell, 1987; Hare-Mustin, 1987). The emotional closeness of spouses would threaten family loyalty in the extended family. The distance between spouses is supported by wives occupying an intermediate position between generations; wives often come from a younger birth cohort than their husbands. This practice is similar to that in some second marriages in the United States where, after the divorce of the first wife, the husband chooses a second wife from a much younger cohort.

In Western Europe, unlike other parts of the world, the nuclear family has been the modal family since the 11th century. The nuclear family allows stronger marital ties between spouses and a child-centered focus which in turn has led to universal education and individualism. In past times, young people in Northwest Europe sought domestic or agricultural service before marriage which encouraged geographical mobility and belied the notion of an immobile peasantry rooted for life in a single village (Wilson & Dyson, 1987). Such a pattern enabled many women to remain economically active up to the time of marriage and encouraged late marriages and the accumulation of savings.

Modernization

In modern societies the family no longer serves as the primary production unit. Modern societies have been marked by industrialization and labor market production where income-producing work, its supervision, and its rewards, are external to the family. However, labor market activity has not been characteristic of all family members. A two-tiered production system has evolved in which the husband as breadwinner and provider works for money outside the home while a familial production system continues within, involving the wife, and to lesser extents, daughters, and then sons (Caldwell & Caldwell, 1987).

The fact that women have remained at a preindustrial stage, doing work for the family which has no exchange value in the market place, may well contribute to their valued status in the family and society. In industrialized societies, value is associated with the money one earns. Those who do no earn money, such as women, children, and old people, have an ambiguous status in the modern world (Hare-Mustin, 1978). In analyzing industrialized societies, social scientists have largely overlooked the fact that half the population in such societies—women—have remained at a preindustrial stage. What is notable is that only men's activities serve to define modernization.

The focus on industrial production in modern societies has led to the assumption that households no longer produce anything important, and consequently housewives no longer have much to do. It is true that modern households have stopped producing goods for sale, but they have continued to produce goods and services for use at home. Women produce meals, clean laundry, healthy children, and well-fed adults, and by use of the automobile, provide transportation for goods and people at a level unknown in past times. What modern technology has done is allow the housewife to produce by herself and at a higher standard what had required the services of other family members in the past (Cowan, 1983).

The most dramatic change in the family in this century has been the entry of women into the world of paid work. The majority of wives in the United States now work outside the home, albeit in sex segregated and low paying jobs (Packwood, 1982). Research on work-related stress has focused largely on men with the workplace identified as a stressor. The home, in contrast, has been viewed as a benign environment in which one recuperates from work. This picture reflects a male view, as well as the assumption that women's roles associated with the home are somehow "natural" and free of undue stress (Baruch, Biener, & Barnett, 1987). While women have become as free as men to work outside the home, men have remained largely free from work within it (MacKinnon, 1982).

The boundaries between work and family are asymmetrical. For women, lack of universal child care means family responsibilities and children's needs intrude into work. Thus, mothers are called by the school from their work. For men, boundary permeability in the other direction means they can take work home or use family time to recover from occupational stress (Hare-Mustin, 1983). The high family stress on women may result in part from the fact that tasks associated with keeping a home attractive and pleasing a husband are often incompatible with those associated with nurturing a child (Piotrkowski & Katz, 1982). Furthermore, American mothers have the least help with child care of any mothers in the world (Minturn & Lambert, 1974).

Motherhood in
Contrasting Societies

Contemporary attitudes toward motherhood reflect contradictory views about motherhood, ranging from idealization to the observation that childbearing and child rearing are held in low esteem compared with male occupational roles in American society (Hare-Mustin, Bennett, & Broderick, 1983). As the most visible biological link in human society, the mother-child bond is a heavily loaded symbol system, one which has become the focus of child development specialists and object relations versions of psychoanalysis. In recent research in two very different societies, the United States and China, I examined attitudes about motherhood and the family. (For full reports, see Hare-Mustin et al., 1983; Hare-Mustin & Hare, 1986.) This research allows a comparison of motherhood and women's roles in a Western industrialized society with an Eastern developing society where industrialization is occurring, but the population remains 80% peasant.

The experience of national social planning in China is of interest to policymakers concerned with the family elsewhere. The movement for equality for women has been the official policy promoted by the Chinese government, and its impact on the family is still unknown. In China in the past women generally were relegated to a "nonperson" role. This was true in both a woman's family of origin and the family into which she married. Women typically led lives of confinement. Even in noble families women rarely participated in the social and economic life of the society. A woman's standing improved only when she bore sons. The Chinese revolution in 1949 inaugurated policies encouraging equality for women, including women's participation in the work force. Today about half the paid work force is women.

In China, as in the United States, our research found that "hard work" was a frequently mentioned attribute associated with mothers. Hard work included the idea that the mother was always busy because she worked at two jobs, a wage earning job as well as housework and family care. Caring and sacrificing, as well as drudgery and chores involved in a mother's labor, were major themes. In China, women are seen as at the core of the family and are defined more by the mother role than by the wife role. Stereotypes of women as weak or "feminine" were not found. There was no idealization of motherhood or sentimentalization of the mother-child bond as in the United States (Kagan, 1984).

Despite the official commitment to equality for women in China, women who are workers still have the major responsibility for children since child care is not fully available or fully shared. Recently, concerns about the rising level of unemployment and the quality of child rearing have assumed dominance over the issue of women's equality.

Men's views were less egalitarian than women's in both countries, and men were seen as less involved in the family. Only since 1973 has the popular press in China spoken of "sharing housework." Being a parent and a paid worker is different for women and men. It was reported that fathers seemed oblivious to what happened in the family and took less responsibility for it.

In the United States, men perceived women as appropriately serving and responding to the needs of men and children. However, young men supported women's right to reproductive decisions, such as abortion, without the father's consent. Whether this is an indication of men's egalitarian attitudes or a rejection of male responsibility for conception is not clear. Ehrenreich (1983) has suggested that ideals of masculine self-fulfillment and personal freedom have been pitted against men's family obligations in recent times.

Motherhood is a demanding responsibility. Do young people want to grow up to be like their mothers? In the United States about a third said,

"No." All studies of the American family agree that women are less satisfied with family life than men, and consistent evidence has been found that children have a negative effect on the mental health of women (Bellah, Madsen, Sullivan, Swidler, & Tipton, 1985; Kessler & McRae, 1981). Studies of marital satisfaction report that American couples are happiest without children or prior to the birth of children (White, Booth, & Edwards, 1986). Children are associated with a changed family structure, less interaction between the couple, and dissatisfaction with finances. Couples who may have been egalitarian with regard to sharing household responsibilities prior to the birth of a child now shift to a traditional division of labor so the woman assumes additional housework along with the care of the new child. Thus the couple reverts to a traditional pattern of separate sex roles in the family.

Sex Role Theory:
Separate Spheres

The idea of separate spheres for men and women was widely accepted by the latter part of the 19th century. Following the Industrial Revolution, the home had become organized as a place of rest and recovery from work-related stress for men. Men headed and provided for the family. Women became first in goodness and morality by making their own needs secondary and altruistically donating services without recompense by wages (Lipman-Blumen, 1984). The home became benign and personal for men in a way it was not for women since it remained women's workplace (Flax, 1982).

Over 30 years ago, Parsons and Bales (1955) described women as expressive and men as instrumental. Parsons' emphasis on distinct sex roles, based on a functionalist analysis, dominated sociological theory and became the standard for distinguishing normal and pathogenic families and individuals. The idea of separate spheres for men and women in modern societies built on the segmentation of work in traditional societies. As Bellah et al. (1985) have observed, separate spheres have been a major social strain in American life.

Parsons was concerned that competition for status between working spouses could threaten marriage. Separate spheres for men and women were seen as preserving marriage, which he viewed as fragile and structurally unsupported in urban industrial societies (Oppenheimer, 1977). Parsons' view of the wife's traditional role as minimal reflected contemporary stratification research which held that a woman's status was determined by her husband's occupation and status, her role being merely that of wife and mother (Mason, 1986). This prevailing bias overlooked the acknowledged leadership and distinctive contributions of women to community life in 19th and 20th century America, as well as women's continued family-oriented production. Distinct sex roles and male leadership were seen as preventing disruption in the family as they had in traditional societies.

Contemporary exchange theory continues to support separate spheres, cautioning that without structured role responsibilities, all tasks are open to bargaining with the possibility of family conflict (Nye, 1982). Just as functionalism does not question why some relationships exist, exchange theory does not question the different values attached to men's and women's activities or the different choices available to men and women.

Gilligan (1982) has harked back to Parsons' duality, viewing women as relational and men as instrumental. While reasserting as essential some of the gender differences asserted by Freud (1959), Erikson, (1968), and Parsons, she has reversed their value so women's concern with relationships is idealized. In point of fact, men and women alike have been found to be both instrumental and relational. Women's concern with relationships can be understood as the need to please others when one lacks power. The powerful typically advocate rules and rationality while the weak espouse relatedness (Hare-Mustin & Marecek, 1986). Thus, in husband-wife conflicts, husbands use logic, wives call upon caring. But in parent-child conflicts, parents, including mothers, emphasize rules; it is the children who appeal for understanding. Gender and power are confounded; whether one is rational or relational depends on the power one holds rather than on gender per se.

In their feminist versions of object relations theory, Chodorow (1978) and Dinnerstein (1976) were careful to point out that gendered personalities were limiting to both women and men. Nevertheless, their focus on gender differences has been popularized as well as embraced by some feminists along with the view of motherhood as pathogenic. Other feminist theorists like Scott (1985) have questioned the literalness of object relations theories which hold that a small interaction of mother and infant can explain all the differences in social institutions and actions between women and men throughout the world. Psychoanalytic and object relations theories rest on untested assumptions about the primacy of early experience and ignore later events in human development (Kagan, 1984; Lott, 1985).

The Problem of Gender Differences

The conventional meaning assigned to gender is difference. Bifurcating phenomena into two distinct categories is a customary method of analysis.

This has led to an emphasis on male and female as opposites, on comparing and contrasting them, and on the exhaustive cataloguing of differences rather than the exploration of commonalities (Hare-Mustin & Marecek, 1987).

Two forms of bias can emerge in dealing with differences (Hare-Mustin, 1987). Alpha bias, the maximalist position, is the exaggeration of differences between groups such as women and men. Beta bias, the minimalist position, is the denial of differences when they do exist. The term "bias" refers to the systematic inclination to emphasize certain experiences and overlook others.

Alpha Bias

Alpha bias can be seen in psychodynamic theories and Parsons's (Parsons & Bales, 1955) sex role theory. Traditional psychodynamic theories define masculinity as the human norm and sharply contrast female development against this standard based on male anatomy and patriarchal assumptions. Neoanalytic theories like that of Erikson (1968) which is based on male development or like those of Gilligan (1982) and Chodorow (1978) contrast female and male development. Emphasizing differences limits human opportunities for both males and females and fails to explain the gender-based inequality in the family and the disadvantaged economic position of women. Because essentialist theories like Gilligan's do not demand either individual or social change, they are likely to receive ready acceptance, especially in the popular culture.

The exaggeration of gender differences is also evident in Parsons's sex role theory. The very language of sex roles conveys the sense of roles being inflexibly fixed and dichotomous (Thorne, 1982). The idea of separate spheres and the segmentation of work by gender reflects alpha bias, whether women are the carriers of water or 98% of all secretaries and men are sailors or miners. Scanzoni (1979) has drawn attention to the circularity involved in Parsons's justification of male power in the family.

In traditional societies the segmentation of work was highly developed. The value of the managerial and directing functions performed by the old and by males was exaggerated, which, in turn, supported the dominance of older males (Liu & Yu, 1977). This exaggeration of the value of management has persisted in modern times in male-headed households and corporate business structures. Alpha bias is apparent in the value attached to instrumentality and autonomy, the qualities associated with management, which are contrasted with affiliation and expressiveness.

Sex roles represent a false dichotomy and caricatures of human experience (Hare-Mustin & Marecek, 1986). The view of men as autonomous and rational ignores the fact that one can be autonomous only *in relation to* others. Self-reliant men typically have wives to keep their households running and raise their children; secretaries perform support functions at work.

Similarly, the assumption that women cannot think like men and the portrayal of women as nurturing, self-sacrificing, and other-directed ignores the complexity of their experiences (Broughton, 1983). Marrying, bearing children, and rearing them are sources of achievement, not merely sacrifice. Helping others also involves power and may not be valued since helping others confirms their helplessness. The salience of differences between men and women is created by marginalizing and denying similarities.

Beta Bias

Beta bias is characterized by ignoring or minimizing differences. Until the last decade, most psychological research on human behavior and development was based on male subjects (see Levinson, 1978; Vaillant, 1977). Beta bias occurred when such research was incorrectly generalized to apply to women.

The fact that women and men typically live together in the family and separately from their own gender groups obscures their differences. For example, legislation supporting parental work leave in the United States minimizes the unique and dramatic bodily changes that women have undergone in giving birth, changes from which they need to recuperate whereas men do not. Other apparently "neutral" laws such as no-fault divorce laws have benefitted men while resulting in poverty for women. Divorced women and their children have suffered a decline of 73% in living standard at the same time divorced men have experienced an increase of 42% (Weitzman, 1985).

Beta bias is evident in therapists' ignoring the different impact of the social context on men and women and women's multiple roles. In family and marital therapy, equal treatment is not always equitable (Margolin, Talovic, Fernandez, & Onorato, 1983). Many therapists foster inequality when they advocate nonpreferential and nondifferential treatment on the basis of gender. By ignoring differences in power and resources between women and men, therapists using so called "gender-free" approaches in effect support such differences. In a situation of social inequality, "gender-neutral" approaches will preserve the status quo.

Systems and structural family therapists such as those of Haley (1976) and Minuchin (1974) reveal beta bias when they disregard gender and view generation, which is based on age, as the central organizing principle in the family (Hare-Mustin, 1987). The major power differences in all societies are associated with sex, age, race, and class. Within the family, sex and age interact while race and class are typically constant. However, the only attribute which is immutable is sex. Age will change. Class can change. One can even imagine a world where the category of race disappears through intermarriage, but there is no way to eradicate the category of sex.

By omitting gender, systems therapists have maintained a neutered version of cybernetic theory (Libow, 1985). But, parents are not interchangeable parts in the family system. Furthermore, husbands and wives may not be of the same age cohort, a difference which supports the male authority in the family and puts the woman between the generations of father and children. This complex interaction of age and gender may better explain some of the problems in the family than current family systems theories.

The schema of alpha and beta bias provides a framework for evaluating theories about gender differences and the family. What this schema makes apparent is that just as the emphasis on differences can result in discrimination, the ignoring of differences can perpetuate gender inequality.

Sex Roles: Implications for the Future

The nature of the world is to be complex, but we assume we can understand better by simplifying. Sex role stereotypes are such simplifications. Sex role theory provides a conceptual framework that emphasizes the equal and opposite nature of men and women. The idea of gender opposition is not a result of faulty definitions but of an ideology which encourages differences. Wilden (1972) has suggested that this "error" has its source in the dominant group's interest in preserving the status quo.

When women take on both work and family roles, the idea of separate spheres for men's and women's activities and interests is no longer viable. As research in such disparate societies as China and the United States has shown, women continue in their preindustrial family role doing work which has no exchange value in the marketplace even when they enter the paid labor force.

Some social science theorists have tried to develop an additive model of sex roles, others have proposed a resource theory of exchange. Beta bias, the minimizing of differences, is an obvious shortcoming of such approaches. The teleology embedded in functionalist theories and their systemic derivatives cannot account for the subordination of women (Elshtain, 1982). The contribution of women's family work continues to be minimized, perhaps because it is hard to measure, perhaps because it does not directly produce income. What follows is that women's role overload, the total hours of family work and paid work of employed wives, is also minimized. In fact, the average of 35 hours a week of housework and 40 hours of paid work add up to a week even sweatshops cannot match. As Cowan (1983) has reported, being a "working mother" is virtually a guarantee of being overworked and perpetually exhausted.

A further shortcoming of the model of gender opposition is that it disregards not only women's dual roles but also women's dual socialization. Subordinate groups always experience dual socialization, that of their own group and that needed to survive in a society whose themes and rules are those of the dominant group. Women are socialized in the female subsystem with one set of values, as well as the dominant male system with another set of values. The contradictory nature of these values produces further stress on women. Contemporary theories have obscured this dual socialization. In sum, the assumption that industrialized societies have egalitarian patterns in the family which have displaced the male-centered patterns of agrarian societies does not fit the evidence (Burr, Hill, Nye, & Reiss, 1979).

Family Theory and Practice

Despite the expansion of family studies in the last two decades, no social science discipline has concerned itself with studying how families actually function (Handel, 1985). Psychology has focused on parent-child relations. Sociology has focused on marriage and the family as institutions. Anthropology has focused on the family as part of the kinship system. It has remained, for the most part, to the field of family therapy to take on the task of studying how families function. However, family therapists often have not recognized the extent to which they have been limited by cultural norms: the salience given male work activities in Western society, the ideal of autonomy as a therapeutic goal, and the assumption that personal efforts can produce change regardless of the larger social context. Therapists have been found to consistently blame mothers for family problems and to view nontraditional sex roles as pathogenic (Caplan & Hall-McCorquodale, 1985). These kinds of attitudes need to be examined in training and practice.

Recently there has been a renewed emphasis on separate spheres and separate qualities of men and women by some feminist therapists who seek to affirm the value of "women's culture." The problem remains that men's and women's differences become exaggerated and their similarities overlooked when personality characteristics are associated with gender. The simplifications inherent in gender stereotypes lead to hierarchies, to one set of characteristics being viewed as superior to the other. These then become goals for therapy, defining what is normal. Thus we have attempts in therapy to make up for the presumed deficits which women and men suffer. What is still needed is a change in the broader context of individuals' lives so that nontraditional patterns will be supported in the larger society when they are encouraged in therapy.

In family and marital therapy, strategic and systems approaches have emphasized differentiation, power, and hierarchy. These themes are also part of other family therapy approaches more concerned with expressiveness or more closely related to psychodynamic theories. The epistemological ferment currently occurring in the family therapy field has largely disregarded the question of gender, so it provides few guidelines in this regard for therapists (Hare-Mustin, 1987).

Although the contemporary family takes many different forms, no new model has emerged in family therapy to replace the idealized family of the past with its separate spheres for men and women. Therapists working with couples need to be aware of the problems of dealing with gender differences. Research on American couples has drawn attention to certain patterns associated with gender (Blumstein & Schwartz, 1983). Although a therapist may seek to foster sharing housework as a laudable goal in couple therapy, if the ultimate responsibility for housework remains assigned to the woman, little change may occur. Therapists need to recognize the extent to which the contribution of women's family work tends to be minimized by women as well as men. On the other hand, men who participate in household work have been found to exaggerate their own contribution; thus, men who "help" have claimed they average 3–4 hours a day washing dishes (Schwartz, 1987), an amount any housewife would recognize as incredible.

Therapeutic guidelines for dealing with gender issues have addressed some of the myths about gender roles and women's lives (Hare-Mustin, 1978, 1980; Margolin et al., 1983; Weiner & Boss, 1985). Attention is also needed to social policies relating to work and family roles. As long as women's employment opportunities are largely restricted to jobs involving low pay and little autonomy, such jobs will not provide enhanced self-esteem and well-being. As long as the contributions of women's family roles are minimized, the negative effects of family-related stress will also go unacknowledged.

Conclusion

Ultimately the search to define gender is the search to define women. Because man is the hidden referent in our culture, "women can only aspire to be as good as a man; there is no point trying to be as good as a woman" (Spender, 1984, p. 201). However, the search to define gender has reified and reinforced differences, revealing what Harding (1986) calls the defensively dualistic knowledge characteristic of male-dominant social orders. It is in the interest of any dominant group to maintain its difference from others.

Women's and men's relations are not symmetrical, but sex role theory continues to equate two spheres which are not separate, equal, and opposite. In modern societies, women do not occupy only one sphere; they increasingly operate in both spheres. A false symmetry based on family production models in traditional societies obscures women's dual roles and work overload. Our therapeutic models, as well as models for social change and public policy, are based on a pattern of gender differences which does not exist. What is needed is a new theory that not only can deal with the complex and dual nature of women's experiences but also can acknowledge the asymmetry and biases in the relationships and responsibilities of women and men.

Notes

This paper was prepared during the author's term as Research Fellow at the Population Institute of the East-West Center, Honolulu, Hawaii.

References

Baruch, G. K., Biener, L., & Barnett, R. C. (1987). Women and gender in research on work and family stress. *American Psychologist, 42,* 130–136.

Bellah, R. N., Madsen, R., Sullivan, W. M., Swidler, A., & Tipton, S. M. (1985). *Habits of the heart.* New York: Harper and Row.

Blumstein, P., & Schwartz, P. (1983). *American couples: Money, work, and sex.* New York: Morrow.

Broughton, J. M. (1983). Women's rationality and men's virtues: A critique of gender dualism in Gilligan's theory of moral development. *Social Research, 50,* 597–642.

Bulatao, R. A., & Fawcett, J. T. (1983). *Influences on childbearing intentions across the fertility career: Demographic and socioeconomic factors and the value of children* (No. 60-F). Honolulu, HI: East-West Population Institute.

Burr, W. R., Hill, R., Nye, F. I., & Reiss, I. L. (Eds.). (1979). *Contemporary theories about the family: Research-based theories, Vol. 1.* New York: Free Press.

Caldwell, J. C., & Caldwell, P. (1987, January). *Family systems: Their viability and vulnerability: A study of intergenerational transactions and their demographic implications.* Paper presented at the International Union for the Scientific Study of Population Seminar on Changing Family Structures and Life Courses in Less Developed Countries, East-West Population Institute, Honolulu, HI.

Caplan, P. J., & Hall-McCorquodale, I. (1985). Mother-blaming in major clinical journals. *American Journal of Orthopsychiatry, 55,* 345–353.

Chodorow, N. (1978). *The reproduction of mothering*. Berkeley: University of California Press.

Cowan, R. S. (1983). *More work for mother: The ironies of household technology from open hearth to microwave*. New York: Basic Books.

Dinnerstein, D. (1976). *The mermaid and the minotaur: Sexual arrangements and the human malaise*. New York: Harper and Row.

Ehrenreich, B. (1983). *The hearts of men: American dreams and the flight from commitment*. Garden City, NY: Doubleday.

Elshtain, J. B. (1982). "Thank heaven for little girls": The dialectics of development. In J. B. Elshtain (Ed.), *The family in political thought* (pp. 288–351). Amherst: University of Massachusetts Press.

Erikson, E. H. (1968). *Identity, youth, and crisis*. New York: Norton.

Flax, J. (1982). The family in contemporary feminist thought: A critical review. In J. Elshtain (Ed.), *The family in political thought* (pp. 223–253). Amherst: University of Massachusetts Press.

Freud, S. (1959). *Collected papers*. New York: Basic Books.

Gilligan, C. (1982). *In a different voice*. Cambridge: Harvard University Press.

Haley, J. (1976). *Problem-solving therapy*. San Francisco: Jossey-Bass.

Handel, G. (1985). Introduction. In G. Handel (Ed.), *The psychological interior of the family* (3rd ed.) (pp. xi–xiv). New York: Aldine.

Harding, S. (1986). The instability of the analytical categories of feminist theory. *Signs: Journal of Women in Culture and Society, 11*, 645–664.

Hare-Mustin, R. T. (1978). A feminist approach to family therapy. *Family Process, 17*, 181–194.

Hare-Mustin, R. T. (1980). Family therapy may be dangerous for your health. *Professional Psychology, 11*, 935–938.

Hare-Mustin, R. T. (1983). An appraisal of the relationship between women and psychotherapy: 80 years after the case of Dora. *American Psychologist, 38*, 594–601.

Hare-Mustin, R. T. (1987). The problem of gender in family therapy theory. *Family Process, 26*, 15–27.

Hare-Mustin, R. T., Bennett, S. K., & Broderick, P. C. (1983). Attitude toward motherhood: Gender, generational, and religious comparisons. *Sex Roles, 9*, 643–661.

Hare-Mustin, R. T., & Hare, S. E. (1986). Family change and the concept of motherhood in China. *Journal of Family Issues, 7*, 67–82.

Hare-Mustin, R. T., & Marecek, J. (1986). Autonomy and gender: Some questions for therapists. *Psychotherapy, 23*, 205–212.

Hare-Mustin, R. T., & Marecek, J. (1987, March). *Gender and meaning: The construction of differences*. Paper presented at the meeting of the American Orthopsychiatric Association, Washington, DC.

Kagan, J. (1984). *The nature of the child*. New York: Basic Books.

Kessler, R. C., & McRae, J. A., Jr. (1981). Trends in the relationship between sex and psychological distress: 1957–1976. *American Sociological Review, 46*, 443–452.

Levinson, D. J. (1978). *The seasons of a man's life*. New York: Knopf.

Libow, J. A. (1985). Gender and sex role issues as family secrets. *Journal of Strategic and Systemic Therapies, 4*(2), 32–41.

Lipman-Blumen, J. (1984). *Gender roles and power.* Englewood Cliffs, NJ: Prentice-Hall.

Liu, W., & Yu, E. S. H. (1977). Variations in women's roles and family life under the socialist regime in China. *Journal of Comparative Family Studies, 8,* 201–215.

Lott, B. (1985). The potential enrichment of social/personality psychology through feminist research and vice versa. *American Psychologist, 40,* 155–164.

MacKinnon, C. A. (1982). Feminism, Marxism, method, and the state: An agenda for theory. *Signs: Journal of Women in Culture and Society, 7,* 515–544.

Margolin, G., Talovic, S., Fernandez, V., & Onorato, R. (1983). Sex role considerations and behavioral marital therapy: Equal does not mean identical. *Journal of Marital and Family Therapy, 9,* 131–145.

Mason, K. O. (1986). The status of women: Conceptual and methodological issues in demographic studies. *Sociological Forum, 1,* 284–300.

Minturn, L., & Lambert, W. W. (1974). *Mothers of six cultures: Antecedents of child rearing.* New York: John Wiley and Sons.

Minuchin, S. (1974). *Families and family therapy.* Cambridge: Harvard University Press.

Nye, F. I. (1982). *Family relationships: Rewards and costs.* Beverly Hills, CA: Sage Publications.

Oppenheimer, V. K. (1977). The sociology of women's economic role in the family. *American Sociological Review, 42,* 387–406.

Packwood, R. (1982, July 1). The equal rights amendment. *Congressional Record.* Washington, DC.

Parsons, T., & Bales, R. F. (1955). *Family, socialization, and interaction process.* Glencoe, IL: Free Press.

Piotrkowski, C. S., & Katz, M. H. (1982). Women's work and personal relations with the family. In P. W. Berman & E. R. Ramey (Eds.), *Women: A developmental perspective* (Publication No. 82–2298, pp. 221–235). Bethesda, MD: National Institute of Health.

Scanzoni, J. (1979). Social processes and power in families. In W. R. Burr, R. Hill, F. I. Nye, & I. L. Reiss (Eds.), *Contemporary theories about the family: Research-based theories, Vol. 1* (pp. 295–316). New York: Free Press.

Schwartz, P. (1987, June). *American couples: The intimate struggle for power.* Paper presented at the Meeting of the American Family Therapy Association, Chicago, IL.

Scott, J. (1985, December). *Is gender a useful category of historical analysis?* Paper presented at the meeting of the American Historical Association, New York, NY.

Spender, D. (1984). Defining reality: A powerful tool. In C. Kramarae, M. Schulz, & W. M. O'Barr (Eds.), *Language and power* (pp. 194–205). Beverly Hills, CA: Sage Publications.

Thorne, B. (1982). Feminist rethinking of the family: An overview. In B. Thorne & M. Yalom (Eds.), *Rethinking the family: Some feminist questions* (pp. 1–24). New York: Longman.

Vaillant, G. E. (1977). *Adaptation to life*. Boston: Little Brown.

Watzlawick, P. (Ed.). (1984). *The invented reality: Contributions to constructivism*. New York: Norton.

Weiner, J. P., & Boss, P. (1985). Exploring gender bias against women: Ethics for marriage and family therapy. *Counseling and Values, 30*, 9–23.

Weitzman, L. J. (1985). *The divorce revolution: The unexpected social and economic consequences for women and children in America*. New York: Free Press.

White, L. K., Booth, A., & Edwards, J. N. (1986). Children and marital happiness: Why the negative correlation? *Journal of Family Issues, 7*, 131–147.

Wilden, A. (1972). *System and structure: Essays in communication and exchange*. London: Tavistock Publications.

Wilson, C., & Dyson, T. (1987, January). *Family systems and cultural change: Perspectives from past and present*. Paper presented at the International Union for the Scientific Study of Population Seminar on Changing Family Structures and Life Courses in Less Developed Countries, East-West Population Institute, Honolulu, HI.

PART 4
WOMEN-INCLUSIVE PSYCHOLOGY: NEW ANSWERS, NEW QUESTIONS

Whether or not we have transformed the discipline of psychology, and whether or not we would like to, remain empirical and political questions. . . . At the level of theory, methods, politics, and activism, it is safe to say that feminist psychology has interrupted the discipline. (Fine & Gordon, 1989, p. 146)

In a sense, of course, merely interrupting the discipline is transformative; the hegemony of psychology's long-standing paradigmatic commitments is disrupted by the impact of this change of mind sufficiently powerful to challenge its legitimacy as arbiter of truth. Yet still, "We exist at moments, at the margins and among ourselves" (Fine & Gordon, 1989, p. 146). Beyond the (almost self-evident) implication that interruption *is* transformation lies the deeper question: Can feminist psychology effect a thoroughgoing alteration in the assumptions, the structures, and the practices of this discipline that have heretofore proven so exclusive of women? And how do we translate the disruption within psychology into the social action that a feminist politic envisions?

Having explored in the previous part the reconstruction of psychology wrought by the infusion of feminist consciousness, we now turn inward to query feminist psychology itself, to reflect on the implications for the discipline and for ourselves of the process to date. Questions arise: Are we doing psychology differently, asking new questions, fundamentally shaking the foundations of the discipline, or are we (inadvertently, to be sure) reproducing the very forms we strive to disrupt? If, as the constructionist approach demands, all knowledge (including feminist knowledge) is context-dependent, is it possible for us to step back from our own knowledge production to assess the forces that frame our own work? Are our understandings truly liberated—from the delimiting assumptions of psychology's self-definition, from the constraints of socially constructed "truths" about gender? And what does the feminist psychology of today have to offer to the social and political agendas that stimulated its emergence, the issues raised by Weisstein and others two decades ago?

Evidence that feminist psychology has "interrupted" the discipline, generating new understandings, is found in the very title of the article that introduces this part: "Doing Gender." This is disruption revealed in discourse: "gender" used to be a noun. In this article, Candace West and Don Zimmerman offered an excellent discussion of the conceptual and historical evolution of considerations of gender in social science literature, depicting the movement from gender seen as synonymous with sex, through gender regarded as a quality of individuals, to current (constructionist) notions of gender as process. The analysis that was undertaken here amounts to a historically informed deconstruction of gender understandings and ranges among the variety of approaches that have been used in attempting to understand this construct. West and Zimmerman's work revealed gender to be a complex, complicated, and conceptually rich construction, which itself acts to shape our understanding of human experience, even as that experience shapes gender. It is a view of gender far removed from its earlier rendition as a simple, dichotomous, empirically accessible trait.

The breadth and depth of gender's impact on psychological understandings was striking in this analysis, as West and Zimmerman examined research and theory dealing with relationships among sex, gender display, sex categorization, and gender, challenging the conceptual myopia that had directed much previous work. They offered in place of these earlier versions of gender a process-oriented approach that defines gender as an interactive event, as a verb rather than a noun. It is from this conception of gender as something one does that the authors launched their challenge to feminist psychology, calling attention to the practical necessity for "doing gender"—the personal demand that one "do gender"—and the sociopolitical ramifications of that prescription. "The doing of gender," they argue, "is undertaken by women and men whose competence as members of society is hostage to its production. . . . [Gender is] an emergent feature of social situations: both as outcome of and a rationale for various social arrangements and a means of legitimating one of the most fundamental divisions of society" (1987, p. 126).

Compulsory adherence to this pervasive requirement that one do gender (and do it properly) both legitimates the process of gender and normalizes gendered institutions and practices, granting them an aura of "naturalness." In order for feminist aims to be achieved, West and Zimmerman argued, it is necessary to challenge traditional forms on both interpersonal and institutional levels, for both serve to justify and reproduce existing gender arrangements. Thus, while a recognition of gender's location in social interchange on its face liberates us from the easy sexism of psychodynamic and biological attributions, it nevertheless does not free us from the delimiting power of gender prescriptions. Reconstructing gender as process begins but does not complete the feminist project in psychology.

The question of the role played by feminist psychology in producing social change is a vexing one. Traditional understandings of women did not, of course, support either personal or institutional change toward improving women's lot. Yet our own efforts in this direction have often generated as many new concerns as they have alleviated existing ones. Arnold Kahn and Janice Yoder explored this quandary, suggesting that much work in the psychology of women has served not to enhance women's position but to reinforce traditional (if reconceptualized) understandings of women and their place in society. This phenomenon, the authors argued, reflects the reality that scholars in this area are as much products of their professional and sociopolitical surround as are other psychologists.

As the major impediment to a politically active, progressive, feminist psychology, Kahn and Yoder implicated psychology's penchant for locating the determinants of behavior and experience within the individual. This preference for internal attribution, the authors pointed out, is reinforced by societal norms that value independence, idealizing the self-contained individual and reifying the notion of individual responsibility for one's fate. This theme, an echo from our earlier discussions, sounds persistently through work in the psychology of women, which has routinely joined in placing the etiology of women's experience squarely in traits attributed to them as individuals. When such individualistic theories form the ground for work in the psychology of women, the outcome is a body of research and theory that serves to maintain the status quo, arguing for changes within individual women and disregarding the historical, social, and political forces that in fact shape women's experience.

Further, Kahn and Yoder asserted, insofar as feminist psychologists are themselves products of disciplinary and societal conditioning, they are exposed to the foundational assumption of gender understandings—namely, that women and men are fundamentally different. Their embeddedness in this understanding results in work that reproduces this same belief. Ironically, this tendency may render the psychology of women a force for conservatism rather than progress, for personal change strategies rather than social activism. To return to West and Zimmerman's theme, if gender is presumed to be a quality of individuals, the contexts that shape its performance are neglected, and person attribution reinforces the presumption of gender as a trait, a noun rather than a verb—a conclusion that vitiates feminist social analysis.

The possibility that (presumably) feminist psychology could support antifeminist outcomes is a paradox in need of analysis. Celia Kitzinger's article undertook one critical aspect of this analysis, exploring the notion of power and its implications for feminist psychology and calling uncomfortable attention to the unexamined political implications of feminist construals of power. Kitzinger's article amounted to a deconstruction of the notion of power in feminist writings, both lay and professional, pointing up the paradox of power portrayed as evil (male power) and power presented as good (female self-empowerment).

The unfortunate consequence of this bifurcated construal of the meaning of power, Kitzinger argued, lies in its implicit accommodation to (even support for) the status quo. Women portrayed as carriers of socialized, patriarchal self-denigration are women responsible for altering their own experience: "Because the problem of male power is now located inside *women's heads*, the solution to male power is located there too" (1991, p. 118). To the extent that women are seen as victims of (evil) male power, to the extent that their own power (empowerment) is seen as internally evoked, generated, or discovered, women are rendered individually, intrapsychically responsible for their own salvation—and their own victimization. Herein lies the risk in feminist psychology's failure thoroughly to deconstruct the meaning of power and oppression in women's lives: the appeal to intrapsychic qualities (fear of success, external locus of control, and so forth) as the determinants of women's experience amounts to victim blaming and distracts from the analysis of power structures that in truth undergird women's oppression.

The construal of power as something internal and possessed by the individual is a peculiarly Western notion, one historically and politically situated in a societal milieu that is at base patriarchal. Thus, any attempt to conceptualize women as "powerful," Kitzinger insisted, necessarily comes face to face with a paradox: to grant power to the powerless is oxymoronic. The "power" attributed to women (that is, the expectation for self-empowerment) serves in fact to maintain their powerlessness by making them responsible for their own situation, thus protecting patriarchal power asymmetries. The invocation of women's potential for self-empowerment charges women to seize (their own, personal, internal) power, thus rendering mute politically feminist critiques of institutionalized, misogynist power structures. Kitzinger cautioned that even postmodernism itself, in many ways a useful tool for examining psychology's inherent androcentrism, must not be so eagerly embraced that a vision of "the material reality of women's oppression" (1991, p. 126) is lost to the intellectual elegance and institutional acceptability of poststructuralist analysis.

Challenges such as those raised by Kahn and Yoder and by Kitzinger oblige feminist psychologists to reflect on the situatedness of our own work. Feminist psychology, too, this work avers, is shaped by professional, political, and sociohistorical influences. Is feminist psychology unknowingly reflective, even reproductive, of the very fetters it strives to throw off? Or, alternatively, is feminist psychology indeed generating a new view of human experience, a view enriched by women's unique vision as marginalized participants in that experience and in psychology?

Probably both; feminist psychology is product of its own milieu as well as producer of a new perspective. Attempts to tease out the intricate reciprocity between feminist psychology and its multifaceted contextual surround raise critical questions: In what ways is feminist psychology altering the discipline, even as it reflects and reproduces the contexts of its own generation? Is feminist psychology no more free than the rest of psychology from the bonds of traditionalism (but only more blind to their impediment)? Has mainstream psychology changed (even if it is equally blind to such change) as a result of the challenges of feminist psychology? If we have not thoroughly reconstructed psychology because of our own embeddedness in its forms, have we applied sufficient pressure to its foundations so that the field will be transformed by feminist scholarship? Is it possible to preserve feminist political commitments while participating in a discipline that is by definition devoted to individual subjectivities? Or, as Fine and Gordon asked, "Is feminist psychology an inherent contradiction?" (1989, p. 147); are the foundational underpinnings of psychology so intrinsically antifeminist that the only way to do feminism is to escape the discipline?

Each of the articles included up to this point was grounded, either explicitly or by interpretation, in a constructionist approach to gender. But constructionism is itself only one rendition of the meaning of knowledge; it is itself a construction. Accordingly (and paradoxically), one can, from a constructionist perspective, challenge the legitimacy of constructionism. A series of questions arises: Is this approach to knowledge itself a product of the sociohistorical milieu in which it has emerged? (A constructionist must answer yes.) And if so, might even this construal of knowledge (and of gender) reflect the impact of the very social forces it calls us to abrogate? (A constructionist must answer yes.) And, if so, might not constructionism itself embody the very assumptions, firmly rooted in current sociopolitical and disciplinary milieus, that have served to marginalize women? (Again, yes.) In other words, to paraphrase Shields, might constructionism play handmaiden to social forces, not supporting but threatening the feminist agenda? This is the challenge raised by Erica Burman, as discomfiting closure to this final section of readings.

Burman couched her discussion in terms of deconstruction, an approach that stresses the need to dismantle existing understandings, to expose the tacit assumptions and the contextual situatedness that underlie their deployment. Her arguments are clearly applicable to constructionism as presented here. Although Burman recognized the potential gains for feminism of a (de)constructionist position, her clear and powerful alliance was against a constructionist perspective, for she saw it as potentially lethal for the ultimate aims of feminist psychology.

Burman's most fundamental disagreement with constructionism lay in what she regarded as its inherently apolitical nature. If so-called knowledge is constructed in, and always contingent upon, particular contexts, then each rendition of truth can be seen as equally legitimate, as a response to distinctive contextual parameters. Where there is no outside arbiter of truth, no particular political agenda can be privileged over any other; misogynist tolerance for bigotry is as "true" as is feminist sensitivity to diversity. Although deconstruction may serve our (feminist) purposes in exposing the exclusionary agendas of mainstream psychology, it prohibits our claim to any understanding that is necessarily more enlightened.

Further, in an argument that parallels current debates about "essentialism" and constructionism in the psychology of gender (e.g., Fuss, 1989; Nicholson, 1990), Burman pointed out that sensitivity to the defining impact of context can overreach its goal. If context is sufficiently deconstructed, we discover that every individual has her or his own distinctive context, with commonality thoroughly a casualty of this deconstructive process. The costs to feminist psychology of this dismantling of community are two. First, it invalidates any sense of shared reality among women. If we reify context to the point of generating entirely individualized persons, then "identity politics" at its ultimate reigns and collective activity is impossible, for the concept of a collective of such individualistic "realities" is inherently paradoxical. Second, this deconstruction of context places the locus of one's (a woman's) experience and behavior within her (unique) self, thus inuring us to the reality of contexts that in fact shape her life. Invoking what is by now a familiar theme, Burman argued that we may become blind to the misogynist consequences of social institutions through our intense focus on individual context, individual experience.

This is a paradox for constructionism in general, for the postmodern project is, in part, to dissolve the modernist reverence for the self-contained individual, the legacy of liberal humanism, in order to validate the ultimate contextuality of human experience. Thus, it appears that this agenda might contain the seeds of its own demise, the very focus of specificity of context leading in a circle back to the individual identity. In feminist terms, the personal becomes the political only to become once again thoroughly personalized.

Burman explored for all their ramifications the dilemmas inherent in efforts to meld constructionism, which she saw as depoliticizing, and feminism. Burman abjured any possibility of a radical feminist politic if we operate from a constructionist perspective; such attempts are doomed to fail as diversionary rather than truly transformative engagements with the field. Indeed, the very strengths of deconstruction become its dangers, because the tools used to deconstruct not only dismantle the existing order but also destroy crucial building blocks for the new.

Burman's article is a thought-provoking exposé of the complexities of constructionism; it revealed an approach whose compelling intuitive and intellectual appeal may mask unforeseen detriment for feminist psychology. Although Burman's critique is not the only one of this genre (see also Fuss, 1989; Squire, 1989), it is nonetheless at this juncture a relatively faint voice among the chorus of advocates for deconstruction. Replies to the concerns voiced by Burman have been articulated as well (e.g., Gergen, 1988; Yeatman, 1990), and the debate is far from being resolved. Burman's article alerted us to the fact that gender remains a terribly complex issue; that women's place in the past, present, and future of psychology is far from assured and far from defined; and that what seems so promising a mechanism for coming to an understanding of those facts—postmodernism in its various forms—must also be scrutinized for the very dynamic it alerts us to: the insidious impact of unexamined context.

References

Fine, Michelle A., & Gordon, Susan M. (1989). Feminist transformations of/despite psychology. In Mary Crawford & Margaret Gentry (Eds.), *Gender and thought: Psychological perspectives* (pp. 146–174). New York: Springer-Verlag.

Fuss, Diana. (1989). *Essentially speaking: Feminism, nature and difference.* New York: Routledge.

Gergen, Kenneth J. (1988). Feminist critique of science and the challenge of social epistemology. In Mary M. Gergen (Ed.), *Feminist thought and the structure of knowledge* (pp. 27–48). New York: New York University Press.

Kitzinger, Celia. (1991). Feminism, psychology and the paradox of power. *Feminism and Psychology, 1,* 111–129.

Nicholson, Linda J. (Ed.). (1990). *Feminism/Postmodernism.* New York: Routledge.

Squire, Corrine. (1989). *Significant differences: Feminism in psychology.* London: Routledge.

West, Candace, & Zimmerman, Don. (1987). Doing gender. *Gender & Society, 1,* 125–151.

Yeatman, Anna. (1990). A feminist theory of social differentiation. In Linda J. Nicholson (Ed.), *Feminism/Postmodernism* (pp. 281–299). New York: Routledge.

14

DOING GENDER

Candace West and
Don H. Zimmerman

In the beginning, there was sex and there was gender. Those of us who taught courses in the area in the late 1960s and early 1970s were careful to distinguish one from the other. Sex, we told students, was what was ascribed by biology: anatomy, hormones, and physiology. Gender, we said, was an achieved status: that which is constructed through psychological, cultural, and social means. To introduce the difference between the two, we drew on singular case studies of hermaphrodites (Money 1968, 1974; Money and Ehrhardt 1972) and anthropological investigations of "strange and exotic tribes" (Mead 1963, 1968).

Inevitably (and understandably), in the ensuing weeks of each term, our students became confused. Sex hardly seemed a "given" in the context of research that illustrated the sometimes ambiguous and often conflicting criteria for its ascription. And gender seemed much less an "achievement" in the context of the anthropological, psychological, and social imperatives we studied—the division of labor, the formation of gender identities, and the social subordination of women by men. Moreover, the received doctrine of gender socialization theories conveyed the strong message that while gender may be "achieved," by about age five it was certainly fixed, unvarying, and static—much like sex.

Since about 1975, the confusion has intensified and spread far beyond our individual classrooms. For one thing, we learned that the relationship between biological and cultural processes was far more complex—and reflexive—than we previously had supposed (Rossi 1984, especially pp. 10–14). For another, we discovered that certain structural arrangements, for example, between work and family, actually produce or enable some capacities, such as to mother, that we formerly associated with biology (Chodorow 1978 versus Firestone 1970). In the midst of all this, the notion of gender as a recurring achievement somehow fell by the wayside.

Our purpose in this article is to propose an ethnomethodologically informed, and therefore distinctively sociological, understanding of gender as a routine, methodical, and recurring accomplishment. We contend that the "doing" of gender is undertaken by women and men whose competence as members of society is hostage to its production. Doing gender involves a complex of socially guided perceptual, interactional, and micro-political activities that cast particular pursuits as expressions of masculine and feminine "natures."

When we view gender as an accomplishment, an achieved property of situated conduct, our attention shifts from matters internal to the individual and focuses on interactional and, ultimately, institutional are-nas. In one sense, of course, it is individuals who "do" gender. But it is a situated doing, carried out in the virtual or real presence of others who are presumed to be oriented to its production. Rather than as a property of individuals, we conceive of gender as an emergent feature of social situations: both as an outcome of and a rationale for various social arrangements and as a means of legitimating one of the most fundamental divisions of society.

To advance our argument, we undertake a critical examination of what sociologists have meant by *gender*, including its treatment as a role enactment in the conventional sense and as a "display" in Goffman's (1976) terminology. Both *gender role* and *gender display* focus on behavioral aspects of being a woman or a man (as opposed, for example, to biological differences between the two). However, we contend that the notion of gender as a role obscures the work that is involved in producing gender in everyday activities, while the notion of gender as a display relegates it to the periphery of interaction. We argue instead that participants in interaction organize their various and manifold activities to reflect or express gender, and they are disposed to perceive the behavior of others in a similar light.

To elaborate our proposal, we suggest at the outset that important but often overlooked distinctions be observed among *sex*, *sex category*, and *gender*. *Sex* is a determination made through the application of socially agreed upon biological criteria for classifying persons as females or males.[1] The criteria for classification can be genitalia at birth or chromosomal typing before birth, and they do not necessarily agree with one another. Placement in a *sex category* is achieved through application of the sex criteria, but in everyday life, categorization is established and sustained by the socially required identificatory displays that proclaim one's mem-bership in one or the other category. In this sense, one's sex category presumes one's sex and stands as proxy for it in many situations, but sex and sex category can vary independently; that is, it is possible to claim membership in a sex category even when the sex criteria are lacking. *Gender*, in contrast, is the activity of managing situated conduct in light of normative conceptions of attitudes and activities appropriate for one's sex category. Gender activities emerge from and bolster claims to membership in a sex category.

We contend that recognition of the analytical independence of sex, sex category, and gender is essential for understanding the relationships among these elements and the interactional work involved in "being" a gendered person in society. While our primary aim is theoretical, there will be occasion to discuss fruitful directions for empirical research following from the formulation of gender that we propose.

We begin with an assessment of the received meaning of gender, particularly in relation to the roots of this notion in presumed biological differences between women and men.

Perspectives on Sex and Gender

In Western societies, the accepted cultural perspective on gender views women and men as naturally and unequivocally defined categories of being (Garfinkel 1967, pp. 116–18) with distinctive psychological and behavioral propensities that can be predicted from their reproductive functions. Competent adult members of these societies see differences between the two as fundamental and enduring—differences seemingly supported by the division of labor into women's and men's work and an often elaborate differentiation of feminine and masculine attitudes and behaviors that are prominent features of social organization. Things are the way they are by virtue of the fact that men are men and women are women—a division perceived to be natural and rooted in biology, producing in turn profound psychological, behavioral, and social consequences. The structural arrangements of a society are presumed to be responsive to these differences.

Analyses of sex and gender in the social sciences, though less likely to accept uncritically the naive biological determinism of the view just presented, often retain a conception of sex-linked behaviors and traits as essential properties of individuals (for good reviews, see Hochschild 1973; Tresemer 1975; Thorne 1980; Henley 1985). The "sex differences approach" (Thorne 1980) is more commonly attributed to psychologists than to sociologists, but the survey researcher who determines the "gender" of respondents on the basis of the sound of their voices over the telephone is also making trait-oriented assumptions. Reducing gender to a fixed set of psychological traits or to a unitary "variable" precludes serious consideration of the ways it is used to structure distinct domains of social experience (Stacey and Thorne 1985, pp. 307–8).

Taking a different tack, role theory has attended to the social construction of gender categories, called "sex roles" or, more recently, "gender roles" and has analyzed how these are learned and enacted. Beginning with Linton (1936) and continuing through the works of Parsons (Parsons 1951; Parsons and Bales 1955) and Komarovsky (1946, 1950), role theory has emphasized the social and dynamic aspect of role construction and enactment (Thorne 1980; Connell 1983). But at the level of face-to-face interaction, the application of role theory to gender poses problems of its own (for good reviews and critiques, see Connell 1983, 1985; Kessler, Ashendon, Connell, and Dowsett 1985; Lopata and Thorne 1978; Thorne 1980; Stacey and Thorne 1985). Roles are *situated* identities—assumed and relinquished as the situation demands—rather than *master identities* (Hughes 1945), such as sex category, that cut across situations. Unlike most roles, such as "nurse," "doctor," and "patient" or "professor" and "student," gender has no specific site or organizational context.

Moreover, many roles are already gender marked, so that special qualifiers—such as "female doctor" or "male nurse"—must be added to exceptions to the rule. Thorne (1980) observes that conceptualizing gender as a role makes it difficult to assess its influence on other roles and reduces its explanatory usefulness in discussions of power and inequality. Drawing on Rubin (1975), Thorne calls for a reconceptualization of women and men as distinct social groups, constituted in "concrete, historically changing—and generally unequal—social relationships" (Thorne 1980, p. 11).

We argue that gender is not a set of traits, nor a variable, nor a role, but the product of social doings of some sort. What then is the social doing of gender? It is more than the continuous creation of the meaning of gender through human actions (Gerson and Peiss 1985). We claim that gender itself is constituted through interaction.[2] To develop the implications of our claim, we turn to Goffman's (1976) account of "gender display." Our object here is to explore how gender might be exhibited or portrayed through interaction, and thus be seen as "natural," while it is being produced as a socially organized achievement.

Gender Display

Goffman contends that when human beings interact with others in their environment, they assume that each possesses an "essential nature"—a nature that can be discerned through the "natural signs given off or expressed by them" (1976, p. 75). Femininity and masculinity are regarded as "prototypes of essential expression—something that can be conveyed fleetingly in any social situation and yet something that strikes at the most basic characterization of the individual" (1976, p. 75). The means through which we provide such expressions are "perfunctory, conventionalized acts" (1976, p. 69), which convey to others our regard for them, indicate our alignment in an encounter, and tentatively establish the terms of contact for that social situation. But they are also regarded as expressive behavior, testimony to our "essential natures."

Goffman (1976, pp. 69–70) sees *displays* as highly conventionalized behaviors structured as two-part exchanges of the statement-reply type, in which the presence or absence of symmetry can establish deference or dominance. These rituals are viewed as distinct from but articulated with more consequential activities, such as performing tasks or engaging in discourse. Hence, we have what he terms the "scheduling" of displays at junctures in activities, such as the beginning or end, to avoid interfering with the activities themselves. Goffman (1976, p. 69) formulates *gender display* as follows:

> If gender be defined as the culturally established correlates of sex (whether in consequence of biology or learning), then gender display refers to convention- alized portrayals of these correlates.

These gendered expressions might reveal clues to the underlying, fundamental dimensions of the female and male, but they are, in Goffman's view, optional performances. Masculine courtesies may or may not be offered and, if offered, may or may not be declined (1976, p. 71). Moreover, human beings "themselves employ the term 'expression', and conduct themselves to fit their own notions of expressivity" (1976, p. 75). Gender depictions are less a consequence of our "essential sexual natures" than interactional portrayals of what we would like to convey about sexual natures, using conventionalized gestures. Our *human* nature gives us the ability to learn to produce and recognize masculine and feminine gender displays—"a capacity [we] have by virtue of being persons, not males and females" (1976, p. 76).

Upon first inspection, it would appear that Goffman's formulation offers an engaging sociological corrective to existing formulations of gender. In his view, gender is a socially scripted dramatization of the culture's *idealization* of feminine and masculine natures, played for an audience that is well schooled in the presentational idiom. To continue the metaphor, there are scheduled performances presented in special locations, and like plays, they constitute introductions to or time out from more serious activities.

There are fundamental equivocations in this perspective. By segregating gender display from the serious business of interaction, Goffman obscures the effects of gender on a wide range of human activities. Gender is not merely something that happens in the nooks and crannies of interaction, fitted in here and there and not interfering with the serious business of life. While it is plausible to contend that gender displays—construed as conventionalized expressions—are optional, it does not seem plausible to say that we have the option of being seen by others as female or male.

It is necessary to move beyond the notion of gender display to consider what is involved in doing gender as an ongoing activity embedded in everyday interaction. Toward this end, we return to the distinctions among sex, sex category, and gender introduced earlier.

Sex, Sex Category, and Gender

Garfinkel's (1967, pp. 118–40) case study of Agnes, a transsexual raised as a boy who adopted a female identity at age 17 and underwent a sex reassignment operation several years later, demonstrates how gender is created through interaction and at the same time structures interaction. Agnes, whom Garfinkel characterized as a "practical methodologist," developed a number of procedures for passing as a "normal, natural female" both prior to and after her surgery. She had the practical task of managing the fact that she possessed male genitalia and that she lacked the social resources a girl's biography would presumably provide in everyday interaction. In short, she needed to display herself as a woman, simultaneously learning what it was to be a woman. Of necessity, this full-time pursuit took place at a time when most people's gender would be well-accredited and routinized. Agnes had to consciously contrive what the vast majority of women do without thinking. She was not "faking" what "real" women do naturally. She was obliged to analyze and figure out how to act within socially structured circumstances and conceptions of femininity that women born with appropriate biological credentials come to take for granted early on. As in the case of others who must "pass," such as transvestites, Kabuki actors, or Dustin Hoffman's "Tootsie," Agnes's case makes visible what culture has made invisible—the accomplishment of gender.

Garfinkel's (1967) discussion of Agnes does not explicitly separate three analytically distinct, although empirically overlapping, concepts—sex, sex category, and gender.

Sex

Agnes did not possess the socially agreed upon biological criteria for classification as a member of the female *sex*. Still, Agnes regarded herself as a female, albeit a female with a penis, which a woman ought not to possess. The penis, she insisted, was a "mistake" in need of remedy (Garfinkel 1967, pp. 126–27, 131–32). Like other competent members of our culture, Agnes honored the notion that there *are* "essential" biological criteria that unequivocally distinguish females from males. However, if we move away from the commonsense viewpoint, we discover that the reliability of these criteria is not beyond question (Money and Brennan 1968; Money and Erhardt 1972; Money and Ogunro 1974; Money and Tucker 1975). Moreover, other cultures have acknowledged the existence of "cross-genders" (Blackwood 1984; Williams 1986) and the possibility of more than two sexes (Hill 1935; Martin and Voorhies 1975, pp. 84–107; but see also Cucchiari 1981, pp. 32–35).

More central to our argument is Kessler and McKenna's (1978, pp. 1–6) point that genitalia are conventionally hidden from public inspection in everyday life; yet we continue through our social rounds to "observe" a world of two naturally, normally sexed persons. It is the *presumption* that essential criteria exist and would or should be there if looked for that provides the basis for sex categorization. Drawing on Garfinkel, Kessler and McKenna argue that "female" and "male" are cultural events—products of what they term the "gender attribution process"—rather than some collection of traits, behaviors, or even physical attributes. Illustratively they cite the child who, viewing a picture of someone clad in a suit and a tie, contends, "It's a man, because he has a pee-pee" (Kessler and McKenna 1978, p. 154). Translation: "He must have a pee-pee [an essential characteristic] because I see the *insignia* of a suit and tie." Neither initial sex assignment (pronouncement at birth as a female or male) nor the actual existence of essential criteria for that assignment (possession of a clitoris and vagina or penis and testicles) has much—if anything—to do with the identification of sex category in everyday life. There, Kessler and McKenna note, we operate with a moral certainty of a world of two sexes. We do not think, "Most persons with penises are men, but some may not be" or "Most persons who dress as men have penises." Rather, we take it for granted that sex and sex category are congruent—that knowing the latter, we can deduce the rest.

Sex Categorization

Agnes's claim to the categorical status of female, which she sustained by appropriate identificatory displays and other characteristics, could be *discredited* before her transsexual operation if her possession of a penis became known and after by her surgically constructed genitalia (see Raymond 1979, pp. 37, 138). In this regard, Agnes had to be continually alert to actual or potential threats to the security of her sex category. Her problem was not so much living up to some prototype of essential femininity but preserving her categorization as female. This task was made easy for her by a very powerful resource, namely, the process of commonsense categorization in everyday life.

The categorization of members of society into indigenous categories such as "girl" or "boy," or "woman" or "man," operates in a distinctively social way. The act of categorization does not involve a positive test, in the sense of a well-defined set of criteria that must be explicitly satisfied prior to making an identification. Rather, the application of membership categories relies on an "if-can" test in everyday interaction (Sacks 1972, pp. 332–35). This test stipulates that if people *can be seen* as members of relevant categories, *then categorize them that way.* That is, use the category that seems appropriate, except in the presence of discrepant information or obvious features that would rule out its use. This procedure is quite in keeping with the attitude of everyday life, which has us take appearances at face value unless we have special reason to doubt (Schutz 1943; Garfinkel 1967, pp. 272–77; Bernstein 1986).[3] It should be added that it is precisely when we have special reason to doubt that the issue of applying rigorous criteria arises, but it is rare, outside legal or bureaucratic contexts, to encounter insistence on positive tests (Garfinkel 1967, pp. 262–83; Wilson 1970).

Agnes's initial resource was the predisposition of those she encountered to take her appearance (her figure, clothing, hair style, and so on), as the undoubted appearance of a normal female. Her further resource was our cultural perspective on the properties of "natural, normally sexed persons." Garfinkel (1967, pp. 122–28) notes that in everyday life, we live in a world of two—and only two—sexes. This arrangement has a moral status, in that we include ourselves and others in it as "essentially, originally, in the first place, always have been, always will be, once and for all, in the final analysis, either 'male' or 'female'" (Garfinkel 1967, p. 122).

Consider the following case:

> This issue reminds me of a visit I made to a computer store a couple of years ago. The person who answered my questions was truly a *salesperson.* I could not categorize him/her as a woman or a man. What did I look for? (1) Facial hair: She/he was smooth skinned, but some men have little or no facial hair. (This varies by race, Native Americans and Blacks often have none.) (2) Breasts: She/he was wearing a loose shirt that hung from his/her shoulders.

And, as many women who suffered through a 1950s' adolescence know to their shame, women are often flat-chested. (3) Shoulders: His/hers were small and round for a man, broad for a woman. (4) Hands: Long and slender fingers, knuckles a bit large for a woman, small for a man. (5) Voice: Middle range, unexpressive for a woman, not at all the exaggerated tones some gay males affect. (6) His/her treatment of me: Gave off no signs that would let me know if I were of the same or different sex as this person. There were not even any signs that he/she knew his/her sex would be difficult to categorize and I wondered about that even as I did my best to hide these questions so I would not embarrass him/her while we talked of computer paper. I left still not knowing the sex of my salesperson, and was disturbed by that unanswered question (child of my culture that I am). (Diane Margolis, personal communication)

What can this case tell us about situations such as Agnes's (cf. Morris 1974; Richards 1983) or the process of sex categorization in general? First, we infer from this description that the computer salesclerk's identificatory display was ambiguous, since she or he was not dressed or adorned in an unequivocally female or male fashion. It is when such a display *fails* to provide grounds for categorization that factors such as facial hair or tone of voice are assessed to determine membership in a sex category. Second, beyond the fact that this incident could be recalled after "a couple of years," the customer was not only "disturbed" by the ambiguity of the salesclerk's category but also assumed that to acknowledge this ambiguity would be embarrassing to the salesclerk. Not only do we want to know the sex category of those around us (to see it at a glance, perhaps), but we presume that others are displaying it for us, in as decisive a fashion as they can.

Gender

Agnes attempted to be "120 percent female" (Garfinkel 1967, p. 129), that is, unquestionably in all ways and at all times feminine. She thought she could protect herself from disclosure before and after surgical intervention by comporting herself in a feminine manner, but she also could have given herself away by overdoing her performance. Sex categorization and the accomplishment of gender are not the same. Agnes's categorization could be secure or suspect, but did not depend on whether or not she lived up to some ideal conception of femininity. Women can be seen as unfeminine, but that does not make them "unfemale." Agnes faced an ongoing task of *being* a woman—something beyond style of dress (an identificatory display) or allowing men to light her cigarette (a gender display). Her problem was to produce configurations of behavior that would be seen by others as normative gender behavior.

Agnes's strategy of "secret apprenticeship," through which she learned expected feminine decorum by carefully attending to her fiancé's criticisms of other women, was one means of masking incompetencies and simultaneously acquiring the needed skills (Garfinkel 1967, pp. 146–147). It was through her fiancé that Agnes learned that sunbathing on the lawn in front of her apartment was "offensive" (because it put her on display to other men). She also learned from his critiques of other women that she should not insist on having things her way and that she should not offer her opinions or claim equality with men (Garfinkel 1967, pp. 147–148). (Like other women in our society, Agnes learned something about power in the course of her "education.")

Popular culture abounds with books and magazines that compile idealized depictions of relations between women and men. Those focused on the etiquette of dating or prevailing standards of feminine comportment are meant to be of practical help in these matters. However, the use of any such source *as a manual of procedure* requires the assumption that doing gender merely involves making use of discrete, well-defined bundles of behavior that can simply be plugged into interactional situations to produce recognizable enactments of masculinity and femininity. The man "does" being masculine by, for example, taking the woman's arm to guide her across a street, and she "does" being feminine by consenting to be guided and not initiating such behavior with a man.

Agnes could perhaps have used such sources as manuals, but, we contend, doing gender is not so easily regimented (Mithers 1982; Morris 1974). Such sources may list and describe the sorts of behaviors that mark or display gender, but they are necessarily incomplete (Garfinkel 1967, pp. 66–75; Wieder 1974, pp. 183–214; Zimmerman and Wieder 1970, pp. 285–98). And to be successful, marking or displaying gender must be finely fitted to situations and modified or transformed as the occasion demands. Doing gender consists of managing such occasions so that, whatever the particulars, the outcome is seen and seeable in context as gender-appropriate or, as the case may be, gender-*in*appropriate, that is, *accountable.*

Gender and Accountability

As Heritage (1984, pp. 136–37) notes, members of society regularly engage in "descriptive accountings of states of affairs to one another," and such accounts are both serious and consequential. These descriptions name, characterize, formulate, explain, excuse, excoriate, or merely take notice of some circumstance or activity and thus place it within some social framework (locating it relative to other activities, like and unlike).

Such descriptions are themselves accountable, and societal members orient to the fact that their activities are subject to comment. Actions are often designed with an eye to their accountability, that is, how they might look and how they might be characterized. The notion of accountability also encompasses those actions undertaken so that they are specifically unremarkable and thus not worthy of more than a passing remark, because they are seen to being accord with culturally approved standards.

Heritage (1984, p. 179) observes that the process of rendering something accountable is interactional in character:

> [This] permits actors to design their actions in relation to their circumstances so as to permit others, by methodically taking account of circumstances, to recognize the action for what it is.

The key word here is *circumstances.* One circumstance that attends virtually all actions is the sex category of the actor. As Garfinkel (1967, p. 118) comments:

> [T]he work and socially structured occasions of sexual passing were obstinately unyielding to [Agnes's] attempts to routinize the grounds of daily activities. This obstinacy points to the *omnirelevance* of sexual status to affairs of daily life as an invariant but unnoticed background in the texture of relevances that compose the changing actual scenes of everyday life. (italics added)

If sex category is omnirelevant (or even approaches being so), then a person engaged in virtually any activity may be held accountable for performance of that activity as a *woman* or a *man,* and their incumbency in one or the other sex category can be used to legitimate or discredit their other activities (Berger, Cohen, and Zelditch 1972; Berger, Conner, and Fisek 1974; Berger, Fisek, Norman, and Zelditch 1977; Humphreys and Berger 1981). Accordingly, virtually any activity can be assessed as to its womanly or manly nature. And note, to "do" gender is not always to live up to normative conceptions of femininity or masculinity; it is to engage in behavior *at the risk of gender assessment.* While it is individuals who do gender, the enterprise is fundamentally interactional and institutional in character, for accountability is a feature of social relationships and its idiom is drawn from the institutional arena in which those relationships are enacted. If this be the case, can we ever *not* do gender? Insofar as a society is partitioned by "essential" differences between women and men and placement in a sex category is both relevant and enforced, doing gender is unavoidable.

Resources for Doing Gender

Doing gender means creating differences between girls and boys and women and men, differences that are not natural, essential, or biological. Once the differences have been constructed, they are used to reinforce the "essentialness" of gender. In a delightful account of the "arrangement between the sexes," Goffman (1977) observes the creation of a variety of institutionalized frameworks through which our "natural, normal sexedness" can be enacted. The physical features of social setting provide one obvious resource for the expression of our "essential" differences. For example, the sex segregation of North American public bathrooms distinguishes "ladies" from "gentlemen" in matters held to be fundamentally biological, even though both "are somewhat similar in the question of waste products and their elimination" (Goffman 1977, p. 315). These settings are furnished with dimorphic equipment (such as urinals for men or elaborate grooming facilities for women), even though both sexes may achieve the same ends through the same means (and apparently do so in the privacy of their own homes). To be stressed here is the fact that:

> The *functioning* of sex-differentiated organs is involved, but there is nothing in this functioning that biologically recommends segregation; *that* arrangement is a totally cultural matter . . . toilet segregation is presented as a natural consequence of the difference between the sex-classes when in fact it is a means of honoring, if not producing, this difference. (Goffman 1977, p. 316)

Standardized social occasions also provide stages for evocations of the "essential female and male natures." Goffman cites organized sports as one such institutionalized framework for the expression of manliness. There, those qualities that ought "properly" to be associated with masculinity, such as endurance, strength, and competitive spirit, are celebrated by all parties concerned—participants, who may be seen to demonstrate such traits, and spectators, who applaud their demonstrations from the safety of the sidelines (1977, p. 322).

Assortative mating practices among heterosexual couples afford still further means to create and maintain differences between women and men. For example, even though size, strength, and age tend to be normally distributed among females and males (with considerable overlap between them), selective pairing ensures couples in which boys and men are visibly bigger, stronger, and older (if not "wiser") than the girls and women with whom they are paired. So, should situations emerge in which greater size, strength, or experience is called for, boys and men will be ever ready to display it and girls and women, to appreciate its display (Goffman 1977, p. 321; West and Iritani 1985).

Gender may be routinely fashioned in a variety of situations that seem conventionally expressive to begin with, such as those that present "helpless" women next to heavy objects or flat tires. But, as Goffman notes, heavy, messy, and precarious concerns can be constructed from *any* social situation, "even though by standards set in other settings, this may involve something that is light, clean, and safe" (Goffman 1977, p. 324). Given these resources, it is clear that *any* interactional situation sets the stage for depictions of "essential" sexual natures. In sum, these situations "do not so much allow for the expression of natural differences as for the production of that difference itself" (Goffman 1977, p. 324).

Many situations are not clearly sex categorized to begin with, nor is what transpires within them obviously gender relevant. Yet any social encounter can be pressed into service in the interests of doing gender. Thus, Fishman's (1978) research on casual conversations found an asymmetrical "division of labor" in talk between heterosexual intimates. Women had to ask more questions, fill more silences, and use more attention-getting beginnings in order to be heard. Her conclusions are particularly pertinent here:

> Since interactional work is related to what constitutes being a woman, with what a woman *is*, the idea that it *is* work is obscured. The work is not seen as what women do, but as part of what they are. (Fishman 1978, p. 405)

We would argue that it is precisely such labor that helps to constitute the essential nature of women *as* women in interactional contexts (West and Zimmerman 1983, pp. 109–11; but see also Kollock, Blumstein, and Schwartz 1985).

Individuals have many social identities that may be donned or shed, muted or made more salient, depending on the situation. One may be a friend, spouse, professional, citizen, and many other things to many different people—or, to the same person at different times. But we are always women or men—unless we shift into another sex category. What this means is that our identificatory displays will provide an ever-available resource for doing gender under an infinitely diverse set of circumstances.

Some occasions are organized to routinely display and celebrate behaviors that are conventionally linked to one or the other sex category. On such occasions, everyone knows his or her place in the interactional scheme of things. If an individual identified as a member of one sex category engages in behavior usually associated with the other category, this routinization is challenged. Hughes (1945, p. 356) provides an illustration of such a dilemma:

[A] young woman . . . became part of that virile profession, engineering. The designer of an airplane is expected to go up on the maiden flight of the first plane built according to the design. He [sic] then gives a dinner to the engineers and workmen who worked on the new plane. The dinner is naturally a stag party. The young woman in question designed a plane. Her co-workers urged her not to take the risk—for which, presumably, men only are fit—of the maiden voyage. They were, in effect, asking her to be a lady instead of an engineer. She chose to be an engineer. She then gave the party and paid for it like a man. After food and the first round of toasts, she left like a lady.

On this occasion, parties reached an accommodation that allowed a woman to engage in presumptively masculine behaviors. However, we note that in the end, this compromise permitted demonstration of her "essential" femininity, through accountably "ladylike" behavior.

Hughes (1945, p. 357) suggests that such contradictions may be countered by managing interactions on a very narrow basis, for example, "keeping the relationship formal and specific." But the heart of the matter is that even—perhaps, especially—if the relationship is a formal one, gender is still something one is accountable for. Thus a woman physician (notice the special qualifier in her case) may be accorded respect for her skill and even addressed by an appropriate title. Nonetheless, she is subject to evaluation in terms of normative conceptions of appropriate attitudes and activities for her sex category and under pressure to prove that she is an "essentially" feminine being, despite appearances to the contrary (West 1984, pp. 97–101). Her sex category is used to discredit her participation in important clinical activities (Lorber 1984, pp. 52–54), while her involvement in medicine is used to discredit her commitment to her responsibilities as a wife and mother (Bourne and Wikler 1978, pp. 435–37). Simultaneously, her exclusion from the physician colleague community is maintained and her accountability *as a woman* is ensured.

In this context, "role conflict" can be viewed as a dynamic aspect of our current "arrangement between the sexes" (Goffman 1977), an arrangement that provides for occasions on which persons of a particular sex category can "see" quite clearly that they are out of place and that if they were not there, their current troubles would not exist. What is at stake is, from the standpoint of interaction, the management of our "essential" natures, and from the standpoint of the individual, the continuing accomplishment of gender. If, as we have argued, sex category is omnirelevant, then any occasion, conflicted or not, offers the resources for doing gender.

We have sought to show that sex category and gender are managed properties of conduct that are contrived with respect to the fact that others will judge and respond to us in particular ways. We have claimed that a person's gender is not simply an aspect of what one is, but, more fundamentally, it is something that one *does*, and does recurrently, in interaction with others.

What are the consequences of this theoretical formulation? If, for example, individuals strive to achieve gender in encounters with others, how does a culture instill the need to achieve it? What is the relationship between the production of gender at the level of interaction and such institutional arrangements as the division of labor in society? And, perhaps most important, how does doing gender contribute to the subordination of women by men?

Research Agendas

To bring the social production of gender under empirical scrutiny, we might begin at the beginning, with a reconsideration of the process through which societal members acquire the requisite categorical apparatus and other skills to become gendered human beings.

Recruitment to Gender Identities

The conventional approach to the process of becoming girls and boys has been sex-role socialization. In recent years, recurring problems arising from this approach have been linked to inadequacies inherent in role theory *per se*—its emphasis on "consensus, stability and continuity" (Stacey and Thorne 1985, p. 307), its ahistorical and depoliticizing focus (Thorne 1980, p. 9; Stacey and Thorne 1985, p. 307), and the fact that its "social" dimension relies on "a general assumption that people choose to maintain existing customs" (Connell 1985, p. 263).

In contrast, Cahill (1982, 1986a, 1986b) analyzes the experiences of preschool children using a social model of recruitment into normally gendered identities. Cahill argues that categorization practices are fundamental to learning and displaying feminine and masculine behavior. Initially, he observes, children are primarily concerned with distinguishing between themselves and others on the basis of social competence. Categorically, their concern resolves itself into the opposition of "girl/boy" classification versus "baby" classification (the latter designating children whose social behavior is problematic and who must be closely supervised). It is children's concern with being seen as socially competent that evokes their initial claims to gender identities:

> During the exploratory stage of children's socialization . . they learn that only two social identities are routinely available to them, the identity of "baby," or, depending on the configuration of their external genitalia, either "big boy" or "big girl." Moreover, others subtly inform them that the identity of "baby"

is a discrediting one. When, for example, children engage in disapproved behavior, they are often told "You're a baby" or "Be a big boy." In effect, these typical verbal responses to young children's behavior convey to them that they must behaviorally choose between the discrediting identity of "baby" and their anatomically determined sex identity. (Cahill 1986a, p. 175)

Subsequently, little boys appropriate the gender ideal of "efficaciousness," that is, being able to affect the physical and social environment through the exercise of physical strength or appropriate skills. In contrast, little girls learn to value "appearance," that is, managing themselves as ornamental objects. Both classes of children learn that the recognition and use of sex categorization in interaction are not optional, but mandatory (see also Bem 1983).

Being a "girl" or a "boy" then, is not only being more competent than a "baby," but also being competently female or male, that is, learning to produce behavioral displays of one's "essential" female or male identity. In this respect, the task of four- to five-year-old children is very similar to Agnes's:

For example, the following interaction occurred on a preschool playground. A 55-month-old boy (D) was attempting to unfasten the clasp of a necklace when a preschool aide walked over to him.

A: Do you want to put that on?
D: No. It's for girls.
A: You don't have to be a girl to wear things around your neck. Kings wear things around their necks. You could pretend you're a king.
D: I'm not a king. I'm a boy. (Cahill 1986a, p. 176)

As Cahill notes of this example, although D may have been unclear as to the sex status of a king's identity, he was obviously aware that necklaces are used to announce the identity "girl." Having claimed the identity "boy" and having developed a behavioral commitment to it, he was leery of any display that might furnish grounds for questioning his claim.

In this way, new members of society come to be involved in a *self-regulating process* as they begin to monitor their own and others' conduct with regard to its gender implications. The "recruitment" process involves not only the appropriation of gender ideals (by the valuation of those ideals as proper ways of being and behaving) but also *gender identities* that are important to individuals and that they strive to maintain. Thus gender differences, or the sociocultural shaping of "essential female and male natures," achieve the status of objective facts. They are rendered normal, natural features of persons and provide the tacit rationale for differing fates of women and men within the social order.

Additional studies of children's play activities as routine occasions for the expression of gender-appropriate behavior can yield new insights into how our "essential natures" are constructed. In particular, the transition from what Cahill (1986a) terms "apprentice participation" in the sex-segregated worlds that are common among elementary school children to "bona fide participation" in the heterosexual world so frightening to adolescents is likely to be a keystone in our understanding of the recruitment process (Thorne 1986; Thorne and Luria 1986).

Gender and the Division of Labor

Whenever people face issues of *allocation*—who is to do what, get what, plan or execute action, direct or be directed, incumbency in significant social categories such as "female" and "male" seems to become pointedly relevant. How such issues are resolved conditions the exhibition, dramatization, or celebration of one's "essential nature" as a woman or man.

Berk (1985) offers elegant demonstration of this point in her investigation of the allocation of household labor and the attitudes of married couples toward the division of household tasks. Berk found little variation in either the actual distribution of tasks or perceptions of equity in regard to that distribution. Wives, even when employed outside the home, do the vast majority of household and child-care tasks. Moreover, both wives and husbands tend to perceive this as a "fair" arrangement. Noting the failure of conventional sociological and economic theories to explain this seeming contradiction, Berk contends that something more complex is involved than rational arrangements for the production of household goods and services:

> Hardly a question simply of who has more time, or whose time is worth more, who has more skill or more power, it is clear that a complicated relationship between the structure of work imperatives and the structure of normative expectations attached to work as *gendered* determines the ultimate allocation of members' time to work and home. (Berk 1985, pp. 195–96)

She notes, for example, that the most important factor influencing wives' contribution of labor is the total amount of work demanded or expected by the household; such demands had no bearing on husbands' contributions. Wives reported various rationales (their own and their husbands') that justified their level of contribution and, as a general matter, underscored the presumption that wives are essentially responsible for household production.

Berk (1985, p. 201) contends that it is difficult to see how people "could rationally establish the arrangements that they do solely for the production of household goods and services"—much less, how people could consider them "fair." She argues that our current arrangements for the domestic division of labor support *two* production processes: household goods and services (meals, clean children, and so on) and, at the same time, gender. As she puts it:

> Simultaneously, members "do" gender, as they "do" housework and child care, and what [has] been called the division of labor provides for the joint production of household labor and gender; it is the mechanism by which both the material and symbolic products of the household are realized. (1985, p. 201)

It is not simply that household labor is designated as "women's work," but that for a woman to engage in it and a man not to engage in it is to draw on and exhibit the "essential nature" of each. What is produced and reproduced is not merely the activity and artifact of domestic life, but the material embodiment of wifely and husbandly roles, and derivatively, of womanly and manly conduct (see Beer 1983, pp. 70–89). What are also frequently produced and reproduced are the dominant and subordinate statuses of the sex categories.

How does gender get done in work settings outside the home, where dominance and subordination are themes of overarching importance? Hochschild's (1983) analysis of the work of flight attendants offer some promising insights. She found that the occupation of flight attendant consisted of something altogether different for women than for men:

> As the company's main shock absorbers against "mishandled" passengers, their own feelings are more frequently subjected to rough treatment. In addition, a day's exposure to people who resist authority in a woman is a different experience than it is for a man. . . . In this respect, it is a disadvantage to be a woman. And in this case, they are not simply women in the biological sense. They are also a highly visible distillation of middle-class American notions of femininity. They symbolize Woman. Insofar as the category "female" is mentally associated with having less status and authority, female flight attendants are more readily classified as "really" females than other females are. (Hochschild 1983, p. 175)

In performing what Hochschild terms the "emotional labor" necessary to maintain airline profits, women flight attendants simultaneously produce enactments of their "essential" femininity.

Sex and Sexuality

What is the relationship between doing gender and a culture's pre-scription of "obligatory heterosexuality" (Rubin 1975; Rich 1980)? As Frye (1983, p. 22) observes, the monitoring of sexual feelings in relation to other appropriately sexed persons requires the ready recognition of such persons "before one can allow one's heart to beat or one's blood to flow in erotic enjoyment of that person." The appearance of heterosexuality is produced through emphatic and unambiguous indicators of one's sex, layered on in ever more conclusive fashion (Frye 1983, p. 24). Thus, lesbians and gay men concerned with passing as heterosexuals can rely on these indicators for camouflage; in contrast, those who would avoid the assumption of heterosexuality may foster ambiguous indicators of their categorical status through their dress, behaviors, and style. But "ambiguous" sex indicators are sex indicators nonetheless. If one wishes to be recognized as a lesbian (or heterosexual woman), one must first establish a categorical status as female. Even as popular images portray lesbians as "females who are not feminine" (Frye 1983, p. 129), the accountability of persons for their "normal, natural sexedness" is preserved.

Nor is accountability threatened by the existence of "sex-change operations"—presumably, the most radical challenge to our cultural per-spective on sex and gender. Although no one coerces transsexuals into hormone therapy, electrolysis, or surgery, the alternatives available to them are undeniably constrained:

> When the transsexual experts maintain that they use transsexual procedures only with people who ask for them, and who prove that they can "pass," they obscure the social reality. Given patriarchy's prescription that one must be *either* masculine or feminine, free choice is conditioned. (Raymond 1979, p. 135, italics added)

The physical reconstruction of sex criteria pays ultimate tribute to the "essentialness" of our sexual natures—as women *or* as men.

Gender, Power, and Social Change

Let us return to the question: Can we avoid doing gender? Earlier, we proposed that insofar as sex category is used as a fundamental criterion for differentiation, doing gender is unavoidable. It is unavoidable because of the social consequences of sex-category membership: the allocation of power and resources not only in the domestic, economic, and political domains but also in the broad arena of interpersonal relations. In virtually any situation, one's sex category can be relevant, and one's performance as an incumbent of that category (i.e., gender) can be subjected to evaluation. Maintaining such pervasive and faithful assignment of lifetime status requires legitimation.

But doing gender also renders the social arrangements based on sex category accountable as normal and natural, that is, legitimate ways of organizing social life. differences between women and men that are created by this process can then be portrayed as fundamental and enduring dispositions. In this light, the institutional arrangements of a society can be seen as responsive to the differences—the social order being merely an accommodation to the natural order. Thus if, in doing gender, men are also doing dominance and women are doing deference (cf. Goffman 1967, pp. 47–95), the resultant social order, which supposedly reflects "natural differences," is a powerful reinforcer and legitimator of hierarchical arrangements. Frye observes:

> For efficient subordination, what's wanted is that the structure not appear to be a cultural artifact kept in place by human decision or custom, but that it appear *natural*—that it appear to be quite a direct consequence of facts about the beast which are beyond the scope of human manipulation. . . . That we are trained to behave so differently as women and men, and to behave so differently toward women and men, itself contributes mightily to the appearance of extreme dimorphism, but also, the *ways* we act as women and men, and the *ways* we act toward women and men, mold our bodies and our minds to the shape of subordination and dominance. We do become what we practice being. (Frye 1983, p. 34)

If we do gender appropriately, we simultaneously sustain, reproduce, and render legitimate the institutional arrangements that are based on sex category. If we fail to do gender appropriately, we as individuals—not the institutional arrangements—may be called to account (for our character, motives, and predispositions).

Social movements such as feminism can provide the ideology and impetus to question existing arrangements, and the social support for individuals to explore alternatives to them. Legislative changes, such as that proposed by the Equal Rights Amendment, can also weaken the accountability of conduct to sex category, thereby affording the possibility of more widespread loosening of accountability in general. To be sure, equality under the law does not guarantee equality in other arenas. As Lorber (1986, p. 577) points out, assurance of "scrupulous equality of categories of people considered essentially different needs constant monitoring." What such proposed changes *can* do is provide the warrant for asking why, if we wish to treat women and men as equals, there needs to be two sex categories at all (see Lorber 1986, p. 577).

The sex category/gender relationship links the institutional and interactional levels, a coupling that legitimates social arrangements based on sex category and reproduces their asymmetry in face-to-face interaction. Doing gender furnishes the interactional scaffolding of social structure, along with a built-in mechanism of social control. In appreciating the institutional forces that maintain distinctions between women and men, we must not lose sight of the interactional validation of those distinctions that confers upon them their sense of "naturalness" and "rightness."

Social change, then, must be pursued both at the institutional and cultural level of sex category and at the interactional level of gender. Such a conclusion is hardly novel. Nevertheless, we suggest that it is important to recognize that the analytical distinction between institutional and interactional spheres does not pose an either/or choice when it comes to the question of effecting social change. Reconceptualizing gender not as a simple property of individuals but as an integral dynamic of social orders implies a new perspective on the entire network of gender relations:

> [T]he social subordination of women, and the cultural practices which help sustain it; the politics of sexual object-choice, and particularly the oppression of homosexual people; the sexual division of labor, the formation of character and motive, so far as they are organized as femininity and masculinity; the role of the body in social relations, especially the politics of childbirth; and the nature of strategies of sexual liberation movements. (Connell 1985, p. 261)

Gender is a powerful ideological device, which produces, reproduces, and legitimates the choices and limits that are predicated on sex category. An understanding of how gender is produced in social situations will afford clarification of the interactional scaffolding of social structure and the social control processes that sustain it.

Notes

This article is based in part on a paper presented at the Annual Meeting of the American Sociological Association, Chicago, September 1977. For their helpful suggestions and encouragement, we thank Lynda Ames, Bettina Aptheker, Steven Clayman, Judith Gerson, the late Erving Goffman, Marilyn Lester, Judith Lorber, Robin Lloyd, Wayne Mellinger, Beth E. Schneider, Barrie Thorne, Thomas P. Wilson, and most especially, Sarah Fenstermaker Berk.

1. This definition understates many complexities involved in the relationship between biology and culture (Jaggar 1983, pp. 106–13). However, our point is that

the determination of an individual's sex classification is a *social* process through and through.

2. This is not to say that gender is a singular "thing," omnipresent in the same form historically or in every situation. Because normative conceptions of appropriate attitudes and activities for sex categories can vary across cultures and historical moments, the management of situated conduct in light of these expectations can take many different forms.

3. Bernstein (1986) reports an unusual case of espionage in which a man passing as a woman convinced a lover that he/she had given birth to "their" child, who, the lover, thought, "looked like" him.

References

Beer, William R. 1983. *Househusbands: Men and Housework in American Families.* New York: Praeger.

Bem, Sandra L. 1983. "Gender Schema Theory and Its Implications for Child Development: Raising Gender-Aschematic Children in a Gender-Schematic Society." *Signs: Journal of Women in Culture and Society* 8:598–616.

Berger, Joseph, Bernard P. Cohen, and Morris Zelditch, Jr. 1972. "Status Characteristics and Social Interaction." *American Sociological Review* 37:241–55.

Berger, Joseph, Thomas L. Conner, and M. Hamit Fisek, eds. 1974. *Expectation States Theory: A Theoretical Research Program.* Cambridge: Winthrop.

Berger, Joseph, M. Hamit Fisek, Robert Z. Norman, and Morris Zelditch, Jr. 1977. *Status Characteristics and Social Interaction: An Expectation States Approach.* New York: Elsevier.

Berk, Sarah F. 1985. *The Gender Factory: The Apportionment of Work in American Households.* New York: Plenum.

Bernstein, Richard. 1986. "France Jails 2 in Odd Case of Espionage." *New York Times* (May 11).

Blackwood, Evelyn. 1984. "Sexuality and Gender in Certain Native American Tribes: The Case of Cross-Gender Females." *Signs: Journal of Women in Culture and Society* 10:27–42.

Bourne, Patricia G., and Norma J. Wikler. 1978. "Commitment and the Cultural Mandate: Women in Medicine." *Social Problems* 25:430–40.

Cahill, Spencer E. 1982. "Becoming Boys and Girls." Ph.D. dissertation, Department of Sociology, University of California, Santa Barbara.

———. 1986a. "Childhood Socialization as Recruitment Process: Some Lessons from the Study of Gender Development." Pp. 163–86 in *Sociological Studies of Child Development,* edited by P. Adler and P. Adler. Greenwich, CT: JAI Press.

———. 1986b. "Language Practices and Self-Definition: The Case of Gender Identity Acquisition." *The Sociological Quarterly* 27:295–311.

Chodorow, Nancy. 1978. *The Reproduction of Mothering: Psychoanalysis and the Sociology of Gender.* Los Angeles: University of California Press.

Connell, R. W. 1983. *Which Way Is Up?* Sydney: Allen & Unwin.

———. 1985. "Theorizing Gender." *Sociology* 19:260–72.

Cucchiari, Salvatore. 1981. "The Gender Revolution and the Transition from Bisexual Horde to Patrilocal Band: The Origins of Gender Hierarchy." Pp. 31–79 in *Sexual Meanings: The Cultural Construction of Gender and Sexuality*, edited by S. B. Ortner and H. Whitehead. New York: Cambridge.

Firestone, Shulamith. 1970. *The Dialectic of Sex: The Case for Feminist Revolution.* New York: William Morrow.

Fishman, Pamela. 1978. "Interaction: The Work Women Do." *Social Problems* 25:397–406.

Frye, Marilyn. 1983. *The Politics of Reality: Essays in Feminist Theory.* Trumansburg, NY: The Crossing Press.

Garfinkel, Harold. 1967. *Studies in Ethnomethodology.* Englewood Cliffs, NJ: Prentice-Hall.

Gerson, Judith M., and Kathy Peiss. 1985. "Boundaries, Negotiation, Consciousness: Reconceptualizing Gender Relations." *Social Problems* 32:317–31.

Goffman, Erving. 1967 (1956). "The Nature of Deference and Demeanor." Pp. 47–95 in *Interactional Ritual.* New York: Anchor/Doubleday.

———. 1976. "Gender Display." *Studies in the Anthropology of Visual Communication* 3:69–77.

———. 1977. "The Arrangement Between the Sexes." *Theory and Society* 4:301–31.

Henley, Nancy M. 1985. "Psychology and Gender." *Signs: Journal of Women in Culture and Society* 11:101–119.

Heritage, John. 1984. *Garfinkel and Ethnomethodology.* Cambridge, England: Polity Press.

Hill, W. W. 1935. "The Status of the Hermaphrodite and Transvestite in Navaho Culture." *American Anthropologist* 37:273–79.

Hochschild, Arlie R. 1973. "A Review of Sex Roles Research." *American Journal of Sociology* 78:1011–29.

———. 1983. *The Managed Heart: Commercialization of Human Feeling.* Berkeley: University of California Press.

Hughes, Everett C. 1945. "Dilemmas and Contradictions of Status." *American Journal of Sociology* 50:353–59.

Humphreys, Paul, and Joseph Berger. 1981. "Theoretical Consequences of the Status Characteristics Formulation." *American Journal of Sociology* 86:953–83.

Jaggar, Alison M. 1983. *Feminist Politics and Human Nature.* Totowa, NJ: Rowman & Allanheld.

Kessler, S., D. J. Ashendon, R. W. Connell, and G. W. Dowsett. 1985. "Gender Relations in Secondary Schooling." *Sociology of Education* 58:34–48.

Kessler, Suzanne J., and Wendy McKenna. 1978. *Gender: An Ethnomethodological Approach.* New York: Wiley.

Kollock, Peter, Philip Blumstein, and Pepper Schwartz. 1985. "Sex and Power in Interaction." *American Sociological Review* 50:34–46.

Komarovsky, Mirra. 1946. "Cultural Contradictions and Sex Roles." *American Journal of Sociology* 52:184–89.

———. 1950. "Functional Analysis of Sex Roles." *American Sociological Review* 15:508–16.

Linton, Ralph. 1936. *The Study of Man.* New York: Appleton-Century.

Lopata, Helen Z., and Barrie Thorne. 1978. "On the Term 'Sex Roles.'" *Signs: Journal of Women in Culture and Society* 3:718–21.

Lorber, Judith. 1984. *Women Physicians: Careers, Status and Power.* New York: Tavistock.

————. 1986. "Dismantling Noah's Ark." *Sex Roles* 14:567–80.

Martin, M. Kay, and Barbara Voorheis. 1975. *Female of the Species.* New York: Columbia University Press.

Mead, Margaret. 1963. *Sex and Temperament.* New York: Dell.

————. 1968. *Male and Female.* New York: Dell.

Mithers, Carol L. 1982. "My Life as a Man." *The Village Voice* 27 (October 5):1ff.

Money, John. 1968. *Sex Errors of the Body.* Baltimore: Johns Hopkins.

————. 1974. "Prenatal Hormones and Postnatal Sexualization in Gender Identity Differentiation." Pp. 221–95 in *Nebraska Symposium on Motivation,* Vol. 21, edited by J. K. Cole and R. Dienstbier. Lincoln: University of Nebraska Press.

———— and John G. Brennan. 1968. "Sexual Dimorphism in the Psychology of Female Transsexuals." *Journal of Nervous and Mental Disease* 147:487–99.

———— and Anke, A. Erhardt. 1972. *Man and Woman/Boy and Girl.* Baltimore: John Hopkins.

———— and Charles Ogunro. 1974. "Behavioral Sexology: Ten Cases of Genetic Male Intersexuality with Impaired Prenatal and Pubertal Androgenization," *Archives of Sexual Behavior* 3:181–206.

———— and Patricia Tucker. 1975. *Sexual Signatures.* Boston: Little, Brown.

Morris, Jan. 1974. *Conundrum.* New York: Harcourt Brace Jovanovich.

Parsons, Talcott. 1951. *The Social System.* New York: Free Press.

———— and Robert F. Bales. 1955. *Family, Socialization and Interaction Process.* New York: Free Press.

Raymond, Janice G. 1979. *The Transsexual Empire.* Boston: Beacon.

Rich, Adrienne. 1980. "Compulsory Heterosexuality and Lesbian Existence." *Signs: Journal of Women in Culture and Society* 5:631–60.

Richards, Renee (with John Ames). 1983. *Second Serve: The Renee Richards Story.* New York: Stein and Day.

Rossi, Alice. 1984. "Gender and Parenthood." *American Sociological Review* 49:1–19.

Rubin, Gayle. 1975. "The Traffic in Women: Notes on the 'Political Economy' of Sex." Pp. 157–210 in *Toward an Anthropology of Women,* edited by R. Reiter. New York: Monthly Review Press.

Sacks, Harvey. 1972. "On the Analyzability of Stories by Children." Pp. 325–45 in *Directions in Sociolinguistics,* edited by J. J. Gumperz and D. Hymes. New York: Holt, Rinehart & Winston.

Schutz, Alfred. 1943. "The Problem of Rationality in the Social World." *Economics* 10:130–49.

Stacey, Judith, and Barrie Thorne. 1985. "The Missing Feminist Revolution in Sociology." *Social Problems* 32:301–16.

Thorne, Barrie. 1980. "Gender . . . How Is It Best Conceptualized?" Unpublished manuscript.

———. 1986. "Girls and Boys Together . . . But Mostly Apart: Gender Arrangements in Elementary Schools." Pp. 167–82 in *Relationships and Development*,
edited by W. Hartup and Z. Rubin. Hillsdale, NJ: Lawrence Erlbaum.

——— and Zella Luria. 1986. "Sexuality and Gender in Children's Daily Worlds."
Social Problems 33:176–90.

Tresemer, David. 1975. "Assumptions Made About Gender Roles." Pp. 308–39 in
Another Voice: Feminist Perspectives on Social Life and Social Science, edited by
M. Millman and R. M. Kanter. New York: Anchor/Doubleday.

West, Candace. 1984. "When the Doctor is a 'Lady': Power, Status and Gender in
Physician-Patient Encounters." *Symbolic Interaction* 7:87–106.

——— and Bonita Iritani. 1985. "Gender Politics in Mate Selection: The Male-
Older Norm." Paper presented at the Annual Meeting of the American
Sociological Association, August, Washington, DC.

——— and Don H. Zimmerman. 1983. "Small Insults: A Study of Interruptions
in Conversations Between Unacquainted Persons." Pp. 102–17 in *Language,
Gender and Society*, edited by B. Thorne, C. Kramarae, and N. Henley. Rowley,
MA: Newbury House.

Wieder, D. Lawrence. 1974. *Language and Social Reality: The Case of Telling the
Convict Code*. The Hague: Mouton.

Williams, Walter L. 1986. *The Spirit and the Flesh: Sexual Diversity in American
Indian Culture*. Boston: Beacon.

Wilson, Thomas P. 1970. "Conceptions of Interaction and Forms of Sociological
Explanation." *American Sociological Review* 35:697–710.

Zimmerman, Don H., and D. Lawrence Wieder. 1970. "Ethnomethodology and the
Problem of Order: Comment on Denzin." Pp. 287–95 in *Understanding
Everyday Life*, edited by J. Denzin. Chicago: Aldine.

15

THE PSYCHOLOGY OF WOMEN AND CONSERVATISM: REDISCOVERING SOCIAL CHANGE

Arnold S. Kahn
and Janice D. Yoder

Sociologists and political scientists categorize the contemporary feminist or women's movement as a social movement (Freeman, 1975, 1989). At its core, the feminist movement is a civil rights movement (Eisenstein, 1984), a movement for gender equality that in many ways parallels movements for racial equality, rights of disabled persons, equality for lesbians and gays, and all other struggles for rights and privileges in a society that discriminates on a number of bases.[1]

Psychology of women as a distinct field within psychology grew out of the feminist social movement of the 1960s and 1970s. Three events gave formal recognition to this area of psychology: the formation of the Association of Women in Psychology in 1969 and of Division 35 in 1973 and the publication of *Psychology of Women Quarterly* in 1977. However, the link between these three exemplars of women's scholarship within psychology and the sociopolitical actions of the popular women's movement appears to have deteriorated in some areas. We believe that it is time to rejuvenate the relationship between the public policy issues of the women's movement and the scholarship and practice of the psychology of women.

The women's movement is a social movement aimed at eliminating gender-based oppression. It is a sociopolitical movement demanding im-

Arnold S. Kahn and Janice D. Yoder, "The Psychology of Women and Conservatism: Rediscovering Social Change." *Psychology of Women Quarterly*, 13, 417–432. Copyright 1989 by Cambridge University Press. Reprinted by permission.

provements at every level of society: individual, interpersonal, organizational, and societal/cultural. We will argue that the often individualistic orientation of psychology and, more specifically, of the psychology of women can inhibit social movements by inadvertently supporting the status quo. However, with careful reassessment this need not be the case. We envision a psychology of women that will contribute substantially to the future of the women's movement.

We will look at individualism and conservatism in psychology overall and will examine these forces in the psychology of women. Next, we will turn to the causes and consequences of conservatism in the psychology of women. Finally, we will offer an alternative construction that is aimed at contributing to the ongoing women's movement.

Psychology and Conservatism

In a recent article, Prilleltensky (1989) made a convincing case that, rather than helping to foster social change, psychology as a discipline plays a major role in maintaining the status quo in society. He asserted that although psychologists often strive to promote human welfare, they in fact more frequently exert a conservative force that hinders change.

Prilleltensky suggested two reasons for psychology's failure to improve society. First, psychology maintains a strong, pervasive focus on the individual as he or she exists at the moment. Such a focus does not allow psychologists to easily examine the historical and cultural context surrounding the individual and, therefore, minimizes the impact the latter might have in shaping behavior (cf. Sarason, 1981). This individual focus, Prilleltensky suggested, leads psychologists to look for determinants of behavior within, rather than outside, the individual and directs attention to the individual as the source of change. Thus, attempts are made to improve human welfare by changing individuals without concomitant societal change. Such a perspective ignores the role of the social order as a potent determinant of an individual's current situation and directs attention away from viewing changes in society as a mechanism for producing changes in behavior (cf. Albee, 1986; Caplan & Nelson, 1973; Ryan, 1971).

A second cause of psychology's conservatism, according to Prilleltensky, resides in the socialization of psychologists and the culture and circumstances in which psychology is practiced (cf. Sarason, 1981). Like all American citizens, psychologists have been inculcated with a variety of values and beliefs (e.g., "the basic social order is good and should not be questioned," and "people are responsible for their fates"). Furthermore, a variety of institutions from governmental funding agencies to universities and scholarly journals continue to reinforce these values. These values are steeped in a highly individualistic philosophy—that outcomes are due to people's own actions and that people get what they deserve. Thus, the well-socialized psychologist typically ignores the impact of the social order in shaping and maintaining behavior (Albee, 1986; Caplan & Nelson, 1973; Ryan, 1971; Sarason, 1981).

In his paper, Prilleltensky (1989) demonstrated how the behavioral, organic, humanistic, and cognitive perspectives in psychology all envision social change through individual action that does not challenge basic social values. He pointed to the psychology of women as one field of psychology that has begun to break out of this conservatism. Prilleltensky's view certainly is bolstered by a number of feminist psychologists who have pointed out the potentially biased policy implications of focusing on sex differences (e.g., Parlee, 1979; Sherif, 1979; Unger, 1983). However, we believe Prilleltensky was premature in his characterization of much of the psychology of women.

Contrary to Prilleltensky's representation of the psychology of women in the 1980s, individualistic theories that focus on the personality of women have flourished (Fine, 1985). We believe that the field of the psychology of women has fallen prey to the same forces that have affected psychology more generally. Increasingly, the field has examined women (and men) without regard to the social, historical, and political contexts surrounding gender. We will argue that this has important implications for how the field of psychology views women, the research conducted on gender, and the kinds of public policy recommendations that emerge from our research.

Psychology of Women and Conservatism

Although the psychology of women began with (and to some extent still retains) the lofty goal of changing society so that women are empowered, we believe it not only has failed to meet that goal, but may no longer be striving toward it. Paralleling the biases of psychology as a whole (Prilleltensky, 1989), the psychology of women focuses on person-based causes of gender differences between women and men rather than on social, historical, and cultural forces that underlie these apparent behavioral differences. Furthermore, we believe that the cause of this state of affairs is not solely the difficulties inherent in social change, but the actions of many feminist psychologists. Too many psychologists, whether consciously or not, assume that women and men are basically different and subsequently, attempt to document "valid" gender differences. Their systematic attempt to discover and explain gender differences in individual-istic terms often replace efforts to focus on the position of women within a social, historical, and cultural context. We believe such a focus produces research and theory that ultimately support, rather than challenge, existing social policies.

The "Alpha Bias" Bias

Conservatism in the psychology of women is reflected in what Hare-Mustin and Marecek (1988) referred to as "alpha bias." Examining gender from a social-constructionist position (Gergen, 1985), Hare-Mustin and Marecek suggested that the extent to which women and men are similar or different is unknowable, but how we construe gender has important research and policy implications. They noted that psychologists (and others) can construe women and men either as being basically different, the alpha bias, or basically the same, the "beta bias." They note that alpha bias is the perspective from which most psychologists represent gender and point out that envisioning women as inherently and basically different from men has the consequence of focusing psychologists' attention on the personalities of women and men rather than on the social order.

The Case of Achievement. By all objective measures, women appear to achieve less than men; women tend to have lower status jobs that pay less, and they earn less than men when equally qualified for and occupying the same position (England & McCreary, 1987). Furthermore, women are more likely than men to be unemployed and underemployed (Nieva & Gutek, 1981) and to be living below the poverty level (Russo & Denmark, 1984). Unlike men, women are viewed as not making major contributions to the arts and sciences.

The question of interest to psychologists is why women appear not to have achieved to the extent men have in the public sphere. One direction would be to look at achievement opportunities as they have existed historically for women and as they currently exist, as well as to examine what happens to women (and men) when they attempt to achieve. Such an examination would reveal a number of potential external factors such as job discrimination (Nieva & Gutek, 1981), sexual harassment (Gutek, 1985), lack of role models (Yoder, Adams, Grove, & Priest, 1985), and the devaluation of women's performance (Hagen & Kahn, 1975; Spence, Helmreich, & Stapp, 1975). Also evident would be the biases of historians (Giddings, 1984), lack of affordable day care (Gerson, 1985; Hewlett, 1986), and ineffective birth control (Luker, 1984). A focus on these external, societal, and structural factors would likely lead to suggestions for societal change in an effort to improve the status of women.

Although a few psychologists have adopted this perspective, far greater numbers have looked at women themselves to discover the "deficiencies" that inhibit their achievement. Examples of this trend, both within and outside of psychology, include achievement motivation, fear of success, the Impostor Phenomenon, and the Mommy Track.

Early work in the area of achievement motivation suggested that women achieve less than men because they are less motivated to achieve success—a personality deficit in women (Veroff, 1969; Veroff, Wilcox, & Atkinson, 1953). In contrast, more recent research has suggested that women and men do not differ in their motivations to achieve (e.g., Spence & Helmreich, 1983).

The next influential explanation came from Matina Horner (1968, 1970) who proposed that women had a diminished achievement orientation relative to that of men because women have developed, as a stable personality characteristic, a motive to avoid success. The attribution of such a personality trait clearly blames women's apparent lack of achievement on themselves. A very sizable literature on this topic subsequently has questioned whether fear of success is a personality trait. It has been suggested that fear of success might best be viewed as a situational variable—both women and men avoid striving for success in areas in which success has negative outcomes (Condry & Dyer, 1976; Deaux, 1976; Paludi, 1984; Tresemer, 1976).

As fear of success explanations waned, the Impostor Phenomenon came into vogue to explain women's lack of achievement (Clance & Imes, 1978). According to this notion, although some women succeed, they do not internalize a sense of success and feel they have fooled everyone. In other words, they feel like "impostors." The anxiety and guilt experienced by these women, an internal barrier to success, was presumed to limit subsequent achievement. Clance and O'Toole (1987) cited a series of dissertations to document that men experience the phenomenon as frequently as women; however, they continued to assert that the Impostor Phenomenon limits women's achievements more than men's (p. 53).

Each of these attempts to explain women's "failure" to achieve successes comparable to those of men places the blame for failure squarely on the shoulders of women who are less motivated, fear success, or shrink as impostors. Each captured the spotlight of the mass media in its heyday (Dowling, 1981; Harvey, 1987; Krueger, 1975) then quietly faded from public view as discrediting research evidence mounted. Yet, each was eventually replaced by a more contemporary version of the same old person-based saw.

The most recent manifestation of this individualism is the concept of what has been dubbed by the popular press as the Mommy Track (Schwartz, 1989). Schwartz proposed that separate and unequal tracks be created:

one for exclusively career-oriented women (and for men); the other for those workers who seek to blend career and parenting (read: mothering). We know that career tracks as currently defined conflict with parental responsibilities and desires (Gerson, 1985). Schwartz, the president and founder of Catalyst, attempted to resolve this conflict with the best of liberal feminist intentions. But, instead, she produced a perfect example of what happens when alpha bias is drawn upon to shape organizational policies.

The concept of a Mommy Track assumes that women and men are inherently different; unlike men, when women biologically reproduce, they lose their career commitment. Because mothers differ from other workers (men and childless women), mothers need to adapt. It never questions a workplace that demands total immersion from both female and male workers. Nothing is done to restructure the workplace to be compatible with parenting (or any other type of extra-work activity, for that matter).

Alpha bias is not limited to theory and research on achievement; it appears throughout the psychology of women. A highly visible example is Gilligan's work on gender differences in morality (Gilligan, 1982; Gilligan, Ward, Taylor, & Bardige, 1989). Although a great deal of research has failed to support the notion that women and men differ in their conception of morality (Freedman, Robinson, & Friedman, 1987; Gibbs, Arnold, & Burkhart, 1984; Smetana, 1984; Thoma, 1986; Walker, 1984), the presumed truth of the gender difference in morality remains strong and popular (Csikszentmihaly, 1989). Other theories that demonstrate alpha bias include the works of Belenky, Clinchy, Goldberger, and Tarule (1986) on cognitive development and Benbow and Stanley (1980, 1983) on mathematical reasoning ability.

Causes of Conservatism
in the Psychology of Women

Why has the psychology of women demonstrated this conservative drift despite its original goal of social change? Certainly feminist psychologists are not immune to the forces Prilleltensky (1989) and others (Albee, 1986; Sarason, 1981) have noted. Like their nonfeminist colleagues, feminist psychologists have been trained throughout their undergraduate and graduate educations to view human behavior from an individualist perspective, and this perspective has been reinforced by journal editors, tenure review committees, and funding agencies. Likewise, feminist psychologists share many of the core societal beliefs and values with the general population of which they are a part.

These explanations, while clearly part of the picture, seem insufficient in light of the feminist movement's strong actions toward social change in a variety of areas from abortion to the Equal Rights Amendment. We believe part of the problem lies with gender stereotypes. One of the core beliefs of our society is that men and women are basically different—the "opposite" sexes. This, of course, is a restatement of the alpha bias (Hare-Mustin & Marecek, 1988). The contents of these presumed gender differences are well-known by children and adults and constitute what are frequently referred to as gender stereotypes or what Deaux (Deaux & Kite, 1987; Deaux & Major, 1987) has labeled "gender belief systems." We believe many in the field of the psychology of women assume, consciously or not, the stereotype of women to be a relatively accurate portrayal of what women (and men) are really like. This belief that women and men are basically different leads psychologists to look for such differences.

Stereotypes

The stereotype of women has been studied extensively and has been shown to contain a cluster of traits denoting warmth, expressiveness, affiliation, nurturance, and an absence of stereotypical masculine qualities (achievement, autonomy, dominance, and aggressiveness) (Ashmore & Del Boca, 1981; Broverman, Vogel, Broverman, Clarkson, & Rosenkrantz, 1972; Williams & Best, 1982). Although the warmth-expressive qualities seen as characteristic of women and the instrumental qualities perceived as characteristic of men are not opposites and can be possessed by the same individual (Bem, 1974; Spence & Helmreich, 1978), most people view them as bipolar opposites (Storms, 1979).

The explanations of many psychologists for women's lack of achievement demonstrates the operation of this stereotype: lacking the motivation to achieve, fearing success, believing oneself to be an impostor, and wishing to care for children all portray women in a fashion consistent with their stereotype—high in nurturance and warmth, low on competence (Broverman et al., 1972; Deaux & Kite, 1987). Likewise, theories such as those of Gilligan (1982) and Belenky et al. (1986) view women as possessing special characteristics that are consistent with the stereotype and lacking the instrumental characteristics seen as typical of men. In their search to understand the behavior of women, these investigators have not considered the historical, political, and cultural forces that might shape and reinforce certain behavior patterns in women and men. Rather, they assume there is something about women and men, either in their biology or their early socialization, that makes them irreversibly different.

Chodorow (1978) also saw women as possessing special characteristics consistent with the feminine stereotype. However, recognizing the histor-

ical, political, and cultural forces that shape socialization processes, Chodorow theorized that contemporary sex-role development is the result of
postindustrial labor market influences on the modern family. Hence,
Chodorow regarded a social force, capitalism, not socialization practices
per se, as the ultimate cause of stereotyped sex-role development.

Interestingly, reviews and summaries by psychologists of Chodorow's
(1978) ideas misread her work as a socialization theory (e.g., Belenky et
al., 1986; Gilligan, 1982; Gump, 1979; Williams, 1987; Young-Eisendrath
& Wiedemann, 1987). They focus almost solely on Chodorow's identification of the mother's role in reproducing stereotyped sex roles. They also
largely ignore the cultural and historical context in which Chodorow
placed her theory. This readiness to individualize and de-historicize the
development of gender further illustrates our assertion that the field of
psychology all too often exhibits a conservative bias.

Consequences of the
Individualistic Approach

In agreement with others who adopt a social-constructionist perspective (Gergen, 1985; Hare-Mustin & Marecek, 1988; Sampson, 1985; Unger,
1983, 1989), we believe the issue is not the extent to which gender
differences actually exist. Indeed, from this perspective the answer is not
knowable. However, the current practice of many in the psychology of
women—who assume that gender differences are large, stable, and inherent in biology or very early socialization—has important consequences
for public policy on issues relevant to women's lives.

Others have written about the consequences of ignoring the social
context and focusing exclusively on the individual (Albee, 1986; Caplan
& Nelson, 1973; Prilleltensky, 1989; Sarason, 1981). Looking at psychology
in general, Prilleltensky (1989) summed it up cogently:

> Psychology is instrumental in maintaining the societal status quo by (a)
> endorsing and reflecting dominant social values, (b) disseminating those
> values in the persuasive form of so-called value-free scientific statements, and
> (c) providing an asocial image of the human being, which in turn portrays
> the individual as essentially independent from sociohistorical circumstances.
> (p. 800)

Looking at the field of the psychology of women, there are two important
consequences of adopting an individualistic approach: blaming the victim
and asserting the immutability of difference.

Blaming the Victim

In a patriarchal society, a focus on gender differences typically reveals that women seem to possess fewer of those qualities valued most in the society. Gender stereotypes themselves are replete with examples. In a society that values instrumentality, men are viewed as independent, active, competitive, and confident. In a society that devalues emotionality and nurturance, women are regarded as stereotypically helpful, kind, understanding, and warm (Spence & Helmreich, 1978).

Such differences between the sexes easily can be viewed as "deficiencies" in women. This clearly is seen in the explanations for women's lack of achievement: women's lack of achievement motivation, their excessive fear of success, their lack of self-confidence, or their desire for children. Each draws upon a quality presumed to exist within women that is responsible for their lack of achievement. To make women more successful, they have to change; they have to want to achieve more, or to stop fearing success, or to better internalize their successes, or to stop wanting to raise children. The historical, cultural, and structural aspects of society that continue to oppress women are left unexamined (Lott, 1981, 1988; Mednick, 1987; Ryan, 1971).

The Immutability of
Person-Based Differences

As Mednick (1987) pointed out, theories such as those proposed by Gilligan (1982), Belenky et al. (1986), Benbow and Stanley (1980, 1982, 1983), and others presume either inherent, biological, or early socialization causes for gender differences. This necessarily implies that the differences are permanent and will resist change. Thus, efforts to improve the status of women are unlikely to be attempted.

The conservatism of biological explanations is readily apparent. For example, if hormones are linked to aggressiveness, the only way to change the aggressiveness of an individual would be to biologically alter his or her hormonal balance. Surrealistic scenarios such as this obviously mediate against biologically determined gender equality.

The immutability of socialized gender differences is less readily apparent. According to this explanation of gender differences, early socialization shapes personality traits, characteristics that are by definition relatively stable and unchanging. To change an adult's already formed traits requires re-socialization. For example, in the area of aggressiveness, assertiveness training became the rage of professional women in the 1970s and early 1980s (Baer, 1976; Zuker, 1983). But, it was soon pointed out that as long as gender stereotypes persisted, what was regarded as assertiveness in men was readily re-interpreted as "bitchiness" in women (Kanter, 1977).

Another possibility is to abandon the already socialized and turn our attention to the new generation that is currently undergoing its initial socialization. The problem here, as with re-socialization, is that socialization itself is by definition an internalization of societal values. Hence, nonsexist socialization cannot take place within a sexist society. Even the most egalitarian parents realize that their ability to control their child's beliefs is limited; peers, teachers, television, and so on all exert some influence.

Overall then, biological and socialization explanations of gender differences, both of which draw upon an individualistic approach, offer limited hope of individual and, ultimately, societal change. Since the women's movement is committed to such change, these explanations do not contribute to this movement.

Social Forces and Beta Bias

The beta bias assumes that women and men are basically similar (Hare-Mustin & Marecek, 1988). From this perspective, apparent gender differences simply reflect social forces that differentially affect women and men. When these social forces are changed so that they influence both genders similarly, the behavioral differences disappear.

There is a great deal of psychological and sociological evidence to support this logic. For example, when women and men leaders are released from the stereotypic definitions of leadership that pervade the laboratory, they exhibit similar leadership styles in the field (Hollander & Yoder, 1980; Osborn & Vicars, 1976). When the advancement opportunities of men are depressed, they take on work behaviors similar to those of women with limited promotional possibilities (Kanter, 1977). Recent experimental work is social psychology has shown no gender differences in supposedly gender-linked behaviors, such as displays of interpersonal power (Dovidio, Brown, Heltman, Ellyson, & Keating, 1988) and interpersonal sensitivity (Snodgrass, 1985), when situational expectations for stereotypic behavior are absent.

If researchers assume that social forces cause behavior, the search for causal explanations proceeds much differently than if they adopt an individualistic orientation. For example, we have examined the Impostor Phenomenon as an explanation for why women have achieved limited success in managerial positions. The gender difference in question here is the paucity of women in top management relative to middle management. The Impostor Phenomenon is used to argue that women opt out of advancement to the highest echelons because they question their own abilities to work at this level. Clearly, this explanation draws upon a personality deficiency in women that does not exist for most men (i.e., a true gender difference—the alpha bias).

An equally plausible explanation envisions a "glass ceiling," a discriminatory barrier that is designed to permit only limited success by women. A researcher's choice to pursue one potential explanation over the other will lead to quite different research projects. We already have examined the implications of pursuing the former. The latter approach avoids these pitfalls and opens up possibilities for initiating social change consonant with the goals of the women's movement. In sum, then, we regard assumptions about social, external causality, and beta bias as mutually reinforcing.

Social Forces and Alpha Bias

Other authors have sought to blend the alpha bias with causal explanations that explore social forces (Eagly, 1987; Eagly & Steffan, 1984). Eagly (1987) has argued persuasively that the stereotype of women does contain some truth (alpha bias); for example, women are more communal and less instrumental than men. However, this stereotype derives from the social and occupational roles typically held by women and men. Thus, women are more communal than men because they are more likely to be found in roles such as mother or nurse that require communal behavior. Women are not naturally more communal and less instrumental than men, but have become this way because of the place of gender within the social order.

Eagly (1987) is in agreement with us that gender differences are caused by social forces, but has argued that such differences are real and therefore psychologists should study them in order to determine their causes. She also is aware of the potential policy implications of focusing on gender differences, but does not believe that "acknowledgment by social scientists of existing sex differences invites discrimination against women or any other particular consequence" (p. 5).

There are two important differences between our position and that of scholars who blend alpha bias with causality rooted in social forces. First, based on a social constructionist point of view, we believe that gender is a social construct and that its true nature is unknowable.

Second, we believe—and have attempted to document—that assuming the validity of gender differences does have a negative impact on women in that it thwarts the primary goal of the women's movement. The alpha bias, even though cloaked in social explanations, ultimately can revert back to the person-based explanations of either biology or socialization. Using Eagly's example of women's communal orientation, we are left with a question concerning why women choose communal roles in the first place.

The alpha and beta biases suggest two distinct possibilities. Research characterized by alpha bias assumes that something different about women and men causes their differential selection of roles. This internal difference must be rooted in either biology or socialization. In contrast, an argument drawing on beta bias might assume that if women make rational choices about the social acceptability of roles appropriate for their gender, then women avoid instrumental roles because of anticipated discrimination (a social force). If this discrimination disappeared, women (and men) would choose roles freely and there would be no gender difference in role selection. (To posit differences in choices here again leads us to ask why and we eventually will end up with a biological or socialization explanation.) Thus, it appears that alpha bias simply puts a social forces mediator between an initial biological or socialization cause and the effect of a gender difference. The end result is a combination of alpha bias and person-based causality, the consequences of which we examined earlier in this article.

A Psychology of Women
in the Service of Women

How can we create a psychology of women that will foster, rather than inhibit, social change aimed at improving the status of women? How can we avoid the tendency to look at gender differences and explain the behavior of women (and men) in terms of their personalities? Prilleltensky (1989) suggested two necessary processes for psychology to work effectively toward social change: (a) becoming aware of the social, economic, and cultural forces that shape our lives, and (b) having an image of the ideal society that would maximize the welfare of its members. In terms of the psychology of women, these two processes are: (a) becoming aware of the various external forces that shape the behavior of women, and (b) having an image of the kind of society that would maximize women's well-being. Research on the psychology of women can contribute to these two processes.

Like other feminist scholars (e.g., Sherif, 1979; Unger, 1983), we firmly believe that research on the psychology of women cannot be value-free. Whatever course researchers pursue, they are making assumptions about the validity and causes of gender "differences." Our preference is to favor beta bias and to search for social forces that create apparent gender differences. By identifying these social forces, psychologists can contribute a research-based agenda to the women's movement.

This concentration on social causality obviously suits social psychology, but it does not necessarily invalidate other psychological contributions. For example, socialization research is important to the extent that it identifies social forces that underlie sexist socialization practices (e.g., biased parental attitudes, advertising, postindustrial capitalism) (Chodorow, 1978). To the extent that psychology can document the impact on the individual of sexist social forces, it can contribute substantially to a social movement.

In summary, a psychology of women that assumes that women and men are naturally different (alpha bias) or that differences are caused by factors internal to individuals (i.e., biological or socialized) is necessarily supportive of the status quo and, hence, antithetical to a women's movement. In contrast, we believe that a psychology that assumes apparent gender differences are the result of differential social forces supports a women's movement by identifying targets for social change.

Notes

The authors wish to thank Jeanne Marecek and two anonymous reviewers for their help.

1. An alternative view envisions the women's movement as a revolutionary movement (Marger, 1987) designed to end the oppression of women by replacing the existing social structure (Hooks, 1984). Whether the women's movement is considered reformational or revolutionary, although important ideologically and in practice, does not matter in the present article, since both perspectives share a common focus on changing social institutions. This focus is at the crux of the present arguments.

References

Albee, G. W. (1986). Toward a just society: Lessons from observations on the primary prevention of psychopathology. *American Psychologist, 41,* 891–898.

Ashmore, R. D., & Del Boca, F. K. (1981). Conceptual approaches to stereotypes and stereotyping. In D. L. Hamilton (Ed.), *Cognitive processes in stereotyping and intergroup behavior.* Hillsdale, NJ: Erlbaum.

Baer, J. L. (1976). *How to be an assertive, not aggressive, woman in life, in love, and on the job: A total guide to self-assertiveness.* New York: Rawson.

Bem, S. L. (1974). The measurement of psychological androgyny. *Journal of Consulting and Clinical Psychology, 42,* 155–162.

Belenky, M. F., Clinchy, B. M., Goldberger, N. R., & Tarule, J. M. (1986). *Women's ways of knowing: The development of self, voice, and mind.* New York: Basic.

Benbow, C. P., & Stanley, J. C. (1980). Sex differences in mathematics ability: Fact or artifact? *Science, 210,* 1262–1264.

Benbow, C. P., & Stanley, J. C. (1982). Consequences in high school and college of sex differences in mathematical reasoning ability: A longitudinal perspective. *American Educational Research Journal, 19,* 598–622.

Benbow, C. P., & Stanley, J. C. (1983). Sex differences in mathematical reasoning ability: More facts. *Science, 222,* 1029–1031.

Broverman, I. K., Vogel, S. R., Broverman, D. M., Clarkson, F. E., & Rosenkrantz, P. S. (1972). Sex-role stereotypes: A current appraisal. *Journal of Social Issues, 28,* 59–78.

Caplan, N., & Nelson, S. D. (1973). On being useful: The nature and consequences of psychological research on social problems. *American Psychologist, 28,* 199–211.

Chodorow, N. J. (1978). *The reproduction of mothering.* Berkeley: University of California Press.

Clance, P. R., & Imes, S. A. (1978). The impostor phenomenon in high achieving women: Dynamics and therapeutic intervention. *Psychotherapy: Theory, Research and Practice, 15,* 241–247.

Clance, P. R., & O'Toole, M. A. (1987). The impostor phenomenon: An internal barrier to empowerment and achievement. *Women and Therapy, 6*(3), 51–64.

Condry, J., & Dyer, S. (1976). Fear of success: Attribution of cause to the victim. *Journal of Social Issues, 32,* 63–84.

Csikszentmihaly, M. (1989, May 28). More ways than one to be good [Review of Mapping the moral domain: A contribution of women's thinking to psychological theory and education]. *New York Times Book Review,* p. 6.

Deaux, K. (1976). *The behavior of women and men.* Monterey, CA: Brooks/Cole.

Deaux, K., & Kite, M. E. (1987). Thinking about gender. In B. B. Hess & M. M. Ferree (Eds.), *Analyzing gender: A handbook of social science research* (pp. 92–117). Newbury Park, CA: Sage.

Deaux, K., & Major, B. (1987). Putting gender into context: An interactive model of gender-related behavior. *Psychological Review, 94,* 369–389.

Dovidio, J. F., Brown, C. E., Heltman, K., Ellyson, S. L., & Keating, C. F. (1988). Power displays between women and men in discussions of gender-linked tasks: A multichannel study. *Journal of Personality and Social Psychology, 55,* 580–587.

Dowling, C. (1981). *The Cinderella complex: Women's hidden fear of independence.* New York: Summit.

Eagly, A. H. (1987). *Sex differences in social behavior: A social-role interpretation.* Hillsdale, NJ: Erlbaum.

Eagly, A. H., & Steffan, V. J. (1984). Gender stereotypes stem from the distribution of women and men into social roles. *Journal of Personality and Social Psychology, 46,* 735–754.

Eisenstein, Z. R. (1984). *Feminism and sexual equality: Crisis in liberal America.* New York: Monthly Review Press.

England, P., & McCreary, L. (1987). Gender inequality in paid employment. In B. B. Hess and M. M. Ferree (Eds.), *Analyzing gender: A handbook of social science research* (pp. 286–320). Newbury Park, CA: Sage.

Fine, M. (1985). Reflections on a feminist psychology of women: Paradoxes and prospects. *Psychology of Women Quarterly, 9,* 167–183.

Freedman, W. J., Robinson, A. B., & Friedman, B. L. (1987). Sex differences in moral judgments? A test of Gilligan's theory. *Psychology of Women Quarterly, 11,* 37–46.

Freeman, J. (1975). *The politics of women's liberation.* New York: McKay.

Freeman, J. (1989). *Women: A feminist perspective* (4th ed.). Mountain View, CA: Mayfield.

Gergen, K. J. (1985). The social constructionist movement in modern psychology. *American Psychologist, 40,* 266–275.

Gerson, K. (1985). *Hard choices: How women decide about work, career, and motherhood.* Berkeley: University of California Press.

Gibbs, J. C., Arnold, K. D., & Burkhart, J. E. (1984). Sex differences in the expression of moral judgment. *Child Development, 55,* 1040–1043.

Giddings, P. (1984). *When and where I enter: The impact of black women on race and sex in America.* New York: Bantam.

Gilligan, C. (1982). *In a different voice: Psychological theory and women's development.* Cambridge, MA: Harvard University Press.

Gilligan, C., Ward, J. V., Taylor, J. M., & Bardige, B. (Eds.). (1989). *Mapping the moral domain: A contribution of women's thinking to psychological theory and education.* Cambridge, MA: Harvard University Press.

Gump, J. P. (1979). Gender differences: Their genesis and regeneration [Review of *The reproduction of mothering: Psychoanalysis and the sociology of gender*]. *Contemporary Psychology, 24,* 657–658.

Gutek, B. A. (1985). *Sex and the workplace.* San Francisco: Jossey-Bass.

Hagen, R. I., & Kahn, A. (1975). Discrimination against competent women. *Journal of Applied Social Psychology, 5,* 362–376.

Hare-Mustin, R. T., & Marecek, J. (1988). The meaning of difference: Gender theory, postmodernism, and psychology. *American Psychologist, 43,* 455–464.

Harvey, C. V. (1987). *Women and self-confidence: How to take charge of your life.* Joliet, IL: Positive Press.

Hewlett, S. A. (1986). *A lesser life: The myth of women's liberation in America.* New York: William Morrow.

Hollander, E. P., & Yoder, J. D. (1980). Some issues in comparing women and men as leaders. *Basic and Applied Social Psychology, 1,* 267–280.

Hooks, B. (1984). *Feminist theory: From margin to center.* Boston, MA: South End Press.

Horner, M. J. (1968). *Sex differences in achievement motivation and performance in competitive-noncompetitive situations.* Unpublished doctoral dissertation, University of Michigan.

Horner, M. J. (1970). Femininity and successful achievement: A basic inconsistency. In J. M. Bardwick, E. Douvan, M. S. Horner, & D. Gutman (Eds.), *Feminine personality and conflict.* Belmont, CA: Brooks/Cole.

Kanter, R. M. (1977). *Men and women of the corporation.* New York: Basic.

Krueger, D. W. (1975). *Success and the fear of success in women.* New York: Harper & Row.

Lott, B. (1981). A feminist critique of androgyny: Toward the elimination of gender attributions for learned behavior. In C. Mayo & N. Henley (Eds.), *Gender and nonverbal behavior* (pp. 171–180). New York: Springer.

Lott, B. (1988). Separate spheres revisited. *Contemporary Social Psychology, 13,* 55–62.

Luker, K. (1984). *Abortion and the politics of motherhood.* Berkeley: University of California Press.

Marger, M. N. (1987). *Elites and masses* (2nd ed.). Belmont, CA: Wadsworth.

Mednick, M. T. (1987). On the politics of psychological constructs: Stop the bandwagon, I want to get off. *American Psychologist, 44,* 1118–1123.

Nieva, V. F., & Gutek, B. A. (1981). *Women and work: A psychological perspective.* New York: Praeger.

Osborn, R. N., & Vicars, W. M. (1976). Sex stereotypes: An artifact in leader behavior and subordinate satisfaction. *Academy of Management Journal, 19,* 439–449.

Paludi, M. A. (1984). Impact of androgynous and traditional sex-role orientations on evaluations of successful performance. *Psychology of Women Quarterly, 8,* 370–375.

Parlee, M. B. (1979). Psychology and women. *Signs, 5,* 121–133.

Prilleltensky, I. (1989). Psychology and the status quo. *American Psychologist, 44,* 795–802.

Russo, N. F., & Denmark, F. L. (1984). Women, psychology, and public policy: Selected issues. *American Psychologist, 39,* 1161–1165.

Ryan, W. (1971). *Blaming the victim.* New York: Pantheon.

Sampson, E. E. (1985). The decentralization of identity: Toward a revised concept of personal and social order. *American Psychologist, 40,* 1203–1211.

Sarason, S. B. (1981). An asocial psychology and a misdirected clinical psychology. *American Psychologist, 36,* 827–836.

Schwartz, F. N. (1989). Management women and the new facts of life. *Harvard Business Review, 89,* 65–76.

Sherif, C. W. (1979). Bias in psychology. In J. A. Sherman & E. T. Beck (Eds.), *The prism of sex: Essays in the sociology of knowledge* (pp. 93–133). Madison: University of Wisconsin Press.

Smetana, J. G. (1984). Morality and gender: A commentary on Prat, Golding, and Hunter. *Merrill-Palmer Quarterly, 30,* 341–348.

Snodgrass, S. E. (1985). Women's intuition: The effect of subordinate role on interpersonal sensitivity. *Journal of Personality and Social Psychology, 49,* 146–155.

Spence, J. T., & Helmreich, R. L. (1978). *Masculinity and femininity: Their psychological dimensions, correlates, and antecedents.* Austin: The University of Texas Press.

Spence, J. T., & Helmreich, R. L. (1983). Achievement-related motives and behaviors. In J. T. Spence (Ed.), *Achievement and achievement motives* (pp. 7–68). San Francisco, CA: Freeman.

Spence, J. T., Helmreich, R., & Stapp, J. (1975). Likability, sex-role congruence of interest, and competence: It all depends on how you ask. *Journal of Applied Social Psychology, 5,* 93–109.

Storms, M. D. (1979). Sex role identity and its relationship to sex role attributes and sex role stereotypes. *Journal of Personality and Social Psychology, 37,* 1779–1789.

Thoma, S. (1986). Estimating gender differences in the comprehension and preferences of moral issues. *Developmental Review, 6,* 165–180.

Tresemer, D. (1976). Do women fear success? *Signs, 1,* 863–874.

Unger, R. K. (1983). Through the looking glass: No wonderland yet! The reciprocal relationship between methodology and models of reality. *Psychology of Women Quarterly, 8,* 9–32.

Unger, R. K. (1989). Psychological, feminist, and personal epistemology: Transcending contradiction. In M. M. Gergen (Ed.), *Feminist thought and the structure of knowledge* (pp. 124–141). New York: New York University Press.

Veroff, J. (1969). Social comparison and the development of achievement motivation. In C. P. Smith (Ed.), *Achievement-related behaviors in children.* New York: Russell Sage.

Veroff, J., Wilcox, S., & Atkinson, J. W. (1953). The achievement motive in high school and college age women. *Journal of Abnormal and Social Psychology, 43,* 108–119.

Walker, L. J. (1984). Sex differences in the development of moral reasoning: A critical review. *Child Development, 55,* 677–691.

Williams, J. E., & Best, D. L. (1982). *Measuring sex stereotypes: A 30-nation study.* Newbury Park, CA: Sage.

Williams, J. H. (1987). *Psychology of women* (3rd ed.). New York: Norton.

Yoder, J. D., Adams, J., Grove, S., & Priest, R. F. (1985). To teach is to learn: Overcoming tokenism with mentors. *Psychology of Women Quarterly, 9,* 119–131.

Young-Eisendrath, P., & Wiedemann, F. L. (1987). *Female authority: Empowering women through psychotherapy.* New York: Guilford.

Zuker, E. (1983). *Mastering assertiveness skills: Power and positive influence at work.* New York: American Management Association.

16
FEMINISM, PSYCHOLOGY, AND THE PARADOX OF POWER

Celia Kitzinger

Power is a word we are all familiar with: we talk about 'will power', 'staying power', 'personal power', 'political power' and the 'powers that be'; the need for checks and balances on power, the responsibilities of power, the abdication of power, the abuse of power, power plays, power games, power dressing; and we know the popular slogans: black power, power to the people, sisterhood is powerful. But what *is* power? Who has it (and how can we tell)? How do we conceptualize and use 'power' as feminists, and as psychologists?

When it comes to answering questions like these, psychology (as usual) arrives late on the scene. Power has been a central concern within other disciplines for a very long time: Aristotle classified political systems according to their internal distribution of power. Machiavelli instructed his prince on how to seize and secure power. Hobbes considered desire for power to be the wellspring of human behaviour. Many philosophers, political scientists, sociologists and anthropologists have placed power centre-stage. Bertrand Russell (1938: 9) claims that 'the fundamental concept in social science is Power, in the same sense in which Energy is the fundamental concept in physics'. According to the sociologist Steven Lukes (1977: 29), 'no social theory merits serious attention that fails to retain an ever present sense of the dialectics of power and structure'.

Approaching the *psychological* literature, it is striking, first, how little the concept of 'power' features. As Rachel Perkins [1991] illustrates in her analysis of clinical psychology, and Erica Burman [1991] documents through a discussion of development psychology, the discipline as a whole is deeply implicated in the maintenance and reproduction of power relation-

Reprinted with permission from Celia Kitzinger, "Feminism, Psychology and the Paradox of Power." *Feminism and Psychology*, 1, 111–129. Copyright 1991, Sage Publications Ltd.

ships which it persistently refuses to make explicit—indeed actively obscures: 'at times, it is as if power were a social obscenity' (Billig et al.,
1988: 147). Secondly, it is striking how naively the concept is typically
used when it does feature in psychological research—in the sense that
there is no apparent awareness of the theoretical debates current in other
disciplines, and 'power' is conceptualized in positivist terms as something
directly observable and measurable, a property possessed by discrete
individuals, an internalized 'motive' which can be measured and then
correlated with other variables in the hope of psychological enlightenment.
For example, in one classic psychological study of power, high scores on
the 'power motive' were (for men) positively correlated with ownership
of sports cars, number of credit cards possessed, and with the likelihood
of their illegally removing towels from motel rooms at the end of their
stay (Winter, 1973).

But whatever the problems in conceptualizing power within the
discipline as a whole, one might expect that *feminist* psychologists would
seriously address the issue. Feminism is, after all, a movement devoted to
the transformation of unequal power relationships. This paper explores
the concept of power as it is used within feminist theory—both within
and beyond psychology; it discusses some of the paradoxes of power
within feminist thinking and the political implications of our different
analyses.

First, the concept of 'power' (certainly in the sense of social and
political power) is simply absent in much feminist psychology. Often, the
word (or its synonyms) is not used at all. Power does not, for example,
appear in the index of Mary Roth Walsh's (1987) *The Psychology of Women*
nor in Corinne Squire's (1989) *Significant Differences: Feminism in Psychology*. Some feminists have pointed out that explicitly political terms tend
to be avoided by successful feminist academics: words like 'patriarchy',
'woman-hating' or 'oppression' are eschewed in favour of 'inequality of
opportunity', 'prejudice' or 'discrimination' (Taking Liberties Collective,
1989: 138). Looking through much of the feminist psychological literature,
it would appear that 'power' falls into the same category. Certainly my
own experience is that when I use the language of power and politics, and
draw on concepts rooted in my understanding of women's oppression,
what I write is labelled 'polemical' or 'political'—and as being in some
sense 'not real psychology' (see Kitzinger, 1990a, for a detailed analysis).
In other words, one reason for the relative absence of concepts of 'power'
and 'powerlessness' from feminist psychology may be because the norms
of academic psychology militate against the use of such overtly political
language.

Second, if the notion of 'power' *is* used, it often functions as a
rhetorical flourish rather than as an integral part of the research. There is

a tradition, in feminist psychology, of ending research and review papers with a caveat about the 'social and political context of male power', but most feminist psychological research does not apply an understanding of this context to the research design or data analysis itself. Consequently, concepts of 'power' (or 'patriarchy' or 'male supremacy') too often have only the status of backdrops or props to a psychological discussion and are not explored in their own right. For example, a chapter in an edited book on feminist psychology ends with these sentences: 'Individual psychological change is not enough. Social change is also required if women's "hysterical misery" is to be converted not only into "common unhappiness", but into the happiness women need, want, and desire' (Sayers, 1986: 37). All well and good—but the entire chapter deals with the problem of individual psychological change for women under headings like 'Repression and Neurosis', 'Introjection and Depression' and 'Projection and Paranoia'. There is a sense of course, in which that is all feminist psychology can do if it is to remain 'psychology'. The (usually) implicit story it commonly tells goes something like this:

> Yes, there are social and political features which cause women's unhappiness, but here, in this chapter, this article, this book, we are talking about the personal and individual ways in which women can deal with their misery, and this is not to *deny* structural and political power, but to *choose a different focus* here, because to do otherwise would be to do sociology, or political theory—and we are psychologists, and this individual and personal focus is our particular area of expertise.

Remaining within the disciplinary confines of 'psychology', then, this has to be the story. This means that the concept of (male) 'power' is often used in feminist psychology as a quality which does not have to be explained, but can be invoked as a dustbin term to summarize a state of affairs. Just as some people invoke 'God' and others invoke 'Nature' at the point where their ability to explain the world runs out, so some feminist psychology invokes 'male power' as a pseudo-explanation. For example, another psychology of women text poses, in the last chapter, the question: 'Why has the female always been defined in male terms?', and the author responds to her own question: 'The answer can be expressed in one word: *power*' (Rohrbaugh, 1981, 463). Without further analysis or exploration this statement is, in effect, tautological: by 'power' she *means* the ability of one group (men) to define another group (women) in their own terms. 'Power' is a convenient way of *summarizing* the situation, but fails to *explain* it. The concept, as Latour (1984) points out, is too often used as 'a pliable and empty term . . . a stopgap solution to cover our ignorance'.

In failing adequately to conceptualize and explore the subject of power, feminist psychology, then, reflects *psychology's* failings. But it also, I think reflects *feminism's*. This leads me to my third point. There is a profound ambivalence about power within feminist theory. On the one hand, feminists have often relied upon a characterization of power as something evil, dangerous and corrupting—a male activity or preoccupation with control and domination which results in violence, rape, the stockpiling of nuclear weapons and the destruction of the planet. 'Power' here clearly carries negative connotations: it is not something any self-respecting feminist would want to get involved with. (In fact, some writers have made the [highly controversial] suggestion that much feminist behaviour can be interpreted as part of an effort to *avoid* the exercise of power— behaviours like downward mobility, opposition to leadership and insistence on collective working, for example [cf. Hartsock, 1983].) On the other hand, we have said that 'sisterhood is powerful', produced feminist books with titles like *Helping Ourselves to Power* (Slipman, 1986), *Womanpower* (Manis, 1984) or *Women of Power* (King, 1989), spoken of women's power as positive, creative, life-affirming, and stated that feminism is a revolutionary movement intending to use political power to transform society. On the surface it looks as though there is a double standard here: male power bad, female power good.

One way of resolving the apparent paradox is by claiming that power in and of itself is neutral—that it is how you *use* power that matters. (Men have obviously used power for evil ends, and it is an act of faith to claim that women would use it better.) As a discursive move, this conveniently shifts attention away from the concept of power (now implicitly defined as a neutral possession), and the concept itself remains tacit and untheorized.

The danger then is that, in leaving the concept of power relatively untheorized, we run the risk of accepting definitions of power which are directly counter to our interests as feminists: we become victims of the categories provided by patriarchy. The concept of 'power' is socially constructed. Anthropological research suggests that there are cultures (Muslim Swahili society is one) in which there is no word for 'power', arguing that the concept is part of *our* (white western) representational model and not suited to cross-cultural comparison since it means that 'we end up asking how do *they* do *our* politics' (Fardon, 1985: 10). Moreover, its complexities of meaning, even in western discourse, are illustrated by the existence of many centuries of debate as to its proper definition— sufficient that many theorists now accept that 'power' (like 'justice' or 'beauty') is an essentially contested concept—meaning, in other words, not just that there is a diversity of operational definitions of power, but that these conceptual disputes cannot be settled by recourse to 'the facts'—

that the concept is ineradicably evaluative (Lukes, 1977). What is necessary, then, is not to seek some elusive 'correct' or 'objective' definition, but rather to locate the different discourses within which power-talk is embedded, to examine the rhetorical functions of different conceptualizations of power, and their sociopolitical implications and effects. In short, we need to deconstruct the different ways in which 'power' is understood within psychology and within feminism, and to construct *our own* theories of power and powerlessness in terms which are useful to us as feminists.

This is, in fact, a frequent explanation for the apparent characterization of 'male power bad', 'female power good' described above. In other words, women (it is said) are eschewing *male* definitions of power and constructing our own alternatives. Male power is bad because male definitions of power rely on concepts of domination, control and coercion. Female power is good because it is a different kind of power. 'Power is also being redefined. Women often explain with care that we mean power to control our lives but not to dominate others' (Steinem, 1983: 156). Lesbian feminist philosopher, Sarah Lucia Hoagland, claims that:

> When men consider questions of power, they focus on state authority, police and armed forces, control of economic resources, control of technology and hierarchy and chain of command. . . . 'Power over' is a matter of dominance and subordination, of bending others to our will. . . . It is the power of control. . . . (Hoagland, 1988: 114).

Lesbians, she suggests, are developing a different understanding of power, which she calls 'power-from-within': this conceptualization of power represents it as 'a matter of centering and remaining steady in our environment as we choose how we direct our energy. Power-from-within is the power of ability, of choice and engagement. It is creative; and hence it is an affecting and transforming power, but not a controlling power' (Hoagland, 1988: 118). The claim is, then, that there are two competing definitions of power, a 'bad' male one and a 'good' female one.

What are we to make of this claim? One obvious response is to point out that feminists who make this claim are quite simply *wrong* in their version of what men understand by 'power'. Many men (at least, male philosophers and political scientists) do *not* represent 'power' merely as external coercion and dominance, or as located primarily in the police, armed forces, and so on. Bertrand Russell (1938), Noam Chomsky (cf. Kitzinger, 1989a), Stephen Lukes (1974) and Michel Foucault (1980) are amongst the more eminent men who have (in their very different ways) stressed that power is *much* more than this naked, overt, visible power, and have emphasized the pervasive and insidious manifestations of power through propaganda, through ideology and false consciousness, and through the technologies of subjectivity (the media, the mental 'health' industry). Another obvious response is to point out that in *claiming* that women's understanding of power is different from that of men, feminists are repeating (albeit with a different value judgement attached) identical claims made by men from Aristotle through Rousseau to Freud about women's different and (implicitly or explicitly) inferior understandings of political issues like justice, ethics and power. Within psychology, the classic study by David McClelland (1975) analyses male and female fantasies of power and concludes that power is 'conceptualized by men as assertion and aggression, by women as nurturance'. So those feminists who *do* assert that men's and women's concepts of power are quite different are hardly making an original claim. In any event, my interest lies not in addressing the empirical issue of whether or not male and female concepts of power are different (nor in making value judgements about whose is objectively 'best') but rather in asking the questions: What *are* the implicit definitions of power underlying feminist theorizing and what are their political implications? With what different functions and meanings do feminists (and feminist psychologists) invest the word 'power'—both male power and female power?

Because power is rarely given an explicit definition in feminist theory, in asking these questions it is necessary to read off those definitions from the way in which the word is used in practice. In so doing, I explore the notions of power underlying two, at first sight contradictory, feminist positions: the arguments that women are *powerless*, and the arguments that women are *powerful*.

There is, in much feminist discourse, a repeated evocation of images of female helplessness, victimization and powerlessness. One set of claims central to this approach relies on the observation that women's lives are determined and ordered externally to us: that we are subjected to rape, murder and other forms of male violence, or to the threat of all these. This form of male power has as direct and immediate an impact over the bodies of its subjects as physical force and coercion. Male power is conceptualized as taking things away from women—our lives, our sexual autonomy, our rights over our bodies, our freedom to walk the streets at night. Male power appropriates women: 'men feed on women's stolen energy, dismember our heritage, erase our traditions' (Daly, 1978). This is a form of power which Foucault (1984: 259) labels 'sovereign' power: 'Power in this instance', he says, 'was essentially a right of seizure: of things, time, bodies, and ultimately life itself.' It is this kind of power that is exercised against long-term mental patients, especially women, who are not only deprived of their liberty, but also given second-class positions (compared with men) within the mental health services (Perkins, 1991: 131–9).

But rooted in this same understanding of 'sovereign power', a parallel image of *female power* is set against the image of female victimization. Many feminists who have taken this approach argue that 'women have always wielded more power than has been apparent, and aspects of women's lives which appear to be restrictive may actually be enabling' (Greene and Kahn, 1985: 8). Many women feel degraded by and angry about feminist theories which present them only in the role of powerless victim: one writer about her work in the sex industry argues that 'it borders on the criminal for feminists to perpetuate the insulting stereotype of sex workers as degraded victims. . . . Sex work at the extreme represents a courageous choice and the conscious determination of the world's poorest women to survive. The prostitute, then, is a fighter and survivor; to reduce her to a pitiable victim is inexcusable' (Roberts, 1990). 'Where ever there is male power', says Dale Spender (1984: 210), 'there has been female resistance'; and she objects to the term 'phallic power', preferring to substitute the term 'willy waggling', on the grounds that 'a mean and petulant antagonist is easier to deal with than a grand enemy' (Spender, 1984: 210). According to this argument, to accept oppression as the meaning of our lives as women is to overlook the threat we pose—worse, makes us complicit with the victimizers. Power is not something only men possess, not 'a property, stamped all the way through like a stick of rock with the definition "men only"' (Miles, 1985: 81). Women's powers are 'the powers of the weak' (Janeway, 1980)—the exercise of personal agency under oppression. Some historians argue, for example, that the supposed 'sexual repression' of Victorian women provided them with a means of control over reproduction and an opportunity for resisting compulsory heterosexuality (e.g. Jeffreys, 1985), and some anthropologists suggest that male fear of menstruation, and women's retreat to menstrual huts, has been engineered by women for similar purposes (e.g. Kitzinger, S., 1978). Against men's overt powers are set women's covert powers, and a celebration of women's survival and achievement against the odds.

Another, more 'psychological' set of claims about female powerlessness relies on the argument that rape, violence and other forms of explicit exclusion, appropriation and coercion are only the most obvious forms of male power. Women are damaged, mutilated, not just physically but also psychologically: our minds, our very selves, are warped by patriarchy. Marge Piercy compares women to bonsai trees, that might have grown eighty feet tall on the side of a mountain, but are carefully pruned to nine inches high:

With living creatures
one must begin very early
to dwarf their growth:

the bound feet,
the crippled brain
the hair in curlers,
the hands you
love to touch.

In this analysis, the monolithic brutality of male power has reduced women almost to the status of non-persons: indeed, Mary Daly (1978) describes women as 'moronized', 'robotized', 'the puppets of Papa' and 'fembots'. Language like this certainly reinforces the image of female powerlessness: it suggests that women are so indoctrinated, conditioned and brainwashed that we are incapable of taking power even in those areas where we might be offered it.

One definition of power, common in much of the older sociological and philosophical literatures, is power as the freedom to act as you choose (e.g. Nagel, 1975; Russell, 1938: 25). The problem is that if the female self under male domination is riddled through and through with false desires, then women's 'choices' too are constructed under male supremacy. There is a fundamental paradox in insisting on women's 'right to choose' while simultaneously characterizing women's choices (or a subset of them) as determined by the internalized dictates of male power (a paradox discussed by, amongst others, Cartledge, 1983; Hoagland, 1988; Kitzinger, 1988). One difficulty with the latter position is that it forecloses the possibility of women acting autonomously (except possibly for a minority of women with raised consciousnesses). As one writer argues, such accounts:

> . . . are implicitly divisive and threatening. They are divisive because they have a tendency to divide women into two camps; those who have and those who have not shaken the dust of patriarchal conditioning from their feet. And they are threatening, because it is offensive and undermining to be told that the life one has led has merely been one of servility, that it has not been of truly 'human' value, that one has been a 'fembot' or a 'puppet' (Grimshaw, 1988: 97).

It is this implicit conception of power, however, that is very common in feminist psychology: and when it surfaces here another difficulty becomes apparent. Because the problem of male power is now located *inside women's heads*, the solution to male power is located there too. Feminist psychologists describe the effects of male power on women's minds—our alleged loss of self-esteem, self-hatred, internalized sexism and homophobia, inferiority complex, fear of success—and then attempt to 'cure' women, (or, to use the preferred language, 'empower' women) from their own position as women who know better. The target of resistance to male power becomes women's minds.

Colette Dowling, author of *The Cinderella Complex*, argues that women suffer from a fear of independence and sit around waiting for a prince to come and rescue them. In constructing her argument, she draws heavily on psychological research into women's alleged 'fear of success' and 'external locus of control', on psychological analyses of women's allegedly 'deferential' and 'helpless' body language and self-deprecating verbal style. Using such research, much of it produced by feminist psychologists (e.g. Judith Bardwick, Janet Hyde, Jean Baker Miller) she describes women as 'vulnerable', 'unsure', 'crippled', 'frightened', 'helpless', 'fearful', 'passive' and 'dependent'. She too was once like this. Then she discovered therapy. She says:

> We have only one real shot at 'liberation' and that is to emancipate ourselves from within. *It is the thesis of this book that personal psychological dependency— the deep wish to be taken care of by others—is the chief force holding women down today* (Dowling, 1981: 27, emphasis in original).

And you thought it was patriarchy!

The core problem, as I see it, with this conception of 'power' is *not* just that it is humiliating for women to be described in this way. It *may* indeed feel humiliating, despairing, shocking, to acknowledge the extent and pervasiveness of our oppression. The experience of becoming a feminist is not, necessarily, one of joyous recognition of women's power:

> My entry to the women's movement has led to feelings of vulnerability, despair, and shock. That cannot be denied. For identifying with women, instead of men, means taking on, in part, the notion of one's powerlessness, victimisation, and lack of resources. In my own head, for example, I was much less exposed to the danger of rape when I believed that the women who were raped contributed to it in some way, for after all there was no way *I* would provoke or initiate such an attack. Recognising now that *all* women are potentially rape victims, that most rapists are known to their victims, that the object of rape is domination, I no longer have that (false) security that it won't happen to me (Spender 1984: 211).

As Leah Fritz (1979: 237) has argued, 'feminists eschew false pride. For a slave to be a victim, to *admit* she is a victim, is not ignominious.' (Of course, claiming your *own* victimhood is one thing—labelling other women as victims while believing [openly or secretly] that *you* have escaped or transcended most or all of the 'conditioning' or 'brainwashing' is quite another; cf. Hanish, 1971; Leon, 1978; Price, 1972; all early second-wave feminists who produced searing critiques of 'feminist psychology's' line on 'sex role socialization' and 'conditioning', in part on these grounds.) Nor do I think the central problem with this account of female powerlessness lies, as others (e.g. Grimshaw, 1988: 96) suggest, in its overly monolithic account of male power: in some ways the 'conditioning' line *under*estimates male power, by suggesting that if only women understood they were free, they would be—as though there are no real social penalties and punishments attached to stepping out of line, and methods for enforcing conformity.

I think the core problem with this version of power lies in its conceptualization of authenticity or selfhood for women. If power is seen as imposing 'false' consciousness, inauthentic desires and preferences upon women, then there is a concept of a true authentic inner self, which can spontaneously generate its own actions and free choices, a self that *could be free* of external influences. It is this image of an authentic self that is promoted in a great deal of US psychology which aims to liberate 'the child within'—the free spirit, untouched by social oppression. It is this image that provides feminist psychologists with a discourse of female *power* which is set against the opposing discourse of female powerlessness.

Many feminists represent women's power as arising out of our 're-claiming' this essential inner self, our authentic womanhood and spiritual creativity—the power within. Power is represented as 'standing for the first time inside the self' (Morgan, 1989: 330); a woman is powerful when she 'enters her own psychic and psychological space . . . beyond patriarchy's midnight' (p. 329). A recent book, *Woman of Power*, was given that title, the author says,

> . . . because I feel these women are connected in some way to a spiritual source of inspiration and knowledge. To me, spirit comes through one's heart and intuition. I believe they have learned to honour their own wisdom and therein lies their power (King, 1989: 2).

'Power' here means 'learning to honour your own wisdom' and being 'connected to a spiritual source of inspiration'. The same book has maxims telling you how *you* too can be 'a woman of power', e.g.:

> Follow your compass of joy. . . . Discover your vocation of destiny . . . find your life partners and do the work together in resonance with the evolution of our planet as a whole.

A feminist magazine, called *Woman of Power*, states as its editorial philosophy that:

Our power as women arises from our understanding of interconnectedness: with all people, all forms of life, the earth, and the cycles and seasons of nature and our lives (1987: 1).

'Power', in this formulation, is simply 'an understanding'. This same magazine includes, amongst articles with titles like, 'Reclaiming the Spirit of Life', 'Restoring the Goddess', and 'The Wise Woman Tradition' contributions from Jean Baker Miller (author of the classic *Toward a New Psychology of Women*, 1976), and Laura Brown, a clinical psychologist at the University of Washington. According to Laura Brown:

> . . . part of what I do with the people I work with in therapy is to point out to them that they are already powerful in ways that the culture does not define as being powerful (quoted in Malina, 1987).

Power, then, is an awareness, an understanding, a realization *that you already have power*, albeit power that the culture does not recognize.

Browsing through the bookstall at the Association for Women in Psychology (AWP) annual conference in Arizona (March, 1990), I jotted down the following titles: they give a flavour of the task faced by women who want this type of 'power', and make very clear where that power is located: *Journey into Me; The Journey Within; Healing the Child Within; A Gift to Myself; How to Accept Yourself; How to Live Your Own Life.*

Or, instead of resorting to self-help books in your search for power, you can try feminist therapists. (The following quotations are taken from publicity material distributed at the AWP annual conference in Arizona.) How about joining a 'Woman's Healing Circle' where you can 'reclaim the loving power of the Goddess, bloom forth in the eternal dance of cosmic circle's renewal' with Sonia Ganz, PhD, who (after listing her academic qualifications) describes herself as 'Keeper of the flame, weaving Her Golden Net of Great Mystery and Magick in the Global Dance of Women's Healing Circles': she 'creates ceremonies and rituals, she calls and invokes the Wise Woman Within You' (advertising flier). Sage Freechild, a professional counsellor and bodywork therapist, who specializes in creative visualization and guided meditation, wants to help her clients 'reach a centered place. . . . Through the integration of physical, mental, and spiritual energies, clients are empowered to make clearer choices based on full awareness' (advertising flier). A poster advertising a 'Women in Power' seminar facilitated by a 'spiritual psychologist, healer, and founder of the Inner Light Center of Sedona, who playfully and lovingly assists people in moving from fear into their power and full potential' announces that the seminar will enable participants to:

- Expand Your Limits
- Remove Unconscious Blocks
- Rewrite the Script of Your Life to Recreate a New You
- Learn to Receive Love, Money & Inner Peace
- Understand Unconscious Hopes and Fears Which Govern Your Relationships
- Learn the Truth About Your Personal Laws.

Lest all this sound like the wildest excesses of US individualism run amok, a fringe psychobabble without relevance to feminist psychology overall, let me refer you to the same themes in writings widely read and acclaimed within mainstream feminist psychology, like Carol Gilligan's *In a Different Voice* and Belenky et al.'s *Women's Ways of Knowing*. Gilligan (1972) uses the myth of Persephone, kidnapped and raped by the King of the Under-world, as symbolizing *women's power* (!) and draws heavily on a psychological study by David McClelland (entitled *Power: The Inner Experience*) in claiming (like him) that women experience power through nurturance, care and connection. Belenky and her colleagues open their book with the following statement:

> In this book we describe the ways of knowing that women have cultivated and learned to value, ways we have come to believe are powerful but have been neglected and denigrated [*sic*] by the dominant intellectual ethos of our time.

These ways of knowing turn out to be intuitive, subjective, rooted in 'the inner voice', 'the inner expert', 'connected knowing' and involving 'the reclamation of the self'. When feminist psychologists reject positivism, they frequently resort to this type of subjective, internal, semi-mystical alternative.

The problem with this conception of power is that, in turning the spotlight on women's power as residing inside the self, other sources of our power (and powerlessness) are plunged into darkness.

If women are so powerful, then it is your own fault if you got raped, or battered, or if you have not received love, money and inner peace. Louise Hay, author of *You Can Heal Your Life*, makes this explicit in her explanation of how to cure yourself of cancer and AIDS through the power of positive thinking. According to her 'the mental patterns that create AIDS are similar to those that create cancer (deep hurt, resentment, and self-hatred), although it has the added factor of sexual guilt' (cf. King, 1989: 139):

We are each 100 percent responsible for all of our experiences. Every thought we think is creating our future. We create every so-called 'illness' in our body. The point of power is always in the present moment. Everyone suffers from self-hated and guilt. It's only a thought and a thought can be changed. Self-approval and self-acceptance in the now are the key to positive changes (quoted in King, 1989: 135).

The notion of 'empowerment', which is *much* more common in feminist psychology than the notion of 'power', relies on developing in women this sense of personal agency. It attempts to create in women a certain state of mind (feeling powerful, competent, worthy of esteem, able to make free choices and influence their world) *while leaving the structural conditions unchanged*. One feminist therapist states explicitly that her purpose is to help women to find ways of 'enacting one's wholeness within the context of society as it is' (Heriot, 1985: 27).

Obviously a sense of personal empowerment can sometimes make us feel much better about ourselves than does a passive fatalism about life, but I think we should be concerned about the near-exclusive focus on 'empowerment' in psychology—a catchword applied to a host of therapeutic techniques. 'Empowerment' carries good vibes—is personal, internal, private, subjective experience—but insofar as this represents the extent of psychology's engagement with the concept of 'power', we need, at the very least to think carefully about its political implications. Drawing upon psychological research allegedly proving that rapists, when shown videos of women in crowds or dangerous situations, tend to pick out the same women as potential victims, a journalist writing in *New Woman* magazine, argues that there is 'a victim look': if you get raped it is your own fault for projecting the wrong image and for having the wrong kind of beliefs about power. Power, she says is internal—a belief in yourself, not something you exert in the world outside—and women who attract rapists lack the proper mental set: 'a victim is someone who feels she doesn't have power' (Morris, 1990). When, as psychologists, we focus on power as an internal individualistic possession, we permit and encourage precisely these kinds of victim-blaming accounts. Jenny Kitzinger (1990) has analysed the political implication of the child sexual abuse prevention programmes that focus on 'empowering' children by telling them they have the right to say 'no': children are told to 'speak up, say no', that 'you're in charge', and taught catchy jingles like 'My body's nobody's body but mine'. Power is seen in individualistic terms as something that can be 'claimed' or 'given away' by a five-year-old. A follow-up study found that, after one prevention programme, children were *more* likely to believe that if they were abused it was their own fault: victimization was seen as evidence of collusion. This is a logical outcome of the messages conveyed in these (and similar) programmes. 'Telling children that they "have" certain rights', she says 'is not enough. They need some idea of the forces which deny them those rights and ways of fighting back. Powerlessness is *not* "all in the mind"' (Kitzinger, J., 1990).

Interestingly, feminist psychologists recognize this when they write about their *own* experiences of power and powerlessness as psychologists. Such discussions are remarkable for their absence of internal, private, individualized explanations for women's powerlessness: they focus almost exclusively on structural and political constraints. One excellent chapter describes the struggle of women psychologists to achieve representation within the national psychological societies, especially the British Psychological Society (BPS) (Wilkinson, 1990). Not once does the author ascribe women's difficulties in achieving representation to their lack of confidence, external locus of control, learned helplessness, fear of success or need for 'assertiveness training' or 'empowering' therapy. Nor does she suggest that men's power in the BPS is compensated for by women psychologists' superior moral and spiritual power. Instead, she focuses on the organization of disciplinary structures, the dominance of the positivist mode of inquiry, and the patriarchal nature of the BPS. As she recounts, the initial proposal for a Psychology of Women section within the BPS was rejected. Eighteen months later, the second proposal was accepted. How does Sue Wilkinson explain this? Not once does she suggest that in the interim she and her colleagues had removed their unconscious blocs, rewritten the scripts of their lives, and understood the symbolic hopes and personal fears which governed their relationships. Instead, she explains it in terms of having 'learnt a great deal about the procedures and practices of the BPS as an extremely patriarchal, bureaucratic institution', having 'rewritten the proposal using successful section proposals as a model of academic respectability', and sought letters of support from 'big name individuals in the field'. In other words, they learned to play the system.

Feminist psychologists, then, do have access to an explicitly political discourse of power. This discourse is rarely used, however, except when feminist psychologists are writing about their *own* power struggles within the discipline of psychology. And then it becomes, of necessity, a 'socio-political' rather than a 'psychological' analysis (cf. the earlier unpublished version of Sue Wilkinson's paper subtitled 'A *Socio-political* Analysis of Institutional Constraints on Scholarship and Action').

Finally, a very different conceptualization of power is emerging from a minority of feminist psychologists (e.g. Burman, 1990; Kitzinger, 1987; Morawski, 1988; Walkerdine and Lucey, 1989) who draw on (even as they criticize) post-structuralist approaches, especially as represented by the work of Foucault. An important feature of Foucault's (1984: 60–1) analysis of power is his observation that power is not simply repressive and prohibitive—something external to the individual which prevents action and suppresses full human development: rather power is *productive*, that is, produces our very concepts of individuality, of full human development, our knowledge of the world. To take an example from my own work (Kitzinger, 1987, 1989b), patriarchal power does not simply forbid lesbianism and punish lesbians, it also (through sexological and psychological theorizing) constructs and regulates lesbian identities.

The central focus of post-structuralism is on language. Our sense of who we are and who we can be—our identities and subjectivities—are, according to post-structuralism, constituted by the language we use, through a myriad of 'discursive practices' (practices of talk, text, writing, representation) which position us in the world. The identities and subjectivities we evolve are due not to something intrinsic 'in' us (an essential, true, inner 'female' or 'lesbian' self), but are defined by the categories made available to us in the language we use, and by the meanings and contents ascribed to those categories. Power is implicated in attempts to define these categories and their meanings, to privilege some identities at the expense of others. Hence, power is not simply something which represses and denies individual identity, but rather promotes, cultivates and nurtures (particular types of) identity. Power is not a force which acts on individuals from the outside, at a distance: it is intimately involved in the construction of the individual and her sense of selfhood. Power and knowledge, then, are inextricably connected and 'psychology occupies a key role in the maintenance and regulation of prevailing power relations and gendered arrangements' (Burman, 1990): knowledge is itself a form of politics.

One feature of this conception of power is its inherently unstable expression: it exists not as a monolithic, all-encompassing strategy, but as shifting terrain of professional and everyday discourses. Female experience, the central focus of much feminist analysis, is itself structured by the social relations, knowledge and language of a patriarchal culture. The notion of the free, autonomous, self-fulfilled and authentic woman possessed of a personal power innocent of coercion—an ideal which informs most feminist psychological engagement with the concept of power—is simply an individualist myth which actively obscures the operation of power. When feminist psychologists attempt to foster the development of this kind of 'self' in themselves or in other women (through 'empowerment') instead of challenging the operation of power they participate in it.

The main strengths of this approach for feminist psychologists concerned adequately to conceptualize 'power' lie, I think, in two areas: first, in emphasizing the role of psychology in reproducing and maintaining existing power relations; and, second, in addressing an explicit *politics* of subjectivity. Together, these two overlapping emphases on the role of disciplinary power in constituting subjective experience, challenge both the feminist psychologist's often trite 'acceptance' and 'validation' of all women's inner experience as the final test of theory and arbiter of truth *and* her arrogant notion that, by virtue of her own raised consciousness, she can 'explain' (away) other women's accounts as rooted in patriarchal conditioning. Insofar as post-structuralism has introduced into feminist psychology some understanding of psychology's own location and operation as a 'technology of subjectivity' and of the extent to which our experience as women and as lesbians is determined and constituted by power, it has been of (albeit limited) value. The central irony is, of course, that varying expressions of these ideas (as well as competing notions about women's 'essential' selves, and parallel discussions about the material effects of male power and female resistance) have been around within grassroots feminism for a very long time, and in a much more accessible and politically relevant form. It is an indictment of 'feminist psychology' that its proponents apparently can avail themselves of these ideas only when presented with them in the form of 'fancy theory' (Morawski, 1988: 184) permeated with the 'strange cult of obscurantism' (Clegg, 1989: 152) that surrounds post-structuralism. There is too the danger that, in drawing on post-structuralism rather than grassroots feminism for an analysis of women's power and powerlessness, 'feminist psychologists' are simply mimicking prestigious male-centred theory in order to secure their own position within manned academia.

But the problems for feminists in drawing on post-structuralism for understandings of power and powerlessness go well beyond the inaccessibility and rampant mystification of the language within which the theory is couched. Post-structuralism embraces a pluralist view of power which militates against the identification of any particular group (e.g. men) as 'powerful'. As Erica Burman points out:

> The overall problem concerns the approach's inability to ally itself with any explicit political position; and following from this, a deliberate distancing and 'deconstruction' of any progressive political program. . . . For deconstruction to join forces with feminism and socialism would be to prioritise particular textual readings in a way that is utterly antithetical to its intent (Burman, 1990: 210–11).

Post-structuralism offers a 'legitimate' academic framework within which feminist academics can write with apparent credibility. But in deferring to what Burman (1990: 213) describes as post-structuralism's '"facilitating" mantle', we are made rationally invisible as *feminists*, and our work is appropriated by and 'incorporated' within a male-defined theoretical position. Moreover, in directing our attention to the technology of symbolic power (representation, discourse, language, the text), post-structuralism turns our attention away from (even when it does not explicitly deny the existence of) the material realities of women's oppression. We cannot stop rape, murder, sexual abuse and oppressive legislation simply by changing symbolic representations of them. Some writers, inspired by post-structuralism's focus on discourse and subjectivity, seem not to realize this, and are now suggesting that 'the notion of power should be abandoned' (Latour, 1984), that we should 'dispense with the term power and begin to talk instead of regulatory practices of the self' (Miller, 1987: 17). To abandon the word 'power', to replace it with euphemisms which disguise the violence of our oppression and the courage of our resistance, is antithetical to feminist politics.

As feminists it is important to address the concept of power and to clarify the meanings we intend by it. Contending concepts are not morally and politically neutral. How we conceptualize power reflects in part what it is we think requires explanation and what we consider a good explanation of it. It affects the questions we can ask about male power, and about female power, and where we are likely to look for the answers. Finally, it behooves us to select our definitions of power with care because the definitions we decide to use reflect and construct our practical strategies—our feminist vision, our feminist politics.

Notes

An abbreviated version of this paper was presented at the British Psychological Society Annual Conference in Swansea (April, 1990) as part of the Psychology of Women Section Symposium, convened by the author and entitled 'Power and Powerlessness: Developing Theory and Practice'. I am grateful to the other symposium participants, Erica Burman, Jenny Kitzinger, Paula Nicolson and Rachel Perkins, for stimulating discussions on the topic and I appreciate the editorial suggestions offered by Chris Griffin and Sue Wilkinson. I extend special thanks to both Jenny Kitzinger and Sheila Kitzinger for their detailed criticism of earlier drafts of this paper, which was written while the author was in the Department of Psychology at the Polytechnic of East London.

References

Belenky, M. F., Clinchy, B. M., Goldberger, N. R., and Tarule, J. M. (1986) *Women's Ways of Knowing: The Development of Self, Voice and Mind*. New York: Basic Books.
Billig, M., Condor, S., Edwards, D., Gane, M., Middleton, D., and Radley, A. R. (1988) *Ideological Dilemmas*. London: Sage.

Burman, E. (1990) 'Differing with Deconstruction: A Feminist Critique', in I. Parker and J. Shotter (eds) *Deconstructing Social Psychology*. London: Routledge.

Burman, E. (1991) 'Power, gender and developmental psychology', *Feminism & Psychology* 1(1):141–54.

Cartledge, S. (1983) 'Duty and Desire: Creating a Feminist Morality', in S. Cartledge and Joanna Ryan (eds) *Sex and Love: New Thoughts on Old Contradictions*. London: The Women's Press.

Clegg, S. R. (1989) *Frameworks of Power*. London: Sage.

Daly, M. (1978) *Gyn/Ecology: The Metaethics of Radical Feminism*. London: The Women's Press.

Dowling, C. (1981) *The Cinderella Complex: Women's Hidden Fear of Independence*. London: Fontana.

Fardon, R. (1985) 'Introduction: A Sense of Relevance', in R. Fardon (ed.) *Power and Knowledge: Anthropological and Sociological Approaches*. Edinburgh: Scottish Academic Press.

Foucault, M. (1980) In C. Gordon (ed.) *Power/Knowledge: Selected Interviews and Other Writings 1972–1977*. Brighton: Harvester.

Foucault, M. (1984) *The History of Sexuality*. Harmondsworth: Peregrine.

Foucault, M. (1986) 'Disciplinary Power and Subjection', in S. Lukes (ed.) *Power*. Oxford: Blackwell.

Fritz, L. (1979) *Dreamers and Dealers: An Intimate Appraisal of the Women's Movement*. Boston: Beacon Press.

Gilligan, C. (1972) *In a Different Voice*. Harvard: Cambridge University Press.

Grimshaw, J. (1988) 'Autonomy and Identity in Feminist Thinking', in M. Griffiths and M. Whitford (eds) *Feminist Perspectives in Philosophy*. London: Macmillan.

Hanish, C. (1971) 'Male Psychology: A Myth to Keep Women in Their Place', reprinted in Redstockings (ed.) *Feminist Revolution*. New York: Random House, 1978.

Hartsock, N. (1983) *Money, Sex, and Power: Toward a Feminist Historical Materialism*. New York: Longman.

Heriot, J. (1985) 'The Double Bind: Healing the Split', in J. H. Robbins, and R. J. Siegel (eds) *Women Changing Therapy: New Assessments, Values and Strategies in Feminist Therapy*. New York: Harrington Park Press.

Hoagland, S. L. (1988) *Lesbian Ethics: Toward New Value*. Palo Alto, CA: Institute of Lesbian Studies.

Janeway, E. (1980) *Powers of the Weak*. New York: Alfred A. Knopf.

Jeffreys, S. (1985) *The Spinster and Her Enemies: Feminism and Sexuality 1880–1930*. London: Pandora.

King, L. (1989) *Women of Power*. Berkeley, CA: Celestial Arts.

Kitzinger, C. (1987) *The Social Construction of Lesbianism*. London: Sage.

Kitzinger, C. (1988) 'Sexuality: Cause, Choice and Construction', *Lesbian and Gay Socialist* 15: 18–19.

Kitzinger, C. (1989a) 'Noam Chomsky: American Dissident', Profile in *The Psychologist*, May: 206–8.

Kitzinger, C. (1989b) 'Liberal Humanism as an Ideology of Social Control: The Regulation of Lesbian Identities', in J. Shotter and K. Gergen (eds) *Texts of Identity*. London: Sage.

Kitzinger, C. (1990a) 'Resisting the Discipline', in E. Burman (ed.) *Feminists and Psychological Practice*, pp. 119–36. London: Sage.

Kitzinger, J. (1990) 'Who are You Kidding? Power and Child Sexual Abuse Prevention Programs', unpublished paper, available from AIDS-Media Unit, University of Glasgow.

Kitzinger, S. (1978) *Women as Mothers*. London: Fontana.

Latour, B. (1984) 'The Powers of Association', in J. Law (ed.) *Power, Action and Belief: A New Sociology of Knowledge*. Sociological Review Monographs 32. London: Routledge & Kegan Paul.

Leon, B. (1978) 'Consequences of the Conditioning Line', in Redstockings (ed.) *Feminist Revolution*. New York: Random House, 1978.

Lukes, S. (1974) *Power: A Radical View*. London: Macmillan.

Lukes, S. (1977) 'On the Relativity of Power', in S. C. Brown (ed.) *Philosophical Disputes in the Social Sciences*. Brighton: Harvester Press.

Malina, D. (1987) 'On Integrity and Integration: Towards a Feminist Vision of Psychology', *Women of Power: A Magazine of Feminism, Spirituality and Politics* 5: 14–17.

Manis, L. G. (1984) *Womanpower: A Manual for Workshops in Personal Effectiveness*. Cranston, RI: Carroll Press.

McClelland, D. C. (1975) *Power: The Inner Experience*. Irvington: New York.

Miles, R. (1985) *Women and Power*. London: Macdonald.

Miller, P. (1987) *Domination and Power*. London: Routledge & Kegan Paul.

Morawski, J. (1988) 'Impasse in Feminist Thought', in M. M. Gergen (ed.) *Feminist Thought and the Structure of Knowledge*. New York: New York University Press.

Morgan, R. (1989) *The Demon Lover: On the Sexuality of Terrorism*. New York: Norton.

Morris, M. (1990) 'Is It Within Your Power?', *New Woman* (July): 58–60.

Nagel, J. H. (1975) *The Descriptive Analysis of Power*. New Haven: Yale University Press.

Perkins, R. E. (1991) 'Women With Long-term Mental Health Problems: Issues of Power and Powerlessness', *Feminism & Psychology* 1(1): 131–9.

Price, C. (1972) 'Up Against Conditioning', reprinted in Redstockings (ed.) *Feminist Revolution*. New York: Random House, 1978.

Roberts, N. (1990) 'The Making of Pornography' (Letter), *Spare Rib* 214 (July): 4.

Rohrbaugh, J. B. (1981) *Women: Psychology's Puzzle*. London: Abacus/Sphere.

Russell, B. (1938) *Power: A New Social Analysis*. London: Unwin Books.

Sayers, J. (1986) 'Sexual Identity and Difference: Psychoanalytic Perspectives', in S. Wilkinson (ed.) *Feminist Social Psychology: Developing Theory and Practice*. Milton Keynes: Open University Press.

Slipman, S. (1986) *Helping Ourselves to Power: A Handbook for Women on the Skills of Public Life*. Oxford: Pergamon.

Spender, D. (1984) in R. Rowland (ed.) *Women Who Do and Women Who Don't Join the Women's Movement*. London: Routledge & Kegan Paul.

Steinem, G. (1983) 'Words and Change', in *Outrageous Acts and Everyday Rebellions*. London: Flamingo/Fontana.

Squire, C. (1989) *Significant Differences: Feminism in Psychology*. London: Routledge.

Taking Liberties Collective (1989) *Learning the Hard Way: Women's Oppression in Men's Education*. London: Macmillan.

Walkerdine, V. and Lucey, H. (1989) *Democracy in the Kitchen: Regulating Mothers and Socialising Daughters*. London: Virago.

Walsh, M. R., ed. (1987) *The Psychology of Women*. New Haven: Yale University Press.

Wilkinson, S. (1990) Part 1 of S. Wilkinson and J. Burns, 'Women Organizing within Psychology: Two Accounts', in E. Burman (ed.) *Feminists and Psychological Practice*, pp. 140–51. London: Sage.

Winter, D. (1973) *The Power Motive*. New York: Free Press.

17
DIFFERING WITH DECONSTRUCTION: A FEMINIST CRITIQUE

Erica Burman

As [*Deconstructing Social Psychology*] testifies, deconstruction, and associated post-structuralist ideas have been used in psychology in a number of ways. As a feminist I have felt wary and even hostile to these approaches, and not only because of the complexity and commitment to theory that its deployment presupposed. In this chapter I outline the political challenges presented by deconstruction, not only those through which they are used to critique psychology, but also the difficulties that the use of these methods present to the maintenance of a progressive politics. It is worth, however, briefly summarising deconstruction's progressive possibilities before moving on to look at the problems.

Promises

1. Attention is drawn to the materiality of language: discourse is seen as constitutive of and linked to practice, hence it is possible to theorise psychology's relationship to social practices as both reflective and productive. Rose (1985), for example, highlights how the domain of 'individual psychology', focused around the key concepts of 'ability' and 'temperament', developed to provide the technology to segregate and classify people through personality and intelligence testing; to differentiate the 'fit' from the 'feebleminded', and to diagnose indications of 'degeneracy'

and 'delinquency'. Thus its subsequent history traces the struggle to legitimise that 'expertise', to maintain its monopoly on its administration.

2. The approach succeeds in relativising psychology, and highlighting the historical variability of discursive relations. This affords a clearer method and perspective of theorising our own positions in relation to psychological practices, and enables us to identify progressive or reactionary features of discourses according to our purposes. For example, the 'human rights' discourse of 'normalisation' which is so prevalent in mental handicap can be seen to be gender insensitive (Adcock and Newbigging 1990); the discourse of protection and violation of innocence surrounding child abuse denies childhood sexuality and correspondingly positions a 'knowing' child as culpable (Kitzinger 1988); the child-centered discourse of 'natural needs' can skate over issues of school racism as 'adolescent peer group problems' (Warren 1988).

3. Deconstruction focuses on dominance, contradiction and difference: in highlighting the multiplicity of positions afforded by competing discourses and their contradictory effects, it enables us to envisage ways of disrupting the dominant discourse and to construct positions of resistance. So, for example, Steedman (1982) points out how young girls can use their extending symbolic repertoire to reflect upon and transcend their social positions; Walden and Walkerdine (1982) highlight the gendered culture of early education as providing an environment in which girls are supported and encouraged to be successful (in marked contrast with later schooling); and Hudson (1984) suggests that young women adopt the discourse of 'adolescence' as a strategy to escape the more confining definitions of behaviour and opportunities permitted by 'femininity'.

4. Deconstruction also introduces a politics of subjectivity: This accounts for the dynamics of subordination, including female 'narcissism' and even 'masochism' as constructed through cultural forces, and it has prompted powerful analyses of pornography and media representations of women, as well as more theoretical analysis of women's excursion from systems of representation as their constitutive feature. This work is empowering in so far as it avoids positioning women as passive victims. Now women are beginning to challenge the traditional relations and idealised images set up in technologies of representation (Spence 1986). Moreover, these accounts highlight the absences, resistances and denials of psychology as a gendered practice.

5. When Foucault's (1979a) work is brought in, it provides a description of power. What we can gain, then, from post-structuralist critiques in psychology is a framework to trace, theorise and talk about the power relations it both participates in and gives rise to. So, for example, Walkerdine (1981) accounts for a group of three-year-old boys' verbal sexual harassment of their nursery school teacher in terms of their strategic

adoption of masculine discourse, which positions them as dominant in relation to a female teacher, to counter their otherwise subordinate position as pupils. The teacher, however is disempowered from resisting through her subscription to a 'child-centred' pedagogy which positions her as powerless to interfere in the 'natural' course of children's development. Three major issues follow from this analysis: first, the child-centred model, arising out of post-Darwinian evolutionary theory, presents an asocial model of development as an organic unfolding of inherent abilities (Venn and Walkerdine 1978) which denies or neglects gender relations and specificities (Urwin 1986). Second, drawing attention to the gendered culture of early (and in different ways later) education has implications for our understanding of the relative progress and achievements of girls and boys. Third, the discourse of child-centredness, with its notions of 'readiness', 'treating each child as an individual', 'learning through play', and 'interest-driven learning' accords so little agency to teachers or schools as responsible for children's educational progress that the only explanation available to account for failure is one which lapses into a cultural or class deficit model (Sharp and Green 1975). Hence 'progressive education' as enshrined in the 'positive discriminatory' policies of the Plowden Report is shown to slip into victim blaming, taking the child as responsible for their disadvantage and treating this as an unalterable quality of the individual which is unamenable to intervention.

These, then are some of the powerful analyses made available by deconstruction and post-structuralism. Yet despite the powerful practical and conceptual apparatus these offer to a feminist critique of psychology, there are also areas in which post-structuralists and fellow travellers and the now attendant culture of deconstruction—postmodernity—are fundamentally at variance with this project.

Conflicts and Commonalities

The overall problem concerns the approach's inability to ally itself with any explicit political position; and following from this, a deliberate distancing and 'deconstruction' of any progressive political program. Indeed, a key feature of 'deconstruction' is its explicit critique and proscription of any commitment to a conception of history as moving forwards. Teleology is seen as one of the key characteristics of the modernist movement it seeks to deconstruct, and all utopias are branded as idealist, unattainable, and metaphysical. This is all very well when we want to use deconstruction to highlight the underlying political program of psychology as reproducing and perpetuating a liberal humanist ideology of the rational uniform subject. Here deconstruction allows us to highlight the default politics at work, the cultural imperialism, the individualisation and denial of oppression, and ultimately the reinstatement of the mind-body, self-other, emotion-reason oppositions that have structured western philosophy and politics since the 'coincidental meeting' of Descartes and capitalism. Unfortunately it also rules out building a feminist or socialist politics into the deconstructive enterprise. For deconstruction to join forces with feminism and socialism would be to prioritise particular textual readings in a way that is utterly antithetical to its intent.

This issue has largely been elaborated in terms of current debates about the nature of postmodernity and the future of socialism. Drawing upon Lyotard's (1984) distinction between 'grand' and 'little narratives', we can see that there are continuities as well as conflicts between feminism and deconstruction. This opposition between narratives mirrors a tension within feminism, that of the problem of integrating the 'little stories' of individual women with the wider narratives of history and patriarchy—a tension heightened by the fact that a feminist politics is premised on the necessity and possibility of articulating the two (hence 'the personal is political'). Marxist analyses have also addressed this issue by trying to link the history of the working classes and understanding of capitalism with the activities of the workers. But while in Marxism the tension between the personal and the grand narrative is bridged or articulated primarily through notions of a 'vanguard' (with all the problems this entails), feminism goes further by threatening (deconstructing) the opposition through developing new ways of organising. In this way feminism can be seen to problematise the heirarchical nature of most left organisations and Marxist politics, showing how they are in danger of reproducing precisely those inequalities they are against.

However, there is one area where feminism's partiality for the personal may lead it into the same political cul-de-sac as deconstruction. In particular we can notice continuities between the cultural corollary of deconstruction, postmodernism, and current tendencies in feminism. Just as the post-modern subject is said to be caught in a static series of presents rather than history, capable only of pastiche rather than parody, pleasure rather than politics, is individualised rather than collective, so too we can interpret and evaluate 'identity politics' as leading towards an individualisation and depoliticisation of experience with a corresponding shift from questions of oppression to identity (Bourne 1987; Burman, in press).

Dilemmas

Not only are there conceptual problems in trying to mesh together feminism and deconstruction, but there are also more immediate tactical dilemmas that feminist involvement in deconstruction poses. Much of the impetus for the deconstructive enterprise in psychology, as elsewhere, has come from feminists. However, there is a danger that deconstruction may be appropriating feminist critiques, through claiming to incorporate and thus rendering irrationally invisible a specifically feminist contribution and project. In social psychology this is illustrated through the ways feminist research and methodological critiques have been assimilated into 'new paradigm' research, which draws heavily on, but rarely acknowledges, a much longer tradition of feminist work. As Reason and Rowan put it, in a section of their introduction entitled 'The feminism issue', '. . . there seems to be a real danger that in new paradigm research men will take a "female" view of looking at the world, and turn it into another "male way of seeing it"' (Reason and Rowan 1981: xxiii). Indeed, it is interesting that this danger was highlighted by the (male) editors of a 'handbook' of 'new research methods' which was guilty of precisely this inadvertent disenfranchisement of feminist research, and even more significant that in the follow-up book (Reason 1988) neither 'feminism' nor 'feminist research' appear in the index and the only references are in fact cited within a general rubric of 'post-positivism' (Reason 1988: 3).

This argument has parallels in the broader arena in which deconstruction critiques arise before gradually percolating into psychology. It may have taken the insights of post-structuralist psychoanalysis to *theorise* women's subversion of the patriarchal order, but this powerful critique is predicated on the prior existence of women's resistance. Psychoanalysis may have facilitated *recognition* of women's oppositional relation to as well as (and by virtue of) our exclusion from dominant systems of representation. Drawing on Irigaray's (1977) analysis of the speculum as the symbol of how masculine practices are shaped by the feminine void they seek to master, we might even go further to posit the category of the feminine as their suppressed/repressed constituting force. However, there is no reason why feminists should necessarily defer to a theoretical framework such as deconstruction simply because it lends some credence or legitimacy to our demands. Nor is it clear that these analyses of 'femininity' necessarily have anything to do with feminist politics unless they are linked to theories of both resistance and change. Indeed, deconstruction could well become a new technology to colonise women's critical and revolutionary potential.

While it may be tactically useful to adopt deconstructive approaches for progressive political projects, this could be done at the expense of failing to advance the underlying feminist and radical project through lack of explicit commitment to it. Hence we marginalise those feminists who do not seek refuge under deconstruction's 'facilitating' mantle, and at the same time surrender the expression of our own motivations to be cast within its own terms. This raises then the question of dangers from within of being recuperated into a new kind of orthodoxy or subject position.

Dangers

The main danger deconstruction holds for feminists is that of depoliticisation. There are a number of subtle ways in which this possibility arises, some of which I have already touched upon. Here I want to concentrate on one main issue: the political consequences of deconstruction's celebration of 'difference'.

Difference (with '*différance*') is perhaps the key term in the deconstructive lexicon (Derrida 1982b); its methodology is to adopt the devalued term of the opposition it identifies to highlight the metaphysical dynamic of its construction. However, just as 'affirmative' movements have their limitations as political strategy, so too the principal danger with deconstruction is that difference may become a substitute rather than a starting point for resistance. Hence it is in relation to this issue that debates about deconstruction and feminism are most closely intertwined.

The post-structuralist package of Derrida, Foucault and Lacan offers critiques and insights into the constitution of dominant patriarchal discourses and constructions of feminine positions, but leaves feminists in some confusion as to what action follows from this analysis of women's relation to the symbolic. As Toril Moi's (1985) account of Kristeva's analysis of the implications of post-Lacanian psychoanalysis for feminism points out, there are three possible avenues for feminist politics. The first of these, women's demands for equal access to the symbolic order, can broadly be equated with 'equal opportunities'. This is liberal feminism, where equality is defined in terms of male (patriarchal) norms, and as such is clearly insufficient to dismantle patriarchy. The second position is that of radical feminism, where women reject the male symbolic order in the name of difference. This glorification of the (formerly devalued term of) femininity can be seen as congruent with the practice of deconstruction, and is epitomised in the writing of Hélène Cixous. However, this position, through its undoubtedly empowering celebration of women's bodily and psychological qualities, lapses into biologism and essentialism, and treats difference as universal and timeless. Equally, as Moi's critique of Irigaray demonstrates, ignoring material and historical specificities of women's relation to power permits the essentialisation of women's experiences, reduces us to our bodies, individualises our struggles and positions us as uniformly powerless within the dominant order so that resistance from within cannot be envisaged.

This is perhaps the primary danger of deconstructive critiques, a danger that is acknowledged in wider discussions of post-modernism where the subject is depicted as alienated from a collective politics, as able to sustain only a momentary criticality, and as ultimately stranded in a timeless present that maintains and constitutes itself only by carnival-esque allusion to past genres (Jameson 1984). At the theoretical level, we have seen how deconstruction is fundamentally committed to a liberal pluralism which renders each of its deconstructive readings as equally valid, and paralyses political motivation. Again, there are some connec-tions to be made with contemporary debates in the women's movement, most notably around theorising differences of culture and heritage through 'identity politics', and the politics and ethics of women's sexuality as in addressing sado-masochism.

Deconstruction, like some varieties of feminism, seeks to undo or reject the dichotomy between masculine and feminine by demonstrating its metaphysical (and, for feminists, political) basis (this is Moi's third position). As Moi points out, while it is *politically* essential that feminists defend women as women to counteract our oppression as women under patriarchy, 'an "undeconstructed" form of "stage two" feminism, unaware of the metaphysical nature of gender identities, runs the risk of . . . uncritically taking over the very metaphysical categories set up by patriar-chy in order to keep women in their places, despite attempts to attach new feminist values to these categories' (1985: 13).

Dilutions

As well as its inherently problematic nature for radicals, there are also difficulties associated with introducing post-structuralist ideas into social psychology. I will confine myself to two examples here.

The psychological concept of 'androgyny' is perhaps the shining example of the career of an undeconstructed critique of 'masculinity' and 'femininity', yet which nevertheless anticipates some of deconstruction's rhetoric. Formulated as a way of escaping the restrictive confines of polarised psychological sex roles, it has been hailed as a visionary promise of what life without sex typing could be like. What it notably fails to theorise though, through its equal valuing of qualities traditionally asso-ciated with masculinity and femininity, is the initial inequality of gendered positions. It thus renders oppression as simply a feature of individual incompetence or unwillingness to change (Carrigan *et al.* 1987). Like postmodernism, 'androgyny' needs to be seen in the context of the market needs of late capitalism, and that this is recognised (even welcomed) by its advocates is seen by one of the paradigmatic examples of androgynous behaviour offered by Bem (1976): the ability to sack an employee 'with sensitivity' (Billig 1982). This is no rejection of the masculinity/femininity distinction as metaphysical, but a simple exploitation and construction of human potential to meet the demands of capital.

Second, one of the primary routes by which deconstruction has found its way into social psychology has been through 'discourse analysis'. Perhaps the paradigmatic case of the consequences of this is the construction and reception of Potter and Wetherell's *Discourse and Social Psychology* (1987), which has created a first legitimate foothold for post-structuralist critiques in mainstream social psychology. The book holds within itself a number of contradictory positions, sometimes claiming that the role of discourse analysis is to comment on and critique social psychology, and at other times asserting that it is part and parcel of the proper business of social psychology. Moreover, the sample analyses of transcripts reveal a reluctance to deconstruct their own discourse as researchers (Bowers 1988). So far so good: strategy may prevail over logic; sometimes there are good reasons for not wanting to entirely undermine authorial authority, particularly when seeking to make a credible case for innovation. However, it would have been better to acknowledge properly the post-structuralist inspiration for their approach. Although Foucault and Derrida are briefly cited, the potential of discourse analysis to surprise, disrupt and unsettle psychology is instead safely attributed to developments in ethnomethodology, ordinary language philosophy and linguistics. (Psychoanalysis, let alone Lacan, does not get a mention.) Deconstruction may be watered down to such an extent that it can easily be assimilated into prevailing paradigms, and renders even more difficult the project to bring the full force of these critiques to bear on the practice of psychology.

Diversions

There is a further sense in which post-structuralism could be seen to be diversionary rather than simply dangerous, particularly in the seduction of form. (Of course, this reintroduction of the form-content opposition is heresy to deconstruction.) It is easy to be hypnotised by the aesthetic of argument, to create a kind of conceptual analysis for pleasure rather than for politics (indeed such is the dynamic of deconstruction proper). Just as anti-nuclear activists can become fascinated by the details of the horror of weapons of mass destruction, so too we can become so absorbed in analysing the technology of symbolic domination that we come to treat the discursive as a *purely* symbolic relation, and forget the material and historical basis of oppression.

Of course, this argument could be turned against me to suggest that the account I have presented here is motivated by an unconscious desire simply to deconstruct deconstruction rather than subject it to a thoroughgoing political critique. But how are we to judge? Am I answerable to history? To a wider community of feminists? Or, as current vogue would have it, to my therapist (should I have one—should I have one?)? Perhaps speculation of this kind is symptomatic of the priority individual reflection is accorded over action through a politics informed by deconstruction. At the very least, the lack of specification of a political accountability should be good grounds for suspicion.

Deconstruction's avowed focus on the materiality of discourse can have other effects too: it is easy to over-interpret interventions at the level of discourse as necessarily having political implications and to divert political projects into discursive ones, misrecognising full-blown political resistance in every momentary contradiction.

At a wider level, the cultural correlate of deconstruction in wider society, postmodernism, is characterised by a political apathy and disengagement that itself mocks politics as 'post'. This resignation and indifference should lead us to be wary of the current moves to see in popular culture and consumption a 'political' resistance. Further, the contemporary left rhetoric of 'new times' and, still worse, 'new realism' can be seen to reflect the same political fatalism and preoccupation with ephemera that postmodernism engenders.

Converses and Conclusions

Given the arguments and issues outlined in this chapter, it is not surprising that the feminist response to post-structuralist ideas in the social sciences is far from uniform. Some feminists are in the forefront of developing deconstructive techniques and some give it an enthusiastic reception as a political tool (Weedon 1987), while others find it possible to develop a progressive political practice within psychology without invoking a post-structuralist framework (Sayers 1986), or are actively hostile to it as an elitist and intellectualist substitute for politics (Stanley and Wise 1983).

As far as social psychology is concerned, like Humpty Dumpty, deconstruction takes it apart and refuses to let it be reconstituted. Rather, it comments on the political undesirability and theoretical impossibility of such an enterprise. For to 'reconstruct' psychology is to tie it to the limits of our current vision, to foreclose possibilities for change, and to return us to a static and essential social psychology that counters any genuinely historical and materialist analysis.

At the level of theory, deconstruction seems to be a sharp but dangerous tool. The political impasses and consequences of a commitment to the deconstructive enterprise seem to take away as much as they offer.

In fact the problems and pitfalls of post-structuralism as a whole for a radical critique of social psychology derive from precisely those features which I outlined at the beginning as potentially most promising: highlighting the materiality of language carries with it the danger of tackling the representation at the expense of engaging with the political reality; using the multiplicity of readings to indicate ideological operation of dominant discourses opens the project up to liberal pluralism; acclaiming the subject's multiple positioning in discourse as facilitating contradiction and resistance also presents the prospect of fragmentation and incipient dissipation of political energies; and focusing on a politics of subjectivity can lead to a celebration of difference rather than a galvanising into action.

In terms of practice, the recent history of the uptake of these ideas in British psychology provides some instructive lessons. While they were initially circulated through the shortlived but influential radical journal *Ideology and Consciousness* (later *I & C*) in the late 1970s, they were first collected together to mount a sustained and specific critique of psychology in *Changing the Subject* (Henriques *et al.* 1984). The reception and effects of this book present in microcosm the dilemmas posed by post-structuralism in psychology. A striking feature is its highly uncharacteristic publishing history: like any other book, its sales started with an initial peak which gradually declined, but unlike many others it has reproduced this pattern several times over the last five years, almost as though it is rediscovered by successive cohorts of radical psychologists. However the dangers of producing a 'new orthodoxy' which simply replaces the old were epitomised by what, with hindsight, sound like complacent and mistaken claims made for it as marking a new era in psychology (Ingleby 1984). Nevertheless the book, and the ideas contained within it, did become the focus of debate by some psychologists, although others found the meetings alienating, academic and insufficiently linked to action. Ultimately the networks created have largely become a forum for postgraduates doing similar research, hence reinstating with an over-elaborate if potentially progressive theory the traditional division of labour and interests between academics and practitioners. The endeavours that have tried to follow the real political reverberations in psychology accompanying deconstruction have so far been dogged by its theoretical reputation, which has, paradoxically—in terms of the substance of the ideas—foreclosed further radical political developments.

Post-Word

As I finish this chapter, I am no longer certain whether my account has dispensed with deconstruction by showing some of its political impasses; or has in fact reinstated it through employing deconstructive methods to highlight its own limitations. Have I deconstructed my own resistance to deconstruction through using its methodology to critique it? Or still yet fallen prey to the charge of subordinating a feminist politics to deconstruction? Or both of these?

I suggested earlier that the danger of deconstruction is that it invites us to let difference stand in for political action. Writing now at the brink of the 1990s and in the middle of third-term Thatcher Britain, understanding 'race', class, and sex subject positions in relation to power is more than academic. And yet I am drawn back to the question that the political critique both afforded and problematised by deconstruction poses for feminists: How can we resist the seductiveness of difference? Should we resist post-structuralism or can we appropriate its analysis of sexual difference to inform our own struggles? If post-structuralism has anything useful to tell us it can illuminate the processes of objectification and idealism that construct and maintain prevailing (patriarchal) power relations. To take up deconstruction's interpretation of difference and *différance* poses two major challenges to a feminist politics: to re-envisage subject positions that are capable of change beyond merely reproducing the inverse of what they are not; and to take seriously our own claims that discourses are practices which lie beyond as well as within language.

Deconstruction offers a notion of difference that resists closure and is always provisional. Yet part of the very popularity of its ideas must be understood in terms of its emergence at a particular juncture in late capitalism. Indeed it is the very discourse of discourse that makes it possible to speak of its effects. Rather than allowing deconstruction to function as a defence, a displacement used to defer political engagement, a feminist position on deconstruction, as with every other dominant social/symbolic practice, can only be one of a strategic marginality and subversion.

Note

I would like to thank Jonathan Potter for his helpful comments on an earlier version of this chapter.

References

Adcock, C. and Newbigging, K. (1990). 'Women in the shadows: clinical psychology, women and feminism', in E. Burman (ed.) *Feminists and Psychological Practice*, London: Sage.

Bem, S. (1976). 'Probing the promise of androgyny', in A. G. Kaplan and J. P. Bean (eds) *Beyond Sex Roles: Reading Towards a Psychology of Androgyny*, Boston: Little, Brown and Co.

Billig, M. (1982). *Ideology and Social Psychology: Extension, Moderation and Contradiction*, Oxford: Basil Blackwell.

Bourne, J. (1987). 'Homeland of the mind: Jewish feminism and identity politics', *Race and Class* 29(1):1–24.

Bowers, J. M. (1988) 'Review essay on *Discourse and Social Psychology*', *British Journal of Social Psychology* 27:185–192.

Burman, E. (in press) 'Identity crisis, political cop-out or cultural affirmation?: the Jewish feminism debate', in G. Chester and others *An Anthology of British Jewish Feminist Writing*, London: Women's Press.

Carrigan, T., Connell, B. and Lee, J. (1987) 'The "sex-role" framework and the sociology of masculinity', in G. Weiner and M. Arnot (eds) *Gender Under Scrutiny: New Inquiries in Education*, London: Hutchinson.

Derrida, J. (1982). *Positions*, London: Athlone Press.

Foucault, M. (1979) *The History of Sexuality. Vol. I: An Introduction*, London: Allen Jane.

Henriques, J., Holloway, W., Urwin, C., Venn, C., and Walkerdine, W. (1984) *Changing the Subject: Psychology, Social Regulation and Subjectivity*, London: Methuen.

Hudson, B. (1984) 'Femininity and adolescence', in A. McRobie and M. Nava (eds) *Gender and Generation*, Basingstoke: Macmillan.

Ingleby, D. (1984) 'Development in social context', Paper given at British Psychological Society Developmental Psychology Section Conference, University of Lancaster.

Irigaray, L. (1977) 'Women's exile', *Ideology and Consciousness* 1:62–76.

Jameson, F. (1984) 'Postmodernism, or the cultural logic of late capitalism', *New Left Review* 146:53–92.

Kitzinger, C. (1988) 'Defending innocence: ideologies of childhood', *Feminist Review* 28:77–87.

Lyotard, J. -F. (1984) *The Postmodern Condition: A Report on Knowledge*, Manchester: Manchester University Press.

Moi, T. (1985) *Sexual/Textual Politics: Feminist Literary Theory*, London: Methuen.

Potter, J. and Wetherell, M. (1987) *Discourse and Social Psychology: Beyond Attitudes and Behaviour*, London: Sage.

Reason, P. (ed.) (1988) *Human Inquiry in Action: Developments in New Paradigm Research*, London: Sage.

Reason, P. and Rowan, J. (eds) (1981) *Human Inquiry: A Sourcebook of New Paradigm Research*, London: Sage.

Rose, N. (1985) *The Psychological Complex*, London: Routledge & Kegan Paul.

Sayers, J. (1986) *Sexual Contradictions: Psychology, Psychoanalysis, and Feminism*, London: Tavistock.

Sharp, R. and Green, A. (1975) *Education and Social Control*, London: Routledge & Kegan Paul.

Spence, J. (1986). *Putting Myself in the Picture*, London: Camden Press.

Stanley, L. and Wise, S. (1983) *Breaking Out: Feminist Consciousness and Feminist Research*, London: Routledge & Kegan Paul.

Steedman, C. (1982) *The Tidy House: Little Girls' Writing*, London: Virago.

Urwin, C. (1986). 'Developmental psychology and psychoanalysis: splitting the difference', in M. Richards and P. Light (eds) *Children of Social Worlds*, Cambridge: Polity Press.

Venn, C. and Walkerdine, V. (1978) 'The acquisition and production of knowledge: Piaget's theory reconsidered', *Ideology and Consciousness* 3:67–94.

Walden, R. and Walkerdine, V. (1982) *Girls and Mathematics: the Early Years*, Bedford Way Papers, Institute of Education, University of London.

Walkerdine, V. (1981) 'Sex, power and pedagogy', *Screen Education*, 38:14–21.

Warren, K. (1988) ' "The child as problem" or "the child with needs": a discourse analysis of a school case conference', unpublished B.Sc. (Hons) Psychology Project, Manchester Polytechnic.

Weedon, C. (1987) *Feminist Practice and Post-structuralist Theory*, Oxford: Basil Blackwell.

ABOUT THE BOOK
AND EDITOR

This book uses a constructionist approach to explore the place of women in psychology, both as participants in the discipline and as subjects of psychological theory, research, and practice. The book provides an explanation of the principles of social constructionism and then utilizes this model as a tool for discovering the influences that have shaped psychology's treatment of women.

Certainly recent works have addressed the construction of gender, but this is the first to apply the constructionist lens to psychology itself. It asks how the social construction of gender has interacted, both historically and at present, with the sociohistorical forces that shape psychology. It is the intersection of these two understandings—accepted "truths" about the nature of gender and psychology's own understanding of its role—that has framed women's place in the discipline.

Utilizing readings from a variety of sources, the book explicates women's place in psychology, from early misogynist to recent feminist attempts to understand the psychology of women. This exploration reveals the tacit assumptions about gender and about psychology that traditionally have acted in concert to discount, demean, marginalize, and misrepresent women's experience. Recent feminist psychology is given an equally thorough review, demonstrating that feminist thought must also be conscientiously queried lest we inadvertently reproduce the very forms we strive to dismantle.

Janis S. Bohan is professor of psychology at Metropolitan State College of Denver.

ABOUT THE CONTRIBUTORS

Erica Burman is lecturer in psychology at Manchester Polytechnic in the United Kingdom.

Mary Crawford is professor of psychology and women's studies at West Chester University.

Laurel Furumoto is professor of psychology at Wellesley College.

Kathleen Grady is president of the Massachusetts Institute of Behavioral Medicine.

Rachel T. Hare-Mustin is professor of psychology at Villanova University.

Arnold S. Kahn is professor of psychology at James Madison University.

Celia Kitzinger is lecturer in psychology at the University of Surrey in the United Kingdom.

Bernice Lott is professor of psychology at the University of Rhode Island.

Jeanne Marecek is professor of psychology at Swarthmore College.

Jill G. Morawski is associate professor of psychology at Wesleyan University.

Elizabeth Scarborough is dean of Liberal Arts and Sciences at Indiana University at South Bend.

Carolyn Wood Sherif (1922–1982) was formerly professor of psychology at Pennsylvania State University.

Stephanie Shields is professor of psychology at the University of California at Davis.

Rhoda Kesler Unger is professor of psychology and director of the honors program at Montclair State College.

Barbara Strudler Wallston (1943–1987) was formerly professor of psychology at George Peabody College for Teachers, Vanderbilt University.

Naomi Weisstein lives and works in New York City.

Candace West is professor of sociology at the University of California, Santa Cruz.

Michele Andrisin Wittig is professor of psychology at California State University, Northbridge.

Janice D. Yoder is associate professor of psychology at the University of Wisconsin at Milwaukee.

Don H. Zimmerman is professor of sociology at the University of California, Santa Barbara.